THE DEFINITIVE ILLUSTRATED
ENCYCLOPEDIA of
ROCK

Publisher and Creative Director: Nick Wells
Project Editor: Sara Robson
Commissioning Editor: Polly Willis
Designer: Michael Spender
Picture Research: Gemma Walters
Production: Kelly Fenlon, Chris Herbert and Claire Walker

Special thanks to: Joe Cushley, Jason Draper, Catherine Emslie, Jake Jackson,
Karen Fitzpatrick and Rosanna Singler

First Published 2006 by
FLAME TREE PUBLISHING
Crabtree Hall, Crabtree Lane
Fulham, London, SW6 6TY
United Kingdom

www.flametreepublishing.com

Music information site: www.musicfirebox.com

10 09

3 5 7 9 10 8 6 4

Flame Tree is part of the Foundry Creative Media Company Limited

The CIP record for this book is available from the British Library.

Hardback ISBN: 978-1-84451-521-9
Hardback Special ISBN: 978-1-84786-730-8
Paperback ISBN: 978-1-84451-996-5

Printed in China

THE DEFINITIVE ILLUSTRATED
ENCYCLOPEDIA OF
ROCK

Richard Buskin, Alan Clayson, Joe Cushley, Rusty Cutchin, Jason Draper, Hugh Fielder,
Mike Gent, Michael Heatley, Jake Kennedy, Colin Salter, Ian Shirley, John Tobler

General Editor: Michael Heatley
Foreword by Scotty Moore

FLAME TREE
PUBLISHING

Contents

THE SEVENTIES

THE EIGHTIES

HOW TO USE THIS BOOK

The Definitive Illustrated Encyclopedia of Rock is a rip-roaring ride through the history of rock'n'roll. From a heady cocktail of blues, country, jazz and gospel, the new music of the early 1950s broke loose and became the hypnotic familiar of modern youth. The book will lead you through the subsequent decades, illuminating the styles, influences and moods, through to the major artists and finally a comprehensive list of artists (singers, musicians and producers) in each relevant era.

Rock draws from a seductive melting pot of influences – it is impossible not to dive into the myriad pop, blues, dance, jazz, funk, rap, country, hip-hop, folk, reggae, gospel, world, soul and R&B artists that dance alongside their rockier counterparts in telling the story of Rock Music. The book tracks the fusions of social, political and cultural changes, which both informed and was reflected by the music, gathering pace with accelerating technological and media progress. Such advances have increased the contact between different musical forms and stretched the distance between the traditional, simple music making and today's complex industry of internet, mp3s, CD and clubs, where the sheer diversity of available music would astonish anyone who lived through the first years of rock'n'roll, just 50 years ago.

SECTION OPENER

Each section is set in its cultural context, and given a glimpse into what was going on behind the scenes that served to influence the musical highs and lows of the decade.

SOURCES & SOUNDS

These pages offer more detail about the decade – what was new, what was exciting, what was in and what was out, and tries to figure out why that was. Helpful cross-references enable you to follow threads of interest throughout the book.

SUBSECTION

Some of the decades – namely the 1960s and 1970s – have been broken into the main musical genres, highlighting the massive divergences of the musical and cultural themes.

KEY ARTISTS

These artists carry the musical torch for their generation and so provide the main features for each era. Classic Recordings, key album covers and great quotes help to get under the skin of the artists' music.

A-Z OF ARTISTS

Although they did not quite make into the Key Artists pages, these are the artists that formed the musical backbone of each decade.

LIST OF ARTISTS

These lists, at the end of each decade, offer a comprehensive list of all the major artists, from those included in the Key Artists and A–Z sections, to the many others who contributed to the mood of the decade. The list gives a brief idea of each artist's origins and main period of influence.

Foreword

I've been in music most of my life and have worked with some great musicians, like Elvis and Keith Richards and Eric Clapton. But when I first started, after I came out of the Navy, all I had in mind to do was start a little band and pick up some work at the weekends, and maybe some sessions from Sam Phillips at his studio on Union Avenue, to go with my job as a milliner. Well, I got a band, The Starlite Wranglers, and we released a record on Sun which probably sold about a dozen copies. But I got friends with Sam and we used to go and sit in Miss Taylor's restaurant next door to the studio and talk about everything. And somehow, through Sam and his secretary, Marion Keisker we fixed up an audition with this new kid, Elvis Presley. We were in the studio and were nearly done – Bill Black, the bassist and me had to work the next day – then just as we were about to pack up, Elvis started goofing around on the old Arthur 'Big Boy' Crudup tune, 'That's All Right', and we just fell in behind. We just thought it was still the audition when Sam told us to do it again, we didn't realize that was going to be Elvis's first record!

Some people say my second solo on 'Hound Dog' is the first rock'n'roll guitar solo, or one of the greatest, or whatever, but that was a bit of an accident too! We'd done it and done it and done it. I don't know how many takes. And Elvis said, 'let's do one more'. I was as mad as heck, and I thought, to hell with it. There was no beating around the bush with that one! I always tried to do something different on the solos, to keep an improvized feel. I suppose that might have come from the jazz guitarists I liked, such as Tal Farlow. But I grew up listening to and playing all sorts: B.B. King; Chet Atkins; blues; country; jazz; all sorts. I guess it came from that Triangle of Mojo; New Orleans; Memphis; Nashville; where it all got mixed up. I'd never claim to be a great musician, but I always listened to a song and tried to play what was appropriate. I tried to keep an open mind, not just play a bunch of notes. I'd listen and try and do something a bit different, put my own mark on it.

After Elvis went into the Army I started working as an engineer and producer. I'd always watched and listened wherever we'd recorded and picked up things along the way. I ended up working for Sam again at his new Memphis studio. We did a lot of soundalike recordings, and for that you had to take the songs apart. That's how I came in contact with The Beatles and The Rolling Stones. To me they were in the same vein as us when we started out in '54. They took it and hit us right back in the face with it. I loved it! When I played with Keith Richards later, it seemed like we'd known each other for ever. He said to me, 'everyone wanted to be Elvis, I wanted to be you!'. I guess maybe I opened the door for them; that's sort of what George Harrison and Mark Knopfler said to me, too.

I hung-up my guitar after a solo album and went to work at my Nashville studio, Music City Recorders where I engineered Ringo Starr's *Beaucoups Of Blues* in 1970, among many others, and then freelance. I just loved being around music in any form. I started to play live again in the early 1990s with The Jordanaires and Carl Perkins. I still play and record, but it's not really a business for me anymore. Unfortunately, there's too much business around. There always has been. It's what ruined Elvis, having to do all those crappy songs in those movies. It's always about the bottom line. I was inducted into the Rock And Roll Hall Of Fame's new Sideman category in 2000, but they seem to have let that slip, which is a great shame. Everything comes down to money. There should be Halls Of Fame for engineers and writers and so on.

You can dig deep here in this encyclopedia. It mentions everyone involved not just the stars, which can only be a good thing. I hope you get as much enjoyment out of the music and reading about it as I have.

Scotty Moore
2006

Legendary guitarist Winfield Scott 'Scotty' Moore (left).

Introduction OF ROCK

Perhaps this introduction should start with a disclaimer. Though you are holding an encyclopedia of rock music in your hands, this book includes artists who would never use that four-letter term to identify themselves. So if you are offended by the idea of reading about Eminem as well as Pink Floyd, then please return the book to the shelf!

Music may not have changed the world in the way the peace-loving hippies of the 1960s hoped, but has certainly exerted an influence. Its multicultural, multiracial roots have encouraged acceptance of people's differences. Those differences have in turn helped make some distinctive music, and that is fully reflected in these pages.

The roots of rock music lie in black music. Just as rap has transcended the colour barrier, so it is harder than ever in the twenty-first century to place artists and their music in boxes or categories. When Run-DMC and Aerosmith brought rock and rap together back in 1986 their rock-rap fusion was considered unusual; since then, careers have been built on such cross-fertilization.

Then there are figures like Madonna, constantly reinventing herself and moving from genre to genre. Samplers also mix and match by extracting musical phrases from well-known songs and building others around them, with the result that classics have enjoyed a new life and reached a new audience. All this makes the imposition of genres more and more difficult, if not futile – hence our reliance on decades to split up the artists in these pages.

The history of popular music has been one of innovation followed by imitation – critics would say there is more of the latter than the former. Just as a guitarist will learn their instrument through playing existing songs, so these will come out sounding different to the original and perhaps suggest a new avenue of exploration.

Our Sources & Sounds articles at the beginning of each chapter are intended to join up some of the dots and suggest strands that have continued, mutated and evolved through the decades. The Roots chapter reflects the country and blues musics that came together to form Elvis Presley's brand of rock'n'roll – the spark that lit the fuse for the musical and cultural explosion that followed.

The relation between black and white music gradually disappeared – disco was perhaps the first sub-genre where the identity of the artist involved was irrelevant, and that has now been followed by rave, trance and other dancefloor-aimed classifications. Rock and dance first mixed in the 1960s with Sly and The Family Stone, and the inter-relation has become more intimate in subsequent years.

The choice of Key Artists is, inevitably, a subjective one and will stir most controversy. Indeed, only the likes of Elvis and The Beatles are likely to poll unanimous approval. In an era of text-message voting

and Internet discussion, you will unfortunately have to live with our choices. The death of Syd Barrett, the original singer of Pink Floyd, during the preparation of our book reminded us that today's established supergroups were yesterday's innovators.

Some, of course, die young, as did Jimi Hendrix and Kurt Cobain, both sons of Seattle. Part of the fascination of the likes of Eminem and Babyshambles' Pete Doherty lies in what might be considered their seemingly self-destructive urges. Yet in an era when Keith Richards can still make headlines for falling out of a tree – in the 1960s it was urinating in a petrol-station forecourt – there will always be room for the rebel.

Music has always had a bearing on fashion, cinema and other aspects of popular culture. That ongoing process continues today, and has been accelerated – if not exaggerated – by the 24-hour availability of music television. Once upon a time, record purchasers might not have been certain even what race the recording artist was – now they will not only have seen them perform on the small screen but may also have digested every possible piece of personal information via the Internet. The demise of Britain's TV music showcase *Top Of The Pops* in 2006 showed an era had ended: the future is still unfolding.

Ten years ago, you would have bought this book in a bookshop. Now you may have purchased it through an Internet bookseller. In the same way, the means by which music is purchased has changed with the advent of the World Wide Web.

The way we listen to music has also changed. Today's consumers are as likely to listen through a computer or, if on the move, MP3 player as a stereo system, making this perhaps more of a solitary experience. Similarly, festivals seem to be ways of big acts reaching the maximum number of people through the least effort expended rather than the sense of community such efforts used to engender.

But rock music, like the world at large, is ever-changing. This book's extensive lists and cross-references can be your route map. Its carefully researched illustrations add the all-important visual dimension, leaving you to supply your record/CD/MP3 collection to complete the total picture.

One final disclaimer: if you find your bank account overstretched after following our writers' listening recommendations, we cannot be held responsible. With that warning in mind, read and enjoy!

Michael Heatley
2006

ROOTS

Rock'n'roll did not spring fully formed from Memphis in the shape of Elvis Presley but was the coming together of several different roots musics. Country, jazz, doo-wop and the blues had all enjoyed significant audiences in their own right, and all would have a bearing on the sounds to come.

The music scenes across America had been local or, at best regional. But just as the advance of radio beamed entertainment to new audiences, the migratory nature of life made American cities centres of musical change. As wartime industries demanded labour, so rural workers would bring themselves and their tastes to town. Clubs were opened to serve their leisure needs, and record labels surely followed.

Instruments were developing on which to play the music, notably the electric guitar that Leo Fender was on the point of perfecting in 1949. His Esquire, later renamed Telecaster, became the industry standard as rock amplified itself and prepared to make itself heard, loudly and proudly. A new era beckoned.

Sources & Sounds

The creation of rock'n'roll changed youth culture as we know it. But whether you consider the era began with Bill Haley's 'Rock Around The Clock', which reached No. 1 in the US charts in May 1955, Elvis Presley's bursting out of Sun Studios in Memphis with 'That's All Right' the previous year or his hip-swivelling to a national US audience a couple of years later, there is little doubt that when the genie came out of the bottle it would not be put back in.

Mixing It Up

The twin musical ingredients that led to the explosion that was rock'n'roll were blues and country. The former was an urban phenomenon, or certainly became one as the black migration from the southern states to the cities grew in number. Country and western also grew in popularity to transcend its regional beginnings. A music that had been hitherto passed down the generations through the folk tradition was now reaching new audiences with the help of radio. It created national celebrities in cowboy singers like Gene Autry and Roy Rogers and, by the end of the 1940s, had enjoyed a number of million-selling releases.

The divide between the musics was, quite simply, the colour bar. It was not usual for white youth to listen to and enjoy black or black-influenced music, nor for blacks to listen to country. Radio stations, likewise, remained exclusive, but performers like Bill Haley, with his country-music background, helped smudge the line between them. His inspiration to move from ballads to boogie was bluesman Joe Turner, who had relocated from Kansas to New York in 1939 and helped spark a boogie-woogie craze. His 'Shake, Rattle And Roll' became an early rock'n'roll anthem in Haley's hands in 1954 – a pattern that would be repeated when Big Mama Thornton's 'Hound Dog' was covered by Elvis Presley in 1956.

Rhythm and blues had started life in the worksongs of the oppressed blacks, been refined into rural blues and then exported to the great industrial cities of the north and west. The war effort sped up that process. The music of such now-legendary guitar and vocal performers as Big Bill Broonzy would become more widely appreciated, and the likes of the much-travelled John Lee Hooker would make a bigger mark in Detroit than in his native Mississippi. With his cherry red Gibson electric guitar, he was the archetypal urban bluesman.

Breaking Through

The blues phenomenon had largely been ignored by the major labels, so a string of independents sprung up to fill the gap: King, Chess, Aladdin, Specialty and Modern were just a handful. Chess was the label that afforded Jackie Brenston the opportunity to record what was arguably the first rock'n'roll record, 'Rocket 88', in 1951.

The crucial early breakthrough to the white mainstream was made by black vocal groups like The Dominoes and The Orioles, whose harmony-coated hits 'Sixty Minute Man' (1951) and 'Crying In The

> *'Rock'n'roll... smells phoney and false. It is sung, played and written for the most part by cretinous goons.'*
>
> Frank Sinatra

Right

Although rock'n'roll has its roots in the heady synthesis of black and white cultures in the early 1950s, its most recognizable origins reach back to the late nineteenth century when black migrant workers sang old plantation melodies mixed with white music hall ditties, church songs and show tunes.

🚗 *see Introduction pp 12* 🚗 *see A–Z of Artists pp 18* 🚗 *see List of Artists pp 31*

15

📼 **CLASSIC**
RECORDINGS

1931
Jimmie Rodgers: 'Mule Skinner Blues'

1936
Robert Johnson: 'Terraplane Blues'

1948
Muddy Waters: 'I Can't Be Satisfied'

Far Left

Hank Williams' 1953 recording of 'Weary Blues From Waiting' was a hit in the last year of his life. He represents a significant strand of the influences that created the rock'n'roll phenomenon in the 1950s.

Left

Gene Autry

Below

Kansas City's Big Joe Turner was a blues shouter turned boogie-woogie man, and it was his version of 'Shake, Rattle and Roll' that was cleaned up to become Bill Haley and The Comets' 1950s hit.

Chapel' (1953) appealed to a white audience. Interestingly, Bill Haley covered some of the black blues artists like Ruth Brown whose music was initially considered too hard-edged to 'cross over'.

Louis Jordan was the James Brown of his day, the figurehead of raucous black music whose innovations included adding an electric guitar to his line-up in the mid-1940s. His influence was to be heard in later acts like Little Richard and Screamin' Jay Hawkins, while Milt Gabler, the man who produced him, went on to work with Bill Haley, taking Jordan's patented shuffle rhythm with him. Jordan notched up many entries on *Billboard's* 'race' chart (the name changed to R&B in 1949.)

Nashville To Cashville

Country music was firmly established on American radio by the 1930s, the Grand Ole Opry being broadcast across the nation from the music's spiritual home in Nashville. The Delmore Brothers hillbilly duo were the progenitors of The Everly Brothers, drawing from gospel and Appalachian folk, as did the Carter family whose family tree would one day encompass Johnny Cash. The Delmores were also leaning

📻 *see* Bill Haley pp 48   📻 *see* Elvis Presley pp 52   📻 *see* Little Richard pp 66   📻 *see* Screamin' Jay Hawkins pp 70

increasingly towards uptempo material that reflected
Western swing and boogie-woogie. By the end of 1947,
they were using electric guitars and drums.

Electric instrumentation, in the hands of
pioneers like Ernest Tubb, had helped county music
be heard in the noisy bars and juke joints where it
was played live. Another variation that edged the
music towards what we now term rock was Western
swing, a genre synonymous with Bob Wills. His fusion
of jazz and country found a ready audience of dancers.
Dancing and movement would also be the major
audience reaction to rock.

Hard-living Hank Williams was country music's
first superstar. It is astounding that he enjoyed so much
success and influence in such a short life: he was only
29 when he passed away on New Year's Day, 1953.
Yet even then the songs he wrote were already being
covered by more mainstream acts, albeit in a far more
refined way so that they were purveyed by the so-called
'hillbilly Shakespeare'.

Let The Good Times Roll

Chess Records was formed by Polish immigrant
brothers Phil and Leonard Chess to promote the work
of Muddy Waters, whose records they realized would
sell to the audience that flocked to their Chicago
nightclub. Using future Sun boss Sam Phillips as talent
scout they found Howlin' Wolf, whose work along with
that of Little Walter, Bo Diddley and Chuck Berry
would influence a wave of 1960s rock bands like The
Animals, Fleetwood Mac and The Rolling Stones.

While the 1930s had been the years of
depression, there was now a new post-war generation
of white youth unwilling to submit to the cultural

see Introduction pp 12   *see A–Z of Artists pp 18*   *see List of Artists pp 31*

straitjackets of its parents: films like 1953's *The Wild One* and James Dean's *Rebel Without A Cause* (1955) gave them their first role models, while it was when 'Rock Around The Clock' was included on the

soundtrack to the film *The Blackboard Jungle* (1955) that it took off in a big way. Rationing, austerity and the recent strictures of wartime life were anathema to this new generation. They were living in a free world, albeit one that would increasingly be overshadowed by the nuclear arms race. Why not live each day as if it were their last?

When he founded Sun Studios and its retail arm, Sun Records, in Memphis, Sam Phillips had dreamed of finding a white singer who could sing the blues. If he could do this, he believed, he would break down the racial barriers that shackled black artists just as surely as they had been by their slave-masters. That man, of course, was Elvis Presley, whose story is told in the 1950s chapter of this book. Now read about the artists who provided the roots of the rock'n'roll revolution.

Above

The walls of many of Nashville's bars are still covered by the memorabilia of gigs and shows from previous decades, some stretching back to the 1930s.

Left

In the 1930s and 1940s the blues was a street phenomenon, moving from the fields of the south to industrial towns further north like Chicago. Brass instruments, played for church songs and jazz were critical in shaping the big sounds that were adopted by the rock'n'rollers.

see Howlin' Wolf pp 21   *see* The Rolling Stones pp 96   *see* The Animals pp 102   *see* Fleetwood Mac pp 106

A-Z of Artists ROOTS

Bill Black Combo
(Instrumental group, 1958–65)
Bassist Black helped create the rockabilly sound on Elvis Presley's Sun recordings and in the singer's live performances from 1954–58 with guitarist Scotty Moore and drummer D.J. Fontana. Ironically, Black became better known commercially through a string of instrumental hits with The Bill Black Combo, a group he formed after leaving Presley in a dispute over wages. The Combo's hits included 'Smokie', 'White Silver Sands' and 'Josephine'. Black died of a brain tumour in 1965.

Jackie Brenston
(Saxophone, vocals, 1930–79)
Jackie Brenston recorded arguably the first rock'n'roll record with 1951's 'Rocket 88', an R&B boogie that featured Ike Turner's Kings Of Rhythm, of which Brenston was a member. 'Rocket 88' (by Jackie Brenston and His Delta Cats) stayed at the top of the R&B charts for over a month, but Brenston never recaptured the energy on later recordings. He remained with Turner's group until 1962, and then left the music business.

Big Bill Broonzy
(Guitar, vocals, 1893–1958)
A powerful guitarist and prolific composer, Big Bill Broonzy linked the Mississippi delta blues of Robert Johnson with the electrified Chicago sound of Muddy Waters and others. Broonzy was recognized early on by the nascent folk music movement in the 1940s. Underappreciated in America, he gained a wide following in Europe through live performances and made lasting impressions on guitarists like George Harrison and Eric Clapton, who recorded Broonzy's 'Key To The Highway'.

Ruth Brown
(Vocals, b. 1928)
Beginning in 1949 Ruth Brown's soulful voice put Atlantic Records on the map with a string of R&B classics like 'So Long', 'Teardrops In My Eyes' and

see Introduction pp 12   see Sources & Sounds pp 14

Far Left

Big Bill Broonzy first recorded
as a self-accompanied singer
in 1929, and recorded over
350 compositions.

Above Left

In the late 1950s, Bill Black
became one of the first bass
players to use the electric
bass in popular music in
'Jailhouse Rock'.

Left

Owing to the seemingly
endless string of hits enjoyed
by Ruth Brown on Atlantic
Records, the then fledgling
label came to be known as
'The House That Ruth Built'.

'(Mama) He Treats Your Daughter Mean'. Two-dozen
hits later in 1960 Brown left the music business,
enduring difficult times before resurging in the mid-
1970s as a Broadway star. Her attempts to regain unpaid
royalties led to the formation of the Rhythm and Blues
Foundation, which helps struggling R&B artists.

The Carter Family
(Vocal/instrumental group, 1915–56)
The Carter Family was the first vocal group to become
country music stars. Consisting of A.P. Carter, his wife
Sara and their sister-in-law Maybelle, The Carter
Family's simple harmonies and unique guitar-based
arrangements supplanted the bluegrass-oriented
'hillbilly' music of rural America. The family's sound
gave new life to British and Appalachian traditionals
and made country standards of songs like 'Wabash
Cannonball', 'Will The Circle Be Unbroken',
'Wildwood Flower' and 'Keep On The Sunny Side'.

The Delmore Brothers
(Vocal group, 1931–52)
The Delmore Brothers (Alton and Rabon) were
a precursor to sibling vocal groups like The Everly
Brothers. The Delmores' sound, which
incorporated fast electric guitar parts and bluesy
harmonica riffs, foreshadowed the crossover
appeal of later rockabilly and country rock
bands. Embracing elements of western swing
and boogie-woogie in the late 1940s,
The Delmores recorded multiple songs
like 'Hillbilly Boogie' and 'Freight Train
Boogie', but their biggest hit was the slower
'Blues, Stay Away From My Door'.

see Muddy Waters pp 24   *see* The Everly Brothers pp 46   *see* Elvis Presley pp 52   *see* The Yardbirds pp 117

who attracted singers like Clyde McPhatter and Jackie Wilson to the group. The Dominoes' biggest R&B hit was the raunchy '60-Minute Man'. The group's version of 'Stardust' reached No. 12 on the pop charts in 1957. Ward's strict-disciplinarian ways led to a high turnover rate. McPhatter became lead singer of The Drifters and Wilson developed a legendary solo career.

Lionel Hampton
(Vibraphone, 1930–90)

Vibraphonist Lionel Hampton's long career included roles as sideman, bandleader, and cultural force that extended beyond the jazz world. Beginning as a drummer, he switched to vibes at the suggestion of Louis Armstrong, and then broke the colour barrier as a member of Benny Goodman's legendary big band. Hampton's own groups melded swing with R&B, and he was instrumental in developing the career of Dinah Washington, as well as numerous jazz greats.

Above

In November 1955, Bo Diddley appeared on the *Ed Sullivan Show*, the first African-American to do so.

Bo Diddley
(Guitar, vocals, b. 1928)

Born Ellas Bates in McComb, Mississippi, Bo Diddley developed his guitar skills and stage persona in Chicago. He had his first guitar by the age of 10. By 1951, at 23, he was a regular in clubs on Chicago's South Side. By 1955 he was signed to Checker, a spinoff of Chess Records. His debut single was a two-sided gem that featured his compositions 'Bo Diddley' and 'I'm A Man'.

The single gave the world the 'Bo Diddley beat', a staccato rhythm that was picked up and used in hits by Buddy Holly ('Not Fade Away') and The Who ('Magic Bus'), among others. Diddley was also known for his 'cigar box' guitar, which he first designed and built in 1945 while in school. Diddley's songs, like 'You Don't Love Me', 'Pretty Thing', 'Diddy Wah Diddy', 'Who Do You Love?' and 'Mona', reflect the energy and drive of early rock'n'roll.

Right

Pictured here in 1969, Lionel Hampton has been credited with popularizing the vibraphone as a jazz instrument.

The Dominoes
(Vocal group, 1950–65)

The Dominoes were an R&B/pop vocal group led by Billy Ward, a child prodigy and army choir director

W.C. Handy
(Archivist, bandleader, 1873–1958)

W.C. Handy, who led string quartets, brass bands and minstrel-show groups, was a major force in exposing the blues of southern blacks to a mainstream audience. In Memphis in the 1910s Handy, who would become known as the Father of the Blues, emerged with recordings of his compositions 'Yellow Dog Blues', 'The Memphis Blues' and 'The St Louis Blues', one of the most widely recorded songs in history. In 1917, Handy composed 'Beale Street Blues'.

In 1918, Handy moved to New York, and established his publishing company on Broadway. Eventually he copyrighted over 150 songs of secular

see *Introduction* pp 12   see *Sources & Sounds* pp 14

and religious material, while continuing to record. In 1926, he wrote *Blues: An Anthology*, for which he compiled sheet music for the most famous blues songs and attempted to explain their origins. He would compile other anthologies and write his autobiography before losing his eyesight by 1943. He died in 1958.

John Lee Hooker
(Guitar, vocals, 1917–2001)

As a youth in Mississippi blues superstar John Lee Hooker was exposed to blues musicians by his step father. After living in Memphis and Cincinnati he gravitated to Detroit in 1943, where he recorded the single 'Boogie Chillen'. It reached the top of the R&B charts in 1948. Follow-ups included the hits 'Hobo Blues', 'Hoogie Boogie' and 'Crawling King Snake Blues'. Throughout the 1950s Hooker often recorded under pseudonyms like Delta John, Birmingham Sam and Little Pork Chops.

Hooker's mournful voice and droning guitar had an enormous influence on British rock bands like The Yardbirds and The Animals, who covered his 'Boom Boom' in 1964. Hooker continued label hopping through the 1960s and had a major success with 1970's 'Hooker 'n' Heat', teaming with the band Canned Heat. He won a Grammy for the star-studded album *The Healer* in 1989. Hooker continued recording into the 1990s and collaborating with rock artists.

Howlin' Wolf
(Guitar, vocals, 1910–76)

Howlin' Wolf was born Chester Burnett in West Point, Mississippi, and learned the blues from Charley Patton and harmonica from Sonny Boy Williamson, who married his half-sister. After the Army, he began performing around West Memphis, Arkansas, wowing fans with his aggressive vocals and newfangled electric guitar. Promoting himself on local radio, he was heard by Sam Phillips, who cut Wolf's first sides at Phillips' Memphis Recording Service. Phillips leased the results to Chess, and Wolf was on his way.

For Chess, Wolf had hits with 'Evil' and 'Smokestack Lightnin''. But his career headed to a new level in 1960, when he was teamed with writer Willie Dixon. The combination produced a spate of mid-1960s hits, including 'I Ain't Superstitious', 'Back Door

Man', 'Spoonful' and 'Wang Dang Doodle'. Wolf toured Europe and became an inspiration to The Rolling Stones, whose version of 'The Red Rooster' reached No. 1 in Britain. Wolf's material was also recorded by The Doors, Cream and Jeff Beck. Wolf's later solo albums were not as successful, and in the 1970s his health began to fail. He died in a Veterans' Administration Hospital in 1976.

Above

John Lee Hooker made his first recording in 1948, and went on to record over 100 albums.

see Dinah Washington pp 29   *see* The Rolling Stones pp 96   *see* The Animals pp 102   *see* The Yardbirds pp 117

The Ink Spots

(Vocal group, 1931–52)

The Ink Spots were the inspiration for many black vocal groups who emerged in the doo-wop era. The group's tight, mellow harmonies helped them achieve wide crossover appeal. Anchored by the romantic crooning of tenor Bill Kenny and supported by Charlie Fuqua, Deek Watson and bass Hoppy Jones, the Indianapolis natives caught fire in 1939 with the ballad 'If I Didn't Care'. The Spots followed this up with 'My Prayer', ' 'We Three', 'Maybe' and numerous other hits.

Robert Johnson

(Guitar, vocals, 1911–38)

Despite recording only 29 songs in his short life, bluesman Johnson is a mythical figure and one of the most influential guitarists in the history of music. Born in Hazlehurst, Mississippi, in 1911, Johnson learned guitar from players like Charlie Patton and Son House and supported himself on the road from the Mississippi and Arkansas deltas to the big towns of St Louis, Detroit, Chicago, and elsewhere.

Johnson's myth includes stories that he sold his soul to the devil and that he was tormented by nightmares of hellhounds until his untimely death from pneumonia after being poisoned by a jealous husband. But Johnson's true power came from an intense desire to excel and a ferocious work ethic. His first hit 'Terraplane Blues' floored listeners with its haunting vocals and guitar technique. Subsequent hits, like 'Cross Road Blues', 'Love In Vain' and 'Sweet Home Chicago', have influenced guitarists everywhere and been regularly remade by modern bands.

Louis Jordan

(Bandleader, saxophonist, 1908–75)

During the big-band era saxophonist Jordan was burning up the R&B charts with his small group, The Tympany Five. Jordan's music combined jazz and blues with salty, jive-talking humour. People called the sound 'jump blues' or 'jumpin' jive', and from 1942 to 1951, Jordan scored 57 R&B chart hits. Jordan's best-loved songs include 'Choo Choo Ch'Boogie', 'Ain't Nobody Here But Us Chickens' and 'Saturday Night

see Introduction pp 12   *see* Sources & Sounds pp 14

Moon Mullican

(Piano, vocals, 1909–67)

Mullican was a versatile Texas pianist and vocalist who influenced Jerry Lee Lewis and others with pre-rock pounders like 'Cherokee Boogie' and western-swing gems like 'Don't Ever Take My Picture Down', but was perhaps even more influential behind the scenes of his 30-year career. Widely acknowledged to be the co-writer of Hank Williams' 'Jambalaya', Mullican summoned up many of that song's Cajun references for his own highly stylized version of the traditional waltz, 'Jolie Blon'.

Far Left

Robert Johnson's sound was new, full of raw emotion, and one that continues to influence musicians today.

Left

Clyde McPhatter

Below

Amos Milburn

Fish Fry'. Bill Haley and Chuck Berry each cited Jordan as a major influence, while Joe Jackson cut a 1981 album of his music, suitably titled *Jumpin' Jive*.

Clyde McPhatter

(Vocals, 1932–72)

McPhatter was among the first singers to make the transition from gospel singer to R&B and pop star, and his emotional singing set the stage for vocalists like Jackie Wilson and Smokey Robinson. McPhatter started out with Billy Ward's Dominoes, and left in 1953 to form and lead The Drifters. His Drifters hits included 'Money Honey' and 'Honey Love'. During a successful solo career, he recorded his biggest hit, 'A Lover's Question'.

Amos Milburn

(Piano, vocals, 1927–80)

Milburn was a Houston pianist whose rollicking piano-playing and versatile singing was a major influence on Fats Domino and others. Milburn's first hit was the 1948 party classic 'Chicken Shack Boogie'. Milburn could croon a soulful ballad, but made a bigger impact with horn-driven material such as 'Roomin' House Boogie' and 'Sax Shack Boogie', along with several songs about liquor like 'Thinking And Drinking' and the much-covered 'One Scotch, One Bourbon, One Beer'.

see Chuck Berry pp 38   see Bill Haley pp 48   see Fats Domino pp 61   see Jerry Lee Lewis pp 66

Muddy Waters

(Guitar, vocals, 1915–83)

Born McKinley Morgenfield in Mississippi, Muddy Waters was first recorded by musicologist Alan Lomax. Waters' first recording for Lomax, 'I Be's Troubled', would become his first hit when he recorded it in Chicago as 'I Can't Be Satisfied' (1948). By 1951, Waters was on the R&B charts consistently with tunes like 'Louisiana Blues', and 'Long Distance Call'.

In 1952, he created the smash 'She Moves Me', and later came 'I'm Your Hoochie Coochie Man' and 'I'm Ready'. Bo Diddley borrowed a Waters beat for 'I'm a Man' in 1955, and then Waters reworked the idea into 'Mannish Boy'. In 1956, Waters had three more R&B smashes, but as rock'n'roll developed he became a blues elder statesman to followers like The Rolling Stones (named after a Waters tune) Johnny Winter and Eric Clapton. Waters continued performing to acclaim and releasing albums to mixed results into the 1980s.

The Orioles

(Vocal group, 1948–54)

The Orioles were one of the first R&B vocal groups. Led by vocalist Sonny Til, the Baltimore-based group hit No. 1 in 1948 with 'It's Too Soon To Know', and followed it up with the Top 10 'Lonely Christmas' and 'Tell Me So', their second No. 1. In 1950, a car accident would kill guitarist Tommy Gaither and injure singers George Nelson and Johnny Reed, but the group would return with hits like 'Baby Please Don't Go', and 'Crying In The Chapel', later covered by Elvis. Til would continue to perform and record with various line-ups until his death in 1981.

Les Paul

(Guitar, b. 1915)

At 13 Lester Polfus was playing country music semi-professionally and working on sound-related inventions. In the 1930s and 1940s, he worked his way from Wisconsin to New York, eventually playing for blues shouter Georgia White and bandleader Fred Waring before settling in Hollywood and working with Bing Crosby and others. Paul also developed ideas for an electric guitar design and new recording techniques like multi-tracking.

see Introduction pp 12   *see* Sources & Sounds pp 14

Paul's interests converged when with his wife, singer Colleen Summers, whom Paul renamed Mary Ford, he recorded several albums of standards such as 'How High The Moon' and 'Vaya Con Dios'. Both became No. 1 hits and spotlighted Paul's pioneering use of overdubbing, which created a futuristic sound nicely modulated by Ford's voice. Les Paul's namesake guitar would become synonymous with rock, and Paul would continue performing into his 90s, achieving iconic status for his contributions to the music world.

The Penguins
(Vocal group, 1954–59)
The Penguins were an early West Coast doo-wop group formed in 1954, when the group's members were all attending Fremont High School in Los Angeles. Tenor Curtis Williams created the song 'Earth Angel' with two other vocalists. The song, which was going to be a B-side, became a national hit, spending three weeks at the top of the R&B charts and reaching No. 8 on the pop charts. The Penguins could not sustain their success and disbanded in 1959.

Lloyd Price
(Vocals, b. 1933)
Growing up outside New Orleans, Lloyd Price was exposed to music through the jukebox in his mother's fish-fry joint. At 18, the crossover-ready performer recorded a version of 'Lawdy Miss Clawdy' that became a runaway hit and spawned a slew of successful follow-ups. Price's 'Stagger Lee' topped both the R&B and pop lists in 1958. In 1959, his 'Personality' was an unapologetic pop success. Price was an able businessman and turned away from performing in the 1970s.

Professor Longhair
(Piano, 1918–80)
A New Orleans native, Roy Byrd brought an irresistible Caribbean feel to his piano-playing. The shaggy-haired Byrd got the nickname Professor Longhair from a club owner in 1948. Longhair first recorded his signature 'Mardi Gras In New Orleans' in 1949, the national R&B hit 'Bald Head' in 1950, and 'Tipitina' in 1953. Longhair endured tough times in the 1960s but enjoyed a resurgence in the 1970s. His work influenced Fats Domino, Allen Toussaint and many others.

Above
Professor Longhair, or 'the Bach of Rock and Roll', performing at the Newport Jazz Festival in 1973.

Far Left
Muddy Waters had an illustrious career, and was an inspiration to countless musicians from every genre.

🎸 *see* Bo Diddley pp 20 🎸 *see* Cream pp 92 🎸 *see* The Rolling Stones pp 96 🎸 *see* Johnny Winter pp 151

Johnnie Ray

(Vocals, 1927–90)

Johnnie Ray's emotional delivery made him stand out in a crowd of early 1950s crooners, especially among young girls. The Oregon native was signed to Columbia's R&B subsidiary Okeh Records. But his big hit, 'Cry', a million-seller that featured a typically overwrought performance and background vocals by The Four Lads, had little to do with R&B.

Although Ray's reign as an object of teen-girl obsession was short-lived, his style set the stage for over-the-top singers to come.

Jimmie Rodgers

(Vocals, 1897–1933)

Jimmie Rodgers, 'The Singing Brakeman', struggled against poor health and the rigours of the road to forge a new American folk music that would influence country music for generations. Rodgers wrote songs like 'T.B. Blues', 'Travelin' Blues', 'Train Whistle Blues' and his 13 'blue yodels'. Rodgers' voice and inherent honesty attracted legions of listeners.

Rodgers developed his guitar-playing and lyrics during 10 years working on southern and western railroads. Despite a diagnosis of tuberculosis in 1924, he alternated railroad jobs with music work. When he was signed to RCA his 'Blue Yodel' became a major hit, followed by 'Way Out On The Mountain', 'Blue Yodel No. 4' and 'In The Jailhouse Now'. The financial rewards from the work were short-lived, however, and during the Depression Rodgers' T.B. overcame him. He died of a lung haemorrhage in 1933. Rogers was the first artist inducted into The Country Music Hall Of Fame.

Bessie Smith

(Vocals, 1894–1937)

Bessie Smith was the first blues recording star during the form's initial heyday in the 'jazz age' of the 1920s. A protégé of the great Ma Rainey, Smith and her booming, sorrowful voice took the East Coast by storm in stage shows in the 1920s. Signed to Columbia Records, she scored with 'Downhearted Blues', 'Nobody Knows You When You're Down And Out' and others. Smith died in a car accident in Mississippi in 1937.

Hank Snow

(Vocals, 1914–99)

Hank Snow ran away from his Canadian home at 12 to join the Merchant Marine. Wanderlust would inform his great 'travelling' songs, 'I'm Movin' On' and 'I've Been Everywhere'. A disciple of Jimmie Rodgers, Snow would bill himself as the Yodelling Ranger, until his developing baritone made him better suited for ballads like 'Hello Love', a hit when Snow was 60. Snow's songs about the road would influence Johnny Cash and Willie Nelson.

Below

Johnnie Ray had an over-the-top, emotional performance style that was later associated with rock'n'roll.

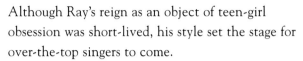 *see* Introduction pp 12 *see* Sources & Sounds pp 14

Big Mama Thornton

(Vocals, 1926–84)

Willie Mae 'Big Mama' Thornton had a big, no-nonsense voice perfect for the blues, yet she was able to manage only one big R&B hit with a song that soon became associated with Elvis Presley, leaving her original version in the dust. Thornton's recording of 'Hound Dog' topped *Billboard's* R&B chart for seven weeks in 1953. Thornton would record and perform into the 1970s, but never achieve similar success.

Big Joe Turner

(Vocals, 1911–85)

Big Joe Turner's tenure as 'Boss of the Blues' is dominated by one song, 'Shake, Rattle And Roll', which became an early rock'n'roll anthem as recorded by white artists Bill Haley and Elvis Presley. But Turner's long career and legacy of R&B hits includes boogies like 'Roll 'Em Pete', the seminal blues of 'Cherry Red', and rollicking ribald romps like 'My Gal's A Jockey' and 'Battle Of The Blues' a duet with Wynonie Harris.

Above

Although his musical career lasted only six years, the 113 songs Jimmie Rodgers recorded have hardly ever been out of print.

see Bill Haley pp 48   *see* Elvis Presley pp 52   *see* Johnny Cash pp 59   *see* Janis Joplin pp 142

T-Bone Walker
(Guitar, vocals, 1910–75)

Dallas-bred Aaron Walker was soloing on electric guitar as early as 1940, setting a trend that would eventually be the most commonplace image in rock music. B.B. King marvelled at Walker's ability to play while holding the guitar away from his body. Walker left Texas in the 1930s and alternated between sessions and performances in Los Angeles, Chicago and, later, Europe as he advanced the instrumental appeal of blues.

Walker's peak years were the 1940s and 1950s. He found work in LA as a dancer and singer, and used both skills in his own shows when he formed his own group. Working for multiple labels like Capitol, Black & White, Imperial and Atlantic, T-Bone wowed fans with potent jams like 'Mean Old World', 'T-Bone Shuffle', 'Strollin' With Bones' and the immortal 'Stormy Monday'. Late in life Walker won a Grammy for 'Good Feelin'', a 1970 LP.

Dinah Washington
(Vocals, 1924–63)

Dinah Washington influenced countless R&B and jazz singers, including Nancy Wilson and Esther Phillips. Born Ruth Lee Jones, the young singer moved quickly from her gospel roots to become a pro pianist, big band singer with Lionel Hampton and jazz and blues solo artist. After Washington's 'What A Diff'rence A Day Makes' became a major national hit, she stuck with a formula of orchestrated pop. An accidental overdose killed her at 39.

Hank Williams
(Singer/songwriter, 1923–53)

Insofar as rock has been shaped by country music, it has been shaped by Hank Williams. Williams, a superstar at 25 and dead at 29, set standards for popular as well as country music, and was a virtual hit songwriting machine. Yet, like several young rock stars who followed him, he was unable to manage stardom and drifted into alcoholism and addiction.

Williams started out performing around his native Alabama. He landed a spot on a local radio station, and was signed to MGM Records by 1947. By 1951 his songs were being covered by the biggest mainstream artists, and Hank was appearing with them on stage and television to sing hits like 'Your Cheatin' Heart', 'Cold Cold Heart', 'Jambalaya' and 'Hey Good Lookin''. But his life and career collapsed after his divorce from his manager/wife Audrey, and he died in the back of his car on New Year's Eve, 1952.

Above
Hank Williams' songs form the mainstay of country music, and have been covered by rock and pop artists.

see B.B. King pp 65   see The Animals pp 102   see The Yardbirds pp 117   see Bob Dylan pp 126

Sonny Boy Williamson

(Harmonica, vocals, 1899–1965)

The career of Mississippi's Sonny Boy Williamson
began as a case of identity theft. A 1930s delta
bluesman named 'Rice' Miller had landed a starring
spot on the blues radio show *King Biscuit Time*. The
sponsor had Miller pose as Chicago harmonica star
John Lee 'Sonny Boy' Williamson. The deception
worked in rural America, and, when John Lee was
murdered in 1948, Miller declared himself 'the
original Sonny Boy'.

Sonny Boy II had his own vocal and harp style
and would prove himself one of the greatest bluesmen of
all. The sides he cut for Trumpet and Chess in the 1950s
showcase him at full power on signature songs like
'Eyesight To The Blind', 'Don't Start Me To Talkin'' and
'Help Me'. The early 1960s folk revival and exposure in
Europe made Williamson a star there and a big influence
on The Yardbirds and The Animals. Williamson always
returned, however, to the *King Biscuit* show.

Bob Wills

(Bandleader, fiddle, 1905–75)

Between 1929 and 1931 Bob Wills assembled his first
western-swing band, The Light Crust Doughboys, later
rechristened The Texas Playboys. By 1940, with its hit
single 'New San Antonio Rose', it was filling concert
halls across the country. The band's biggest hit, 'New
Spanish Two Step', spent 16 weeks at No. 1. The hit
'Faded Love' became a standard. Wills bucked traditions
to fuse two genres and create one of the most popular
bands in America.

List of Artists

Entries appear in the following order: name, music style, year(s) of popularity, type of artist, country of origin

Abshire, Nathan, Chicago Blues, 1940s-1980s, Artist, American
Acuff, Roy, Honky Tonk, 1930s-1960s, Artist, American
Almanac Singers, Traditional Folk; Political Folk & Protest Songs, 1940s, Artist, American
Ammons, Albert, Boogie-Woogie, 1920s-1940s, Artist, American
Ammons, Gene, Bebop; Hard Bop, 1940s-1970s, Artist, American
Anderson, Ernestine, Northern Soul, 1940s-, Artist, American
Arnold, Eddy, The Nashville Sound; Cowboy Music; Honky Tonk, 1940s-1990s, Artist, American
Arnold, Kokomo, Chicago Blues, 1930s-1940s, Artist, American
Atkins, Chet, The Nashville Sound, 1940s-1990s, Artist, American
Babbitt, Milton, Electro, 1940s-1990s, Artist, American
Baker, Edythe, Boogie-Woogie, 1920s, Artist, American
Bartholomew, Dave, Rhythm & Blues, 1940s-1990s, Artist; Songwriter, American
Basie, Count, Boogie-Woogie, 1920s-1980s, Artist, American
Bellson, Louie, Swing; Bebop, 1940s-1990s, Artist, American
Big Maybelle, Piedmont Blues; Jump Blues; Rhythm & Blues, 1940s-1960s, Artist, American
Big Three Trio, The, Chicago Blues, 1940s-1950s, Artist, American
Blackwell, Scrapper, Chicago Blues, 1920s-1930s; 1950s-1960s, Artist, American
Blakey, Art, Hard Bop, 1940s-1990s, Artist, American
Bond, Johnny, Country Rock, 1940s-1970s, Artist, American
Boogie-Woogie Red, Boogie-Woogie, 1940s-1970s, Artist, American
Bostic, Earl, Rhythm & Blues, 1930s-1960s, Artist, American
Boyd, Eddie, Chicago Blues, 1940s-1980s, Artist; Songwriter, American
Bradshaw, Tiny, Jump Blues; Rhythm & Blues, 1930s-1950s, Artist, American
Brenston, Jackie, Jump Blues; Rhythm & Blues, 1940s-1960s, Artist, American
Brooks, Hadda, Boogie-Woogie, 1940s-1960s, Artist, American
Broonzy, Big Bill, Delta/Country Blues; Chicago Blues, 1920s-1950s, Artist, American
Brown, Lee, Piedmont Blues; Boogie-Woogie, 1930s-1940s, Artist, American
Brown, Ray, Bebop, 1940s-, Artist, American
Brown, Ruth, Jump Blues; Rhythm & Blues; The Classic Soul Era; 1940s-1960s; 1980s-1990s, Artist, American
Bruner, Cliff, Honky Tonk; Western Swing, 1930s-1940s, Artist, American
Bryant, Felice, The Nashville Sound, 1940s-1950s, Songwriter; Composer, American
Bryany, Boudleaux, Country Rock; 1950s Pop, Rock'n'Roll, 1940s-1970s, Artist; Songwriter, American
Byas, Don, Swing; Bebop, 1930s-1970s, Artist, American
Cage, John, Electro, 1930s-1990s, Composer, American
Callender, Red, Cool Jazz; Swing; Bebop, 1940s-1980s, Artist, American
Candoli, Conte, Cool Jazz; Bebop, 1940s-1990s, Artist, American
Carr, Leroy, Boogie-Woogie, 1920s-1930s, Artist; Songwriter, American
Carter Family, The, Early & Old-Time Country, 1920s-1960s, Artist, American
Charles, Ray, Rhythm & Blues; The Classic Soul Era 1940s-1980s, Artist, American
Christian, Charlie, Swing; Bebop, 1930s-1940s, Artist, American
Clarke, Kenny, Bebop, 1940s-1980s, Artist, American
Clovers, The, Doo-Wop; Rhythm & Blues, 1940s-1950s, Artist, American
Cohn, Al, Bebop; Cool Jazz, 1940s-1980s, Artist, American
Cole, Nat King, Swing, 1930s-1960s, Artist, American
Colyer, Ken, Skiffle; New Orleans Jazz, 1940s-1980s, Artist, British
Cooke, Sam, Rhythm & Blues; The Classic Soul Era, 1940s-1960s, Artist, American
Cooper, Bob, Cool Jazz; Hard Bop, 1940s-1990s, Artist, American
Copas, Cowboy, Honky Tonk, 1940s-1960s, Artist, American
Counce, Curtis, Hard Bop, 1940s-1960s, Artist, American
Criss, Sonny, Hard Bop, 1940s-1970s, Artist, American
Crudup, Arthur 'Big Boy', Delta/Country Blues; Rhythm & Blues, 1940s-1970s, Artist, American
Dameron, Tadd, Bebop, 1940s-1960s, Composer; Songwriter; Artist, American
Davenport, Charles 'Cow Cow', Boogie-Woogie, 1920s-1950s, Artist, American
Davis, Blind John, Boogie-Woogie, 1930s-1950s, Artist, American
Davis, Eddie 'Lockjaw', Bebop; Hard Bop, 1940s-1980s, Artist, American
Davis, James, Modern Electric Blues, 1930s-1980s, Artist, American
Davis, Miles, Bebop; Hard Bop; Cool Jazz; Jazz Rock; Fusion, 1940s-1990s, Artist; Composer, American
DeFranco, Buddy, Bebop, 1940s-1990s, Artist, American
Delmore Brothers, The, Honky Tonk; Early & Old-Time Country, 1930s-1950s, Artist, American
Dixon, Floyd, Jump Blues; Rhythm & Blues, 1940s-1970s; 1990s, Artist, American
Dixon, Willie, Jump Blues; Chicago Blues, 1940s-1990s, Artist; Songwriter; Producer, American
Domino, Fats, Rock'n'Roll; Louisiana Blues; Rhythm & Blues, 1940s-1990s, Artist, American
Donegan, Dorothy, Boogie-Woogie, 1940s-1990s, Artist, American
Dorham, Kenny, Hard Bop, 1940s-1970s, Artist, American
Dorough, Bob, Cool Jazz; Bebop; Swing, 1940s-, Artist, American
Dupree, Champion Jack, Louisiana Blues; Rhythm & Blues, 1940s-1990s, Artist, American
Duskin, Big Joe, Boogie-Woogie, 1940s-1980s, Artist, American
Eckstine, Billy, Bebop, 1940s-1980s, Artist, American
Edwards, Honeyboy, Modern Electric Blues, 1940s-, Artist, American
Edwards, Teddy, Bebop; Hard Bop, 1940s-, Artist, American
Ellis, Herb, Swing; Bebop, 1940s-1990s, Artist, American
Ennis, Seamus, Irish Folk, 1930s-1980s, Artist, Irish
Evans, Gil, Cool Jazz; Fusion, 1940s-1980s, Artist, Canadian
Fitzgerald, Ella, Swing; Bebop, 1930s-1990s, Artist, American
Flanagan, Tommy, Bebop; Hard Bop, 1940s-1990s, Artist, American
Foley, Red, Honky Tonk; Bluegrass, 1940s-1960s, Artist, American
Forest City Joe, Chicago Blues, 1940s-1950s, Artist, American
Freeman, Russ, Cool Jazz; Bebop, 1940s-1980s, Artist, American
Gant, Cecil, Jump Blues; Rhythm & Blues, 1940s-1950s, Artist, American
Garner, Erroll, Bebop; Swing, 1940s-1970s, Artist, American
Getz, Stan, Cool Jazz; Hard Bop, 1940s-1990s, Artist, American
Gillespie, Dizzy, Bebop, 1930s-1990s, Artist, American
Giuffre, Jimmy, Bebop; Cool Jazz, 1940s-, Artist, American
Gordon, Dexter, Bebop; Hard Bop, 1940s-1980s, Artist, American
Granz, Norman, Bebop, 1940s-1990s, Artist, American
Gray, Wardell, Bebop; Swing, 1940s-1950s, Artist, American
Green, Bunky, Hard Bop, 1940s-1980s, Artist, American
Grey, Al, Bebop; Swing, 1940s-1990s, Artist, American
Griffin, Johnny, Bebop; Hard Bop, 1940s-, Artist, American
Grimes, Tiny, Bebop, 1940s-1970s, Artist, American
Guthrie, Woody, Traditional Folk; Political Folk & Protest Songs, 1930s-1960s, Artist, American
Haig, Al, Bebop, 1940s-1980s, Artist, American
Hampton, Lionel, Jump Blues; Swing, 1920s-1990s, Artist, American
Handy, W.C., Delta/Country Blues, 1900s-1920s, Songwriter; Artist, American
Harewood, Al, Bebop, 1940s-1960s, Artist, American
Harris, Wynonie, Jump Blues; Rhythm & Blues, 1940s-1960s, Artist, American
Harrison, Lou, Fusion and Jazz Rock, 1940s-1990s, Artist, American
Hawkins, Coleman, Swing; Bebop, 1920s-1960s, Artist, American
Hawkins, Roy, Jump Blues; Rhythm & Blues, 1940s-1950s, Artist, American
Haynes, Roy, Bebop; Hard Bop, 1940s-, Artist, American
Heard, J. C. , Swing; Bebop, 1940s-1980s, Artist, American
Heath, Albert 'Tootie', Hard Bop, 1940s-1990s, Artist, American
Heath, Jimmy, Hard Bop, 1940s-1990s, Artist, American
Heath, Percy, Bebop; Hard Bop; Cool Jazz, 1940s-1990s, Artist, American
Hendricks, Jon, Bebop, 1940s-, Artist, American
Holiday, Billie, Piedmont Blues; Rhythm & Blues, 1930s-1950s, Artist, American
Hollywood Flames, Doo-Wop, 1940s-1960s, Artist, American
Hooker, John Lee, Chicago Blues, 1940s-1990s, Artist; Songwriter, American
Hope, Elmo, Hard Bop; Bebop, 1940s-1960s, Artist; Composer, American
Hope, Stan, Hard Bop, 1940s-1990s, Artist, American
Horton, Big Walter 'Shakey', Chicago Blues, 1940s-1980s, Artist, American
Howlin' Wolf, Chicago Blues, 1930s-1970s, Artist, American
Hunter, Alberta, Rhythm & Blues, 1920s-1980s, Artist, American
Ink Spots, The Classic Soul Era, 1930s-1960s, Artist, American
Ives, Burl, Traditional Folk; Folk Pop, 1940s-1960s, Artist, American
Jackson, Bull Moose, Jump Blues; Rhythm & Blues, 1940s-1950s, Artist, American
Jackson, Milt, Bebop; Hard Bop, 1940s-1990s, Artist, American
Jackson, Willis 'Gator', Soul Jazz; Hard Bop, 1940s-1980s, Artist, American
Jacquet, Illinois, Swing; Bebop, 1940s-1990s, Artist, American
Jazz at the Philharmonic, Swing; Bebop, 1940s-1980s, Artist, American
Johnson, Budd, Swing; Bebop, 1930s-1980s, Artist, American
Johnson, Buddy, Jump Blues; Rhythm & Blues, 1930s-1960s, Artist; Songwriter, American
Johnson, Ella, Piedmont Blues; Jump Blues; Rhythm & Blues, 1940s-1950s, Artist, American
Johnson, J. J., Bebop; Hard Bop, 1940s-1990s, Artist, American
Johnson, Pete, Boogie-Woogie, 1920s-1960s, Artist, American
Johnson, Robert, Delta/Country Blues, 1930s, Artist; Songwriter, American
Jones, Little Johnny, Chicago Blues; Boogie-Woogie, 1940s-1960s, Artist, American
Jordan, Duke, Bebop; Hard Bop, 1940s-1990s, Artist, American
Jordan, Louis, Jump Blues; Swing, 1930s-1970s, Artist, American
Jordanaires, The, The Nashville Sound, 1940s-, Artist, American
Kessel, Barney, Bebop; Cool Jazz, 1940s-, Artist, American
King, B.B., Modern Electric Blues; Rhythm & Blues, 1940s-, Artist, American
Lara, Agustin, Latin, 1920s-1960s, Artist, Mexican
Lecuona, Ernesto, Latin, 1920s-1960s, Artist, Cuban
Levy, Lou, Cool Jazz; Bebop, 1940s-1990s, Artist, American
Lewis, John, Bebop; Cool Jazz, 1940s-, Artist, American
Lewis, Meade 'Lux', Boogie-Woogie, 1930s-1960s, Artist, American
Lewis, Mel, Bebop, 1940s-1980s, Artist, American
Liggins, Jimmy, Jump Blues; Rhythm & Blues, 1940s-1950s, Artist, American
Liggins, Joe, Jump Blues; Rhythm & Blues, 1940s-1950s, Artist, American
Little Walter, Chicago Blues, 1940s-1960s, Artist; Songwriter, American
Littlefield, Little Willie, Jump Blues; Boogie-Woogie; Rhythm & Blues, 1940s-1990s, Artist, American
Locklin, Hank, The Nashville Sound, Honky Tonk, 1940s-1970s, Artist, American
Lockwood, Robert Jr., Delta/Country Blues; Chicago Blues, 1930s-, Artist, American
Lutcher, Joe, Rhythm & Blues, 1940s-1950s, Artist, American
Manne, Shelley, Bebop; Cool Jazz, 1940s-1980s, Artist, American
Maphis, Joe, Honky Tonk, 1940s-1980s, Artist, American
Marmarosa, Dodo, Bebop, 1940s-1960s, Artist, American
Mayfield, Percy, Jump Blues; Rhythm & Blues, 1940s-1970s, Artist, American
McGhee, Howard, Bebop; Hard Bop, 1940s-1980s, Artist, American
McKibbon, Al, Bebop; Hard Bop, 1940s-1990s, Artist, American
McNeely, Big Jay, Jump Blues, Rhythm & Blues, 1940s-1990s, Artist, American
Meade, Donna, Honky Tonk, 1920s, Artist, American
Memphis Minnie, Delta/Country Blues; Chicago Blues, 1920s-1950s, Artist, American
Memphis Slim, Boogie-Woogie, 1930s-1980s, Artist, American
Merriweather, Big Maceo, Chicago Blues, 1930s-1950s, Artist, American
Milburn, Amos, Jump Blues; Rhythm & Blues, 1940s-1960s, Artist, American
Milton, Roy, Jump Blues; Rhythm & Blues, 1940s-1980s, Artist, American
Mingus, Charles, Bebop; Hard Bop, 1940s-1970s, Artist; Composer, American
Monk, Thelonious, Bebop; Modal Jazz; Hard Bop, 1940s-1970s, Artist, American
Montgomery, Little Brother, Boogie-Woogie, 1930s-1970s, Artist, American
Montgomery, Wes, Hard Bop, 1940s-1960s, Artist, American
Moody, James, Bebop; Hard Bop, 1940s-, Artist, American
Moon Mullican; Honky Tonk; Western Swing, 1940s-1960s, Artist, American
Muddy Waters; Delta/Country Blues; Chicago Blues, 1940s-1980s, Artist, American
Navarro, Fats, Bebop, 1940s-1950s, Artist, American
Nighthawk, Robert, Chicago Blues, 1930s-1960s, Artist, American
Nix, Willie, Chicago Blues, 1940s-1970s, Artist, American
O'Day, Anita, Swing; Bebop, 1940s-1990s, Artist, American
O'Farrill, Chico, Latin Jazz; Bebop, 1940s-1970s, Artist, Cuban
Orioles, The, Doo-Wop; Rhythm & Blues, 1940s-1960s, Artist, American
Otis, Johnny, Jump Blues; Rhythm & Blues; The Classic Soul Era, 1940s-1990s, Artist, American
Partch, Harry, Fusion and Jazz Rock, 1920s-1970s, Artist, American
Paul, Les, 1950s Pop; Swing; Blues Rock; Hard Rock, 1930s-1960s; 1970s; 1980s, Artist, American
Pepper, Art, Bebop; Hard Bop; Cool Jazz, 1940s-1980s, Artist, American
Perkins, Pinetop, Boogie-Woogie; Chicago Blues, 1940s-, Artist, American
Peterson, Oscar, Swing; Bebop, 1940s-, Artist, Canadian
Pettiford, Oscar, Bebop, 1940s-1950s, Artist, American
Pomus, Doc, 1960s Pop, 1940s-1960s, Artist, American
Potter, Tommy, Bebop, 1940s-1950s, Artist, American
Powell, Bud, Bebop, 1940s-1960s, Artist; Composer, American
Previn, André, Cool Jazz; Bebop, 1940s-, Artist, French
Price, Sammy, Boogie-Woogie; Jump Blues, 1920s-1980s, Artist, American
Prima, Louis, Jump Blues, Rhythm & Blues, 1930s-1970s, Artist, American
Professor Longhair, Louisiana Blues; The Classic Soul Era, 1940s-1980s, Artist; Songwriter, American
Pryor, Snooky, Chicago Blues, 1940s-1990s, Artist, American
Quebec, Ike, Hard Bop; Soul Jazz; Swing, 1940s-1960s, Artist, American
Raeburn, Boyd, Bebop, 1940s-1950s, Artist, American
Ravens, The, Doo-Wop; Rhythm & Blues, 1940s-1950s, Artist, American
Red Rodney, Bebop; Hard Bop, 1940s-1990s, Artist, American
Rich, Buddy, Bebop; Swing, 1940s-1980s, Artist, American
Roach, Max, Bebop; Hard Bop, 1940s-1990s, Artist, American
Robins, The, Doo-Wop; Rhythm & Blues, 1940s-1950s, Artist, American
Rodgers, Jimmy, Early & Old-Time Country, 1920s-1930s, Artist; Songwriter, American
Roland, Walter, Boogie-Woogie; Delta/Country Blues, 1930s, Artist, American
Rollins, Sonny, Bebop; Hard Bop, 1940s-, Artist; Composer, American
Rouse, Charlie, Hard Bop, 1940s-1980s, Artist, American
Royal, Ernie, Bebop; Swing, 1940s-1980s, Artist, American
Russell, Curly, Bebop, 1940s-1950s, Artist, American
Scott, Raymond, Electro, 1930s-1980s, Artist; Composer, American
Seeger, Pete, Traditional Folk; Folk Songs; Political Folk & Protest Songs; The Folk Revival, 1940s-, Artist, American
Shaw, Robert, Boogie-Woogie, 1930s; 1960s-1980s, Artist, American
Shearing, George, Cool Jazz; Bebop, 1930s-1990s, Artist, British
Sims, Zoot, Bebop; Cool Jazz, 1940s-1980s, Artist, American
Slack, Freddie, Boogie-Woogie, 1940s-1950s, Artist, American
Smith, Bessie, Delta/Country Blues; New Orleans Jazz, 1920s-1930s, Artist, American
Smith, Clarence 'Pine Top', Boogie-Woogie, 1920s, Artist, American
Smith, George 'Harmonica', Modern Electric Blues, 1940s-1980s, Artist, American
Smith, Jabbo, Bebop, 1920s-1970s, Artist, American
Snow, Hank, Honky Tonk; Cowboy Music, 1930s-1980s, Artist, Canadian
Solis, Javier, Latin, 1940s-1960s, Artist, Mexican
Speckled Red, Boogie-Woogie, 1920s-1930s, Artist, American
Stitt, Sonny, Bebop, 1940s-1980s, Artist, American
Sykes, Roosevelt, Chicago Blues, 1920s-1980s, Artist, American
Tampa Red, Chicago Blues, 1920s-1960s, Artist, American
Taylor, Billy, Bebop; Hard Bop; Swing, 1940s-, Artist, American
Temple, Johnnie 'Geechie', Delta/Country Blues; Chicago Blues, 1930s-1950s, Artist, American
Thompson, Hank, Honky Tonk; Western Swing, 1940s-1990s, Artist, American
Thompson, Lucky, Bebop; Hard Bop, 1940s-1970s, Artist, American
Thornton, Big Momma, Rhythm & Blues, 1940s-1970s, Artist, American
Tillman, Floyd, Honky Tonk, 1940s-1970s, Artist, American
Tormé, Mel, Swing; Bebop, 1940s-1990s, Artist, American
Treniers, The, Jump Blues; Rhythm & Blues, 1940s-1980s, Artist, American
Tristano, Lennie, Cool Jazz; Bebop, 1940s-1960s, Artist, American
Tubb, Ernest, Honky Tonk, 1930s-1980s, Artist, American
Turner, Big Joe, Rock'n'Roll; Jump Blues; Rhythm & Blues; Swing, 1930s-1980s, Artist, American
Turner, Zeb, Boogie-Woogie, 1940s-1950s, Artist, American
Varese, Edgar, Electro, 1920s-1960s, Composer, French
Vaughan, Sarah, Bebop; Cool Jazz, 1940s-1980s, Artist, American
Vinson, Eddie 'Cleanhead', Jump Blues; Rhythm & Blues; Bebop, 1940s-1980s, Artist, American
Walker, Billy, Western Swing; Honky Tonk, 1940s-1990s, Artist, American
Walker, T-Bone, Texas Blues, 1920s-1970s, Artist; Songwriter; American
Wallington, George, Bebop, 1940s-1960s, Artist, American
Weavers, The, Traditional Folk; Political Folk & Protest Songs; The Folk Revival, 1940s-1960s, Artist, American
Wells, Kitty, The Nashville Sound; Honky Tonk, 1940s-1980s, Artist, American
Wess, Frank, Swing; Cool Jazz; Bebop, 1940s-, Artist, American
White, Josh, Political Folk & Protest Songs, 1920s-1960s, Artist, American
Whitman, Slim, Folk Pop, 1940s-1980s, Artist, American
Williams, Hank, Honky Tonk, 1940s-1950s, Artist, American
Williams, Lester, Rhythm & Blues, 1940s-1950s, Artist, American
Williams, Mary Lou, Swing; Bebop, 1920s-1970s, Artist; Composer, American
Williamson, Homesick James, Chicago Blues, 1930s-1990s, Artist, American
Williamson, Sonny Boy (I), Delta/Country Blues, 1930s-1940s, Artist, American
Williamson, Sonny Boy (II), Chicago Blues, 1930s-1960s, Artist; Songwriter, American
Wills, Bob, Western Swing, 1930s-1970s, Artist; Songwriter. American
Wilson, Gerald, Swing; Bebop, 1940s-1990s, Artist; Composer, American
Winding, Kai, Bebop, 1940s-1970s, Artist, American
Yancey, Jimmy, Boogie Woogie, 1930s-1950s, Artist, American

see John Lee Hooker pp 19 *see* Muddy Waters pp 22 *see* Bessie Smith pp 26 *see* Hank Williams pp 29

THE FIFTIES

The 1950s was the decade when the straitjacket imposed by the recent world war was loosened a little – and rock took full advantage. The Sun studios in Memphis and Chess Records in Chicago were the places to be as the likes of Elvis, Jerry Lee Lewis and Chuck Berry turned the existing generation gap into a chasm.

Though he did not always appear in vision, Bill Haley reaped the rewards as rock helped Hollywood bring in the younger generation – even if a few seats were slashed in the process. Television, which by the end of the decade would be well established, offered another medium by which to reach willing youth and scandalize their parents. Elvis was initially cut off at the waist by over-zealous cameramen, but the power to shock remained.

While the music publishers of Tin Pan Alley had controlled the writing and recording of music, teenage subjects were addressed in lyrics for the first time by rock's new songwriters. Chuck Berry's songs of romance, frustration and homework appealed to white and black, male and female alike, while the Brill Building turned out similar quality pop from the pens of Neil Sedaka, Carole King and others.

Britain began its rock'n'roll odyssey via skiffle, using acoustic and/or home-made instruments. Paul McCartney and John Lennon were among the followers of skiffle king Lonnie Donegan. The electric guitar was still a rarity, but when Brian Rankin got hold of a real Fender Stratocaster from the States he was on his way to becoming Britain's first guitar hero, fronting The Shadows as Hank B. Marvin.

Sources & Sounds

34

KEY ARTISTS

Chuck Berry

Ray Charles

Lonnie Donegan

The Everly Brothers

Bill Haley

Buddy Holly

Elvis Presley

Right and Below
Dancing, drinking and flirting in dance halls and bars, the youth of the 1950s started to strike out from the austerity of their parents' generation and were determined to have a good time.

'Let's face it – rock'n'roll is bigger than all of us.'
Alan Freed

The 1950s was the decade when rock'n'roll crossed the globe like a tidal wave. The music first hit Britain, where it inspired an enthusiastic reaction, then the rest of the world. And if the language in which it was sung was universally English, the combination of minimal lyrics and driving beat swiftly made rock'n'roll universally acceptable.

Shock Around The Clock

To the world's youth, that is. The powers that be immediately smelt trouble: Indonesia and Argentina were quick to ban the new music in 1957, while South Africa's regime employed troops with tear gas to stop rock fans rioting. The fact the music had emerged from black roots was, doubtless, coincidental.

Germany proved a fertile breeding ground for rock. The nation that lost the Second World War was now occupied by American forces, and their tastes would help make the former Fatherland an early convert to the rock cause. Though Elvis Presley's arrival in the country on national service was in a strictly non-singing capacity, the less inhibited Little Richard was one of many regular Stateside visitors. And it would not be long before The Beatles would use the clubs of Hamburg to work up their world-beating stage act.

see Introduction pp 32 *see Key Artists pp 38* *see A–Z of Artists pp 56* *see List of Artists pp 74*

Sun-Rise

But it was the Sun Records' studio in Memphis, Tennessee, that had been the real launch-pad for rock. Even though label founder Sam Phillips sold Elvis Presley's contract to RCA Victor to ease crippling debts and stave off the immediate danger of bankruptcy, he knew even then that he had other irons in the fire – namely pianist Jerry Lee Lewis, Carl Perkins and Johnny Cash, all of whom would enjoy long and influential careers.

Bill Haley smudged the boundaries of the colour bar, playing country with a blues beat and covering blues songs with a down-home twang. But when it came to versatility Ray Charles was hard to beat. Bringing churchy call and response vocals to popular music, he would eventually veer off into country and western, proving that no material was off limits. Being both blind and black was no barrier to his towering talent … little wonder Stevie Wonder was among those hanging on his every note.

By the end of the 1950s, however, rock'n'roll had inevitably already lost some of its shock value, with impresarios and theatre owners waking up fast to its money-making potential. In the States, Buddy Holly's ill-fated Winter Dance Party tour was drawing sizeable crowds, the 1,500 people at its last port of call, Clear Lake, Iowa, contrasting well with the town's population of 30,000.

The Teen Revolution

While traditional composers had written about romance from an adult viewpoint, teenage emotions were now taking pride of place. Other topics included the twin teenage banes of parents and school, and these caught the ear and imagination of a new generation less inclined to knuckle under to authority as their parents had been.

The previously mentioned Buddy Holly was one of rock's first singer/songwriters, penning his own breathy paeans to teen life, while The Everly Brothers had the writing team of Felice and Boudleaux Bryant to lean on. Don and Phil's charming harmonies were crucial in shaping the 1960s sounds of The Beatles and Hollies, to name just two of many groups.

A series of attractive US male singers emerged to service the new audience, such as Paul Anka, Ricky Nelson and Pat Boone. Television helped promote Nelson as a 'safer' version of Elvis, while Boone, the clean-cut, God-fearing boy-next-door, also starred in

◼ CLASSIC RECORDINGS

1951
Johnny Ray: 'Cry'

1955
Little Richard: 'Tutti Frutti'

1956
Elvis Presley: 'Hound Dog'

1957
The Everly Brothers: 'Wake Up Little Susie'

1958
Chuck Berry: 'Johnny B. Goode'

Left
Dion and The Belmonts, a doo-wop band from the Bronx, had a major hit with 'A Teenager In Love'. They were characteristic of the male groups of the 1950s.

Below
The flamboyant Alan Freed was the first to coin the term rock'n'roll. He championed the vital, vibrant beat of the new sound.

🎸 *see* Carl Perkins pp 68 🎸 *see* The Beatles pp 88 🎸 *see* The Hollies pp 109 🎸 *see* Stevie Wonder pp 162

Above

In the UK, skiffle groups breathed life into local bars with their guitars, tea chests and simple percussion. The home spun feel of the music gave a warmth and vitality to the songs.

several teen-orientated films. Not to be outdone, Connie Francis and Brenda Lee told of romance from a female perspective.

The Rock'n'Roll Gospel

Girl groups would not emerge until the following decade, but there were many doo-wop-influenced male vocal combos already out there like Dion and The Belmonts and Frankie Valli and The Four Seasons. Often drawn from immigrant Italian or Hispanic stock, they made the transition from street-corner harmonizing to the hit parade in style. Their black counterparts like The Drifters and Coasters successfully sanitized rhythm and blues with help from white writers Leiber and Stoller.

see Introduction pp 32   *see* Key Artists pp 38   *see* A–Z of Artists pp 56   *see* List of Artists pp 74

The rock'n'roll gospel was being spread by the likes of DJ Alan Freed, instigator of a number of 'rock exploitation' movies, and Dick Clark whose *American Bandstand* TV show, broadcast nationally from Philadelphia from 1957 onwards, was influential enough to spawn a local 'scene' from which the likes of Frankie Avalon, Fabian and Bobby Rydell sprung. All were fresh-faced Italian-American teen idols with varying degrees of natural talent. Instrumentalist Duane Eddy recorded for Philadelphia's Jamie label, proving influential with his 'twangy guitar'.

Singled Out

The 78-rpm shellac record had been the standard method of sound reproduction until Columbia Records pioneered the 12-inch album, playing at 33 $\frac{1}{3}$-rpm (revolutions per minute), in 1948. RCA offered a competing format, a 45-rpm, seven-inch disc that would come to be known as the single; this went on sale the following year. In order to make up ground on the longer-playing 12-inch, RCA also introduced the 'auto-changer' by which means several singles could be stacked over the turntable and played in succession.

Having been knocked out by Elvis Presley, Britain got off the canvas and mounted a fightback in an attempt to prove that home-grown music could stand on its own two feet. The skiffle boom, led by Lonnie Donegan, established local 'scenes' based around coffee bars. Many of Britain's most successful rock names of the late 1950s and 1960s would start their musical lives in skiffle groups, playing acoustic guitars, tea-chest bass or home-made percussion.

Singing For Britain

Another answer came in the shape of home-grown Elvis 'clones' like Terry Dene, Marty Wilde, Vince Eager and Dickie Pride, whose careers were launched by impresario Larry Parnes. They would enjoy brief fame before the 1960s beat boom swept everything aside.

Cliff Richard was the survivor who proved the rule. Born in Lucknow, India, but raised in Britain, his 'fairy godfather' was Jack Good, a seminal figure in the development of British rock who devised the 6.5 *Special* TV programme, which first aired in 1957. He encouraged Cliff to drop his guitar and shave off his Presley-esque sideburns, suggesting he move in a way the newspapers of the time considered 'depraved'.

A slight curl of the lip proved equally popular with teens, to whom press disapproval made Cliff even more desirable. Good's new TV show, *Oh Boy!*, gave Cliff and backing group The Shadows the exposure they needed, and suddenly, after their debut in late 1958, they were on their way to stardom, courtesy of 'Move It'. But by June 1960, Cliff and The Shadows were residents at the London Palladium in an old-fashioned 'variety show', just as role model Elvis Presley would be neutered by the restrictions and conventions of Hollywood.

Billy Fury, Joe Brown and Johnny Kidd were rare examples of 'credible' British rockers. Fury and Brown (who played lead guitar) combined on 'The Sound Of Fury', a fine if belated example of Britain trying to emulate authentic American rock'n'roll. Kidd had already registered hits like 'Please Don't Touch', and 'Restless' before the single 'Shakin' All Over' hit No. 1 just after the decade ended.

As far as the 1950s went, America held all the aces. But British beat, and The Beatles, would soon attempt to redress the balance.

Above
The US led the way with the rock explosion of the 1950s but there were some notable exceptions, with Johnny Kidd and his band entertaining the UK with hits such as 'Please Don't Touch'.

Above
As the 1950s ended, the dancing became more abandoned as the young generation gained confidence in their newly-realized freedom.

see Lonnie Donegan pp 44   see Dion and The Belmonts pp 61   see Duane Eddy pp 62   see Cliff Richard pp 69

Chuck Berry

CLASSIC RECORDINGS

1955
'Maybellene'

1956
'Roll Over Beethoven',
'Too Much Monkey
Business'

1958
'Sweet Little Sixteen',
'Johnny B Goode'

1963
Chuck Berry

1964
'Nadine', 'No Particular
Place To Go', 'You Never
Can Tell'

1965
'The Promised Land'

1971
San Francisco Dues

1972
'My Ding-A-Ling'

Right
The ingenious songs of Chuck
Berry combined clever and witty
lyrics with fast-moving tunes
and intricate guitar playing.

*'[My mama] said, "You and
Elvis are pretty good, but
you're no Chuck Berry."'*

Jerry Lee Lewis

Far Right
Berry was the first rock and
roller to write words that were
relevant and entertaining to
his young white audience
without alienating his core
black audience.

Charles Edward Anderson Berry, known to all as Chuck, was born in St Louis, Missouri, on 18 October 1926, at the family's home in Goode Avenue. The local gospel choir used it for their rehearsals and there was a well-employed piano in situ. Berry began learning the guitar in his mid-teens. At 17 he was involved in a string of robberies which led to a tough jail sentence, and he was released on his twenty-first birthday.

A Long Apprenticeship

On release, Berry played pick-up gigs wherever he could, while studying to be a hairdresser and looking after his wife and children. On 30 December 1952,

he got a call from piano-player Johnnie Johnson who had a gig at the Cosmopolitan Club in East St Louis. It soon began to live up to its name, becoming a haunt for both blacks and whites. Berry was used to playing white bars, and started to introduce country songs alongside the blues and standards that Johnson's band played. While Elvis was a hillbilly singer who sang the blues, Berry was a bluesman who sang hillbilly. They both ended up with the same result. Rock'n'roll.

In early 1955, he saw Muddy Waters in Chicago and afterwards asked his advice on getting a record deal. The great man recommended going to see Leonard Chess. Berry did just that and was asked if he had a demo. He returned to St Louis and made one with Johnson and Ebby Hardy, their regular drummer.

see Introduction pp 32   *see Sources & Sounds pp 34*   *see A–Z of Artists pp 56*

Chess Mate

Both Leonard Chess and bassist/fixer Willie Dixon were intrigued by the sound of Berry's 'Ida May', which he had developed from country bopper Bob Wills's 'Ida Red'. But they counselled a further bit of disguise, and the song became 'Maybellene', recorded at Chess Records on 21 May 1955. Around this time the band also stopped being the Johnnie Johnson Trio and became Chuck Berry's. The song appealed to both races, naturally, and stormed up all three American charts: pop, country and R&B, reaching No. 5 on the one that mattered most – the *Billboard* Hot 100 chart – several months before Elvis appeared as a national star.

The band soon set out on the hardly glamorous, endless rounds of touring, though sell-out residencies at one of DJ Alan Freed's promotions at the Paramount in New York, and at Harlem's legendary Apollo Theatre were highlights. It was around this time that Berry started bringing the house down with his trademark duck walk. 'Thirty Days', a hurriedly issued follow-up did not fare so well, and it was not until mid-1956 that another classic Berry composition, 'Roll Over Beethoven', breached the US Top 30. Berry's juices were in full flow. He could afford to consign the superb 'Brown Eyed Handsome Man' to the B-side of 'Too Much Monkey Business' (which became the template for Dylan's 'Subterranean Homesick Blues'). Almost unbelievably the single did not chart, though Buddy Holly soon recorded a cover of 'Brown Eyed…'. The next track, 'You Can't Catch Me' (1957), scraped into the Top 30. It was another ode to automobiles, and it inspired John Lennon's 'Come Together'. After this slew of scintillating, but hardly chart-busting singles, 'School Day' became a bona fide smash. It reached No. 3 in the US and gave Berry his first UK hit. Berry was in his thirties, but seemed to be able to describe teenage life to a tee. With his witty vignettes of American life, explored in verses dense with evocative imagery and metrical complexity, he was well on his way to becoming the first poet of the new sound; and his paean to the genre, 'Rock And Roll Music', became his next hit.

Berry Business

By this time Berry had bought his Club Bandstand and the land for Berry Park and set up Chuck Berry Music. He did not want to be cheated as he had been in the early days, though he was not averse to making sure he paid his backing musicians as little as possible. This included the loyal, if often inebriated, Johnnie Johnson – his former boss and, some say, co-composer of many of his songs.

🚗 *see* Muddy Waters pp 24 🚗 *see* Buddy Holly pp 50 🚗 *see* Alan Freed pp 63 🚗 *see* Bob Dylan pp 126

After School Sessions was both Berry and Chess Records' first LP, released in 1958, his best chart year by far. It also saw 'Sweet Little Sixteen' – with its list of place names guaranteeing sales in those locations – attaining No. 2 in the US, and No. 16, appropriately enough, in the UK. The semi-autobiographical 'Johnny B Goode' (the surname in honour of his birthplace) came next, strolling to No. 8 in America. Berry borrowed heavily for this one. Carl Hogan, a guitarist with Louis Jordan, played an intro on the 1946 song, 'Ain't That Just Like A Woman', that is practically note for note the drive Berry used.

In 1959, his standards were just as high, but his chart placings began to slip. The extraordinarily strong pairing of 'Back In The USA' and 'Memphis, Tennessee' barely scraped into the Top 40. The answer to his own 'Johnny B Goode', entitled 'Bye Bye Johnny', had a prophetic ring. Berry had been harassed

by the police for the last few years, but he did not help matters by bringing a 14-year-old Apache girl from Mexico to work at his St Louis club. A racist judge added to the problems, and after legal delays, Berry spent two more years in jail for transporting a minor for immoral purposes. However, his time inside from February 1962 to October 1963 was put to good use: studying law and writing the string of hits that would re-establish him.

Back In The UK

The Beatles, whose Hamburg sets were crammed with Berry originals, and The Rolling Stones, whose first single 'Come On' was a Chuck original, already knew all about him. 1963's eponymous compilation spread the word further, going to No. 12 in Britain. 'Memphis, Tennessee' went to No. 6, and 'No Particular Place To Go' to No. 3. 'Nadine', 'Run, Rudolph, Run' and 'You

see Introduction pp 32   *see* Sources & Sounds pp 34   *see* A–Z of Artists pp 56

Never Can Tell' (later to be used so effectively on the *Pulp Fiction* (1994) soundtrack by Quentin Tarantino), also scored. This burst of brilliance also revitalized his career in his homeland. In May 1964, Berry toured the UK to a tumultuous reception. His return trip in early 1965 was a different matter, plagued by the clock-watching indifference that would mar a lot of future performances.

In June 1966, Berry signed with Mercury Records and the decline in his output was obvious. In fact, all the company really wanted him to do was re-record his classics so they had rights to the titles, though *Chuck Berry In Memphis* (1967) was a half-decent set.

Berry began to play rock'n'roll revival shows, including Toronto, where Lennon and the Plastic Ono Band headlined. In 1972, Lennon invited Berry to be a guest on American TV's *The Mike Douglas Show* which he was co-hosting. He introduced him by saying: 'If you ever tried to give rock'n'roll another name, you might call it Chuck Berry.'

In 1970, Berry returned to Chess and came up with 'Tulane' and *San Francisco Dues* (1971), his finest work for years. In 1972, he recorded a live gig at the Lanchester Arts Festival in Coventry which resulted in his biggest, but by no stretch, finest hit. 'My Ding A Ling', a risqué novelty number, was a transatlantic No. 1. In the same year Berry played a triumphant gig at Wembley Stadium with many of his fellow rock'n'roll pioneers.

Hail! Hail! Rock'n'Roll!

Berry produced little new material in the 1970s and ended the decade in jail again on tax charges. Despite a bizarre collaboration with Shabba Ranks in 1994 on 'Go Shabba Go' his long promised new album has not materialized. In 1986, he was in the first rank of artists to be inducted into the Rock And Roll Hall Of Fame. The man who inducted him, Keith Richards, based a career on Berry's guitar style, though that style, in turn, had been based on forefathers such as Charlie Christian and T-Bone Walker. 1986 coincided with Berry's sixtieth birthday, and Richards organized a huge celebratory bash, filmed in its entirety, in the documentary *Hail! Hail! Rock'n'Roll*; a fascinating tribute to a great showman (when he felt like it), the greatest lyricist of his era and a huge influence on all who followed.

see T-Bone Walker pp 29   see The Beatles pp 88   see The Rolling Stones pp 96   see The Beach Boys pp 120

Ray Charles

Key Artists

'I was born with music inside me. That's the only explanation I know of.'
Ray Charles

Above
As well as R&B, Ray Charles has successfully turned his hand to a number of musical styles, including blues, gospel, pop, country, jazz and early rock'n'roll.

Born Ray Charles Robinson on 23 September 1930 in Albany, Georgia, Charles suffered from glaucoma from the age of five and was blind by the time he was seven. His mother was unable to look after him and he moved away to the Institute for the Blind, Deaf and Dumb in St Augustine, Florida. He learned to play piano (he had already been taught some basics by local musician Wylie Pitman), organ, clarinet and saxophone and to read music in Braille. When he was 14 his mother died, and the following year he went to live with friends of hers in Jacksonville.

From Florida To Seattle
Charles started finding gigs around Jacksonville, then moved to Orlando and Tampa, playing piano or sax and working out arrangements for whoever would hire him; he even learned to yodel with country

outfit The Florida Playboys. At the time he was obsessed with Nat 'King' Cole's smooth vocals and jazzy piano, and modelled himself pretty wholeheartedly on his style.

He then chose to move to Seattle, as it was diametrically across the US from Florida. He arrived in March 1948, and the trio he assembled soon had a residency at the Rocking Chair nightclub, where Jack Lauderdale signed him to his Downbeat label. His debut single, 'Confession Blues' (1949) became an R&B hit. Around this time he started using the surname Charles, to avoid confusion with the boxer Sugar Ray Robinson. Downbeat became Swingtime and Ray joined up with the imprint's premier draw: sophisticated bluesman, Lowell Fulson. He sang and played piano in his band between 1950 and 1952, but was increasingly restless in this subordinate position. As luck would have it, Lauderdale sold Ray's contract to Atlantic Records.

🔊 *see Introduction pp 32* 🔊 *see Sources & Sounds pp 34* 🔊 *see A–Z of Artists pp 56*

From Cole To Soul

Atlantic had been set up by Ahmet Ertegun in 1947 and had a good reputation for R&B, scoring hits with Ruth Brown, Joe Turner and the original Drifters. Ray's first recording session came in 1952. He was still very much beholden to Cole and only minor hits ensued with 'Mess Around' and 'It Should've Been Me'. Around this time he played with the highly emotive blues guitarist Guitar Slim, on the now classic 'The Things I Used To Do', and some of Slim's raw emotion seemed to rub off on Charles.

He recorded 'I Got A Woman', on 18 November 1954. The tune was based on a gospel song, but, in singing his mildly raunchy lyrics in an unfettered, 'churchy' fashion, he laid the groundwork for soul music. Tracks such as 'Hallelujah I Love Her So' and 1959's 'What'd I Say' – with his female backing singers The Raelettes very much a feature – built on this foundation.

'The Genius'

Ray Charles was not to be confined by genre, however. He recorded jazz using Duke Ellington and Count Basie's musicians – with his friend Quincy Jones arranging – on one side of *The Genius Of Ray Charles* (1959), and string-laden pop on the other. In 1960, he signed to ABC-Paramount. The strong-willed Charles had wanted more control over his career and his new contract gave him just that. He founded his own record label, Tangerine, and achieved chart success with a pair of US No. 1s, 'Georgia On My Mind' and 'Hit The Road Jack'.

Not content with his achievements, Ray returned to the country sounds he had heard on the Grand Ole Opry radio show as a child, and produced the crossover classic *Modern Sounds In Country And Western Music* (1962), which became his only US No. 1 album, and yielded another chart-topper in 'I Can't Stop Loving You'. He recorded further country and pop albums throughout the decade. Charles reacted to soul's rising social awareness with fine albums *A Message From The People* (1972) and *Renaissance* (1975), and nearly stole the film *The Blues Brothers* (1980) with a stunning street performance of 'Shake Your Tail Feather'. He was also prominent on 1985's USA For Africa single 'We Are The World'.

Charles died on 10 June 2004, and tributes poured in. His posthumous album *Genius Loves Company* (2004), featured duets with the likes of Gladys Knight, Willie Nelson and Norah Jones, while Jamie Foxx won a deserved Oscar for his uncannily accurate portrayal in the Hollywood biopic, *Ray* (2004).

Above

During his prodigious career, Charles won 12 Grammy Awards and a Lifetime Achievement Award.

see B.B. King pp 65   see Gladys Knight and The Pips pp 172   see Elton John pp 232   see Norah Jones pp 401

Lonnie Donegan Key Artists

**⊙⊙ CLASSIC
RECORDINGS**

1955
'Rock Island Line'

1956
*Lonnie Donegan
Showcase LP*

1958
'The Grand Coolee Dam'

1962
'I'll Never Fall In Love
Again'

1999
Muleskinner Blues

2000
*The Skiffle Sessions:
Live In Belfast*

'The shows weren't
organized at all.
They just happened.'

Lonnie Donegan

Above Right

Lonnie Donegan was the first
major star of British pop,
notching up 28 Top 30 hits
during the early 1950s.

Donegan was born in Glasgow, the son of a professional violinist, on 29 April 1931. The family moved to the east end of London when Tony, as he was then known, was two. He finally got the guitar he craved in his early teens. He attended his first jazz club soon after and was smitten by singer Beryl Bryden – their paths would cross again. He was also influenced by seeing black American singer, Josh White, in concert. Donegan began playing in various bands, but was interrupted by his national service in 1949. His spell abroad exposed him to American forces radio, and broadened his knowledge of jazz, blues and folk.

The Birth Of The Beat

Donegan fell in with fellow musician Chris Barber. They performed together in Ken Colyer's trad outfit,

but Colyer was a purist and essentially ousted himself from his own band. Barber took charge. Lonnie (who had got his nickname when a compere mixed him up with one of Donegan's heroes, blues musician Lonnie Johnson), was encouraged to develop an act based around his exuberant performance of various American roots songs, often employing improvized instruments such as a tea-chest bass and washboard. These cameos became extremely popular in the band's breaks between sets; Donegan called it 'mongrel music'. On 13 July 1954, just a few days after Elvis's first Sun Studios session, he recorded a couple of tracks for the Barber band's Decca debut album, *New Orleans Joys*, with Beryl Bryden on washboard. 'Rock Island Line', an old Leadbelly number, and 'John Henry' a traditional Afro-American ballad, were released as a single in late 1955, and went to No. 8 in the UK, and

🎙️ *see Introduction pp 32* 🎙️ *see Sources & Sounds pp 34* 🎙️ *see A–Z of Artists pp 56*

to the same position in the US charts, when it was issued there the following February. He was a US Top 10 artist before Presley! The effect on the youth of Britain was electrifying. This was do-it-yourself music, and sales of acoustic guitars went through the roof. John Lennon formed The Quarrymen skiffle band in Liverpool in 1957, Pete Townshend and Roger Daltrey became The Detours. Homegrown British rock music began in Lonnie's wake.

The King Of Skiffle

Follow-up single, 'Digging My Potatoes', (another Leadbelly cover), was banned by the BBC for its supposed innuendo, and Donegan's cachet rose even higher. Now signed to Pye, 'Lost John' backed with 'Stewball', repeated the formula, and his enthusiastic, expressive vocals took it to No. 2. He toured to America, releasing an album entitled *An Englishman Sings American Folk Songs* (he was actually Scottish-Irish by birth), and appeared on the Perry Como show in a skit with then-actor Ronald Reagan. Woody Allen debuted on the same programme. Essentially, he was making the Americans aware of their own heritage.

Lonnie chalked up his first No. 1 with 'Cumberland Gap' and followed it with another, 'Gamblin' Man' (both 1957). The hits kept flowing with the likes of 'The Grand Coolee Dam' and 'Tom Dooley' (both 1958), but he started introducing numbers that had more to do with British music-hall traditions into his repertoire, such as 'Does Your Chewing Gum Lose Its Flavour On The Bedpost Overnight?' and 'My Old Man's A Dustman' (1960, another chart-topper). Some saw this as a cheapening of his act, though he finished his chart career with a nice symmetry. He released another Leadbelly number, 'Pick A Bale Of Cotton' in autumn 1962, a handful of weeks before The Beatles, who had been so inspired by him, took over the decade.

Putting On The Style

Donegan worked through the next 15 years, singing and acting, but the new folk revival did not take to him, and his old popular fanbase had grown-up. Then in 1978, Adam Faith organized a line-up of his fans including Ringo Starr, Brian May, Ronnie Wood and Elton John, who contributed to a Donegan album

called, *Putting On The Style*. Lonnie had a flourishing final few years. He toured again with Chris Barber; British DJ John Peel booked him as one of his favourite artists for his Meltdown Festival in 1998, and in 1999, he released *Muleskinner Blues*, with special guest Van Morrison, another long-time aficionado. Donegan, Barber and Morrison reconvened for *The Skiffle Sessions: Live In Belfast* (2000), which went to No. 14. Donegan died on 3 November 2002 in the middle of another stint on the road.

Below
Donegan's 1955 hit, 'Rock Island Line', was the first debut record to go gold in Britain.

🎙 *see* The Beatles pp 88   🎙 *see* The Who pp 100   🎙 *see* Van Morrison pp 219   🎙 *see* Elton John pp 232

The Everly Brothers

'Don and Phil used proper English and I just thought they were a cut above … intellectually and education-wise.'

Chet Atkins

The Everlys were born into a country music family; Don on 1 February 1937 in Brownie, Kentucky; Phil in Chicago – where father Ike had moved to play in bands with his brothers – on 19 January 1939. The family moved to Shenandoah, Iowa, to a regular slot on a local radio station, and Ike and Margaret's young sons soon started performing with them on the Everly Family Radio Show. Their career choice had been made.

Nashville Next

With the family settled in Knoxville, Tennessee, Ike used his friendship with legendary guitarist Chet Atkins to get his boys a foothold in the Nashville music business. Atkins introduced them to Wesley Rose of the influential Acuff-Rose publishing partnership. Don managed to place a song with Kitty Wells, which sold reasonably well, but times were tough. They released a straight country single in early 1956 on Columbia, but it flopped, and it was not until Rose persuaded Archie Bleyer at Cadence to take them on that their star rose.

He teamed them with the songwriting couple Felice and Boudleaux Bryant, and in mid-1957 the pop-rockabilly of 'Bye Bye Love' zoomed to No. 2 in the US,

6 in the UK. It contained all the elements that made the Everlys. The audience could hear the Kentucky /Appalachian deep country origins of the close harmonies – with Don taking the melody. These had been handed down from other sibling groups such as The Delmore and Louvin Brothers; and yet there was a freshness to their approach, and a strong acknowledgement of rock'n'roll that pointed forwards.

This is evident in the fine Little Richard and Gene Vincent covers on their excellent self-titled debut album (1958). It is interesting to note that when Vincent re-recorded 'Be-Bop-A-Lula' he followed the Everlys' up-tempo arrangement to a tee. Their influence on The Beatles (The Everlys' version of Ray Charles' 'Leave My Woman Alone' is a prime example), The Byrds, The Beach Boys, and Simon & Garfunkel is obvious from the earliest days, as hit followed hit; the mildly risqué 'Wake Up Little Susie' (1957), the heavenly ballad 'All I Have To Do Dream', the humorous 'Bird Dog' (both 1958) and the first self-penned smash '('Til) I Kissed You (1959)'. But a bitter split with manager Wesley Rose, however, heralded a move to the newly founded Warner Brothers recording wing on a much-trumpeted, million-dollar 10-year contract.

Brothers With Warner

Their first offering at the new label was the moody psychodrama of 'Cathy's Clown' (1960), fleshed out by far more echo than they had used previously. Further big sellers ensued, 'Lucille' (1960), 'Walk Right Back', innovative pop epic 'Temptation' (both 1961) and albums *It's Everly Time!* (1960) and *A Date With The Everly Brothers* (1961). But troubles loomed. They aborted their projected film career; had to serve a six-month stint in the US Marines; Don became reliant on drugs (and collapsed before a gig at one point); the British Invasion stole their chart thunder; and their bust-up with the powerful Rose meant that they had trouble getting hold of songs from the best Nashville writers.

🎸 *see Introduction pp 32* 🎸 *see Sources & Sounds pp 34* 🎸 *see A–Z of Artists pp 56*

Appropriately, since they had inspired many British groups, they still had hits in the UK ('The Price Of Love' and 'Love Is Strange', both 1965) and recorded an album, *Two Yanks In England* with The Hollies, whose sound had essentially been shaped by the brothers.

Another album, *Roots* (1968) was a trailblazing country rock collection, but at that time nothing of theirs would shift. They drifted on until a gig at Knotts Berry Farm California, in July 1973, when a drunken Don insulted his brother. Long-running grievances erupted, and the normally placid Phil stormed off. They did not play together again for 10 years.

Solo And Reunited

Both did some good solo work; Phil his *Star Spangled Springer* (1973) set, and Don his *Brother Juke Box* (1977). It took their father's funeral to reconcile them. Their emotional, live double album *The Everly Brothers' Reunion Concert* recorded at the Royal Albert Hall in September 1983, saw them back in the charts. An eponymous follow-up LP (*EB 84* in the US) with a Paul McCartney-written single, 'On The Wings Of A Nightingale', was also successful. They continued to tour and record, their considerable powers pretty much undiminished, until 2001.

Above

The brothers' music helped bridge the gap between rock and country music in a way that appealed to fans of both genres.

see The Delmore Brothers pp 19   *see* The Beach Boys pp 120   *see* The Byrds pp 124   *see* Simon and Garfunkel pp 147

Bill Haley

Key Artists

⊙⊙ CLASSIC RECORDINGS

1952
'Rock The Joint'

1953
'Crazy, Man, Crazy'

1954
'Shake, Rattle And Roll',
'Rock Around The Clock'

1955
'Razzle Dazzle'

1956
'See You Later, Alligator'

1971
Rock Around The Country

'The music is the main thing and it's just as easy to write acceptable words.'
Bill Haley

Above Right
The curl Haley wore to draw people's attention from his blind eye sparked a kiss-curl craze during the 1950s.

William John Clifton Haley was born on 6 July 1925 in Highland Park, Detroit, and raised near Chester, Pennsylvania. His parents were both musical, and he got his first proper guitar when he was 13. Even though he was blind in one eye and shy about his disability (he later tried to distract from it with his trademark kiss-curl), he started playing local shows.

A Professional Yodeller

In his late teens he joined a working country and western band, The Downhomers, and was styled Yodeling Bill Haley. He then fronted The Four Aces Of Western Swing, and landed a job back home on radio station WPWA in Chester, forming the

Saddlemen there. His show was scheduled after a black R&B programme called Judge Rhythm's Court. Here he first heard 'Rocket 88' by Jackie Brenston and His Delta Cats – which was actually Ike Turner's band – and recorded it in 1951 with the Saddlemen: the first cover of what is often considered the first rock'n'roll record. Haley started working R&B songs into his set alongside the rocking (but white) country boogie styles they already played. In April 1952, they released a version of Jimmy Preston's R&B hit 'Rock The Joint'. They signed to Dave Miller's Essex label where, under the name Bill Haley with Haley's Comets, 'Crazy Man Crazy,' a Haley original, became the first charting rock'n'roll record in history, going to No. 15. But the follow-ups were weak, and Miller did not like a song that Haley kept pushing....

🎞 *see Introduction pp 32* 🎞 *see Sources & Sounds pp 34* 🎞 *see A–Z of Artists pp 56*

The Father Of Rock'n'Roll

Milt Gabler at Decca had overseen the career of Louis Jordan whose jump-jive style has a strong claim as an ancestor of rock'n'roll. He signed Haley and set a recording date for 12 April 1954. They spent most of the session working on 'Thirteen Women', allowing only two takes of 'Rock Around The Clock' by Jimmy DeKnight and Max C. Freedman. Time enough for Danny Cedrone to lay down the exact same – but still scintillating – guitar solo he had played on 'Rock The Joint' two years previously. The track was more popular than the A-side but hardly set the world alight. Instead the genial, and let us not forget, talented Haley went to No. 12 in summer 1954 with a raucous version of Big Joe Turner's 'Shake Rattle And Roll' (this became his first UK hit in late 1954).

But the wheels of fate were turning. The actor Glen Ford's son had bought 'Thirteen Women'. His father's producer was looking for a song to capture the mood of disaffected youth in a new film, *Blackboard Jungle*. 'Rock Around The Clock' fitted the bill. When the movie came out in 1955, the track stormed to No. 1 – and stayed there.

Haley and his band appeared in films, *Rock Around The Clock* and *Don't Knock The Rock* (both 1956), and had further big hits with 'Rock-A-Beatin' Boogie' (1955), 'See You Later, Alligator' and 'The Saints Rock'n'Roll' (both 1956), and they toured Britain to a riotous (literally) reception in 1957. (UK fans sent 'Rock Around The Clock' into the charts on its three different issues, 1954, 1968 and 1974). But, there was a new generation – the Presleys, Cochrans and Berrys – following in his pioneering footsteps. The Comets goofed around wildly on stage, but they were not exactly sexy; and some of Haley's repertoire was not the strongest.

Rocking Around The World

Haley's last US hit came in late 1959 with 'Skokiaan (The South African Song)'. He then decamped to Mexico, where he scored hits as the King of Twist! He spent the next years touring, finding some success with Richard Nader's Rock'n'Roll Revival Shows.

In 1971, a deal with Swedish label Sonet linked Haley with blues historian Samuel Charters as his producer, and he delivered a superb album.

Rock Around The Country showcased excellent versions of 'Me And Bobby McGhee', Joe South's 'Games That People Play' and Creedence's 'Travelin' Band'. Unfortunately it did not sell.

Haley managed a final British gig at the Royal Variety Performance in late 1979, but he was not a well man. After a difficult illness – he was suffering from a brain tumour – he died on 9 February 1981 in Harlingen, Texas.

Below

Haley and His Comets succeeded in translating black rhythm and blues into a form that adolescent white audiences could understand.

see Jackie Brenston pp 18   see Louis Jordan pp 22   see Big Joe Turner pp 27   see Chuck Berry pp 38

Buddy Holly

Key Artists

▣ CLASSIC RECORDINGS

1957
'That'll Be The Day',
'Peggy Sue',
'Not Fade Away'

1958
The Chirping Crickets,
'Words Of Love'

1959
'It Doesn't Matter
Anymore', 'Crying,
Waiting, Hoping'

1960
'True Love Ways'

*'We like this kind of
music. Jazz is strictly
for stay-at-homes.'*
Buddy Holly on rock'n'roll music

Above
Holly with The Crickets,
with whom he co-wrote
several of his most
memorable songs.

Buddy Holly was born Charles Hardin Holley in Lubbock, Texas, on 7 September 1936. Buddy got a guitar in his mid-teens and started practising with friend, Bob Montgomery. They liked country and western but also had predilection for the blues. An Elvis gig in Lubbock in early 1955 alerted them to new possibilities. Buddy and Bob, as they called themselves, played local radio stations and were making a reputation; but when agent Eddie Crandall managed to get Holly a deal with Decca in Nashville, after seeing him support Bill Haley, Bob was not included. Guitarist Sonny Curtis, bassist Don Guess and drummer Jerry Allison joined the line-up.

A False Start And A New Dawn

Holly recorded under the auspices of legendary producer Owen Bradley, and released 'Blue Days, Black Nights' in July 1956. It did well enough to earn another couple of dates in the studio. 'Modern Don Juan' appeared in late 1956 to a muted response. Bradley, steeped in country, did not quite know what to do with this new rock'n'roll sound.

Holly returned to Norman Petty's studio in Clovis, New Mexico, where he had previously recorded some demos. Petty had a well-equipped operation. As at Sun Studio in Memphis there was no time-limit on sessions, and as at Sun, Petty had developed his own echo technology.

Buddy had apparently been talking about their future fame, and Allison, quoting from the recent film, *The Searchers*, had answered with the catchphrase of John Wayne's character – 'That'll be the day…'. This became the title of The Crickets' first hit, released in its demo form by Coral. It went to the US No. 1 in summer 1957.

Hitting the market with songs under the band's moniker and with his own name became the norm. It doubled the chance of airplay. This dual success continued with 'Peggy Sue', a Holly track; then a couple of Crickets' releases, 'Oh Boy' backed with

'Not Fade Away' (one of the strongest pairings in rock history) and 'Maybe Baby'; followed by two Holly numbers, 'Listen To Me' and 'Rave On'. In the midst of this the band were touring heavily with a new bassist and guitarist, Joe B. Mauldin and Niki Sullivan – notably on the 'Biggest Show Of Stars For '57' package, with Chuck Berry, The Everlys and Fats Domino, amongst many others. The sessions at Clovis also bore fruit in two of the finest albums of the era, *The Chirping Crickets* in November 1957 (March 1958 in the UK) and *Buddy Holly* in March 1958 (July 1958, UK). 'Words Of Love', from the latter, and 'Peggy Sue' both used pioneering overdubbing and double-tracking techniques. More evidence of both Petty and Holly's willingness to experiment.

📻 *see Introduction pp 32* 📻 *see Sources & Sounds pp 34* 📻 *see A–Z of Artists pp 56*

The Star Shines On

In March 1958, Buddy and The Crickets toured Britain, and two avid spectators at their Liverpool gig were teenagers John Lennon and Paul McCartney. Several years on their compositions rang with Holly's influence. McCartney would later buy the publishing rights to Holly's song catalogue.

On their return things began to change. In the summer Holly recorded without The Crickets for the first time, and also taped demos of songs he wanted The Everly Brothers to use. In August, he married Maria Elena Santiago. Around this time he also helped out on the unknown Waylon Jennings' first single. Holly then acquiesced to a session with a string accompaniment that Petty had been badgering him to do. This took place in New York in October and resulted in 'True Love Ways',

and the two songs which would make up his final single, 'It Doesn't Matter Anymore' and 'Raining In My Heart'. Later in October, tensions came to a head between Holly and Petty over various matters, including royalties, and they went their separate ways. The Crickets stayed with Norman, to Holly's surprise and disappointment.

In the new year, Buddy got a band together to headline the 'Winter Dance Party' tour. After a gig at Clear Lake Iowa, Buddy had chartered a plane, as the tour bus was proving unreliable. Holly, Ritchie Valens and the Big Bopper died when the flight crashed in snowy conditions on 3 February 1959.

So much potential unfulfilled, but a legacy left that would influence rockers and singer/songwriters alike, from Bob Dylan to Elvis Costello, from The Rolling Stones to Paul Simon.

Below
Buddy Holly was probably the first rock'n'roll artist to concern himself with virtually every aspect of his music including arranging and record production.

see The Everly Brothers pp 46   see The Beatles pp 88   see Bob Dylan pp 126   see Elvis Costello pp 256

Elvis Presley

Key Artists

'There have been a lotta tough guys. There have been pretenders. And there have been contenders. But there is only one king.'

Bruce Springsteen

Right
Perhaps the ultimate pop icon, Elvis Presley brought attitude and sexuality into the mainstream at a time when it was far from acceptable.

Elvis Aaron Presley was born in his family's shot-gun shack in Tupelo, Mississippi, on 8 January 1935. His twin brother died at birth, and his mother doted on her sole son. He showed musical aptitude early, and loved to sing at the local First Assembly of God church. His mother, Gladys and father, Vernon, moved to Memphis when Elvis was 13, first to a run-down area, then to good public housing at Lauderdale Courts. Throughout his childhood and adolescence, Elvis would drink in music of every variety, anything from Dean Martin to Arthur 'Big Boy' Crudup, from the Blackwood Brothers Quartet to Mario Lanza; and, according to some stories, he secretly frequented the black clubs on Beale Street. Ike Turner for one, remembers sneaking him into a West Memphis night-spot and hiding him behind his piano.

The Rising Son

Presley graduated from Humes High School and went to work first at M.B. Parker Machinists' shop. He may have heard about Sam Phillips's Sun Studio from an article in the local paper about The Prisonaires, a group of convicts who had recorded there in mid-1953. In summer 1953, he presented himself at 706 Union Avenue, and taking advantage of their $3.98 offer, recorded 'My Happiness' and 'That's When Your Heartaches Begin'. He returned in January 1954, obviously trying to catch the ear of Mr Phillips. Sam's secretary, Marion Keisker, suggested Presley to Phillips when Sam was looking for someone to demo a particular song, and the man who had already taped Howlin' Wolf and B.B. King on the premises agreed to give him a try. It did not go smoothly but Phillips persevered, putting him together with two other hungry, if slightly older musicians; guitarist Scotty Moore, serious but talented, and Bill Black, a bassist and natural clown.

Their session on 5 July 1954, seemed to be going nowhere until Elvis started messing around on an old Arthur Crudup blues number, 'That's All Right'; attacking it with punky vigour. Phillips knew that this was the combination of country and blues, sung by a charismatic young white man, he had been searching for. They recorded a hopped-up version of Bill Monroe's bluegrass classic 'Blue Moon Of Kentucky' to complete the single and rush-released it as Sun 209

see Introduction pp 32 *see Sources & Sounds pp 34* *see A–Z of Artists pp 56*

on 17 July 1954. It lit up the Memphis area, and it soon became apparent that Elvis had the live act to promote this new and exhilarating hybrid. Four more Sun records followed the same blueprint over the next year; country song one side, R&B the other, all backed by Moore's fine rockabilly guitar and Black's slapped bass. Excitement grew exponentially amongst fans – helped immensely by the band's weekly slot on the *Louisiana Hayride* radio show. 'I Forgot To Remember To Forget', the flip side to the awesome blues power of 'Mystery Train' – the final Sun single, even made the Top 10 of the national country charts. The calculating Colonel Tom Parker, who already looked after country star Hank Snow, became Presley's manager, and Elvis's contract with Sun was sold on to RCA in late 1955 for $35,000 – a large amount of money for a struggling concern such as Sam's.

The King Of Rock'n'Roll

Elvis went into RCA's Nashville Studios on 10 January 1956, two days after he officially entered adulthood. Black and Moore were there with him, a star in his own right, alongside session-men, Floyd Cramer on piano and guitarist Chet Atkins. Presley was unfazed and laid down the charged melancholia of 'Heartbreak Hotel', which became his first No. 1, and several tracks for his self-titled first album. His appearance on Tommy Dorsey's national TV show fuelled the fire, and a stream of high quality rock'n'roll, leavened with a slightly more poppy approach, hit the singles charts: 'I Want You I Need You, I Love You', 'Hound Dog', 'Too Much' and 'All Shook Up', all went to the US No. 1 slot within a year and a half of his RCA debut. And that is without including 'Love Me Tender' (1956) from the film of the same name and '(Let Me Be Your) Teddy Bear' from *Loving You* (1957), his first two movies. He completed a celluloid quartet, with the more than passable *Jailhouse Rock* (1957) and *King Creole* (1958), before a turn of events that would redefine Presley as an all-American hero, or mark the end of his career as a rebel figure, depending on your viewpoint. Elvis was drafted into the US Army in March 1958.

Films, Films, Films

While he was serving in Germany, Elvis suffered the loss of his beloved mother. When he was demobbed

in March 1960, he seemed to have grown-up, but that was not all to the good. He guested on Frank Sinatra's ABC TV show, proving that he could handle Ol' Blue Eyes's material, 'Witchcraft', but Frank was not quite so good with Elvis' new single, 'Stuck On You'. This was a far cry from his appearances on the *Ed Sullivan Show* when cameras were ordered to cut his youth-corrupting, pelvis-swivels from the shot. In April 1961, he appeared at a benefit gig for the US Navy, his last public appearance for seven years. Estimable tracks still

emerged – 'Mess Of Blues' (1960), 'Return To Sender' (1962) – (and *Elvis Is Back!* (1960) is a very good album), but they were outnumbered by the tracks from the often awful films he made – 'Wooden Heart' (1964), 'Do The Clam' (1965), and average orchestral pop. In May 1967, he married Priscilla Beaulieu, and in February 1968, their daughter Lisa Marie was born.

Return Of The King

Elvis was not entirely happy with his career at this point and neither were his public. The hits were getting smaller. His return to form can be traced to his gospel album, *How Great Thou Art* (1967), which reached

Above

Presley was able to sound alternately raucous, gospel-tinged, crooner-like, countrified and bluesy.

🎸 *see Bill Black Combo pp 18* 🎸 *see Howlin' Wolf pp 21* 🎸 *see Big Mama Thornton pp 27* 🎸 *see Chet Atkins pp 56*

Above and Right

Despite Presley's risqué onstage moves, he was really a sweet, home-loving boy; the fact he was considered corruptive only furthered his iconic status.

His white-suited finale singing 'If I Can Dream' is one of the great moments in rock performance. Elvis moved straight on to some of his finest recorded work at producer Chip Moman's American studio in Memphis. *From Elvis In Memphis* (1969) yielded the surprisingly political, 'In The Ghetto'. The glorious 'Suspicious Minds' (1969) then gave him his first No. 1 for over four years. In 1971, he continued his golden run by issuing one of his very best collections, *Elvis Country*, which revisited some of his downhome musical influences.

Presley returned to regular live performance, first at the International Hotel in Las Vegas, where he opened an incredibly successful season of shows on 31 July 1969 with a classy line-up of backing musicians who included James Burton (guitar), Jerry Scheff (bass), Ronnie Tutt (drums) and The Sweet Inspirations (backing vocals). This period of spell-binding live shows was captured on the documentary, *Elvis: That's The Way It Is* (1970); the live satellite broadcast, *Aloha From Hawaii* (1973); and on the album, *Elvis: As Recorded At Madison Square Garden* (1972).

The Final Years

Priscilla left Graceland in late 1971, and it affected Elvis badly. His consumption of prescription drugs increased massively, and his live shows often suffered; and he was doing a lot of them. He had financial worries as well as personal ones, and so had to keep on the touring treadmill. Presley had his last Top 20 US hit – before the posthumous triumph of 'Way Down' – with 'Promised Land' in late 1974. He was admitted to hospital at least three times in 1975, which also marked his last session in a recording studio. From then on he laid down his tracks at Graceland. But he kept performing on the road, taping a final pair of shows for a CBS *Elvis In Concert* special in June 1977. His drug-ravaged body, however, had had enough, and on 16 August 1977, he died of heart failure at his Graceland home.

Elvis was the first and ultimate rock star, as well as playing a massive part in creating the 'rock' that he was 'star' of. He was the most charismatic performer in popular music history, and one of the most talented; and his latest number one, a 2005 remix of 1968's 'A Little Less Conversation', proves that he still lives.

back to his roots, and the superb 'Guitar Man' (1968). But it was the June NBC TV show, which became known as the 1968 *Comeback Special* that relaunched his career. Dressed in a stunning black leather outfit and reunited with Scotty Moore, he seemed on top of his game, running through gems from his back catalogue with a fervour he had not mustered for years.

🔊 *see Introduction pp 32* 🔊 *see Sources & Sounds pp 34* 🔊 *see A–Z of Artists pp 56*

A-Z of Artists

Paul Anka
(Singer/songwriter, b. 1941)
Born in Canada of Lebanese parents, Anka was a child prodigy, whose chart career started with 1957's multi-million selling UK/US No. 1, 'Diana' (written about the family babysitter). 1959's 'Lonely Boy', another US No. 1 was another of his 53 US hit singles by 1983. Rarely a rocker, he duetted with protégée Odia Coates on his third US chart-topper, 1974's sentimental '(You're) Having My Baby'. Anka also wrote 'It Doesn't Matter Anymore', a big Buddy Holly hit, and British lyrics to Frank Sinatra's 'My Way' signature tune.

Chet Atkins
(Guitar, producer, 1924–2001)
Tennessee-born Chester Burton Atkins, whose father was a music teacher, was one of the most influential twentieth-century guitarists, and was initially influenced by the finger and thumb-picking country-style playing of Merle Travis. Signed to RCA from 1947, he made scores of mainly instrumental albums, and in 1955 became the head of RCA's new Nashville studio, producing artists signed to the label, and working with numerous country artists, including Don Gibson, Waylon Jennings, Elvis Presley and Jim Reeves. He also produced for pop artists such as Perry Como, and was recognized by Gretsch guitars, who named their Chet Atkins Country Gentleman model after him. One of his most significant signings to RCA was successful black country singer Charley Pride, as few black acts were tolerated in Nashville. Atkins also made duet albums with notable pickers like Les Paul, Jerry Reed and Mark Knopfler (1992's 'Neck And Neck').

Frankie Avalon
(Trumpet, vocals, b. 1939)
As rock'n'roll lost its way in the late 1950s, good looks replaced musical ability and Philadelphia-born Francis Avalon became a teen idol via a series of forgettable pop hits like 1959's million-selling US No. 1, 'Venus'. Frequent exposure on the *American Bandstand* TV show produced two dozen US hits by 1962, and Avalon co-starred with Annette Funicello in teenage beach movies, later guesting in 1978's *Grease*.

Right
20-30
20-30 word caption to go here
20-30 word caption to go here
word caption to go here
word caption to go
20-30 word caption to go

see Introduction pp 32   *see* Sources & Sounds pp 34   *see* Key Artists pp 38

Harry Belafonte
(Vocals, b. 1927)

57

Born in Harlem to Caribbean parents, the young Belafonte lived in Jamaica for five years. Multi-talented, he starred on stage and screen (in *Carmen Jones*, 1954), becoming a folk singer in 1955. He led a brief calypso craze with 'Jamaica Farewell', 'Mary's Boy Child' and the million-selling 'Banana Boat (Day-O)'. The title song from 1957's *Island In The Sun*, in which he starred, was his final hit single. However, he sold millions of LPs: *Belafonte* and *Calypso* (both 1956) topped the US chart. Regarded as a black elder statesman, he was behind 1985's USA For Africa single, 'We Are The World'.

Far Left

Mark Knoplfer and George Harrison are among those infuenced by Chet Atkins.

Far Left

Clean-cut smoothie Frankie Avalon.

Below

Doo-wopper Hank Ballard brought a mixture of gospel influences and raunchy R&B to the vocal group that he joined in 1953.

LaVern Baker
(Vocals, b. 1929)

Chicago-born Delores Williams sang in church choirs, but after bandleader Fletcher Henderson discovered her, she became the first black torch singer of the rock era, and in 1953, was one of the early artists signed to Atlantic Records. Many of her 20 US R&B hits were novelty items, including her 1957 No. 1, 'Jim Dandy', but several, like 1955's 'Tweedle Dee', were successfully covered for white audiences by Georgia Gibbs, and Baker unjustly lost out.

Hank Ballard
(Bandleader, vocals, b. 1936)

Alabama-raised Henry 'Hank' Ballard fronted The Midnighters (previously The Royals). 1954 brought the Detroit group four big US R&B hits with risqué lyrics about a fictitious 'Annie'. In 1960, the group released the original version of 'The Twist', written by Ballard, but the younger, more photogenic Chubby Checker took the million sales and the glory. It is said that James Brown's wild stage show was influenced by Ballard, who later worked in Brown's revue.

see Les Paul pp 24   see Buddy Holly pp 50   see James Brown pp 154   see Chubby Checker pp 167

The Big Bopper

(Disc jockey, singer/songwriter, 1930–59)

Jiles Perry (J.P.) Richardson, a Texan disc jockey, who wrote Johnny Preston's million-selling 1960 'Running Bear' hit, also adopted the moniker The Big Bopper, a loudmouth novelty act whose big 1958 hit was the lecherous 'Chantilly Lace'. Probably the least talented of the three stars whose plane came down on a winter tour of the Midwest, he became most famous for dying with Buddy Holly.

Pat Boone

(Vocals, b. 1934)

Supposedly directly descended from US pioneer Daniel Boone, Florida-born Charles Eugene Boone's 55th US hit, 'Speedy Gonzalez', in 1962 followed 10 million-sellers and six US No. 1s since 1955. His early hits were tame white versions of black R&B hits by Fats Domino ('Ain't That A Shame'), Little Richard ('Tutti Frutti' and 'Long Tall Sally') and The Flamingos ('I'll Be Home', Boone's 1956 five-week UK No. 1). With black acts effectively banned from white American radio, Boone, wearing trademark 'white buck' shoes, was Elvis Presley's safer rival in the 1950s. He married Shirley, daughter of country star Red Foley, in 1956, and sang the theme to the movie, *Friendly Persuasion* (1956), starred in and sang the movie themes to *Bernadine* and *April Love* (both 1957), but was not a rock'n'roller. Graduating to family TV shows and later, religion, he was arguably overshadowed in 1977 by his daughter, Debbie Boone's platinum single 'You Light Up My Life', which topped the US chart for 10 weeks.

Joe Brown

(Guitar, vocals, b. 1941)

Discovered by TV producer Jack Good, guitarist Brown backed visiting American stars including Eddie Cochran and Gene Vincent, before launching his own career as a rocking Cockney with a handful of UK hit singles, before The Beatles changed the world. After appearing in British pop films and London theatre, Brown formed 1970s country rock combo Brown's Home Brew. His daughter, Sam Brown, had a brief late 1980s UK chart career.

see Sources & Sounds pp 34   see Key Artists pp 38

Johnny and Dorsey Burnette
(Vocal duo, 1958–61)

The Memphis-born brothers Dorsey (1932–79) and
Johnny (1934–64) were both successful amateur boxers
and formed the Rock And Roll Trio c. 1953 with
guitarist Paul Burlison. Their rockabilly, too wild for
the time, was later regarded as seminal, and the
Burnettes moved to California, where they began
songwriting (Ricky Nelson scored hits with their songs,
'It's Late' and 'Waitin' In School') and restarted
recording careers. Dorsey sang country, Johnny pop
with four US Top 20 hits in 1960–61 before he died
in a boating accident.

Freddie Cannon
(Vocals, b. 1940)

Massachusetts-born Frederick Picariello got his
nickname Freddy 'Boom Boom' Cannon from the bass
drum sound on his hits, which began in 1959 with
'Tallahassee Lassie', a US Top 10 item written by his
mother. His only million-seller, the same year's 'Way
Down Yonder In New Orleans', continued his place-
name fixation, but thereafter his hits became smaller
until 1962's 'Palisades Park' restored him to the US Top
3. With over 20 hits by 1965, Cannon was respected,
but ultimately unable to change with musical tastes.

Johnny Cash
(Guitar, singer/songwriter, 1932–2003)

Arkansas-born Cash enjoyed a 49-year career
involving several periods of huge popularity. After
USAF service, he formed a trio with Luther Perkins
(guitar) and Marshall Chapman (bass). Auditioning
for Sam Phillips at Sun Records in Memphis, Cash
played rockabilly, scoring more than 20 US country
hits and several US pop hits before signing with
Columbia/CBS in late 1958, when he became among
the biggest country music attractions, remaining with
the label until 1987. Cash became an American
treasure during the 1960s, particularly after recording
live albums at *Folsom Prison* (1968) and *San Quentin*
(1969), which both went triple platinum.
In 1968, he married June Carter (of The Carter
Family), and they fronted a hugely popular live revue
for many years. After 1976, further mainstream
success seemed an impossibility, until producer Rick
Rubin offered to produce him; 1994's *American
Recordings* was the first of four Grammy-winning
albums on Rubin's label. Cash's daughter, Rosanne,
keeps the Cash name popular.

Above

Johnny Cash, the 'Man In Black'.

Far Left

Crooner Pat Boone sold more
records than anyone except
Elvis in the 1950s.

🎙 *see Eddie Cochran pp 60* 🎙 *see Fats Domino pp 61* 🎙 *see Little Richard pp 66* 🎙 *see Gene Vincent pp 72*

'Searchin'' (1957, US Top 3), 'Yakety Yak' (1958, US No. 1/UK Top 20), 'Charlie Brown' (1959, US Top 3 /UK Top 10) and 'Poison Ivy' (US Top 10/ UK Top 20, later covered by The Rolling Stones). Tracks featured sax player King Curtis. Hits ended in early 1960s.

Eddie Cochran

(Guitar, singer/songwriter, 1938–60)

Oklahoma-born Cochran was a rising star of rock'n'roll, guest-starring in 1956's 'The Girl Can't Help It', the best ever rock movie. He wrote songs with lyrics that spoke to teenagers like 1958's 'Summertime Blues' (US Top 10/UK Top 20) and 1959's 'C'mon Everybody' (UK Top 10). After dying in a car crash while on tour in Britain with Gene Vincent, his UK popularity increased, with 1960's 'Three Steps To Heaven' topping the UK charts. After Presley and Holly, Cochran is probably the best-loved US rock'n'roll star in Britain, and among his other hits were 1959's 'Teenage Heaven' and 'Something Else' and his excellent cover of the Ray Charles classic, 'Hallelujah I Love Her So'. 1960's *Eddie Cochran Memorial Album* made the Top 10 of the UK album chart.

Danny and The Juniors

(Vocal group, 1955–present)

Originally known as The Juvenaires, this doo-wop group was formed in 1955 while members Danny Rapp, Frank Maffei, Joe Terranova and Dave White were still at high school in Philadelphia. They signed to Singular Records, owned by Artie Singer, and made the 1957 million-seller 'At The Hop', which topped the US singles chart for seven weeks on ABC-Paramount, and made the UK Top 3. Originally titled 'Do The Bop', it was written by Singer, White and Joe Madara. A similar 1958 follow-up, 'Rock & Roll Is Here To Stay', made the US Top 20. Rapp apparently committed suicide in 1983, but the group continued billed as Danny and The Juniors Featuring Joe Terry.

The Coasters

(Vocal group, 1955–61)

Formed in 1955 in Los Angeles by ex-members of The Robins: Carl Gardner and Bobby Nunn, with Billy Guy and Leon Hughes, plus Adolph Jacobs (guitar), The Coasters were a black act enjoying popularity across the colour divide. Produced by white New Yorkers Jerry Leiber and Mike Stoller, who also wrote their often humorous hits, they scored with million-sellers

Bobby Darin

(Singer/songwriter, 1936–73)

Aged 20, New York-born Walden Robert Cassotto's chart career started with the novelty million-seller, 'Splish Splash'. Leading The Rinky Dinks, he next charted with 'Early In The Morning' (later a hit for

see Introduction pp 32   *see* Sources & Sounds pp 34   *see* Key Artists pp 38

Buddy Holly), and in 1957 'Queen Of The Hop' also sold a million. His major breakthrough was 1959's million-selling 'Dream Lover', followed by his Sinatra-esque US/UK No. 1 cover of 'Mack The Knife', the first of several revamped oldies and novelties. He starred in *Come September* (1961) with his wife, Sandra Dee. When his popularity fell as British beat predominated, he became a troubadour, singing Tim Hardin songs from 1966–67, but died during heart surgery. Kevin Spacey's 2004 biopic *Beyond The Sea* helped keep the memory alive.

Dion and The Belmonts

(Vocal group, 1958–present)
Formed in New York's Bronx in 1958 by Dion DiMucci, Angelo D'Aleo, Carlo Mastangelo and Fred Milano, this doo-wop group had had several US hits by 1960, including 1959's 'A Teenager In Love', also a UK hit. Dion went solo in 1960, scoring more US hits, the biggest 1961's million-selling US No. 1, 'Runaround Sue', but label changes and drug addiction limited his big hits to the million-selling 1968 hit, 'Abraham, Martin & John'. Periodic reunions with The Belmonts,

1975's Phil Spector-produced 'Born To Be With You' and 1989's Dave Edmunds-produced 'Yo Frankie' confirmed his legendary status.

Fats Domino

(Piano, singer/songwriter, b. 1928)
Signed to Imperial Records, New Orleans-born Antoine Domino's first million-seller, 'The Fat Man' (1949) began a run of over 60 US pop and R&B hits by 1964, many written by Domino with Dave Bartholomew. Other million-selling classics included 'Ain't That A Shame' (1955), 'Bo Weevil', 'I'm In Love Again' and 'Blueberry Hill (all 1956), 'Blue Monday' (featured in *The Girl Can't Help It*) and 'I'm Walkin'' (both 1957) and 'Whole Lotta Loving' (1958). Domino's secret appears to be that he has never changed, his smoky Louisiana accent above his percussive piano-playing, making him instantly recognizable. Twist king Ernest Evans used the name Chubby Checker in polite emulation. Domino's last US hit was a 1968 cover of 'Lady Madonna' by The Beatles, who apparently wrote the song in Domino's style. In September 2005, Domino made international news bulletins when his house was destroyed by Hurricane Katrina, but happily survived.

Left
As well as being one of the most popular rock'n'roll teen idols of the decade, Bobby Darin was a versatile performer and actor, who was successful in other musical genres such as, folk, country, pop and jazz.

Below
The best-selling African-American singer of the 1950s and early 1960s, Fats Domino is renowned for his individualistic piano playing with its boogie-woogie influences.

🚗 *see* Ray Charles pp 42 🚗 *see* The Beatles pp 88 🚗 *see* Tim Hardin pp 141 🚗 *see* Chubby Checker pp 167

The Drifters
(Vocal group, 1953–present)

Formed in 1953, various versions of The Drifters have existed ever since. Among the significant members of the group among the dozens who have been involved are Clyde McPhatter (lead vocalist 1953–54), Johnny Moore (lead vocalist 1955–57, 1963–78, 1985–98), Ben E. King (lead vocalist 1958–60, 1981–85) and Rudy Lewis (lead vocalist 1960–64). Signed to Atlantic Records from 1953–72, The Drifters' biggest hits with McPhatter were 'Money Honey' (1953) and 'Honey Love' (1954). Manager George Treadwell owned the group name, and after Moore left in 1957, disbanded the group, replacing them with The Five Crowns (including Ben E. King), which he renamed The Drifters, who released 1959's million-sellers 'There Goes My Baby' and 'Dance With Me' (produced by Leiber and Stoller) and 1960's US No. 1 'Save The Last Dance For Me'. Leiber and Stoller also produced the group with Rudy Lewis singing lead, and hits continued with 1962's 'Up On The Roof' and 1964's 'Under The Boardwalk', until Lewis died of a heart attack. Moore took over lead vocals for less soulful hits

including 'Saturday Night At The Movies' (1964), but US pop hits ended in 1966. When Treadwell died, his wife, Faye, took control, and signed the group to Bell Records, for whom they made several ersatz UK soul hits from 1972. King's return restored some credibility.

Duane Eddy
(Guitar, b. 1938)

With producer/co-writer Lee Hazlewood, Eddy scored 20 US hits between 1958 and 1961, showcasing his 'twangy' guitar on the Jamie label, part-owned by Hazlewood. Eddy's US Top 10 hits were 1958's 'Rebel Rouser', 1959's 'Forty Miles Of Bad Road' and 1960's 'Because They're Young'. After signing with RCA in 1962, his appeal largely left him, his biggest hit being 1962's US Top 20 '(Dance With The) Guitar Man'. After a 20-year plus US chart absence, he returned as featured instrumentalist on a revival of his 1960 'Peter Gunn' hit by The Art Of Noise.

Adam Faith
(Vocals, 1940–2003)

London-born Terence Nelhams sang in skiffle group The Worried Men, before changing his name at UK TV guru Jack Good's suggestion. After early flops, arranger John Barry provided string backing for 1959's UK No. 1 'What Do You Want', while 1960's follow-up 'Poor Me' also topped the chart, and Faith accumulated 22 more hits by 1966. In 1972, he discovered Leo Sayer, and in 1974, starred with David

🎙 *see Introduction pp 32* 🎙 *see Sources & Sounds pp 34* 🎙 *see Key Artists pp 38*

Above

Californian Etta James is a
blues, jazz, R&B and gospel
singer who received her first
professional vocal training
at the tender age of five at
St Paul's Baptist Church in
Los Angeles.

Essex in *Stardust*. 1988 brought TV stardom as *Budgie*, and in 1993, he starred with Zoe Wanamaker in the *Love Hurts* TV series. During the early 1990s, he provided investment advice in the *Daily Mail*.

Connie Francis
(Vocals, b. 1938)
New Jersey-born Concetta Franconero appeared on Arthur Godfrey's TV talent show, and while still at university, signed to MGM Records. 1958's UK chart topper, 'Who's Sorry Now' was the first of eight mainly sentimental million-selling US hits, including 1959's 'Among My Souvenirs', and 1960's 'Everybody's Somebody's Fool', the first of three US No. 1s. Her second UK No. 1, 1958's 'Stupid Cupid', only made the US Top 20, but was one of 56 US hits before 1970. Her career was interrupted in 1974, when she was victim of a sex attack, but she returned to performing in 1978.

Alan Freed
(Disc jockey, 1922–65)
Freed, the DJ who gave rock'n'roll its name, fronted Moondog's Rock'n'Roll Party at Cleveland's WJW radio station, where he programmed mainly black R&B plus some early white rock'n'roll records. His vocal jive delighted his audience, and he also appeared in several early rock'n'roll exploitation movies, including *Rock Around The Clock*, *Rock, Rock, Rock* (both 1956) and others. He accepted a songwriting credit on Chuck Berry's 'Maybellene' in exchange for helping to make it a hit, and was accused of payola, after which he died an alcoholic accused of income tax evasion.

Etta James
(Vocals, b. 1938)
Los Angeles-born Jamesetta Hawkins was discovered by Johnny Otis, who helped her write her first US R&B hit (and four-week chart-topper), 1955's 'The Wallflower', an 'answer record' to Hank Ballard's 'Work With Me Annie'. Her 1960 breakthrough came with four US Hot 100 singles, including two duets with Harvey Fuqua of The Moonglows. Crossover R&B hits continued through the 1960s, but heroin addiction cramped her style. Her biggest hit was 1967's 'Tell Mama' (US Top 30), and the same year's 'I'd Rather Go Blind' (covered by Britain's Chicken Shack) is arguably this latter-day anti-drug campaigner's best-known song.

see Clyde McPhatter pp 23   see Johnny Otis pp 68   see Chuck Berry pp 167   see Ben E. King pp 172

Little Willie John

(Vocals, 1937–68)

Arkansas-born William Edgar John, who moved to Detroit as a child, was signed to King Records from 1955. A string of US R&B Top 20 hits followed, several of which crossed over to the US pop chart. He is said to have influenced many major soul singers of the 1960s, and his best-known hits included 'Need Your Love So Bad' (1956, covered by Fleetwood Mac), and 'Fever' (1956, US R&B No. 1/US pop Top 30, later covered with great success by Peggy Lee). John, whose sister was Mable John (once of The Raelettes, Ray Charles' vocal backing group), was convicted of manslaughter in 1966, and died of a heart attack in Washington State Prison.

Johnny and The Hurricanes

(Vocal/instrumental group, 1958–61)

Formed in Ohio in 1958 by John Pocisk (aka Johnny Paris, saxophone), Paul Tesluk (organ), Dave Yorko (guitar), Lionel Mattice (bass) and Tony Kaye (drums, replaced by Don Staczek on 'Red River Rock' and by Bo Savich), the group accumulated nine US hits between 1959 and 1961, the biggest of which was 1959's 'Red River Rock', a rocked-up version of 'Red River Valley'. The formula for their hits, most of which were dominated by Tesluk's organ, was to play well-known tunes in rock'n'roll style (e.g. 'Blue Tail Fly' became 1960's US Top 20 hit, 'Beatnik Fly'). The group disbanded in 1961, reputedly due to exhaustion from continual touring. John Pocisk, who performed until 2005, died in 2006.

Above
Surf-pop duo Jan and Dean first began singing together after football practice at high school, and their first stage performance was as The Barons at a school dance.

Jan and Dean

(Vocal duo, 1957–66)

In 1957, at Los Angeles high school, Jan Berry (1941–2004) and Dean Torrence (b. 1940), together with Bruce Johnston (later of The Beach Boys), drummer Sandy Nelson and Arnie Ginsburg, formed The Barons. Berry, Torrence and Ginsburg recorded 'Jennie Lee' (about a local stripper), which was released in 1958 and credited to Jan and Arnie, as Torrence was in the US Army reserves. Although it made the US Top 10, other Jan and Arnie singles flopped, and as Torrence returned, Ginsburg departed. With initial help from Lou Adler and Herb Alpert, Jan and Dean made surfing-style records. Their biggest hit was 1963 US No. 1, 'Surf City', co-written by Berry and Beach Boy Brian Wilson, while Torrence sang on 1966 Beach Boys hit, 'Barbara Ann'. Also in 1966, Berry was seriously injured in a car crash, signalling the end of the duo as chart contenders.

Right
Johnny and The Hurricanes developed a strong following in Europe, and in the early 1960s were supported at a show at the Star Club in Hamburg by a little-known band named The Beatles.

see Introduction pp 32 · see Sources & Sounds pp 34 · see Key Artists pp 38

Johnny Kidd and The Pirates

(Vocal/instrumental group, 1959–67)

Londoner Frederick Heath was vocalist/leader of one of the first credible UK beat groups. Wearing a patch over a defective eye, he became Johnny Kidd, and his backing group (guitarist Alan Caddy, Brian Gregg on bass and drummer Clem Cattini) The Pirates. Ten UK hits between 1959 and 1964 included chart-topping 'Shakin' All Over' (1960) and 'I'll Never Get Over You' (1963, Top 5). When The Pirates left Kidd in 1961, later joining The Tornados, they were replaced by Frank Farley (drums), John Spence (bass) and Mick Green (guitar). Kidd died in a car crash, and became a cult hero.

B.B. King

(Guitar, vocals, b. 1925)

Riley B. King, from Indianola, Mississippi, is arguably the last surviving authentic blues artist. Orphaned, he took up guitar aged 15, turning professional after US military service. In 1947, he moved to Memphis and lived with cousin Bukka White. There, he worked on a local radio station, acquiring his B.B. ('Blues Boy') epithet, also working with Bobby Bland and Johnny Ace. First recording in 1949, his breakthrough came with 1951's four-week US R&B chart-topper 'Three O'Clock Blues'. R&B hits continued, but after signing with ABC-Paramount circa 1964, he regularly crossed over to the US pop singles chart, also making the US pop album chart from 1968, with big albums like *Live And Well* and *Completely Well* (both 1959), *Live In Cook County Jail* (1971) and 1974's gold-certified *Together For The First Time … Live with Bobby Bland*. King toured relentlessly, and was said to have played 300 gigs per year between the mid-1950s and the late 1970s. Widely regarded as a true legend, King still performs and records, and has frequently guested with younger blues guitarists such as Eric Clapton, even sharing a 1989 minor US hit single, 'When Love Comes To Town', with U2.

The Kingston Trio

(Vocal/instrumental group, 1958–67)

Between 1958, when they formed, and 1963, The Kingston Trio, comprising Dave Guard (vocals, banjo) and vocalists/guitarists Bob Shane and Nick Reynolds released 17 albums, 10 of which made the US Top 3,

and seven of which were certified gold. Wearing matching striped shirts and with short hair, parents and middle-class kids in America saw them as the acceptable and non-threatening face of popular music. The career of the trio, who regarded their music as folk, even if it somehow lacked the political bite of The Weavers, took off in late 1958 with the US No. 1 'Tom Dooley', although later hit singles were few, but LPs were another story. Guard left in 1961, and was replaced by John Stewart (b. 1939). The arrival of The Beatles pushed them down the ladder and the group disbanded in 1967.

Above
B.B. King has called each of his guitars 'Lucille' since the day in 1949 when he nearly lost his precious Gibson L-30 guitar in a fire allegedly started by a woman named Lucille.

see Fleetwood Mac pp 107   *see* The Tornados pp 116   *see* The Beach Boys pp 120   *see* U2 pp 284

Buddy Knox

(Guitar, vocals, b. 1933)

Texas-born Knox formed The Rhythm Orchids at
West Texas State high school with Jimmy Bowen (bass,
vocals). 'Party Doll' (by Knox) and 'I'm Stickin' With
You' (by Bowen), recorded by Norman Petty, which
possibly influenced Buddy Holly to choose Petty as his
producer, were released as the two sides of a 1957
million-selling single. Thereafter, Knox managed lesser
hits until 1961, but Bowen became a label executive
and remains a much in-demand record producer.

Brenda Lee

(Vocals, b. 1944)

The diminutive Georgia-born Brenda Tarpley turned
professional aged six, and was known as 'Little Miss
Dynamite', debuting on the US pop and country charts
in early 1957. 1959's 'Sweet Nothin's', a sexy rocker,
was her first US Top 5 hit, and her biggest success
came with 1960's million-selling US No. 1 ballad,
'I'm Sorry'. 'Rockin' Around The Christmas Tree' was
another 1960 million-seller, and she accumulated over
50 US pop hits by the end of the decade, also releasing
20 UK hits by 1965.

Jerry Lee Lewis

(Piano, vocals, b. 1935)

After signing to Sun Records
in 1957, Louisiana-born
rock'n'roller Lewis, noted for
his percussive piano style,
opened his account with two
million-selling US Top 3 hits,
'Whole Lot Of Shakin' Going
On' and 'Great Balls Of Fire'
(both 1957), but caused
major media controversy
during a 1958 UK tour when
it was discovered that his
wife, who was also his cousin,
was 13 years old (legal in
parts of the US, unacceptable
in the UK). This blighted his
pop career, but from the late
1960s onwards, he combined
the rockabilly that made him
famous with country music, becoming a major US
star with over 60 US country hits, many making the
Top 10, including his chart-topping 1972 revival of
'Chantilly Lace'. Now over 70, Lewis continues to
tour, and remains one of the greatest early
rock'n'rollers. Dennis Quaid played him in 1989's
Great Balls Of Fire movie.

Little Richard

(Piano, vocals, b. 1932)

Georgia-born Richard Penniman, who combines frantic
vocals with uninhibited pianistics, was one of 12
children. Raised in a religious family, he started recording
for RCA in 1951 after winning a talent contest. Chart
success followed his signing with Specialty Records,
where Bumps Blackwell produced a series of classic
rock'n'roll tracks between 1955 and 1958, including
1955's 'Tutti Frutti', 1956's million-selling 'Long Tall
Sally' and 'Rip It Up', 1957's 'Lucille' and 'Keep A
Knockin'' and 1958's 'Good Golly Miss Molly',

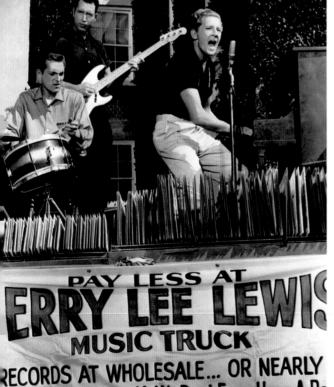

PAY LESS AT
ERRY LEE LEWIS
MUSIC TRUCK
RECORDS AT WHOLESALE... OR NEARLY

see Introduction pp 32   *see* Sources & Sounds pp 34   *see* Key Artists pp 38

among others. While touring Australia in 1957, he abandoned the music business, apparently after seeing the Russian Sputnik space rocket, which he felt was a divine sign to change his behaviour. He studied to become a preacher, only recording gospel music but returned to the fray in the mid-1960s. While he remained a dynamic live performer and an undoubted legend, his records rarely matched his 1950s rock'n'roll hits.

Frankie Lymon and The Teenagers
(Vocal group, 1955–present)
New Yorker Lymon was invited to join a school vocal group with Sherman Gaines (1940–78), Jimmy Merchant, Joe Negroni and Herman Santiago. Before finding Lymon, the others, who were known as The Premiers, were working on a song they had written, but needed a soprano lead voice, a vacancy Lymon filled. The result was the 1956 million-selling US Top 10 hit, 'Why Do Fools Fall In Love', which also topped the UK chart. The group managed a few more minor hits from 1956–57, the best being 1957's UK Top 5 hit, 'Baby Baby', but without the novelty aspect, the group were in decline. Lymon made the US chart with 1960's 'Little Bitty Pretty One', but drug problems resulted in his early death. Later, both The Beach Boys and Diana Ross recorded 'Why Do Fools Fall In Love', and clearly The Jackson Five were strongly influenced by The Teenagers.

The Moonglows
(Vocal group, 1952–60, 1972–present)
Formed in 1952 in Cleveland, Ohio, this doo-wop outfit comprised Harvey Fuqua, Bobby Lester, Alexander 'Pete' Graves, Prentiss Barnes and guitarist Billy Johnson. Originally called The Crazy Sounds, they changed their name at Alan Freed's suggestion. After several minor singles, they signed with Chess Records in 1954, when they released their first hit, 'Sincerely', which credited Freed as co-writer of the song. Six further US R&B Top 20 hits followed by 1958, the last of which, 'Ten Commandments Of Love', is regarded as their classic. Fuqua, whose uncle, Charlie Fuqua, was a member of the Ink Spots, left in 1958. He then joined Motown as producer and songwriter for The (Detroit) Spinners, among others.

see The Ink Spots pp 22   see The Detroit Spinners pp 168   see The Jacksons pp 172   see Diana Ross and The Supremes pp 176

Above

Despite being a teenage idol, Ricky Nelson had a strong musical background, and enjoyed working with a variety of highly regarded musicians, such as The Jordanaires and Johnny and Dorsey Burnette.

Ricky Nelson

(Vocals, 1940–85)

Born into a showbiz family – his father was bandleader Ozzie Nelson – Eric Hilliard Nelson starred in the the radio show and TV sitcom, *The Adventures Of Ozzie & Harriet*, with his family. In 1956, a girlfriend told him she preferred Elvis Presley, so he made a record. 1957's million-selling 'I'm Walking'/'A Teenager's Romance' started a career that produced over 50 US hits by 1973, including more million-sellers: 1957's 'Be-Bop Baby' and 'Stood Up', 1958's 'Believe What You Say', US No. 1 'Poor Little Fool' and 'Lonesome Tears' and 1961's 'Travelin' Man'. A 1963 label change brought fewer and smaller hits, as the teenage pop star Ricky became the grown-up country rock star Rick. His last million-seller was 1972's 'Garden Party' and he died in a plane crash.

Roy Orbison

(Singer/songwriter, 1936–88)

Right

Johnny Otis was an A&R man and an influential disk jockey as well as a performer and composer; and as well as 'discovering' many artists, his 'Every Beat Of My Heart' would go on to be a huge hit for Gladys Knight.

Born in Texas, the high-voiced Orbison first recorded with Norman Petty, but his first US chart success was 1956's rockabilly 'Ooby Dooby' on Sun Records. After writing 'Claudette' (a 1957 hit for The Everly Brothers), he became a Nashville songwriter for Acuff-Rose, and restarted his recording career with 1960's million-selling ballad, 'Only The Lonely', setting a pattern for many later woebegone hits, including 1961's US No. 1, 'Running Scared', 1964's UK No. 1, 'It's Over' and US and UK No. 1, 'Oh Pretty Woman'. A 1965 label change and evolution of pop music saw his US hits end in 1967, and his UK hits in 1969, while he was beset with family tragedies. In 1988,

he joined The Traveling Wilburys with George Harrison, Bob Dylan, Tom Petty and Jeff Lynne, who all held him in high esteem, but he died of a heart attack before he could take real advantage of his restored popularity.

Johnny Otis

(Bandleader, singer/songwriter, b. 1921)

Of Greek parentage, California-born John Veliotes topped the US R&B chart twice in 1950 with 'Double Crossing Blues' and 'Mistrustin' Blues', both credited to The Johnny Otis Orchestra. After moving from Berkeley to Los Angeles, he supposedly discovered such notable R&B vocalists as 'Little' Esther Phillips, Willie Mae 'Big Mama' Thornton, Etta James, Sugar Pie DeSanto, Hank Ballard, Jackie Wilson and Little Willie John, as well as The Robins (who became The Coasters), all of whom were featured vocalists in his band. More US R&B hits followed, the first one to cross over being 1958's 'Willie And The Hand Jive' (US Top 10). Cliff Richard covered the song in the UK where Otis was already known for his noisy 1957 UK Top 3 hit, 'Ma, He's Making Eyes At Me', featuring vocalist Marie Adams. A veritable R&B pioneer, the Otis tradition is being maintained by his singer/guitarist son, Shuggie Otis (b. 1953).

Carl Perkins

(Guitar, vocals, 1932–88)

Tennessee-born Perkins was a rockabilly pioneer. Signed to Sun Records in 1955, he is most famous for 1956's US country chart-topper/US Pop Top 3/UK Top 10 'Blue Suede Shoes'. On his way to New York for a

🎙 *see Introduction pp 32* 🎙 *see Sources & Sounds pp 34* 🎙 *see Key Artists pp 38*

TV appearance, Perkins was involved in a serious car crash, and a 1956 Elvis Presley cover version of the song was a million-seller. Perkins was sidelined and despite continuing to record, never again reached the US Top 50. As George Harrison was a big fan, The Beatles covered the Perkins compositions 'Honey Don't', 'Matchbox' and 'Everybody's Trying To Be My Baby', but attempts to revive his career were generally fruitless, and he played in the Johnny Cash touring show for 10 years from 1965, eventually dying of throat cancer.

The Platters

(Vocal group, 1953–present)

Manager/producer Buck Ram formed The Platters in Los Angeles in 1953 with original members Tony Williams (lead vocalist), David Lynch (tenor), Alex Hodge (baritone), replaced by Paul Robi, Herb Reed (bass) and Zola Taylor. Signed to Mercury Records, their smooth harmonies brought hits with 1955's million-selling 'Only You (And You Alone)', followed two months later by a second US chart-topper, 'The Great Pretender'. Appearing in several rock'n'roll exploitation movies, the group released 'My Prayer' (1956), which also topped the US chart, and 1958 brought two more US No. 1s, 'Twilight Time' and 'Smoke Gets In Your Eyes'. After 40 US hits by 1967 and numerous personnel changes, many Platters line-ups with few, if any, original members remain active.

Cliff Richard

(Vocals, b. 1940)

Born Harry Webb in India, Cliff Richard is the ultimate British pop star, with over 100 UK hit singles to his credit since 1958, when 'Move It', widely regarded as the first credible British rock'n'roll record, reached the UK Top 3. More than a dozen UK No. 1s include 1959's 'Living Doll' and 'Travellin' Light', 'The Young Ones' (1962) and 'Summer Holiday' (1963), both title songs of movies in which Richard starred with The Shadows, his backing group until 1968. Circa 1966, he publicly proclaimed that he was a Christian, and has since released both religious and secular records. After a number of his singles failed to chart during the 1970s, he returned in 1979 with his 11th UK No. 1, 'We Don't Talk Anymore'. More recent chart-toppers include the Christmas singles: 1988's 'Mistletoe And Wine' and 1999's 'The Millennium Prayer'. Cliff Richard, initially the British answer to Elvis Presley, remains Britain's foremost domestic pop star, but remains largely unknown in the US.

Left
The Platters were one of the most successful vocal groups of the early 1950s and were the first rock'n'roll group to have a Top 10 US album.

Below
Cliff Richard was the first artist in Britain to emulate the Presley look. His hair- and dress-style mimicked the teen-idol's, and he adopted a rock attitude when performing: rarely looking directly at the camera or audience, or even smiling.

see Etta James pp 63   *see* The Beatles pp 88   *see* Bob Dylan pp 126   *see* Tom Petty pp 310

Jack Scott
(Singer/songwriter, b. 1936)

Canadian Jack Scafone Jr. has enjoyed hits on three record labels since his 1958 breakthrough with the US Top 3 rock ballad, 'My True Love', whose full throttle rock'n'roll flipside, 'Leroy', also peaked just outside the US Top 10. When Scott left Carlton Records in 1959, after nine US hits in 18 months, he signed with Top Rank Records, instantly producing another US Top 5, 'What In The World's Come Over You'. He signed with Capitol Records in 1961 and was subsequently regarded as a country artist, although his early classics remain timeless.

Screamin' Jay Hawkins
(Vocals, b. 1929)

Ohio-born ex-Golden Gloves champion boxer Jalacy Hawkins evolved a stage show in which his props included a coffin and a skull, and although he never actually achieved any hit records, his larger-than-life stage show brought him great popularity. He also co-wrote 'I Put A Spell On You', a song which was a UK hit for Nina Simone, Alan Price (ex-The Animals) and Bryan Ferry. Hawkins was surely a role model for Screaming Lord Sutch, Arthur Brown and others.

Neil Sedaka
(Piano, singer/songwriter, b. 1939)

New York-born Sedaka started writing songs as a teenager with lyricist Howard Greenfield. They wrote many hits for Sedaka, including 1959's 'Oh Carol', 1961's 'Happy Birthday Sweet Sixteen' and 1962's US No. 1 , 'Breaking Up Is Hard To Do'. The early 1970s saw a Sedaka renaissance when he made two albums

Above

Prolific songwriter Neil Sedaka.

Right

Screamin' Jay Hawkins originally intended to become an opera singer, but his lack of success led him to the career of blues pianist, singer and wildly theatrical performer.

Far Right

Many considered Tommy Steele Britain's answer to Elvis Presley.

Bobby Rydell
(Vocals, b. 1942)

Philadelphia-born Robert Ridarelli regularly appeared on Paul Whiteman's TV talent show, and played with Frankie Avalon in Rocco and The Saints, before signing with the local Cameo label in 1959. His biggest success was 1960's million-selling US Top 3 hit, 'Wild One', although the same year's 'Volare' (US Top 5) has aged better. Probably appreciated more for his good looks than his vocal prowess, Rydell accumulated 30 US hits by 1965.

see Introduction pp 32   see Sources & Sounds pp 34   see Key Artists pp 38

with what would become 10CC, followed with another US No. 1, 'Laughter In The Rain' (1974). 1975 brought a third US chart-topper, 'Bad Blood'. Sedaka and Greenfield also wrote 'Is This The Way To Amarillo', a major hit for Tony Christie.

The Shadows
(Instrumental/vocal group, 1958–2004)
Formed in 1958 by Newcastle teenagers Hank B. Marvin (lead guitar) and Bruce Welch (rhythm guitar), the friends became the backbone of Cliff Richard's backing group, The Drifters, who were joined later in 1958 by Terence 'Jet' Harris (bass guitar) and Tony Meehan (drums). In 1959, the group became The Shadows and continued to back Richard until 1968, when the line-up included John Rostill (bass) and Brian Bennett (drums). By this time they had accumulated 26 UK hits including five UK No. 1s, among them 1961's 'Kon-Tiki', and 1962's 'Wonderful Land'. The Shadows have reformed spasmodically since 1974, but performed farewell tours in the twenty-first century.

Tommy Steele
(Vocals, b. 1936)
Born Thomas Hicks, Steele began playing ersatz British rock'n'roll at the London 2I's coffee bar. Spotted by Fleet Street photographer John Kennedy, who became his manager, Steele co-wrote 'Rock With The Caveman' with Lionel Bart, and the single made the UK Top 20. In 1957, Steele covered 'Singing The Blues', which topped the UK chart. Later that year the biopic, *The Tommy Steele Story*, was released, and Steele released more hits until 1961, when he moved into the thespian world, starring in stage and screen hits such as *Half A Sixpence* (1965), *The Happiest Millionaire* (1967) and *Finian's Rainbow* (1968).

Conway Twitty
(Vocals, 1933–93)
Mississippi-born Harold Jenkins, who changed his name in 1957 to reflect the place names of Conway, Arkansas, and Twitty, Texas, started his career as a rock'n'roll singer in the late 1950s, scoring his biggest hit in 1958 with 'It's Only Make Believe', continuing in 1959 with 'Mona Lisa' and a second US million-

seller, 'Lonely Blue Boy'. In 1965, Twitty moved into country music and became one of the most successful country acts of all time with 40 US country No. 1s, including five duets with Loretta Lynn.

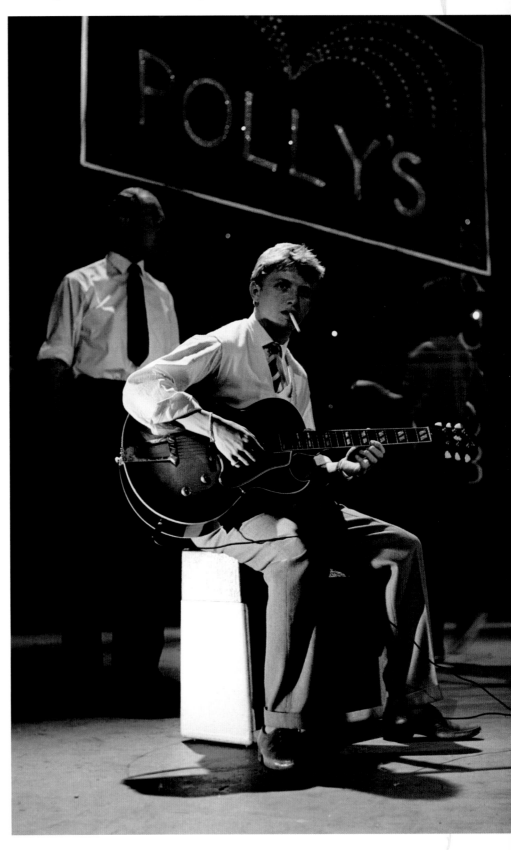

🎵 *see Frankie Avalon pp 56*   🎵 *see Cliff Richard pp 69*   🎵 *see Screaming Lord Sutch pp 114*   🎵 *see 10CC pp 244*

Bob Bogle (bass), Don Wilson (guitar) and Howie Johnson (drums), the group's first and best-known hit was 'Walk Don't Run', which they heard played by Chet Atkins and was written by jazz guitarist Johnny Smith. Two more US Top 10 hits, 1964's 'Walk Don't Run '64' and 1969's 'Hawaii Five-O', were almost irrelevant, as The Ventures were superstars in Japan, where they have reputedly released over 100 original albums. The current line-up is McGee (lead guitar, Wilson (guitar), Bogle (bass) and Leon Taylor.

Gene Vincent
(Vocals, 1935–71)
Virginia-born Eugene Vincent Craddock, who wore a steel leg brace after a 1953 motorcycle crash and used it as a stage prop, fronted The Blue Caps: Cliff Gallup (lead guitar), Willie Williams (rhythm guitar), Jack Neal (double bass), and Dickie Harrell (drums). Gallup's lead guitar work on Vincent's early recordings has been admired by innumerable rock'n'roll players. Vincent's classic is his 1956 debut hit, 'Be-Bop-A-Lula', which he and the Blue Caps memorably performed in the 1956 rock'n'roll movie *The Girl Can't Help It*. Surprisingly, Vincent released more hits in the UK than the US, and he suffered further injury in the 1960 car crash in Britain that killed Eddie Cochran. This led to alcohol problems, and a once-great rocker turned to country music in the last decade of his life.

Above

Ritchie Valens was a completely self-taught musician whose playing was full of improvisation and exciting riffs.

Far Right

Jackie Wilson had a unique singing voice that enabled him to cross easily into the pop charts.

Right

Gene Vincent grew up listening to country, R&B and gospel, and by the time he received his first guitar aged 12 was playing along with his black neighbours on his parents' porch.

Ritchie Valens
(Guitar, vocals, 1941–59)
In 1958, California-born Richard Valenzuela had already released the million-selling 'Donna' as well as two other US hits, 'Come On Let's Go' and 'La Bamba', and was close to becoming a major star when he died in the air crash that also killed Buddy Holly and The Big Bopper. In the 1980s, Hispanic-American quintet Los Lobos topped the US chart with their revival of 'La Bamba', the title tune of the feature film of the life of Valens.

The Ventures
(Instrumental group, 1960–present)
Formed in Seattle by Nokie Edwards (lead guitar),

see Introduction pp 32   *see* Sources & Sounds pp 34   *see* Key Artists pp 38

Marty Wilde

(Singer/songwriter, b. 1939)

London-born Reginald Smith enjoyed 15 UK hit singles between 1958 and 1962. He appeared regularly on early British TV pop shows: 6.5 *Special* and *Oh Boy*, and was the star of *Boy Meets Girls*, where he met and married his wife, a member of The Vernons Girls, but marriage affected his popularity. Arguably the closest home-grown rival to Cliff Richard at the time, Wilde appeared in the West End musical, *Bye Bye Birdie*, before success as a songwriter with three 1968 UK hits: The Casuals' 'Jesamine', Status Quo's 'Ice In The Sun' and Lulu's 'I'm A Tiger'. In the early 1980s, his daughter, Kim Wilde, was successful with the assistance of dad and brother Ricky.

Chuck Willis

(Singer/songwriter, 1928–58)

Known as 'The Sheik Of The Stroll', Atlanta-born Harold Willis was a rising star, with a string of US R&B hits to his credit, the biggest 1957's R&B No. 1, 'C.C. Rider', which also made the US pop Top 20. Signed to Okeh Records between 1952 and 1954, his career took off in 1956, when he signed with Atlantic, for whom he made a second posthumous R&B chart-topper, 1958's ironically titled 'What Am I Living For', dying of peritonitis after a stomach ulcer.

Jackie Wilson

(Singer/songwriter 1934–84)

Detroit-born Jackie Wilson, an ex-amateur boxer, sang with gospel groups before replacing Clyde McPhatter in Billy Ward & The Dominoes in 1953. His first solo success came with 1957's UK and US hit, Reet Petite', co-written by Berry Gordy Jr., who went on to found Motown Records. His first US Top 40 hit was 1958's 'To Be Loved', and his first US Top 10 single was 1958's 'Lonely Teardrops', also co-written by Gordy. Wilson's dynamic stage show vastly increased his popularity, and by 1972, he had accumulated over 50 US pop hits, the biggest being 1960's 'Night', while arguably the best-known was 1967's '(Your Love Keeps Lifting Me) Higher And Higher'. By 1970, the hits had diminished, and in 1972, he suffered a massive heart attack while on stage in New Jersey, and remained hospitalized in a coma for the rest of his life. The same year, Van Morrison had a minor hit single with a tribute song titled 'Jackie Wilson Said (I'm In Heaven When You Smile)'.

see Chet Atkins pp 56   *see* Berry Gordy pp 171   *see* Van Morrison pp 219   *see* Status Quo pp 222

List of Artists

Entries appear in the following order: name, music style, year(s) of popularity, type of artist, country of origin

Ace, Johnny, Rhythm & Blues, 1950s, Artist, American
Adams, Faye, Piedmont Blues; Jump Blues; Rhythm & Blues, 1950s-1960s, Artist, American
Adams, Johnny, The Classic Soul Era; Rhythm & Blues, 1950s-1990s, Artist, American
Adams, Pepper, Hard Bop, 1950s-1980s, Artist, American
Adderley, Cannonball, Hard Bop, 1950s-1970s, Artist, American
Adderley, Nat, Hard Bop, 1950s-1990s, Artist, American
Adkins, Hasil, Rockabilly, 1950s-1990s, Artist, American
Aitken, Laurel, Ska; Roots, 1950s-1990s, Artist, Jamaican
All Day Long, The Classic Soul Era, 1950s, Artist, American
Allison, Mose, Hard Bop, 1950s-, Artist, American
Alphonso, Rolando, Ska; Roots; Rock Steady, 1950s-1970s, Artist, Cuban
Alston, Shirley, The Classic Soul Era, 1950s-1970s, Artist; Songwriter, American
Amram, David, Fusion and Jazz Rock; Latin Jazz; Bebop, 1950s-1990s, Artist; Composer, American
Andrews, Lee, and the Hearts, Doo-Wop, 1950s, Artist, American
Anka, Paul, 1950s Pop, 1950s-, Artist, Canadian
Arnold, Billy Boy, Chicago Blues, 1950s-, Artist, American
Avalon, Frankie, 1950s Pop, 1950s-1970s, Artist, American
Bachelors, The, Irish Folk; Folk Pop, 1950s-1980s, Artist, Irish
Baez, Joan, 1950s Pop Singer/Songwriters; Traditional Folk; Folk Rock; Political Folk & Protest Songs; The Folk Revival, 1950s-, Artist; Songwriter, American
Baker, Lavern, Rhythm & Blues; Jump Blues; The Classic Soul Era; 1950s-1960s; 1980s-1990s, Artist, American
Baker, Mickey, Rhythm & Blues; Piedmont Blues 1950s-1970s, Artist, American
Baldry, Long John, British Blues; Blues Rock, 1950s-, Artist, British
Ballard, Hank, Rhythm & Blues; Northern Soul, 1950s-1990s, Artist; Songwriter, American
Barnum, H. B., The Classic Soul Era, 1950s-1960s, Producer; Artist, American
Barron, Kenny, Hard Bop, 1950s-, Artist, American
Beck, Joe, Fusion, 1950s-, Artist, American
Bell, Thom, Urban Soul, 1950s-1990s, Producer; Artist, American
Belmonts, The, Doo-Wop, 1950s-1970s, Artist, American
Belvin, Jesse, The Classic Soul Era, 1950s, Artist, American
Bennett, Lou, The Classic Soul Era, 1950s-1980s, Artist, American
Benton, Brook, Rhythm & Blues, 1950s-1970s, Artist, American
Berry, Chuck, Rock'n'Roll, 1950s-1980s, Artist; Songwriter, American
Berry, Richard, Rhythm & Blues, 1950s-1960s, Artist, American
Big Bopper, The, Rock'n'Roll, 1950s, Artist, American
Bill Black Combo, Rock'n'Roll; Rockabilly, 1950s-1960s, Artist, American
Bill Haley and his Comets, Rock'n'Roll, 1950s-1960s, Artist, American
Black, Bill, The Classic Soul Era, 1950s-1960s, Artist, American
Blackwell, Otis, Piedmont Blues, 1950s-1970s, Songwriter; Artist, American
Bland, Bobby 'Blue', The Classic Soul Era; Texas Blues; Rhythm & Blues, 1950s-, Artist, American
Blue, Little Joe, Jump Blues; Modern Electric Blues, 1950s-1980s, Artist, American
Bo, Eddie, Rhythm & Blues, 1950s-, Artist, American
Bob and Earl, Rock'n'Roll, 1950s-1960s, Artist, American
Bobettes, The, 1950s Pop, 1950s-1970s, Artist, American
Booker, James, The Classic Soul Era; Boogie-Woogie; Louisianna Blues 1950s-1980s, Artist, American
Boone, Pat, 1950s Pop, 1950s-1990s, Artist, American
Brim, John, Chicago Blues, 1950s-1960s; 1990s, Artist, American
Brooks, Lonnie, Modern Electric Blues, 1950s-1990s, Artist, American
Brooks, Tina, Hard Bop, 1950s-1960s, Artist, American
Brown, Clifford, Hard Bop; Bebop, 1950s, Artist, American
Brown, James, Funk; Funk Soul; Rhythm & Blues, 1950s-1980s, Artist; Songwriter, American
Brown, Jim Ed, The Nashville Sound; Honky Tonk, 1950s-1990s, Artist, American
Brown, Nappy, Jump Blues; Rhythm & Blues, 1950s-1960s; 1980s-1990s, Artist, American
Bryant, Ray, Soul Jazz; Swing; Bebop, 1950s-, Artist, American
Bryant, Rusty, Soul Jazz; Hard Bop, 1950s-1980s, Artist, American
Budwig, Monty, Cool Jazz; Bebop, 1950s-1990s, Artist, American
Burgess, Sonny, Rockabilly, 1950s-1990s, Artist, American
Burke, Solomon, The Classic Soul Era, 1950s-, Artist, American
Burnette, Johnny, Rockabilly, 1950s-1960s, Artist; Songwriter, American
Burrell, Kenny, Bebop; Hard Bop; Cool Jazz, 1950s-, Artist, American
Butler, Jerry, 1950s Pop, Northern Soul; Rhythm & Blues, 1950s-1990s, Artist, American
Byrd, Donald, Funk; Hard Bop; Fusion, 1950s-, Artist, American
Cadets, The, Doo-Wop; Rhythm & Blues, 1950s-1960s, Artist, American
Cadillacs, The, Doo-Wop, 1950s-1960s; 1990s, Artist, American
Cannon, Freddy, Rock'n'Roll, 1950s-1980s, Artist, American
Capris, The, Doo-Wop, 1950s; 1980s, Artist, American
Carr, Sister Wynona, Jump Blues; Rhythm & Blues, 1950s, Artist, American
Carter, Betty, Bebop, 1950s-1990s, Artist, American
Cash, Johnny, Rockabilly; Rock'n'Roll; Mainstream Country; Country Rock, 1950s-, Artist, American
Cellos, The, Doo-Wop, 1950s, Artist, American
Chambers, Paul, Hard Bop, 1950s-1960s, Artist, American
Chantels, The, Doo-Wop; Funk Soul, 1950s-1960s, Artist, American
Chase, Lincoln, The Classic Soul Era, 1950s-1970s, Artist; Songwriter, American
Cherry, Don, Free Jazz; Fusion and Jazz Rock, 1950s-1990s, Artist, American
Chords, The, Doo-Wop, 1950s-1960s, Artist, American
Clark, Dee, Northern Soul; Rhythm & Blues, 1950s-1980s, Artist, American
Clark, Sonny, Bebop; Hard Bop, 1950s-1960s, Artist, American
Clearwater, Eddy, Modern Electric Blues; Rhythm & Blues; Chicago Blues, 1950s-, Artist, American
Cleftones, The, Doo-Wop, 1950s-1960s, Artist, American
Cline, Patsy, The Nashville Sound, 1950s-1960s, Artist, American
Coasters, The, Doo-Wop; Rock'n'Roll; Rhythm & Blues, 1950s-1970s, Artist, American
Cobb, Jimmy, Hard Bop, 1950s-, Artist, American
Cochran, Eddie, Rock'n'Roll; Rockabilly, 1950s, Artist, American
Coleman, George, Hard Bop, 1950s-, Artist, American
Coles, Johnny, Hard Bop, 1950s-1990s, Artist, American
Collins Kids, The, Rockabilly, 1950s-1960s, Artist, American

Collins, Albert, Texas Blues; Modern Electric Blues, 1950s-1990s, Artist; Songwriter, American
Collins, Judy, Folk Rock; The Folk Revival; 1950s Pop Singer/Songwriters, 1950s-, Artist; Songwriter, American
Collins, Tommy, Honky Tonk, 1950s-1970s, Artist; Songwriter, American
Coltrane, John, Modal Jazz; Free Jazz; Hard Bop, 1950s-1960s, Artist, American
Cookie and the Cupcakes, Rhythm & Blues, 1950s-1960s, Artist, American
Cookies, The, 1950s Pop, 1950s-1960s, Artist, American
Cortez, Dave 'Baby', The Classic Soul Era, 1950s-1970s, Artist, American
Cotton, Elizabeth, Rhythm & Blues, 1950s-1980s, Artist; Composer, American
Cotton, James, Modern Electric Blues; Chicago Blues, 1950s-, Artist, American
Cramer, Floyd, The Nashville Sound, 1950s-1990s, Artist, American
Crawford, Hank, Soul Jazz; Hard Bop, 1950s-1990s, Artist, American
Crests, The, Doo-Wop, 1950s-1960s, Artist, American
Crew-Cuts, The, Rhythm & Blues; Doo-Wop, 1950s-1960s, Artist, Canadian

Crickets, The, Rock'n'Roll; Rockabilly, 1950s-1980s, Artist, American
Crows, The, Doo-Wop, 1950s, Artist, American
Cruz, Celia, Latin; Latin Jazz, 1950s-, Artist, Cuban
Cuba, Joe, Latin; Latin Jazz, 1950s-1970s; 1990s, Artist, American
Curtis, King, The Classic Soul Era, 1950s-1970s, Artist, American
Dale, Larry, Piedmont Blues; Rhythm & Blues, 1950s-1960s, Artist, American
Danny and the Juniors, Rhythm & Blues, 1950s-1960s, Artist, American
Darin, Bobby, Folk Rock; 1950s Pop, 1950s-1970s, Artist, American
Davis, Richard, Hard Bop, 1950s-, Artist, American
Davis, Walter Jr, Bebop; Hard Bop, 1950s; 1970s-1980s, Artist, American
Dawson, Ronnie, Rockabilly, 1950s-1960s, Artist, American
Day, Bobby, Doo-Wop; Rock'n'Roll, 1950s, Artist, American
Dells, The, 1950s Pop; Urban Soul, 1950s-1990s, Artist, American
Del-Vikings, The, Doo-Wop, 1950s-1960s, Artist, American
Detroit Spinners, The, The Classic Soul Era; Rhythm & Blues, 1950s-, Artist, American

Dexter, Al, The Nashville Sound; Honky Tonk; Cowboy Music, 1950s-1960s, Artist; Songwriter, American
Diamonds, The, Doo-Wop, 1950s-1970s, Artist, Canadian
Diddley, Bo, Rock'n'Roll; Rhythm & Blues; Chicago Blues, 1950s-, Artist, American
Dion and the Belmonts, Doo-Wop, 1950s, Artist, American
Dion, Doo-Wop; Rock'n'Roll, 1950s-, Artist, American
Dominoes, Rhythm & Blues, 1950s-1960s, Artist, American
Don and Dewey, Rhythm & Blues, 1950s-1960s, Artist, American
Donaldson, Lou, Bebop; Hard Bop, 1950s-, Artist, American
Donegan, Lonnie, Skiffle; Rockabilly; UK Folk, 1950s-1990s, Artist, British
Drew, Kenny, Hard Bop, 1950s-1990s, Artist, American
Drifters, The, Doo-Wop; Rhythm & Blues; The Classic Soul Era, 1950s-1990s, Artist, American
Du Droppers, The, Rhythm & Blues, 1950s, Artist, American

Duke, Douglas, The Classic Soul Era, 1950s, Artist, American
Duncan, Johnny, Skiffle, 1950s-1970s, Artist, British
Duvivier, George, Swing; Bebop, 1950s-1990s, Artist, American
Eardley, Jon, Cool Jazz; Bebop, 1950s-1970s, Artists, American
Eccles, Clancy, Rock Steady; Ska, 1950s-1980s, Artist, Jamaican
Eddy, Duane, Rock'n'Roll, 1950s-1980s, Artist, American
Edsels, The, Doo-Wop, 1950s-1960s, Artist, American
Egan, Willie, Boogie-Woogie, 1950s, Artist, American
El Dorados, The, Doo-Wop, 1950s; 1990s, Artist, American
Elbert, Donnie, The Classic Soul Era, 1950s-1970s, Artist, American
Elliot, Ramblin' Jack, Traditional Folk; The Folk Revival, 1950s, Artist, American
Elliott, Don, Cool Jazz; Swing; Fusion, 1950s-1970s, Artist, American
Ellis, Alton, Ska; Rock Steady, 1950s-, Artist, Jamaican
Erteghun, Armet, Funk Soul, 1950s-1960s, Producer, Turkish
Ervin, Booker, Hard Bop, 1950s-1960s, Artist, American
Esquires, The, The Classic Soul Era, 1950s-1990s, Artist, American
Everett, Betty, The Classic Soul Era, 1950s-1970s, Artist, American
Everly Brothers, The, Country Rock; Folk Rock; Rock'n'Roll; Rockabilly, 1950s-1990s, Artist, American
Fabian, 1950s Pop, 1950s-1970s, Artist, American
Fagerquist, Don, Cool Jazz; Bebop, 1950s, Artist, American
Faith, Adam, 1950s Pop, 1950s-1990s, Artist, British
Falcon, The, The Classic Soul Era, 1950s-1960s, Artist, American
Farlow, Tal, Bebop; Cool Jazz, 1950s-1990s, Artist, American
Farmer, Art, Bebop; Hard Bop; Cool Jazz, 1950s-1990s, Artist, American
Feathers, Charlie, Rockabilly, 1950s-1990s, Artist; Songwriter, American
Ferguson, Maynard, Hard Bop, 1950s-1990s, Artist, Canadian
Fireballs, The, Rock'n'Roll, 1950s-1960s, Artist, American
Five Keys, The, Doo-Wop; Piedmont Blues, 1950s-1960s, Artist, American
Five Royales, The, Rhythm & Blues, 1950s-1960s, Artist, American
Five Satins, The, Doo-Wop, 1950s-1960s, Artist, American
Flamingos, The, Doo-Wop, 1950s-1960s, Artist, American
Fleetwoods, The, Rhythm & Blues; Doo-Wop, 1950s-1970s, Artist, American
Fontana, Carl, Cool Jazz; Bebop, 1950s-1990s, Artist, American
Ford, Frankie, Louisiana Blues, 1950s-, Artist, American
Foster, Frank, Hard Bop; Swing, 1950s-1990s, Artist, American
Four Freshmen, The, 1950s Pop, 1950s-1990s, Artist, American
Four Preps, The, 1950s Pop, 1950s-1960s, Artist, American
Four Tops, The, The Classic Soul Era, 1950s-1980s, Artist, American
Francis, Connie, Rock'n'Roll, 1950s-, Artist, American
Frankie Lymon and the Teenagers, Doo-Wop, 1950s-1960s, Artist, American
Franklin, Aretha, The Classical Soul Era, 1950s-1990s, Artist, American
Frazier, Dallas, The Nashville Sound; Honky Tonk, 1950s-1970s, Artist; Composer; Songwriter, American
Freeman, Bobby, Northern Soul, 1950s-1960s, Artist, American
Freeman, Ernie, The Classic Soul Era, 1950s-1960s, Producer, American
Freeman, Stan, Cool Jazz; Swing; Bebop, 1950s-1960s, Artist, American
Frizzell, Lefty, Honky Tonk, 1950s-1970s, Artist; Songwriter, American
Frost, Frank, Modern Electric Blues, 1950s-1990s, Artist, American
Fuller, Curtis, Hard Bop, 1950s-1990s, Artist, American
Funicello, Annette, 1950s Pop, 1950s-1980s, Artist, American
Fury, Billy, 1950s Pop; Rock'n'Roll, 1950s-1980s, Artist, British
Garland, Red, Hard Bop, 1950s-1980s, Artist, American
Gaye, Marvin, The Classic Soul Era; Urban Soul, 1950s-1980s, Artist, American
Gibbs, Terry, Bebop, 1950s-1990s, Artist, American
Gilmore, John, Free Jazz; Bebop, 1950s-1990s, Artist, American
Golson, Benny, Hard Bop, 1950s-, Artist; Composer, American
Gonsalves, Paul, Swing; Bebop, 1950s-1970s, Artist, American
Green, Benny, Swing; Bebop, 1950s-1960s, Artist, American
Green, Grant, Hard Bop, 1950s-1970s, Artist, American
Gryce, Gigi, Hard Bop, 1950s-1970s, Artist, American
Guitar Shorty, Modern Electric Blues, 1950s-, Artist, American
Gullin, Lars, Cool Jazz; Bebop, 1950s-1970s, Swedish,
Haden, Charlie, Free Jazz; Hard Bop, 1950s-, Artist, American
Haley, Bill, Rock'n'Roll; Rockabilly; Western Swing, 1950s-1970s, Artist, American
Hallyday, Johnny, Rock'n'Roll, 1950s, Artist, French
Hamilton, Jimmy, Bebop; Swing, 1950s-1990s, Artist, American
Hampton, Slide, Bebop; Hard Bop, 1950s-, Artist; Composer, American
Hare, Pat, Modern Electric Blues, 1950s-1960s, Artist, American
Harper, Toni, Boogie-Woogie; Rhythm & Blues, 1950s-1960s, Artist, American
Harptones, The, Doo-Wop, 1950s-1990s, Artist, American
Harris, Barry, Bebop, 1950s-, Artist, American
Harris, Benny, Bebop, 1950s-, Artist, American
Harris, Gene, Soul Jazz; Hard Bop; Fusion, 1950s-1990s, Artist, American
Harrison, Wilbert, Rhythm & Blues, 1950s-1970s, Artist, American
Hawes, Hampton, Bebop; Hard Bop, 1950s-1970s, Artist, American
Hawkins, Dale, Rockabilly; Rock'n'Roll, 1950s-1990s, Artist, American
Hawkins, Hawkshaw, Honky Tonk, 1950s-1960s, Artist, American
Hawkins, Ronnie, Rockabilly; Rock'n'Roll, 1950s-1980s, Artist, American
Hawkins, Screamin' Jay, Funk Soul, 1950s-1990s, Artist, American
Hayes, Louis, Hard Bop, 1950s-, Artist, American
Heap, Jimmy, Honky Tonk; Western Swing, 1950s-1970s, Artist, American
Henry, Pierre, Electro, 1950s-1990s, Artist; Composer, French
Higgins, Billy, Hard Bop; Free Jazz, 1950s-1990s, Artist, American
Higgins, Chuck, The Classic Soul Era, 1950s-1960s, Artist, American
Holloway, Red, Soul Jazz; Swing; Bebop, 1950s-, Artist, American
Holly, Buddy, Rock'n'Roll; Rockabilly, 1950s, Artist; Songwriter, American
Holman, Eddie, The Classic Soul Era, 1950s-1970s,Artist, American
Holmes, Richard 'Groove', Soul Jazz; Hard Bop, 1950s-1990s, Artist, American
Holt, Redd, Funk Soul, 1950s-1970s, Artist, American
Hooker, Earl, Delta/Country Blues; Chicago Blues, 1950s-1970s, Artist, American
Hopkins, Lightnin', Texas Blues, 1950s-1970s, Artist, American
Horn, Paul, Fusion and Jazz Rock; Hard Bop, 1950s-, Artist, American
Hornets, The, Doo-Wop, 1950s, Artist, American
Horton, Johnny, Rockabilly; The Nashville Sound; Honky Tonk, 1950s-1960s, Artist, American
Howard, Harlan, Honky Tonk, 1950s-1980s, Artist; Composer, American
Hughes, Joe 'Guitar', Texas Blues; Modern Electric Blues, 1950s-, Artist, American
Husky, Ferlin, The Nashville Sound; Honky Tonk, 1950s-1990s, Artist, American
Impalas, The, Doo-Wop, 1950s, Artist, American
Impressions, The, 1950s Pop; Northern Soul, 1950s-1970s, Artist, American
Isley Brothers, The, Funk; Funk Soul; Rhythm & Blues; The Classic Soul Era, 1950s-, Artist, American
Jacks, The, Doo-Wop; Rhythm & Blues, 1950s-1960s, Artist, American
Jackson, Stonewall, The Nashville Sound; Honky Tonk, 1950s-1980s, Artist, American
Jackson, Wanda, Rockabilly, 1950s-1990s, Artist, American
James, Elmore, Chicago Blues, 1950s-1960s, Artist; Songwriter, American
James, Etta, Rhythm & Blues; The Classic Soul Era, 1950s-, Artist, American
Jan and Dean, Surf; Doo-Wop; Rock'n'Roll, 1950s-1960s, Artist, American
Jefferson, Eddie, Bebop, 1950s-1970s, Artist; Songwriter, American
Jennings, Waylon, The Outlaw Movement, 1950-, Artist, American
Jive Five, The, Doo-Wop, 1950s-1990s, Artist, American
Jobim, Antonio Carlos, Brazilian Jazz; Fusion and Jazz Rock; Latin Jazz, 1950s-1990s, Artist, Brazilian
Johnnie Ray and the Four Lads, Rhythm & Blues; Rock'n'Roll, 1950s, Artist, American
Johnny and the Hurricanes, Rock'n'Roll, 1950s-1960s, Artist, American
Johnny Kidd and the Pirates, Rock'n'Roll, 1950s-1960s, Artist, American
Johnson, Johnnie, Boogie-Woogie; Rhythm & Blues, 1950s-1990s, Artist, American
Johnson, Marv, The Classic Soul Era; Northern Soul; Rhythm & Blues, 1950s-1960s, Artist, American
Johnson, Syl, Northern Soul, 1950s-, Artist, American
Jolly, Pete, Cool Jazz; Bebop, 1950s-1990s, Artist, American
Jones, George, The Nashville Sound; Honky Tonk, 1950s-, Artist, American
Jones, Hank, Swing; Bebop, 1950s-1990s, Artist, American
Jones, Jimmy, Doo-Wop; Rock'n'Roll, 1950s-1960s, Artist; Songwriter, American
Jones, Philly Joe, Hard Bop, 1950s-, Artist, American
Jones, Quincy, Urban Soul; Swing; Bebop, 1950s-, Producer; Artist; Composer, American
Jones, Sam, Hard Bop, 1950s-1980s, Artist, American
Jones, Thad, Bebop; Hard Bop, 1950s-1980s, Artist; Composer; Producer, American
Jordan, Clifford, Hard Bop, 1950s-1990s, Artist, American
Julian, Don, Rhythm & Blues, 1950s-1970s, Artist, American
Kelly, Wynton, Hard Bop, 1950s-1970s, Artist, American
King Curtis, Rhythm & Blues; Piedmont Blues, 1950s-1970s, Artist, American
King, Earl, Funk Soul, 1950s-, Artist, American
King, Freddie, Texas Blues; Rhythm & Blues; Modern Electric Blues, 1950s-1970s, Artist, American
Kingston Trio, The, Traditional Folk; The Folk Revival; Folk Pop, 1950s-1990s, Artist, American
Knox, Buddy, Rockabilly; Rock'n'Roll, 1950s-1980s, Artist, American
Lambert, Henricks and Ross, Bebop, 1950s-1960s, Artist, American
Land, Harold, Hard Bop, 1950s-, Artist, American
Larks, The, Doo-Wop, 1950s-1970s, Artist, American
Lateef, Yusef, Hard Bop, 1950s-, Artist, American
Laws, Hubert, Hard Bop, 1950s-1990s, Artist, American
Lazy Lester, Modern Electric Blues, 1950s-, Artist, American
Lee, Brenda, The Nashville Sound, 1950s-1990s, Artist, American
Leiber and Stoller, Rhythm & Blues; Rock'n'Roll; 1950s Pop, 1950s-1960s, Songwriter, American
Lenoir, J. B., Chicago Blues, 1950s-1960s, Artist, American
Levey, Stan, Cool Jazz; Bebop, 1950s, Artist, American
Lewis, Jerry Lee, Rock'n'Roll; Rockabilly; Honky Tonk, 1950s-, Artist, American
Lewis, Ramsey, Soul Jazz, 1950s-1990s, Artist, American
Lighthouse All-Stars, The, Cool Jazz; Bebop, 1950s, Artist, American
Little Anthony and the Imperials, Doo-Wop, 1950s-1970s, Artist, American
Little Milton, The Classic Soul Era; Modern Electric Blues; Rhythm & Blues, 1950s-, Artist, American
Little Richard, Rock'n'Roll; Rhythm & Blues, 1950s-1990s, Artist, American
Little Wille John, Rhythm Blues; The Classic Soul Era, 1950s-1960s, Artist, American
Little, Booker, Hard Bop, 1950s-1960s, Artist, American
Lonesome Sundown, Chicago Blues, 1950s-1970s, Artist, American
Long, Shorty, The Classic Soul Era, 1950s-1960s, Artist, American
Love, Darlene, 1950s Pop, 1950s-1970s, Artist, American
Lowe, John 'Duff', Skiffle; Rock'n'Roll, 1950s, Artist, British
Lucier, Alvin, Electro, 1950s-, Composer, American
Lymon, Frankie, Doo-Wop, 1950s-1960s, Artist, American
Lynne, Gloria, Northern Soul, 1950s-1990s, Artist, American
Mabon, Willie, Chicago Blues; Rhythm & Blues, 1950s-1980s, Artist, American
Magic Sam, Modern Electric Blues; Chicago Blues, 1950s-1960s, Artist, American
Mance, Junior, Soul Jazz; Bebop, 1950s-, Artist, American
Mann, Carl, Rock'n'Roll; Rockabilly, 1950s-1980s, Artist, American
March, Little Peggy, 1950s Pop, 1950s-1980s, Artist, American
Mariano, Charlie, Bebop, 1950s-, Artist, American
Martin, George, British Invasion; Merseybeat, 1950s-1990s, Producer, British
Martin, Janis, Rockabilly; Rock'n'Roll, 1950s-1960s, Artist, American
Marvin, Hank B., 1960s Pop; British Invasion, 1950s-, Artist, British
Mayfield, Curtis, Funk; Funk Soul, 1950s-1990s, Artist, American
McCain, Jerry 'Boogie', Modern Electric Blues, 1950s-1960s; 1980s-, Artist; Songwriter, American
McCracklin, Jimmy, Jump Blues; Rhythm & Blues, 1950s-1990s, Artist, American
McDuff, Jack, Soul Jazz; Hard Bop, 1950s-1990s, Artist, American
McFarland, Gary, Hard Bop, 1950s-1990s, Artist; Composer, American
McLean, Jackie, Hard Bop, 1950s-, Artist, American
McPhatter, Clyde, Rhythm & Blues; The Classic Soul Era, 1950s-1960s, Artist, American
McPherson, Charles, Bebop; Hard Bop, 1950s-1990s, Artist, American
Melle, Gil, Hard Bop; Bebop; Cool Jazz, 1950s-1990s, Artist; Composer, American
Melvin, Harold, and the Bluenotes, Urban Soul, 1950s, Artist, American
Mickey and Sylvia, Rhythm & Blues, 1950s-1960s, Artist, American
Mighty Hannibal, The, Funk Soul, 1950s-1990s, Artist; Producer, American
Miller, Roger, The Nashville Sound; Honky Tonk, 1950s-1980s, Artist; Songwriter, American
Mimms, Garnet, The Classic Soul Era, 1950s-1970s, Artist, American
Miracles, The, The Classic Soul Era; Urban Soul, 1950s-1990s, Artist, American
Mitchell, Blue, Hard Bop, 1950s-1970s, Artist, American
Mitchell, Chad, Traditional Folk; The Folk Revival; Folk Pop, 1950s-1990s, Artist, American
Mitchell, Red, Cool Jazz; Hard Bop, 1950s-1990s, Artist, American
Mobley, Hank, Hard Bop, 1950s-1970s, Artist, American
Monotones, The, Doo-Wop, 1950s, Artist, American
Monterose, J. R., Hard Bop, 1950s-1980s, Artist, American
Moonglows, The, Doo-Wop; Rhythm & Blues, 1950s, Artist, American
Moore, Merrill, Boogie-Woogie; Rhythm & Blues, 1950s-1970s, Artist, American
Moore, Scotty, Rockabilly; Rock'n'Roll, 1950s-1990s, Artist, American
Morello, Joe, Cool Jazz; Hard Bop, 1950s-1990s, Artist, American
Morgan, Frank, Hard Bop; Bebop, 1950s-1990s, Artist, American
Morgan, Lee, Hard Bop, 1950s-1970s, Artist, American
Morton, Shadow, 1950s Pop; 1950s Pop Singer/Songwriter, 1950s-1960s, Producer, American
Mystics, The, Doo-Wop, 1950s-1970s, Artist, American
Nash, Johnny, Reggae Pop, 1950s-1970s, Artist, American
Nathan, Syd, Urban Soul, 1950s-1960s, Producer, American
Nelson, Jimmy, Jump Blues; Rhythm & Blues, 1950s-1960s, Artist, American
Nelson, Oliver, Hard Bop, 1950s-1970s, Artist; Composer, American
Nelson, Ricky, Country Rock; Rock'n'Roll; Rockabilly, 1950s-1980s, Artist, American
Nelson, Willie, The Outlaw Movement; Mainstream Country, 1950s-, Artist; Songwriter, American
Neville, Art, Funk Soul, 1950s-1990s, Artist, American
Newborn, Phineas, Hard Bop, 1950s-1980s, Artist, American
Newman, David 'Fathead', Soul Jazz; Hard Bop, 1950s-, Artist, American
Newsom, Tommy, Cool Jazz; Bebop, 1950s-, Artist, American
Nichols, Herbie, Dixieland Revival; Swing; Bebop, 1950s, Artist; Composer, American
Niehaus, Lennie, Cool Jazz; Bebop, 1950s-1990s, Artist, American
O'Day, Molly, Honky Tonk, 1950s-1970s, Artist, American
Orbison, Roy, 1950s Pop; Rockabilly; Rock'n'Roll, 1950s-1980s, Artist, American
Owens, Buck, Mainstream Country; Honky Tonk, 1950s-1980s, Artist, American
Paich, Marty, Bebop; Cool Jazz, 1950s-1990s, Artist, American
Palmer, Earl, Rhythm & Blues, 1950s-, Artist, American
Paragons, The, Doo-Wop, 1950s-1960s, Artist, American
Parker, Junior, Rhythm & Blues, 1950s-1970s, Artist, American
Pass, Joe, Bebop; Hard Bop, 1950s-1990s, Artist, American
Payne, Cecil, Bebop; Hard Bop, 1950s-, Artist, American
Pearson, Duke, Hard Bop, 1950s-1970s, Producer; Artist, American
Penguins, The, Doo-Wop, 1950_, Artist, American
Perkins, Bill, Cool Jazz; Hard Bop, 1950s-, Artist, American
Perkins, Carl, Rock'n'Roll; Rockabilly, 1950s-1990s, Artist, American
Phillips, Esther, 1950s Pop; Rhythm & Blues, 1950s-1970s, Artist, American
Piano Red, Boogie-Woogie, 1950s-1960s, Artist, American
Pierce, Webb, Honky Tonk, 1950s-1980s, Artist, American
Platters, The, Doo-Wop, 1950s-1960s, Artist, American
Poni-Tails, The, 1950s Pop, 1950s, Artist, American
Poole, Brian, and the Tremeloes, British Invasion; 1950s Pop, 1950s-1980s, Artist, British
Powers, Johnny, Rockabilly; Rock'n'Roll, 1950s-1990s, Artist, American
Presley, Elvis, Rock'n'Roll; Rockabilly, 1950s-1970s, Artist, American
Price, Lloyd, Rock'n'Roll; Rhythm & Blues; The Classic Soul Era, 1950s-1960s; 1980s, Artist; Producer, American
Price, Ray, The Nashville Sound; Honky Tonk, 1950s-, Artist, American
Prystock, Red, Jump Blues; Rhythm & Blues, 1950s-1960s, Artist, American
Ray, Johnnie, 1950s Pop; Rhythm & Blues, 1950s-1960s, Artist, American
Red, Sonny, Hard Bop, 1950s-1970s, Artist, American
Redd, Freddie, Hard Bop, 1950s-1990s, Composer; Artist, American
Reed, Jimmy, Chicago Blues; Rhythm & Blues, 1950s-1970s, Artist, American
Reeves, Jim, The Nashville Sound, 1950s-1960s, Artist, American
Reid, Duke, Ska; Roots, 1950s-1970s, Producer, Jamaica
Rich, Charlie, Rockabilly; The Nashville Sound, 1950s-1990s, Artist, American
Richard, Cliff, 1950s Pop; Rock'n'Roll, 1950s-, Artist, British
Richardson, Jerome, Cool Jazz; Hard Bop, 1950s-1990s, Artist, American
Riley, Billy Lee, Rockabilly, 1950s-1990s, Artist, American
Rivera, Hector, Funk Soul, 1950s-1970s, Artist; Composer, American
Robertson, Robbie, Rock'n'Roll; Alternative/Indie Rock, 1950s-1990s, Artist, Canadian
Robinson, Smokey, The Classic Soul Era, 1950s-1980s, Artist; Producer; Songwriter, American
Roca, Pete la, Latin Jazz; Hard Bop, 1950s-1990s, Artist, American
Rodgers, Jimmy F., Folk Pop, 1950s-1970s, Artist, American
Rogers, Jimmy, Chicago Blues, 1950s-1990s, Artist, American
Rooftop Singers, Traditional Folk; Folk Pop; The Folk Revival, 1950s-1960s, Artist, American
Rowles, Jimmy, Bebop; Swing, 1950s-1990s, Artist, American
Ruff, Willie, Hard Bop; Bebop, 1950s-1990s, Artist, American
Rumsey, Howard, Cool Jazz; Bebop, 1950s-1960s, Artist, American
Rush, Otis, Chicago Blues, 1950s-1990s, Artist, American
Rydell, Bobby, Rock'n'Roll, 1950s-1960s, Artist, American
Sahm, Doug, Delta/Country Rock; Blues Rock, 1950s-1990s, Artist; Songwriter, American
Salvador, Sal, Cool Jazz; Bebop, 1950s-1990s, Artist, American
Schifrin, Lalo, Bebop, 1950s-, Composer; Artist, Argentinean
Scott, Jack, Rockabilly; Rock'n'Roll, 1950s-1970s, Artist, American
Scott, Shirley, Soul Jazz; Hard Bop, 1950s-1990s, Artist, American
Sedaka, Neil, 1950s Pop, 1950s-1990s, Artist, American
Self, Ronnie, Rockabilly, 1950s-1960s, Artist, American
Shank, Bud, Cool Jazz; Hard Bop, 1950s-, Artist, American
Sheldon, Jack, Bebop, 1950s-, Artist, American
Shepard, Jean, Honky Tonk, 1950s-1990s, Artist, American
Shihab, Sahib, Bebop; Hard Bop, 1950s-1990s, Artist, American
Shirelles, The, 1950s Pop; Funk Soul, 1950s-1990s, Artist, American
Shirley and Lee, Rhythm & Blues, 1950s-1960s, Artist, American
Silhouettes, The, Doo-Wop, 1950s-1960s, Artist, American
Silver, Horace, Hard Bop; Fusion, 1950s-, Artist, American
Skyliners, The, Doo-Wop, 1950s-1960s, Artist, American
Slim, T. V., Delta/Country Blues; Rhythm & Blues, 1950s-1960s, Artist, American
Slim, Tarheel, Rhythm & Blues, 1950s-1970s, Artist, American
Smith, Carl, Western Swing; Honky Tonk, 1950s-1980s, Artist, American
Smith, Jimmy, Hard Bop, 1950s-, Artist, American
Smith, Louis, Hard Bop, 1950s-, Artist, American
Smith, Warren, Rockabilly, 1950s-1980s, Artist, American
Smokey Robinson, The Classic Soul Era, 1950s-1980s, Artist; Producer; Songwriter, American
Sovine, Red, Honky Tonk; Early & Old-Time Country, 1950s-1970s, Artist, American
Spaniels, The, Doo-Wop; Rhythm & Blues, 1950s-1970s, Artist, American
Spann, Otis, Chicago Blues, 1950s-1960s, Artist, American
Spiders, The, Rhythm & Blues, 1950s, Artist, American
Staple Singers, The, The Classic Soul Era, 1950s-1990s, Artist, American
Staples, Pops; Rhythm & Blues; Gospel, 1950s-1990s, Artist, American
Steele, Tommy, Skiffle; Rock'n'Roll, 1950s-1960s, Artist, British
Stockhausen, Karlheinz, Electro, 1950s-1990s, Composer, German
Strong, Nolan, Rhythm & Blues, 1950s-1960s, Artist, American
Sumlin, Hubert, Chicago Blues; Modern Electric Blues, 1950s-, Artist, American
Tate, Grady, Hard Bop, 1950s-1990s, Artist, American
Taylor, Art, Bebop; Hard Bop, 1950s-1990s, Artist, American
Taylor, Eddie, Modern Electric Blues; Rhythm & Blues, 1950s-1980s, Artist, American
Taylor, Johnnie, The Classic Soul Era; Funk Soul, 1950s-1990s, Artist, American
Taylor, Ted, Northern Soul, 1950s-1970s, Artist, American
Tee, Richard, Funk Soul, 1950s-1990s, Artist, American
Terry, Clark, Bebop; Swing, 1950s-, Artist, American
Thielemans, Toots, Brazilian Jazz; Latin Jazz; Swing; Bebop, 1950s-, Artist, Belgian
Thigpen, Ed, Bebop; Hard Bop, 1950s-1990s, Artist, American
Thomas, Rockin' Tabby, Chicago Blues, 1950s-1990s, Artist, American
Tillotson, Johnny, 1950s Pop, 1950s-1960s, Artist, American
Timmons, Bobby, Soul Jazz; Hard Bop, 1950s-1960s, Composer; Artist, American
Toussaint, Allen, The Classic Soul Era; Louisiana Blues, 1950s-1990s, Producer; Artist, American
Turner, Ike, Rhythm & Blues, 1950s-, Producer; Songwriter; Artist, American
Turner, Titus, Piedmont Blues; Jump Blues; Rhythm & Blues, 1950s-1970s, Artist, American
Twitty, Conway, Rockabilly; The Nashville Sound, 1950s-1990s, Artist, American
Valens, Ritchie, Rock'n'Roll, 1950s, Artist, American
Vaughan, Ivan, Skiffle; Rock'n'Roll, 1950s, Artist, British
Vee, Bobby, 1950s Pop, 1950s-1990s, Artist, American
Vincent, Gene, Rock'n'Roll; Rockabilly, 1950s-1970s, Artist, American
Vipers Skiffle Group, The, Skiffle, 1950s-1960s, Artist, British
Waldron, Mal, Hard Bop, 1950s-, Artist, American
Walton, Cedar, Hard Bop, 1950s-, Artist; Composer, American
Ward, Billy, Rhythm & Blues, 1950s, Artist, American
Washington, Baby, Urban Soul, 1950s-1970s, Artist, American
Watson, Johnny 'Guitar', Modern Electric Blues; Texas Blues; Rhythm & Blues, 1950s-1990s, Artist, American
Webb, Boogie Bill, Rhythm & Blues; Country Blues, 1950s-1980s, Artist, American
Wells, Junior, Chicago Blues; Modern Electric Blues, 1950s-1990s, Artist, American
Weston, Randy, Hard Bop, 1950s-1990s, Artist, American
Whalley, Nigel, Skiffle; Rock'n'Roll, 1950s, Artist, British
Wiggins, Gerald, Swing; Bebop, 1950s-1990s, Artist, American
Wilde, Marty, Rock'n'Roll, 1950s-1980s, Artist, British
Wilkin, Marijohn, Outlaw County; Honky Tonk, 1950s-1970s, Artist; Songwriter, American
Wilkins, Ernie, Bebop; Swing, 1950s-1990s, Artist, American
Williams and Watson, The Classic Soul Era, 1950s-1970s, Artist, American
Williams, André, Rhythm & Blues, 1950s-1970s; 1990s-, Artist, American
Williams, Larry, Rock'n'Roll; Rhythm & Blues, 1950s-1970s, Artist, American
Williams, Otis, Doo-Wop, 1950s-1970s, Artist, American
Williamson, Claude, Cool Jazz; Bebop, 1950s-1990s, Artist, American
Willis, Chuck, Rhythm & Blues, 1950s, Artist, American
Wilson, Jackie, 1960s Pop; Rhythm & Blues; The Classic Soul Era, 1950s-1970s, Artist, American
Woods, Phil, Bebop; Hard Bop, 1950s-, Artist, American
Wray, Link, Rock'n'Roll, 1950s-1990s, Artist, American
Yarbrough, Glenn, Traditional Folk; The Folk Revival; Folk Pop, 1950s-1990s, Artist, American
Young, Faron, The Nashville Sound, Honky Tonk, 1950s-1990s, Artist, American
Zawinul, Joe, Fusion; Fusion and Jazz Rock; Soul Jazz; Hard Bop, 1950s-1990s, Artist, Austrian

see Chuck Berry pp 38 *see* Ray Charles pp 42 *see* Bill Haley pp 48 *see* Buddy Holly pp 50 *see* Elvis Presley pp 52

THE SIXTIES

Popular music's most influential decade saw British and American rock develop in parallel, the creative torch passing across the Atlantic to The Beatles, then returning as the West Coast rock boom reflected the influence of drugs on music.

In rock, guitar was now the undisputed focus of the music with 'axe heroes' like Clapton, Hendrix, Townshend and Page all inspiring a generation of followers. Meanwhile, soul music was enjoying halcyon days thanks to the twin crucibles of Motown in Detroit and Stax in Memphis both delivering dancehall-filling music.

The recording studio itself became an instrument, being used to complement the music created and add new dimensions to it. Producers like Phil Spector and George Martin became celebrities in their own right thanks to their respective work with The Beatles and West Coast girl groups like The Crystals and The Ronettes.

Of the various tribes that existed, the hippies and their ethos of 'peace and love' was the most widely reflected in music. Major festivals created a sense of community: the Monterey International Pop Festival in 1967 allowing Otis Redding access to a white audience and Jimi Hendrix the chance to impress his fellow Americans. Woodstock, held two years later, entered legend thanks to a feature film, but the optimism of the era was fast evaporating even then.

Sources & Sounds

78

'Back in those days, all us skinny white British kids were trying to look cool and sound black. And there was Hendrix, the ultimate in black cool. Everything he did was natural and perfect.'

Ronnie Wood, The Rolling Stones

Above and Right

The era which began the subdued images in black and white surged to the end of the 60s with a blaze of psychedelic colour, expressed through the intensely creative music and fantastic light shows at ever more elaborate gigs.

It was the decade that began with a whimper and ended with a bang. The 1960s saw rock not only come of age but also become the pre-eminent cultural force, its impact and importance outstripping anything the worlds of fashion, film, art and literature could muster and, in turn, informing all of them.

By 1960–61, the original rock'n'roll explosion had lost its impetus. Elvis had emerged from the US Army bound for Hollywood, while the energy and excess of Little Richard and Jerry Lee Lewis had given way to softer, more harmonious sounds from industry created stars. But the 1960s would peak in an explosion of energy, colour and creativity that has never been equalled since as figures like Jimi Hendrix, Janis Joplin and Mick Jagger reclaimed rock as a vibrant, fiercely anti-Establishment force.

see Introduction pp 76   *see UK Rock pp 86*   *see US Rock pp 118*   *see Soul pp 152*

Stateside Influence

Throughout the 1960s a number of scenes co-existed around the world, all of which would feed into each other to create a 'big bang' effect in youth culture. In Southern California, the surf craze owed its soundtrack to Dick Dale, Jan and Dean and, most importantly, The Beach Boys. Led by Brian Wilson, the family-based group took Chuck Berry rhythms, harmony pop and twanging guitars and moulded them into a glorious West Coast sound, which they would then develop into something more complex.

Five thousand miles from sunny California, the dingy clubs of London saw young bands influenced by American jazz and blues began to develop their own exciting style of music. A crop of new groups emerged from under the wing of older players like Cyril Davies and Alexis Korner; The Rolling Stones, The Pretty Things and The Yardbirds were all heavily influenced by the primal beat and sexually explicit lyrics of old blues masters such as Bo Diddley, Muddy Waters and Howlin' Wolf.

From The Soul

But American black music did not just influence young, English, middle-class, white boys. The decade saw the birth of soul music, a mixture of gospel and rhythm and blues that had begun to emerge in the late 1950s and would flower in the 1960s as a major force in its own right. Soul was different in the way it utilized gospel music, placing more emphasis on vocals and the way it brought together secular and religious themes. Solomon Burke's first recordings for New York's Atlantic Records perfected the soul sound in the wake of pioneers like James Brown, Ray Charles and Sam Cooke. But it was Stax Records in Memphis that became synonymous with the term.

Stax issued hit records by Otis Redding, Wilson Pickett and Joe Tex and by their house band Booker T and The MGs – though they were later rivalled by a run of fabulous singles by the Queen of Soul, Aretha Franklin for Atlantic. The Memphis scene was further enhanced by the Muscle Shoals studio in the neighbouring town of Florence, Alabama,

📼 CLASSIC RECORDINGS

1964
The Beatles:
A Hard Day's Night

1965
Bob Dylan:
Highway 61 Revisited

1966
The Beach Boys:
Pet Sounds

1967
Jimi Hendrix:
Are You Experienced?

Below
Aretha Franklin at the Muscle Shoals Studios, where carefully crafted pop songs were created and given to the best voices of the era.

🎧 see Ray Charles pp 42 🎧 see The Rolling Stones pp 96 🎧 see The Beach Boys pp 120 🎧 see Aretha Franklin pp 156

a hotbed of musical activity, which enjoyed a close
relationship with Stax and from where many of the
label's later hits emerged. Not all black music emerged
from a 'stable', as maverick Sly Stone showed with his
multi-gender, multi-racial band the Family Stone.

But arguably the most successful black music
concern of the decade was Tamla Motown. Set up by
Berry Gordy Jr. in 1959 with a loan of $8,000, Motown
was more than just another record label – Gordy's
dream was to produce music from the ghetto with a
dance beat that would become mainstream, with its
own unique sound. Taking its name from a Debbie
Reynolds film, *Tammy,* and Motor Town – Detroit was
the home of Ford Motors – Gordy got lucky when he
hooked up with a group called The Miracles. It was
their lead singer Smokey Robinson (later Gordy's
number two) who persuaded him to press and
distribute his own records.

Gordy never looked back as Motown became
a studio and, using one of the most successful
songwriting teams ever in Holland, Dozier and
Holland, created worldwide hits for the likes of The
Supremes, Four Tops, Martha and The Vandellas,

Marvin Gaye and The Temptations. Another name,
Stevie Wonder, would mature from teen sensation to
mature genius over the years to come and would
remain with Motown – on his own terms – into the
next millennium.

The Fab Four

But there was one band and one city in particular that
that stamped their mark indelibly on the world at large
and fired the public imagination – four lads from
Liverpool by the name of The Beatles. Their influence

🎸 *see Introduction pp 76* 🎸 *see UK Rock pp 86* 🎸 *see US Rock pp 118* 🎸 *see Soul pp 152*

on pop and rock was all-encompassing. Over the course of the decade The Fab Four, as they were christened by an eager press, were to prove that there was longevity in the pop phenomenon.

Groomed by manager Brian Epstein, the quartet quickly graduated from the clubs of Hamburg's notorious Reeperbahn to the world's living rooms, attracting not just a teenage but family audiences as their records gate-crashed the Top 10 on both sides of the Atlantic. They created a pop catalogue that remains unrivalled today, their tunes discussed in detail by serious music critics.

Just as The Beatles crossed international boundaries, their home town of Liverpool and the club that launched them, the Cavern, momentarily became the epicentre of the pop world. Fellow Liverpool acts such as The Searchers, Gerry and The Pacemakers and The Swinging Blue Jeans led the way, and most of the big cities in the UK would be rocked by the ensuing beat boom. Every youngster wanted to play the guitar, it seemed, and a crop of regional heroes soon emerged. Manchester provided the likes of The Hollies, Hermann's Hermits and Freddie and The Dreamers, Newcastle's contribution was the tougher sound of The Animals, whilst Birmingham's wake-up call brought out such bands as The Move and The Moody Blues, acts that would go on to play a prominent part in the 1970s rock scene.

The Mods And The Rockers

Black music was popular with an emergent youth cult in Britain known as the Mods, a rebellious group of young men and women who favoured the latest fashions from the Carnaby Street and Swinging London scenes, amphetamines and motor scooters (as opposed to their arch-rivals the Rockers whose predilection was for old-style leather jackets and motorbikes). The seaside towns of the English south coast became the backdrop for skirmishes between the two groups.

Out of mod culture would emerge some of the greatest English rock bands of all time notably The Who, The Small Faces and The Kinks, who would meld their early rhythm and blues influences with a peculiarly British style that owed a lot to the old music-hall tradition to write sublime songs that perfectly defined the mood and character of the country. In turn, these bands would head off to the US to find varying

degrees of fame and fortune. Known as the British Invasion, they became the ambassadors of a new youth culture and were welcomed with open arms by an equally dissatisfied American youth looking for a change of values and lifestyle.

The Beat Goes On

One of the most fertile home-grown scenes in the US in the early part of the decade was the folk movement whose home was in the bohemian area of New York City. Greenwich Village had long been a centre for arty types, especially from the 1950s onwards when the beat poets like Allen Ginsberg and Jack Kerouac rose to prominence. In the early 1960s, it was home to the beatniks – anybody who wanted to play guitar and sing like the great Woody Guthrie or Leadbelly and who was influenced by the burgeoning civil rights movement.

Below
Carnaby Street, in London's west end, became the focus of fashionable youth ready to experiment with style, music and drugs.

see The Beatles pp 88   see The Who pp 100   see The Animals pp 102   see Stevie Wonder pp 162

Above

Beatniks represented a generations' quest for liberation and choice. Their exploration of altruism above materialism can be found in many different strands of 1960s music, from the protest songs of Bob Dylan to later hits of The Beatles.

The Byrds' first single released in early summer of 1965, a version of Dylan's 'Mr Tambourine Man', started off the folk rock phenomenon; there were many imitators like Sonny and Cher and Barry McGuire, but over the next few years McGuinn and company would become one of the most influential groups in the history of rock as they experimented with jazz, Indian music, electronics and country.

Far Out

The all-out revolution in American popular music that followed not only drew on different traditional forms, but was also inspired by the prevailing political climate such as the escalating war in Vietnam and by the advent of a new 'wonder drug', LSD. The music's epicentre swung from Liverpool back to America and to another city by the sea, San Francisco. A place with strong bohemian traditions, Frisco was a liberal town and it was there that novelist Ken Kesey – who had undergone tests by the US government for a mind-expanding drug called lysergic acid and found it beneficial – staged the first 'Acid Tests' with his troupe, The Merry Pranksters.

LSD, as it became known, quickly caught on, especially amongst young kids living there smitten with the folk rock boom happening down the coast in Los Angeles and eager to plug in. Bands like The Beau Brummels and The Charlatans were the first acts around the city to play a form of electric folk, but it was a second wave that captured the imagination of the media at large – notably Jefferson Airplane – who took folk-rock on to its next stage, bringing folk, blues and elements of pop together with the kind of improvizational ability enjoyed by jazz players such as John Coltrane and Miles Davis.

Many talented singer/songwriters came out of the coffee houses and folk clubs along Bleeker Street – but all were overshadowed by the 1960s' greatest spokesman, Bob Dylan. The former Robert Zimmerman took his direction from Woody Guthrie and Charley Patten and shaped his very own musical vision, one initially caught up in the civil rights movement but which quickly developed into a poetic vision, as much like his namesake Dylan Thomas or Baudelaire as it was Guthrie.

Dylan had already issued a number of recordings by the time The Beatles and the Stones were making their presence felt on his side of the Atlantic and many young American kids were picking up on both Dylan's articulate, very relevant songs and the punchy beat of the Brits. None more so than Jim McGuinn, Gene Clarke and David Crosby, three young men in Los Angeles whose vision was to take folk music and merge it with the new sound of electric guitars.

Right

The light shows pioneered by Jefferson Airplane reflected the drug-enhanced experience of 1960s culture.

see Introduction pp 76   see UK Rock pp 86   see US Rock pp 118   see Soul pp 152

They were soon at the heart of a new scene joined by fellow locals Country Joe and The Fish, Quicksilver Messenger Service, Big Brother and The Holding Company, Moby Grape and The Grateful Dead. If their LA counterparts like Love, Spirit and The Doors excelled at making the most of the studio environment, the San Francisco bands were at their best when they took off on long, spacey explorations, jamming on numbers often over half an hour in length. It was all a far cry from the two and a half-minute pop songs of earlier in the decade.

The Summer Of Love

By 1967, the San Francisco sound had become the backdrop to the Summer of Love. Kids across the planet rejected their parents' values and joined together to grow their hair long and espouse brotherly love instead of supporting the expansionist war the Americans were fighting in south-east Asia. The hippie movement had arrived.

Indeed, by the middle of the decade rock was developing at a rate never witnessed before or since. Dylan went electric, alienating some of his more

Below
Country Joe and The Fish specialized in rambling jams rather than three-minute pop songs.

see The Byrds pp 124   see Bob Dylan pp 126   see The Doors pp 140   see Jefferson Airplane pp 142

traditional fans, while The Beatles quit touring, left their army of screaming devotees behind and concentrated on composition and working in the studio, capturing the *zeitgeist* with *Sgt. Pepper's Lonely Hearts Club Band* (1967). The same year, 1967, saw Lou Reed's Velvet Underground cut their own eponymous art rock masterpiece in New York under the aegis of Pop Art guru Andy Warhol.

At the same time the San Franciscans were experimenting with new sounds, attempting to simulate the sounds of a drug 'trip' with their music,

Below

The Avalon Ballroom in San Francisco was one of a new breed of smart dance halls that created special effects and light shows for a drug-enhanced generation.

their British counterparts were also undergoing a complete sea change. Guitar technology in particular was improving constantly with bigger, better and louder amplification coming on to the scene. This was the era of the fuzz box, the wah-wah pedal and the Marshall stack, embraced by a new breed of British guitarist like Jeff Beck, Eric Clapton and Jimmy Page.

An Electric Revolution

The revolution in electric guitar-playing was about to be kick-started by the arrival in London in autumn 1966 of a young black musician, Jimi Hendrix, who took the sound of blues guitar out of the Mississippi delta and launched it into space. Writing tunes that combined LSD-inspired lyrics with other-worldly sounds from his guitar (often achieved by means of feedback), Jimi and his band The Experience were the children of a new tomorrow. During the few short years he was alive, Hendrix became one of the most influential figures in rock.

New types of club sprang up to cater for the new music and the new audience: the grubby little venues that had been such a feature of the beat era were replaced by more elaborate environments such as the Avalon and Fillmore ballrooms in the US and places like the UFO club in London. One feature of these venues never before witnessed was the advent of the light show, where all kinds of images were projected behind the musicians and often on to the audiences in an attempt to recreate the effects of LSD.

One band that pioneered the mixed-media concept and took rock off in yet another direction was Cambridge's Pink Floyd. Led by Syd Barrett, a talented songwriter who took the band into the singles charts, the group's forte was long spacey numbers like 'Interstellar Overdrive', which combined electronics with ethereal keyboard sounds, drones and pounding drums and atonal guitar licks to create a 'far-out' psychedelic effect. Rock began to look to the avant-garde for inspiration and bands like The Soft Machine, Frank Zappa's Mothers Of Invention and Captain Beefheart and His Magic Band became the order of the day.

New Vibrations

Rock as a cultural phenomenon was now separating from 'pop'. The grip of Tin Pan Alley had been

see Introduction pp 76 see UK Rock pp 86 see US Rock pp 118 see Soul pp 152

loosened and bands were now, for the most part, writing their own material. Groups like The Tremeloes in the UK and The Ohio Express in the US still filled the Top 20, as did the 'made-for-TV' Monkees, but many musicians who had started their careers as chart bands were now taking music in a direction never before dreamt of.

The 45-rpm single was no longer perceived as the most important medium by which to reach the public – the long-playing (LP) album now held sway. The Beatles and Cream used their pre-eminent position to release double albums, while The Who, whose Pete Townshend had created many classic three-minute singles, was now attempting to break new ground with their epic rock opera *Tommy* (1969).

The sleeves in which records were clothed became almost as important as the music itself. In the States, Rick Griffin's mind-blowing artwork graced the sleeves of LPs by The Grateful Dead; rising underground cartoonist Robert Crumb designed the cover for Big Brother's *Cheap Thrills* (1968), while in the UK Martin Sharpe's day-glo designs decorated sleeves for Cream. Tired of screaming girls who did not listen to the music anyway, The Small Faces released one of the most evocative records of the time and arguably the first concept LP, *Ogden's Nut Gone Flake* (1968), in a circular sleeve – then promptly split up in a bid to be taken more seriously!

Above
Woodstock in New York – the most memorable of 1960s festivals – featured Jimi Hendrix, The Who, Joan Baez and Crosby, Stills, Nash & Young. It remains one of the key memories of the era.

The End Of The Love-In?

The late 1960s saw live music events grow in size as hundreds of thousands of fans got together in tribal gatherings: the Human Be-In in San Francisco and Monterey Pop further down the coast. There were the big Isle of Wight Festivals, free concerts in Hyde Park and, biggest of all, the Woodstock Festival in upstate New York in the summer of 1969. Yet despite all the optimism and figures like John Lennon and Jim Morrison speaking out for the love generation, the 1960s ended on a sour note with The Beatles in disarray, a disillusioned Dylan making a country and western album, and a death at the Altamont Festival when Hell's Angels security guards clashed with an audience member.

After the excesses of psychedelia came a return to roots by musicians on both sides of the Atlantic, all of whom were influenced by the likes of The Byrds *Sweetheart Of The Rodeo* (1968), The Band's *Music From Big Pink* (1968) and Fairport Convention's *Liege And Lief* (1969). In fact the biggest-selling rock bands in 1969 were Berkeley; California's Creedence Clearwater Revival with their evocative songs extolling simple American values; and Fleetwood Mac, a British quintet who had weathered the blues boom of the previous year to forge a style that encompassed not only blues but folk, classical and the San Franciscan love of extemporization.

The 1960s had been a decade that had achieved so much but, as the 1970s dawned, excess, disillusionment and death replaced the celebration of life and its vibrant spirit. The pendulum was swinging once again….

Left
Cream's synthesis of blues and jazz created a coruscating power rock trio. They fed off the massive cultural shifts experienced by a generation of youth that was exposed, for the first time, to an astonishing breadth of musical influences.

 *see* Jimi Hendrix pp 132 *see* The Velvet Underground pp 134 *see* Pink Floyd pp 204 *see* Jeff Beck pp 212

SIXTIES UK ROCK

The 1960s was the decade that saw British teenagers who had suddenly been empowered by the records of Elvis and his compatriots buy guitars and follow in Presley's footsteps. British bands picked up the musical torch that crossed the Atlantic and took rock music to another level: The Beatles and The Kinks relied on smart songwriting while The Stones, The Who and Cream turned up the volume for maximum effect. The last-named trio of Clapton, Bruce and Baker laid the foundations for the rock decade that followed with their over-amplified blues licks and virtuoso soloing, yet themselves barely lasted a couple of years before burning out.

Britain led the world with bands that brought jazz, folk, classical themes and orchestras into the mix. Jethro Tull, Fairport Convention, Procol Harum and The Moody Blues would all enjoy long careers that lasted into the twenty-first century, proving that the new music was no here today, gone tomorrow fad the older generation hoped it would be.

From A–Z, Amen Corner to The Zombies, British rock was never to be fresher or more varied as the decade when the blank pages of history were inscribed in many different hues.

The Beatles

CLASSIC RECORDINGS

1963
'Please Please Me',
'She Loves You',
'I Want To Hold Your
Hand', *With The Beatles*

1964
A Hard Day's Night,
'I Feel Fine'

1965
'Day Tripper'/'We Can
Work It Out', *Rubber Soul*

1966
Revolver

1967
'Penny Lane'/'Strawberry
Fields Forever', *Sgt.
Pepper's Lonely Hearts
Club Band*, 'Hello
Goodbye'/'I Am The
Walrus'

1968
'Lady Madonna', *The
Beatles*, 'Hey Jude'

1969
Abbey Road

1994–96
Live At The BBC,
Anthology 1, *Anthology 2*,
Anthology 3

Above
The advent of The Beatles
changed the course of music
history irrevocably. Their
catchy songs and loveable
marketability opened the
doors for a new era of British
pop music.

Consisting of John Lennon (1940–80) on rhythm guitar, Paul McCartney (b. 18 June 1942) on bass, George Harrison (1943–2001) on lead guitar and Ringo Starr (b. Richard Starkey, 7 July 1940) on drums, The Beatles evolved from Lennon's grammar school skiffle group The Quarry Men to become the most successful, acclaimed and influential act in the history of popular music.

Liverpool Beginnings

Born and raised in the seaport city of Liverpool, northwest England, John, Paul, George and Ringo had no formal musical education, yet from their earliest years they were steeped in the traditions of British music hall, as well as the sounds of pre- and post-war popular music that emanated from the radio. In addition, the blues and country & western records that local sailors brought home from their trips to America meant that, by the time Elvis Presley's

'Heartbreak Hotel' (1956) inspired a generation of teens to acquire instruments and mould themselves in his likeness, the soon-to-be Fab Four had absorbed an eclectic array of influences that would one day resurface in their own recordings.

The Quarry Men were among the thousands of groups that sprang up all over Britain in the wake of the Lonnie Donegan-inspired skiffle boom, which enabled cash-strapped teenagers to emulate their idols with a variety of rudimentary instruments. Yet, just as the craze was dying down the following year, Lennon's amateurish band received a boost via his recruitment of the younger but more instrumentally adept Paul McCartney, and the subsequent departure of its less talented and committed members. Elvis, Chuck Berry, Little Richard, Jerry Lee Lewis, Buddy Holly, Gene Vincent and Eddie Cochran were among the contemporary American artists whose material they now covered in their homegrown style, and shortly after McCartney's young school chum

 *see* Introduction pp 86   *see* Sources & Sounds pp 78   *see* A–Z of Artists pp 102

George Harrison joined the fold in 1958, the group comprised just them and Lennon as its core members, performing at parties and in small venues both with and without a makeshift drummer.

Too Much Monkey Business

After a fallow period featuring few gigs and a revolving door of drummers, the summer of 1960 marked the first of several turning points for the band, which had quickly gone through several name changes, including The Silver Beetles, The Beatals, The Silver Beatles and, finally, The Beatles, a musical twist on Buddy Holly's Crickets. Lennon had persuaded his art-college friend Stuart Sutcliffe to fill in on bass, despite the fact that Sutcliffe's considerable talent with the paintbrush did not extend to much musical ability, and that August, on the eve of an extended club engagement in Hamburg, West Germany, a full-time drummer at last augmented the line-up in the form of Pete Best.

Although Best's withdrawn personality did not really gel with the more outgoing nature of his colleagues, he at least provided the band with some much needed stability while his good looks attracted the attention of female fans. For it was in Hamburg that The Beatles really came of age, fusing as a unit during long, gruelling sessions onstage, where they had to learn to improvise, extend their repertoire and really put on a show, both musically and physically, for their demanding German audiences.

Seventeen-year-old Harrison was eventually deported for being underage, and Best and McCartney followed him in short order after being arrested for a spot of juvenile delinquency. But when John, Paul, George, Stu and Pete made their reappearance on the Liverpool club circuit at the end of 1960, they were virtually unrecognizable from the unruly bunch of no-hopers who had departed for Germany just a few months earlier. Suddenly, they were a local phenomenon,

Below

Although recorded in one day, The Beatles' debut album *Please Please Me* (1963) topped the UK chart for 30 weeks, making them the most popular act ever seen in Britain.

see Chuck Berry pp 38   *see* Lonnie Donegan pp 44   *see* Jerry Lee Lewis pp 66   *see* Little Richard pp 66

wowing audiences with their new powerhouse brand of rock'n'roll, tight group harmonies and John and Paul's dynamic personalities. Stu Sutcliffe quit the group after a second Hamburg stint in the spring of 1961, preferring to remain there with his photographer girlfriend Astrid Kirchherr – he would tragically die of a brain haemorrhage the following year – yet this only served to strengthen the remaining foursome, with McCartney taking over on bass.

> 'We don't like their sound, and guitar music is on the way out.'
>
> Decca Recording Company
> rejecting The Beatles, 1962

Above

With the release of 'I Want To Hold Your Hand' in 1963 Beatlemania swept the US. Selling one million copies in just 10 days, the song became the band's best-selling single.

One of The Beatles favoured venues – and the one with which they would for ever be associated – was the now-legendary Cavern Club. A dank and musty warehouse cellar that served as the spiritual home of the so-called 'Merseybeat' scene, it was here that another turning point took place in November 1961, when a local record retailer by the name of Brian Epstein witnessed one of the group's energetic if undisciplined performances, interspersing their musical numbers with onstage swearing, smoking and drinking. This was unconventional behaviour during an era of smooth, clean-cut pop idols such as Fabian, Frankie Avalon and Cliff Richard, yet The Beatles never believed in adhering to the rules. Clad in tight-fitting leather outfits and now sporting unusual 'moptop' hairdos – aside from Pete Best, who opted to retain the slicked-back rocker look – they went their own route ... until Epstein became their manager.

Bigger Than Elvis

Although totally inexperienced in managerial terms, it was Epstein who quickly persuaded his charges that, if they wanted success, they would need to adopt a far more professional and disciplined approach: turn up for gigs on time, cut out the onstage smoking and drinking, and discard the rough and ready rocker look in favour of the sharp suits, shirts and ties that were befitting stars of the day. In return, he secured The Beatles more money via better bookings while doing the rounds of London record companies in search of a prized contract. In 1962, the major labels still were not interested in groups from north of the nation's capital and they all ignored Epstein's assertion that 'One day these boys will be bigger than Elvis' ... save for the last one he approached, EMI's small Parlophone label, run by George Martin, the producer of mostly comedy and orchestral recordings. Intrigued as much by their captivating personalities as by their musical ability, Martin signed The Beatles and both parties would never look back.

Still, one more change had to take place before history could be made. Informed that George Martin was less than impressed with Pete Best's drumming, and feeling no allegiance to a man who had provided them with stability while remaining something of an outsider, John, Paul and George conspired with Brian Epstein to oust Pete from the group in one of rock's most notorious and shoddily handled sackings. In his place, on the eve of fame, they installed Ringo Starr, the popularly sad-eyed and charismatic drummer with another well-liked Liverpudlian outfit, Rory Storm and The Hurricanes, who had sat in with The Beatles on several occasions when Pete Best was not available. Now the stage was set for one of the most remarkable and unforgettable periods in the annals of popular music.

Beatlemania

During the next seven years, the Fab Four scaled heights that were unprecedented even by Elvis Presley's standards; critically, commercially and, most enduring of all, artistically. Since the early days of their collaboration, Lennon and McCartney had written songs both separately and together, and while few of these had surpassed the standard of the group's workmanlike first single, 'Love Me Do', once they had

see Introduction pp 86   *see* Sources & Sounds pp 78   *see* A–Z of Artists pp 102

a record company consistently demanding new material the pair went into another gear, producing songs of incredible range and increasing sophistication. From the infectious early likes of 'Please Please Me', 'She Loves You' and 'I Want To Hold Your Hand' that helped the band conquer Britain in 1963 amid hysterical fan scenes of what the press aptly termed 'Beatlemania', through hits such as 'A Hard Day's Night' (the title of their first, highly acclaimed film), 'Can't Buy Me Love' and 'I Feel Fine' that saw them slay America and the rest of the world during the halcyon year of 1964, The Beatles operated as a totally self-contained unit, leading the 'British Invasion' that opened the doors for numerous other homegrown acts to gatecrash the seemingly impenetrable US charts.

As Beatlemania ran its course and the group members became jaded with the trappings of fame and non-stop concert, TV and radio appearances, they quit the road, withdrew to the EMI Studios on Abbey Road and embarked on the second and artistically even more remarkable phase of their career. Between 1966 and 1969, drawing on personal experiences, socio-cultural influences, Harrison's immersion in Indian music and philosophy, and Lennon's prodigious ingestion of mind-bending drugs, they produced recordings of breathtaking scope, originality, imagination, technological innovation, and musical and (sometimes) lyrical sophistication. From the albums *Revolver* (1966), *Sgt. Pepper's Lonely Hearts Club Band* (1967), *The Beatles* (a.k.a. *The White Album*, 1968) and *Abbey Road* (1969) to landmark singles like 'Eleanor Rigby', 'Strawberry Fields Forever', 'Hey Jude' and Harrison's 'Something', The Beatles created a body of work that transcended Brian Epstein's 1967 drug overdose death and their subsequent bitter squabbles to leave a musical legacy that, more than 35 years after the band's demise, still has a solid grip on the mass consciousness.

Above

Helping to pioneer more advanced, multi-layered arrangements in pop, The Beatles were also instrumental in developing folk rock, hard rock and psychedelia.

see Elvis Presley pp 52   *see* Frankie Avalon pp 56   *see* Cliff Richard pp 69   *see* Gene Vincent pp 72

📼 CLASSIC RECORDINGS

1966
Fresh Cream, 'I Feel Free'

1967
Disraeli Gears

1968
Wheels Of Fire

1969
Goodbye

1970
Live Cream, Vol. 1

1972
Live Cream, Vol. 2

2003
BBC Sessions

Above

With all band members having a reputation for being a virtuoso on his respective instrument, Cream was the first 'supergroup'.

'I've always wanted the sound of Muddy Waters' early records – only louder.'

Eric Clapton

The first and arguably most famous of hard rock's much touted 'supergroups', Cream comprised Eric Clapton (born Eric Patrick Clapp, 30 March 1945) on guitar/vocals, Jack Bruce (born 14 May 1943) on bass/harmonica/keyboards/vocals and Ginger Baker (born Peter Edward Baker, 19 August 1939) on drums, a trio who achieved lasting fame courtesy of their technically virtuosic, jam-and-solo-laden concerts and four psychedelia-fueled blues rock albums during the space of less than two and a half years.

Producing and performing music that would have been inconceivable during the first half of the decade, Cream was very much a product of the late 1960s, when artistic innovation was continually extending the pop/rock envelope. That is why few outside the group could have foreseen the results when its members first got together in 1966.

Straight Blues And Jazz-Based R&B

Eric Clapton had been a member of the pre-fame, R&B/blues-based Yardbirds, quitting in early 1965 due to his dissatisfaction with the more commercial, pop-oriented direction that the band was taking with tracks such as 'For Your Love', and thereafter he had spent the better part of a year playing straight Chicago-style blues and establishing his reputation on the burgeoning British blues scene with John Mayall's Bluesbreakers. However, while graffiti asserting that 'Clapton is God' began appearing on walls all over London, the man himself was ready to move on yet again, forming a band

🔊 *see Introduction pp 86*   🔊 *see Sources & Sounds pp 78*   🔊 *see A–Z of Artists pp 102*

with multi-instrumentalist Jack Bruce – who had also been a brief part of the Bluesbreakers' ever-evolving line-up – as well as with Ginger Baker.

Bruce and Baker had known each other since 1962, when the former had relocated to the English capital from his native Scotland to play bass with Alexis Korner's seminal Blues Incorporated. Baker had replaced drummer Charlie Watts in that line-up, and by 1963 Baker, Bruce and Blues Inc. saxophonist/organist Graham Bond had teamed up with sax player Dick Heckstall-Smith to form the jazz-based, R&B-oriented Graham Bond Organization. Still, the musical compatibility that Baker and Bruce enjoyed never extended to their personal relationship, which was characterized by onstage fights and even damage to each other's instruments, and it was after the drummer had ousted him from the group that Bruce joined The Bluesbreakers, and then Manfred Mann. All of which makes the two antagonists' agreement to reunite as part of Cream quite remarkable. However, when Clapton and Baker decided to form their own group in early 1966, one that would hopefully provide them with a real outlet for their improvisational skills, the guitarist persuaded his new collaborator that it was worth overlooking personal differences in light of Jack Bruce's undeniable musical talent. And for a time that turned out to be the case.

Virtuosity And Self-Indulgence

Signed to Robert Stigwood's Reaction Records, the trio's debut album *Fresh Cream*, recorded in the summer of 1966, made the UK Top 10 following its release that December. Clapton's superb blues guitar was perfectly complemented by Bruce's powerful vocals and inventive playing of both the bass and harmonica, while Baker jumped to the fore on his self-penned 'Toad'. In concert, the band would perform a 15-minute version of this track, 13 minutes of which was Baker's drum solo, thus setting the tone for the kind of stunning virtuosity that some critics would view as overblown self-indulgence.

Bruce penned half of the songs on *Fresh Cream*, and he repeated the feat on 1967's *Disraeli Gears* – sometimes in conjunction with lyricist Pete Brown – while Clapton was credited as a co-writer on three of the album's most famous tracks, 'Strange Brew', 'Tales Of Brave Ulysses' and 'Sunshine Of Your Love', the group's

first Stateside hit single. Released shortly after Cream's concerts at Bill Graham's Fillmore Auditorium in San Francisco had set the pattern for them performing extended live versions of their studio recordings, this album blitzed listeners with a welter of awesome instrumentals, multi-layered textures and dazzling effects.

The process continued with the altogether more patchy *Wheels Of Fire* (1968), a studio-and-stage two-album set that contained both the band's worst excesses and some of its finest moments, not least Jack Bruce's superb 'White Room' and the covers of Robert Johnson's 'Crossroads' and Albert King's 'Born Under A Bad Sign'. However, while the record topped the US charts and the group was established as one of the world's top live attractions, the group members shocked everybody by deciding to call it a day. For one thing, they felt trapped by the 'supergroup' tag and all its attendant expectations, and for another, Clapton was bored with playing power-rock and tired of refereeing the ongoing disputes between Bruce and Baker. The posthumous *Goodbye* album, featuring the classic Clapton/George Harrison composition 'Badge', served as a suitable epitaph upon its release in January 1969, and Clapton and Baker then showed they had not learned their lesson when comprising one half of the even more short-lived Blind Faith venture. A brief reunion occurred in 2005.

Below
Despite only lasting for three years, Cream's first three albums are widely accepted as both blues rock classics and milestones in the birth of rock music.

🚗 *see* Robert Johnson pp 22   🚗 *see* Blind Faith pp 103   🚗 *see* John Mayall pp 111   🚗 *see* The Yardbirds pp 117

The Kinks

Key Artists

📼 CLASSIC RECORDINGS

1964
'You Really Got Me', 'All Day And All Of The Night'

1965
'Tired Of Waiting For You'

1966
'Dedicated Follower Of Fashion', 'A Well Respected Man', 'Sunny Afternoon', *Face To Face*

1967
'Waterloo Sunset'

1968
'Days', *The Kinks Are The Village Green Preservation Society*

1969
Arthur (Or The Decline And Fall Of The British Empire)

1970
Lola Versus Powerman And The Money-Go-Round, Part One

'I want people to be entertained and have a good time as well as there being an undercurrent message hopefully that might be helpful to people.'

Dave Davies

Above

The songs of The Kinks paired Ray Davies' quick-witted, observant lyrics with his brother Dave's powerful guitar style.

One of the more popular bands of the 'British Invasion' and a considerable influence on both 1970s heavy metal outfits and 1990s groups such as Blur and Oasis, The Kinks went through numerous line-up changes but were always led by singer/songwriter Ray Davies (born 21 June 1944), while his brother Dave (born 3 February 1947) supplied the band's signature rock guitar sound.

Raw Unbridled Energy

Born and raised in Muswell Hill, North London, the Davies boys were a little younger than many of their contemporaries on the mid-1960s scene, Dave being only 16 when he and Ray formed an R&B outfit named The Ravens with schoolfriend Pete Quaife (born 31 December 1943) on bass and Mickey Willet on drums. Willet was quickly replaced by Mick Avory

(born 15 February 1944), previously a member of the fledgling Rolling Stones, just as the group was signed to Pye Records courtesy of American producer Shel Talmy and changed its name to The Kinks.

Talmy, as later evidenced by his production of The Who's debut album and first three singles, had a penchant for capturing raw, unbridled energy on tape, and this was clearly the case when, following a couple of unsuccessful releases, The Kinks' 'You Really Got Me' stormed its way to the top of the UK charts in 1964 and made the US Top 10. Featuring Ray's idiosyncratic vocal style, the metal-ish, high-volume record was truly distinguished by Dave's fierce, distorted, proto-punk power chords – purportedly achieved by him sticking knitting needles into his amplifier – and wild, unrestrained solo, and the formula was repeated on 'All Day And All Of The Night', which peaked at No. 2 in Britain and No. 7 in the US.

Big In Britain, Banned In America

Up to this point, noted session drummer Bobby Graham had played on The Kinks' records while Mick Avory provided additional percussion, but hereafter Avory would assume his rightful place and by 1965 the band had recorded a couple of so-so albums and several EPs while making non-stop concert and TV appearances. However, things ground to an untimely halt in America during the summer of that year when the group was banned from re-entering the country following a tour marred by conflicts with promoters over money and concert venues.

The ban would last four years, during which time Ray Davies' compositions would become more introspective and whimsically English – as characterized by such classic UK hits as 'Dedicated Follower Of Fashion', 'Sunny Afternoon', 'Dead End Street', 'Waterloo Sunset', 'Autumn Almanac' and 'Days' – while disputes with his publishing company, the band's management and even its members (including some notorious onstage fights) would contribute to his nervous breakdown.

📼 *see Introduction pp 86* 📼 *see Sources & Sounds pp 78* 📼 *see A–Z of Artists pp 102*

As The Kinks grew increasingly out of touch with a contemporary scene that was replete with psychedelia and social upheaval, they released critically acclaimed albums of great artistry: *The Village Green Preservation Society* (1968), a nostalgic reflection on Ray's favoured English traditions, was succeeded thematically by the magnificent 1969 concept album *Arthur (Or The Decline And Fall Of The British Empire)*. Unfortunately, sales were modest, and Pete Quaife quit the band after the failure of *Village Green* and was replaced by John Dalton, while the addition of keyboardist John Gosling following the release of *Arthur* turned The Kinks into a five-piece setup.

Revival

The 1970 album *Lola Versus The Powerman And The Money-Go-Round, Part One*, on which Ray Davies vented brilliantly against the music industry, proved to be a surprise financial and critical success, spawning hit singles in the form of the satirical 'Lola' and 'Apeman' (the band's last UK Top 10). Thereafter, with The Kinks signed to RCA, things took a downturn as Davies flirted with rock opera and theatrical projects, before he then returned to commercial form following the group's affiliation with Arista in 1976. For the next seven years, through various line-up changes, The Kinks enjoyed renewed success in America, both on the album charts with *Sleepwalker* (1977), *Misfits* (1978), *Low Budget* (1979) and the aptly titled *Give The People What They Want* (1981), and on the road, touring arenas to sellout crowds.

The group had come a long way in 20 years, culminating with the overtly commercial 'Come Dancing' single that peaked at No. 6 in the US and No. 12 in the UK in the spring of 1983, followed by the *State Of Confusion* album that made No. 12 in America. Seven years later The Kinks were inducted into The Rock And Roll Hall Of Fame.

Above

By the mid-1960s The Kinks were drawing heavily from British music hall and traditional pop, as well as incorporating elements of country, blues and folk into their sound.

see The Rolling Stones pp 96   see The Who pp 100   see Blur pp 342   see Oasis pp 360

The
Rolling Stones

UK ROCK
Key Artists

CLASSIC RECORDINGS

1964
'Little Red Rooster',
The Rolling Stones

1965
'(I Can't Get No)
Satisfaction', 'Get Off Of
My Cloud'

1966
Aftermath

1967
Between The Buttons

1968
'Jumpin' Jack Flash',
Beggars Banquet

1969
'Honky Tonk Women',
Let It Bleed

1971
Sticky Fingers

1972
Exile On Main St.

1978
Some Girls

1981
Tattoo You

2005
A Bigger Bang

In its classic line-up, featuring singer/songwriter Mick Jagger (born 26 July 1943), guitarist/ songwriter Keith Richards (born 18 December 1943), guitarist/multi-instrumentalist Brian Jones (1942–69), bass player Bill Wyman (born William Perks, 24 October 1936) and drummer Charlie Watts (born 2 July 1941), what came to be acclaimed and self-proclaimed as 'The World's Greatest Rock'n'Roll Band' first achieved success and notoriety as a loutish, parentally disapproved, blues rock counterpoint to the equally contrived happy-go-lucky image of The Beatles.

Blues And Jazz Beginnings

Having first met as South London schoolboys, Jagger and Richards were reintroduced to one another at the start of the 1960s by mutual friend Dick Taylor, with whom London School of Economics student Jagger played in a blues outfit named Little Boy Blue and The Blue Boys. Richards subsequently joined the band, and he and Jagger also made guest appearances for Alexis Korner's Blues Inc, befriending its drummer Charlie Watts as well as erstwhile member Brian Jones.

A high school dropout with a penchant for fathering illegitimate children and a passion for jazz and the blues, Jones was trying to form a band of his own when he met Jagger and Richards. He had already recruited keyboard player Ian Stewart, and within a short time Mick and Keith joined the fold, along with Dick Taylor on bass and future Kinks drummer Mick Avory. Having previously recorded a demo tape that was rejected by EMI, the band made its debut at

Right

Inspired by the likes of Muddy Waters and Howlin' Wolf, The Rolling Stones started out playing covers of blues songs, which were largely unknown to British audiences.

see Introduction pp 86   *see Sources & Sounds pp 78*   *see A–Z of Artists pp 102*

London's Marquee Club on 12 July 1962, as The Rollin'
Stones, a name that Brian adapted from the Muddy
Waters song 'Rollin' Stone Blues'. Nevertheless, Taylor
was a guitarist rather than a bass player, and within a
few weeks he quit – later forming The Pretty Things –
and was replaced by Bill Wyman who, although several
years older than his new colleagues, reportedly got the
gig because he had his own amplifier. When Mick
Avory also left the band, his place was taken by Tony
Chapman (who had actually drummed on the
aforementioned EMI-rejected demo), but this
association did not work out and in January 1963 the
Stones recruited jazz aficionado Charlie Watts.

Bad Boy Image

Dates at venues such as Ken Colyer's Studio 51, the
Ealing Jazz Club and Eel Pie Island coincided with
an eight-month residency at Giorgio Gomelsky's
Crawdaddy Club, located inside the Station Hotel in
Richmond, South London. It was here that, in April
1963, The Stones were checked out by a sharp young
wheeler-dealer named Andrew Loog Oldham and signed
to a management contract. Previously a publicist for
Beatles' manager Brian Epstein, Oldham knew little
about music but everything about promotion, and after
The Stones secured a record contract with Decca on the
strength of a recommendation by George Harrison to
A&R executive Dick Rowe (who had once made the
fateful decision of turning down The Fab Four), Oldham
immediately forced conservative-looking Ian Stewart
out of the official line-up – staying on as a roadie and
contributor on keyboards, Stewart would remain a
largely sight-unseen sixth Stone until his death in 1985.

Next, while The Rolling Stones released their
first two R&B-flavoured singles, a cover of Chuck
Berry's 'Come On' and the Lennon/McCartney-
donated 'I Wanna Be Your Man', Oldham flirted with
moulding them in The Beatles' lovable, smiling, clean-
cut image. Then he thought better of it and, in a
masterstroke, cast them as the anti-Fabs. 'Would you
let your daughter marry a Rolling Stone?' was the main
thrust of Oldham's ingenious press campaign, and his
charges ran with it; Bill standing stoically onstage while
Charlie looked bemused, Keith looked indifferent,
Brian's impish smile betrayed his angelic appearance,
and Mick grabbed everyone's attention by way of his

macho strutting, camp dance moves and, by early 1960s
standards, unconventionally laid-back attitude, staring
at his audiences and straight into the TV cameras as if
to say, 'Take it or leave it'.

Offstage, from many parents' point of view,
things only got worse, as The Stones seemingly
challenged the Establishment by flaunting their bad-boy
image, culminating in several notorious and widely
reported incidents. There was, for example, Mick, Keith
and Bill's March 1965 arrest for 'insulting behaviour',
after they had been denied access to the toilet at a
petrol station and proceeded to urinate against a wall.
And then there was the February 1967 raid on Keith's
Redlands estate in which the police alleged they found
amphetamines, marijuana and Mick's girlfriend
Marianne Faithfull wearing 'nothing but a fur rug'.
Mick and Keith's respective three- and twelve-month
prison sentences were overturned on appeal.

Above
A rebellious, bad-boy image
helped propel The Rolling
Stones from a modern blues
outfit to 'The Greatest Rock
and Roll Band in the World'
as billed on their infamous
1969 US tour.

see Muddy Waters pp 24   see Chuck Berry pp 38   see Marianne Faithfull pp 106   see Alexis Korner pp 111

Above

Breaking away from their blues roots, the mid-1960s saw The Rolling Stones develop their signature style of big, bluesy riffs and wry, sardonic lyrics.

Experimentation And Tragedy

In the recording studio it was a different story, with The Stones going from strength to strength as the 1960s began to swing and Andrew Oldham compelled Mick and Keith to write their own material in order to earn more for themselves and his publishing company. So it was that, after 1964 saw the band enjoy UK chart-topping success with covers of 'It's All Over Now' and 'Little Red Rooster', as well as with an eponymous debut album that included the first Jagger/Richards composition, 'Tell Me', they kicked off 1965 with the self-penned No. 1 'The Last Time' and followed this up with the worldwide smash that would become their anthem, '(I Can't Get No) Satisfaction', as well as the chart-topping 'Get Off Of My Cloud'.

Experimentation reared its head in 1966 with a variety of instruments on the groundbreaking *Aftermath* album (the first to contain all-original material), Brian's sitar-playing on the No. 1 'Paint It Black' single, and the hallucinogen-inspired psychedelia of 'Have You Seen Your Mother, Baby, Standing In The Shadow?' The even more experimental *Between The Buttons* album followed in 1967, along with the controversially suggestive 'Let's Spend The Night Together' single – Jagger rolled his eyes while obliged to sing 'let's spend *some time*

see Introduction pp 86   *see* Sources & Sounds pp 78   *see* A–Z of Artists pp 102

together' on US TV's family oriented *Ed Sullivan Show* – but that December's release of the Sgt. Pepperish *Their Satanic Majesties Request* album simply confirmed for many that beads, bells and flower power just did not suit the bad boys of blues-based rock'n'roll.

Loog Oldham, who had been credited as the band's producer up to and including *Between The Buttons*, was soon out of the managerial picture, and with Allen Klein now taking his place and Jimmy Miller assuming the production reins, The Stones returned to form with the superb 'Jumpin' Jack Flash' single and musically eclectic *Beggar's Banquet* LP (both 1968). Behind the scenes, however, all was not well. Brian Jones resented Jagger's and Richards' increasing domination of the band that he had founded (not to mention Richards stealing his girlfriend Anita Pallenberg), and his chronic drug addiction prevented him from contributing in the studio. On 9 June 1969, Jones officially quit the band, yet in actual fact he was fired since there was no way The Stones could tour with him in the line-up. Mick Taylor, formerly of John Mayall's Bluesbreakers, was drafted in his place, but just over three weeks later Brian Jones was found drowned in his swimming pool, and, although his death was ruled an accident, there would be subsequent rumours that he was murdered.

The *Let It Bleed* album and 'Honky Tonk Women' single (both 1969) maintained the run of chart success, yet tragedy continued to dog the band when a free concert staged at the Altamont Speedway resulted in the death of a young black fan, Meredith Hunter, at the hands of Hell's Angels 'security guards' just as The Stones were in the middle of 'Sympathy For The Devil'. They would not perform the song live again for several years, and in the interim, while Jagger immersed himself more and more in the jet-set lifestyle and Richards retreated into his own drug-induced nightmare, increased tensions between the two often adversely affected the quality of product released on their Rolling Stones Records label.

Redefining The Standards

Still, there were flashes of the old genius with singles like 'Brown Sugar' and 'Angie', as well as the double-album *Exile On Main Street* (1972), which many would eventually hail as the band's masterpiece despite its

initial critical drubbing. That same year, The Stones undertook a US tour that organizer Pete Rudge described as 'more like the Normandy landing', and thereafter, throughout the rest of the decade and right up to the present day, the band would continue to lead the way and continually redefine the standards for lavish, large-scale stadium tours.

Mick Taylor left the group and was replaced by Faces guitarist Ron Wood in 1974, and Bill Wyman departed in 1991. Yet, despite Mick Jagger's 1975 assertion that he would 'rather be dead than singing 'Satisfaction' when I'm forty-five,' he continues to break that pledge and, as evidenced by mid-period and later albums like *Some Girls* (1978), *Tattoo You* (1981), *Steel Wheels* (1989), *Voodoo Lounge* (1994) and most specifically *A Bigger Bang* (2005), he and his colleagues can still turn out worthy material and rock with the best of them.

Below
With the release of '(I Can't Get No) Satisfaction' in the summer of 1965, which topped the US *Billboard* 'Hot 100', The Rolling Stones were elevated to the level of superstardom.

see The Beatles pp 88   see The Who pp 100   see John Mayall pp 111   see The Small Faces pp 114

📼 CLASSIC RECORDINGS

1965
'I Can't Explain', 'My Generation', 'The Kids Are Alright'

1966
'Substitute'

1967
'I Can See For Miles'

1969
Tommy, 'Pinball Wizard'

1971
Who's Next, 'Won't Get Fooled Again'

1973
Quadrophenia

1978
Who Are You

'The Who … smashed through every door in the uncharted hallway of rock'n'roll without leaving much more than some debris for the rest of us to lay claim to.' Eddie Vedder, Pearl Jam

Right
Famed for smashing up instruments and inventing the rock opera, The Who produced some of the greatest singles of the 1960s, none of which ever hit the UK or US No. 1 spot.

Originally comprising Pete Townshend (born 19 May 1945) on guitar, Roger Daltrey (born 1 March 1944) on vocals, John Entwistle (1944–2002) on bass and Keith Moon (1947–78) on drums, The Who virtually exploded onto the mid-1960s scene in a blaze of power rock that placed them at the forefront of the mod movement. Reinforced by Townshend's songwriting, and a stage act that saw him leap into the air, strike ear-shattering chords with a swirling windmill motion and smash his guitar, as Daltrey, swaggering menacingly, swung his microphone like a lasso, Moon went berserk on the drums and Entwistle stood without motion or expression, this London outfit helped define teen rebellion while continually pushing the sonic envelope.

From Detours To High Numbers

After meeting in their native Shepherds Bush neighbourhood during their early teens, Townshend and Entwistle joined a Dixieland band in which the former played banjo and the latter played trumpet. They then formed a rock'n'roll outfit, before Entwistle left in 1962 to join a band named The Detours that included Roger Daltrey in its line-up. Daltrey replaced Colin Dawson on lead vocals shortly after Townshend joined as a rhythm guitarist, and that same year, 1963, drummer Doug Sandom was replaced by one Keith Moon. In early 1964, The Detours became The Who, and while still semi-professional they secured regular bookings at London's Marquee club. It was there that Townshend, frustrated with the sound system, first smashed one of his guitars, and where the group caught the attention of manager Peter Meaden. With Meaden at the helm, The Who became The High Numbers, adopted a sharp mod image and released the Meaden-penned single 'I'm The Face'/'Zoot Suit'. The record sank without a trace and took Meaden with it, to be replaced by Chris Stamp and Kit Lambert while The High Numbers reverted to

The Who and built a sturdy following courtesy of their animated stage performances and solid R&B repertoire.

The Mod Years

A contract with Decca Records placed the band with Kinks' producer Shel Talmy, a relationship that yielded the UK hit singles 'I Can't Explain', 'Anyway, Anyhow, Anywhere' and 'My Generation', featuring Daltrey alternately stuttering and belting out Townshend's lyrics, including the anthemic wreckless-youth line, 'I hope I die before I get old'. Onstage this message was reinforced not only by Townshend's guitar-smashing antics, but also by Keith Moon regularly demolishing his kit, and the string of UK Top 10 hits continued in 1966 with 'Substitute', although this marked the end of The Who's collaboration with Shel Talmy.

🎞 *see Introduction pp 86* 🎞 *see Sources & Sounds pp 78* 🎞 *see A–Z of Artists pp 102*

Kit Lambert now took over the production reins, and in 1967 the band at last achieved American success when *Happy Jack* (originally titled *A Quick One* in Britain) cracked the Top 40 and 'I Can See For Miles' made the Top 10, resulting in the band's dynamic appearance at the Monterey Pop Festival in June of that year. The Who had finally arrived, yet the mod movement was winding down, prompting Pete Townshend to regroup and compose what many consider to be his masterpiece, the rock opera *Tommy* (1969).

Neo-Classical Rock

Released to widespread acclaim and huge sales, the double album about a deaf, dumb and blind child was performed in its entirety during The Who's 1969 tour, which included prestigious dates at the London Coliseum and New York's Metropolitan Opera House, and it would later resurface as a play, a 1975 movie starring Daltrey, and a 1993 Broadway musical. As a logical progression to the serious critical attention lavished on The Beatles' masterpiece *Sgt. Pepper* album, *Tommy* transformed rock into a neo-classical artform.

Thereafter, The Who would not find it easy to live up to *Tommy*'s reputation, although the band still enjoyed considerable success with further hit singles and acclaimed albums such as *Who's Next* (1971), *Quadrophenia* (1973) and *Who Are You* (1978). The latter turned out to be its last outing with Keith Moon, whose famously debauched sex, drugs and rock'n'roll lifestyle caught up with him at the age of just 31. And although there would be more recordings and numerous tours with others filling Moon's larger-than-life shoes – even stretching beyond John Entwistle's death in 2002 – Townshend, Daltrey and Entwistle would subsequently concede that The Who really died along with its enigmatic, manically virtuosic drummer.

Below

Although they later moved into rock territory, The Who was originally marketed as a mod band. Their status as mods was amplified by Pete Townshend's irreverent attitude.

see The Beatles pp 88   see The Kinks pp 94   see David Bowie pp 196   see U2 pp 284

Amen Corner
(Vocal group, 1966–70)
This horn-laden outfit from south Wales had gained a formidable reputation for exacting musical standards and a natural vitality when they reached the UK Top 20 with 1967's funereal-paced 'Gin House Blues'. More nakedly commercial hits included a No. 1 with '(If Paradise Is) Half As Nice' (which was covered by The Dave Clark Five for the US market). Following disbandment, Andy Fairweather-Low (vocals) had qualified success with, first, Fairweather and then as a solo attraction.

The Animals
(Vocal/instrumental group, 1962–66)
After million-selling 'House Of The Rising Sun' in 1964, Tyneside's Eric Burdon (vocals), Hilton Valentine (guitar), Alan Price (keyboards), Chas Chandler (bass) and John Steel (drums) racked up further international smashes and by 1965, music press popularity polls had them breathing down the necks of The Beatles and The Rolling Stones. Price then left to pursue a solo career

and was replaced by Dave Rowberry from The Mike Cotton Sound. It was business as usual for The Animals until they disbanded after 1966's 'Don't Bring Me Down' fell from the Top 20. Burdon was persuaded to front a New Animals, who racked up hits of a psychedelic tinge. The old line-up reassembled for periodic reunion concerts and for two albums – 1976's *Before We Were So Rudely Interrupted* and, more notably, *Ark* in 1983, which they promoted – along with a re-released 'House Of The Rising Sun' – on a world tour.

Badfinger
(Vocal/instrumental group, 1965–75)
Although their best-known work was released in the 1970s, Badfinger had been around since 1965 as The Iveys in their native north Wales. In 1966, they toured the UK backing David Garrick. Signed to the Apple Records label in 1968 as The Beatles' potential successors, Tom Evans (bass), Mike Gibbins (drums), Pete Ham (guitar, piano, vocals) and Joey Molland (guitar, replacing Ron Griffiths) released their first album as Badfinger, *Magic Christian Music*, containing songs from the Peter Sellers film of that name along with new music, in 1970. 'Come And Get It', a single written by Paul McCartney, had all the hallmarks of a Fab Four classic.

A track from 1970's *No Dice*, 'Without You', was taken to the top of the UK/US charts by Harry Nilsson (and, two decades later by Mariah Carey) but frustrations with management and lack of funds led co-writer Pete Ham to commit suicide in 1975. In 1983, Tom Evans followed suit, making the band's story one of the most tragic in rock history.

Cliff Bennett and The Rebel-Rousers
(Vocal group, 1961–69)
If admired as a bandleader, Bennett was also one of few white UK singers able to take on black pop without losing the overriding passion. After six flop singles, covers of The Drifters' 'One Way Love' and 'I'll Take You Home' reached Nos. 9 and 42 respectively, but it was to

be nearly two years before a return to the charts with their biggest and final hit, 1966's 'Got To Get You Into My Life', a Beatles number produced by Paul McCartney.

Blind Faith
(Vocal/instrumental group, 1969)

Billed as 'the supergroup of all times', Steve Winwood (keyboards, vocals), Eric Clapton (guitar), Rick Grech (bass) and Ginger Baker (drums) were an amalgam of ex-members of Cream, Traffic and Family. Launched with a free concert in London's Hyde Park, they broke up after a troubled US tour. Winwood then reformed a Traffic that was to recruit Grech in 1970, while Clapton recorded a solo album and Baker formed the percussion-heavy Airforce.

The Bonzo Dog Doo-Dah Band
(Comedy group, 1962–69)

Though they scored their only big hit, 'I'm The Urban Spaceman', two years later, this London band, led by Vivian Stanshall (vocals, euphonium) and Neil Innes (vocals, guitar), had run in the same pack as The New Vaudeville Band, Whistling Jack Smith and other leading lights of a 1966 craze for olde-tyme whimsy. They were also musical forerunners of the strain of comedy that culminated with *Monty Python's Flying Circus* (1969).

Petula Clark
(Vocals, b. 1932)

A celebrity on radio and celluloid since her teens, Clark first penetrated the UK chart in 1954 with 'The Little Shoemaker' and scored the first of two No. 1s with 1961's 'Sailor'. Following a French cover of this by Dalida, she was invited to perform in Paris and became as well-known *sur le continent* as she was at home. After 1967's million-selling 'This Is My Song', hits became sporadic, though she made the UK Top 10 – with a disco remake of 1964's 'Downtown' – as late as 1988.

Above
With almost 70 million records sold worldwide, Petula Clark remains the most successful British solo artist of all time.

Left
The Bonzo Dog Doo Dah Band's debut album *Gorilla* (1967) parodied the band's jazz roots and featured some of the most deliberately hopeless jazz playing ever recorded.

see The Drifters pp 62   *see* The Beatles pp 88   *see* Cream pp 92   *see* The Dave Clark Five pp 104

Joe Cocker
(Vocals, b. 1944)

A UK Top 50 entry with 1968's self-penned 'Marjorine' prefaced a sweaty and chart-topping overhaul of The Beatles' 'With A Little Help From My Friends'. This domestic success was not repeated in North America. Nevertheless, he became a bigger star there following a show-stealing performance at Woodstock (1969) and hit revivals in 1970 of The Beatles' 'She Came In Through The Bathroom Window', The Box Tops' 'The Letter' and 'Cry Me A River', Julie London's signature tune. After a tour as *de jure* leader of the oversubscribed Mad Dogs And Englishmen troupe of Hollywood 'supersidemen' and their associates plus what was left of his English backing group, The Grease Band, progress was erratic

Below

Best remembered for his outlandish performances, British rock'n'roller Arthur Brown earned the distinction of being the only music artist to be banned from performing in the US.

until 1983 when 'Up Where We Belong', a duet with Jennifer Warnes, was a US No. 1 and reached the Top 10 in Britain. Since then, he has settled down to regular tour-album-tour sandwiches as a rock treasure guaranteed well-paid work for as long as he can stand.

The Crazy World Of Arthur Brown
(Vocal group, 1966–68)

With an alarming stage act and a debut single, 'Devil's Grip', paving the way, 1968's 'Fire!' was a No. 1 in Britain and came within an ace of doing the same in the US. However, after a fraught North American tour the group split. Vocalist Brown then travelled down many artistic avenues, most conspicuously as leader of Kingdom Come and as the Priest in 1975's film version of The Who's rock opera *Tommy*. He remains an active performer and recording artist.

The Creation
(Vocal/instrumental group, 1965–68)

This most striking of London's 'Mod' groups climaxed their act with vocalist Kenny Pickett splashing an action painting on to a canvas that was then set alight, and lead guitarist Eddie Phillips pioneered the scraping of a violin bow across a fretboard, most conspicuously on 1966's 'Painter Man', a modest chart foray at home that went to the top in West Germany. After disbandment in 1968, Pickett co-wrote sentimental 'Grandad', a UK No. 1 for actor Clive Dunn in 1971.

The Dave Clark Five
(Vocal/instrumental group, 1961–70)

Prior to the issue of an instrumental single, 'Chaquita', in 1962, this London combo underwent fundamental personnel reshuffles that resulted in a line-up that remained stable for the rest of its career. Then Dave Clark (drums), Lenny Davidson (guitar), Denis Payton (saxophone), Rick Huxley (bass) and Mike Smith (vocals, keyboards) switched their stylistic emphasis to music with vocals. After a 1964 chart-topper, 'Glad All Over' and its 'Bits And Pieces' follow-up – both written by Smith and Clark – the group racked up heftier achievements in the States as a foremost 'British Invasion' act. Their only major film, *Having A Wild Weekend* (UK title: *Catch Us If You Can*) was a box-office triumph, and – also in 1965 – 'Over And

see Introduction pp 86   see Sources & Sounds pp 78   see Key Artists pp 88

Left
Heavily promoted as having a 'cleaner' image than The Beatles, The Dave Clark Five were the so-called second group of the British Invasion.

Over' was a US No. 1, but many later releases were characterized by bandwagon-jumping. Clark's main public activities since have been 1970s recordings with Smith as 'Dave Clark And Friends', promoting repackagings of The Five's hits, and 1987's *Time* musical, praised mostly for its spectacular visual effects.

Donovan
(Guitar, vocals, b. 1946)
After 'Catch The Wind' and 'Colours' charted in 1965, this projected English 'answer' to Bob Dylan lost impetus until he mined a seam of 'sunshine' pop with such as 'Sunshine Superman' – a US No. 1 – and 'Jennifer Juniper'. After 'Atlantis' foundered in 1968's UK Top 30, he bounced back briefly with 'Goo Goo Barabajagal (Love Is Hot)', a liaison with The Jeff Beck Group. Since then, only a 1990 comedy revival of 'Jennifer Jumiper' (with Singing Corner) has been even a minor hit.

The Edgar Broughton Band
(Vocal/instrumental group, 1966–76)
If received with some affection when they reformed in the 1990s, Broughton (vocals, guitar) and his boys – Arthur Grant (bass) and Steve Broughton (drums) – will be remembered more for a rabble-rousing non-song, 'Out Demons Out', one of two Top 40 entries that typified the musical articulation of issues political and social that had secured this Warwickshire hard rock combo their high standing in Britain's agitprop circles. Yet the Band were not so 'alternative' that they could not be great fun too.

Fairport Convention
(Vocal group, 1967–present)
Not so much a premier folk rock ensemble as one of the most English of veteran rock bands, they formed in London in 1967 in a vague image of Jefferson Airplane, but traditional folk pervaded a second LP, *What We Did On Our Holidays* (1969), on which singer Sandy Denny debuted) and those that followed. Representatives of all line-ups have pitched in at Cropredy, the annual festival over which the group have presided since the early 1980s.

Below
Emerging from the British folk scene, Donovan's successful blend of folk, jazz, pop and psychedelia along with a hippy image earned him a huge international following.

🎸 *see* The Who pp 100 🎸 *see* Bob Dylan pp 126 🎸 *see* Jefferson Airplane pp 142 🎸 *see* Jeff Beck pp 212

Marianne Faithfull

(Vocals, b. 1947)

After 1964's 'As Tears Go By' – written by Rolling Stones Mick Jagger (her then-boyfriend) and Keith Richards – climbed high in the UK and US charts, a winning streak was protracted with songs of like lightweight persuasion until Faithfull's innocent schoolgirl image was tarnished for ever by frank and public opinions on free love and her involvement in Stones drug busts. Nonetheless, she staged a remarkable comeback in the late 1970s with a voice grippingly shorn of former soprano purity.

Georgie Fame

(Keyboards, vocals, b. 1943)

Real name Clive Powell, his million-selling 'Yeah Yeah' in 1964 triggered a chart run that included two more UK No. 1s in the self-composed 'Get Away' and – also a US Top 10 entry – 1967's 'Ballad Of Bonnie And Clyde'. Though there have been no more hits since 1971's 'Rosetta' (with ex-Animal Alan Price), Fame is now financially secure without any – but he continues to take occasional pot-shots at the charts. In the 1990s, he was most often seen in the bands of Van Morrison and Bill Wyman.

Family

(Vocal/instrumental group, 1966–73)

In 1967, Family became popular on London's 'underground' circuit. Not the least of their distinctions was singer Roger Chapman's nanny-goat vibrato (which you either liked or you did not) other stalwarts were Charlie Whitney (guitar) and Rob Townsend (drums). UK Top 30 singles 'No Mule's Fool', 'Strange Band', 'In My Own Time' and 'Burlesque' were but a surface manifestation of Family's entries into the album lists, of which 1973's valedictory *It's Only A Movie* was the last.

Chris Farlowe

(Vocals, b. 1940)

Real name John Deighton, Farlowe's strangled gasps and anguished roars were X-factors of 1966's 'Out Of Time', produced and co-written by Mick Jagger. Its rise to the top in Britain demonstrated that all this north Londoner needed was the right song. Yet even material as sturdy as 1967's 'Handbags And Gladrags' – a hit decades later for The Stereophonics – and stints with Atomic Rooster and Colosseum somehow could not put him back on his perch. A reissued 'Out Of Time' was a minor hit in 1975.

Fleetwood Mac

(Vocal/instrumental group, 1967–present)

Peter Green (vocals, guitar) had been a star of John Mayall's Bluesbreakers in which John McVie (bass) and Mick Fleetwood (drums) had toiled less visibly. On leaving Mayall in 1967, the three became 'Peter Green's Fleetwood Mac' after enlisting guitarist Jeremy Spencer. Later, a third guitarist, Danny Kirwan, was

see Introduction pp 86   see Sources & Sounds pp 78   see Key Artists pp 88

107

US No. 1 with 20-month-old 'I'm Telling You Now', and amassing advance orders of 142,000 (the biggest in record label Mercury's history) for a debut US album. Much of their appeal lay in trademark comic antics centred on bespectacled, geeky Freddie Garrity (vocals) – though it was noticeable that none of his ensemble's smashes were with songs designed specifically to be funny, apart from 1965's US-only 'Do The Freddie'. Nevertheless, latter-day output encompassed a larger proportion of humorous material such as an entire LP of Disney film songs and 1971's 'Susan's Tuba', which was a huge hit in France if nowhere else. All roads led to the nostalgia trail, and one-shot singles like self-penned 'I'm A Singer In A Sixties Band' by a solo Garrity, who was writing an autobiography when he died after a long illness in 2006.

Left
Peter Green's Fleetwood Mac of the late 1960s and early 1970s was a straight-up blues rock band playing blues classics.

Below
Based around the comic antics of frontman Freddy Garrity, Freddy and The Dreamers enjoyed success in the US, riding the wave of the British Invasion.

added. The outfit began moving away from its blues core with 'Albatross', 'Oh Well' and other hits penned by Green. His exit – and that of Spencer – in 1970 brought the group to its knees, despite the enlistment of McVie's wife, Christine Perfect (vocals, keyboards) from Chicken Shack. More upheavals preceded a relocation to California by the mid-1970s. After long 'wilderness years', Green managed a qualified comeback as a concert attraction in the 1990s.

Wayne Fontana and The Mindbenders
(Vocal group, 1963–68)
This Manchester group's fifth single, 'Um Um Um Um Um Um', in the domestic Top 10 was harbinger of a US breakthrough with 1965's million-selling 'Game Of Love'. With the comparative failure of subsequent releases came a rancorous parting of singer and backing combo. The Mindbenders (with future 10CC mainstay Eric Stewart on lead vocal) made the most immediate impact with 1966's 'Groovy Kind Of Love' while Fontana notched up his biggest solo hit with 'Pamela Pamela' that same year.

Freddie and The Dreamers
(Vocal group, 1961–2002)
A debut single, 1963's 'If You Gotta Make A Fool Of Somebody', began a two-year British chart run for this Manchester outfit. Moreover, as their fortunes subsided at home, they caught on in North America, scoring a

see The Rolling Stones pp 96   *see* Atomic Rooster pp 211   *see* Van Morrison pp 219   *see* The Stereophonics pp 367

Billy Fury
(Vocals, 1940–83)

This fated Liverpudlian was on a par with Cliff Richard as a British Elvis Presley, enjoying 11 Top 10 hits before vanishing into a cabaret nether-world. Though dogged by severe ill health, he resurfaced as a typecast rock'n'roll singer in the 1973 movie *That'll Be The Day*. As he may have wished, he died with a record in the charts – 1983's 'Devil Or Angel' – although he was unable either to begin a scheduled tour or complete *The Only One*, intended as a farewell album.

Gerry and The Pacemakers
(Vocal/instrumental group, 1959–present)

In 1963, this Liverpool act's first three singles – 'How Do You Do It', 'I Like It' and 'You'll Never Walk Alone' – all reached the top in Britain, a hitherto unmatched feat. Self-composed 'I'm The One' almost made it four in a row but times got harder after 'Don't Let The Sun Catch You Crying' seized up at No. 6, though it did establish the group in North America.

Backed by new Pacemakers, Gerry Marsden (vocals, guitar) became a popular draw on Swinging Sixties nostalgia revues.

The Graham Bond Organization
(Vocal/instrumental group 1963–68)

Though Dick Heckstall-Smith (saxophone), Jack Bruce (vocals, bass) and John McLaughlin (guitar) became respective mainstays of Colosseum, Cream and The Mahavishnu Orchestra, it is too sweeping to say that this group was most notable for those members who went on to greater success. The late Bond (vocals, keyboards, saxophone) was one of the most proficient musicians of his day, but it was consolidation rather than development of a jazzy take on R&B that was to be his Organization's downfall.

The Herd
(Vocal group, 1965–71)

This London outfit reached No. 6 in Britain with funereal 'From The Underworld'. Its soundalike

see Introduction pp 86 *see Sources & Sounds pp 78* *see Key Artists pp 88*

follow-up 'Paradise Lost' was a lesser UK smash, but singing guitarist Peter Frampton was to be *Rave!* magazine's 'Face Of '68'. While 'I Don't Want Our Loving To Die' returned them to the Top 10, that was that for The Herd as far as the record-buying public was concerned. Nevertheless, they soldiered on for two more years after the injurious defection of Frampton to Humble Pie in 1969.

Herman's Hermits
(Vocal group, 1964–present)
Peter 'Herman' Noone (vocals) had been a TV soap-opera actor before the group's maiden single, 1965's 'I'm Into Something Good', was a hit both at home and in the States where 'Hermania' was manifested by high Hot 100 climbs for such as 'Silhouettes', 'Mrs Brown You've Got A Lovely Daughter' and 'Listen People' before a predictable decline when new sensations – notably The Monkees – arrived. Turning back on the European market, Herman's Hermits managed a few more chart strikes before Noone went solo in 1971.

The Hollies
(Vocal/instrumental group, 1962–present)
The sound of Manchester's most acclaimed beat group hinged on the jazz sensibility of Bobby Elliott (drums) and, more so, on the breathtaking chorale of Allan Clarke (vocals), Tony Hicks (guitar, vocals) and Graham Nash (vocals, guitar) who, under the pseudonym 'L. Ransford', also composed many of an unbroken series of smashes from 1963 to 1968. Yet it was a non-original, 1966's 'Look Through Any Window', that broke The Hollies in the US. Though reliant more on outside writers after Nash left to form

the Crosby, Stills and Nash 'supergroup', the run of hits continued up to 1974's 'The Air That I Breathe', and, as late as 1983, 'Stop In The Name Of Love' swept into the US Top 20. Moreover, via its use in a TV commercial, a re-release of 1969's 'He Ain't Heavy (He's My Brother)' was a domestic No. 1 in 1988. Clarke retired, but Hicks and Elliott soldiered on into the new millennium.

The Incredible String Band
(Vocal/instrumental group, 1966–74)
On breaking free of the Scottish folk circuit, singing multi-instrumentalists Robin Williamson and Mike Heron charmed a wider world with homespun modal harmonies and exotic Gaelic mysticism that reconciled the pibroch with the sitar. They peaked commercially in 1968 with *The Hangman's Beautiful Daughter* in the UK album Top 10. Later output relied more on instrumentation less quaint to rock consumers, but the long chromatic melodies and harmonic daredevilry remained intriguing and influential on Led Zeppelin and others.

Left
With a unique blend of pop and flower power, teen idols The Herd chalked up several UK hits from 1967–68.

Below
Herman's Hermits' smooth, pleasant pop rock, roughly the British Invasion equivalent of easy listening, set the band apart from most of their contemporaries.

see Crosby, Stills and Nash pp 140   *see* The Monkees pp 145   *see* Led Zeppelin pp 200   *see* Humble Pie pp 217

Jethro Tull

(Vocal/instrumental group, 1967–present)

While this group – originally Ian Anderson (vocals, flute), Mick Abrahams (guitar), Glenn Cornick (bass) and Clive Bunker (drums) – rose on the crest of the British 'blues boom' in the late 1960s, they absorbed many other musical idioms, principally via composer Anderson. The image of his matted hair, vagrant attire and antics with his flute during early TV appearances was not easily forgotten, for, as well as being a popular album act, especially after the second one, *Stand Up* (1969), sold well in North America, they were also mainstream pop stars by 1969 when 'Living In The Past' all but topped the UK chart. Such entries, however, dried up by 1971 when *Aqualung*, a 'concept' album, appeared. By the 1980s, the group had become Anderson and Martin Barre (guitar) plus backing musicians whose living depended mostly upon US consumers' continued liking for 1987's Grammy-winning *Crest Of A Knave* and whatever other albums the financially secure Anderson chose to record.

Tom Jones

(Vocals, b. 1940)

This Welshman's piledriving but flexible baritone was first heard by the world at large on 1965's 'It's Not Unusual', a UK No. 1 that also reached the Top 10 in the States. A lean period ended with 'Green Green Grass Of Home' at the top at home and high in the US Hot 100. Further hits stretched to the early 1970s, partly because the magnificence of his voice was able to ride roughshod over indifferent material, like 1971's 'Puppet Man'. In any case, chart entries had become mere sideshows now that he had found an apparent niche as a tuxedo-ed Las Vegas cabaret performer. Nonetheless, a return to the charts after a 10-year absence with 1987's 'The Boy From Nowhere' and a re-issued 'It's Not Unusual' brought much of the aura of a fresh sensation to teenage consumers. Suddenly hip, he had another smash in 1990 with a version of Prince's 'Kiss'; starred in a TV documentary by former Sex Pistols svengali, Malcolm McLaren, and recorded with Robbie Williams, The Stereophonics, Wyclef Jean and other modern chart contenders, intrigued by his unquiet journey to old age and, in 2006, a knighthood.

🎸 *see Introduction pp 86*   🎸 *see Sources & Sounds pp 78*   🎸 *see Key Artists pp 88*

Alexis Korner
(Guitar, vocals, 1928–84)

The late 'Godfather of British blues' emerged from London's traditional jazz scene to found Blues Incorporated in 1962. Among those passing through the ranks of this loose if inspirational amalgam were subsequent members of The Rolling Stones, Cream and Led Zeppelin. In the late 1960s, Korner too made the charts as singer with CCS, whose biggest hit, a cover of Led Zeppelin's 'Whole Lotta Love' became the theme tune to BBC television's *Top Of The Pops*.

Manfred Mann
(Vocal/instrumental group, 1962–69)

This multifaceted ensemble – Paul Jones (vocals, harmonica), Mike Vickers (guitar, woodwinds), Manfred Mann (keyboards), Dave Richmond (bass) and Mike Hugg (drums) – first reached the national Top 20 with 1963's '54321'. After Richmond was replaced by Tom McGuinness, there was hardly any let up of hits, both home and overseas, including a US chart-topper with 'Do Wah Diddy Diddy', despite other personnel changes. Some of the most enduring tracks were written by Bob Dylan who considered Manfred Mann the most proficient exponents of his work. Indeed, the group scored a million-seller with his 'Mighty Quinn' after McGuinness switched to guitar and Mike D'Abo superceded Jones in 1966. All former members of the group achieved further success as recording artists, most remarkably Jones with two fast UK Top 5 penetrations; McGuinness, doing the same with his McGuinness-Flint unit, and Mann, whose progressive Earth Band enjoyed a longer run of hits in the 1970s.

Marmalade
(Vocal group, 1966–present)

As Dean Ford and The Gaylords, this Glaswegian outfit struggled until a change of name and a subsequent hit in Holland with 1967's psychedelic 'I See The Rain'. Tenacity was rewarded even more the following June when they cracked the British Top 10 at last with 'Lovin' Things' and began a four-year chart run. The twin peaks of this high summer of Scottish pop were 1968's reggaefied 'Ob-la-di Ob-la-da', a Beatles cover, at No. 1, and 'Reflections Of My Life', their only major US chartbuster.

John Mayall
(Multi-instrumentalist, vocals, b. 1933)

When he was a Manchester art student in the late 1940s, blues record sessions evolved into successful attempts at reproducing the sounds himself, so much so that he dared a stage debut in a city club in 1950. In the decades that followed, Mayall carved a niche of true individuality in perhaps pop's most stylized form, re-inventing it from all manner of new angles: duetting with Chicago bluesman Paul Butterfield on a 1967 British EP; with a big band on 1968's *Bare Wires* album; and without a drummer for 1969's near-acoustic *The Turning Point*. From the mid-1960s, his albums had been making inroads into the UK list, and his accompanying Bluesbreakers cradled many stars-in-waiting, among them guitar heroes Eric Clapton and Peter Green. Initially modest success in the States prompted an uprooting to California in 1968, and a preponderance of North American hirelings in the 1970s. He is still a reliable concert attraction and new albums remain worthwhile marketing exercises.

Above

Born out of the British blues boom sweeping London in the early 1960s, Manfred Mann ranked among the most adept of the British Invasion acts.

see Fleetwood Mac pp 106   see Bob Dylan pp 126   see Prince pp 282   see Robbie Williams pp 371

The Moody Blues
(Vocal/instrumental group, 1964–present)

Though 'Go Now' was a worldwide smash in 1965, later singles were much less successful for Denny Laine (vocals, guitar), Mike Pinder (keyboards), Ray Thomas, (woodwinds, percussion), Clint Warwick (bass) and Graeme Edge (drums), veterans of several beat groups from the British Midlands. With the departures of the late Warwick and Laine (later in Paul McCartney's Wings), the group were sagging on the ropes by 1967. However, with the respective enlistments of John Lodge and Justin Hayward, they revived with 'Nights In White Satin', the hit 45 from *Days Of Future Passed*, an ambitious concept LP with orchestra. Consequent albums refined a grandiose style so nebulous in scope that such diverse units as Yes, King Crimson and Roxy Music were all cited erroneously as variants of The Moody Blues prototype. Following a sabbatical for solo projects in the mid-1970s, the group reassembled for 1978's *Octave* and further albums that have tended to sell steadily if unremarkably.

The Move
(Vocal/instrumental group, 1966–71)

Carl Wayne (vocals), Roy Wood (guitar), Trevor Burton (guitar), Chris 'Ace' Kefford (bass) and Bev Bevan (drums) burst forth from Birmingham with a run of memorable UK hit singles, including a No. 1 with 1968's 'Blackberry Way'. All were composed by Wood who had taken over as lead singer by 1970 when The Move consisted only of him, Bevan and, from The Idle Race, guitarist Jeff Lynne who was to rival Wood as chief songwriter when the group evolved into The Electric Light Orchestra by 1972.

The Nice
(Instrumental group, 1966–70)

After 1968's *The Thoughts Of Emerlist Davjack*, their first LP, David O'List (guitar) left, and Keith Emerson (keyboards), Lee Jackson (bass) and Brian Davison (drums) chose to trade in adaptations of classical pieces as well as more contemporary material, notably 1968's hit arrangement of 'America' from *West Side Story*, plus solid originals that had an endearing quality that would be lacking in the 'technoflash' pomp-rock of the next decade when Emerson was the 'E' in ELP.

Pentangle
(Vocal/instrumental group, 1967–73)

Formed by acoustic guitar virtuosos John Renbourn and Bert Jansch, it also included Jacqui McShee (vocals), Danny Thompson (bass) and Terry Cox (drums). Described by one critic as 'the missing link between folk, jazz, blues and pop', Pentangle were considered the

Below

The Moody Blues are best known for their fusion of classical and pop music, as heard on the seminal 1967 album *Days Of Future Passed*.

see **Introduction pp 86**   *see* **Sources & Sounds pp 78**   *see* **Key Artists pp 88**

– unarguably the first 'rock opera' – and 1969's *Parachute*, *Rolling Stone* magazine's Album Of The Year.

Procol Harum

(Vocal/instrumental group, 1966–present)
Propelled by the 'holy' organ of Matthew Fisher, 'A Whiter Shade Of Pale' spent six weeks at No. 1 in Britain and rose high in the US Hot 100 during 1967's flower-power summer. The 'Homburg' follow-up – also written by Gary Brooker (vocals, piano) and lyricist Keith Reid – was almost as big a hit worldwide, but further chart strikes were less impressive until a reissue of evergreen 'A Whiter Shade Of Pale' restored them to the domestic Top 20 in 1972. Guitarist Robin Trower and drummer B.J. Wilson were other sometime members.

Left

British folk rock band Pentangle achieved their greatest commercial success in 1969 thanks to the surprise hit single 'Light Flight', which was used for a TV drama series.

most sophisticated outfit within the commercial folk movement after they crept into the UK singles Top 50 with 1969's 'Once I Had A Sweetheart', and completed the first of several successful tours of North America.

The Pretty Things

(Vocal/instrumental group, 1963–present)
Phil May (vocals) and ex-Rolling Stone Dick Taylor (guitar) formed this London R&B outfit in 1963. A long-haired reprobate image held instant appeal and they made the UK Top 20 with 'Don't Bring Me Down' and 'Honey I Need'. A few minor hits later, they signed off the singles chart for ever in 1966, and sales did not match critical acclaim for such as *S.F. Sorrow* (1968)

The Searchers

(Vocal/instrumental group, 1961–present)
Tidy harmonies and restrained fretboard interaction became stylistic trademarks after Tony Jackson (bass), John McNally (guitar) and Mike Pender (guitar) with Chris Curtis (drums) had a UK No. 1 with 'Sweets For My Sweet' in 1963. This precipitated further hits over the next two years. Belated success in the States was followed by personnel changes and commercial decline, though years on the cabaret trail were punctuated by two well-received albums of new material in the late 1970s.

Below

With a style built around an eclectic mix of blues-based rock riffs and grand classical themes, Procol Harum became one of the most popular prog rock bands.

see Emerson, Lake and Palmer pp 214   see Electric Light Orchestra pp 238   see Paul McCartney and Wings pp 241

Above
One of the original British psychedelic groups, The Soft Machine was instrumental in the birth of both prog rock and jazz rock.

The Small Faces
(Vocal/instrumental group, 1965–69)
After entering the UK Top 20 with 1965's 'Whatcha Gonna Do About It', this pre-eminent mod group – Steve Marriott (vocals, guitar), Jimmy Winston (keyboards), Ronnie Lane (bass, vocals) and Kenney Jones (drums) – suffered a miss with self-composed 'I Got Mine'; replaced Winston with Ian McLagan, and got back on course with chart-topping 'All Or Nothing' and lesser hits before a post-1967 creative peak with 'Here Come The Nice', 'Itchycoo Park', 'Tin Soldier', and 'Lazy Sunday', which summed up The Small Faces dialectic in its blend of R&B, psychedelia and Cockney chirpiness. 'Itchycoo Park' was the vehicle of a US advance that was thwarted by Marriott's departure to form the Humble Pie supergroup. The others rallied by teaming up with Ron Wood (guitar) and Rod Stewart (vocals) from The Jeff Beck Group as 'The Faces'. A brief Small Faces reunion in the late 1970s was notable for market indifference towards two comeback albums against UK Top 40 placings for re-promoted 1960s singles.

Right
Whilst not a talented singer or musician, Screaming Lord Sutch released several horror themed singles in the UK in the 1960s, the post popular of which being 'Jack The Ripper'.

The Soft Machine
(Vocal/instrumental group, 1965–75)
At the dawning of the age of Aquarius, The Soft Machine – their ever-changing line-up based around Robert Wyatt (drums) and Mike Ratledge (organ)

– rivalled Pink Floyd as London's prime exponents of psychedelic rock, mainly through use of complex time signatures, a stubbornly English lyricism and the creation of musical moods through open-ended improvisation. A later, jazzier edition of the group reached the UK album chart in the early 1970s, relying less on instinct and thrilling margin of error than technical precision.

Al Stewart
(Guitar, vocals, b. 1945)
Once lead guitarist with Bournemouth's Tony Blackburn and The Rovers, Stewart's commercial discography as a solo artist commenced with a 1966 Xerox of a Yardbirds LP track, 'Turn Into Earth'. Very bound up in himself lyrically, he impinged on national consciousness via mild media uproar over his insertion of a rude word in autobiographical 'Love Chronicles', title track of a 1969 album. As a post-Woodstock singer/songwriter, he penetrated the US Top 10 with 1976's 'Year Of The Cat'.

Screaming Lord Sutch
(Vocals, 1940–99)
The most famous English pop star who never had a hit – and the country's longest-serving political leader – accrued instant national notoriety for a ghoulish stage act that would be reflected in 1963's 'Jack The Ripper', his best-remembered single. A small army of famous musicians, among them personnel from Led Zeppelin,

see Introduction pp 86   see Sources & Sounds pp 78   see Key Artists pp 88

assisted on 1970's *Lord Sutch And Heavy Friends* (1970) album, on which a controlled, melodic vein of heavy metal underlined a witty if gruesome lyricism.

The Swinging Blue Jeans
(Vocal group, 1958–present)
1963's 'Hippy Hippy Shake' came close to topping the UK chart, and it was to be one of the first examples of Merseybeat to enter the US Top 30. After a soundalike follow-up, 'Good Golly Miss Molly', peaked at a domestic No. 11, further hits were sporadic, though 1964's 'You're No Good' was nearly as big as 'Hippy Hippy Shake' in Europe. By the late 1960s, their very name had become a burden, but it was to keep them in well-paid work when pop's history became as marketable as its present.

Them
(Vocal/instrumental group, 1963–66)
This Irish R&B group entered the UK Top 10 in 1965 with 'Baby Please Don't Go' and 'Here Comes The Night'. The latter also made the US Top 40, as did 'Mystic Eyes'. However, a self-written B-side, 'Gloria', was to be their most renowned number after it became a US garage band standard. It was, however, a mismanaged tour of North America that proved the last straw for Van Morrison (vocals, harmonica), who commenced a climb to international solo stardom.

Tomorrow
(Vocal/instrumental group, 1966–68)
Though they wowed hippy audiences at 'happenings' in London during the watershed year of 1967, this did not translate into chart placings for 'My White Bicycle' and 'Revolution', now regarded as psychedelic classics. Yet singer Keith West alone had a hit with 'Excerpt From A Teenage Opera' from an intended album and stage show. However, the 'Sam' follow-up barely touched the Top 40 and the project was abandoned. Steve Howe (guitar) became a founder member of Yes.

Above

With a simmering sound dominated by organ riffs, lean guitars and the tough vocals of Van Morrison, Them had a considerable influence on bands like The Doors.

see The Yardbirds pp 117   see Led Zeppelin pp 200   see Pink Floyd pp 204   see Yes pp 225

The Tornados
(Instrumental group, 1961–66)

After a flop with 'Love And Fury', they raced to No. 1 with 1962's ethereal 'Telstar'. This quintessential British instrumental did likewise in the US Hot 100, though further progress there was checked when executive politics caused the cancellation of a tour. Three more singles made 1963's domestic Top 20 before The Tornados became *passé* with the coming of Merseybeat. Sales dwindled, too, through releases that either repeated old ideas or made token concessions to current trends.

Traffic
(Vocal/instrumental group, 1966–75)

From various also-ran beat groups, Dave Mason (vocals, guitar), Chris Wood (woodwinds) and Jim Capaldi (drums) joined forces with Steve Winwood (vocals, keyboards, guitar) of The Spencer Davis Group. Though 'Paper Sun' and 'Hole In My Shoe', and the *Dear Mr Fantasy* (1967) LP, all charted in Britain, tensions between Winwood and Mason caused the latter's brief exit early in 1968 and a permanent one after a second album, *Traffic* (1968). Capaldi and Wood's help during subsequent sessions for a proposed solo offering by Winwood came to be issued in 1970 as a Traffic album, *John Barleycorn Must Die*. The group reached a commercial summit with 1971's million-selling *Low Spark Of High-Heeled Boys* before an over-reliance on long-winded improvisations failed to mask a creative bankruptcy, though there was a return to form with 1974's *When The Eagle Flies* finale. In 1994, Winwood and the late Capaldi reformed Traffic for an album, *Far From Home* and correlated concerts.

Below

Largely considered an interim band for British artist Steve Winwood, Traffic forged a highly successful path through the rock scene of the late 1960s and early 1970s.

see Introduction pp 86   see Sources & Sounds pp 78   see Key Artists pp 88

The Tremeloes

(Vocal/instrumental group, 1962–present)
After eight UK chartbusters as singer Brian Poole's backing combo, 1967's 'Here Comes My Baby' precipitated a golden age for Chip Hawkes (vocals, bass), Alan Blakely (guitar, keyboards, vocals), Ricky West (guitar, vocals) and Dave Munden (drums). 1967's 'Silence Is Golden', a British No. 1, was to be their biggest US hit. A third global smash, 'Even The Bad Times Are Good', was followed by domestic triumphs before a Top 40 finale with 1971's country-flavoured 'Hello Buddy'.

The Troggs

(Vocal group, 1964–present)
After 'Wild Thing' charged into the UK chart in 1966; its follow-up, 'With A Girl Like You', penned by mainstay Reg Presley (vocals), actually seized the top spot. These were smashes in North America, too. Intermittent successes later and the recurrence of Troggs numbers in the repertoires of countless US garage bands were a solid foundation for a lucrative post-Top 40 career that has embraced a link-up with REM for 1991's *Athens To Andover* album, and a 1994 chart-topping hit revival of 1967's 'Love Is All Around' by Wet Wet Wet.

The Yardbirds

(Vocal/instrumental group, 1963–68)
The nurtured prowess of successive lead guitarists Eric Clapton (until 1965), Jeff Beck and Jimmy Page helped make The Yardbirds one of the most innovative rock groups of the 1960s. More discreetly influential, however, were more permanent members: Keith Relf (vocals, harmonica), Chris Dreja (rhythm guitar), Paul Samwell-Smith (bass) and Jim McCarty (drums), especially after 1965's 'For Your Love' came within an ace of topping both the British and US charts, and began two years of hits that combined musical adventure and instant familiarity. In 1966, Samwell-Smith left, and Page agreed to play bass until Dreja was able to take over. Beck and Page then functioned as joint lead guitarists until the former's departure in the middle of a harrowing US tour. With an increased stake in The Yardbirds' fortunes, Page suggested the hiring of mainstream pop producer Mickie Most for the releases that preceded a final performance until McCarty and Dreja reformed the group in 1995.

Below
With a unique sound dominated by Colin Blunstone's melodic vocals and Rod Argent's jazz-influenced piano, The Zombies are a favourite of music critics.

The Zombies

(Vocal/instrumental group, 1962–69)
1964's 'She's Not There' nestled uneasily among more extrovert offerings of the day in the UK Top 20. It also topped the US Hot 100 and smaller hits followed for Colin Blunstone (vocals), Paul Atkinson (guitar), Rod Argent (keyboards), Paul Arnold (bass) and Hugh Grundy (drums). Furthermore, The Zombies had actually disbanded when 1969's 'Time Of The Season' put them suddenly back near No. 1 in the US again, with commensurate sales for a final album, *Odessey And Oracle* [sic] (1968).

Left
Hailed as an inspiration for garage rock and punk rock, The Troggs chalked up a number of hits in the UK and US, including their most famous song, 'Wild Thing'.

see Cream pp 92   see Jeff Beck pp 212   see R.E.M. pp 338   see Wet Wet Wet pp 371

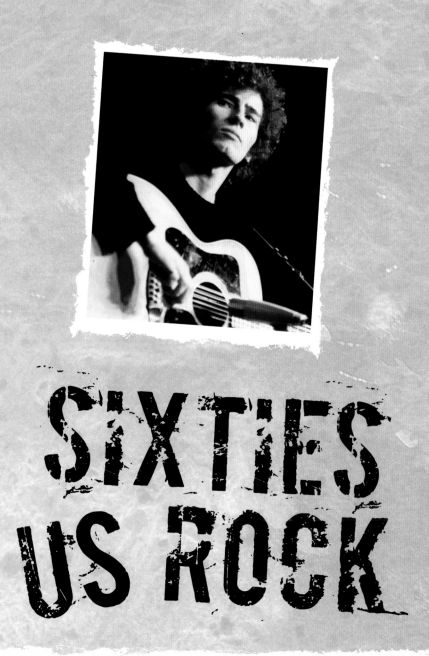

SIXTIES US ROCK

With the exception of Bob Dylan, American popular music post-Elvis was no great shakes. It would take until 1965 when The Byrds and Sonny and Cher re-established the Stateside stranglehold via their varying brands of folk rock that The Beatles and The Stones even looked worried. There would be no holding America after that: The Beach Boys morphed from twee surfing popsters into the US Beatles, while The Grateful Dead led the hippie charge.

Seattle's Jimi Hendrix went to London to find fame to inspire a host of imitators worldwide, while vocal harmonies, rather than the electric guitar, would prove the foundation for success for Crosby, Stills and Nash, Love and The Association.

The Doors and Jefferson Airplane posed anti-Establishment questions in an era when the Vietnam draft cast a mighty shadow, while maverick talents like Frank Zappa, albino bluesman Johnny Winter and, of course, Bob Dylan, exerted an influence out of proportion to their record sales.

But when it came to influence, it was New York's Velvet Underground, whose banana-cover first album emerged around the same time as *Sgt. Pepper* (1967), who would prove one of the decade's most significant acts. Their mentor, Andy Warhol, might have been surprised how long their 15 minutes of fame lasted....

The
Beach Boys

Key Artists

CLASSIC RECORDINGS

1962
'Surfin' Safari'

1963
'Surfer Girl'
'In My Room'

1964
'Fun, Fun, Fun'
'I Get Around'
'Don't Worry Baby'

1965
'Help Me Rhonda'
'California Girls'

1966
Pet Sounds
'Good Vibrations'

1967
'Heroes And Villains'

1971
'Surf's Up'

America's most successful pop group, graduating from fun-in-the-California-sun surf and hot-rod songs to multi-textured, intricately arranged numbers of exquisite harmonic structure, The Beach Boys initially achieved fame with a line-up consisting of the Wilson brothers, Brian (born 20 June 1942), Dennis (1944–83) and Carl (1946–98), together with their cousin Mike Love (born 15 March 1941) and Brian's high school friend Al Jardine (born 3 September 1942).

'Hey, surfing's getting really big. You guys ought to write a song about it.'

Dennis Wilson to brother Brian and Mike Love, 1961

Above

The Beach Boys got together in 1961, consisting of the Wilson brothers, cousin Mike Love and friend Al Jardine, and practised their harmonies round the Wilson family piano.

Harmonizing Together

1950s vocal outfits such as The Four Freshmen and The Hi-Lo's were the inspiration for Brian to form his own group and write songs that stand among the most beautiful and sophisticated in all of popular music, largely built around stunning five-part harmonies. And it was the surfing of middle brother Dennis that served as the starting point for the lyrical content.

Growing up in Hawthorne, a Los Angeles suburb just a few miles from the Pacific Ocean, the Wilsons and their cousin Love were well versed in harmonizing together by the time that Jardine joined

the fold and his mother helped rent instruments and book studio time for the teens to record 'Surfin'', co-written by Brian and Love. Without any formal training, Carl took up the guitar, Brian and Jardine alternated on bass, Dennis drummed in rudimentary fashion and Love was the main lead vocalist, while the brothers' abrasive, bullying father, Murry Wilson, relied on his experience as a song plugger to manage the fledgling band, initially named The Pendletones in homage to their preferred Pendleton shirts.

Released on the tiny local Candix label in 1961, 'Surfin'' climbed to No. 75 on the Billboard chart and helped secure the renamed Beach Boys a contract with Capitol Records. However, disappointed with the low returns earned on the nearly-hit record, Jardine made what could have been one of rock's most disastrous decisions – and there have been plenty of those – when he quit the band to pursue a dentistry degree. In his place, The Beach Boys recruited another friend, 15-year-old David Marks, and set about recording their first album, *Surfin' Safari*, which was released in late 1962 along with a single comprising the title track and, as its B-side, '409', which made the Top 20 and helped ignite the surf-rock craze while setting the early pattern for pairing a surf song with one about hot rodding.

Rapidly Growing Abilities

As the band caught fire on first a local and then a national level, Capitol began demanding new material at a frenetic rate, placing a huge burden on Brian and necessitating plenty of filler in order for The Beach Boys to record and release no less than four more albums by the end of 1963. Still, there were numerous classic tracks along the way, including 'Catch A Wave', 'Little Deuce Coupe', and the sublime harmony-laced ballads 'Surfer Girl' and 'In My Room', all of which displayed Brian's rapidly growing abilities as a songwriter, arranger and producer, the latter heavily influenced by his admiration for Phil Spector and his much-vaunted 'Wall of Sound'.

see Introduction pp 118 ⊞ see Sources & Sounds pp 78 ⊞ see A–Z of Artists pp 136

Jardine was offered a second chance when he was asked to reclaim his job from Marks, and The Beach Boys' fortunes continued through 1964 as they held their own against the onslaught of Beatlemania and the British Invasion courtesy of several new albums, a string of infectious hit singles – 'Fun, Fun, Fun', chart-topper 'I Get Around' and 'Dance, Dance, Dance' – and beautifully composed, produced and performed tracks like 'Don't Worry Baby', 'The Warmth Of The Sun', 'Girls On The Beach' and 'All Summer Long'. The ongoing pressure to deliver was too much for Brian, however, and that December, while on tour with the band, he suffered a nervous breakdown and opted to quit the road for good.

While his place was taken first by seasoned guitarist Glen Campbell and then on a permanent basis by multi-instrumentalist Bruce Johnston (born 24 June 1944), Brian focused on his songwriting which, as illustrated by tracks like 'When I Grow Up (To Be A Man)' and the chart-topping 'Help Me, Rhonda', was moving away from sun-and-sea-drenched teen themes into far more contemplative and introspective areas. What's more, the overbearing Murry Wilson was fired as the band's manager, and while the guys were on tour Brian took the opportunity to employ the cream of LA's session musicians – most of them culled from Phil Spector's famed 'Wrecking Crew' – to record backing tracks to his exact specifications, before Mike, Carl, Dennis and Jardine then added their vocals.

Below

Their success in early 1963 lead to the release of two further albums *Surfer Girl* and *Little Deuce Coupe*, and by 1964 they spread their wings internationally with a tour in Australia.

🎙 *see* The Beatles pp 88   🎙 *see* The Mamas and The Papas pp 143   🎙 *see* Phil Spector pp 177

The results were self-evident, both in the consistent quality of material on March 1965's *Today!* album, and the highly sophisticated production on one of Brian's masterpieces, 'California Girls', with its stunning harmonies and brilliant musical arrangement, where vocals and instruments blend symphonically and seamlessly in a fashion worthy of Phil Spector's most classic productions. As it turned out, this was only a precursor of what was to come next.

Competing With The Beatles

Simultaneously awed and inspired by The Beatles' late 1965 *Rubber Soul* album, Brian immediately took it upon himself to outdo the compositional and recorded achievements of the Fab Four, and in collaboration with lyricist Tony Asher he came up with some of his most beautiful and timeless material. Songs such as 'Wouldn't It Be Nice' (with its multi-layered harmonies), 'God Only Knows' (featuring Carl's

see Introduction pp 118   *see* Sources & Sounds pp 78   *see* A–Z of Artists pp 136

angelically majestic lead vocal), 'Caroline No', 'You Still Believe In Me', 'Don't Talk (Put Your Head On My Shoulder)' and 'I Just Wasn't Made For These Times' revealed not only the extent of Brian's talent as a writer and arranger, but also a maturity that belied his 23 years. All appeared together, along with classic cuts like 'Sloop John B', on 1966's *Pet Sounds* album that, with its plethora of unconventional sounds and unusual instruments, was a *tour de force* of the 1960s.

Hailed worldwide and a No. 2 best-seller in the UK, *Pet Sounds* was a surprising failure with the American public, which evidently still expected to hear The Beach Boys singing about the sun and the surf. And although Brian then produced one of the all time greatest singles in the form of the chart-topping, theremin-flavoured 'Good Vibrations', an effects-filled track that he withheld from *Pet Sounds* in order to spend six months (and $50,000) perfecting its intricately assembled, multi-sectional structure, the aforementioned attitude prevailed among his bandmates when they got wind of the totally non-commercial route that he was taking with his/the group's next project, *Dumb Angel*.

In the summer of 1966, spurred on by the standard of material and depth of acid-induced vision on The Beatles' tremendous *Revolver* album, Brian embarked on what he intended to be his avant-pop masterpiece while himself ingesting copious amounts of marijuana and LSD. Van Dyke Parks was recruited to contribute suitably offbeat, sometimes unfathomable lyrics, but with the mind-bending effects of the drugs, self-imposed pressure, and negative vibes from concerned colleagues and record company execs, the musical results became as fragmented and disjointed as his own fractured vision. In May 1967, having totally lost the plot after 10 months of intense work, Brian shelved the now re-titled *SMiLE* project and, with the release of The Beatles' landmark *Sgt. Pepper* album just a couple of weeks later, basically admitted defeat and withdrew.

Dynamic Concert Performances

Brian had engaged in an ego battle of his own making and lost. And thereafter, while he increasingly confined himself to the bedroom of his Bel Air mansion, The Beach Boys often soldiered on without their chief

creative force. Some of the material intended for *SMiLE* – such as 'Heroes And Villains' – was either remixed or reworked for the moderate *Smiley Smile* (1967) LP, and although albums such as *Wild Honey* (1967), *Sunflower* (1970), *Surf's Up* (1971) and *Love You* (1977) would contain definite moments of magic (many of them still instigated by Brian), the band's ability to influence and inspire was a thing of the past as its future lay mainly in dynamic concert performances, surviving even Dennis's drink-and-drugs problems and 1983 drowning.

Carl's death from brain cancer in 1998 effectively put an end to The Beach Boys, yet Love and Bruce Johnston maintain rights to the name and still tour with their own band under that banner. More surprisingly, Brian Wilson's live re-creation of *SMiLE* toured the world in 2004.

Below
The year 2006 marks the 40th anniversary of what is universally acclaimed as the perfect pop album, *Pet Sounds* (1966) – the happy, harmonious, sun-kissed sound epitomizing feel-good music.

🎸 *see* The Rolling Stones pp 96 🎸 *see* Paul McCartney and Wings pp 214 🎸 *see* John Lennon pp 218

The Byrds

124

'I really dig The Byrds.
I think they are the most
underrated – in their original
form – pop group.'

Bruce Johnston, The Beach Boys

Above

'Dylan meets The Beatles'
is once how Roger McGuinn
described The Byrds: the
melodic pop vibe of The
Beatles infused with the
edgy lyricism of Bob Dylan,
resulting in a genre branded
folk rock.

Melding folk with rock, smooth harmonies with jangling guitars, The Byrds enjoyed a short period during the mid-1960s when they were not only publicly acclaimed by their two biggest influences, Bob Dylan and The Beatles, but when they themselves also influenced those icons.

Acoustic Folk Pop

Jim McGuinn (born James Joseph McGuinn III, 13 July 1942), David Crosby (born 14 August 1941) and Gene Clark (1944–91) were all seasoned folk musicians when, inspired by the sounds of the 'British Invasion', they teamed up in Los Angeles in early 1964 to form an acoustic folk pop group named The Jet Set. Managed by Crosby's friend, producer Jim Dickson, the trio recorded a demo that secured them a deal with Elektra Records, and after undergoing an Anglicized name change to The Beefeaters they released a flop single titled 'Please Let Me Love You'. Session musicians assisted them in that endeavour, but Dickson now suggested that, with

McGuinn, Crosby and Clark each singing and playing acoustic 12-string guitars, the group should recruit their own bass player and drummer.

To that end, Dickson knew a bluegrass mandolin player named Chris Hillman (born 4 December 1944) and, confident of his abilities, inserted him on bass even though he had never played the instrument. The same applied to conga player Michael Clarke (1946–93), who filled the other spot even though he did not really know how to play the drums – his facial similarity to The Rolling Stones' Brian Jones was enough to land him the job. Indeed, it was what McGuinn later described as a group 'pilgrimage' to see The Beatles' movie *A Hard Day's Night* that determined not only the appearance but, more importantly, the trademark sound of the outfit that would soon rename itself The Byrds.

Twelve-String Electric Sound

Utilizing a $5,000 loan and the trade-in of McGuinn's now-redundant banjo and acoustic guitar, the group invested in a Rickenbacker 12-string electric for him just like the one they saw and heard George Harrison

see Introduction pp 118   *see* Sources & Sounds pp 78   *see* A–Z of Artists pp 136

play, as well as a Gretsch six-string electric guitar for Crosby, a Gibson bass for Hillman, Ludwig drums for Clarke, three Epiphone amplifiers and five black suits with velvet collars. Clark, who would subsequently be the main composer and, along with McGuinn, handle many of the lead vocals, was basically relegated to the tambourine. Nevertheless, after The Byrds moved to the Columbia label in late 1964, McGuinn was the only one of them to play an instrument on their first release, accompanied by members of Phil Spector's famed 'Wrecking Crew': Hal Blaine on drums, Larry Knechtel on bass, Jerry Cole and Bill Pitman on guitars, and Leon Russell on electric piano.

The song they played was a shortened version of Bob Dylan's 'Mr Tambourine Man', rearranged from a 2/4 time signature to a more Beatle-ish 4/4, and distinguished by McGuinn's Bach-like Rickenbacker guitar intro, his laid-back, Dylanish vocal delivery and Crosby's and Clark's high harmonies. Eventually released on 5 June 1965, the single hit the top of the US charts just three weeks later and was quickly followed by another similarly revamped Dylan cover, 'All I Really Want To Do', and a chart-topping interpretation of Pete Seeger's 'Turn! Turn! Turn!'. By now, all of the band members were playing on the records, including their stunning debut album *Mr Tambourine Man*, released that same summer of 1965, and including such Byrds classics as Clark's 'I'll Feel A Whole Lot Better' and their version of Pete Seeger's 'The Bells Of Rhymney', whose jangling guitar riff was in turn adapted by George Harrison for his *Rubber Soul* contribution 'If I Needed Someone'.

Psychedelic Folk Rock

The Beatles publicly proclaimed The Byrds to be their favourite American band, while Bob Dylan not only endorsed their covers of his material but actually followed their lead into folk rock. The April 1966 single 'Eight Miles High' heralded in the era of psychedelic rock, although co-composer Clark quit the band shortly thereafter due to his fear of flying and the others' resentment of the extra income that his songwriting was earning him. 'Eight Miles High' was banned by many radio stations for its alleged drug references and turned out to be The Byrds' last Top 20 US single, even though they continued to enjoy

success as a quartet with the innovative *Fifth Dimension* (1966) and *Younger Than Yesterday* (1967) albums.

1967 was the year that Jim turned into Roger McGuinn, after an Indonesian guru asserted that a new name would vibrate better with the universe. Apparently it did not vibrate better with either Crosby or Clarke, both of whom departed the band due to musical and personal differences, leaving McGuinn and Hillman to pick up the pieces with a variety of new musicians. These included Gram Parsons, who was on hand to record one of the first major country rock albums, *Sweetheart Of The Rodeo* in 1968. However, this signalled the end of the classic Byrds' sound, and by 1973, following a one-album reunion of the original quintet, the end of the band itself.

Above

Acclaimed for their versions of 'Mr Tambourine Man' and 'Turn! Turn! Turn!', The Byrds' finest moment was 'Eight Miles High' (1966). Controversy ensued because of the song's alleged drug references.

see The Beatles pp 88   see The Rolling Stones pp 96   see Bob Dylan pp 126   see The Flying Burrito Brothers pp 214

Bob Dylan

'If Woody Guthrie set the bar for American songwriters, Bob Dylan jumped right over it.'

John Mellencamp

Above
Bob Dylan's documentarian lyrical style of the early 1960s struck a chord with the feelings of the unrest experienced by many Americans of the time.

Next to The Beatles, Bob Dylan was the most influential artist of his generation, writing and performing songs whose poetic, sometimes-abstract, often-philosophical lyrics of astute commentary and therapeutic introspection spoke to the masses during an era of social unrest, political upheaval and radical change. While cross-pollinating folk and country with electric rock, Dylan elevated the role of the singer/songwriter and, in so doing, introduced an entirely new dimension to popular music.

From Zimmerman To Dylan

Born Robert Allen Zimmerman in Duluth, Minnesota, on 24 May 1941, and raised from age seven in nearby Hibbing, the future icon learned to play guitar and harmonica as a child while influenced by radio broadcasts of country, blues and, during his mid-teens, rock'n'roll. This, in turn, led to his participation in several high-school rock bands, yet while studying art at the University of Minnesota in Minneapolis a burgeoning interest in American folk music precipitated Zimmerman taking the name of Welsh poet Dylan Thomas and, as Bob Dylan, performing on the local folk music circuit, as well as at other venues during brief trips to Denver and Chicago. (He would legally change his name in August 1962.)

Having quit college at the end of his freshman year to become a full-time musician, Dylan was returning from Chicago to Minneapolis in January 1961 when he decided to head for New York City. While performing in a number of Greenwich Village coffee houses, he also took the time to visit his music idol Woody Guthrie, the socially-conscious singer/composer of 'This Land Is Your Land' and numerous protest songs, who was in a New Jersey hospital dying from hereditary neurological disorder Huntington's chorea. That April, Dylan opened for bluesman John Lee Hooker at Gerde's Folk City, and on the strength of a growing Village buzz about the young artist, as well as a good review by *New York Times* critic Robert Shelton following a September gig at the same venue, A&R exec John Hammond signed Bob Dylan to Columbia Records and produced his eponymous first album.

That record, released in March 1962, reflected Dylan's live repertoire, with just a couple of original compositions among an assortment of folk, blues and gospel standards. However, it was a totally different story by the time *The Freewheelin' Bob Dylan* was released in May 1963, a cover of 'Corrine, Corrina' standing alone amid a dozen self-penned tracks, including some solid gold songs of love ('Girl From The North Country'), lost love ('Don't Think Twice, It's Alright') and protest ('Blowin' In The Wind' and 'A Hard Rain's A-Gonna Fall'). Given the political

📻 see Introduction pp 118   📻 see Sources & Sounds pp 78   📻 see A–Z of Artists pp 136

climate of the times, the last two songs attracted the most attention, 'A Hard Rain's A-Gonna Fall' conjuring brutal images of nuclear Armageddon while 'Blowin' In The Wind', with its heartfelt call for change, brought Dylan's name to everyone's attention when Peter, Paul and Mary's version became an international chart-topper in the summer of 1963.

Broadened Appeal

Given Dylan's idiosyncratic, nasal style of singing – expressive and evocative in the ears of his followers, discordant and largely incomprehensible in the minds of many other people – the more conventional, pop renditions of his songs made them more accessible and helped broaden his appeal. This was the case when Dylan embarked on a relationship with the reigning Queen of

Folk, Joan Baez, who invited him onstage during her concerts and recorded several of his songs, prefiguring numerous other successful pop-oriented covers by the likes of The Hollies, Herman's Hermits, Judy Collins, Sonny and Cher, Manfred Mann, The Turtles and, most famously, The Byrds, during the next few years.

In the meantime, while Dylan's influence was spreading on both sides of the Atlantic, with rock contemporaries like John Lennon transitioning from boy-loses-girl themes to ones of far more personal expression, Dylan's own songwriting was advancing at a rapid rate. The January 1964 release of *The Times They Are A-Changin'* continued the cycle of protest songs, its outstanding title track sounding a warning to parents and politicians about the crumbling status quo, yet just eight months later *Another Side Of Bob Dylan* proved to

Below

In 1965, Dylan surprised his traditional audience with the huge commercial success of the fully fledged rock'n'roll album *Highway 61 Revisited*.

see **The Beatles** pp 88　　see **The Byrds** pp 124　　see **Joan Baez** pp 136　　see *Peter, Paul and Mary* pp 145

be just that; partly more romantic, invariably more poetic, with greater depth and imagery to both the music and the lyrics in such classics as 'All I Really Want To Do', 'Chimes Of Freedom', 'My Back Pages' and 'It Ain't Me Babe'.

Influenced by The Beatles as well as the rock'n'roll of his teen years, Dylan now opted to go for broke and explore the much broader possibilities of electric folk rock. Given the musical genre in which he had established himself and cultivated a huge following, this was a giant artistic leap, bound to shock both fans and critics alike.

Fiery Folk Rock

Bringing It All Back Home, released in March 1965, exploded the image of Bob Dylan as a latter day Woody Guthrie by projecting him into the pop mainstream, its first side featuring the main man backed by a heavily amplified five-piece band and tearing his way through numbers like 'Maggie's Farm' and 'Subterranean Homesick Blues', whose Chuck Berry-type melody and repetitive, bridge-less arrangement melded brilliantly with the poetic lyrics and Dylan's staccato, rapid-fire vocal delivery. This was not the smooth folk rock of The Byrds, but an altogether more fiery brand.

Indeed, the song that had already provided that group with its first and biggest hit, 'Mr Tambourine Man', appeared in its full, unexpurgated form on the all-acoustic second side of the record, alongside gems like 'It's Alright, Ma (I'm Only Bleeding)' and 'It's All Over Now, Baby Blue' that revealed their composer eschewing social commentary in favour of the increasingly fashionable personal expression.

Dylan rammed home his message that summer at the Newport Folk Festival, where his electrified performance with members of The Paul Butterfield Blues Band drew boos from many in the crowd. The same applied at the Forest Hills tennis stadium shortly afterwards, and at the Manchester Free Trade Hall in England the following year, where someone called him a 'Judas', prompting Dylan to brand his detractor a 'liar'.

Still, by then the main man was largely past caring, having secured a massive worldwide audience with his breakthrough single, 'Like a Rolling Stone', which peaked at No. 2 on the US charts (behind The

see Introduction pp 118   *see* Sources & Sounds pp 78   *see* A–Z of Artists pp 136

Beatles' 'Help!') and, at just over six minutes, was roughly twice the length of conventional releases. Dylan was redefining the parameters of popular music.

'Like A Rolling Stone' was the curtain raiser to August 1965's *Highway 61 Revisited*, whose music veered between the blues of 'It Takes A Lot To Laugh, It Takes A Train To Cry' and the all-out rock of the title track and 'Tombstone Blues'. Lyrically, Dylan was now a streetwise beat poet, and this was an image that he would stick with, reaching its apotheosis on arguably his finest record, the double album *Blonde On Blonde* (1966).

Supported in the studio as on the road by rockabilly singer Ronnie Hawkins' former backing group The Hawks (renamed The Band a couple of years later), Dylan wove a texture that combined his favourite musical genres – folk, rock, country and blues – with surreal imagery and witty wordplay on tracks such as 'Rainy Day Women #12 & 35' and 'Stuck Inside Of Mobile With The Memphis Blues Again'. Yet there was also a tender beauty to songs like 'Visions Of Johanna', 'I Want You', 'Just Like A Woman' and 'Sad Eyed Lady Of The Lowlands'.

Calmer Waters Of Country Rock

On 29 July 1966, just over two months after *Blonde On Blonde*'s release, Dylan suffered a near-fatal motorcycle accident near his home in Woodstock, New York, and thereafter he was a changed man. Following several months of recording demos with The Hawks (widely bootlegged, they would be released as *The Basement Tapes* a decade later), The *John Wesley Harding* (1967) and *Nashville Skyline* (1969) albums signalled Dylan's foray into the much calmer waters of country rock. The latter even spawned a Top 10 single in the form of 'Lay Lady Lay', whose surprisingly melodic vocal encouraged radio airplay.

Although 1970's *Self Portrait* incited the first uniformly critical drubbing of Dylan's career, the new decade saw him sustain a fairly high degree of success (if not as much influence) with the albums *New Morning* (1970), *Planet Waves* (1974), *Blood On The Tracks* (1975), *Desire* (1976), *Street Legal* (1978) and *Slow Train Coming* (1979). The latter followed on the heels of his conversion from Judaism to Christianity, yet two subsequent born-again projects were met with derision

and thereafter the Jewish re-convert made the artistically wise decision to keep religion out of his music.

Since 1988, Dylan has fronted what has come to be known as his 'Never Ending Tour' of the globe, while returning to form in the studio on such highlights as *Oh Mercy* (1989), the acoustic folk record *World Gone Wrong* (1993), the multi-Grammy-winning *Time Out Of Mind* (1997) and *Love And Theft* (2001). He remains one of the world's most formidable and relevant artists.

Below and Far Left
Dylan's contribution to music is immeasurable. 'Like A Rolling Stone' of 1965 was named the No. 1 song of all time by *Rolling Stone* magazine.

see Chuck Berry pp 38   see The Band pp 136   see Joni Mitchell pp 146   see Sonny and Cher pp 148

CLASSIC RECORDINGS

1967
The Grateful Dead

1968
Anthem Of The Sun

1969
Aoxomoxoa
Live/Dead

1970
Workingman's Dead
American Beauty

1972
Europe '72

1973
Wake Of The Flood

1974
From The Mars Hotel

1987
In The Dark

'Well, when I'm writing the music, I just follow my fingers, and follow the thread that hopefully emerges in the music.'

Bob Weir

Above

The late Jerry Garcia, lead guitarist of The Grateful Dead, co-wrote some of the band's most memorable songs, such as 'Touch Of Grey' (their only Top 10 hit).

Rock's most famous and celebrated hippie band, known more for its anything-goes, drug-hazed concerts and legions of 'Deadhead' fans than for its body of studio work, The Grateful Dead grew out of a union between singer/songwriter/ lead guitarist Jerry Garcia (1942–95), songwriter/rhythm guitarist Bob Weir (born 16 October 1947) and keyboardist/singer Ron 'Pigpen' McKernan (1946–73). They were to become the poster boys of the psychedelic scene that flourished in San Francisco during the mid to late 1960s.

Electric Warlocks

Garcia had played banjo in a number of bluegrass and jug bands when, in 1964, he first teamed up with blues/gospel enthusiast McKernan to form Mother McCree's Uptown Jug Champions, recruiting folk devotee Weir and several other musicians along the way. McKernan then persuaded Garcia and Weir to go electric, and it was as the amplified Warlocks that, in July 1965, they began performing around the Bay Area with classically trained avant-garde/electronica graduate Phil Lesh (born 15 March 1940) on bass and Bill Kreutzmann (born 7 April 1946) on drums.

As the house band at Ken Kesey's notorious LSD parties (before the drug was banned), The

see Introduction pp 118   *see* Sources & Sounds pp 78   *see* A–Z of Artists pp 136

Warlocks turned into The Grateful Dead at the year's end, and after moving into a communal house located at 710 Ashbury Street they quickly built a firm fan following courtesy of numerous free concerts at which they combined folk and country with blues. Following a short-lived deal with MGM, the band was picked up by Warner Brothers. In March 1967 they released an eponymous debut album that, despite providing some indication as to the band's eclecticism, failed to reproduce the range and excitement of its live performances. *Anthem of the Sun*, released in July 1968, went a considerable way towards correcting that problem with its psychedelically improvisational sound collages, thanks in large part to the addition of a rock-solid second drummer, Mickey Hart (born 11 September 1943), and avant-garde second keyboard player Tom Constanten (born 19 March 1944).

Free-Form Improvisation

Nevertheless, although the aural experimentation continued to sometimes-stunning effect on 1969's *Aoxomoxoa*, with its Garcia-penned, hallucinogen-fuelled songs boasting suitably abstract lyrics by new non-performance band member, poet Robert Hunter (born 23 June 1941), it was not until the in-concert double-album *Live/Dead* was released later that year that record buyers finally got to hear what the group was truly all about. Here were the free-form improvisational skills of the musicians in their unexpurgated, virtuosic glory, highlighted by the extended jam 'The Eleven', a barnstorming 15-plus-minute cover of '(Turn On Your) Lovelight' and, most significantly, a 23-plus-minute version of 'Dark Star', the ultimate Grateful Dead trip.

Back in the studio, the band recorded two classic albums in 1970 that represented a drastic change of pace and direction, contrasting sharply with its onstage act. Both the all-acoustic *Workingman's Dead* and the seminal *American Beauty* saw the Dead exploring their country, folk and blues roots in superb and remarkably restrained fashion, their stripped down, more succinct arrangements exposing the beauty of songs such as 'Uncle John's Band' (their first radio hit), 'Casey Jones', 'Sugar Magnolia' and 'Truckin'', and providing The Dead with core material for all future concert appearances.

Deadheads On The Increase

Indeed, the live work would gather momentum with each passing year, as the Deadheads kept increasing in numbers along with their use of drugs at the group's shows. Not that the band members were immune to the effects of substance abuse themselves. McKernan's chronic alcoholism resulted in his death from liver failure at the age of just 26, and Garcia was already in the midst of his long and ultimately unsuccesful battle with drug addiction.

Keith Godchaux (1948–80) replaced McKernan on keyboards, while his wife Donna Jean (born Donna Jean Thatcher, 22 August 1947) was recruited to sing backing vocals prior to 1973's *Wake Of The Flood*, 1974's *Grateful Dead From The Mars Hotel* and 1975's *Blues For Allah* albums, all released on the band's own label and their last good records for more than a decade. The Godchauxs' own substance abuse problems would lead to their dismissal in 1979, a year before Keith's death in a car accident, while his replacement Brent Mydland (1952–90) would be around for just over a decade before he died from a drug overdose.

Above
The Grateful Dead released their first live 16-track recording, *Live Dead*, in 1969, which showcases their experimental jazz rock style.

In the meantime, The Grateful Dead became, out of nowhere, shockingly radio and TV-friendly, courtesy of the band's highest-selling album, 1987's *In The Dark*, that also spawned its only-ever Top 10 single, 'Touch Of Gray'. At this point, The Dead's cult popularity went mainstream and already massive ticket sales went through the roof; yet this ongoing success was time-limited. Following Mydland's death – the third fatality of a Dead keyboardist (no pun intended) – his place was taken by ex-Tube Vince Welnick (1951–2006) as well as by part-time member Bruce Hornsby, and the band continued performing to sell-out crowds until Garcia's 1995 death from a heart attack while attending a drug abuse treatment centre in Northern California.

see The Band pp 136   *see* Lovin' Spoonful pp 143   *see* The Allman Brothers pp 211

Jimi Hendrix

Key Artists

With his pioneering use of fuzz, feedback and distortion in tandem with a God-given talent, Jimi Hendrix expanded and redefined the range of the electric guitar, and in so doing he became one of rock's greatest superstars, all within the space of just four years.

Changing Names

Born in Seattle, Washington, on 27 November 1942, the left-handed Johnny Allen Hendrix (renamed James Marshall by his father Al Hendrix in 1946) taught himself to play guitar while drawing on blues influences such as Robert Johnson, Howlin' Wolf, Muddy Waters, T-Bone Walker and B.B. King, as well as soul legend Curtis Mayfield and early rockers like Buddy Holly. He played in a couple of high-school bands, as well as for another outfit during a US Army stint that ended with his November 1962 discharge due to injury, at which point he began working as a session guitarist under the names of both Maurice and Jimmy James.

Assignments followed with the soul/R&B likes of Sam Cooke, King Curtis, Ike and Tina Turner, The Isley Brothers, Little Richard and John Hammond Jr., before Hendrix opted to switch from sideman to lead guitarist in his own band, Jimmy James and The Blue Flames. Playing gigs around New York City's Greenwich Village throughout late 1965 and much of 1966, Hendrix was spotted by Animals' bassist Chas Chandler during a performance at Café Wha? in July of that year, and a couple of months later Chandler persuaded him to relocate to London, which back then represented the centre of the creative/ cultural universe.

Instant Fame

After quitting The Animals, and in partnership with the group's manager, Mike Jeffery, Chandler signed Hendrix to a management contract and helped create The Jimi Hendrix Experience, with guitarist Noel

'He played his own s***, he didn't play nobody else's stuff like they do now. Jimi was original.'

Albert Collins

Above
The left-handed Jimi Hendrix played a re-strung right-handed Fender Stratocaster guitar upside-down.

Far Right
Hendrix, the 'semi-demigod' as described by *Life* magazine.

Redding (1945–2003) on bass and the highly talented Mitch Mitchell (born John Mitchell, 9 June 1947) on drums. Within weeks, the trio's performances were creating a major buzz on the London scene, and they also hit the UK Top 10 three times during the first half of 1967 with the singles 'Hey Joe', 'Purple Haze' and 'The Wind Cries Mary', all produced by Chas Chandler and included on Hendrix's outstanding debut album *Are You Experienced?* (1967).

Displaying not only the artist's stunningly virtuosic talents as a guitarist, which melded an assortment of high-volume sonic effects with lightning-fast fingerwork, but also the breadth of his previously unknown abilities as a songwriter, this record ran the gamut from tender ballads to mind-blowing, psychedelic fusions of rock, pop, blues and soul, all wed to Hendrix's distinctively husky vocals. And together with his

see Introduction pp 118   *see* Sources & Sounds pp 78   *see* A–Z of Artists pp 136

sensational appearance at the Monterey Pop Festival in June 1967, it made him a superstar in his home country as well as overseas, just nine months after he had left.

Pushing The Technological Envelope

Onstage the innately shy Hendrix ignited audiences with his breathtaking musicianship and willingness to put on a show, featuring such antics as setting fire to his guitar, while in the studio engineer Eddie Kramer helped realize Jimi's sonic vision by pushing the technological envelope to its absolute limits, as evidenced on *Axis: Bold As Love* (1967) and the double-album *Electric Ladyland* (1968), including self-penned tracks like 'Little Wing', 'Voodoo Chile' and 'Crosstown Traffic', as well as his definitive cover of Bob Dylan's 'All Along The Watchtower'.

Opting to return to America halfway through the *Electric Ladyland* sessions, Hendrix also parted ways with Chas Chandler, the co-producer having grown tired of his protégé's increasingly time-consuming approach to recording and penchant for populating the studio with assorted friends and hangers-on. Hereafter, the last two years of Jimi's life would be characterized by personal and professional unrest. He folded The Experience in June 1969 and formed the funkier, all-black Band Of Gypsies with old Army colleague/musical sidekick Billy Cox on bass and Buddy Miles (born George Miles, 5 September 1947) on drums.

This was the trio that appeared at Woodstock – where Hendrix's erratic performance was salvaged by his unforgettable and then-controversial rendition of 'The Star Spangled Banner' – and on the self-titled live album that was culled from performances at New York's Fillmore East on New Year's Eve, 1969, and New Year's Day, 1970. Nevertheless, The Gypsies' standard of musicianship could not match that contributed by Mitch Mitchell and Noel Redding.

The Jimi Hendrix Experience was briefly reformed in early 1970 before Billy Cox again replaced Redding on bass to tour the world with Hendrix and Mitchell while work was in progress on a fourth album, tentatively titled *First Rays Of The New Rising Sun*. Hendrix's death in London from drugs-related causes on 18 September of that year would prevent its completion, yet the extant tracks and numerous other unreleased recordings would posthumously see the light of day.

see Buddy Holly pp 50   see The Animals pp 102   see Bob Dylan pp 126   see Sam Cooke pp 168

The Velvet Underground

134

📼 **CLASSIC RECORDINGS**

1967
The Velvet Underground And Nico
White Light/White Heat

1969
The Velvet Underground

1970
Loaded

1974
1969: Velvet Underground Live

'We're musical primitives.'
John Cale

Above
The year 1967 saw the release of *White Light/White Heat* and is one of the 'harshest, loudest records ever released'. 'Sister Ray' from the album is one of the most significant songs of the time.

Offbeat, daring, challenging, provocative, sometimes outrageous, always different, during the wildly experimental and progressive second half of the 1960s The Velvet Underground was the avant-rock outfit par excellence. Although not commercially successful, they produced groundbreaking music that would subsequently cultivate a strong cult following while heavily influencing the punk/new-wave generation.

Acclaim And Disdain

Eschewing conventional melodies and pop-style lyrics in favour of dour, rigidly constructed songs about sadomasochism, sexual deviance, drugs, despair and the harsh, often sordid reality of urban life on the fringes, The Velvets attracted acclaim and disdain in roughly equal measure. And for this they were primarily indebted to lead singer/songwriter/guitarist Lou Reed (born Lewis Allen Reed, 2 March 1942), whose uncompromising blend of rock'n'roll with poetically sing-speak narratives delved into territories that were previously *verboten*.

A pop-grounded musician who had dabbled in avant-garde jazz, Reed met an ideal colleague in John Cale (born 9 March 1942), a classically trained multi-instrumentalist who had left his native Wales in 1963 to immerse himself in New York City's underground scene. It was shortly after he had played an 18-hour piano recital with experimental composer John Cage and collaborated with minimalist La Monte Young in The Dream Syndicate that Cale hooked up with Reed to pursue his growing love for rock'n'roll. Both were interested in trying to merge rock with the avant-garde, and they took their first step in this direction after Reed and some fellow studio musicians recorded 'The Ostrich', an off-key dance-song parody that Reed had co-composed while doing his day job as a staff songwriter for the budget Pickwick label.

Boasting a B-side called 'Sneaky Pete', this forgettable single was credited to The Primitives, and to promote it Reed enlisted Cale, avant-garde sculptor Tony Conrad and sculptor Walter DeMaria (playing drums) for some 1964 live appearances. Like Cale, Conrad had been in The Dream Syndicate, so both

📻 *see Introduction pp 118* 📻 *see Sources & Sounds pp 78* 📻 *see A–Z of Artists pp 136*

men were on the same page when Reed informed them that 'The Ostrich' simply required all strings to be tuned to a single note – welcome to minimalist rock'n'roll.

Warhol's Protégés

By 1965, The Primitives had evolved into The Velvet Underground; their name taken from an erotic novel, with Cale contributing bass guitar, viola and organ while Reed's friend Sterling Morrison (1942–95) played guitar and, following a brief tenure by Angus MacLise, Maureen Tucker (born 26 August 1944) filled the drummer's role. A young promoter named Al Aronowitz obtained them a residency at Café Bizarre in Greenwich Village, and it was there, while The Velvets were performing numbers such as 'Venus in Furs', 'Heroin', 'I'm Waiting For The Man', 'All Tomorrow's Parties' and 'The Black Angel's Death Song', that Pop Art guru Andy Warhol took in one of their shows and decided to manage them.

Under Warhol's guidance, and against the band members' better judgment, former model and current Warhol Factory superstar Nico (born Christa Paffgen, 1938–88) was added to the line-up, contributing dusky lead vocals on some of her specially written material when the group performed as part of a multi-media experience dubbed the 'Exploding Plastic Inevitable', featuring films, fetish dancers and a light show. Warhol then secured his protégés a contract with MGM's Verve label and, in the spring of 1966, produced their first album, *The Velvet Underground And Nico* (also known as 'The Banana Album' courtesy of his own cover art). This record's brilliantly eclectic collection of songs – many culled from their aforementioned live set – failed to ignite sales or light up radio dials upon its release in January 1967, but it would have an indelible influence on subsequent generations of offbeat musos and performance artists.

Musical Pandemonium

Nico went her own way later that year and Warhol was also out of the picture when The Velvets recorded their second album, *White Light, White Heat*, which was even more extreme and less commercially viable than their previous outing, offering its few listeners a half-dozen abrasive, ultra-high-volume tracks epitomized by the record's closer, 'Sister Ray', a 17-minute exercise in

musical pandemonium, where the band members seemingly tried to outdo each other in terms of the noise they were creating, while Lou Reed belted out lyrics dealing with drugs, oral sex and murder. It was strictly for purists.

Not that The Velvets' instruments were the only things clashing. Reed and Cale were engaged in their own battle for artistic control, resulting in Cale's ousting from the band in 1968 and replacement by Doug Yule (born 25 February 1947), who contributed bass, organ and vocals to the group's third album, *The Velvet Underground* (1969), which represented an about-face from all that had gone before. Its quieter, more basic rock approach was also seen on 1970's *Loaded* with relatively conventional and commercial tracks like 'Sweet Jane' and 'Rock And Roll'.

Below
Maureen 'Moe' Tucker (centre right) became The Velvet Underground's drummer in 1965. Her distinct drumming style – done standing up – was a vital component of the band's free-form, chaotic sound.

Reed, however, quit just before the album's release and he was soon followed by Morrison and Tucker, leaving Yule to front a band that was The Velvet Underground in name only by the time of its final release, the abysmal *Squeeze*, in 1973.

see Pink Floyd pp 204   see The Ramones pp 250   see The Sex Pistols pp 252   see Nirvana pp 334

The Association

(Vocal group, 1965–75)

Modelled on the Beach Boys and Four Seasons, and planting feet in both the easy-listening and hippy camps, this Californian sextet's domestic chart career began with 1966's 'Along Comes Mary'. Next up were 'Cherish' and 'Pandora's Golden Heebie Jeebies'. After 'Windy' reached No. 1 and 'Never My Love' did nearly the same, The Association enjoyed another two domestic smashes in 1968, 'Everything That Touches You' and 'Time For Livin'' (their only UK Top 40 strike).

Joan Baez

(Guitar, vocals, b. 1941)

Of Mexican and Irish extraction, Baez was the surprise hit of 1959's Newport Folk Festival. With her pure soprano and deft way with an acoustic six-string, she was thus well-placed to become one of North America's leading folk music ambassadors via ongoing international tours and albums that appealed initially

to an intellectual fringe. However, after the civil rights movement fused with folk songs as 'protest', she and Bob Dylan emerged as the genre's Royal Couple, and she scored in the UK singles list throughout 1965 with anthemic 'We Shall Overcome', 'There But For Fortune', Dylan's 'It's All Over Now Baby Blue' and 'Farewell Angelina'. She would wait until 1971 for her biggest global smash, a cover of The Band's 'The Night They Drove Old Dixie Down'. Earlier, her version of 'What Have They Done To The Rain' had served as a useful 1964 demo for The Searchers' hit just as that of 'Babe I'm Gonna Leave You' would for Led Zeppelin's debut album in 1968.

The Band

(Vocal/instrumental group, 1960–76)

1968's *Music From Big Pink* was, like most subsequent Band albums, a true blend of electric folklore nurtured over rough nights in Canadian palais with rock'n'roller Ronnie Hawkins before Robbie Robertson (guitar), Richard Manuel (piano, vocals), Rick Danko (bass), Garth Hudson (organ, saxophone) and Levon Helm (drums) landed a job backing Bob Dylan, who would be in an all-star cast at *The Last Waltz*, a 1976 concert film that marked The Band's farewell to the road.

Blood, Sweat and Tears

(Vocal/instrumental group, 1967–present)

They were the most famous rock equivalent of a 'brass band' – founder member Al Kooper's own description. With a sensational horn section always high in the mix, 1968's *Child Is Father To The Man* established them a musicianly act that was to serve as role model for Colosseum and The Average White Band and the more sophisticated US jazz rock of Weather Report and Return To Forever. On keyboards and lead vocals, Kooper was responsible for self-penned items on this debut album. Yet the group survived his exit later that year by adopting a more mainstream approach, chiefly via the recruitment of London-born, Canadian-raised David Clayton-Thomas, a singer of aggressively

🎸 *see Introduction pp 118* 🎸 *see Sources & Sounds pp 78* 🎸 *see Key Artists pp 120*

masculine bent, who dominated a million-selling second LP, *Blood Sweat And Tears*, and its 45 rpm spin-offs 'You've Made Me So Very Happy' and 'Spinning Wheel', which both climbed to No. 2 in the US Hot 100. Four more hits followed, but the outfit proved incapable of major commercial recovery after 'Go Down Gamblin'' fell from its apogee of No. 32 in 1971.

Mike Bloomfield
(Guitar, 1943–81)
Once a mainstay of Chicago's Paul Butterfield Blues Band and the shorter-lived Electric Flag, Bloomfield was a prime mover in an apparent shift towards recognition for individual players rather than groups in the late 1960s. Joined by guitarist Steve Stills and organist Al Kooper, his modestly titled *Super Session* was the best-selling CBS album of 1968. An in-concert offering with Kooper and a solo album, *It's Not Killing Me*, was followed by a drug-addled artistic decline.

Gary 'US' Bonds
(Vocals, b. 1939)
This former church chorister from Virginia reached global Top 20s in 1961 with call-and-response 'New Orleans'. While its 'Not Me' follow-up flopped, 'Quarter To Three' topped the US chart. Further US-only hits included 1962's 'Seven Day Weekend', his last before the patronage of Bruce Springsteen facilitated a commercial revival in the early 1980s, both home and abroad. This included a minor UK hit with 'Jole Blon' – the Cajun 'national anthem' – and a return to the domestic Top 20 with 'This Little Girl'.

Above

A white American blues artist, Michael Bloomfield's most famous work is the album *East-West* (1966), which experimented with the fusion of blues and Indian-style raga music.

Left

Pioneers in the field of jazz rock, Blood, Sweat and Tears had massive success with their 1969 album of the same name – it spent two years in the US charts, seven weeks of which were at No. 1.

see The Beach Boys pp 120   *see* Bob Dylan pp 126   *see* Bruce Springsteen pp 222   *see* Average White Band pp 236

Above

In 1968, Tim Buckley produced *Dream Letter: Live in London 1968* recorded from the live performance in Queen Elizabeth Hall, London.

Tim Buckley

(Guitar, vocals, 1947–75)

As one of a bohemian clique of singer/songwriters in mid-1960s New York, he developed a style of *de rigueur* melancholy introspection that was jazzier and more daring than most – though this was moderated on his first three albums. However, after 1970's transitional *Blue Afternoon*, offerings like *Lorca* and *Starsailor* were virtually free-form – though there was a return to more conventional song structure for later releases. Buckley died of a heroin overdose, leaving son Jeff to posterity.

Right

Short-lived yet highly original, Buffalo Springfield only made three albums; the first album *Buffalo Springfield* reached No. 5 in the *Billboard* charts.

Buffalo Springfield

(Vocal/instrumental group, 1966–68)

Migrating from New York to Los Angeles, Steve Stills and Richie Furey rehearsed with a third singing guitarist, Canadian Neil Young, who recommended Bruce Palmer (bass) and Dewey Martin (drums). 1967's *Buffalo Springfield* was remarkable for an acoustic bias and clever vocal harmonies. A hit single, 'For What It's Worth', and healthy sales for two further albums did not forestall a rancourous split – though two of them were to form half of Crosby, Stills, Nash and Young.

🔊 *see Introduction pp 118* 🔊 *see Sources & Sounds pp 78* 🔊 *see Key Artists pp 120*

Canned Heat
(Vocal/instrumental group, 1967–present)

Much of this good-time blues outfit's allure lay in the disparate natures of its late front men: jocular Bob 'Bear' Hite (vocals) and intense Al 'Blind Owl' Wilson (vocals, harmonica, guitar). 1968's *Boogie With Canned Heat* and its attendant 'On The Road Again' hit established them as a world-class act. 'Goin' Up The Country' and 1970's 'Let's Work Together' were also smashes, but the group became more renowned for reliable entertainment at outdoor festivals under the leadership of long-time drummer Fito de la Parra.

Patsy Cline
(Vocals, 1932–63)

The late Cline, who died in a plane crash, was Nashville's queen of the heartbreak ballad who, it was said, could 'cry on both sides of the microphone'. She was catapulted from obscurity through a performance of her maiden single (and, soon, first hit), 'Walking After Midnight', on a TV talent contest in 1957. While the former Virginia Hemsley scored heaviest in *Billboard*'s C&W charts, she crossed over into mainstream pop, notably with 1961's 'Crazy'. She was a major influence on kd lang, a star of C&W's 'New Tradition' in the 1990s.

Leonard Cohen
(Guitar, vocals, b. 1934)

Despite a humble vocal endowment, this acclaimed Canadian poet and novelist moved to the States in his mid-30s to make his first essay as a recording artist with 1968's sparsely arranged and all-acoustic *Songs Of Leonard Cohen*, which included the much-covered 'Bird On A Wire'. Reaching out to self-doubting adolescent diarists, it and its successors – notably *Songs From A Room* and 1971's *Songs Of Love And Hate* – were big hits, albeit much less so in North America than Europe, where he was a surprise hit at 1970's Isle of Wight festival, although the gloomy content of many of his compositions had Cohen stereotyped by the media as a merchant of melancholy. After weathering punk, in which his wordy gentility had no place, later albums such as *I'm Your Man* (1988) and *Ten New Songs* (2003) brought him to a new young audience interested in pop of far more depth than the usual.

Country Joe and The Fish
(Vocal/instrumental group, 1965–70)

One of the more doctrinal psychedelic groups that flourished in flower-power San Francisco featured Country Joe McDonald (vocals) and Barry 'Fish' Melton (guitar). Both *Electric Music For The Mind And Body* and *Together* made the US album Top 40, and 'I Feel Like I'm Fixing To Die Rag' was taken up as an anti-Vietnam war anthem. It was also a highlight of the group's appearance at Woodstock, the springboard of McDonald's subsequent solo career.

Below

The dark sound of Leonard Cohen's debut album *Songs Of Leonard Cohen* was widely acclaimed by folk music fans.

🎸 see John Lee Hooker pp 21 🎸 see Crosby, Stills and Nash pp 140 🎸 see Neil Young pp 225 🎸 see Jeff Buckley pp 344

Creedence Clearwater Revival

(Vocal/instrumental group, 1967–72)

If John Fogerty (vocals, guitar), Tom Fogerty (guitar), Stuart Cook (bass) and Doug Clifford (drums) were Californian hippy in appearance, their music harked back to the energy and stylistic cliches of 1950s rock'n'roll, and their spiritual home seemed to be the swamplands of the Deep South, as instanced in titles like 'Born On The Bayou'. After 1969's 'Proud Mary' all but topped the US chart, they reached a global audience too with 'Bad Moon Rising' at No. 1 in Australia and Britain, and comparable figures for the likes of 'Green River', 'Down On The Corner', 'Travelling Band', 'Up Around The Bend' and attendant albums that met favour with heavy rock and mainstream pop fans alike. The winning streak came to an end in 1972. Following disbandment, chief among composer John Fogerty's solo hits was 1975's 'Rockin' All Over The World' – adopted as a signature tune by Status Quo.

Crosby, Stills and Nash

(Vocal/instrumental group, 1968–70)

When on a US tour with The Hollies, Graham Nash (vocals, guitar) had sown the seeds of a 'supergroup' with ex-Byrd Dave Crosby (vocals, guitar) and Steve Stills (vocals, guitar) from Buffalo Springfield. The new combine rehearsed in London for an eponymous album that featured hippy lyricism, flawless vocal harmonies and neo-acoustic backing tracks. Its spin-off single, Nash's 'Marrakesh Express', was a worldwide smash, and, if his trio's warblings were not to everyone's taste, they were well-received at Woodstock – only their second stage appearance – where they were joined by Neil Young, a Buffalo Springfield colleague of Stills, who stayed on for 1970's *Deja Vu*, attributed to Crosby, Stills, Nash and Young. The group broke up the following year to devote themselves principally to solo careers, though the four individuals reunited for Live Aid and a 1988 album, *American Dream*.

Dick Dale

(Guitar, b. 1937)

Backed by The Del-Tones, California's 'King of the Surf Guitar' dented 1962's Hot 100 with 'Let's Go Trippin''. Its immediate follow-ups – also instrumentals – were less successful, but an album, *Surfer's Choice* and its 'Miserlou' single sold moderately well, and he appeared in associated assembly line movies such as 1963's *Beach Party*. When 'Miserlou' was heard over the opening credits to 1994's *Pulp Fiction*, Dale rose anew as an elderly icon of a new generation of fans.

The Doors

(Vocal/instrumental group, 1966–72)

Jim Morrison (vocals) has been the posthumous subject of a movie that fuelled the myth that he *was* The Doors. If his stage antics brought the Los Angeles outfit much publicity – and notoriety – their hits were either team efforts or written by other personnel, namely Ray Manzarek (keyboards), Robbie Kreiger (guitar) and John Densmore (drums). 1967's 'Light My Fire', a US No. 1, was followed by further high placings in both the single and album lists, peaking in 1968 with million-sellers 'Hello I Love You' and 'Touch Me'. Then came a concert in Miami where Morrison was purported to have exposed himself. During a long wait for the scheduled trial, he exiled himself in Paris where he died suddenly in 1971. The Doors disbanded a year later after two albums without him – though they reconvened in 1978 to provide accompaniment on *An American Prayer*, an album centred on tapes of Morrison reciting self-written poems. Since then, action has deferred to debate concerning a more permanent reformation with a new lead singer.

Below

A swamp rock band, Creedance Clearwater Revival had their first big hit with 'Susie Q' from their first album *Creedance Clearwater Revival* released in 1968.

see Introduction pp 118   *see* Sources & Sounds pp 78   *see* Key Artists pp 120

The Four Seasons

(Vocal group, 1961–present)

In 1962, New Jersey session singers Frankie Valli, Tommy
DeVito and Nick Massi plus songwriter Bob Gaudio
issued a single, 'Sherry', as The Four Seasons. With Valli's
shrill falsetto to the fore, it was an international million-
seller. Other such triumphs of the same persuasion
included 'Big Girls Don't Cry', 'Rag Doll' and 1965's
'Let's Hang On'. By 1968, the momentum had slackened,
but the group enjoyed a further brace of chartbusters
during the late 1970s disco boom.

The Fugs

(Vocal group, 1956–69)

Linked culturally to the 1950s beatniks, this burlesque
poetry rock outfit was formed in New York by vocalists
Ed Sanders and Tuli Kupferberg. While their long hair,
anti-everything stance and slapdash musicianship was
shared with chartbusting Anglophile garage bands of
the mid-1960s, The Fugs' uncompromising coverage
of taboo subjects and Kupferberg's middle age precluded
conventional stardom. Since the mid-1980s, there have
been reunion concerts and new albums.

Tim Hardin

(Guitar, vocals, 1940–80)

He is most renowned for other artists' interpretations
of his compositions from the mid-1960s. While Rod
Stewart took 'Reason To Believe' to No. 1 on both
sides of the Atlantic in 1971, the most 'covered'
Hardin opus is 'If I Were A Carpenter', which provided
hits for both Bobby Darin and The Four Tops. 1969
brought his only chart entry, 'Simple Song Of
Freedom', a non-original. 1980's in-concert
Homecoming served as Hardin's epitaph, preceding
as it did his death a few months later.

see Bobby Darin pp 60   *see* The Four Tops pp 170   *see* Status Quo pp 222   *see* Rod Stewart pp 234

Jefferson Airplane

(Vocal/instrumental group, 1965–73)

When the 'classic' line-up of Marty Balin (vocals), Grace Slick (vocals), Paul Kantner (guitar, vocals), Jorma Kaukonen (guitar, vocals) and Skip Spence (drums) found each other, a merger of an oblique form of folk rock with psychedilia ensured acceptance by their native San Francisco's hippy community; 1967 hit singles in 'Somebody To Love' and 'White Rabbit', and albums that were still charting when the group evolved into Jefferson Starship to enjoy another golden age in the 1980s.

Janis Joplin

(Vocals, 1943–70)

During a troubled adolescence in Texas, Joplin sang in regional clubs before a move to California where she emerged as focal point of San Francisco's Big Brother and The Holding Company, sounding weary, cynical and knowing beyond her years. In 1968, she began a solo career that was triumphant and tragic – for, shortly after a drug-induced death in 1970, she topped both the US album and singles chart with, respectively, *Pearl* and 'Me And Bobby McGee'.

Above

Richie Havens' spellbinding opening performance at the 1969 Woodstock Festival led to a series of ovations, prompting an improvisation of 'Motherless Child' that became 'Freedom', an anthem of a generation.

Right

The distinctive blues-inspired rock sound of Janis Joplin saw her lead several bands from 1967 to 1970, the year of her death, which was caused by an overdose of near pure heroin.

Richie Havens

(Guitar, vocals, b. 1941)

His Brooklyn busker's bark and percussive fretboard style was a familiar sound in New York folk clubs in the mid-1960s, mingling a minority of self-compositions with idiosyncratic arrangements of Bob Dylan, Lennon-McCartney, Gordon Lightfoot and other contemporary songwriters. 1967's *Mixed Bag* was the vehicle of an international breakthrough that rebounded on the US with a compelling late-night performance at Woodstock and a Top 20 hit in 1971 with a revival of The Beatles' 'Here Comes The Sun'.

Love

(Vocal/instrumental group, 1965–74)

Love's fusion of jingle-jangling folk rock, surreal lyrics and elements peculiar to themselves was at its purest on 1968's *Forever Changes*, a third album on which songwriting was shared between Bryan Maclean (vocals, guitar) and leader Arthur Lee (vocals, guitar). After decades out of the public eye, and a spell in prison, Lee was as ecstatic as his devotees to perform the entire

see Introduction pp 118   see Sources & Sounds pp 78   see Key Artists pp 120

Forever Changes at London's Royal Festival Hall in 2003. Arthur Lee died in 2006.

The Lovin' Spoonful
(Vocal/instrumental group, 1964–68)

Though New Yorkers, this group – John Sebastian (vocals, guitar, autoharp), Zal Yanovsky (guitar), Steve Boone (bass) and Joe Butler (drums) – had musical roots in rural blues and jug bands – and showbiz evergreens as shown by their grafting of the tune of 1931's 'Got A Date With An Angel' on to 'Daydream', the first of two million-sellers. The second, 'Summer In The City', also in 1966 was a swipe at seasonal humidity. Sebastian's solo career embraced a 1976 US No. 1, 'Welcome Back'.

The Mamas and The Papas
(Vocal group, 1964–68)

Singers Michelle Gilliam, Cass Elliot (real name Naomi Cohen), John Phillips and Denny Doherty had been part of the folk and fringe theatre scene in New York. On trying their luck in Los Angeles – where Phillips had made useful music industry connections – 'California Dreamin'' and 'Monday Monday' were recorded with session musicians underpinning the four's vigorous and contrapuntal chorale. After these each rose high in the US Top 10 in 1966, The Mamas and The Papas reached a global audience too. Further hits

included 'Dedicated To The One I Love' and 'Creeque Alley'. Personal traumas and a vexing run of comparative flops led to disbandment, but all ex-personnel remained in the entertainment industry. However, while Gilliam became a moderately successful film actor, only Elliot sustained any measure of chart success, mainly in Britain where she died in 1974. Twelve years later, Doherty and Phillips with two female vocalists took a Mamas and the Papas on the first of many tours on the 1960s nostalgia circuit.

MC5
(Vocal group, 1968–72)

Michigan's loud and politically resolute MC5 – Rob Tyler (vocals), Wayne Kramer (guitar), Fred 'Sonic' Smith (guitar), Mike Davis (bass) and Dennis Thompson (drums) – were connected with The White Panthers. Riddled with slogan-ridden social comment, rude words and raw musical attack, their three albums may be seen to have pre-empted the more dogmatic punk groups like The Clash and Crass, as well as later acts such as Killing Joke and The Levellers.

Above
The Mamas and The Papas, whose sweet California-sound harmonies remain popular.

Below
MC5 were one of the first, if not *the* first, punk rock band to hit the music scene in the late 1960s.

see The Beatles pp 88   *see* Bob Dylan pp 126   *see* The Clash pp 248   *see* Killing Joke pp 304

144

Below
Perhaps The Monkees could be criticized as being the first-ever 'manufactured' band, yet their music stands testament to their value as representatives of 1960s pop culture.

Joni Mitchell
(Guitar, vocals, b. 1947)

Fairport Convention were among several artists who had already covered her songs when this gifted Canadian soprano's debut LP, *Songs To A Seagull*, appeared in 1968. A move to California coupled with relentless touring assisted the passage of the following year's *Clouds* into the US Top 40. However, it was not until she caught the general tenor of the post Woodstock era that Mitchell truly left the runway with 1970's *Ladies Of The Canyon* and its spin-off hit single, 'Big Yellow Taxi' – as well as a cover of its 'Woodstock' by Matthews' Southern Comfort climbing to No. 1 in Britain. *Blue* and 1974's *Court And Spark* – her first with all-amplified accompaniment – were particularly big sellers before a jazzier approach in the later 1970s

was received less enthusiastically. Since then, artistic and commercial progress has been patchy and have involved ventures into other cultural areas – most conspicuously exhibitions of her paintings in the mid-1990s – and increasingly longer periods of vanishing from the public eye.

Moby Grape
(Vocal/instrumental group, 1966–73)

The Grape, featuring singing guitarists Skip Spence, Jerry Miller and Peter Lewis, plus Bob Mosley (bass) and Don Stevenson (drums) were leading exponents of the psychedelic sounds wafting from California. Heavily over-publicized – as exemplified by the issue of six singles simultaneously – they sneaked into the US Hot 100 in 1967 with 'Omaha', and a 1968 LP, *Wow!*

see Introduction pp 118   *see* Sources & Sounds pp 78   *see* Key Artists pp 120

reached the Top 20 – just. Further headway was patchy, though Spence, once drummer with Jefferson Airplane, achieved cult celebrity via a 1969 solo album, *Oar*.

The Monkees

(Vocal/instrumental group, 1966–69)

Four amenable youths – Mike Nesmith (guitar), Peter Tork (vocals), Mickey Dolenz (drums) and Davy Jones (vocals) – were hired by a Hollywood business conglomerate to play an Anglo-American pop combo in a 1966 TV series that was to be networked worldwide. Success was instant, and an international No. 1 with 'I'm A Believer' precipitated further smashes that continued after the final programme in 1968. Decades later, re-runs of the series struck chords with both pre-teens and their nostalgic parents.

Laura Nyro

(Piano, vocals, 1947–97)

An ill-fated performance at 1967's Monterey Festival arrested the commercial progress of the late New Yorker, whose songs – imaginative fusions of jazz, gospel and folk – were to be covered by the diverse likes of Blood, Sweat and Tears, Fifth Dimension, Three Dog Night, Barbra Streisand and Frank Sinatra, jackpot of all songwriters. A long vinyl silence ended with a 1975 album, *Smile*. There followed another withdrawal from the public eye until a 1988 tour and a correlated album, *Live At The Bottom Line*.

Peter, Paul and Mary

(Vocal/instrumental group, 1961–71)

This merger of three solo artists from New York – Mary Travers (vocals), Paul Stookey (guitar, vocals) and Peter Yarrow (guitar, vocals) – resulted in the first Top 40 appearances of a 'New Left' act. Yet, after an inaugural flush of success with 'Lemon Tree', 'If I Had A Hammer', self-penned 'Puff The Magic Dragon' and a 1963 cover of Bob Dylan's 'Blowing In The Wind', big hits were thin on the ground, though the decade ended with a worldwide smash in John Denver's 'Leavin' On A Jet Plane'.

Gene Pitney

(Vocals, 1941–2006)

This University of Connecticut graduate was first recognized in the music business as a composer of hits

for Ricky Nelson and Bobby Vee. As a performer, Pitney made a US Hot 100 debut with 1961's '(I Wanna) Love My Life Away' before climbing higher with two successive film title songs – 'Town Without Pity' and 'The Man Who Shot Liberty Valence'. Further hits by short-haired, besuited Pitney included 'Only Love Can Break A Heart', 'Twenty-Four Hours From Tulsa', 'I'm Gonna Be Strong' – his biggest UK smash apart from a chart-topping duet of 'Something's Gotten Hold Of My Heart' with Marc Almond in 1989 – 'Princess In Rags', 'Backstage', 'Nobody Needs Your Love' and the 1967 solo blueprint of 'Something's Gotten Hold Of My Heart'. Without exception, they were ballads sung in his trademark piercing nasal tenor. By the 1970s, Top 40 entries were coming less easily to him, but his regular concert tours remained sellouts. Pitney died suddenly on a UK tour in 2006.

P.J. Proby

(Vocals, b. 1938)

Born James Smith, Proby's career began on a Houston radio station in 1949, but by the early 1960s, he was an also-ran, taping demos for the similar-sounding Elvis Presley. However, on uprooting to Britain, a mannered vocal style, picaresque image and scandalous trouser-splitting publicity assisted the passages of 'Hold Me', 'Somewhere', 1967's 'Niki Hoeky' (his only US hit) and other singles into the charts. These remain the cornerstone of a stage act in which he is still the proverbial 'pop singer who can really sing'.

Above

Gene Pitney is one of the few great artists and songwriters that survived the 1960s intact and went on to continue a successful career performing around the world until his death in April 2006.

see Ricky Nelson pp 68   see Fairport Convention pp 105   see Blood, Sweat and Tears pp 136   see Jefferson Airplane pp 142

Tim Rose
(Guitar, vocals, 1940–2002)
Rose was omnipresent in the clubs of New York's vibrantly bohemian Greenwich Village when his arrangement of the murder ballad 'Hey Joe' was covered in 1966 as The Jimi Hendrix Experience's debut single. 'Morning Dew' proved the hardiest of his own compositions via retreads by such as The Jeff Beck Group, The Grateful Dead and, in 2002, Robert Plant. That year, the late Rose issued a final album, *American Son*, a collection with all the virtues and few of the faults of a virtuoso performance.

Santana
(Vocal/instrumental group, 1966–present)
A Latin-American take on what became known as jazz rock, the group led by Mexican Carlos Santana (guitar) were a palpable hit at Woodstock in 1969. This coincided with an eponymous debut album penetrating the US Top 10. An optimum commercial period – embracing US chart-toppers *Abraxas* and *Santana III* – was followed by dwindling success until 'Smooth' from 1999's guest star-studded *Supernatural* spent weeks at No. 1 in the US and elsewhere, sparking off an on-going reversal of fortune.

Above
Although not as well-known as many other artists of the decade, it was Tim Rose's version of 'Hey Joe' that influenced the release and massive success of the single by The Jimi Hendrix Experience.

Right
The Santana Blues Band first found success in the late 1960s with their immensely popular blend of salsa, rock, blues and jazz styles.

The Righteous Brothers
(Vocal duo, 1962–70)
Bill Medley and the late Bobby Hatfield struck gold in 1965 with 'You've Lost That Lovin' Feeling", a simple song inflated by producer Phil Spector's trademark 'wall of sound'. Another year of hits in the same vein closed with Medley going solo. A reunion with Hatfield spawned a US-only smash, 1974's 'Rock And Roll Heaven'. In 1990, a re-release of 1965's 'Unchained Melody' – featured in the movie *Ghost* – topped the UK chart, and 'You've Lost That Lovin" Feeling' made the Top 10 for the third time.

The Seeds
(Vocal/instrumental group, 1965–72)
This Los Angeles 'garage band' comprised Sky Saxon (vocals), Jan Savage (guitar), Daryll Hooper (organ) and Rick Andridge (drums). Slipping into the national Top 40 in 1965, their second single, 'Pushin' Too Hard', triggered further grippingly slipshod exercises

see Introduction pp 118　　*see* Sources & Sounds pp 78　　*see* Key Artists pp 120

prior to 'going psychedelic' in 1967. A desperate in-concert album, *Raw And Alive* signalled the end, but Saxon's solo releases – such as 2005's *Transparency* – have punctuated the decades since.

The Shangri-Las
(Vocal group, 1964–68)
New York schoolgirls Margie and Mary Ann Ganser, and Betty and Mary Weiss were thrust into the US and UK Top 20s with 1964's 'Remember (Walking In The Sand)'. After 'Leader Of The Pack', a teenage morality play, topped the US chart, its mordant theme was investigated from new angles with such as 'Dressed In Black' and world-weary 'Past Present And Future' – though upbeat 'Give Him A Great Big Kiss' broke the formula in 1965. Repromotions of 'Leader Of The Pack' twice climbed the British Top 20 in the 1970s.

Del Shannon
(Guitar, vocals, 1939–91)
Stating his intent with 1961's million-selling – and self-penned – 'Runaway', this square-jawed hunk from Michigan continued an exploration of small town soul-torture with the likes of 'Hats Off To Larry', 'Little Town Flirt' and 'Stranger In Town'. Other chartbusters included 'The Swiss Maid', 'From Me To You' – the first Beatles composition to penetrate the US Hot 100 – a revival of Jimmy Jones's 'Handy Man' and 1964's 'Keep Searchin'', characterized, like some of its predecessors, by swoops into falsetto and a memorable organ interlude. He also reached the national Top 10 by proxy when Peter and Gordon recorded his composition 'I Go To Pieces'. When the hits petered out, he remained a respected figure in the industry, producing Top 10 entries for Smith ('Baby It's You')

and Brian Hyland ('Gypsy Woman'), and remaining a riveting stage performer. He even managed a one-off return to the charts with 'Sea Of Love' nine years before his apparent suicide in 1991.

Simon and Garfunkel
(Vocal duo, 1956–71)
As 'Tom and Jerry', Paul Simon (vocals, guitar) and Art Garfunkel (vocals) had a minor US Hot 100 success as teenagers in 1957 with 'Hey Schoolgirl'. Both attempted to forge solo careers, which took Simon to the UK where he became a reliable draw in the country's folk clubs. Back in the US by 1964, he recorded an album, *Wednesday Morning 3am* with Garfunkel. Its highlight was 'The Sound Of Silence', which was issued (with superimposed backing) as a single to top the US charts. With Simon taking most of the creative initiative, later hits included 'Homeward Bound', 'Mrs Robinson' (from 1968's *The Graduate* film soundtrack) and 'The Boxer'. The new decade began with a No. 1 in both Britain and the States with 'Bridge Over Troubled Water' in which Garfunkel's breathy tenor floated effortlessly over orchestrated accompaniment. Both he and Simon have given good individual accounts of themselves in the charts since, and, if not all smiles, occasional reunions on disc and on stage have proved lucrative.

Left
The 1960s rock'n'roll band The Seeds embody what is garage rock, with their uncontrolled energy and simple, repetitive lyrics.

Below
Simon and Garfunkel are best known and loved for their hits 'The Sound Of Silence', 'Mrs Robinson' and 'Bridge Over Troubled Water'.

see **The Grateful Dead** pp 130 see **Phil Spector** pp 177 see **Jeff Beck** pp 212 see **Paul Simon** pp 221

Above

Husband and wife team
Sonny and Cher hit the big
time in 1965 with the release
of 'I Got You Babe'.

further smashes, both together and as soloists, for two fat years – with Cher's 'Bang Bang' almost but not quite repeating the 'I Got You Babe' miracle. She also scored three US No. 1s in the early 1970s when hits attributed to 'Sonny and Cher' had become intermittent, and the now-married couple were making the most of past glories in a cabaret netherworld and TV series freighted as much with comedy as music. Following divorce in 1976, Cher enjoyed an eventual career revival as both a film actor and solo chart contender. Sonny achieved political office as mayor of Palm Springs before his death in 1998.

Spirit
(Vocal/instrumental group, 1967–71)
Randy California (guitar, vocals) had worked with Jimi Hendrix in New York clubland in 1966 before returning to Los Angeles to form what became Spirit with stepfather Ed Cassidy (drums), songwriter Jay Ferguson (vocals) and Mark Andes (bass). Jazzier than most 'progressive' rock groups, they released four albums of which 1969's *The Family That Plays Together* gained the highest chart placing and included a US hit single, 'I Got A Line On You'. California died in a surfing accident in 1997.

Steppenwolf
(Vocal group, 1967–present)
After they migrated from Toronto to Los Angeles, they scored a million-seller with the 1968 biker anthem, 'Born To Be Wild'. With 'The Pusher', it was also a highlight of 1969's *Easy Rider* film soundtrack. Other hits included self-penned 'Magic Carpet Ride', 'Rock Me' and 1970's 'Hey Lawdy Mama'. Ebbing record sales led to brief disbandment in the mid-1970s, but, with German-born vocalist John Kay (Joachim Krauledat) the only original member, the group remain a potent draw on the 1960s nostalgia circuit, especially in Europe.

Sonny and Cher
(Vocal duo, 1964–76)
Jobbing Hollywood songwriter and arranger Sonny Bono linked up, both professionally and romantically, with Cher La Pier, a session singer, for a handful of misses before striking gold with 1965's chart-topping 'I Got You Babe'. Its vague if fashionable 'protest' tenor, the overnight sensation's proto-hippy appearance and an element of boy-girl ickiness that some find endearing, helped keep the momentum going with

The Steve Miller Band
(Vocal/instrumental group, 1966–86)
A cauldron of blues and psychedelia, 1968's *Children Of The Future* was a US Top 30 entry for a California-based outfit in which the only constant would be Miller (guitar, vocals), though first singer Boz Scaggs enjoyed solo success. Becoming more radio-friendly,

see Introduction pp 118   *see* Sources & Sounds pp 78   *see* Key Artists pp 120

Miller made greater impact from the early 1970s with US chart-toppers 'The Joker', 'Rock 'N' Me' and 1982's 'Abracadabra'. As a postscript, a 1990 re-issue of 'The Joker' went to No. 1 in Britain, thanks to its use in a TV commercial.

The Stooges
(Vocal/instrumental group, 1967–74)
This Detroit quartet's focal point was Iggy Pop (James Osterberg, vocals), fronting Ron Asheton (guitar), Scott Asheton (drums) and Dave Alexander (bass). Tiring of psychedelia, they had dug down to a raw three-chord bedrock for an eponymous maiden album in 1969, promoted with increasingly more manic stage performances at odds with the prevailing 'laid-back'

mood. Two more albums, *Fun House* and 1973's *Raw Power*, were appreciated mostly in retrospect after internal ructions and drug abuse prompted disbandment.

The 13th Floor Elevators
(Vocal/instrumental group, 1965–68)
They surfaced at the tail-end of the 'British Invasion' from a mid-Texas scene as self-contained in its way as Merseybeat had been. 'You're Gonna Miss Me' – from 1966's *The Psychedelic Sounds Of The 13th Floor Elevators* – was a regional hit, but later releases obeyed a law of diminishing returns both artistically and commercially. Today, The Elevators are remembered principally as the group in which Roky Erickson (vocals, guitar) cut his teeth before achieving solo renown.

Above
Steppenwolf are probably most famous for the single 'Born To Be Wild', which found worldwide fame following the release of the movie *Easy Rider*, in which it appeared.

see Jimi Hendrix pp 132   *see* David Bowie pp 196   *see* Boz Scaggs pp 220   *see* Iggy Pop pp 259

Above

The 1967 single 'Happy Together' is the hit that The Turtles are most associated with and over the years has featured in several movies from *Muriel's Wedding* to *Shrek*.

The Turtles
(Vocal group, 1964–70)

With vocalists Howard Kaylan and Mark Volman at the helm, this Californian outfit boarded a 1965 bandwagon that carried a mixed cargo of British beat and folk protest, and gained a US Top 10 breakthrough with Bob Dylan's 'It Ain't Me Babe'. The Turtles also had a jokey side – as instanced by Volman's buffoonery during TV plugs for 1967's 'Happy Together'. Almost as big globally, 'She'd Rather Be With Me' and 1968's 'Elenore' prefaced Volman and Kaylan's absorption (as 'The Phlorescent Leech & Eddie') into Frank Zappa's Mothers Of Invention.

Below

The Walker Brothers had only minor success in the US but reached No. 1 in the UK with the hit singles 'Make It Easy On Yourself' (1965) and 'The Sun Ain't Gonna Shine Anymore' (1966).

Bobby Vee
(Vocals, b. 1943)

The former Robert Velline was prominent among a crop of insipidly handsome boys-next-door who thrived in the early 1960s, having deputized on stage for Buddy Holly the evening after the Texan's fatal plane crash in 1959. Vee's hits included 'Rubber Ball', 'Take Good Care Of My Baby' – a US No. 1 – 'Run To Him' and 'The Night Has A Thousand Eyes'. He enjoyed a brief second wave of US chart entries later in the decade. On recent tours and disc releases, his backing combo has comprised his three sons.

The Walker Brothers
(Vocal/instrumental group, 1964–67)

The unrelated Walkers, Scott Engel (vocals, bass), John Maus (vocals, guitar) and Gary Leeds (drums), sought their fortunes in Britain where 'Love Her' made the Top 20 in 1965. Then came bigger smashes with 'Make It Easy On Yourself', 'My Ship Is Coming In', 'The Sun Ain't Gonna Shine Anymore' and like orchestral ballads with Engel ('Scott Walker') on lead vocals as the trio emerged as the darlings of young ladies in the UK and, to a smaller degree, in the States. However, provoked by both bickering between Engel and Maus, and falling sales, The Brothers went their separate ways. Engel's *Scott* and 1968's chart-topping *Scott 2* albums established him as both the Belgian *chansonnier* Jacques Brel's principal interpreter, and as an intriguing composer in his own right – but neither these nor *Scott 3* and *Scott 4* were the stuff of mainstream pop, and a cynical Engel churned out easy-listening potboilers before a reformed Walker Brothers scored a UK hit in 1976 with 'No Regrets'. There followed three contrasting albums before Engel resumed a snail's-paced solo career.

see Introduction pp 118   *see* Sources & Sounds pp 78   *see* Key Artists pp 120

Frank Zappa

(Guitar, vocals, 1940–93)

In 1964, Zappa formed The Mothers Of Invention, whose albums resembled pop-Dada aural junk-sculptures made from an eclectic heap that, laced with outright craziness, included 1950s pop, jazz, schmaltz and the pioneering tonalities of Stravinsky, Varese and Webern. However, Zappa's intense concern over social issues was never so stifled by burlesque that it could not be taken seriously. 1968's *We're Only In It For The Money* was a chart entry but, too clever for Joe Average, the now greatly augmented Mothers were disbanded in 1970 by Zappa, who then issued *Hot Rats*, a demonstration of his guitar-playing. Later projects drifted towards lavatorial humour, albeit supported by often beautiful melodies. Yet, in the decade before his death in 1993, he went some way towards establishing himself as a 'serious' composer in the same league as Varese and other of his boyhood idols – and as a professional politician, most palpably when the Czech government appointed Zappa its official Trade and Culture Emissary in 1990.

Left

Johnny Winter, the greatly respected American blues guitarist and singer.

Below

Frank Zappa was one of the most creative musicians and composers of his time. He released over 60 albums in his lifetime.

Johnny Winter

(Guitar, vocals, b. 1944)

A lengthy 1968 eulogy in *Rolling Stone* broadened this boss-eyed and albino Texan's work spectrum and placed an eponymous debut album in the national Top 30. Among famous admirers were The Rolling Stones and John Lennon who each proffered songs for his consideration after he began touring beyond North America, backed by ex-members of The McCoys and his brother Edgar (keyboards, saxophone), who went solo in 1970. *Johnny Winter And* and the first of several concert albums entered international charts, but in ratio to Johnny's increasing drug dependency was a deterioration in quality of successive releases from *Still Alive And Well* to 1974's *John Dawson Winter III*. A merger with Edgar for 1976's *Together* collection (mostly rock'n'roll and soul favourites) made commercial sense but, by then, Johnny's time in the sun was past. Even so, a steady flow of albums since – particularly 1987's Grammy-winning *Third Degree* – has showed a regaining of his former fretboard dexterity.

🎸 see Buddy Holly pp 50   🎸 see The Beatles pp 88   🎸 see The Rolling Stones pp 96   🎸 see Bob Dylan pp 126

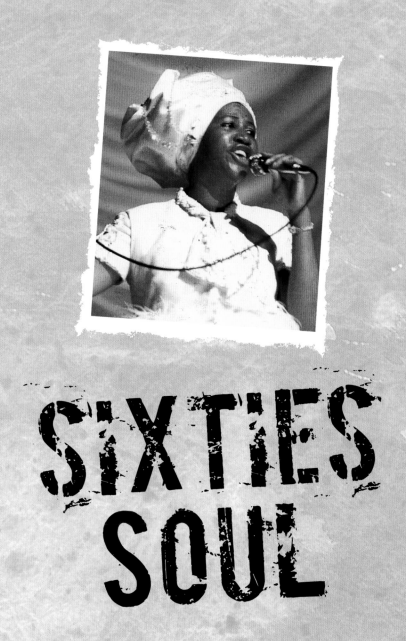

SIXTIES SOUL

One definition of soul music is 'a shared experience, a relationship with the listener'. And in the 1960s it was an experience black and white record-buyers alike clamoured to partake of. The music was measured in songs and singles, the album only becoming a valid currency in the 1970s when artists like Stevie Wonder and Marvin Gaye found the 45 too constricting. Until then the sound of Motown would rule the world, rivalled only by Atlantic and Stax when they got into their stride with Otis Redding and Aretha Franklin.

Soul's links to gospel were obvious, and, having first been made explicit by Ray Charles, were just as audible in the work of Redding and Franklin. James Brown was the major independent soul superstar, paying for his own 1962 live album *Live At The Apollo* when his record company wrongly said it would not sell, and wowing the world with an all-action stage act.

Soul would become somewhat homogenized in the 1970s with the Memphis sound of Hi and Philadelphia International both eager to grab their share of the spotlight and record sales. But with the exception of Al Green, no solo singer would approach the magnificence of a Sam Cooke or Solomon Burke, while the likes of The Supremes, The Impressions and The Four Tops created the template for a myriad of soul wannabes.

James Brown

📼 CLASSIC RECORDINGS

1962
Live At The Apollo

1998
Funky Good Time: The Anthology (The JBs)

2002
The Godfather: The Very Best Of James Brown

'James has more funk in his little finger than most people have in their life.'
Saxophone player Pee Wee Ellis on James Brown

Above
There is no other performer like James Brown: shouting, dancing frenzies and a unique inimitable rhythmical style.

Like many early soul stars James Brown (born in South Carolina on 3 May 1933) came to music through the singing of his local church. He had his first success as frontman of The Famous Flames with the gospel R&B hit 'Please Please Please' in 1956. When 1958's 'Try Me' hit the R&B No. 1 spot the floodgates opened for the man with more entries on the R&B charts than anyone else, and more on the US pop charts than anyone but Elvis.

Try Me

The Flames became part of the James Brown Revue: an all-singing, all-dancing spectacle which played to capacity in black venues throughout America.

The Revue had its own backing band, the JBs, and with them Brown began to make the transition from doo-wop pop to a tougher R&B sound. It was with the Revue that he earned and adopted the title 'hardest working man in show business', reportedly losing 7lbs a night in perspiration through his energized performances. At the same time the JBs built a name as the tightest rhythm section around, a formidable live act captured on *Live At The Apollo*, recorded in 1962 in Harlem at Brown's own expense; his label did not believe live albums sold. The album went to No. 2 in the US charts, an unprecedented crossover for an R&B act, selling over a million copies. It remains the first stop for anyone wanting an insight into the sheer passion and energetic professionalism through which James Brown established himself.

📼 *see Introduction pp 152*   📼 *see Sources & Sounds pp 78*   📼 *see A–Z of Artists pp 166*

Brown was refining a vocal technique of chants and shouts as much as melody, and a musical form using more and more complex rhythms and riffs. The 1964 LP *Out Of Sight*, whose title track, a jazz-organ and brass groove with choppy guitar, was another R&B No. 1. With it, James Brown invented funk.

Reinvigorated by a new recording contract in 1965 and a revised JBs line-up (led by saxophonist Pee Wee Ellis), his next single 'Papa's Got A Brand New Bag' was a worldwide hit, earning Brown his first Grammy. The follow-up 'I Got You (I Feel Good)' cemented the deal, reaching No. 3 and laying the foundation for frequent US pop listings and almost uninterrupted presence in the R&B charts to 1970.

Say It Loud

Brown's success as black businessman and superstar made him a role model for the African-American community. Hits from this time such as 'Say It Loud (I'm Black and I'm Proud)' address the social and racial concerns of young black youth. In April 1969, when race riots broke out in 30 US cities following the assassination of Martin Luther King, James Brown made a national TV address to appeal for calm, which received a ceremonial letter of gratitude from a grateful White House.

In 1971, Brown once again revised the JBs. The new line-up led by trombonist Fred Wesley played a deeper funk than ever, Brown's vocal output becoming ever more abstract and stylized. He sold millions of records, although with less crossover success. The JBs themselves had a successful parallel recording career with funk jams like 'Doing It To Death'. Many former JBs (including bassist Bootsy Collins) graduated to George Clinton's Parliament-Funkadelic stable. There they would define funk in the 1970s just as they had invented it in the 1960s.

Funk Soul Brother

By 1975, both Brown and his band were running out of steam, and a new wave of funk was lapping at their heels led by Clinton, Kool and The Gang and others. Brown was also facing financial and personal difficulties, and attempts to update his sound were less than convincing. A cameo role in the 1980 film *The Blues Brothers*, however, returned him to mainstream

attention, triggering a re-evaluation of his career and a revival of the epithet, 'the godfather of soul'. His comeback eventually saw 1986 single 'Living In America' make the UK and US Top 10s.

That year he was one of the inaugural inductees to The Rock And Roll Hall Of Fame. But just when his fortunes were being revived his personal life disintegrated again, and 1988 saw James Brown arrested five times on drugs and assault charges, and eventually sentenced to six years in prison. When he emerged on parole two years later, it was to a hip-hop world in which his back catalogue was the primary source for a new generation of funk-hungry DJs looking for a good groove to sample. No longer an innovator himself, he continued to inspire others with his energetic performances up until his death on 25th December 2006.

Below

In February 1965, James Brown recorded 'Papa's Got A Brand New Bag', a Top 10 hit that piloted a new era of soul music.

see George Clinton pp 236   see Bootsy Collins pp 237   see Kool and The Gang pp 239   see Michael Jackson pp 276

Aretha Franklin

CLASSIC RECORDINGS

1967
*I Never Loved A Man
The Way I Love You*

1968
Lady Soul

1971
Young, Gifted and Black

1972
Amazing Grace

'I'm gonna make a gospel record and tell Jesus I cannot bear these burdens alone.'

Aretha Franklin

Above

The Queen of Soul, Aretha Franklin, in the early days.

The undisputed Queen of Soul since the title was first applied to her in the late 1960s, Aretha Franklin has been hailed as the greatest soul diva of all time. Possessing a voice of power and passion (and an underrated talent on the piano) she has turned her attention to everything from pop through jazz to classical; but with a grounding in gospel it was in soul music that she found her finest hours and her true home.

The Columbia Years

She was born in Memphis, Tennessee, on 25 March 1942 to parents who were both nationally successful singers. She moved to Detroit with her family in 1949 and made her first recordings at the age of 14 singing hymns in her father's New Bethel Baptist Church, also going on tour with him and her sisters Carolyn and Erma (who would both have successful singing careers of their own).

By 1960, she was tackling secular material, and was signed by John Hammond to Columbia (having also, it is rumoured, been wooed by Motown). Columbia saw her as a crossover pop and jazz artist, and although she had a string of minor hits for them in the early 1960s (the biggest a cover of the Al Jolson standard 'Rock-a-Bye Your Baby With A Dixie Melody'), her talent was generally not well served by the choice of material.

The Atlantic Years

If the Columbia recordings were poorly focused, things came together with laserlike intensity in 1967 when she moved to Atlantic Records. The combination of Aretha Franklin with producer Jerry Wexler, arranger Arif Mardin and the rock-solid R&B of the Muscle Shoals rhythm section lit a fuse that delivered an opening salvo of 10 Top 10 hits for the label in her first two years alone. The very first recording session

see Introduction pp 152 *see* Sources & Sounds pp 78 *see* A–Z of Artists pp 166

resulted in the smouldering gospel-tinged 'I Never Loved A Man (The Way I Love You)', which opened her account at No. 9; the hastily convened second produced one of the defining moments of popular music, her blazing take on Otis Redding's 'Respect'. It was an instant US No. 1, resonating resoundingly with the rising confidence and pride of the black community, which broke her worldwide.

The success of 'Respect' was instrumental in the introduction of a new Grammy Award category in 1967, that of Best Female R&B Vocal, which Aretha won for the next eight years. From the start at Atlantic, and perhaps as the legacy of her Columbia years, she tackled material by an eclectic range of writers from both within the circle of soul and beyond: Goffin and King, Lennon and McCartney, Bacharach and David, Curtis Mayfield and Elton John all received early attention and chart success in her hands. With her gospel roots Aretha was a gifted arranger of vocals on many of her hits, and she and her sister Carolyn also featured in writing credits.

Unusually for a female soul singer at that time, her albums also sold consistently well. Her domination of the charts continued in the early 1970s and included what many consider to be her finest LP, the 1972 live, double gospel set *Amazing Grace*. By the mid-1970s, however, she was beginning to lose her way; experimenting with different producers, the recordings (and the live concerts) became more lavish productions, but the choice of songs was erratic, with some ill-judged departures into disco.

The Later Years

A switch of labels to Arista in 1980 had little initial impact, although a cameo appearance in the film *The Blues Brothers* the same year helped to re-establish the reputation of her world-changing early work. 1985 saw a return to form: a UK Top 10 entry with the anthemic Eurythmics collaboration 'Sisters Are Doin' It For Themselves', and a US No. 1 with 'Freeway Of Love'. Her rousing 1986 duet with George Michael 'I Knew You Were Waiting' was No. 1 in both countries.

With more US pop and R&B hits than any other woman Franklin's status as a soul institution is assured. But rather than see the century out with an untaxing schedule of celebrity duets and compilation releases, she drew admiration in 1998 for *A Rose Is Still A Rose*, on which she worked with contemporary R&B artists (notably on the Lauryn Hill title track). And in 2006 aged 64 she won her 17th Grammy for the Bacharach-David song 'A House Is Not A Home', which she sang on the Luther Vandross tribute album *So Amazing*.

Above
Regarded as one of the best vocalists of all time, Aretha demonstrates why in her 1967 No. 1 hit 'Respect'.

see Otis Redding pp 158   see Eurythmics pp 296   see George Michael pp 307   see Luther Vandross pp 320

Otis Redding

Georgia's finest soul son, Otis Redding's story encapsulates the history of soul music. He was a hard-working performer with special gifts who became a role model of dedication and success, an icon for his African-American peers. In the process he also won the hearts of the white audience with his music, and, by the simple act of singing, played a major role in breaking down racial barriers.

Early Breaks

Otis Redding was born on 9 September 1941, the son of a minister and learned to sing in the gospel choirs of Vineville Baptist Church. By the late 1950s, he was fronting The Upsetters, Little Richard's former backing band; they won the $5 cash prize at the local talent contest so often that they were barred from competing.

In 1960, he started working as a driver (and occasional singer) for Johnny Jenkins and The Pinetoppers. Everything changed in 1962 when he drove Jenkins to an audition in Memphis with Stax Records. With time to spare in the session, Otis was allowed to sing a couple himself, including his own composition 'These Arms Of Mine'. That song persuaded Stax president Jim Stewart to sign him at once to the label's Volt subsidiary. Later featured in the film *Dirty Dancing* (1987), it became Otis' first hit, climbing to No. 20 in the R&B chart in 1963.

Recording with Stax house band Booker T and The MGs, Redding was from the start equally popular in Europe, and The Rolling Stones were early fans, recording two Redding songs 'Pain In My Heart' and 'That's How Strong My Love Is'.

Finding His Voice

1965's 'Mr Pitiful' saw Redding start to make inroads into the pop charts too. Many hits were self-penned, a mixture of towering soul ballads and harder-rocking R&B work-outs. Working within traditional R&B forms, he exploited The MGs' muscular horn

'If you got the feeling, you can sing soul. You just sing from the heart.'

Otis Redding

arrangements and deep, tight rhythm section, and his own strong, pure, classically soulful singing. In 1966, his songwriting talents matured on not one but two classic albums.

Otis Blue (1965), his response to the shooting the previous year of his idol Sam Cooke, included future soul standards 'I've Been Loving You Too Long' and 'Respect' (written by Redding with Stax house guitarist Steve Cropper), and milestone reworkings of the Sam Cooke hit 'Shake' and The Rolling Stones' 'Satisfaction' (written by the Stones in imitation of his style).

Next came *Complete And Unbelievable* (1966) whose hits included 'Fa Fa Fa Fa Fa (Sad Song)', 'My Lover's Prayer' and the song for ever associated with Redding's impassioned heart-wrenching soul voice, 'Try A Little Tenderness'. In December he ended Elvis Presley's 10-year run in the annual *Melody Maker* Poll by being voted Best International Male Vocalist.

📻 *see* Introduction pp 152 📻 *see* Sources & Sounds pp 78 📻 *see* A–Z of Artists pp 166

Meanwhile, Otis Redding was building a formidable name as a live performer: he delivered his songs with the fervour of a gospel preacher, and he had dance moves to rival James Brown. Early in 1967, he came to Britain with the Stax Revue, whose line-up included Arthur Conley (for whom he had written 'Sweet Soul Music') and Carla Thomas (with whom he was about to record a duet album *King And Queen*, yielding the hits 'Tramp' and 'Knock On Wood').

Career High

That summer, with Aretha Franklin's version of his song 'Respect' a worldwide hit and US No. 1, Otis Redding took to the stage in front of the largely white hippy audience at the Monterey Pop Festival. At an event that made the reputations of so many performers, Redding received a rapturous reception for his passionate performance.

On a career high, Redding continued to tour with his on-the-road backing band The Bar-Kays. In early December he recorded some new material at Stax including '(Sittin' On) The Dock Of The Bay', co-written with Steve Cropper and exhibiting a new sensitivity and emotional depth. On 10 December, a day short of three years since the death of Sam Cooke, the tour plane carrying Redding and his band crashed in fog in a lake in Wisconsin, killing him, the pilot and all but one of the Bar-Kays.

'Dock Of The Bay' was a posthumous No. 1 in 1968, winning Best Song and Best R&B Vocal Grammys. Although soul music had lost a widely loved and respected singer, these were not merely sentimental awards. Four subsequent gold discs for CD anthologies, and a Lifetime Achievement Grammy in 1999 testify to the enduring talent and potential that was lost with his death.

Above
Tragically Otis's greatest commercial success came in the posthumous release of '(Sittin' On) The Dock Of The Bay', recorded one month before his death.

see The Rolling Stones pp 96   *see* Aretha Frankin pp 156   *see* Booker T and The MGs pp 166   *see* Sam Cooke pp 168

Sly and The Family Stone

📼 CLASSIC RECORDINGS

1968
Dance To The Music

1969
Stand!

1971
There's A Riot Goin' On

1973
Fresh

The story of Sly Stone (born Sylvester Stewart in Dallas on 15 March 1944) is a classic rock'n'roll tale of ground-breaking success followed by a drug-fuelled downward spiral into unreliability and dissipation. In the 1960s and early 1970s he pioneered a fusion of funk, rock and soul that changed the course of R&B, pop and even jazz. Yet on his induction into The Rock And Roll Hall Of Fame in 1993 he was reportedly found living in sheltered housing; and today he remains largely overlooked in the public's view of popular music history.

Going Up

Sly Stone started playing drums and guitar (aged 4) in the family gospel group, The Stewart Four, in 1948. Growing up he played and sang in the Bay Area, solo and with various groups, and built a large local following as a DJ on two SF radio stations, KSOL and KDIA. In 1964, he became a house producer for Autumn Records, gaining much valuable studio experience.

In 1967, he formed Sly and The Family Stone. Band members – Freddie Stone (guitar), Rose Stone (keyboards), Cynthia Robinson (trumpet), Jerry Martini (sax), Larry Graham (bass), Greg Errico (drums) – came from several racial backgrounds, and they made a big impression on the emerging West Coast psychedelic scene. Their second LP, 1968's *Dance To The Music*, saw the band hit its stride, with an exuberant riot of vocal and instrumental interplay – the free-flowing hippy spirit applied to soul music. Psychedelic Funk was born, and the title track made the US and UK Top 10s.

An early 1969 single 'Everyday People' became the group's first US No. 1 with its engaging chant 'Different strokes for different folks'. It was from their fourth LP, the upbeat masterpiece *Stand!*, an album of joyous psychedelic soul, pop melodies and tight

'He was the true representative of the dream of the crossover between rock and soul and funk and psychedelia.'

Jim Irvin on Sly Stone

Above
'There are two types of black music: black music before Sly Stone, and black music after Sly Stone.' Sly Stone was awarded the R&B Foundation Pioneer Award in 2002.

exchanges between performers both instrumentally and vocally (symbolically giving everyone in this racially integrated unit a voice). Additionally, Stone began addressing social issues with tracks such as 'Don't Call Me Nigger, Whitey' and the title track itself.

Stand! spent over 100 weeks in the charts, selling over two million copies. Their career-defining performance at Woodstock that year stole the show, confirming their reputation as one of the best live acts around.

📻 *see Introduction pp 152* 📻 *see Sources & Sounds pp 78* 📻 *see A–Z of Artists pp 166*

Coming Down

But just as things were coming good they started to go bad. Sly was developing a serious cocaine habit and becoming unpredictable. He missed a third of all the band's shows in 1970; recording deadlines were not met; and although two cheerful singles – 'Hot Fun in the Summertime' and 'Thank You (Falletinme Be Mice Elf Agin)' – and a stop-gap *Greatest Hits* LP all charted well, it was clear that something was seriously wrong.

The much delayed LP, *There's a Riot Goin' On*, that finally emerged in November 1971 was as dark as its predecessor had been bright, the bleary vision of a man disappointed by both his own success and the stalling of the civil rights movement. A musically brilliant expression of the fractured society of the early 1970s after the optimism of the late 1960s, the album and the first single from it ('Family Affair') were the US No. 1s that Christmas.

Sly focused temporarily for 1973's *Fresh*, which continued to address dark themes but with a brighter if not lighter musical touch. It and the accompanying single 'If You Want Me To Stay' made the Top 10. But *Fresh* was Sly Stone's last great album. Succumbing to cocaine, he was competing with (and losing out to) the very bands to whom he had been an inspiration: the likes of the Commodores, the Ohio Players and George Clinton's Parliament. After two disappointing albums the band folded and Sly Stone filed for bankruptcy in 1976.

Down And Out

Stone's cocaine addiction now ruled his life. He made three weak solo albums and a handful of guest appearances (notably on George Clinton's final Funkadelic LP *The Electric Spanking Of War Babies* in 1981). Otherwise Stone's only impact in the 1980s and early 1990s was through a succession of drugs and firearms charges. Sly disappeared for 13 years, fuelling speculation about his mental health and even death, until his re-emergence with a shambolic performance at the 2006 Grammy Awards ceremony triggered rumours of new recordings and even a tour.

Sly Stone's worst habits robbed the music world of a giant talent. His best work, however, changed everything: The Temptations' shift to harder-hitting material at Motown, the assimilation of soul and funk which led to disco, Miles Davis' move to electrification, can all be attributed to his ground-breaking fusion of styles. Sly did it first.

Above

Sly and The Family Stone were one of the first racially integrated bands in music history.

🎸 *see* James Brown pp 154 🎸 *see* The Temptations pp 179 🎸 *see* George Clinton pp 236 🎸 *see* Earth, Wind and Fire pp 238

Stevie Wonder

SOUL
Key Artists

Born Steveland Judkins on 13 May 1950 and blind virtually from birth, the future Little Stevie Wonder was already singing in his local choir at the age of four. By the time he was seven he had mastered the piano, harmonica and drums. In 1961, Ronnie White of The Miracles introduced the child prodigy to the label's founder Berry Gordy, who signed him up immediately to a long-term contract and gave him his stage name. Over the next 20 years he grew to become an icon not just of soul music but of the whole African-American community.

The Formative Years

Early releases made much of his instrumental virtuosity (which now extended to organ and vocals) and of parallels with another blind soulful singer, Ray Charles. Wonder's first two album releases (both in 1962) were *Tribute To Uncle Ray* and *The Jazz Soul Of Little Stevie*.

In 1963, his third single was his breakthrough: an edited version of the largely instrumental 'Fingertips' from live album *The 12-Year Old Genius*. It went to No. 1 in both the pop and the R&B charts in the US, the first live single to do so. The album followed in its wake, Motown's first chart-topping LP and the first time an artist had topped the singles and album charts concurrently.

In 1964, he had his first co-written hit, 'Uptight (Everything's Alright)', a US million-seller, which two years later would open his chart account in the UK. From now on he would write more and more of his output, and in 1968 he was able to claim co-writing credits for half of the album *For Once In My Life*.

The 1960s saw Stevie Wonder's growth in all areas from child star to soul man. He dropped the 'Little' as early as 1964, and his vocal performances developed their trademark tone: pure, full, warm, the soulful embodiment of R&B. He found his voice in other ways too, recording in an ever broader range of musical styles. In 1966, he charted with a striking country'n'gospel arrangement of Bob Dylan's 'Blowin' In The Wind', a hint of Wonder's later strength as a social campaigner. 1967's 'I Was Made To Love Her' blended classic Motown pop with an earthier R&B rhythm section and rootsy gospel backing vocals.

Wonder was one of the very first pop artists to embrace the emerging world of electronic keyboards, and used the hook of the new sounds to good effect on a string of hits such as 1968's 'Shoo Be Doo Be Doo Da Day' (which acknowledged another of R&B's root influences, doo-wop).

> '*Sometimes, I feel I am really blessed to be blind because I probably would not last a minute if I were able to see things.*'
>
> Stevie Wonder

Right

Stevie Wonder continues to be one of the most successful and influential artists in the world, with albums sales of over 100 million units.

see Introduction pp 152   *see* Sources & Sounds pp 78   *see* A–Z of Artists pp 164

Growing Pains

With this rich input of influences and explorations, Stevie Wonder was constantly stretching, and becoming increasingly frustrated by the constraints of Motown's hit-making machine, which still exercised control over his releases. Experimentation was not something that sat easily with a record company where the hit single was king.

1971's album *Where I'm Coming From* was a milestone of maturity – not just a collection of singles and album fillers but a coherent set of compositions, increasingly dominated by Wonder's keyboard arrangements and entirely produced and co-written by him. It generated only one hit single, the melodic but jazzy, mixed-tempo 'If You Really Love Me'. But although not entirely musically successful, it was

Below
The young Stevie Wonder had his first major hit 'Fingertips (Pt. 2)' in 1963 at the age of 13.

🚗 *see* Ray Charles pp 42 🚗 *see* Bob Dylan pp 126 🚗 *see* Berry Gordy pp 171 🚗 *see* Michael Jackson pp 276

Above

Blind from infancy, Stevie Wonder credits his mother for treating him as equally as his other siblings; by an early age he was playing piano, congas and harmonica.

addition to the producing and writing credits Wonder now played all but one of the instruments. The songwriting and arrangements showed a new depth, and his ability to breathe life and warmth into the extensive use of synthesizers would become his defining sound.

Stevie Wonder supported The Rolling Stones on their US tour that summer. This exposed him to a massive new rock audience and carried him over to mainstream pop stardom. His next two singles went to No. 1 in the US (Nos. 11 and 7 in the UK), laying down templates for the twin attacks on which his success would be built: the funk-soul groove and social concerns of 'Superstition' and the deceptively simple ballad 'You Are The Sunshine Of My Life'.

The early 1973 album from which they were drawn, *Talking Book*, was his most well-rounded and personal to date, reflecting the influence of Marvin Gaye's *What's Going On*. It was followed by late 1973's outward-looking *Innervisions*, a powerful and comprehensive discussion of America's early 1970s social confusion, with hit singles 'Higher Ground', 'Living For The City' and 'He's Misstra Know It All'. After surviving a near fatal car crash, no surprise 1974's *Fullfillingness' First Finale* was more introspective but found time for the No. 1 political barb 'You Haven't Done Nothin'' (featuring the Jackson Five on doo-wops). It also saw Wonder further broadening his musical horizons, for example on 'Boogie On Reggae Woman'.

Stevie Wonder's performances on the three albums of 1973–74 earned him a total of nine Grammy Awards, enabling him in 1975 to negotiate with Motown what at the time was the richest ever recording deal: $13 million over seven years. A year later he delivered what still stands as his masterpiece, *Songs In The Key Of Life*. Originally released as a double LP plus bonus EP it was exactly as advertised: a dazzling collection of songs on every aspect of social, political and emotional life in a spectacular array of musical styles and arrangements, a big bold confident work from a man on the top of his form.

It produced a glorious run of hits including two more US No. 1s – the party funk 'I Wish' and a big band jazz tribute to 'Sir Duke' Ellington. Other highlights were 'Another Star' with its swirling Latin rhythms and the beautiful mid-tempo soul ballad 'Isn't She Lovely' (a celebration of the birth of his daughter Aisha).

(as the title suggested) a manifesto for the future.

A month later, on his 21st birthday, his contract with Motown expired. Wonder negotiated a new, stronger deal that gave him increased royalties and allowed him to set up his own production and publishing companies (enabling him to retain the rights to his compositions). Most importantly he also gained complete control of his output, having been impressed by Marvin Gaye's similar move earlier in the year, which had resulted in the powerful *What's Going On*.

The Golden Years

Music Of My Mind, the first fruit of the new deal released early in 1972, demonstrated a further refinement of the whole-album principle, where in

see Introduction pp 152   see Sources & Sounds pp 78   see A–Z of Artists pp 166

It spent a total of 14 weeks at No. 1 in the US and more than a year in the charts (peaking at No. 2 in the UK) and won the singer another five Grammy Awards, confirming his status as the soul performer and composer without equal in the 1970s.

Consolidation

In the years that followed Stevie Wonder struggled to emulate the artistic and commercial pinnacle of *Songs In The Key Of Life*. Discounting a largely instrumental soundtrack album, the first real follow-up, *Hotter Than July* (a 1980 single LP), seemed a little insubstantial after a four-year gap. But it was another strong collection; the 10 tracks yielded four hits including 'Masterblaster', his tribute to Bob Marley, and the album's closing track 'Happy Birthday'.

'Happy Birthday' was Stevie Wonder's upbeat anthem to Martin Luther King Jr. It became the focus of a campaign occupying much of his energy over the next three years, to have the civil rights icon's birthday recognized as a US national holiday. A Bill was eventually passed in 1983.

The early 1980s saw Wonder release only a handful of singles of mixed merit; they included the feisty 'Do I Do' which featured Dizzy Gillespie, but also a decidedly mundane collaboration with Paul McCartney 'Ebony And Ivory', and 'I Just Called To Say I Love You' his biggest-selling single ever but a bland source of despair for his traditional fans.

After another five-year gap, the 1985 set *In Square Circle* showed Wonder comfortably adopting new technologies of keyboard programming. But he had lost momentum. This and its follow-up in 1987, *Characters*, kept him in the chart (notably with the latter's synth-funk 'Skeletons') but having broken new ground throughout the 1970s he now seemed content merely to tread water.

New Respect

Instead, he settled into the role of elder soul statesman, and much of the 1980s was filled with a round of celebrity tribute performances and lifetime-achievement award ceremonies. After another long break, 1995's *Conversation Peace* was a disappointingly detached return to social themes. But the same year, Coolio's UK and US No. 1 'Gangsta's Paradise' updated the *Songs In*

The Key Of Life track 'Pastime Paradise' reminding the public of Wonder's ground-breaking work. He capitalized on the renewed attention by recording a collaboration 'How Come How Long' with contemporary producer-performer Babyface.

In 2005, at the age of 55 he released his first new album for 10 years. A *Time 2 Love* was hailed as his strongest in 25 years – a lyrically thoughtful, mature collection of jazz and R&B, which included duets with his daughter Aisha Morris. It returned him to the singles charts with the stomp-funker 'So What The Fuss', and won him his 21st Grammy for his vocal performance on 'From The Bottom Of My Heart'.

Below

During the late 1960s Stevie Wonder recorded the timeless hits 'I Was Made To Love You', 'For Once In My Life' and 'My Cherie Amour'.

🎙 **see The Rolling Stones pp 96** 🎙 **see Marvin Gaye pp 170** 🎙 **see The Jackson Five pp 172** 🎙 **see Bob Marley pp 240**

P.P. Arnold

(Vocals, b. 1946)

This LA-born former member of The Ikettes was Ike and Tina Turner's backing vocalist. Remaining in London after a UK tour, she signed to Andrew Loog Oldham's Immediate label, capitalizing on Britain's love affair with American soul. She is best known for her 1967 hit, Cat Stevens' 'The First Cut Is The Deepest'. She now enjoys cult status, thanks to several successful collaborations since the 1980s (including The Beatmasters and Ocean Colour Scene). In 2006, she toured with Roger Waters.

Below

Probably best known for their instrumental hit 'Green Onions', Booker T and The MGs were one of the most influential house bands of their time, supporting acts like Otis Redding and Carla Thomas.

Booker T and The MGs

(Vocal/instrumental group, 1962–71)

Stax Records' house band, Booker T also toured and recorded instrumentals in their own right. More than any other group they defined the sound of 1960s soul with their sparse, funky arrangements on hits for other Stax and Atlantic stars like Wilson Pickett, Sam and Dave, and Otis Redding. Booker T. Jones, Stax' sax and

organ prodigy, formed The MGs (Memphis Group) with Steve Cropper (guitar), Donald 'Duck Dunn (bass, replacing Lewis Steinberg) and Al Jackson Jr. (drums).

Their first release, 1963's 'Green Onions' was a US No. 3, eventually charting at No. 7 in the UK on its re-release in 1979. Their 1968 hit 'Soul Limbo' is the BBC's TV cricket theme. Victims of their own success, they split in 1971 because of the demand for their individual services as ace sessioneers. There have been periodic high-profile reformations: in 1992 they backed Bob Dylan at Madison Square Gardens, and in 1993 toured with Neil Young.

Solomon Burke

(Vocals, b. 1940)

A pioneer of soul music, Burke is as a Philadelphia gospel preacher who fused country and western, rock'n'roll, and rhythm and blues to preach through song. He had a string of hits on Atlantic throughout the 1960s, including 'Got To Get You Off My Mind'

🎙 *see Introduction pp 152* 🎙 *see Sources & Sounds pp 78* 🎙 *see Key Artists pp 154*

and 'Everybody Needs Somebody To Love' (covered by The Rolling Stones), although he never charted in the UK. Now hailed as an uncompromising elder statesman of soul, he still records and preaches.

Chubby Checker

(Vocals, b. 1941)

Ernest Evans started out as a Philadelphia novelty act who had his first hit in 1959 as a musical impressionist. In 1960, he recorded a more innocent version of a steamy Hank Ballard B-side, 'The Twist', which made it to the US No. 1, bubbling under for over a year afterwards before, uniquely, returning to the top spot. Many dance-craze singles followed, including the platinum 'Let's Twist Again'. He has had over 50 hits, earning him a place on the R&R revival circuit ever since.

The Chiffons

(Vocal group, 1960–72)

Formed in New York's Bronx by four high school friends (Judy Craig, Barbara Lee Jones, Patricia Bennett and Sylvia Peterson), The Chiffons virtually defined the Girl Group sound with a trio of classic hits in the mid-1960s. 1963's 'He's So Fine' written by manager Ronald Mack was their only No. 1, but the Goffin-King follow-up 'One Fine Day' (originally intended for Little Eva) still hit No. 5 and their last big hit 'Sweet Talking Guy' made the Top 10 in 1965.

Arthur Conley

(Vocals, 1946–2003)

Discovered in 1965 by Otis Redding, Conley shared with him an admiration for Sam Cooke. Redding gets a name-check (twice) in Conley's one big hit, 'Sweet Soul Music' (produced by Redding in 1967), a frantic rock'n'roll work-out with punctuating brass, which exuberantly celebrated the soul greats of the day. Conley was a regular member of the Stax/Volt Soul Revue package that toured America and Europe.

Above

Chubby Checker will always be remembered for 'The Twist' – it made it to No. 1 in September 1960 and again in January 1962.

see Hank Ballard pp 57   see Otis Redding pp 158   see Sam Cooke pp 168   see Wilson Pickett pp 174

Sam Cooke

(Vocals, 1931–64)

With his pure sweet voice, sound business awareness and keen social concerns, Sam Cooke was a key figure in the early development of soul and pop. He was already a star as a member of gospel group The Soul Stirrers when he was sacked in 1956 for releasing a secular solo single. He launched his solo career with a run of exquisite romantic ballads including 'You Send Me' and '(What A) Wonderful World'. A deal with RCA followed, which included his own label and publishing house.

A series of finely crafted pop songs such as 'Chain Gang' and 'Bring It On Home To Me' won him two separate audiences: white teenagers (RCA's target) and black listeners of all ages (to whom he was a role model). In 1963, Dylan's protest songs encouraged him to address civil-rights issues. Cooke recorded the majestic gospel spiritual 'A Change Is Gonna Come', a posthumous hit after his murder in 1964.

The Crystals

(Vocal group, 1961–66)

Barbara Alston, Dee Dee Kennibrew, Mary Thomas, Patricia Wright and Myra Gerrard were discovered recording song demos in the Brill Building by Phil Spector, who was looking for a girl group for his new label Philles Records. His Wall of Sound brought them immortality in teen hits like 'Da Doo Ron Ron' and 'Then He kissed Me'. But pop is fickle: Spector soon moved on to The Ronettes, and soul fans to the girl groups of Motown. The Crystals disbanded in 1966.

The Detroit Spinners

(Vocal group, 1965–80)

Originally a doo-wop group, The Detroit Spinners signed to Motown in 1965 but were overshadowed by the label's excess of talent. Their only big hit there was the Stevie Wonder composition 'It's A Shame'. Switching to Atlantic in 1971 and switching lead singer G.C. Cameron for newcomer Philippe Wynne, they teamed with Philly producer Thom Bell, whose

see Introduction pp 152   *see* Sources & Sounds pp 78   *see* Key Artists pp 154

orchestrations matched their complex harmonies in several chart entries starting with 'Could It Be I'm Falling In Love'. They had a latterday UK No. 1, 1980's 'Working My Way Back To You'.

Lee Dorsey
(Vocals, 1921–86)

Dorsey was a New Orleans veteran who had careers as a sailor, a boxer and a car mechanic before turning to music in 1955. In 1961, he forged a successful partnership with pianist-composer Allen Toussaint with the irresistibly jaunty US R&B No. 1 'Ya Ya'. It set the template of laidback storm-party syncopation and fun which would characterize all his hits. A second bite of the chart cherry in 1965 brought him mainstream pop entries, including 'Holy Cow' and his definitive recording 'Working In A Coalmine' (co-written with Toussaint).

He often recorded and toured with top New Orleans funkers The Meters, and when the hits were not coming he would return to his bodyshop business. A comeback album in 1977 reminded a new generation of his sound, and in 1980 he supported The Clash on tour.

Dr. John
(Piano, singer/songwriter, b. 1942)

A highly respected exponent of Southern R&B, Mac Rebennack had 15 years of recording and production experience as a session player before he released his first LP, 1968's *Gris Gris*. Frequently adding jazz, rock, psychedelia and voodoo to the R&B mix, his prolific output is unpredictably eclectic, although his musical knowledge and connections are impeccable. He was an energetic fundraiser for his home town New Orleans following its destruction by Hurricane Katrina in 2005.

Ahmet Ertegun
(Founder, Atlantic Records, b. 1923)

Ertegun came to the US as son of the Turkish ambassador in 1934 and stayed, founding Atlantic Records in 1947 with brother Nesuhi. Having won the trust of performers with fair contract and royalty dealings, he actively pursued the crossover market in the 1950s, selling black music by Ray Charles and others to a white audience who previously only bought bland cover versions of it. He developed a roster of 1960s soul artists with a distinctive house sound to rival Motown.

Below
Lee Dorsey's laidback New Orlean's R&B style accredited him with two Top 10 hits: 'Ya Ya' in 1961 and 'Working In The Coal Mine' in 1966.

🎙 *see* Ray Charles pp 42   🎙 *see* Stevie Wonder pp 162   🎙 *see* Phil Spector pp 177   🎙 *see* The Clash pp 248

originally meant for Otis Redding; recorded instead by Floyd, it won Stax another R&B No. 1. He is still active on the revival circuit.

The Four Tops
(Vocal group, 1953–present)
Formed in Detroit in 1953, The Four Tops' line-up (Levi Stubbs, Lawrence Payton, Renaldo Benson, Abdul Fakir) remained unchanged for 44 years. Their partnership with Motown production team Holland-Dozier-Holland epitomized the label's 1960s heyday with a run of Top 10s, including No. 1s 'I Can't Help Myself (Sugar Pie, Honey Bunch)' and 'Reach Out I'll Be There'.

Their chart success waned when first Holland-Dozier-Holland left Motown in 1967, and then Motown left Detroit in 1972. The Tops stayed in town, enjoying periodic comebacks with a succession of labels, notably 1981 US R&B No. 1 and UK No. 3 'When She Was My Girl', and UK No. 7 'Loco In Acapulco' from 1988. In 1983, Motown's 25th Anniversary year, they briefly rejoined their old label. Payton died in 1997, and Benson in 2005 (to be replaced by Payton's son). The group still tours.

Marvin Gaye
(Vocals, 1939–84)
Gaye was a soul giant whose career spanned his genre's transition from pop entertainment to social conscience and personal exploration. He signed with Berry Gordy's Motown label in 1961, where his recordings revealed a strong tenor voice with a huge span – three octaves – on songs ranging from R&B mod anthem 'Can I Get A Witness' to the soulful heartache of 'I Heard It Through The Grapevine'.

Above
One of Motown's most successful groups, The Four Tops topped the charts with 'I Can't Help Myself (Sugar Pie Honey Bunch)' in 1965.

Right
Marvin Gaye is regarded by many to have had the best voice of the era.

Eddie Floyd
(Vocals, b. 1935)
Floyd first found fame with the 1950s gospel soulsters The Falcons. After going solo, he eventually migrated to Stax Records as writer and producer; with Steve Cropper he co-wrote '634-5789', a No. 1 R&B hit for Wilson Pickett (who had replaced him in The Falcons). The pair also wrote 'Knock On Wood',

see Introduction pp 152   see Sources & Sounds pp 78   see Key Artists pp 154

He charted with duets too, notably alongside Tammi Terrell. Gaye grieved for a year after Terrell's tragic death, emerging to negotiate artistic control of his work and release 1971's *What's Going On*, routinely regarded as the greatest soul album ever, taking a radical, mature new direction addressing political and social issues. Its follow-up *Let's Get It On* (1973) dealt equally powerfully with more intimate concerns.

Although his creative light never dimmed, his later life was blighted by tax issues, failed marriages, drug dependency and depression. In 1984, his father shot him dead during a family argument.

Berry Gordy

(Founder, Motown Records, b. 1929)

Gordy co-wrote Jackie Wilson's 'Reet Petite' in 1957 while working on Detroit's Ford assembly line and started Motown in 1959 with an $800 loan, creating a factory-like hit-making process. Gordy scouted talented Detroit performers and matched them to equally talented in-house writers and producers. He fostered a family atmosphere of (mostly) friendly rivalry, which earned him the nickname Pops.

Gordy exercised strict control of Motown's output. The emphasis was on crossover hits: Motown's sound, polished up with bright percussion and strings, was prettier than Atlantic's rootsy R&B, for example. Gordy established a charm school for his stars, and packaged them in slick promotional tours, the Motown Revues. It paid off with over 120 Top 20 entries in the 1960s. In Motown's best year, 1966, the release-to-hit ratio was an amazing 75 per cent. Relocating to Los Angeles in 1971, Gordy built Motown into America's biggest black-owned corporation, selling up to MCA in 1988 for $61 million.

Holland-Dozier-Holland

(Songwriting and production team, 1961–75)

Lamont Dozier and brothers Eddie and Brian Holland were all minor Detroit singers when Motown's Berry Gordy combined their talents and redirected them towards songwriting and production. Their output defined the label's sound with a pop-savvy mix of gospel, soul and refined R&B. They wrote over 50 Motown classics, performed by almost every member of the label's roster, and with The Supremes alone they enjoyed five consecutive US No. 1s.

Their bitter departure from Motown in 1967 over artistic and royalty disagreements was Gordy's biggest mistake, triggering a gradual decline in the label's pop pre-eminence. Holland-Dozier-Holland formed their own labels Hot Wax and Invictus, and had some 1970s chart success with Chairmen Of The Board ('Give Me Just A Little More Time') and Freda Payne ('Band Of Gold'). The partnership dissolved in 1973, although all three now run HDH Records, and continue to write, produce and record as individuals.

Below

Holland-Dozier-Holland composed the majority of Motown's great hits for the likes of Marvin Gaye, The Temptations, The Four Tops and The Supremes, earning the decade a reputation as the Golden Era of Soul.

see **Wilson Pickett** pp 174   see **Diana Ross and The Supremes** pp 176   see **Tammi Terrell** pp 179   see **Jackie Wilson** pp 181

Brenda Holloway

(Vocals, b. 1946)

Motown's first West Coast signing (in 1963), charted with 'Every Little Bit Hurts' and supported The Beatles on their 1965 US tour. Deeply religious, she retired in 1968, overlooked at Motown and concerned about pop's hedonism. UK Northern Soul fans never forgot her rich, sensuous voice, and from 1987 she recorded new material in the genre in Britain (collected in 2004's *My Love Is Your Love*), and in 1999 an album of more contemporary songs.

Above

Audiences around the world fell in love with The Jackson Five, their soulful voices and incredible dance moves all the more impressive because of their youth.

The Isley Brothers

(Vocal/instrumental group, 1957–present)

This long-careered family group originally comprised brothers O'Kelly, Rudolph and Ronald who travelled from 1950s gospel to 1980s disco with frequent and influential success. Their early R&B hits 'Shout' (1957) and 'Twist And Shout' (1962) became standards, while their 1964 backing band included the young Jimi Hendrix. They scored only one US success on signing with Motown, 1966's 'This Old Heart Of Mine', and spent much of the decade in Britain (where the song eventually made No. 3 in 1968).

In the 1970s, they merged rock and soul with the hits 'That Lady', 'Summer Breeze' and the uplifting 'Harvest For The World' (UK No. 10), adding brothers

Ernie (guitar) and Marvin (bass) and cousin Chris Jasper (keyboards), but fragmented in the 1980s. Recordings continued, however, and respect from the new generation of R&B artists including R. Kelly revived their fortunes in the 1990s. 2006's star-studded *Baby Makin' Music* was well-received.

The Jackson Five/The Jacksons

(Vocal/instrumental group, 1967–90)

The last great Motown pop group, the brothers Jackson – Jackie, Tito, Marlon, Jermaine and Michael – signed in 1968 and were groomed for a year before their debut single 'I Want You Back' shot to US No. 1, followed by four more chart-toppers in a row including 'ABC' and 'I'll Be There'. The huge teen following for their bubblegum soul led Motown to restrict their growth as songwriters and musicians. Frustrated, the group switched labels in 1975, changing their name because Motown retained rights to the original.

With producers Gamble and Huff they found a new maturity of sound, moving through Philly Soul ('Show You The Way To Go') to self-penned funk ('Blame It On The Boogie'), and climaxing in the masterful 1980 LP *Triumph*. Michael's emerging solo career began to overshadow the family band's (although he still contributed to Jacksons' albums) and they formally disbanded in 1990.

Ben E. King

(Vocals, b. 1938)

Ben E. King was lead singer on The Drifters' 1959 hits, including 'There Goes My Baby' and 'Save The Last Dance For Me'. He quit in 1960 over royalty payments, finding solo success with 1961's 'Spanish Harlem', and co-wrote the follow-up, 'Stand By Me', a US top 5 hit and his meal-ticket recording. King escaped the revival circuit in 1975 with a surprise US disco hit 'Supernatural Thing' and collaborated on the Average White Band's 1977 LP *Benny And Us*. The 1987 film *Stand By Me* sent the song of the same name to UK No. 1.

Gladys Knight and The Pips

(Vocal group, 1952–88)

One of many 1950s doo-wop groups scraping a reputation on the R&B circuit, Gladys Knight and The Pips (brother Merald and cousins William Guest and

Postman' (later covered by The Carpenters) was the label's first US pop No. 1 in 1961. It led to a run of nearly 30 pop and R&B chart entries, from the label's best writers and producers, including Holland-Dozier-Holland and Norman Whitfield.

They were country girls, not ghetto singers; by the mid-1960s they had been replaced in the affections of both Berry Gordy and the public by the label's more polished groups. In 1964, The Marvelettes had turned down a new song 'Where Did Our Love Go', which instead became the first of The Supremes' five No. 1s in a row. After a minor revival of fortune in the late 1960s championed by Smokey Robinson, they folded in 1971.

Left
Gladys Knight and The Pips were great live performers offering impressively choreographed 'fast-stepping' dance routines.

Below
The Marvelettes gave Motown their first No. 1 hit in the US, 'Please Mr Postman'.

Edward Patten) only came to mainstream attention on signing with Motown in 1966, where they had minor hits and the 1967 million-seller original of 'I Heard It Through The Grapevine'. Overlooked by the Motown machine, they switched to Buddah in 1973 just as their 'Neither One Of Us' was climbing to US No. 2.

At Buddah they made their lasting mark with smooth soul ballads: 'Best Thing that Ever Happened To Me', 'The Way We Were' and a US No. 1 cover of Brook Benton's 'Midnight Train To Georgia'. When The Pips retired in 1988, Knight had a UK solo hit with Bond theme 'License To Kill'. In 2005, she won her seventh Grammy for *One Voice*, a gospel release. 2006's *Before Me* was a collection of jazz standards.

Little Eva
(Vocals, 1943–2003)
One of pop's fairy tales. Eva Boyd was baby-sitting for Gerry Goffin and Carole King when they asked her to demo a new dance-craze song, 'The Loco-motion'. It was a 1962 worldwide No. 1, later covered by Kylie Minogue. Follow-up 'Keep Your Hands Off My Baby' also charted. The Crystals' Goffin-King single 'He Hit Me (And It Felt Like A Kiss)' was about Eva's reaction to being beaten by her boyfriend.

The Marvelettes
(Vocal group, 1961–71)
One of Motown's first successful vocal groups comprised Gladys Horton, Georgeanna Tillman, Wanda Young, Katherine Anderson and Juanita Cowart (left 1962). Their first release, 'Please Mr

see Smokey Robinson and The Miracles pp 175   *see* Michael Jackson pp 276   *see* R. Kelly pp 352   *see* Kylie Minogue pp 356

Mayfield went solo in 1970 with a harder funkier sound, which found its greatest release in the 1972 blaxploitation movie soundtrack *Superfly*, containing his biggest hit 'Move On Up'. Paralysed in a stage accident in 1990, he died in 1999. The Impressions disbanded in 1981. Butler is a Chairman Emeritus of the charitable Rhythm and Blues Foundation.

Wilson Pickett
(Vocals, 1941–2006)
After an early career with the seminal R&B group The Falcons (he replaced Eddie Floyd as lead singer), Pickett signed with Atlantic in 1965, recording with Booker T and The MGs at Stax in Memphis, and scored an early hit with 'In The Midnight Hour', first of many successes characterized by mighty horn stabs, vigorous bass lines and his impassioned soul shouting. Next, he worked with The Muscle Shoals band at Fame Studios, and more hits followed, many of them becoming dance band standards, including 'Mustang Sally' and 'Land Of 1000 Dances'.

An album with Philly soul gurus Gamble and Huff kept the hits coming in the early 1970s, but when he quit Atlantic in 1972 the well dried up. A 1987 LP for Motown was a case of wrong place, wrong time. He died in 2006 having made a lasting mark on Southern soul and dance music; The Commitments were among performers at his memorial concert.

Lou Rawls
(Vocals, 1935–2006)
Versatile singer, actor and voiceover artist with gospel roots. The 1960s saw Rawls exploring jazz, blues and pop, finally finding his voice with the 1966 LP *Soulin'* and its hit 'Love Is A Hurtin' Thing'. Naturally gravitating to smooth Philadelphia soul, his best-seller was the lush 1976 No. 2, Gamble and Huff's 'You'll Never Find Another Love Like Mine'. Vocal on civil rights issues, he hosted annual United Negro College Fund telethons from 1980 to his death in 2006.

Martha Reeves and The Vandellas
(Vocal group, 1963–72)
Two lucky breaks for Motown secretary Martha and friends Annette Beard and Rosalind Ashford launched their career: covering for absent backing singers on the

Curtis Mayfield, Jerry Butler and The Impressions
(Vocals/vocal group, 1957–90)
Childhood friends Mayfield and Butler joined Sam Gooden and Arthur and Richard Brooks in The Impressions in 1957, Butler going solo after one hit, 'For Your Precious Love'. In 1967, Butler teamed his distinctive smooth soul voice with producer-writers Gamble and Huff and helped to forge the polished Philadelphia Soul sound with No. 1s like 'Hey Western Union Man'. Under Mayfield The Impressions in the 1960s were the epitome of Chicago soul: light gospel vocals, unusual rhythms and an increasingly explicit expression of civil rights concerns – 'Keep On Pushing', 'People Get Ready', 'We're A Winner'.

see Introduction pp 152 ☞ see Sources & Sounds pp 78 ☞ see Key Artists pp 154

1962 session for Marvin Gaye's 'Stubborn Kind Of Fellow', and taking the lead vocal on 'I'll Have To Let Him Go' when Mary Wells did not show in 1963. Taking their name from raunchy gospel singer Della Reese, the Vandellas were the earthy alternative to Motown's girl-group sophisticates The Supremes, making pop and R&B Top 10s with Holland-Dozier-Holland belters like 'Heatwave', 'Dancing In The Streets' and 'Jimmy Mack'.

By 1967, the pressure to compete took its toll in drug addiction and depression, and The Vandellas dissolved in 1972. After attempts at a solo disco career in the late 1970s, Reeves concentrated on the oldies circuit. Her first album in 24 years, 2004's *Home To You*, found her in remarkably good voice.

Smokey Robinson and The Miracles
(Vocal group, 1958–78)
The Miracles – Smokey Robinson, Claudette Rogers, Bobby Rogers, Ronnie White and Warren Moore – were a cornerstone of Motown's early success. Their 1960 hit 'Shop Around' set the gospel-and-soul tone for the label (later tempered with girl-group pop). Robinson was also a producer and songwriter of great lyricism for other Motown acts, notably Mary Wells, The Temptations and The Marvelettes. He was vice-president of the label from 1961 to its sale in 1988 to MCA.

1967's 'I Second That Emotion' broke the group in Britain. Robinson had already decided to leave before 1970's reissued 'Tears Of A Clown' reached No. 1. Recording thereafter took second place to his vice-presidency, but the 1975 album *The Quiet Storm* lent its name to a new adult-orientated soul genre, in which he topped the charts with 1981's 'Being With You'. The Miracles had one more No. 1 without Robinson, 1976's 'Love Machine', before splitting in 1978.

The Ronettes
(Vocal group, 1963–66)
One Top 10 ('Be My Baby') and one Top 20 hit ('Baby I Love You') do not explain the enduring reputation of The Ronettes, a group of school friends mistaken for a singing act when they queued for entrance to a New York dance club in 1961. Sisters Veronica and Estelle Bennett, with cousin Nedra Talley, became the club's resident vocalists, and in 1963 they succeeded The Crystals as a vehicle for Phil Spector's Wall of Sound.

The Ronettes' real legacy was to change for ever the performer-audience relationship, transforming the third-person musings of The Chiffons' 'He's So Fine' and The Crystals' 'Then *He* Kissed Me' to their own direct 'Baby I Love *You*'. Put simply, it drove the boys wild. Lead singer Ronnie Bennett married Spector, divorcing him in 1974. Recording and touring sporadically since, her 2006 comeback album *Last Of The Rock Stars* was acclaimed by fans and critics.

Below

'Dancing In the Street' (1964) by Martha Reeves and The Vandellas, though intended as an innocent dance song, became an anthem for the civil rights movement.

see The Crystals pp 168   see Marvin Gaye pp 170   see The Temptations pp 179   see Mary Wells pp 181

Diana Ross and The Supremes

(Vocal group, 1961–77)

The jewels in the crown of Motown's golden years, The Supremes' sophisticated act and sound were the TV-friendly face of soul music, winning them 12 No. 1s including a 1964–65 run of five in a row from hitmakers Holland-Dozier-Holland. Many, like: 'You Can't Hurry Love' and 'You Keep Me Hanging On', became pop classics.

The writing team's departure from the label, founder Florence Ballard's ousting from the group and Diana Ross' grooming for solo stardom, all dented the trio's infallibility. But hits continued into the 1970s with 'Stoned Love' and 'River Deep – Mountain High' (their collaboration with childhood friends The Temptations). When third original Mary Wilson left in 1976 The Supremes finally folded. Ross' phenomenal solo career, working with top producers including Chic and The Bee Gees, saw UK hits every single year until 1996, although she was less successful in America.

Jimmy Ruffin

(Vocals, b. 1939)

Cutting his soul teeth with 1950s Detroit group The Four Holidays, Ruffin's early solo career was disrupted by the draft. He broke through on Motown with 1966's towering hit 'What Becomes Of The Broken Hearted' and a handful of follow-ups. His 1980 comeback 'Hold On To My Love' went US Top 10. He became a UK radio host in the 1990s and an anti-drugs campaigner following the 1991 overdose death of his younger brother David, The Temptations' lead singer.

see Introduction pp 152   see Sources & Sounds pp 78   see Key Artists pp 154

Sam and Dave

(Vocal duo, 1965–70)

The original inspiration for The Blues Brothers, Sam Moore and Dave Prater signed to Atlantic in 1965 and recorded a string of energetic soul shouts at Stax under the production team of Isaac Hayes and David Porter, including 'Hold On! I'm Coming' and Southern Soul anthem 'Soul Man'. They split in 1970, personal animosity and drug addictions thwarting several reunions. Prater died in 1988; Moore guested on Bruce Springsteen's *Human Touch* (1992).

Percy Sledge

(Vocals, 1966–68)

Going solo in 1966 after a stint with vocal group The Esquires Combo, Sledge released an independent single, the heartfelt ballad 'When A Man Loves A Woman'. It was snapped up by Atlantic, topping both US pop and US R&B charts and becoming a soul classic. A few follow-ups charted, including 'Warm And Tender Love' and 'Take Time To Know Her', but by the mid-1970s Sledge was working the nostalgia circuit.

Sledge never did much else, but the repeated use of his biggest hit in soundtracks kept him in the public's hearts and minds. When Levis used it in a 1987 UK advertising campaign, the song charted there at No. 2, two places higher than its 1966 listing. Particularly popular in continental Europe and Africa, he still tours, and was inducted to The Rock And Roll Hall Of Fame in 2005.

Phil Spector

(Producer, b. 1940)

Phil Spector devised a studio recording technique he called 'symphonies for the kids', which had considerable success in the 1960s and became known as the Wall of Sound. Characterized by mono production, it had fantastically rich choral and orchestral layering (sometimes as many as 300 musicians) behind the vocals of the titular performers he worked with.

Best remembered for his girl groups The Crystals and The Ronettes (who appear on his classic 1963 LP *A Christmas Gift For You*), he perfected his approach on The Righteous Brothers' 1965 'You've Lost That Lovin' Feeling' and Ike and Tina Turner's 1966 'River Deep – Mountain High'. The latter's US chart failure

Above
The No. 1 single when 'A Man Loves A Woman' by Percy Sledge was the first gold record released by Atlantic Records.

(it reached No. 3 in Britain) shattered Spector, and he became a notoriously eccentric recluse. He has since made rare comebacks (notably with George Harrison and The Ramones). Enduring industry respect for his often-imitated innovations has been overshadowed by his 2003 arrest for murder (to be tried in 2007).

Dusty Springfield

(Vocals, 1939–99)

British-born Springfield (born Mary O'Brien), formerly of The Springfields, showed her affiliation with American girl-group pop on her first outing, 1963's 'I Only Want To Be With You'. Hits by the Brill Building's best songwriting teams (including Bacharach-David and Goffin-King) earned her respect as the finest white soul singer of her era. Her 1969 album *Dusty In Memphis* is now considered a pop soul classic. A 1987 Pet Shop Boys collaboration triggered a successful comeback.

see George Harrison pp 216   *see* Bruce Springsteen pp 222   *see* The Bee Gees pp 230   *see* Tina Turner pp 245

Above

The Staple Singers released an album a year from 1961 to 1978, but their biggest commercial success was in the mid-1960s when they signed with Stax Records.

Edwin Starr
(Vocals, 1942–2003)

Starr's early singing career was interrupted when he was drafted in 1960. He finally broke with 1965 Bond novelty 'Agent Double-O Soul' and its follow-up 'Stop Her On Sight (S.O.S.)'. He had a powerful, rough voice that will be remembered for the 1970 anti-Vietnam hit 'War', originally a Norman Whitfield song for The Temptations. Starr enjoyed a disco comeback in 1979 with two UK Top 10 entries, 'Contact' and 'H.A.P.P.Y. Radio'. He made high-profile guest recordings with Utah Saints (2000) and Jools Holland (2002).

Jim Stewart
(Founder, Stax Records, b. 1930)

Stewart founded Memphis-based Stax Records in 1957 with his sister, Estelle Axton. Local musicians became the house band, Booker T and The MGs. Their backing on many recordings defined the gritty Southern Soul sound. An early hit by Carla Thomas attracted Atlantic, who took options on all Stax releases and sent many of their own acts to record at Stax. Stewart was inducted to The Rock And Roll Hall Of Fame in 2002.

The Staple Singers
(Vocal group, 1968–85)

Roebuck 'Pops' Staples, born 1915, migrated musically and geographically from Mississippi blues to Chicago gospel. In the late 1950s, he was leading a vocal group with his children, and by 1968 had signed with Stax. With lead vocals shared by Pops and daughter Mavis, and backed by Booker T and The MGs or The Muscle Shoals Band they blended gospel, R&B and blues with civil-rights issues on tracks like 'When Will We Be Paid (For The Work We've Done)'. Their uplifting 1972 anthem 'Respect Yourself' struck a chord with the equal rights movement and was a US pop No. 2.

Mavis has periodically recorded solo, most recently a well-received gospel R&B effort, 2004's *Have A Little Faith*. In 1992, aged 77 Pops, a fine blues guitarist, released his first solo album *Peace To The Neighbourhood*. Steeped in tradition and acclaimed a national treasure, he died in 2000.

Right

Barrett Strong performed Motown's first hit 'Money (That's What I Want)', which reached No. 2 in the US in 1960.

Barrett Strong
(Songwriter, b. 1941)

Strong was a Motown staff writer whose own 1960 hit 'Money' helped fund the label's early expansion. His compositions with Norman Whitfield included 'I Heard It Through The Grapevine', and led Motown's forays into more socially aware territory with hits like Edwin Starr's 'War' and many of The Temptations' psychedelic soul outings. Strong won a 1972 Grammy for their 'Papa Was A Rolling Stone', but quit Motown when they abandoned Detroit for LA that year.

 *see* Introduction pp 152   *see* Sources & Sounds pp 78   *see* Key Artists pp 154

The Tams

(Vocal group, 1957–69)

The Tams formed in Atlanta in 1957 and are still touring. They took their name from the tam-o'shanter bonnets they wore on-stage. Their vocal arrangements had a deft, light touch which won them their biggest US hit, 1963's 'What Kind Of Fool Do You Think I Am', although they are best remembered for the 1968 anthem 'Be Young, Be Foolish, Be Happy'. A 1971 reissue of 'Hey Girl Don't Bother Me' was a UK No. 1.

The Temptations

(Vocal group, 1961–present)

Formed in 1961, The Temptations were Motown's leading male group, with smooth harmonies and crisp choreography. Their first big hit, 1965's 'My Girl' was written by Smokey Robinson in reply to his earlier 'My Guy', penned for Mary Wells. From 1967, producer Norman Whitfield gave them a harder edge. Adding psychedelic soul to the Motown pop mix, further hits included 1969's drugs-referencing 'Cloud Nine' and the civil-rights appeal of 1972's epic 'Papa Was A Rolling Stone'.

Several Temptations frontmen have had successful solo careers: David Ruffin (brother of Jimmy) was forced into one, sacked in 1968 for egotism; Eddie Kendricks quit after 1971's 'Just My Imagination', unhappy with the new psychedelic direction; and Dennis Edwards has been in and out three times. Latterday reunions have been plagued by internal disagreements and ill-health. Otis Williams is the only original Temptation in the current line-up, which still tours the oldies circuit.

Above
The classic line-up of The Temptations released the band's signature tune and No. 1 hit 'My Girl' in March 1965.

Tammi Terrell

(Vocals, 1945–70)

After some minor solo success, Terrell was paired with Marvin Gaye; their chemistry as a duo was immediate and led to a string of hits, including 1967's 'Ain't No Mountain High Enough' and 'You're All I Need To Get By'. But Terrell collapsed in Gaye's arms on-stage in 1967, diagnosed with a brain tumour from which she died in 1970 aged 24. Her decline and death drove Gaye to grief-stricken seclusion from which he emerged with his masterpiece, *What's Going On*.

Carla Thomas

(Vocals, b. 1942)

Aged 17, Thomas recorded 'Gee Whiz (Look At His Eyes)', the 1960 track that put Stax Records on the national map with its first Top 10 hit. She went on to become the Queen of Memphis Soul, backed by the talents of producer Isaac Hayes, house band Booker T and The MGs, and her father Rufus. Hits included 'B.A.B.Y.' and battle-of-the-sexes duet 'Tramp' from *King And Queen* (1967), an album recorded with opposite number Otis Redding.

see **Otis Redding** pp 158   see **Booker T and The MGs** pp 166   see **Marvin Gaye** pp 170   see **Smokey Robinson** pp 175

Rufus Thomas

(Vocals, 1917–2001)

Compere, comedian, song and dance man with the Rabbit Foot Minstrels in the 1930s. Thomas sang Sun Records' first national hit 'Bear Cat' in 1953, and repeated the feat regionally for Stax in 1960 on a duet with daughter Carla, 'Cause I Love You'. He had a number of novelty dance hits from then until the early 1970s, including 'Walking The Dog' and 'Do The Funky Chicken', which reflected his vaudeville roots.

vocals when the booked singer did not show. More hits followed, notably 1966's 'How Sweet It Is (To Be Loved By You)' and '(I'm A) Roadrunner'. His sound inspired 1970s saxophonists like Tom Scott, and he memorably guested the solo on Foreigner's 1981 hit 'Urgent'.

Dionne Warwick

(Vocals, b. 1940)

Discovered by Burt Bacharach in 1962 singing backing vocals in a New York studio, Warwick became the muse of the Bacharach-David writing team that made the reputations of both parties. Her first hit that year was their 'Don't Make Me Over', and from then until 1972 when the writers fell out she charted 30 times with their compositions, from 'Anyone Who Had A Heart' to 'I'll Never Fall In Love Again'.

1979's *Dionne*, produced by Barry Manilow, revived her career, as did 1982's *Heartbreaker* with Barry Gibb presiding; the title track and 'All The Love In The World' were Top 10 entries. Following her role on 1985 charity single 'That's What Friends Are For' (co-written by Bacharach), she has concentrated on

Below

Junior Walker's distinctive, idiosyncratic saxophone style supplied Junior Walker and The All Stars with the 1965 Top 10 hit 'Shotgun'.

Junior Walker

(Saxophone, vocals, 1942–95)

Rough bluesy sax player (born Autry DeWalt in Arkansas in 1942) who, with his band The All Stars, signed to Motown in 1964. He first charted the following year with 'Shotgun', having stepped up to perform the

Right

In 1968, Dionne Warwick received her first Grammy Award for 'Do You Know The Way to San Jose?', which reached No. 10 in the US chart.

humanitarian work for AIDS and other causes. Since 2002 she has been UN Ambassador for Food and Agriculture. A 2006 stage musical in Chicago celebrating her career was well-received.

Mary Wells
(Vocals, 1943–92)

One of Motown's first female superstars, Wells was signed when she demo'd a song she had written for Jackie Wilson. Instead it became her own 1961 debut single 'Bye Bye Baby', and reached No. 8 in the R&B chart. Although only her 1964 US pop No. 1 'My Guy' charted in Britain, she had many more hits at home. But after she quit Motown in 1965 she never repeated her early success.

Kim Weston
(Vocals, b. 1939)

Best known for her duets with Marvin Gaye, Weston was also a successful Motown solo artist. She reached R&B No. 2 with 1965's 'Take Me In Your Arms (Rock Me A Little While)', later covered by The Doobie Brothers, and notoriously turned down 'Dancing In The Streets', only to see Martha Reeves take it to No. 1. She had already left Motown when her last duet with Gaye, 1967's 'It Takes Two', became her biggest hit.

Norman Whitfield
(Producer, songwriter, b. 1943)

Whitfield joined Motown as a writer, but his willingness to experiment with other sounds and genres as a producer made him a key player in the growth of Motown beyond its early pop-soul identity. His biggest impact was with The Temptations, whose move to psychedelic soul he directed. He left Motown in 1975 to form Whitfield Records, where his greatest success was with Rose Royce; he won a Grammy for 'Car Wash'.

Jackie Wilson
(Vocals, 1934–84)

With his powerful high vocal range, Jackie Wilson was among the earliest singers to make the transition from R&B to soul. His first single, 1957's 'Reet Petite', was the start of a winning partnership with its writer, young Berry Gordy (although Wilson never recorded for Gordy's Motown label). 'Reet Petite' was actually more successful in Britain, reaching No. 6 (and No. 1 on its Christmas 1986 reissue). Recorded work rarely captured his sexy on-stage energy, which rivalled James Brown – in 1961 he was shot and seriously injured by a frustrated female fan.

1966's '(Your Love Keeps Lifting Me) Higher And Higher' was his last big US hit, although 1972's 'I Get The Sweetest Feeling' made the UK Top 10. The same year Van Morrison wrote his tribute 'Jackie Wilson Said', a 1982 UK No. 5 when covered by Dexy's Midnight Runners. An on-stage heart attack in 1975 left Wilson needing permanent medical care; he died in 1984.

Above Left

Kim Weston's duet with Marvin Gaye, 'It Takes Two Baby', reached No. 14 in the *Billboard* chart in 1966, and remains a classic today.

Above

The energetic stage performances of Jackie Wilson earned him the title of 'Mr Excitement'.

see James Brown pp 154   *see* Martha Reeves and The Vandellas pp 174   *see* Van Morrison pp 219   *see* Rose Royce pp 242

List of Artists

Entries appear in the following order: name, music style, year(s) of popularity, type of artist, country of origin.

? and The Mysterians, US Underground & Garage Rock, 1960s; 1990s-, Artist, American
13th Floor Elevators, Psychedelic Rock, 1960s-1980s, Artist, American
1910 Fruitgum Company, 1960s Pop, 1960s, Artist, American
5th Dimension, 1960s Pop, 1960s-1970s, Artist, American
AB Skhy, Blues Rock, 1960s-1970s, Artist, American
Abyssinians, The, Dub; Roots, 1960s-1990s, Artist, Jamaican
Ackles, David, 1960s Pop Singer/Songwriters, 1960s-1970s, Artist; Songwriter, American
Acklin, Barbara, Northern Soul, 1960s-1970s, Artist, American
Action, The, Mod; British Invasion, 1960s, Artist, British
Alan, Buddy, Country Rock, 1960s-1970s, Artist, American
Alexander, Arthur, The Classic Soul Era; Rhythm & Blues, 1960s-1970s, Artist, American
Alice Cooper, Heavy Metal; Hard Rock, 1960s-, Artist, American
Allison, Luther, Chicago Blues; Modern Electric Blues, 1960s-1990s, Artist, American
Allman Brothers Band, The, Southern Rock; Jam Rock; Blues Rock, 1960s-, Artist, American
Allman, Duane, Southern Rock; Blues Rock, 1960s-1970s, Artist, American
Alpert, Herb, 1960s Pop; Easy Listening, 1960s-, Producer; Artist, American
Always, Billy, Urban Soul, 1960s-1990s, Artist, American
Amen Corner, Mod; British Invasion, 1960s-1970s, Artist, British
Amon Düül, Krautrock, 1960s-1990s, Artist, German
Andersen, Eric, 1960s Pop Singer/Songwriters; Folk Rock; Contemporary Folk, 1960s-, Artist; Songwriter,
Anderson, Kip, The Classic Soul Era, 1960s, Artist, American
Anderson, Miller, Blues Rock, 1960s-1990s, Artist, British
Andrews, Ruby, The Classic Soul Era, 1960s-1970s, Artist, American
Andy, Bob, Rock Steady; Ska, 1960s-1990s, Artist, British
Andy, Horace, Roots; Dub, 1960-, Artist, Jamaican
Angels, The, 1960s Pop, 1960s, Artist, American
Animals, The, Rock'n'Roll; British Invasion; British Blues; Blues Rock, 1960s-1980s, Artist, British
Aphrodite's Child, Prog Rock, 1960s-1970s, Artist, Greek
Arbors, The, 1960s Pop, 1960s, Artist, American
Archies, The, 1960s Pop, 1960s-1970s, Artist, American
Argent, Prog Rock, 1960s-1970s, Artist, British
Arnold, P. P., Urban Soul, 1960s-1980s, Artist, American
Artistics, The, Northern Soul, 1960s-1970s, Artist, American
Ashes, The, Folk Rock, 1960s, Artist, American
Ashton, Gardner and Dyke, Blues Rock, 1960s-1970s, Artist, British
Association, The, 1960s Pop; Wall of Sound, 1960s-1970s, Artist, American
Astors, The, The Classic Soul Era, 1960s, Artist, American
Astronauts, The, Surf, 1960s; 1980-1990s, Artist, American
Atlantics, The, Surf, 1960s-1970s, Artist, Australian
Atomic Rooster, Prog Rock, 1960s-1980s, Artist, British
Auger, Brian, Jazz Rock; Fusion, 1960s-, Artist, British
Autographs, The, Northern Soul, 1960s-1970s, Artist, American
Axelrod, David, Wall of Sound; 1960s Pop, 1960s-, Producer, American
Ayers, Kevin, Prog Rock, 1960s-1990s, Artist, British
Ayers, Roy, Soul Jazz; Fusion, 1960s-, Artist, American
B. Bumble and the Stingers, 1960s Pop, 1960s-1970s, Artist, American
Baby Huey, The Classic Soul Era, 1960s, Artist, American
Bacharach, Burt, 1960s Pop; Wall of Sound; Easy Listening; Lounge Music, 1960s-1990s, Producer; Composer; Songwriter; Artist, American
Bachman-Turner Overdrive, Arena Rock; Hard Rock, 1960s-1980s, Artist, British
Badfinger, 1960s Pop, 1960s-1980s, Artist, British
Bailey, Rene, Northern Soul, 1960s-1970s, Artist, American
Banana Splits, 1960s Pop; Manufactured Pop, 1960s, Artist, American
Band, The, Country Rock; Folk Rock; Rock n Roll, 1960s-1970s; 1990s, Artist, Canadian
Banks, Darrell, The Classic Soul Era, 1960s, Artist, American
Banks, Doug, Northern Soul, 1960s-1970s, Artist, American
Barbarians, The, Pub Rock, 1960s-1970s, Artist, British
Bar-Kays, The, The Classic Soul Era, 1960s-1990s, Artist, American
Barnes, J. J., Northern Soul; The Classic Soul Era, 1960s-1980s, Artist, American
Barnum, Eve, Northern Soul, 1960s-1970s, Artist, American
Barrett, Syd, Psychedelic Rock, 1960s-1970s, Artist, British
Barry and The Remains, US Underground & Garage Rock; Rock'n'Roll, 1960s, Artist, American
Barry, Jeff, 1960s Pop, 1960s-, Producer, American
Bartley, Chris, The Classic Soul Era, 1960s, Artist, American
Bass, Fontella, 1960s Pop; Northern Soul, 1960s-1970s; 1990s-, Artist, American
Beach Boys, The, Surf, 1960s-1990s, Artist, American
Beatles, The, Psychedelic Rock; Folk Rock; Rock'n'Roll; British Invasion; Merseybeat, 1960s-1970s, Artist, British
Beau Brummels, The, Country Rock; Folk Rock; 1960s Pop, 1960s-1970s, Artist, American
Beaver and Krause, Electro, 1960s-1970s, Artist, American
Beck, Jeff, Hard Rock; British Blues; Blues Rock, 1960s-, Artist, British
Bee Gees, The, 1960s Pop; Disco, 1960s-, Artist, British
Bell, Archie, Disco; The Classic Soul Era, 1960s-1970s, Artist; Songwriter, American
Bell, William, Northern Soul, 1960s-, Artist, American
Bennett, Cliff, 1960s Pop, 1960s-1970s, Artist, British
Bennett, Duster, British Blues; Blues Rock, 1960s-1970s, Artist, British
Benson, George, Smooth Jazz; Hard Bop, 1960s-, Artist, American
Benton, Buster, Modern Electric Blues; Chicago Blues, 1960s-1990s, Artist, American
Berns, Bert, British Invasion; 1960s Pop, 1950s-1960s, Producer; Songwriter, American
Berry, Dave, British Invasion, 1960s-1980s, Artist, British
Big Brother and the Holding Company, Blues Rock, 1960s-1990s, Artist, American
Big Three, The, Folk Pop; The Folk Revival, 1960s, Artist, American
Billy J. Kramer and the Dakotas, Merseybeat; The British Invasion, 1960s, Artist, British
Birds, The, British Invasion; Mod, 1960s, Artist, British
Bishop, Elvin, Modern Electric Blues, 1960s-, Artist, American
Bishop, Walter Jr, Bebop; Hard Bop, 1960s-1990s, Artist, American
Black Sabbath, Heavy Metal, 1960s-, Artist, British
Black, Cilla, 1960s Pop; British Invasion, 1960s-1990s, Artist, British
Blackmore, Ritchie, Hard Rock, 1960s-, Artist, British
Blind Faith, Blues Rock; British Blues, 1960s, Artist, British
Blodwyn Pig, Blues Rock, 1960s-1990s, Artist, British
Blood, Sweat and Tears; Jazz Rock, 1960s-1980s, Artist, American
Bloomfield, Michael, Modern Electric Blues; Chicago Blues, 1960s-1980s, Artist, American
Blossom Toes, Psychedelic Rock, 1960s, Artist, British
Blue Cheer, Psychedelic Rock; Hard Rock, 1960s-1990s, Artist, American
Blue Things, The, Folk Rock, 1960s, Artist, American
Blue, David, Folk Rock, 1960s-1970s, Artist; Songwriter, American
Blues Incorporated, British Blues, 1960s, Artist, British
Blues Magoos, The, US Underground & Garage Rock; Psychedelic Rock, 1960s-1970s, Artist, American
Blues Project, The, Blues Rock; Folk Rock, 1960s-1970s, Artist, American
Bo Street Runners, The, Rhythm & Blues, 1960s, Artist, British
Boettcher, Curt, 1960s Pop, 1960s-1970s, Artist, American
Bolan, Marc, Glam Rock & Glitter; Psychedelic Rock; Folk Rock; Rock'n'Roll; 1960s Pop, 1960s-1970s, Artist; Songwriter, British
Bolton, Michael, 1980s Pop, 1980s-, Artist, American
Bond, Graham, British Blues; Blues Rock, 1960s-1970s, Artist, British
Bonds, Gary 'U.S.', Rhythm & Blues; Rock'n'Roll, 1960s-, Artist; Songwriter, American
Bonzo Dog Doo Dah Band, Novelty Songs, 1960s, Artist, British
Booker T. and the MGs, The Classic Soul Era, 1960s-1970s, Artist, American
Boothe, Ken, Roots; Rock Steady, 1960s-1970s, Artist, Jamaican
Bowie, David, Hard Rock; Proto-Punk; Prog Rock; Glam Rock & Glitter; 1960s Pop, 1960s-, Artist, British
Box Tops, The, 1960s Pop, 1960s, Artist, American
Brandywine Singers, The, Folk Pop; The Folk Revival, 1960s, Artist, American
Brass Construction, Funk; Disco; The Classic Soul Era, 1960s-1980s, Artist, American
Brecker Brothers, Fusion, 1960s-1990s, Artist, American
Brecker, Michael, Fusion, 1960s-, Artist, American
Brecker, Randy, Fusion; Hard Bop, 1960s-, Artist, American
Brenda and the Tabulations, The Classic Soul Era, 1960s-1970s, Artist, American
Brewer and Shipley, 1960s-1970s, Folk Rock, Artist, American,
Bristol, Johnny, The Classic Soul Era, 1960s-1980s, Artist, American
Brooklyn Bridge, 1960s Pop, 1960s-1970s, Artist, American
Brown Arthur, Psychedelic Rock, 1960s-1990s, Artist, British
Brown, Glenn, Dub; Dancehall, 1960s-1990s, Artist; Songwriter, American
Brown, Joe, Rock'n'Roll; Country Rock, 1960s-1990s, Artist, British
Brown, Maxine, 1960s Pop; Funk Soul; Rhythm & Blues, 1960s-1970s, Artist, American
Browne, Jackson, 1960s Pop Singer/Songwriters, 1960s-, Artist; Songwriter, American
Bruce and Terry, Surf; 1960s Pop, 1960s, Artist, American
Bruce, Jack, British Blues, 1960s-, Artist, Scottish
Bryant, Don, The Classic Soul Era, 1960s-1990s, Artist, American
Buckinghams, The, 1960s Pop, 1960s; 1990s, Artist, American
Buckley, Tim, Folk Rock; Jazz Rock; 1960s Pop Singer/Songwriters, 1960s-1970s, Artist; Songwriter, American
Budd, Harold, Electro; Ambient, 1960s-, Artist, American
Buffalo Springfield, Country Rock; Folk Rock, 1960s, Artist, American
Bull, Sandy, Folk Rock; Contemporary Rock; Fusion and Jazz Rock, 1960s-1980s, Artist, American
Burdon, Eric, Rock'n'Roll; British Invasion; British Blues; Blues Rock; Funk; Funk Soul, 1960s-2000s, Artist, British
Burnette, Dorsey, Rock'n'Roll; Rockabilly; Country Rock, 1960s-1970s, Artist; Songwriter, American
Burnside, R. L., Delta/Country Blues; Modern Electric Blues, 1960s-, Artist, American
Burton, James, Country Rock; Rockabilly; Rock'n'Roll, 1960s-1970s, Artist, American
Bush, Johnny, Honky Tonk; Western Swing, 1960s-, Artist, American
Butler, Billy, Northern Soul, 1960s-1970s, Artist, American
Butterfield, Paul, Chicago Blues; Blues Rock, 1960s-1980s, Artist, American
Byrd, Bobby, Funk Soul, 1960s-1990s, Artist, American
Byrds, The, Psychedelic Rock; Country Rock; Folk Rock, 1960s-1970s, Artist, American
Cale, John, Proto-Punk; Prog Rock, 1960s-, Artist, British
Callier, Terry, Northern Soul, 1960s-1970s, Artist; Songwriter, American
Cameron, G. C., The Classic Soul Era, 1960s-1990s, Artist, American
Campbell, Glen, Mainstream Country; The Nashville Sound, 1960s-, Artist, American
Can, Prog Rock; Krautrock, 1960s-1990s, Artist, German
Canned Heat, Blues Rock; Modern Electric Blues, 1960s-, Artist, American
Cannon, Ace, The Classic Soul Era, 1960s-1990s, Artist, American
Capaldi, Jim, Psychedelic Rock; Prog Rock, 1960s-, Artist; Songwriter, British
Capitols, The, Urban Soul, 1960s, Artist, American
Captain Beefheart, Psychedelic Rock; Proto-Punk; Prog-Rock; Blues Rock, 1960s-1980s, Artist, American
Caravan, Prog Rock, 1960s-1990s, Artist, British
Carlos, Wendy, Electro, 1960s-, Artist, American
Carlton, Carl, Funk Soul, 1960s-1990s, Artist, American
Carlton, Larry, Fusion; Smooth Jazz, 1960s-, Artist, American
Carpenters, The, 1960s Pop; Easy Listening, 1960s-1980s, Artist, American
Carr, Barbara, Northern Soul, 1960s-1970s, Artist, American
Carr, James, The Classic Soul Era, 1960s-1990s, Artist, American
Carr, Vicki, Latin, 1960s-, Artist, American
Carter, Clarence, The Classic Soul Era, 1960s-1990s, Artist, American
Carter, Mel, The Classic Soul Era, 1960s-1970s, Artist, American
Carter, Ron, Hard Bop, 1960s-, Artist, American
Carthy, Martin, UK Folk; The Folk Revival, 1960s-, Artist, British
Casey, Al, Surf; Rock'n'Roll, 1960s-1970s, Artist, American
Castaways, The, US Underground & Garage Rock, 1960s, Artist, American
Chad and Jeremy, British Invasion; 1960s Pop, 1960s; 1980s, Artist, British
Chairmen Of The Board, The, The Classic Soul Era, 1960s-1970s, Artist, American
Chakachas, Funk Soul, 1960s-1970s, Artist, Belgian
Challengers, The, Surf, 1960s-1970s, Artist, American
Chambers Brothers, The, The Classic Soul Era, 1960s-1970s, Artist, American
Chandler, Gene, Northern Soul, 1960s-1990s, Artist, American
Chantays, The, Surf, 1960s; 1990s, Artist, American
Chapman, Michael, Folk Rock; UK Folk, 1960s-, Artist; Songwriter, British
Charlatans, The, Folk Rock, 1960s, Artist, American
Checker, Chubby, Rock'n'Roll; Rhythm & Blues, 1960s-2000s, Artist, American
Cher, 1960s Pop, 1960s-, Artist, American
Chicago, Melodic Rock; 1960s Pop, 1960s-, Artist, American
Chicken Shack, British Blues; Blues Rock, 1960s-1980s, Artist, British
Chieftains, The, Irish Folk; UK Folk, 1960s-, Artist, Irish
Chiffons, The, 1960s Pop, 1960s-1970s, Artist, American
Chi-Lites, The, Urban Soul, 1960s-1990s, Artist, American
Chocolate Watchband, The, US Underground & Garage Rock; Psychedelic Rock, 1960s; 1990s, Artist, American
Christie, Lou, 1960s Pop, 1960s-1970s, Artist, American
Chrysalis, Folk Rock, 1960s, Artist, American
Clapton, Eric, Hard Rock; British Blues; Blues Rock, 1960s-, Artist; Songwriter, British
Clark, Chris, The Classic Soul Era; Northern Soul, 1960s-1980s, Artist, American
Clark, Gene, Country Rock; Folk Rock, 1960s-1990s, Artist; Songwriter, American
Clark, Petula, British Invasion; 1960s Pop, 1960s-, Artist, British
Clarke, Stanley, Fusion, 1960s-1990s, Artist, American
Clarke, Tony, Northern Soul, 1960s, Artist; Songwriter, American
Classics IV, 1960s Pop, 1960s-1970s, Artist, American
Clay, Otis, The Classic Soul Era, 1960s-1990s, Artist, American
Clayton, Willie, Northern Soul, 1960s-, Artist, American
Clee-Shays, Surf, 1960s, Artist, American
Cliff, Jimmy, Reggae Pop, 1960s-, Artist, Jamaican
Cliff, Jimmy, Reggae Pop, 1960s-, Artist, Jamaican
Climax Blues Band, Blues Rock, 1960s-1990s, Artist, British
Clique, The, 1960s Pop, 1960s, Artist, American
Cochran, Hank, Honky Tonk, 1960s-1990s, Artist, American
Cockburn, Bruce, 1960s Pop Singer/Songwriters; Contemporary Folk, 1960s-1990s, Artist; Songwriter, Canadian
Cocker, Joe, Blues Rock, 1960s-, Artist, British
Cohen, Leonard, Folk Rock; 1960s Pop Singer/Songwriters, 1960s-, Artist; Songwriter, Canadian
Cole, Jerry, Surf, 1960s, Artist, American
Collier, Mitty, Northern Soul, 1960s, Artist, American
Conley, Arthur, The Classic Soul Era, 1960s, Artist, American
Conrad, Tony, Krautrock, 1960s-1970s, Artist, American
Contours, The, The Classic Soul Era, 1960s-1980s, Artist, American
Copeland, Johnny, Modern Electric Blues; Texas Blues, 1960s-1990s, Artist, American
Corea, Chick, Fusion; Free Jazz, 1960s-, Artist; Composer, American
Coryell, Larry, Fusion, 1960s-, Artist, American
Count Five, US Underground & Garage Rock; Psychedelic Rock, 1960s, Artist, American
Country Joe and the Fish, Psychedelic Rock, 1960s-1970s, Artist, American
Covay, Don, The Classic Soul Era, 1960s-, Artist, American
Cowsills, The, 1960s Pop, 1960s-1990s, Artist, American
Cranshaw, Bob, Hard Bop, 1960s-1990s, Artist, American
Crazy Elephant, 1960s Pop; Manufactured Pop, 1960s, Artist, American
Crazy Horse, Hard Rock, 1960s-, Artist, American
Crazy World of Arthur Brown, The, Psychedelic Rock, 1960s, Artist, British
Cream, Hard Rock; Psychedelic Rock; British Blues; Blues Rock, 1960s, Artist, British
Creation, The, Psychedelic Rock; Rock'n'Roll; British Invasion, 1960s, Artist, British
Creedence Clearwater Revival, Southern Rock; Rock'n'Roll, 1960s-1970s, Artist, American
Critters, The, Folk Rock, 1960s, Artist, American
Croce, Jim, 1960s Pop Singer/Songwriters, 1960s-1970s, Artist; Songwriter, American
Cropper, Steve, The Classic Soul Era; Rhythm & Blues, 1960s-1990s, Artist; Songwriter, American
Crosby, Stills and Nash, Folk Rock; 1960s Pop Singer/Songwriters, 1960s-1990s, Artist; Songwriter, American
Crosby, Stills, Nash and Young, Folk Rock; Political Folk & Protest Songs, 1960s-, Artist; Songwriter, American
Crusaders, The, Hard Bop; Soul Jazz; Fusion, 1960s-, Artist, American
Crystals, The, 1960s Pop, 1960s, Artist, American
Cuff Links, The, 1960s Pop; Manufactured Pop, 1960s, Artist, American
Czukay, Holger, Prog Rock; Electro, 1960s-, Artist, German
Daily Flash, The, Folk Rock, 1960s, Artist, American
Dale, Dick, Surf, 1960s-1990s, Artist, American
Daley, Lloyd, Ska, 1960s-1970s, Artist, Jamaican
Dantalion's Chariot, Psychedelic Rock, 1960s, Artist, British
Darling, Eric, The Folk Revival, 1960s-, Artist, American
Dave Clark Five, The, British Invasion, 1960s-1970s, Artist, British
Dave Dee, Dozy, Beaky, Mick and Tich, Rock'n'Roll, 1960s Pop, 1960s-1970s, Artist, British
David, Hal, 1960s Pop, 1960s-1980s, Producer; Songwriter; Artist, American
Davies, Cyril, British Blues, 1960s, Artist, British
Davis, Carl, Northern Soul, 1960s-1970s, Artist, American
Davis, Skeeter, The Nashville Sound; Country Rock, 1960s-1990s, Artist, American
Davis, Tyrone, Urban Soul, 1960s-, Artist, American
Dawkins, Jimmy, Modern Electric Blues; Chicago Blues, 1960s-1990s, Artist, American
Day, Jimmy, Honky Tonk; Western Swing, 1960s; 1990s, Artist, American
Dee, Kiki, The Classic Soul Era, 1960s-1990s, Artist, British
Deep Purple, Hard Rock, 1960s-, Artist, British
DeJohnette, Jack, Fusion, 1960s-, Artist, American
Dekker, Desmond, Ska; Rock Steady, 1960s-, Artist, Jamaican
Delaney and Bonnie, Blues Rock, 1960s-1970s, Artist, American
Delfonics, The, 1960s Pop; Urban Soul, 1960s-1970s, Artist, American
Denny, Sandy, Folk Rock; UK Folk, 1960s-1970s, Artist, British
Denver, John, Folk Rock; 1960s Pop Singer/Songwriters, 1960s-1990s, Artist, American
Denver, Karl, Alternative Folk, 1960s, Artist, British
Deodato, Disco, 1960s-1980s, Artist, Brazilian
DeShannon, Jackie, Folk Rock; 1960s Pop; 1960s Pop Singer/Songwriters, 1960s-1980s, Artist; Songwriter, American
Diamond, Neil, 1960s Pop, 1960s-, Artist, American
Dickens, Hazel, Neo-Traditional Folk; Political Folk & Protest Songs, 1960s-1990s, Artist, American
Diesel Smoke, Honky Tonk, 1960s, Artist, American
Dillard and Clark, Country Rock; Bluegrass, 1960s-1970s; 1990s, Artist, American
Dillards, The, Country Rock; Bluegrass, 1960s-1990s, Artist, American
Din, Hamza el, Fusion and Jazz Rock, 1960s-1990s, Artist, African
Dixie Cups, The, 1960s Pop, 1960s, Artist, American
Dockstader, Tod, Electro; Ambient, 1960s-1970s, Composer, American
Dodd, Clement 'Coxsone', Roots; Rock Steady; Ska, 1960s-1990s, Producer, Jamaican
Dodd, Coxsone, Ska; Rock Steady; Roots, 1960s-1980s, Artist; Producer, Jamaican
Donovan, Psychedelic Rock; Folk Rock; UK Folk; British Invasion; 1960s Pop Singer/Songwriters, 1960s-, Artist; Songwriter, British
Doors, The, Psychedelic Rock; Proto-Punk, 1960s-1970s, Artist, American
Dorsey, Lee, Rhythm & Blues; The Classic Soul Era, 1960s-1980s, Artist, American
Douglas, Steve, Young Country, 1960s, Artist, American
Downliners Sect, The, British Invasion, 1960s-1970s, Artist, British
Dr. Hook, Country Rock; 1960s Pop, 1960s-1970s, Artist, American
Dr. John, Louisiana Blues, 1960s-, Artist, American
Dr. Strangely Strange, Irish Folk; Folk Rock, 1960s-1970s, Artist, Irish
Drake, Nick, Folk Rock; UK Folk; 1960s Pop Singer/Songwriters, 1960s-1970s, Artist; Songwriter, British
Driscoll, Julie, Folk Rock, 1960s-1970s, Artist, British
Drummond, Don, Ska; Rock Steady, 1960s, Artist, Jamaican
Dubliners, The, Irish Folk, 1960s-, Artist, Irish
Dudley, Dave, Honky Tonk, 1960s-, Artist, American
Duke, Doris, The Classic Soul Era, 1960s-1980s, Artist, American
Duke, George, Fusion, 1960s-, Producer; Artist, American
Dupree, Simon, Funk Soul, 1960s, Artist, American
Duprees, The, Doo-Wop, 1960s, Artist, American
Durcal, Rocio, Latin, 1960s-, Artist, Spanish
Dylan, Bob, Country Rock; Political Folk & Protest Songs; Folk Rock; Rock'n'Roll; 1960s Pop Singer/Songwriters, 1960s-, Artist, American
Earland, Charles, Soul Jazz; Hard Bop, 1960s-1990s, Artist, American
Easybeats, The, Rock'n'Roll, 1960s-1980s, Artist, British
Eddie and the Showmen, Surf; Rock'n'Roll, 1960s, Artist, American
Edgar Broughton Band, The, Prog Rock, 1960s; 2000s, Artist, British
Edison Lighthouse, 1960s Pop; Manufactured Pop, 1960s-1970s, Artist, British
Electric Flag, Blues Rock, 1960s-1970s, Artist, American
Electric Prunes, The, Psychedelic Rock; US Underground & Garage Rock, 1960s, Artist, American
Elgins, The, The Classic Soul Era, 1960s, Artist, American
Ellis, Pee Wee, Funk Soul, 1960s-, Artist, American
Ellis, Shirley, The Classic Soul Era, 1960s, Artist, American
Epstein, Brian, British Invasion; Merseybeat, 1960s, Producer, British
Equals, The, 1960s Pop; Funk, 1960s-1980s, Artist, British
Erickson, Roky, Psychedelic Rock, 1960s-, Artist, American
Escovado, Pete, Latin Jazz; Fusion, 1960s-, Artist, American
Essex, The, 1960s Pop, 1960s, Artist, American
Ethiopians, The, Rock Steady, 1960s-1980s, Artist, Jamaican
E-Types, The, US Underground & Garage Rock, 1960s; 1990s, Artist, American
Euphoria, Trance; Techno, 1960s-1970s, Artist, American
Exciters, The, 1960s Pop, 1960s-1970s, Artist, Jamaican
Eyes, The, Mod; British Invasion, 1960s, Artist, British
Fabares, Shelley, 1960s Pop, 1960s, Artist, American
Fairport Convention, Folk Rock; UK Folk, 1960s-1990s, Artist, British
Faithfull, Marianne, 1960s Pop; Folk Rock, 1960s-1970s; 1990s, Artist, British
Fame, Georgie, Rhythm & Blues; Ska, 1960s-2000s, Artist, British
Family, Prog Rock, 1960s-1970s, Artist, British
Fankhauser, Merrell, Prog Rock, 1960s-, Artist, American
Fantastic Baggys, Surf; Rock'n'Roll, 1960s, Artist, American
Fantastic Johnny C., The, The Classic Soul Era, 1960s, Artist, American
Fapardokly, Folk Rock, 1960s, Artist, American
Farina, Richard, The Folk Revival; Folk Rock, 1960s, Artist; Songwriter, American
Farlowe, Chris, Skiffle; Rhythm & Blues, 1960s-1990s, Artist, British
Farr, Gary, The Classic Soul Era, 1960s-1980s, Artist, British
Farrell, Joe, Hard Bop, 1960s-1980s, Artist, American
Fearon, Clinton, Rock Steady; Ska, 1960s, Artist, Jamaican
Feliciano, José, Folk Rock, 1960s-, Artist, Puerto Rican
Five Man Electrical Band, 1960s Pop, 1960s-1970s, Artist, Canadian
Five Stairsteps, The, The Classic Soul Era, 1960s-1970s, Artist, American
Flack, Roberta, Urban Soul, 1960s-, Artist, American
Flamin' Groovies, The, Proto-Punk; Rock'n'Roll, 1960s-1990s, Artist, American
Fleetwood Mac, Prog Rock; 1960s Pop; British Blues; Blues Rock, 1960s-, Artist, British
Fleur de Lys, Les, Psychedelic Rock, 1960s, Artist, British
Flower Pot Men, The, 1960s Pop, 1960s, Artist, British
Floyd, Eddie, The Classic Soul Era, 1960s-1970s, Artist, American
Flying Burrito Brothers, The, Country Rock, 1960s-1990s, Artist, American
Flying Machine, The, 1960s Pop, 1960s, Artist, British
Fontana, Wayne, and the Mindbenders, British Invasion; Merseybeat, 1960s, Artist, British
Ford, Jim, Country Rock, 1960s, Artist; Songwriter, American
Fortunes, The, British Invasion; Merseybeat, 1960s-1980s, Artist, British
Foundations, The, 1960s Pop; Funk Soul, 1960s, Artist, British
Four Seasons, The, 1960s Pop, 1960s-1990s, Artist, American
Fourmost, The, Merseybeat; British Invasion, 1960s, Artist, British
Franklin, Erma, Northern Soul, 1960s, Artist, American
Fred, John, The Classic Soul Era, 1960s, Artist, American
Freddie and the Dreamers, British Invasion; Merseybeat, 1960s, Artist, British
Free Design, The, 1960s Pop; Wall of Sound, 1960s-1970s, Artist, American
Free, Hard Rock; Blues Rock, 1960s-1970s, Artist, British
Friends Of Distinction, The, 1960s Pop; Urban Soul, 1960s-1970s, Artist, American
Fripp, Robert, Prog Rock, 1960s-, Artist, British
Fugs, The, Folk Rock, 1960s-1990s, Artist, American
Fuller, Bobby, Rock'n'Roll; Surf, 1960s, Artist, American
Funk Brothers, The Classic Soul Era, 1960s-1970s, Artist, American
Funkadelic, Funk; Funk Soul, 1960s-1980s, Artist, American
Gabriel, Juan, Latin, 1960s-, Producer; Artist, Mexican
Gallagher and Lyle, 1960s Pop, 1960s-1970s, Artist; Songwriter, British
Gamble and Huff, Disco, 1960s-1980s, Artist, American
Gandalf, Ambient; Electro, 1960s-1990s, Composer; Artist, Austrian
Gants, The, Folk Rock, 1960s, Artist, American
Gary Lewis and the Playboys, 1960s Pop, 1960s, Artist, American
Gaylads, The, Rock Steady, 1960s-1970s, Artist, Jamaican
Genesis, Prog Rock; 1960s Pop, 1960s-1990s, Artist, British
George, Barbara, The Classic Soul Era, 1960s, Artist, American
Gerry and the Pacemakers, British Invasion; Merseybeat, 1960s; 1980s, Artist, British
Gillespie, Dana, Blues Rock, 1960s-2000s, Artist, British
Gillette, Steve, Young Country, 1960s-, Artist, American
Gilley, Mickey, Urban Cowboys; Honky Tonk, 1960s-1990s, Artist, American
Gismonti, Egberto, Brazilian Jazz; Fusion and Jazz Rock, 1960s-1990s, Artist, Brazilian
Gladys Knight and the Pips, The Classic Soul Era; Urban Soul, 1960s-1970s, Artist, American
Glitter, Gary, Glam Rock & Glitter, 1960s-1990s, Artist, British
Goffin, Gerry, 1960s Pop; Funk Soul, 1960s-1970s; 1990s, Songwriter; Artist, American
Golden Earring, Hard Rock; 1960s Pop, 1960s-2000s, Artist, Dutch
Goldsboro, Bobby, 1960s Pop, 1960s-1970s, Artist, American
Gordy, Berry Jr., The Classic Soul Era, 1960s-1980s, Producer, American
Gore, Lesley, 1960s Pop, 1960s-1970s, Artist, American
Gosdin Brothers, Neo-Traditionalists; Bluegrass, 1960s-1990s, Artist, American
Graham Bond Organisation, Rhythm & Blues; Jazz Rock, 1960s, Artist, British
Graham, Larry, Urban Soul; Funk Soul, 1960s-1990s, Artist, American
Grand Funk Railroad, Hard Rock; Arena Rock, 1960s-1990s, Artist, American
Grass Roots, The, 1960s Pop, 1960s-1970s, Artist, American
Grasso, Francis, Disco, 1960s-1980s, Artist, American
Grateful Dead, The, Psychedelic Rock; Jam Rock; Country Rock; Folk Rock, 1960s-1990s, Artist, American
Gray, Dobie, 1960s Pop; The Classic Soul Era, 1960s-1970s, Artist, American
Great Society, Psychedelic Rock, 1960s-1970s, Artist, American
Greaves, R. B., The Classic Soul Era, 1960s-1970s, Artist, British
Green, Al, Urban Soul, 1960s-, Artist, American
Green, Garland, The Classic Soul Era, 1960s-1970s, Artist, American
Greenbaum, Norman, 1960s Pop, 1960s-1970s, Artist, American
Greenfield, Howard, 1960s Pop, 1960s, Composer, American
Greenwich, Ellie, 1960s Pop, 1960s-1970s, Artist; Songwriter, American
Grennan, Winston, Rock Steady; Ska, 1960s-, Artist, Jamaican
Griffiths, Marcia, Dancehall, 1960s-1990s, Artist, Jamaican
Grodes, The, US Underground & Garage Rock, 1960s, Artist, American
Groundhogs, The, Heavy Metal; Psychedelic Rock; Blues Rock, 1960s-1990s, Artist, British
Grusin, Dave, Fusion, 1960s-, Producer; Composer; Artist, American
Guess Who, The, Hard Rock; 1960s Pop, 1960s-1970s; 1990s, Artist, Canadian
Guitar Junior, Chicago Blues, 1960s, Artist, American
Guthrie, Arlo, Political Folk & Protest Songs; Contemporary Folk; Folk Rock, 1960s-1990s, Artist, American
Guy, Buddy, Modern Electric Blues; Chicago Blues, 1960s-, Artist, American
H. P. Lovecraft, Psychedelic Rock; Folk Rock, 1960s, Artist, American
Haack, Bruce, Electro, 1960s-1980s, Producer; Artist, Canadian
Haggard, Merle, Western Swing; Honky Tonk; Mainstream Country, 1960s-, Artist; Songwriter, American
Hammer, Jan, Fusion, 1960s-, Artist, Czech
Hammond, Albert, 1960s Pop Singer/Songwriters, 1960s-1970s, Artist; Songwriter, British
Hammond, John Jr., Blues Rock; Rhythm & Blues, 1960s-, Artist, American
Hancock, Herbie, Funk; Electro; Hard Bop; Modal Jazz; Fusion, 1960s-, Artist; Composer, American
Hardin, Tim, Folk Rock, 1960s-1970s, Artist; Songwriter, American
Harold Melvin and the Blue Notes, Rhythm & Blues; Doo-Wop; Disco, 1960s-1990s, Artist, American
Harper, Roy, Folk Rock; UK Folk, 1960s-, Artist, British
Harpers Bizarre, 1960s Pop; Wall of Sound, 1960s-1970s, Artist, American
Harris, Eddie, Soul Jazz; Hard Bop, 1960s-1990s, Artist, American
Harris, Emmylou, Folk Rock; Alternative Country; Country Rock; Young Country, 1960s-, Artist, American
Harrison, George, Psychedelic Rock; Folk Rock; Rock'n'Roll; British Invasion; Merseybeat, 1960s-2000s, Artist, British
Hathaway, Donny, Urban Soul, 1960s-1990s, Artist, American
Havens, Richie, Folk Rock, 1960s-, Artist; Songwriter, American
Hayes, Isaac, Funk; Funk Soul, 1960s-, Artist; Songwriter, American
Haywood, Leon, Northern Soul, 1960s-1990s, Artist, American
Hazlewood, Lee, Country Rock; 1960s Pop; Wall of Sound, 1960s-1970s; 1990s-, Producer; Songwriter; Artist, American
Head, Roy, The Classic Soul Era, 1960s-1980s, Artist, American
Hearts and Flowers, Folk Rock; Country Rock, 1960s; 1990s, Artist, American
Helm, Levon, Folk Rock, 1960s-, Artist, American
Helms, Don, Cowboy Music; Honky Tonk, 1960s, Artist, American
Henderson, Joe, Hard Bop, 1960s-1990s, Artist, American
Henderson, Willie, The Classic Soul Era, 1960s-1990s, Artist, American
Hendricks, James, The Classic Soul Era, 1960s-1970s, Artist, American
Hendrix, Jimi, Hard Rock; Psychedelic Rock; Blues Rock, 1960s-1970s, Artist; Songwriter, American
Henry Cow, Jazz Rock, 1960s-1970s, Artist, British
Henske, Judy, The Folk Revival; Folk Rock, 1960s-1970s, Artist, American
Heptones, The, Rock Steady; Roots, 1960s-1990s, Artist, Jamaican
Herd, The, Psychedelic Rock, 1960s-1970s, Artist, British
Herman's Hermits, British Invasion; Merseybeat; 1960s Pop, 1960s-1970s, Artist, British
Hester, Carolyn, Traditional Folk; The Folk Revival; Folk Rock, 1960s-1970s; 1990s, Artist, American
Hicks, Dan, Folk Rock; Jazz Rock, 1960s-2000s, Artist, American
Hicks, Joe, The Classic Soul Era, 1960s-1970s, Artist, American
Highwaymen, The, The Folk Revival; Folk Pop, 1960s, Artist, American
Hill, Z. Z., The Classic Soul Era; Modern Electric Blues, 1960s-1980s, Artist, American
Holiday, Jimmy, Northern Soul, 1960s-1970s, Artist; Songwriter, American
Holland, Eddie, The Classic Soul Era, 1960s-1970s, Songwriter; Artist, American
Holland/Dozier/ Holland, The Classic Soul Era, 1960s-1970s, Producer; Songwriter, American
Hollies, The, British Invasion; Merseybeat; 1960s Pop, 1960s-1980s, Artist, British
Holloway, Brenda, The Classic Soul Era, 1960s, Artist, American
Hollywood Argyles, Doo-Wop, 1960s, Artist, American
Holt, John, Reggae Pop, 1960s-, Artist, Jamaican
Holy Modal Rounders, The, Folk Rock, 1960s-1990s, Artist, American
Honeycombs, The, 1960s Pop; British Invasion, 1960s; 1980s, Artist, British
Honeys, The, Surf; 1960s Pop, 1960s; 1980s-1990s, Artist, American
Hopkin, Mary, Folk Rock; 1960s Pop, 1960s-1970s, Artist, British
Hopkins, Nicky, Rock'n'Roll; Hard Rock; Psychedelic Rock; British Invasion, 1960s-1980s, Artist, British
Houston, Thelma, The Classic Soul Era; Urban Soul; Disco, 1960s-1990s, Artist, American
Hubbard, Freddie, Hard Bop; Fusion, 1960s-, Artist, American
Huff, Leon, Urban Soul, 1960s-1980s, Producer; Artist; Composer; Songwriter, American
Hughes, Jimmy, Northern Soul, 1960s-1970s, Artist, American
Human Beinz, The, US Underground & Garage Rock; Psychedelic Rock, 1960s, Artist, American
Humble Pie, Hard Rock; British Blues; Blues Rock, 1960s-1980s, Artist, British
Hunter, Ian, Hard Rock; Proto-Punk; Glam Rock & Glitter, 1960s-, Artist, British
Hunter, Long John, Modern Electric Blues; Texas Blues, 1960s-1990s, Artist, American
Hussain, Zakir, Fusion and Jazz Rock, 1960s-, Artist, Indian
Hutch, Willie, Urban Soul, 1960s-1980s, Artist, American
Hutcherson, Bobby, Hard Bop, 1960s-, Artist, American
Hutchings, Ashley, Skiffle; UK Folk; Traditional Folk, 1960s-, Artist, British
Hyland, Brian, 1960s Pop, 1960s-1970s, Artist, American
Ian and Sylvia, The Folk Revival; Folk Rock; Folk Pop, 1960s-1970s, Artist, Canadian
Ian, Janis, Folk Rock; Contemporary Folk, 1960s-, Artist, American
Ian, Janis, Folk Rock; Contemporary Folk, 1960s-, Artist, American
Ides Of March, The Classic Soul Era, 1960s-1970s; 1990s-, Artist, American
Idle Race, The, Prog Rock; Psychedelic Rock, 1960s-1970s, Artist, British
Ifield, Frank, Mainstream Country, 1960s, Artist, Australian
Iggy Pop, Hard Rock; Proto-Punk, 1960s-1980s, Artist, American
Incredible String Band, The, Psychedelic Rock; Folk Rock; UK Folk, 1960s-, Artist, British
Incredibles, The, The Classic Soul Era, 1960s, Artist, American
Insect Trust, Folk Rock, 1960s-1970s, Artist, American
International Submarine Band, Country Rock, 1960s, Artist, American
Intrigues, The, The Classic Soul Era, 1960s-1970s, Artist, American
Intruders, The, Northern Soul, 1960s-1970s, Artist, American
Intruders, The, US Underground & Garage Rock, 1960s, Artist, American
Iron Butterfly, Psychedelic Rock; Hard Rock, 1960s-1970s, Artist, American
Irvine, Andy, Irish Folk, 1960s-, Artist, British
It's A Beautiful Day, Folk Rock; 1960s Pop, 1960s-1970s, Artist, American
Jackson 5, The, 1960s Pop; The Classic Soul Era, 1960s-1980s, Artist, American
Jackson, Chuck, 1960s Pop; Rhythm & Blues; Urban Soul, 1960s-1990s, Artist, American
Jackson, Deon, The Classic Soul Era, 1960s, Artist, American
Jackson, George, The Classic Soul Era, 1960s-, Artist, American
Jackson, J. J., The Classic Soul Era, 1960s-1970s, Artist, American
Jackson, Walter, Northern Soul, 1960s-1970s, Artist, American
Jaguars, The, US Underground & Garage Rock; Psychedelic Rock, 1960s, Artist, American
Jamaicans, The, Rock Steady, 1960s-1970s, Artist, Jamaican
James Gang, Arena Rock; Hard Rock, 1960s-1970s, Artist, American
James, Bob, Fusion, 1960s-, Artist, American
James, Jimmy, Northern Soul, 1960s-1990s, Artist, Jamaican
James, Tommy, 1960s Pop, 1960s-, Artist, American
Jansch, Bert, Folk Rock; UK Folk, 1960s-, Artist, British
Jara, Victor, Latin; 1960s Pop Singer/Songwriters; Contemporary Folk, 1960s-1970s, Artist; Songwriter, Chilean
Jarrett, Keith, Fusion, 1960s-, Artist, American
Jay and the Americans, Doo-Wop; 1960s Pop, 1960s-1970s, Artist, American
Jaynetts, The, 1960s Pop, 1960s, Artist, American
Jazz Crusaders, The, Soul Jazz; Acid Jazz, 1960s, Artist, American
JBs, The, Funk; Funk Soul, 1960s-1990s, Artist, American
Jefferson Airplane, Psychedelic Rock; Hard Rock; Folk Rock, 1960s-1980s, Artist, American

see Sources & Sounds pp 78 see UK Rock Key Artists pp 88 see US Rock Key Artists pp 120 see Soul Key Artists pp 154

Jellybeans, The, 1960s Pop, 1960s, Artist, American
Jet Harris and Tony Meehan, 1960s Pop; British Invasion, 1960s, Artist, British
Jethro Tull, Prog Rock; Arena Rock; Hard Rock; Folk Rock, 1960s-, Artist, British
Jim and Jean, The Folk Revival; Folk Rock, 1960s, Artist, American
JK and Co., Folk Rock, 1960s, Artist, American
John's Children, Mod; British Invasion, 1960s, Artist, British
Johnson, Gloria, Northern Soul, 1960s-1980s, Artist, American
Johnson, Larry, Modern Electric Blues, 1960s-1970s, Artist, American
Johnson, Ruby, The Classic Soul Era, 1960s, Artist, American
Johnston, Bruce, Surf; Rock'n'Roll, 1960s-1970s, Artist, American
Jones, Elvin, Hard Bop, 1960s-, Artist, American
Jones, Gloria, Northern Soul, 1960s-1980s, Artist, American
Jones, Linda, The Classic Soul Era, 1960s-1970s, Artist, American
Jones, Paul, British Invasion; British Blues, 1960s, Artist, British
Jones, Tom, 1960s Pop, 1960s-, Artist, British
Joplin, Janis, Blues Rock, 1960s-1970s, Artist, American
Journeymen, The Folk Revival; Contemporary Folk; Folk Pop, 1960s, Artist, American
Junior Walker and the All Stars, The Classic Soul Era, 1960s-1970s, Artist, American
Kaleidoscope, Folk Rock, 1960s-1990s, Artist, American
Kasenetz-Katz, 1960s Pop, 1960s-1970s, Artist, American
K-Doe, Ernie, Rhythm & Blues, 1960s-1990s, Artist; Songwriter, American
Kelly, Jo Ann, British Blues, 1960s-1990s, Artist, British
Kelly, Paul, The Classic Soul Era, 1960s-1990s, Artist, American
Kendricks, Eddie, The Classic Soul Era, 1960s-1980s, Artist, American
Kilgore, Merle, Cowboy Music; Country Rock; Honky Tonk, 1960s-1970s, Artist, American
Kim, Andy, 1960s Pop, 1960s-1970s, Artist, Canadian
Kimbrough, Junior, Modern Electric Blues; Delta/Country Blues; 1960s-1990s, Artist, American
King Crimson, Prog Rock, 1960s-, Artist, British
King Floyd, Funk Soul, 1960s-1970s, Artist, American
King Tubby, Dub, 1960s-1980s, Artist; Producer, Jamaican
King, Albert, Modern Electric Blues; Rhythm & Blues, 1960s-1980s, Artist, American
King, Ben E., 1960s Pop; The Classic Soul Era, 1960s-, Artist, American
King, Carole, 1960s Pop; 1960s Pop Singer/Songwriters; The Classic Soul Era, 1960s-, Artist; Songwriter, American
King, Jonathan, 1960s Pop Singer/Songwriters, 1960s-1980s, Songwriter; Producer, British
Kingsley, Gershon, New Age; Ambient; Electro, 1960s, Producer, American
Kingsmen, The, US Underground & Garage Rock, 1960s, Artist, American
Kinks, The, Hard Rock; Rock'n'Roll; British Invasion, 1960s-1990s, Artist, British
Kirkland, Eddie, Modern Electric Blues, 1960s-1990s, Artist, American
Knight, Curtis, The Classic Soul Era, 1960s-1970s, Artist, Dutch
Knight, Gladys, and the Pips, The Classic Soul Era; Urban Soul, 1960s-1970s, Artist, American
Knight, Gladys, 1960s Pop, 1960s-, Artist, American
Knight, Robert, The Classic Soul Era, 1960s, Artist, American
Kool and the Gang, Funk; Funk Soul; Urban Soul, 1960s-1990s, Artist, American
Kooper, Al, Blues Rock; Folk Rock; Jazz Rock, 1960s-, Artist; Songwriter; Producer, American
Korner, Alexis, British Blues; Blues Rock, 1960s-1980s, Artist, Greek
Kossoff, Paul, Hard Rock; Blues Rock, 1960s-1970s, Artist, British
Kottke, Leo, Contemporary Folk, 1960s-1990s, Artist, American
Kramer, Billy J. , Merseybeat; British Invasion, 1960s, Artist, British
La De Das, The, Alternative/Indie Rock, 1960s-1970s, Artist, New Zealander
LaBelle, Patti, and the Bluebelles, Funk Soul, 1960s-1970s, Artist, American
Lance, Major, 1960s Pop; Northern Soul; Urban Soul, 1960s-1980s, Artist, American
Lane, Ronnie, Psychedelic Rock; British Invasion; Mod; Hard Rock; Proto-Punk, 1960s-1990s, Artist, British
Lavette, Betty, Northern Soul; Urban Soul, 1960s-, Artist, American
Leake, Lafayette, Boogie-Woogie, 1960s, Artist, American
Leaves, The, US Underground & Garage Rock; Folk Rock, 1960s, Artist, American
Led Zeppelin, Hard Rock; British Blues; Blues Rock, 1960s-1980s, Artist, British
Lee, Albert, Neo-Traditionalists; Country Rock, 1960s-, Artist, British
Lee, Byron, Dancehall; Ska, 1960s-, Producer; Artist, Jamaican
Lee, Laura, The Classic Soul Era, 1960s-1970s, Artist, American
Left Banke, The, 1960s Pop; Wall of Sound, 1960s-1970s, Artist, American
Lemon Pipers, The, 1960s Pop, 1960s, Artist, American
Lennon, John, Rock'n'Roll; 1960s Pop Singer/Songwriters, 1960s-1980s, Artist; Songwriter, British
Lewis and Clarke Expedition, Folk Rock, 1960s, Artist, American
Lewis, Barbara, 1960s Pop; Funk Soul, 1960s, Artist, American
Lewis, Gary, 1960s Pop, 1960s, Artist, American
Lightfoot, Gordon, Folk Rock; 1960s Pop Singer/Songwriters, 1960s-, Artist; Songwriter, Canadian
Limeliters, The, Traditional Folk; The Folk Revival; Folk Pop, 1960s-1990s, Artist, American
Lind, Bob, Folk Rock, 1960s, Artist; Songwriter, American
Lindisfarne, UK Folk; Folk Rock, 1960s-, Artist, British
Litter, The, US Underground & Garage Rock; Psychedelic Rock, 1960s-1970s, Artist, American
Little Casesar and the Romans, Doo-Wop, 1960s, Artist, American
Little Eva, 1960s Pop, 1960s-1980s, Artist, American
Littlejohn, John, Chicago Blues; Modern Electric Blues, 1960s-1990s, Artist, American
Littles, Hattie, The Classic Soul Era; Urban Soul, 1960s, Artist, American
Lively Ones, The, Surf, 1960s, Artist, American
Liverbirds, The, Merseybeat, 1960s, Artist, British
Los Mockers, Alternative/Indie Rock, 1960s, Artist, Uruguayan
Love Affair, 1960s Pop, 1960s, Artist, British
Love Sculpture, Blues Rock, 1960s-1970s, Artist, British
Love, Mary, Urban Soul, 1960s-1990s, Artist, American
Love, Psychedelic Rock; US Underground & Garage Rock; 1960s Pop; Wall of Sound; Folk Rock, 1960s-1970s, Artist, American
Lovelites, The, Northern Soul, 1960s-1970s, Artist, American
Lovin' Spoonful, The, Folk Rock; 1960s Pop, 1960s-1970s; 1990s, Artist, American
Lulu, British Invasion; 1960s Pop, 1960s-, Artist, British
Luv'd Ones, US Underground & Garage Rock, 1960s, Artist, American
Lynn, Barbara, Northern Soul; Rhythm & Blues; Modern Electric Blues, 1960s-1990s, Artist, American
Lynn, Loretta, Mainstream Country; Honky Tonk, 1960s-, Artist, American
Lynne, Jeff, 1960s Pop; Prog Rock, 1960s-, Artist; Producer, British
Mack, Lonnie, Modern Electric Blues; Rhythm & Blues, 1960s-, Artist, American
Mad Lion, Dancehall, 1960s-, Artist, American
Magnificent Men, The, The Classic Soul Era, 1960s, Artist, American
Main Ingredient, The, Urban Soul, 1960s-1990s, Artist, American
Makem, Tommy, Irish Folk, 1960s-1990s, Artist, Irish
Mamas and the Papas, The, Folk Rock; 1960s Pop, 1960s, Artist, American
Man, Prog Rock; Hard Rock; 1960s-1990s, Artist, British
Mandrill, Funk Soul, 1960s-1980s, Artist, American
Manfred Mann, British Invasion, 1960s-, Artist, British
Mangione, Chuck, Fusion, 1960s-, Artist, American
Manhattans, The, Northern Soul, 1960s-, Artist, American
Mann, Barry, 1960s Pop, 1960s-, Artist; Songwriter, American
Marcels, The, Doo-Wop, 1960s, Artist, American
Margolin, Bob, Modern Electric Blues, 1960s-, Artist, American
Mar-Keys, The, The Classic Soul Era, 1960s-1970s, Artist, American
Markham, Pigmeat, Northern Soul, 1960s, Artist, American
Marley, Bob, Ska; Roots; Rock Steady, 1960s-1980s, Artist, Jamaican
Marmalade, Psychedelic Rock; 1960s Pop, 1960s-1980s, Artist, British
Martha and the Vandellas, 1960s Pop; The Classic Soul Era, 1960s-1970s, Artist, American
Martyn, John, Folk Rock; UK Folk, 1960s-, Artist; Songwriter, British
Marvelettes, The, 1960s Pop; The Classic Soul Era, 1960s-1970s, Artist, American
Marvelows, The, Doo-Wop; The Classic Soul Era, 1960s, Artist, American
Masekela, Hugh, Fusion and Jazz Rock; Soul Jazz, 1960s-, Artist, South African
Mason Proffit, Folk Rock, 1960s-1970s, Artist, American
Masqueraders, The, The Classic Soul Era, 1960s-1970s, Artist, American
Matthews Southern Comfort, UK Folk; Folk Rock, 1960s-1970s, Artist, British
Matthews, Ian, Folk Rock; UK Folk, 1960s-1990s, Artist; Songwriter, British
Mayall, John, British Blues; Blues Rock, 1960s-, Artist, British
Maze, Folk Rock, 1960s, Artist, American
MC5, Hard Rock; Proto-Punk, 1960s-1970s, Artist, American
McCann, Les, Soul Jazz; Hard Bop, 1960s-, Artist, American
McCartney, Paul, Rock'n'Roll; 1960s Pop, 1960s-, Artist, British
McClinton, Delbert, Blues Rock; Modern Electric Blues; Country Rock, 1960s-, Artist, American
McClure, Bobby, Urban Soul, 1960s-1980s, Artist, American
McCook, Tommy, Ska, 1960s-1990s, Artist, American
McCoy, Freddie, The Classic Soul Era, 1960s-1970s, Artist, American
McCoy, Van, Disco; Funk Soul, 1960s-1970s, Artist; Producer; Songwriter, American
McCoys, The, 1960s Pop; Psychedelic Rock; Prog Rock, 1960s-1970s, Artist, American
McDonald, Country Joe, Folk Rock; Political Folk & Protest Songs, 1960s-1990s, Artist; Songwriter, American
McGregor, Freddie, Dancehall; Dub; Roots; 1960s-, Artist; Composer, Jamaican
McGriff, Jimmy, Soul Jazz; Hard Bop, 1960s-, Artist, American
McGuinn, Roger, Psychedelic Rock; Folk Rock; Country Rock, 1960s-, Artist, American
McGuire, Barry, Folk Rock, 1960s-1980s, Artist; Songwriter, American
McKay, Freddie, Rock Steady; Ska, 1960s-1980s, Artist, Jamaican
McKenzie, Scott, Folk Rock, 1960s-1970s, Artist, American
McLaughlin, John, Fusion; Fusion and Jazz Rock, 1960s-, Artist, British
McNair, Barbara, The Classic Soul Era, 1960s, Artist, American
McTell, Ralph, UK Folk, 1960s-, Artist; Songwriter, British
Medicine Head, British Blues, 1960s-1970s; 1990s, Artist, British
Medley, Bill, The Classic Soul Era, 1960s-1990s, Artist, American
Meek, Joe, 1960s Pop, 1960s, Artist, British
Mel and Tim, Northern Soul, 1960s-1970s, Artist, American
Melanie, 1960s Pop; 1960s Pop Singer/Songwriters; Folk Pop, 1960s-, Artist; Songwriter, American
Melodians, The, 1960s-1970s; 1990s, Artist, American,
Memphis Horns, The, Funk Soul; Urban Soul, 1960s-1990s, Artist, American
Meriweather, Roy, The Classic Soul Era, 1960s-, Artist, American
Merry-Go-Round, The, 1960s Pop, 1960s, Artist, American
Merseybeats, The, Merseybeat; British Invasion, 1960s; 1980s, Artist, British
Messina, Jim, Folk Rock, 1960s-1990s, Artist, American
Meters, The, Funk; Funk Soul; Urban Soul; Rhythm & Blues, 1960s-1990s, Artist, American
Mighty Marvelows, The, The Classic Soul Era, 1960s, Artist, American
Miles, Buddy, Blues Rock; Psychedelic Rock; Hard Rock, 1960s-1990s, Artist, American
Millennium, The, 1960s Pop, 1960s, Artist, American
Miller, Steve, Arena Rock; 1960s Pop, 1960s-1990s, Artist; Songwriter, American
Mindbenders, The, Merseybeat; British Invasion, 1960s, Artist, British
Misunderstood, The, US Underground & Garage Rock , 1960s, Artist, American
Mitchell, Joni, Folk Rock, 1960s-, Artist; Songwriter, Canadian
Mitchell, Willie, Northern Soul, 1960s-1980s, Artist, American
Mittoo, Jackie, Ska; Reggae Pop; Rock Steady, 1960s-1980s, Artist, Jamaican
Moby Grape, Psychedelic Rock; Folk Rock, 1960s-1980s, Artist, American
Mojo Men, The, US Underground & Garage Rock; Psychedelic Rock, 1960s, Artist, American
Moments, The, The Classic Soul Era, 1960s-1970s, Artist, American
Money, Zoot, Rock'n'Roll; Psychedelic Rock, 1960s-, Artist, British
Monitors, The, The Classic Soul Era, 1960s, Artist, American
Monkees, The, 1960s Pop, 1960s-1990s, Artist, American
Monks, The, US Underground & Garage Rock, 1960s, Artist, American
Montez, Chris, Rock'n'Roll, 1960s, Artist, American
Moody Blues, The, Prog Rock; British Invasion; Rock'n'Roll, 1960s-, Artist, British
Mooney, Ralph, Honky Tonk, 1960s, Artist, American
Moore, Christy, Irish Folk, 1960s-, Artist; Songwriter, Irish
Moore, Melba, The Classic Soul Era, 1960s-, Artist, American
Moroder, Giorgio, Disco; Urban Soul, 1960s-, Producer; Composer; Artist, Italian
Morrison, Van, Folk Rock; Jazz Rock; 1960s Pop; The Classic Soul Era, 1960s-, Artist; Songwriter, British
Mothers Of Invention, Rhythm & Blues; Doo-Wop; Blues Rock, 1960s-1990s, Artist, American
Mott the Hoople, Hard Rock; Proto-Punk; Glam Rock & Glitter, 1960s-1970s, Artist, British
Mountain, Hard Rock, 1960s-1990s, Artist, American
Mouse and The Traps, US Underground & Garage Rock; Psychedelic Rock, 1960s, Artist, American
Move, The, Prog Rock; Rock'n'Roll; British Invasion, 1960s-1970s, Artist, British
Mowatt, Judy, Roots, 1960s-, Artist, Jamaican
Mud, Glam Rock & Glitter, 1960s-1980s, Artist, British
Mugwumps, Folk Rock, 1960s, Artist, American
Murray, Anne, Country Rock, 1960s-, Artist, Canadian
Murvin, Junior, Roots, 1960s-, Artist, Jamaican
Music Explosion, 1960s Pop, 1960s, Artist, American
Musselwhite, Charlie, Modern Electric Blues, 1960s-, Artist, American
Nashville Teens, The, British Invasion; Rock'n'Roll, 1960s-1980s, Artist, British
Natural Four, The, Northern Soul; Urban Soul, 1960s-1970s, Artist, American
Neil, Fred, Folk Rock, 1960s-1970s, Artist; Songwriter, American
Nelson, Sandy, Rock'n'Roll, 1960s-1970s, Artist, American
Neon Philharmonic, The, 1960s Pop, 1960s, Artist, American
Nero, Frances, Northern Soul; The Classic Soul Era; Urban Soul, 1960s-1990s, Artist, American
Nesmith, Michael, Folk Rock; Country Rock, 1960s-, Artist; Songwriter, American
Neville Brothers, The, Funk; The Classic Soul Era; Rhythm & Blues, 1960s-, Artist, American
Neville, Aaron, 1960s Pop; The Classic Soul Era; Rhythm & Blues, 1960s-, Artist, American
New Birth, Funk Soul, 1960s-1970s, Artist, American
New Christy Minstrels, The, The Folk Revival; Folk Pop, 1960s-1970s, Artist, American
New Colony Six, US Underground & Garage Rock, 1960s, Artist, American
New Riders Of The Purple Sage, The, Country Rock, 1960s-1990s, Artist, American
Newcomers, The, The Classic Soul Era, 1960s-1970s, Artist, American
Newman, Randy, 1960s Pop Singer/Songwriters, 1960s-, Artist; Songwriter, American
Nice, The, Prog Rock, 1960s-1970s, Artist, British
Nichtcrawlers, The, US Underground & Garage Rock; Folk Rock, 1960s, Artist, American
Nico, Folk Rock; Prog Rock; Alternative/Indie Rock, 1960s-1980s, Artist, German
Nilsson, Harry, 1960s Pop; 1960s Pop Singer/Songwriters, 1960s-1990s, Artist; Songwriter, American
Niney The Observer, Dancehall; Dub, 1960s-1990s, Artist, Jamaican
Nirvana (UK), Prog Rock; Psychedelic Rock, 1960s-1990s, Artist, British
Nitty Gritty Dirt Band, Country Rock; Bluegrass, 1960s-, Artist, American
Nobles, Cliff, The Classic Soul Era, 1960s, Artist, American
Notations, The, Northern Soul, 1960s-1970s, Artist, American
NRBQ, Rock'n'Roll, 1960s-, Artist, American
Nugent, Ted, Arena Rock; Hard Rock, 1960s-, Artist, American
Numbers Band, The, Blues Rock, 1960s-1990s, Artist, American
Nyro, Laura, 1960s Pop; 1960s Pop Singer/Songwriters, 1960s-1990s, Artist; Songwriter, American
O'Jays, The, 1960s Pop; Disco; Funk; Urban Soul, 1960s-, Artist, American
Ochs, Phil, Political Folk & Protest Songs; Folk Rock, 1960s-1970s, Artist; Songwriter, American
Ohio Express, 1960s Pop, 1960s, Artist, American
Ohio Players, The, Funk; Funk Soul; Urban Soul, 1960s-1990s, Artist, American
Ollie and the Nightingales, The Classic Soul Era, 1960s-1970s, Artist, American
Olympics, The, The Classic Soul Era; Rhythm & Blues, 1950s-1960s, Artist, British
Originals, The, The Classic Soul Era; Urban Soul, 1960s-1980s, Artist, American
Osmonds, The, 1960s Pop, 1960s-1970s, Artist, American
Otis, Shuggie, Funk Soul, 1960s-1970s, Producer; Artist, American
Outcasts, The, US Underground & Garage Rock, 1960s, Artist, American
Outsiders, The, Psychedelic Rock, 1960s, Artist, Dutch
Ovations, The, The Classic Soul Era, 1960s-1970s, Artist, American
Owens, Bonnie, Honky Tonk, 1960s-1970s, Artist, American
Paragons, The, Rock Steady; Dub, 1960s-1980s, Artist, Jamaican
Parks, Van Dyke, 1960s Pop; Wall of Sound, 1960s-1990s, Artist; Producer, American
Parlan, Horace, Hard Bop, 1960s-, Artist, American
Parsons, Gram, Country Rock, 1960s-1970s, Artist, American
Parton, Dolly, Mainstream Country; Honky Tonk; Young Country, 1960s-, Artist; Songwriter, American
Partridge Family, The, 1960s Pop, 1960s-1970s, Artist, American
Patterson, Bobby, Northern Soul, 1960s-1990s, Artist, American
Patterson, Don, Soul Jazz; Hard Bop, 1960s-1970s, Artist, American
Patton, Big John, Soul Jazz; Hard Bop, 1960s-1990s, Artist, American
Paul Revere and the Raiders, Rock'n'Roll; 1960s Pop, 1960s, Artist, American
Paul Revere and the Raiders, US Underground & Garage Rock, 1960s-1990s, Artist, American
Paxton, Tom, The Folk Revival, 1960s-, Artist; Songwriter, American
Paycheck, Johnny, The Outlaw Movement; Honky Tonk, 1960s-, Artist, American
Payne, Freda, Urban Soul, 1960s-, Artist, American
Peaches and Herb, The Classic Soul Era, 1960s-1990s, Artist, American
Pearls Before Swine, Psychedelic Rock; Folk Rock, 1960s-1970s, Artist, American
Pedersen, Niels-Henning Orsted, Bebop; Hard Bop, 1960s-1990s, Artist, Danish
Peebles, Ann, The Classic Soul Era; Urban Soul, 1960s-1990s, Artist, American
Pena, Ralph, Cool Jazz; Bebop, 1960s, Artist, American
Pentangle, Folk Rock; UK Folk, 1960s-1990s, Artist, British
Perry, Lee 'Scratch', Dub; Roots; Rock Steady, 1960s-, Artist; Producer, Jamaican
Person, Houston, Soul Jazz; Hard Bop; Swing, 1960s-, Artist, American
Persuaders, The, Urban Soul, 1960s-1980s, Artist, American
Peter and Gordon, British Invasion; Merseybeat; 1960s Pop, 1960s, Artist, British
Peter Paul and Mary, Traditional Folk; The Folk Revival; Folk Pop, 1960s-1990s, Artist, American
Phillips, Utah, Traditional Folk; Political Folk & Protest Songs, 1960s-1990s, Artist, American
Piazza, Rod, Jump Blues; Modern Electric Blues, 1960s-, Artist, American
Pickett, Bobby 'Boris', Novelty Songs, 1960s, Artist, American
Pickett, Wilson; The Classic Soul Era, 1960s-1990s, Artist, American
Pink Floyd, Psychedelic Rock; Prog Rock; British Invasion, 1960s-, Artist, British
Pioneers, The, Rock Steady; Roots, 1960s-1970s, Artist, Jamaican
Pitney, Gene, 1960s Pop, 1960s-1980s, Artist, American
Pixies Three, The, 1960s Pop, 1960s, Artist, American
Plant, Robert, Hard Rock; British Blues; Blues Rock, 1960s-, Artist, British
Pleasure Seekers, US Underground & Garage Rock, 1960s, Artist, American
Poco, Prog Rock; Country Rock, 1960s-1990s, Artist, American
Poets, The, British Blues, 1960s-1970s, Artist, British
Ponder, Jimmy, Soul Jazz; Hard Bop, 1960s-, Artist, American
Ponty, Jean-Luc, Fusion, 1960s-, Artist, American
Porter, David, The Classic Soul Era, 1960s-1970s, Producer, American
Powell, Bobby, The Classic Soul Era, 1960s-1970s, Artist, American
Pozo-Seco Singers, The, Folk Pop, 1960s-1970s, Artist, American
Preston, Billy, The Classic Soul Era, 1960s-, Artist, American
Pretty Things, The, Psychedelic Rock; Prog Rock; Hard Rock; Rock'n'Roll; British Invasion, 1960s-, Artist, British
Price, Alan, Rock'n'Roll; British Invasion; British Blues; Blues Rock, 1960s-, Artist, British
Prince Buster, Ska; Rock Steady, 1960s-1990s, Artist, Jamaican
Proby, P.J., British Inavsion, 1960s-1990s, Artist, American
Procol Harum, Psychedelic Rock; Prog Rock, 1960s-1990s, Artist, British
Puckett, Gary, 1960s Pop, 1960s-1970s; 1990s-, Artist, American
Purify, James and Bobby, 1960s Pop, 1960s-1970s, Artist, American
Quicksilver Messenger Service, Psychedelic Rock, 1960s-1990s, Artist, American
Raindrops, The, 1960s Pop; Doo-Wop; Rock'n'Roll, 1960s, Artist, American
Raparata and the Delrons, 1960s Pop, 1960s-1970s, Artist, American
Rare Earth, The Classic Soul Era, 1960s-1970s, Artist, American
Rascals, The, 1960s Pop; The Classic Soul Era, 1960s-1970s, Artist, American
Rationals, The, US Underground & Garage Rock, 1960s-1970s, Artist, American
Rawls, Lou, Urban Soul; The Classic Soul Era, 1960s-, Artist, American
Red Krayola, The, Psychedelic Rock; Prog Rock, 1960s-, Artist, American
Redding, Otis, The Classical Soul Era, 1960s, Artist, American
Reed, Wayman, Hard Bop, 1960s-1980s, Artist, American
Reeves, Martha, The Classic Soul Era, 1960s-1980s; 2000s, Artist, American
Reid, Terry, Hard Rock, 1960s-1990s, Artist; Songwriter, British
Renaissance, Prog Rock, 1960s-, Artist, British
Renay, Diane, 1960s Pop, 1960s, Artist, American
Reynolds, L. J., Urban Soul, 1960s-1990s, Artist, American
Rico, Ska, 1960s-1990s, Artist, Jamaican
Righteous Brothers, The, 1960s Pop; The Classic Soul Era, 1960s-1990s, Artist, American
Rip-Chords, The, Surf; Rockabilly, 1960s, Artist, American
Riperton, Minnie, Northern Soul, 1960s-1970s, Artist, American
Rising Storm, The, US Underground & Garage Rock, 1960s; 1980s, Artist, American
Rising Sun, Folk Rock, 1960s, Artist, American
Rivers, Johnny, 1960s Pop, 1960s-, Artist, American
Rivieras, The, US Underground & Garage Rock, 1960s, Artist, American
Robbins, Hargus 'Pig', Western Swing; The Nashville Sound; Country Rock, 1960s-1990s, Artist, American
Roe, Tommy, 1960s Pop, 1960s-1970s, Artist, American
Rogers, Kenny, Mainstream Country, 1960s-, Artist, American
Rolling Stones, The, Hard Rock; Psychedelic Rock; Rock'n'Roll; British Invasion; Blues Rock, 1960s-, Artist, British
Ronettes, The, 1960s Pop; The Classic Soul Era, 1960s, Artist, American
Ronstadt, Linda, Country Rock; Folk Rock; 1960s Pop, 1960s-, Artist, American
Rose, Tim, Folk Rock; Contemporary Folk, 1960s-1990s, Artist; Songwriter, British
Rosie and the Originals, Rock'n'Roll; 1960s Pop, 1960s, Artist, American
Ross, Diana, 1960s Pop; Disco; The Classic Soul Era; Urban Soul, 1960s-, Artist, American
Ross, Jackie, Northern Soul, 1960s, Artist, American
Rotary Connection, Psychedelic Rock, 1960s-1970s, Artist, American
Roy-C, Urban Soul, 1960s-1990s, Artist, American
Ruby and the Romantics, The Classic Soul Era, 1960s, Artist, American
Ruffin, David, The Classic Soul Era; Urban Soul, 1960s-1980s, Artist, American
Ruffin, Jimmy, The Classic Soul Era; Urban Soul, 1960s-1980s, Artist, American
Rush, Tom, Traditional Folk, 1960s-, Artist; Songwriter, American
Russell, Leon, Rock'n'Roll; 1960s Pop; US Underground & Garage Rock, 1960s-2000s, Artist; Songwriter, American
Ryan, Paul and Barry, 1960s Pop, 1960s, Artist, British
Ryder, Mitch, Rock'n'Roll; The Classic Soul Era, 1960s-, Artist, American
Ryder, Mitch, The Classic Soul Era, 1960s-, Artist, American
Sagittarius, 1960s Pop; Wall of Sound, 1960s, Artist, American
Sain, Oliver, The Classic Soul Era, 1960s-1980s, Artist, American
Saint John, Bridget, Folk Rock, 1960s-1970s, Artist, British
Sainte-Marie, Buffy, Folk Rock; Contemporary Folk; Folk Pop, 1960s-, Artist; Songwriter, Canadian
Sallyangie, The, UK Folk; Folk Rock, 1960s, Artist, British
Sam and Dave, The Classic Soul Era, 1960s-1970s, Artist, American
Sam the Sham and the Pharaohs, Rock'n'Roll, 1960s-1970s, Artist, British
Sample, Joe, Hard Bop; Fusion; Soul Jazz, 1960s-, Artist, American
Samson, Prog Rock, 1960s-1970s, Artist, British
Sanders, Pharaoh, Free Jazz; Hard Bop, 1960s-, Artist, American
Sandpipers, The, The Folk Revival; Folk Pop, 1960s-1970s, Artist, American
Sands, Tommy, Political Folk & Protest Songs; Irish Folk, 1960s-, Artist, Irish
Santana, Hard Rock; Psychedelic Rock; Blues Rock, 1960s-, Artist, American
Savoy Brown, Blues Rock; British Blues, 1960s-, Artist, British
Scaggs, Boz, 1960s Pop, 1960s-, Artist, American
Schulze, Klaus, Krautrock; Electro, 1960s-1990s, Artist, German
Scott, Freddie, Northern Soul, 1960s-1970s, Artist, American
Scott-Adams, Peggy, Modern Electric Blues, 1960s-1970s, Artist, American
Scott-Heron, Gil, Funk Soul; Urban Soul, 1960s-, Artist, American
Screaming Lord Such, Rock'n'Roll, 1960s-1980s, Artist, British
Searchers, The, British Invasion; Merseybeat; Folk Rock, 1960s-, Artist, British
Seeds, The, Psychedelic Rock, 1960s-1970s, Artist, American
Seekers, The, Folk Rock; 1960s Pop, 1960s-1970s, Artist, Australian
Seger, Bob, Hard Rock; Rock'n'Roll; 1960s Pop Singer/Songwriters, 1960s-1990s, Artist; Songwriter, American
Serendipity Singers, Folk Pop; The Folk Revival, 1960s, Artist, American
Sha Na Na, Novelty Songs, 1960s-, Artist, American
Shadows Of Knight, US Underground & Garage Rock, 1960s, Artist, American
Shadows, The, 1960s Pop; British Invasion, 1960s-, Artist, British
Shangri-Las, The, 1960s Pop; Rock'n'Roll, 1960s, Artist, American
Shannon, Del, 1960s Pop; Rock'n'Roll, 1960s-1980s, Artist, American
Shapiro, Helen, 1960s Pop, 1960s, Artist, British
Sharp, Dee Dee, The Classic Soul Era, 1960s-1980s, Artist, American
Shaw, Sandie, British Invasion; 1960s Pop, 1960s-1980s, Artist, British
Shaw, Woody, Hard Bop, 1960s-1980s, Artist, American
Shep and the Limelites, Doo-Wop, 1960s, Artist, American
Shepp, Archie, Free Jazz; Hard Bop, 1960s-, Artist, American
Sheridan, Tony, Rock'n'Roll, 1960s, Artist; Songwriter, British
Sherman, Bobby, 1960s Pop, 1960s-1970s, Artist, American
Shines, Johnny, Delta/Country Blues; Chicago Blues, 1960s-1990s, Artist, American
Shirley, Roy, Rock Steady; Ska, 1960s-1980s, Artist; Composer, Jamaican
Shocking Blue, 1960s Pop, 1960s-1970s, Artist, German
Showmen, The, Northern Soul; Rhythm & Blues, 1960s, Artist, American
Siegel-Schwall Band, Modern Electric Blues, 1960s-1980s, Artist, American
Silver Apples, Proto-Punk; Electro, 1960s; 1990s, Artist, American
Simon and Garfunkel, Folk Rock; 1960s Pop, 1960s-1980s, Artist, American
Simon, Joe, The Classic Soul Era, 1960s-1990s, Artist, American
Simon, Paul, Folk Rock; 1960s Pop Singer/Songwriters, 1960s-, Songwriter; Artist, American
Sinatra, Nancy, 1960s Pop, 1960s-1970s; 1990s, Artist, American
Sir Douglas Quintet, The, Rock'n'Roll, 1960s-1990s, Artist, American
Skatalites, The, Ska; Rock Steady, 1960s-, Artist, Jamaican
Skip Bifferty, Psychedelic Rock, 1960s Pop, 1960s, Artist, British
Sky, Patrick, Irish Folk, 1960s-1990s, Artist, American
Slade, Glam Rock & Glitter, 1960s-1990s, Artist, British
Sledge, Percy, The Classic Soul Era, 1960s-1990s, Artist, American
Sloan, P. F. , Folk Rock; 1960s Pop; 1960s Pop Singer/Songwriters, 1960s-1990s, Artist; Songwriter, American
Sly and the Family Stone, Funk; Funk Soul, 1960s-1980s, Artist, American
Small Faces, The, Psychedelic Rock; British Invasion; Mod, 1960s-1970s, Artist, British
Smith, Lonnie, Soul Jazz; Hard Bop, 1960s-, Artist, American
Smith, Slim, Ska, 1960s-1970s, Artist, Jamaican
Smoke, The, Psychedelic Rock; Mod; British Invasion, 1960s, Artist, British
Soft Machine, The, Psychedelic Rock; Prog Rock; Jazz Rock, 1960s-1990s, Artist, British
Sonics, The, US Underground & Garage Rock; Rock'n'Roll, 1960s, Artist, American
Sonny and Cher, Folk Rock; 1960s Pop, 1960s-1970s, Artist, American
Sopwith Camel, The, 1960s Pop, 1960s-1970s, Artist, American
Sorrows, The, Mod; British Invasion, 1960s, Artist, British
Soul Children, The, The Classic Soul Era, 1960s-1970s, Artist, American
Soul Survivors, The, The Classic Soul Era, 1960s-1970s, Artist, American
Spanky and Our Gang, 1960s Pop, 1960s-1970s, Artist, American
Spector, Phil, Rock'n'Roll; 1960s Pop; The Classic Soul Era, 1960s-1970s, Producer; Songwriter; Artist, American
Spellman, Benny, Rhythm & Blues, 1960s, Artist, American
Spence, Skip, Psychedelic Rock; Folk Rock, 1960s, Artist; Songwriter, American
Spencer David Group, The, British Invasion, 1960s-1990s, Artist, British
Spinners, The, Funk Soul, 1960s-1990s, Artist, American
Spirit, Psychedelic Rock; Prog Rock, 1960s-1990s, Artist, American
Spooky Tooth, Prog Rock; Hard Rock, 1960s-1970s, Artist, British
Spotnicks, The, Rock'n'Roll; Easy Listening, 1960s-1990s, Artist, Swedish
Springfield, Dusty, British Invasion; Urban Soul, 1960s-1990s, Artist, British
Springfield, Rick, 1960s Pop, 1960s-1990s, Artist, Australian
Springfields, The Folk Revival; Folk Pop; Traditional Folk, 1960s, Artist, British
Standells, The, US Underground & Garage Rock, 1960s, Artist, American
Staples, Mavis, Urban Soul, 1960s-1990s, Artist, American
Stardust, Alvin, Glam Rock & Glitter; 1980s Pop, 1960s-1980s, Artist, British
Starr, Edwin, 1960s Pop; The Classic Soul Era; Northern Soul, 1960s-1980s, Artist, American
Starr, Ringo, Rock'n'Roll; British Invasion; Merseybeat, 1960s-, Artist, British
Staton, Candi, Urban Soul, 1960s-, Artist, American
Status Quo, Psychedelic Rock; Hard Rock, 1960s-, Artist, British
Steampacket, Mod; British Invasion; British Blues, 1960s, Artist, British
Steppenwolf, Hard Rock; Psychedelic Rock, 1960s-1990s, Artist, American
Steve Miller Band, The, Blues Rock; Psychedelic Rock, 1960s-1980s, Artist, American
Stevens, Cat, 1960s Pop; 1960s Pop Singer/Songwriters, 1960s-, Artist; Songwriter, British
Stevens, Shakin', Rock'n'Roll; Rockabilly; 1980s Pop, 1960s-1990s, Artist, British
Stewart, Al, Folk Rock; UK Folk; 1960s Pop Singer/Songwriters, 1960s-, Artist; Songwriter, British
Stewart, John, Folk Rock; Contemporary Folk, 1960s-, Artist; Songwriter, American
Stewart, Rod, Hard Rock; Arena Rock; Folk Rock; Rock'n'Roll; 1960s Pop Singer/Songwriters; The Classic Soul Era, 1960s-, Artist; Songwriter, British
Stillroven, The, US Underground & Garage Rock; Prog Rock, 1960s, Artist, American
Stills, Stephen, Folk Rock; 1960s Pop Singer/Songwriters, 1960s-1990s, Artist; Songwriter, American
Stone Poneys, Folk Rock; 1960s Pop, 1960s-1970s, Artist, American
Stooges, The, Hard Rock; Proto-Punk, 1960s-1970s, Artist, American
Strawberry Alarm Clock, 1960s Pop, 1960s-1970s, Artist, American
Strawbs, The, Prog Rock; Folk Rock; UK Folk, 1960s-1980s, Artist, British
Streisand, Barbra, 1960s Pop, 1960s-, Artist, American
Strong, Barrett, The Classic Soul Era, 1960s-1990s, Artist, American
Sunshine Company, 1960s Pop, 1960s, Artist, American
Supremes, The, 1960s Pop; The Classic Soul Era, 1960s-1970s, Artist, American
Surfaris, The, Surf, 1960s-1970s, Artist, American
Swann, Bettye, The Classic Soul Era, 1960s-1970s, Artist, American
Sweet Inspirations, The, The Classic Soul Era, 1960s-1970s, Artist, American
Sweet Thursday, Folk Rock, 1960s, Artist, American
Swinging Blue Jeans, The, British Invasion; Merseybeat, 1960s-1970s, Artist, British
Sylvia, Disco; Urban Soul, 1960s-1980s, Producer; Songwriter; Artist, American
Syndicate Of Sound, US Underground & Garage Rock, 1960s, Artist, American
T Rex, Glam Rock & Glitter, 1960s-1970s, Artist, British
Tages, The, Mod; Rock'n'Roll, 1960s, Artist, Swedish
Taj Mahal, Blues Rock, 1960s-, Artist, American
Tams, The, Northern Soul, 1960s, Artist, American
Tangerine Dream, Prog Rock; Krautrock; Ambient; Electro, 1960s-, Artist, German
Taste, Blues Rock; British Blues, 1960s-1970s, Artist, Irish
Tate, Howard, Northern Soul, 1960s-1980s, Artist, American
Tavares, Disco, 1960s-, Artist, American
Taylor, Bobby, The Classic Soul Era, 1960s-1970s, Artist, Canadian
Taylor, Hound Dog, Chicago Blues, 1960s-1970s, Artist, American
Taylor, James, Urban Soul; 1960s Pop Singer/Songwriters, 1960s-, Artist, American
Taylor, Koko, Modern Electric Blues; Chicago Blues; Rhythm & Blues, 1960s-, Artist, American
Taylor, Little Johnny, The Classic Soul Era, 1960s-1990s, Artist, American
Temptations, The, 1960s Pop; Disco; The Classic Soul Era, 1960s-1990s, Artist, American
Ten Years After, British Blues; Blues Rock, 1960s-1990s, Artist, British
Terrell, Jean, The Classic Soul Era, 1960s-1970s, Artist, American
Terrell, Tammi, The Classic Soul Era, 1960s, Artist, American
Tex, Joe, Funk; Funk Soul, 1960s-1980s, Artist, American
Thee Midniters, US Underground & Garage Rock, 1960s, Artist, American
Them, British Blues; Blues Rock, 1960s, Artist, British
Thomas, B. J., Country Rock, 1960s-1990s, Artist, American
Thomas, Carla, The Classic Soul Era, 1960s-1970s, Artist, American
Thomas, Irma, The Classic Soul Era Rhythm & Blues, 1960s-, Artist, American
Thomas, Rufus, The Classic Soul Era, 1960s-1970s, Artist, American
Thompson, Linda, UK Folk; Folk Rock, 1960s-, Artist; Songwriter, British
Thompson, Richard, Folk Rock; UK Folk, 1960s-1990s, Artist; Songwriter, British
Three Degress, The, The Classic Soul Era; Urban Soul, 1960s-1980s, Artist, American
Three Dog Night, 1960s Pop, 1960s-1980s, Artist, American
Thunderclap Newman, 1960s Pop, 1960s, Artist, British
Tintern Abbey, Psychedelic Rock, 1960s, Artist, British
Tippett, Keith and Julie, Free Jazz; Fusion, 1960s-1990s, Artist, British
Tokens, The, Doo-Wop, 1960s-1970s; 1990s, Artist, American
Tolliver, Charles, Hard Bop, 1960s-1980s, Artist, American
Tom and Jerry, Folk Rock, 1960s, Artist, American
Tommy James and the Shondells, 1960s Pop; Rock'n'Roll, 1960s-1970s, Artist, American
Tomorrow, Psychedelic Rock; 1960s Pop, 1960s, Artist, British
Toots and the Maytals, Rock Steady; Ska, 1960s-1990s, Artist, Jamaican
Tornados, The, Surf; Rock'n'Roll, 1960s; 1990s, Artist, American
Tosh, Peter, Roots, 1960s-1980s, Artist, Jamaican
Townshend, Pete, Hard Rock; Prog Rock, 1960s-, Artist; Songwriter, British
Toys, The, 1960s Pop, 1960s, Artist, American
Traffic, Psychedelic Rock; Prog Rock, 1960s-1970s; 1990s, Artist, British
Trammps, The, Disco; Funk Soul, 1960s-1970s, Artist, American
Tramp, British Blues, 1960s-1970s, Artist, British
Trashmen, The, Rock'n'Roll; Surf, 1960s; 1990s, Artist, American
Tremeloes, The, British Invasion; Rock'n'Roll, 1960s-1980s, Artist, British
Troggs, The, British Invasion; Rock'n'Roll, 1960s-1980s; 1990s, Artist, British
Troy, Doris, Funk Soul, 1960s-1970s, Artist, American
Turner, Ike and Tina, The Classic Soul Era, 1960s-1970s, Artist, American
Turner, Spyder, The Classic Soul Era, 1960s-1970s, Artist, American
Turner, Tina, 1980s Pop; Rhythm & Blues, 1960s-, Artist, American
Turrentine, Stanley, Hard Bop; Fusion, 1960s-1990s, Artist, American
Turtles, The, Folk Rock; 1960s Pop, 1960s, Artist, American
Twice As Much, British Blues, 1960s, Artist, British
Twinkle, British Invasion, 1960s-1970s, Artist, British
Tyner, McCoy, Hard Bop, 1960s-, Artist, American
Undertakers, The, Merseybeat; British Invasion; Rock'n'Roll, 1960s, Artist, British
Uniques, The, The Classic Soul Era, 1960s, Artist, American
United States Of American, The, Psychedelic Rock, 1960s, Artist, American
Unrelated Segments, US Underground & Garage Rock, 1960s, Artist, American
Upsetters, The, Dub; Roots, 1960s-1980s, Artist, Jamaican
U-Roy, Roots; Dub, 1960s-, Artist, Jamaican
Usher, Gary, Surf, 1960s-1970s, Producer; Songwriter; Artist, American
Valentinos, The, Rhythm & Blues, 1960s, Artist, American
Valli, Frankie, 1960s Pop; Disco, 1960s-1970s, Artist, American
Van Der Graf Generator, Prog Rock, 1960s-1970s, Artist, British
Van Dykes, The, The Classic Soul Era, 1960s, Artist, American
Van Zandt, Townes, Alternative Country, 1960s-1990s, Artist; Songwriter, American
Vanilla Fudge, Psychedelic Rock; Hard Rock, 1960s-1980s, Artist, American
Vejtables, The, Folk Rock, 1960s, Artist, American
Velvelettes, The, The Classic Soul Era, 1960s, Artist, American
Velvet Underground, The, Proto-Punk; Rock'n'Roll, 1960s-1970s; 1990s, Artist, American
Velvets, The, Doo-Wop, 1960s, Artist, American
Ventures, The, Surf; Rock'n'Roll, 1960s-, Artist, American
Viceroys, The, Dub, 1960s-1990s, Artist, Jamaican
Vick, Harold, Soul Jazz; Hard Bop, 1960s-1980s, Artist, American
Wailers, The, Rock Steady, 1960s-1990s, Artist, Jamaican
Walker Brothers, The, British Invasion; 1960s Pop, 1960s-1970s, Artist, British
Walker, Cindy, Young Country, 1960s, Artist, American
Walker, Junior, Rhythm & Blues; The Classic Soul Era, 1960s-1980s, Artist, American
Walker, Scott, Alternative/Indie Rock; 1960s Pop; Wall of Sound 1960s-1990s, Artist, American
Wallace Brothers, The, Funk Soul, 1960s, Artist, American
Warwick, Dee Dee, The Classic Soul Era, 1960s-1970s, Artist, American
Warwick, Dionne, 1960s Pop; The Classic Soul Era, 1960s-, Artist, American
Washington, Albert, The Classic Soul Era, 1960s-1990s, Artist; Songwriter, American
Washington, Ella, The Classic Soul Era, 1960s-1970s, Artist, American
Washington, Geno, Northern Soul, 1960s-, Artist, American
Washington, Leroy, Chicago Blues, 1960s, Artist, American
Waters, Roger, Prog Rock; Psychedelic Rock; Folk Rock, 1960s-, Artist, British
Watrous, Bill, Bebop, 1960s-, Artist, American
Watts 103rd Street Rhythm Band, Funk; Funk Soul, 1960s-1970s, Artist, American
Wayfarers Trio, The Folk Revival; Folk Pop, 1960s, Artist, American
We Five, Folk Rock, 1960s, Artist, American
We The People, US Underground & Garage Rock; Psychedelic Rock, 1960s-1970s, Artist, American
Webb, Jimmy, 1960s Pop Singer/Songwriters; 1960s Pop, 1960s-, Artist; Songwriter, American
Webster, Katie, Rhythm & Blues, 1960s; 1980s-1990s, Artist, American
Weil, Cynthia, 1960s Pop, 1960s-, Artist, American
Wells, Mary, 1960s Pop; The Classic Soul Era, 1960s-1980s, Artist, American
Wesley, Fred, Funk Soul, 1960s-1990s, Artist; Songwriter, American
Weston, Kim, The Classic Soul Era, 1960s-, Artist, American
Wet Willie, Southern Rock, 1960s-, Artist; American
Wexler, Jerry, The Classic Soul Era, 1960s-, Producer, American
Whispers, The, Urban Soul, 1960s-1990s, Artist, American
Whitfield, Norman, The Classic Soul Era, 1960s-1970s, Artist, American
Whitney, Marva, Funk Soul, 1960s-1970s, Artist, American
Who, The, Hard Rock; Psychedelic Rock; Rock'n'Roll; British Invasion; Mod, 1960s-, Artist, British
Willette, Baby Face, Soul Jazz; Hard Bop, 1960s, Artist, American
Williams, Buster, Hard Bop, 1960s-, Artist, American
Williams, Don, Country Rock, 1960s-, Artist, American
Williams, Hank Jr., Country Rock, 1960s-, Artist, American
Williams, Maurice, Doo-Wop, 1960s-1980s, Artist, American
Williams, Tony, Fusion; Hard Bop, 1960s-1990s, Artist, American
Williamson, Robin, UK Folk; Folk Rock, 1960s-, Artist, British
Willis, Larry, Fusion, 1960s-, Artist, American
Wilson, Al, Urban Soul, 1960s-1970s, Artist, American
Wilson, Brian, 1960s Pop, 1960s-, Artist; Songwriter; Producer, American
Wilson, Delroy, Reggae Pop; Roots, 1960s-1990s, Artist, Jamaican
Wilson, Mary, The Classic Soul Era, 1960s-1980s, Artist, American
Wilson, Reuben, Soul Jazz; Hard Bop; Fusion, 1960s-1990s, Artist, American
Wimple Winch, Psychedelic Rock, 1960s, Artist, British
Winstons, The, The Classic Soul Era, 1960s-1970s, Artist, American
Winter, Johnny, Blues Rock; Modern Electric Blues, 1960s-, Artist, American
Winter, Paul, Fusion and Jazz Rock, 1960s-, Artist; Producer, American
Womack, Bobby, The Classic Soul Era; Urban Soul, 1960s-, Artist, American
Wonder, Stevie, Funk; The Classic Soul Era, 1960s-, Artist, American
Wood, Brenton, 1960s Pop; Funk Soul, 1960s-1970s; 1990s, Artist, American
Wood, Roy, Glam Rock & Glitter; Hard Rock; Prog Rock, 1960s-, Artist; Songwriter, British
Woods, Bill, Honky Tonk, 1960s, Artist, American
Wright, Charles, Funk Soul, 1960s-1970s, Artist, American
Wright, Edna, The Classic Soul Era , 1960s-1970s, Artist, American
Wright, O. V., The Classic Soul Era, 1960s-1970s, Artist, American
Wyatt, Robert, Psychedelic Rock; Prog Rock; Jazz Rock, 1960s-, Artist, British
Wynne, Philippe, The Classic Soul Era, 1960s-1970s, Artist, American
Yardbirds, The, Psychedelic Rock; Rock'n'Roll; British Invasion; British Blues; Blues Rock, 1960s, Artist, British
Yellow Balloon, 1960s Pop, 1960s, Artist, American
Yes, Prog Rock, 1960s-, Artist, British
Young Rascals, The, 1960s Pop, 1960s-1970s, Artist, American
Young, Kathy, 1960s Pop, 1960s, Artist, American
Young, Larry, Soul Jazz; Hard Bop; Fusion, 1960s-1970s, Artist, American
Young, Mighty Joe, Chicago Blues, 1960s-1990s, Artist, American
Young, Neil, Hard Rock; Country Rock; Folk Rock, 1960s-, Artist; Songwriter, Canadian
Youngbloods, The, Folk Rock; 1960s Pop, 1960s-1970s, Artist, American
Young-Holt Trio/Young-Holt Unlimited, Northern Soul, 1960s, Artist, American
Yuro, Timi, 1960s Pop, 1960s-1970s, Artist, American
Zappa, Frank, Prog Rock; Proto-Punk; Hard Rock; Jazz Rock; Fusion, 1960s-1990s, Artist, American

see The Beatles pp 88 *see* The Rolling Stones pp 96 *see* The Beach Boys pp 120 *see* Bob Dylan pp 126 *see* James Brown pp 154

THE SEVENTIES

After the seismic shifts of the previous decade, the 1970s reflected faster-moving, less permanent crazes, beginning with glam rock and ending with the new wave.

Glam rock saw the likes of Alice Cooper and Kiss taking make-up to extremes, while the comparatively anonymous Eagles and Bruce Springsteen respectively updated the blueprints established the previous decade by country rocker Gram Parsons and singer/songwriter Bob Dylan.

As Motown moved from Detroit to the West Coast, it would be Stevie Wonder and Marvin Gaye who kept black music progressing alongside former Impression Curtis Mayfield. Disco was more faceless if further-reaching, but a true icon of black music appeared from left field in the shape of reggae pioneer Bob Marley.

The introduction of the synthesizer to work alongside the now-established electric guitar fuelled progressive rock as well as influential European groups like Can and Kraftwerk. Progressive music from Yes, Pink Floyd and Mike Oldfield also used keyboards to best-selling effect.

The arrival of punk and its nihilistic philosophy in the mid-1970s gave music a much-needed kick up the backside. Elements like its newspaper cut-up graphics and ripped clothes would have a lasting cultural impart and, while the music was blunt and direct, its plea for social change and racial harmony was as timely as the hippie movement had been a decade previously.

Sources & Sounds

KEY ARTISTS

David Bowie

The Eagles

Led Zeppelin

Pink Floyd

Queen

ABBA

The Bee Gees

Elton John

Rod Stewart

The Clash

The Ramones

The Sex Pistols

Patti Smith

CLASSIC RECORDINGS

1971
Led Zeppelin:
'Stairway To Heaven'

1973
Pink Floyd:
Dark Side of the Moon

1977
The Sex Pistols:
Never Mind The Bollocks

'Ours is the folk music of the technological age.'

Jimmy Page, Led Zeppelin

Above

The 1970s experienced a surge of festivals (such as the Isle of Wight festival above) as the spontaneity of the late 1960s new age events became money-spinning opportunities for big business.

This was the decade that saw popular music turn into one of the biggest money-making industries of recent times – despite oil crises and vinyl shortages, it did not stop promoters, record companies and acts realize their wildest dreams of fame and fortune as sales of records, concert tickets and associated merchandising went through the roof.

Utopian values turned to greed as musicians abandoned their integrity to go for the big bucks. Of course as was the norm, the 1970s only began in earnest a few years in: 1970–71 continued the trends set in the late 1960s. Peace and love had been replaced by profit and the bottom line.

Going One Step Further

The predilection for big outdoor events grew even bigger with huge festivals at Bath, the Isle of Wight,

Lincoln and Weeley in the UK, whilst Watkins Glen in New York State in July 1973 saw upwards of 500,000 music fans come together to see The Band, The Grateful Dead and The Allman Brothers star in what was claimed to be the biggest rock show of all time.

Many musicians who rose to prominence in the 1960s became the rock Establishment of the new decade. Most of the ex-Beatles continued to sell albums and garner column inches, while Dylan returned to form, touring and releasing his 1975 masterpiece *Blood On The Tracks*. He was joined by the likes of ex-Them singer Van Morrison, Crosby, Stills Nash & Young, The Grateful Dead and 1960s outspoken cult figure Frank Zappa as top-grossing US-based acts of the era.

The return-to-roots movement that started with The Band in the late 1960s gathered momentum, especially in the UK where folk rock became hugely

 see Introduction pp 184   *see* Rock pp 194   *see* Pop & Disco pp 226   *see* Punk & New Wave pp 246

popular. Following the example of Fairport Convention, the likes of Steeleye Span and Lindisfarne sold out tours and even scored hits in the Top 20. Even US groups like The Grateful Dead left behind their psychedelic days for the more tranquil waters of backwoods America on albums like *Workingman's Dead* (1970).

Country Rockers And Song-Singers

Indeed, the move towards country and western started by the likes of The Byrds and The Flying Burrito Brothers created a new style of music: country rock. This borrowed heavily from the Nashville sound but was smoothed at the edges to create a more easy-going, radio friendly ambience. Bands like The Eagles hit gold perfecting this style and in their wake came a shoal of soft rock bands. Nashville would become one of the most important cities of the 1970s as country went mainstream via such figures as George Jones, Tammy Wynette and Dolly Parton.

The early 1970s also saw the rise of the singer/songwriter, especially in the US, with Joni Mitchell, Carole King, Jackson Browne, James Taylor and Carly Simon among those matching critical acclaim with high earnings for baring their innermost souls. The UK would match them with Cat Stevens, Rod Stewart and Elton John – artists who had cut their teeth in the 1960s but were now spokespeople for the new 'me generation', writing often very introspective songs from their own viewpoint and experience.

Rock On

Rock in the early 1970s was hard and heavy as perfected by a new breed of British bands like Black Sabbath, Free and Deep Purple, all of whom soared to popularity with mega-selling albums in 1970–71. But undoubtedly the biggest phenomenon was Led Zeppelin who, formed from the ashes of The Yardbirds, became the biggest band on the planet in the 1970s.

The new band had originally thought they would go down like the proverbial 'lead balloon' – yet by 1971 they were outselling practically every other act as their LP *Led Zeppelin IV* demolished the charts on both sides

of the Atlantic with their mixture of bone-crushing riffs, airy acoustic interludes, unbridled sexuality and stunning musicianship. Their 'Stairway To Heaven', which combined all these attributes in one song, became an anthem. And because Zeppelin refused to release singles, in the UK at least, you had to buy the album to get hold of it.

The tastes of the rock audience had swung back to alcohol and downers rather than pot and LSD, and The Rolling Stones remained superstars, producing two of their finest records in *Sticky Fingers* (1971) and *Exile On Main St.* (1972). These were delivered in a style that had not

Left

Folk rockers Steeleye Span proved to be hugely popular in the early years of the 1970s.

Below

Free's Paul Kossoff was a characteristic heavy rocker whose hard-drinking, hard-riffing lifestyle ended in tragedy. Free's classic 'All Right Now' was one of the early soundtracks to the decade.

🔊 *see* The Grateful Dead pp 130   🔊 *see* The Eagles pp 198   🔊 *see* Led Zeppelin pp 200   🔊 *see* Black Sabbath pp 212

Above

The 1970s saw a massive period of experimentation as technology, particularly in the form of the electronic keyboard became a complex and capable instrument in its own right. Bands like Kraftwerk were able to sculpt their synthesizer pop without guitars or drums.

deviated much from their roots of a decade before – rollicking 12-bar blues, top-heavy with slide guitars. Their American counterparts were the likes of The Allman Brothers, Lynyrd Skynryd and The Doobie Brothers who all purveyed no frills basic rock –'heads-down no-nonsense mindless boogie', as British satirists Alberto Y Lost Trios Paranoias put it.

Mega Rock

At the other extreme was 'progressive rock', which took popular music into the realms of opera, classical and electronics. Marrying complex pieces of music with poetic lyrics, the prog rock masters were fond of using full orchestras and the very latest cutting-edge musical instruments such as mellotrons (which replicated the sound of strings), Moog and other synthesizers. Rock became high art as supergroups like Emerson, Lake and Palmer, all gifted musicians, covered classical pieces by the likes of Mussorgsky as well as writing long, complicated suites, and took rock into large arenas and stadiums with often overblown stage shows.

Another act to take this route was Pink Floyd, who lost their arty/underground image of the 1960s to become megastars of the 1970s. Top-selling albums *Dark*

Side Of The Moon (1973) and *Wish You Were Here* (1975) established them as rock colossi, while their elaborate live act featured, at various times, giant inflatable pigs, Spitfire aircraft and the demolition of a huge brick wall. Other kings of prog rock included Yes, King Crimson, Genesis, Jethro Tull, Queen and Mike Oldfield, whose instrumental concept LP *Tubular Bells* came out of left field in 1973 to become a top-selling record.

Whilst pop music had usually emanated from the shores of either Britain or America, another country became a major player in the 1970s: Germany. The country was still split in two following the Second World War and, because of the post-war deprivations, German musicians of the 1970s were of a harder, more radical hue. They played a variety of styles – Amon Duul II from the southern city of Munich purveyed an intense hybrid of spacey, psychedelic West Coast-influenced rock whilst the bands from the *Ruehrgebiet* were more industrial and electronic and became highly influential. From the robotic sounds of Neu and Kraftwerk to the white-noise overkill of Can, their influence would wax stronger and stronger through the late 1970s and onwards. Bowie and others would record in Berlin as the decade went on.

see **Introduction** pp 184   see **Rock** pp 194   see **Pop & Disco** pp 226   see **Punk & New Wave** pp 246

Glam-tastic

The 1970s had seen the advent of glam, which had both its frivolous and serious sides. As early as 1971 the charts were alive with the sounds of Slade, T. Rex and The Sweet, all of whom played a revved-up rock dressed in sequins, sparkle and satin. But glam, despite its teen appeal, had a more serious, theatrical side – its cue taken from a band that only enjoyed cult status in the 1960s but whose influence would reach through the next 30 years and beyond.

The Velvet Underground had stepped out of the shadow of their mentor Andy Warhol and explored the darker side of life. By 1971, most of their key members had left – including leader Lou Reed, whose arrival in London along with another American, ex-Stooges leader Iggy Pop, had a profound effect on British rockers like Mott the Hoople, Roxy Music and David Bowie.

Cross-dressing and a flirtation with the burgeoning gay scenes in both London and New York created an exciting new direction in rock. Bowie, who had already been around for almost 10 years, suddenly caught on with his ambitious concept album *Ziggy Stardust And The Spiders From Mars* (1975). Mascara, lipstick and sexual ambiguity became the order of the day as bands like the New York Dolls followed in his wake – but the chameleon-like Bowie managed to stay one step ahead of the pack, toying with different styles and personas as he went from rock through soul to electronica to become one of the biggest figures of the decade.

A New Black Sound

Black music continued to be a huge force both as an influence and as a mainstream phenomenon. The end of the 1960s had seen the emergence of acts like the Chambers Brothers and Sly and The Family Stone who mixed fiery danceable soul and rhythm and blues with psychedelic effects and radical politics. The 1970s would see the emergence of a more sophisticated but no less radical form of soul as figures like Isaac Hayes, Gil Scott Heron and Curtis Mayfield took the latest sounds of white rock and married them to black politics to enjoy a big crossover appeal. They were joined by such 1960s survivors as The Isley Bros and Stevie Wonder, the latter producing classic progressive soul albums like *Talking Book* (1972) and *Innervisions* (1973).

Above

Gay and lesbian rights became big news in the 1970s and this was reflected in the music of the period, with cross-dressing glam bands and a new found freedom of expression in all musical forms.

Left

Lou Reed, seen here with Andy Warhol, was to have a major effect on 1970s artists like Iggy Pop, Roxy Music and David Bowie.

see Stevie Wonder pp 162   see David Bowie pp 196   see Pink Floyd pp 204   see Emerson, Lake and Palmer pp 214

The Philadelphia sound was now challenging the Motown tradition for domination of the 1970s soul charts, though the latter's Jackson Five carried on where The Four Tops left off. But one of the most interesting outfits to come along was Parliament whose mixture of theatrics, politics, psychedelia and funk broke new barriers. Funk was to become one of the buzzwords of the decade. Taking its cue from 1960s soulster James Brown, funk combined syncopated rhythms, dominant bass lines, sharp rhythm guitars and brass, the style typifying acts as diverse as Earth Wind and Fire, The Meters, The Commodores, Miles Davis and Herbie Hancock.

Below

Parliament created such dance floor favourites as 'Tear The Roof Off The Sucker (Give Up The Funk)', 'Aqua Boogie' and 'Flashlight.'

But in terms of influence there was one style of black music and one figure in particular that changed the face of 1970s music – the sound of reggae and the advent of its most famous ambassador, Bob Marley. There had been a long tradition of music coming out of Jamaica since the 1950s – calypso and mento, followed in the 1960s by bluebeat and ska. But it was reggae with its reliance on skanking rhythms and a tough, slow backbeat that became the most popular. The original Wailers, back in the ghetto of Trenchtown, had been Marley, Peter Tosh and Bunny Livingston, but by the time the group recorded a breakthrough live album in London in 1975 only Marley remained.

Marley soon had a big following, not only of whites but also a young black audience consisting of kids whose parents had arrived in the UK from the Caribbean in the 1950s. The charismatic singer had the knack of communicating a message of universal brotherhood and was soon to unite audiences around the globe, especially after conquering the United States, whilst the music he played informed the direction of many 1960s survivors such as The Stones, Dylan and Eric Clapton. Punks like The Clash also embraced reggae, while new wave trio The Police successfully appropriated its rhythms.

Pop Won't Stop

Pop also continued to sell, thanks to the rise of acts like Elton John, Rod Stewart and Queen all of whom crossed over from rock into the mainstream. The 1970s was also very much the era of teenybopper pop – indeed, the roots of the perennially popular boy-band phenomenon can be traced back to the early 1970s when clean-cut singers like American family The Osmonds took care of the predominantly female teen audience. As the decade progressed they were followed by rougher-hewn home-grown acts like The Bay City Rollers and David Essex.

They may have proved culturally unimportant but the intelligent, original and wholly irresistible pop of Swedish singing quartet ABBA left an indelible mark on the pop scene with a string of catchy, finely crafted tunes such as 1974's Eurovision-winning 'Waterloo'. The decade was seen out with acts embracing disco – artists like Donna Summer and 1960s' rejects The Bee Gees who completely revitalized their career writing a number of disco-based anthems.

 see Introduction pp 184   see Rock pp 194   see Pop & Disco pp 226   see Punk & New Wave pp 246

The Dawn Of Punk

But few saw the storm clouds gathering mid-decade, which heralded one of the most important and drastic sea changes in the history of popular music. Rumours began to circulate in 1975 of a new type of rock that was a return to basics but delivered with such speed and conviction and force that it was like a blow to the head. Punk rock was about to upset the applecart with its simple, basic three-chord guitar attack, delivered without finesse but with the kind of attitude that had not been seen since the 1950s.

Punk did not come out of nowhere – there had always been bands that had delivered their music concisely with a sneer, bite and excitement. 1960s garage rockers like The Standells and The Strangeloves had their tracks collected together as *Nuggets* by Lenny Kaye for Elektra Records as far back as 1972. Kaye was also the guitarist and musical director for poet/singer Patti Smith, whose visionary *Horses* album had been an arms call for a return to simpler guitar rock whilst still possessing a fiery, passionate and poetic heart, and had been declared best album of 1975 by many critics.

Left

Donna Summer may be best-known as a disco diva, but her music had elements of R&B, rock'n'roll and gospel. Her world could not be further from the street chic of punk.

Below

Punks lived by a do-it-yourself attitude, creating their own clothes and even record labels in order to sell their music.

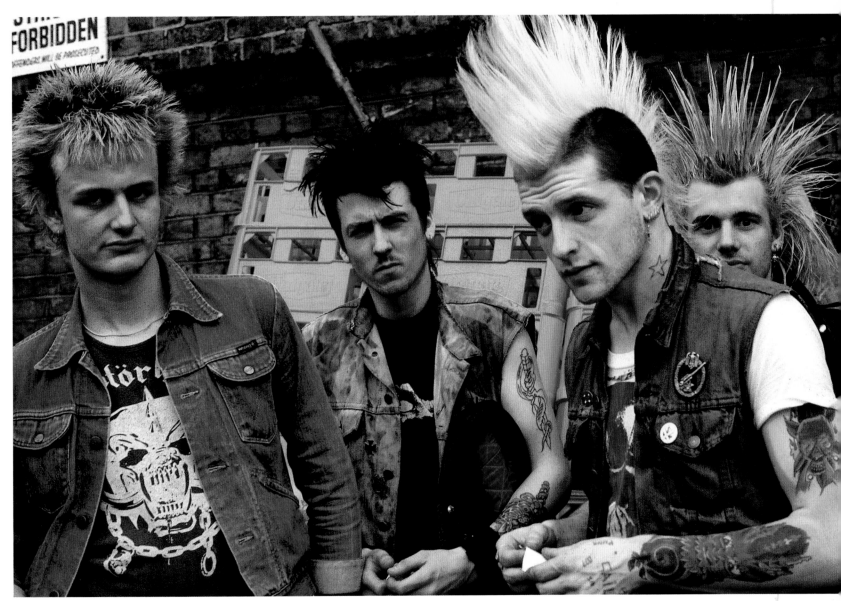

see **Queen** pp 208   see **ABBA** pp 228   see **Bob Marley** pp 240   see **The Police** pp 280

Smith and her band were part of a select, incestuous scene in New York that had congregated at little clubs like CBGBs in the Bowery. It was The Ramones, another member of this clique from the Lower East Side, whose sound was to become the blueprint for a thousand imitators. The cartoon-character-like brothers' snappy, amphetamined anthems caught the imagination of the new 'blank generation', whilst in London manager Malcolm McLaren and designer Vivienne Westwood, influenced by this hotbed of activity in the Big Apple, set about fashioning their own 'punks'.

A Rotten Idea

They created The Sex Pistols, whose look was based on the torn T-shirts of Richard Hell, bassist and writer and another mover/shaker of the NYC scene. But singer Johnny Rotten had his very own ideas – a working-class lad hell bent on rejecting not just British middle-class values but all that the 1970s rock Establishment held so dear. His bug-eyed stare and dishevelled demeanour sent a frisson through the Establishment – though in truth he was as much music-hall jester as he was foul-mouthed rebel.

Things happened swiftly in 1976, the year The Ramones played London's Roundhouse – and many of the capital's pub-rockers, a back-to-basics movement that spawned Dr. Feelgood and Ian Dury's Kilburn and The High Roads, were soon to re-appear as part of the punk boom. Independent labels like Stiff Records were soon in action, issuing records by the likes of the aforementioned Hell and British combo The Damned. However, many of the bigger bands signed to major labels – The Clash were with CBS whilst the Pistols went through EMI and A&M before settling with Virgin. But it did not stop Rotten and company delivering their controversial nihilistic message, a four-letter word row on prime-time TV ensuring their notoriety went before them.

see Introduction pp 184 see Rock pp 194 see Pop & Disco pp 226 see Punk & New Wave pp 246

Bands, labels and venues mushroomed in Britain as teenagers awoke to the filth and the fury of such anthems as 'Anarchy In The UK' and 'No Future' – such was the paranoia engendered by the new revolution that questions were asked in the House of Commons. Inevitably the big labels got in on the act and, slowly but inevitably, punk was watered down to become new wave, sucking in a disparate array of bands in the process.

A New Order

However, the Establishment had momentarily been toppled. Labels like Virgin dropped its hippie bands and only signed outfits with short haircuts and snappy suits. And significantly, as punk rose to a crescendo in the summer of 1977, the death of one rock icon seemed to usher in a new era as an overweight and reactionary Elvis Presley died in sad and bloated circumstances.

The Pistols split in 1978, their bass player Sid Vicious dying of a heroin overdose a year later, but the avalanche they had started could not be stopped. The rock world of the end of the 1970s was completely re-shaped, though ultimately it became even safer than it had been five years before, whilst the DIY example of punk would be adopted by new kids starting out. The scene was characterized by a new order – bands with literate, charismatic frontmen like The Boomtown Rats; Elvis Costello and The Attractions; and Ian Dury and The Blockheads, both the latter escapees from the pub rock era.

Biggest of all the new wavers was Blondie, another veteran of the fertile NYC scene whose figurehead, Debbie Harry, became the most photographed face of 1979 and whose radio-friendly

pop songs climbed the charts one after another, shifting millions of units. Rock's conscience, meanwhile, was safe in the hands of the British 2-Tone bands like The Specials whose music drew on bluebeat and ska but whose vision was informed by inner-city decay, racism and the anti working-class policies of the incoming Thatcher government.

As the Tory party and the US Republicans came to power, the scene was set for the 1980s, an era during which, as one wag put it, it was as if punk never happened.

Left
A broody Bob Geldof in his Boomtown Rats days – frontman of a new wave of late 1970s bands turning out experimental, polished punk.

Below
Debbie Harry, leapt from the platform of CBGBs and forged the new wave pop sound.

see The Ramones pp 250   see The Sex Pistols pp 252   see Blondie pp 256   see The Specials pp 316

SEVENTIES ROCK

The sunshine 1960s were followed by the comparatively grey 1970s. Yet a number of stars of that drab decade started their life in the 1960s. In Britain, the chameleon-like David Bowie suffered several years of obscurity, Status Quo were psychedelic popsters yet to discover 12-bar blues, while Humble Pie was formed by Peter Frampton and Steve Marriott from 1960s pop bands The Herd and Small Faces. Frampton, of course, would go on to find solo acclaim with his multi-platinum *Comes Alive* (1976) album.

Supergroups were very much in vogue. Three-man Emerson, Lake and Palmer came from The Nice, King Crimson and Atomic Rooster, while Led Zeppelin likewise had assembled musicians with an impressive track record – most notably ex-Yardbird Jimmy Page. His former sparring partner Jeff Beck had been there and done that with Rod Stewart, but could not find the right singer to replace him so went the instrumental route.

Leading American acts tended to be souped-up singer/songwriters like Bruce Springsteen and Neil Young, while Southern rock was on the rise in the shape of The Allman Brothers, ZZ Top and Lynyrd Skynyrd. But the inoffensive, country-tinged harmonies of California's Eagles outsold them all.

David Bowie

One of the great chameleon figures in rock, David Bowie has also been among the most influential. Born David Robert Jones on 8 January 1947, his earliest records with The King Bees, The Mannish Boys and The Lower Third were unsuccessful. In 1966 he changed his name to David Bowie and combined his songwriting with an interest in stage and visual arts.

The Rise Of Ziggy Stardust

It was not until 1969 that Bowie caught the British public's imagination with the quirky 'Space Oddity' that became a Top 5 hit soon after the first manned moon landing. Despite fuelling publicity with his androgynous image, Bowie's career continued to stutter with *The Man Who Sold The World* (1971) and *Hunky Dory* (1972) until he created the messianic rock star character Ziggy Stardust. A glam-rock concept album, *The Rise And Fall Of Ziggy Stardust And The Spiders From Mars* (1972) formed the basis of a theatrical live show and was a Top 5 UK album. Such was the interest in Bowie that *Hunky Dory* was revived and got to No. 3. His band – Mick Woodmansey (drums), Trevor Bolder (bass) and especially Mick Ronson (guitar, keyboards, vocals) – were dependable sidekicks.

Aladdin Sane, produced by Tony Visconti who played a significant role in most of Bowie's albums through the 1970s, topped the UK charts in 1973. But just weeks later – on 3 July 1973 – Bowie dramatically killed off Ziggy live on stage in London (recently released on DVD).

> *'From '72 to '76 I was the ultimate rock star. I couldn't have been more a rock star. Anything that had to do with being a rock'n'roll singer was what I was going for.'*
>
> David Bowie

Above and Far Right

Bowie is the master chameleon, constantly re-inventing both his persona and music to the changing moods of the time. Bowie's Aladdin Sane (opposite) perfectly suited the androgenous themes of the early 1970s, while his 'Thin White Duke' period (this page) reflected the more confident, conservatism of the late 1970s.

Going Stateside

After an interlude with *Pin-Ups* (1973), a covers album, Bowie returned with *Diamond Dogs* (1974). The album's bleak, Orwellian theme and the extravagant stage show he devised gave Bowie his American breakthrough, encouraging him to relocate there.

Another stylistic switch based around the soul sound of Philadelphia completed Bowie's American triumph with *Young Americans* (1975), which brought him a US No. 1 single with 'Fame' (co-written with John Lennon). By *Station To Station* (1976) Bowie's stage persona had metamorphosed into the 'Thin White Duke'. During this hectic period Bowie also found time (with assistance from Ronson) to produce seminal albums by Lou Reed, *Transformer* (1972), and Iggy Pop and The Stooges (*Raw Power*, 1973), write and produce Mott The Hoople's 'All The Young Dudes' and star in the film *The Man Who Fell To Earth* (1976).

Frazzled from the perks and pressures of fame, Bowie retreated to seclusion in Berlin later in 1976,

🔊 *see Introduction pp 194* 🔊 *see Sources & Sounds pp 186* 🔊 *see A–Z of Artists pp 210*

studying art and working with pioneering electronic sound musician Brian Eno. The resulting *Low* (1977) was another radically different musical direction, exploring new instrumental and vocal sounds. It was the first of a trilogy with *Heroes* (1977) and *Lodger* (1978). His reputation ensured their success although some fans and critics were getting confused.

Bowie relocated to New York to record the paranoid *Scary Monsters* (1980), updating 'Space Oddity' with 'Ashes To Ashes'. He also collaborated with Queen for their 'Under Pressure' hit and Bing Crosby for the 'Peace On Earth'/'Little Drummer Boy' single, as well as taking the lead role in Broadway play *The Elephant Man*, and writing film themes and soundtracks for *Christiane F* (1981, in which he also appeared) and *Cat People* (1982).

A Lasting Impression

He returned to the mainstream with *Let's Dance* (1983), produced by Chic's Nile Rodgers, which yielded three international hits – 'China Girl', 'Modern Love' and 'Let's Dance', all with innovative videos, and undertook the successful Serious Moonlight world tour. For the rest of the decade Bowie divided his time between music: *Tonight* (1984) and *Never Let Me Down* (1987); duetting with Mick Jagger on 'Dancing In The Street' for Live Aid); acting (*Merry Christmas Mr Lawrence*, *Into The Night*, *Absolute Beginners*, *Labyrinth*); and soundtracks ('The Falcon And The Snowman', 'When The Wind Blows').

In 1989 he formed a band called Tin Machine with the rhythm section from Iggy Pop's band and made two self-titled, rock-oriented albums. But their appeal was limited and Bowie returned to his solo career, and producer Nile Rodgers for the electro-dance styled *Black Tie White Noise* (1993). He continued to experiment with modern musical styles, drawing on industrial rock for *Outside* (1995) with Eno returning as producer, and incorporating jungle beats on *Earthling* (1997). *Hours* (1999, made available as a download before the CD was released), *Heathen* (2002), with Tony Visconti back as producer, and *Reality* (2003) found Bowie in relaxed form, taking facets of his earlier career and updating them. He remains an icon and few rock acts of the past 30 years have been unaffected by his legacy.

see Queen pp 208   see John Lennon pp 218   see Mott The Hoople pp 220   see Nile Rodgers pp 242

The Eagles

The Eagles defined the sound of California in the 1970s and were its most successful exponents. The band formed out of the Los Angeles country rock scene in 1970 when guitarist Glenn Frey (born 6 November 1948), drummer Don Henley (born 22 July 1947), guitarist Bernie Leadon (born 19 July 1947) and bassist Randy Meisner (born 8 March 1946) were recruited as Linda Ronstadt's group for her *Silk Purse* album in 1970.

'Don could sing any song in The Eagles. If it is bluesy it is usually a Don song. If it is light it is usually a Timothy song. If it somewhere in the middle, it is usually a Glenn song.'

Glenn Frey

Above
The laid-back style of The Eagles' early PR shots was in stark contrast to their intense, carefully sculpted songs.

Hitting Solid Gold

Frey had previously played with Bob Seger and J.D. Souther, Leadon with The Flying Burrito Brothers and Dillard-Clark, Meisner with Poco and Ricky Nelson, Henley with Shiloh. They were accomplished musicians and singer/songwriters and after working with Ronstadt they decided to form their own band.

They came to London to record their debut album, *The Eagles* (1972), with producer Glyn Johns (The Rolling Stones, The Who, Steve Miller), polishing the country rock of The Byrds and The Flying Burrito Brothers with a harder sound and carefully arranged harmonies. *The Eagles* went gold in America, spawning three hit singles: 'Witchy Woman', 'Take It Easy' (written by Frey with Jackson Browne) and 'Peaceful Easy Feeling'.

They returned to London for *Desperado* (1973), a conceptual album that drew parallels with cowboy culture and the rock'n'roll lifestyle. It was less successful, although the title track was covered by Linda Ronstadt, The Carpenters and Bonnie Raitt, and 'Tequila Sunrise' became one of their most popular songs. For *On The Border* (1974) The Eagles switched to Los Angeles and producer Bill Szymczyk (who would produced their subsequent albums), adding guitarist Don Felder (born 21 September 1947) to the line-up. Their slicker, sharper sound brought them their first US No. 1 with 'Best Of My Love'. *One Of These Nights* (1975) established The Eagles as one of America's biggest bands. It topped the US charts for five weeks and included three big hits – 'One Of These Nights', 'Lyin' Eyes' and 'Take It To The Limit' – that all charted in the UK along with the album.

Hotel California

The Eagles' increasingly commercial style, spiraling success and internal tensions caused a disaffected Leadon to leave in 1976. He was replaced by guitarist Joe Walsh (born 20 November 1947), who was previously in The James Gang and had released several solo albums.

Hotel California (1976) was The Eagles' pinnacle. Painstakingly recorded, it caught the full decadence of their vision of the American dream in a blaze of guitars, acerbic lyrics and tight harmonies. It was No. 1 in America for eight weeks, produced two No. 1 singles – 'New Kid In Town' and the title track – and won five Grammy Awards.

Meisner bailed out in late 1977. His replacement was bassist Timothy B. Schmit (born 30 October 1947) who had followed Meisner into Poco. But it was another two years before The Eagles completed their next album as their obsessive quest for perfection and strained relations

see Introduction pp 194   *see* Sources & Sounds pp 186   *see* A–Z of Artists pp 210

hampered their creativity. *The Long Run* (1979) continued to break the band's own records, spending nine weeks at No. 1 and featuring three more major hits: 'Heartache Tonight', 'The Long Run' and 'I Can't Tell You Why'. But by the time *Live* (1980) came out the band had broken up, although it was not made official until 1982.

'When Hell Freezes Over'

The group members spent the next decade pursuing solo careers. Henley had a Top 10 hit with 'Leather And Lace', a duet with Stevie Nicks in 1981, followed by 'Dirty Laundry' (1982), 'The Boys Of Summer' and 'All She Wants To Do Is Dance' (1985) and 'The End Of The Innocence' (1989). Frey charted with 'The

One You Love' (1982) and 'Sexy Cat' (1984) before scoring No. 2 hits with 'The Heat Is On' and 'You Belong To The City' (1985). He also embarked on an acting career, making his debut in *Miami Vice*. Whenever Henley was asked when The Eagles would reform he replied, 'When Hell freezes over.'

Hell Freezes Over (1994) was the result of two years inching towards a reunion. There were four new songs including two hits – 'Get Over It' and 'Love Will Keep Us Alive' – plus tracks from the MTV concert that launched their comeback. Since then they have toured periodically. Meanwhile *Eagles: Their Greatest Hits 1971–75* (1975) continues to sell and has already notched up over 28 million copies.

Below
The Eagles' live shows highlighted the power of their perfectly crafted harmonies and the real-life drama of their songwriting.

🚗 *see* The Byrds pp 124 🚗 *see* The Flying Burrito Brothers pp 214 🚗 *see* Linda Ronstadt pp 242

Led Zeppelin

**💿 CLASSIC
RECORDINGS**

1969
Led Zeppelin II
'Whole Lotta Love'

1971
Led Zeppelin IV
'Black Dog'
'Stairway To Heaven'

1973
'No Quarter'

1975
Physical Graffiti
'Kashmir'

'It wasn't supposed to be a pretty thing.'
Robert Plant

Right
Robert Plant in full flight was an incredible sight live. He lived, breathed and revelled in the role as a true rock god.

The biggest heavy metal band of the 1970s, Led Zeppelin left an indelible mark that is still felt a quarter of a century later. The band was put together in London in 1968 by guitarist Jimmy Page (born James Patrick Page, 9 January 1944), singer Robert Plant (born 20 August 1948), bassist John Paul Jones (born John Baldwin, 3 June 1946) and drummer John Bonham (born John Henry Bonham, 31 May 1948).

Beginning Of A Legend

A versatile guitarist, Page was an in-demand session player in the mid-1960s and appeared on countless records and hits. In 1966 he joined The Yardbirds, playing alongside Jeff Beck and taking over when he left in 1967. By early 1968 the band was in decline and Page began planning a new group helped by Yardbirds' road manager Peter Grant. Page's aim was to build on the success that Cream had achieved with their heavy blues rock. When The Yardbirds broke up in the summer of 1968 he recruited Jones, another prominent session musician. They contacted singer Terry Riley who was unavailable but recommended Plant who was in the Midlands group Band Of Joy. He in turn recommended drummer Bonham and Led Zeppelin were born with Grant as their manager.

Their name was donated by The Who's Keith Moon but their first gigs were as The New Yardbirds, fulfilling previously arranged dates in Scandinavia and the UK. They recorded their debut album at London's Olympic Studios in 30 hours for less than £2,000 and Grant took the tapes to America where he negotiated a contract with Atlantic Records that gave the band a £200,000 advance and complete artistic control, unprecedented for an unknown group.

Led Zeppelin (1969) contained heavy, stylized versions of Willie Dixon's 'You Shook Me' and 'I Can't Quit You Baby' and self-written tracks like the frenetic 'Communication Breakdown' and the slow-building, explosive 'Dazed And Confused' that featured Page

playing guitar with a violin bow. The song remained a cornerstone of their set for much of their career, expanded up to 25 minutes.

Set For Success

On the back of relentless touring, which included several major American festivals, *Led Zeppelin* gradually climbed the US and UK album charts, eventually reaching the Top 10 without help from singles or TV appearances (the band deliberately shunned both). As a result, the group remained 'exclusive' to the burgeoning rock audience. When *Led Zeppelin II* was released in November 1969 it quickly rose to No. 1 in the US and UK. *Led Zeppelin II* was recorded at various studios in breaks between tours but was mixed in a single weekend. The opening 'Whole Lotta Love' was Led Zeppelin's manifesto condensed into five and a half minutes – a dynamic riff, vocal preening and a pared-down chorus with guitar echo effects, followed by a crazed middle section. An edited version was put out as a single in America to gain airplay and reached No. 6, but the group refused to allow its release in Britain. In addition to ferocious rockers like 'Heartbreaker' there were expansive acoustic songs like

📻 *see Introduction pp 194*　📻 *see Sources & Sounds pp 186*　📻 *see A–Z of Artists pp 210*

'Ramble On' that pointed towards a future direction for the group.

Led Zeppelin maintained a punishing schedule through 1970 that included their biggest British appearance so far at the Bath Festival in front of 150,000, while fighting off legal threats from the von Zeppelin family in Germany. They took a break to prepare material for their next album at an isolated Welsh cottage called Bron-y-Aur, which was celebrated in several subsequent songs. *Led Zeppelin III* was released in October 1970 with advance orders that sent it to the top of the US and UK charts. It contained the fierce 'Immigrant Song' and the heavyweight blues 'Since I've Been Loving You' but some reviews were critical of the softer, acoustic songs and sales failed to match *Led Zeppelin II*.

At the end of the year the band were back in the studio working on their next album. *Led Zeppelin IV* – the album cover had no title, not even the band's name, just four symbols on the inner sleeve – came out in October 1971 and is widely regarded as their finest album. They successfully blended the various elements of their character – the powerful 'Black Dog' and 'Rock And Roll', the gentler 'Going To California' and the stark 'When The Levee Breaks' – and brought them all together on the epic 'Stairway To Heaven'. Ironically,

Above
Jimmy Page and Robert Plant were perfect foils for each other, both on stage and as songwriters, straining the limits of taste, decency and sheer dramatic noise.

📻 *see* **Cream** pp 92   📻 *see* **The Who** pp 100   📻 *see* **The Yardbirds** pp 117   📻 *see* **Jeff Beck** pp 212

see Introduction pp 194   see Sources & Sounds pp 186   see A–Z of Artists pp 210

Above

During long guitar solos Robert Plant used his trademark howl and inventive vocal styling to accompany the soaring, epic guitar work of Jimmy Page.

the album failed to top the US charts, stalling at No. 2, but overall sales outstripped earlier releases. The album heralded the golden age of Led Zeppelin. They played sell-out tours of Australia, Japan, Britain and Europe. In America they broke box-office records that had been set by The Beatles. *Houses Of The Holy* (1973) was the first album to get a title and again left critics lukewarm, but the crowds who flocked to their concerts had no qualms, making it a No. 1 album around the world.

Ultimate Rock Stars

By now Led Zeppelin were touring America in a private jet with their logo emblazoned on the side, the epitome of rock star chic. They were the biggest grossing act in the world and tales of their rock and roll excesses were already entering folklore. At the beginning of 1974 they formed their own record label, Swansong, and spent much of the year working on the album, taking a break from touring.

They returned with the double album, *Physical Graffiti* (1975), which received universal acclaim, and another massive American tour. Their shows were now running between three and four hours and as a result of renewed interest in their earlier albums, they became the first band to have six albums simultaneously in the *Billboard* Top 200.

Tragedy And Success

In August 1975, while holidaying in Rhodes, Plant was involved in a car accident and suffered multiple fractures of his ankle and elbow, leaving him on crutches for the next six months (his wife had a broken skull and pelvis). Touring plans were cancelled and the band worked instead on their next album, *Presence*, released in April 1976. That was followed by a film and live album, *The Song Remains The Same* (1976) taken from their 1973 New York Madison Square Garden shows.

Led Zeppelin started their first American tour for nearly two years in April 1977 with their popularity undiminished. On 23 July at Oakland Coliseum a security guard was badly beaten, requiring hospital treatment, and the following day Bonham, Grant and two members of the road crew were charged with assault. When the band arrived in New Orleans on 26 July Plant was told that his five-year-old son had died from a sudden and rare stomach infection and the rest of the tour was cancelled. All group operations were suspended until late 1978 when they reconvened to work on a new album, recorded at ABBA's Stockholm studios. *In Through The Out Door* was released in August 1979 and topped the US charts for seven weeks. That month they made their live return at the UK's Knebworth Festival, mounting the biggest rock production yet seen in Britain and playing a three-hour show.

Unledded

In the summer of 1980 they toured Europe and were rehearsing for an American tour when John Bonham was found dead on 25 September, having choked on his own vomit after drinking more than a bottle of vodka. In December the remaining band members announced that they 'could not continue as we were'. An album of unreleased recordings, *Coda*, was issued in 1982. Jones retired from live performances, undertaking various low-key projects. Plant pursued a solo career

releasing eight albums and revisiting his R&B roots with side project The Honeydrippers. Page recorded solo albums and linked up with Paul Rodgers, David Coverdale and The Black Crowes for projects.

In 1985 the three surviving members performed as Led Zeppelin at Live Aid in Philadelphia, with drummers Phil Collins and Tony Thompson. They played together again in 1993 at Atlantic Records' 40th anniversary concert in New York with Bonham's son Jason on drums. In 1994 Page and Plant teamed up for an MTV show, *Unledded*, recorded in Morocco, Wales and London featuring reworked Zeppelin songs with Middle Eastern and North African musical influences. The resulting album, *No Quarter* (1994), was a Top 5 US success. In 1998 they recorded an album of new songs, *Walking Into Clarksdale* that went Top 10.

The Led Zeppelin legacy has been periodically boosted by the *Remasters* compilation (1991) *The Complete Studio Recordings* (1993), the live *How The West Was Won* (2003) and *Led Zeppelin DVD* (2003) featuring film footage from across their career.

Below
Always in the background, drummer John Bonham and bassist John Paul Jones provided the intricate and astonishingly powerful engine to the behemoth that was Led Zeppelin.

see Phil Collins pp 292 *see* The Black Crowes pp 342

Pink Floyd

204

**⌕ CLASSIC
RECORDINGS**

1967
'Arnold Layne'

1971
'One Of These Days'

1973
Dark Side Of The Moon
'Money'

1975
Wish You Were Here
'Wish You Were Here'

1979
The Wall
'Another Brick In The
Wall Part 2'
'Comfortably Numb'

*'For us the most important thing
is to be visual…. We get very upset
if people get bored when we're only
half way through smashing the
second set.'*

Roger Waters

Above

Originally called Tea Set,
the name Pink Floyd was
adopted when the band
found themselves on the
same bill as a band with
the same name.

The band were formed in London in 1965 by
singer/guitarist Syd Barrett (born Roger Keith
Barrett, 6 January 1946, died 7 July 2006), bassist
Roger Waters (born George Roger Waters, 6
September 1944), keyboard player Richard Wright
(born 28 July 1945) and drummer Nick Mason
(born 27 January 1945).

One of the defining albums
of the 1970s, Dark Side Of
The Moon (1973) established
Pink Floyd as the biggest
progressive rock band of the
decade. They have remained
massively popular and their
influence continues to be felt
in rock and ambient music.

Sowing The Seeds

Barrett and Waters had grown up together in
Cambridge before moving to London as students,
playing in various bands. Playing a mixture of R&B
(their name came from an amalgam of blues artists
Pink Anderson and Floyd Council) and primitive
electronic music, enhanced by a psychedelic light
show, they became a big attraction on the London
underground scene in 1966.

Signing to EMI in 1967, the band released two
quirky singles written by Barrett – 'Arnold Layne' and
'See Emily Play' – that made the Top 20 and Top 10
respectively. Barrett also wrote the songs on their
debut album, *Piper At The Gates Of Dawn* (1967),
which made No. 6 in the UK charts, combining a
nursery rhyme musical sensibility with LSD-inspired
imagery. By the end of 1967, however, Barrett's

📻 *see* **Introduction pp 194**   📻 *see* **Sources & Sounds pp 186**   📻 *see* **A–Z of Artists pp 210**

increasingly unstable behaviour was becoming a liability and at the beginning of 1968 the band drafted in another Cambridge friend, David Gilmour (born 6 March 1944), as an additional guitarist. The idea was to ease the pressure on Barrett but this proved impractical and he left in March of that year. He went into seclusion, emerging in 1970 to record two idiosyncratic solo albums, *The Madcap Laughs* and *Barrett* (featuring Waters and Gilmour) before retiring from music.

Pink Floyd's second album, *A Saucerful Of Secrets* (1968), contained a couple of Barrett songs but was dominated by longer, more ambitious numbers like 'Set The Controls For The Heart Of The Sun'. The album was not as successful, although the growing atmospheric element to their music led them to write the soundtrack for the film *More* (1969). *Ummagumma* (1969) was a double album that featured idiosyncratic individual pieces and live tracks. It reached No. 5 but

there was a palpable lack of direction from the band as a new generation of groups swept past them and achieved success in America. *Atom Heart Mother* (1970) restored their credibility. The side-long title track was a classical-rock fusion with an orchestra and choir and laid the seeds for the band's future direction. It gave them their first UK No. 1 album.

Epic Masterpieces

On *Meddle* (1971) Pink Floyd expanded their sound and dynamics on the 23-minute 'Echoes' that linked a series of riffs into an epic masterpiece and the menacing 'One Of These Days'. The album peaked at No. 3 and stayed in the charts for over a year and a half.

Pink Floyd made another soundtrack album, *Obscured By Clouds* (1972), and then spent several months working on their next album. *Dark Side Of The Moon* (1973) was a ground-breaking concept album themed around the pressures of modern life,

Below

Many of Floyd's gigs in the early 1970s were essentially massive jam sessions, which created such atmospheric albums as *Atom Heart Mother* and *Meddle*.

Above

The immense success of *Dark Side Of The Moon* and *Wish You Were Here* marked an increase in confidence in the band, which was reflected in their increasingly extravagant shows.

paranoia and schizophrenia. The band's potent sound and various sound effects highlighted the contrasting imagery of the songs. The album caught the *zeitgeist* and was a soundtrack for stereo's breakthrough into the mass market. But its appeal remains timeless. In the UK it got to No. 2 and spent six years in the charts. In the US it was their first hit album and spent one week at No. 1. But it stayed in the charts for 15 years and was only removed by a technical rule change. Worldwide sales of *Dark Side Of The Moon* are now over 30 million and rising.

Wish You Were Here (1975) explored similar themes of madness and alienation. The 26-minute 'Shine On You Crazy Diamond' that book-ended the album was a tribute to Barrett. In between there was the acerbic 'Welcome To The Machine', the cynical 'Have A Cigar' and the melancholic, acoustic title track. The expectation surrounding the album ensured that it went to No. 1 in Britain and America. By now Waters was exercising increasing dominance over the group and the next album, *Animals* (1977), was a bleak, Orwellian view of the world laid out in three

vitriolic tracks – 'Dogs', 'Pigs (Three Different Ones)' and 'Sheep' – lightened by the acoustic, two-part 'Pigs On The Wing'. By now Pink Floyd's live show had developed into a spectacular production with quadraphonic sound, lights, film, animation and inflatable pigs hovering above the audience. In contrast, the band were deliberately anonymous on stage, focused on the music.

On Top Of The Wall

Pink Floyd's next album was Waters' most ambitious concept. *The Wall* (1979) was a dense double album that dealt with the barriers created by society and individuals. The dark, dramatic soundscape featured the powerful, emotional 'Comfortably Numb' and 'Another Brick In The Wall Part 2', an anti-education rant that was a rare but spectacularly successful single, topping the US charts for four weeks and a UK No. 1. *The Wall* spent 15 weeks at the top of the US album charts. For their live shows Pink Floyd constructed a giant wall across the stage between themselves and the audience and played behind it until the wall tumbled

see Introduction pp 194   see Sources & Sounds pp 186   see A–Z of Artists pp 210

down at the end. The scale of the production meant that concerts were only performed in Los Angeles, New York, London and Dortmund, Germany. However, in 1982 it was turned into the moview *Pink Floyd The Wall* directed by Alan Parker starring Bob Geldof.

But walls were now appearing between the members of Pink Floyd. Wright was fired during the making of the album although he was re-hired for the concerts. And Gilmour and Mason had little input into the next Pink Floyd album, *The Final Cut* (1983), a caustic, heartfelt diatribe by Waters on the futility of war and tyrannical politicians. Although the album went to No. 1 in the UK (*The Wall* had only reached No. 3) it peaked at No. 6 in the US and sold markedly less than previous albums. With no shows forthcoming the band had effectively ceased. In 1984 Gilmour released a solo album, *About Face*, and played a relatively low-key tour while Waters released *The Pros And Cons Of Hitch-Hiking* (1984) featuring Eric Clapton on guitar, and embarked on an arena tour of Europe and America.

A Watershed Period

In 1986 Waters announced that he had left Pink Floyd who were 'a spent force, creatively'. But Gilmour and Mason disagreed and confirmed their intention to continue. A legal battle then ensued over rights to the name. The next Pink Floyd album, *A Momentary Lapse Of Reason* (1987) restored Wright alongside Gilmour and Mason, although not full-time until legal issues were resolved. The album featured Gilmour songs (with co-writers) and made No. 3 in the UK and US. The band played a stadium tour of America and Europe that was captured on the live *Delicate Sound Of Thunder* (1987), which got to No. 11 in the US and UK.

Waters, meanwhile, released *Radio KAOS* (1987) and *Amused To Death* (1992). He also staged a massive production of *The Wall* on the site of the recently demolished Berlin Wall in 1990. Among the artists who took part were Van Morrison, Bryan Adams, Joni Mitchell, Sinead O'Connor, Marianne Faithfull, Cyndi Lauper, The Scorpions and members of The Band.

Reaching A Meltdown

Pink Floyd returned in 1994 with *The Division Bell*, another No. 1 album in the US and UK. The subsequent tour was lavish, even by Pink Floyd

standards, and included a complete performance of *Dark Side Of The Moon*. It was seen by over five million people and was again documented on the live *Pulse* (1995) – also No. 1 in the US and UK.

After the tour, Pink Floyd was wound down with Gilmour becoming increasingly reluctant to revive the band. In 2001 he played a solo concert as part of London's Meltdown Festival that he repeated the following year. He then began recording an album, the UK chart-topping *On An Island* (2006). Waters meanwhile undertook an 'In The Flesh' world tour in

2002 and worked on an opera, *Ca Ira* (2005). But apart from business dealings over a live album of *The Wall* – *Is There Anybody Out There?* (2000) – and the *Echoes* retrospective (2001) there was no contact between Waters and Gilmour.

So it was a considerable surprise in June 2005 when Bob Geldof announced that Pink Floyd – with Waters, Gilmour, Wright and Mason – would be appearing at the Live 8 Festival in London on 2 July, televised worldwide. They played a 25-minute set and dedicated 'Wish You Were Here' to their founder and mentor Syd Barrett. A year later – on 7 July 2006 – Barrett died from complications arising from diabetes.

Above
Nick Mason's self-deprecating drumming style enabled the band to explore long slow movements of music that saw subtle changes of mood of classical proportions.

see Marianne Faithfull pp 106   see The Band pp 136   see Joni Mitchell pp 144   see Van Morrison pp 219

Queen

208

*'A concert is not a live
rendition of our album.
It's a theatrical event.'*

Freddie Mercury

Right

Freddie Mercury was a
glamorous, flamboyant
frontman, who filled the
stage with his histrionic
vocal pyrotechnics.

Far Right

Queen were a perfectly
balanced, democratic band,
each member allowing the
others to express themselves
as much as they desired.

The gorgeously flamboyant Queen were formed in 1970 in London by singer Freddie Mercury (born Farrolch Bulsara, 5 September 1946), guitarist Brian May (born 19 July 1947), and drummer Roger Taylor (born Roger Meddows-Taylor, 26 July 1949), with bassist John Deacon (born 19 August 1951) completing the line up in 1971. They spent two years developing their style while they remained at college, playing few gigs. But once they started touring after the release of *Queen* (1973) their live performances – and Mercury's extrovert personality – quickly won them a loyal following.

Operatic Epics And Rock Anthems

Queen II (1974) gave the band their first UK hit with 'Seven Seas Of Rhye' but it was the tight harmonies and dynamic playing of 'Killer Queen' from their third album, *Sheer Heart Attack* (1974) that really caught the band's character and marked them out from the fading glam rock wave.

Queen delivered the *coup de grace* in 1975 with 'Bohemian Rhapsody', a six-minute epic that blended operatic vocals with metal guitars. The single, boosted by a ground-breaking video, stormed the British charts, staying at No. 1 for nine weeks. The equally extravagant album, *A Night At The Opera* (1975) also topped the UK charts and was a big international success. *A Day At The Races* (1976) maintained the momentum with the bombastic 'Tie Your Mother Down' and the compressed 'Somebody To Love' – while *News Of The World* (1977) featured two of rock's greatest anthems: 'We Will Rock You' and 'We Are The Champions'.

Jazz, Pop, Rock And Disco

By now Queen concerts were stadium rallies with the audience playing its part, conducted by the ever more flamboyant Mercury. *Live Killers* (1979) caught the full force of Queen's show. It followed the ambitious *Jazz* (1978) that ranged from metal to pop and included the

playful 'Fat Bottomed Girls' and the sporty 'Bicycle Race'.

The Game (1980) was a deliberate pop album. It was a UK No. 1 and their biggest US success, topping the charts for five weeks with two No. 1

see Introduction pp 194   *see Sources & Sounds pp 186*   *see A–Z of Artists pp 210*

singles – the jaunty 'Crazy Little Thing Called Love' and the feisty 'Another One Bites The Dust'. *Greatest Hits* (1981), featuring their latest triumph, 'Flash', the theme song to the *Flash Gordon* movie, was a massive worldwide success, not least in the UK where it stayed in the charts for nearly eight years. 1981 also saw the band tour South America, opening up the continent as a rock market. But concerts in apartheid South Africa caused problems when the band found themselves on the United Nations cultural blacklist.

Band members took time out for solo projects before the next Queen album, *Hot Space* (1982), which flirted with disco and funk and featured a collaboration with David Bowie, 'Under Pressure'. *The Works* (1984) was a broader musical sweep embracing synth pop ('Radio Ga Ga'), hard rock ('Hammer To Fall') and pop ('I Want To Break Free'). The following year they were one of the highlights of Live Aid. *A Kind Of Magic* (1986) included 'One Vision' and Queen played a major tour, climaxing at the UK's Knebworth Festival in August. It was the last show they played. The band took another sabbatical (Freddie Mercury collaborated with opera diva Montserrat Caballe for the melodramatic 'Barcelona') and it was three years before *The Miracle* (1989), which featured 'I Want It All' and 'Breakthru'.

Mercury's Genius Is Cruelly Halted

Rumours were already circulating about Mercury's health and the group chose not to tour but returned to the studio to record another album. *Innuendo* (1991) included 'Headlong' and the grandiose 'The Show Must Go On'. Mercury continued to deny increasing speculation on his health until November 1991 when he announced that he had AIDS. Two days later, on 24 November, he died at his London home.

In April 1992, the remaining Queen members staged A Concert For Life at London's Wembley Stadium, joined by Elton John, George Michael, David Bowie, Guns N' Roses, Metallica and Spinal Tap. That year Queen's iconic status became assured when 'Bohemian Rhapsody' was memorably featured in the *Wayne's World* movie. *Made In Heaven* (1995) was an album of songs recorded with Mercury shortly before he died. It debuted at No. 1 and became Queen's best-selling studio album. Periodically, the remaining group members revive the band for a project. In 2005 and 2006 they toured with former Free and Bad Company vocalist Paul Rogers. But everyone knows Freddie Mercury can never be replaced.

🎸 *see David Bowie pp 196*   🎸 *see Elton John pp 232*   🎸 *see Guns N'Roses pp 298*   🎸 *see Metallica pp 332*

A-Z of Artists

Aerosmith
(Vocal group, 1973–present)

This best-selling American heavy rock band, frequently compared to The Rolling Stones and Led Zeppelin, centred on the relationship between principal members Steven Tyler (vocals) and Joe Perry (guitar). The pair came together in Boston, Massachusetts, with Joey Kramer (drums), Brad Whitford (guitar) and Tom Hamilton (bass). Their first album *Aerosmith* (1973) was an immediate success, paving the way for the multi-platinum *Toys In The Attic* (1974) and *Rocks* (1975).

Antagonism between Tyler and Perry led to the latter's departure in 1980, to be replaced by Jimmy Crespo. Differences were set aside four years later when Perry returned to the fold. The band's profile was raised by the ground-breaking collaboration with rappers Run DMC on the single 'Walk This Way', leading to a triumphant resurgence in Aerosmith's fortunes with *Permanent Vacation* (1987), *Pump* (1989) and *Get A Grip* (1993). Aerosmith were a key influence on 1990s American hard rock.

Above
AC/DC's appeal lay in their direct and unfussy hard rock.

AC/DC
(Vocal group, 1973–present)

A hard-rocking quintet whose no frills approach garnered them a huge following, AC/DC were formed in Sydney in 1973 by expatriate Scottish brothers Angus and Malcolm Young (both guitar). Bon Scott became lead singer in 1974. After two Antipodes-only albums, the band moved to America where their fifth album for Atlantic Records, *Highway To Hell* (1979), produced by Mutt Lange, established them in the big league, selling over six million copies. Its title track became a rock radio anthem.

The hard-living Scott died from alcoholic poisoning in London in February 1980 and was replaced by former Geordie singer Brian Johnson. The transition was seamless; AC/DC's first album with Johnson *Back In Black* (1980) provided their only UK No. 1. With a revolving cast of drummers and bassists, AC/DC have stuck to a winning formula, eschewing the vagaries of fashion in favour of direct, audience-pleasing rock'n'roll.

Right
Steve Tyler and Joe Perry propelled Aerosmith to the very tip of American rock, where their influence is still felt today.

see Introduction pp 194   see Sources & Sounds pp 186   see Key Artists pp 196

Alice Cooper

(Vocals, b. 1948)

Although over time the name Alice Cooper came
to attach itself to singer Vincent Furnier, it originally
applied to the rock band that he fronted, the classic
line-up of which comprised Cooper, Glen Buxton
(guitar), Michael Bruce (guitar), Dennis Dunaway
(bass) and Neal Smith (drums). After recording
two albums for Frank Zappa's Straight label, the
band relocated from California back to Detroit,
developing the outrageous stage act for which
Cooper became infamous.

    The 1972 single and album, *School's Out*
made Cooper a major star in America and Britain,
where his outrageous image and theatrics fitted
in well with the glam rock scene. 1973's *Billion
Dollar Babies* was a transatlantic No. 1 and his last
work with the original band members. After several
more hits, Cooper succumbed to alcoholism in the
late 1970s and his star waned until the success of
the 1989 album *Trash* and single 'Poison' resurrected
his career.

The Allman Brothers

(Vocal group, 1969–76, 1978–82, 1989–present)

A southern American blues-rock band comprising
Duane Allman (guitar), Gregg Allman (vocals, organ),
Dickey Betts (guitar, vocals), Berry Oakley (bass),
Butch Trucks and Jai Johanny 'Jaimoe' Johanson (both
drums). The Allmans' incendiary double lead guitar
sound was captured on *Live At The Fillmore East*
(1971). Despite the deaths of Duane Allman (in 1971)
and Oakley (in 1972) in eerily similar motorcycle
accidents, the band played on.

Atomic Rooster

(Vocal group, 1969–73, 1980–83)

A British progressive rock band founded by ex-Crazy
World of Arthur Brown members Vincent Crane
(organ) and Carl Palmer (drums), plus bassist Nick
Graham. After one self-titled album in 1970, Palmer
and Graham left and were replaced by John Cann
(guitar, vocals) and Paul Hammond (drums), scoring
two UK hit singles 'Tomorrow Night' and 'Devil's
Answer' but fragmenting after two albums, Atomic
Rooster finally folded after one further LP.

Bachman-Turner Overdrive

(Vocal group, 1973–84)

This hard-driving Canadian rock band were assembled
by former Guess Who members Randy Bachman
(guitar, vocals) and Chad Allen (keyboards) with
Robbie Bachman (drums) and Fred Turner (bass).
Third brother Tim Bachman soon replaced Allan and
the band's commercial breakthrough came with
Bachman-Turner Overdrive II (1974) and the US hit
'Takin' Care Of Business'. In Britain, they are best
remembered for the 1975 single 'You Ain't Seen
Nothing Yet'.

Above

Atomic Rooster originally
included Carl Palmer of
Emerson, Lake and Palmer.
Their classic recordings though
came after his departure.

see The Rolling Stones pp 96   *see* The Crazy World Of Arthur Brown pp 104   *see* Led Zeppelin pp 200   *see* Run-DMC pp 312

Jeff Beck

(Guitar, vocals, b. 1944)

Regarded as one of Britain's finest rock guitarists, Beck left The Yardbirds in 1968 to form the Jeff Beck Group, initially featuring Rod Stewart on vocals. The band's second incarnation made two ground-breaking albums that mixed rock and pop with jazz and R&B. In 1972, the guitarist became part of the short-lived power trio Beck, Bogert and Appice before making an all-instrumental jazz-fusion album *Blow By Blow* (1975) and a collaborative work with keyboardist Jan Hammer, 1976's *Wired*. After a live album with Hammer's group in 1977, Beck did not record again until 1980's *There And Back*.

His career in the 1980s and 1990s was sporadic, littered with guest appearances, notably on Tina Turner's *Private Dancer* (1984) and Jimmy Page and Robert Plant's *Honeydrippers Vol. 1* (1984). Latterly, he has developed a new style, mixing electronics with his familiar blues-rock playing.

Black Sabbath

(Vocal group, 1970–present)

Pioneers of heavy metal, Sabbath hailed from Birmingham, England and comprised John 'Ozzy' Osbourne (vocals), Tony Iommi (guitar), Terence 'Geezer' Butler (bass), and Bill Ward (drums). Their second album's title track 'Paranoid' was a rare hit single as Black Sabbath's reputation was built on a series of 1970s albums featuring doom-laden lyrics set to downtuned guitar. Osbourne was fired in 1979, finally rejoining his colleagues in 1997.

see Introduction pp 194   *see* Sources & Sounds pp 186   *see* Key Artists pp 196

Liebezeit (drums) and, briefly, David Johnson (flute). American singer Malcolm Mooney joined for Can's debut album *Monster Movie* (1969), which showcased the band's lengthy, hypnotic improvisations, underpinned by cyclical, repetitive drumming.

Mooney left in 1971 and the band recorded three albums with his replacement, Japanese singer Kenji 'Damo' Suzuki, *Tago Mago* (1971), *Ege Bamyasi* (1972) and *Future Days* (1973), which edged towards ambient music. Can established a significant following in Britain and in 1976, achieved a minor hit with 'I Want More' by which time Suzuki had departed leaving Schmidt and Karoli to share vocals. The recruitment of less sympathetic musicians had a deleterious effect on Can's music hastening 1979's split.

Boston

(Vocal group, 1976–present)

A mainstream American rock band whose meticulously layered music was largely the brainchild of songwriter, guitarist and producer Tom Scholz, Boston's line-up was completed by Brad Delp (vocals), Barry Goudreau (guitar), Sib Hashian (drums) and Fran Sheehan (bass). The all-conquering first album *Boston* released in 1976 became the biggest-selling debut of all time and yielded the hit single 'More Than A Feeling'. Ever the perfectionist, Scholz considered the follow up, *Don't Look Back*, which appeared in 1978 – when a two-year gap between albums was regarded as excessive – to be a rush job for which he blamed record company Epic. Exactly duplicating its predecessor's formula, the album sold seven million copies.

Eight years later, Boston's next album, *Third Stage* (1986), emerged boasting the US No. 1 single 'Amanda'. For 1994's *Walk On* Delp was replaced as vocalist by Fran Cosmo, although he returned for *Corporate America* (2002).

Can

(Vocal group, 1969–79)

An experimental German outfit, Can were significantly influential on both rock and dance music. The band was founded by students of avant-garde composer Karlheinz Stockhausen: Holger Czukay (bass) and Irmin Schmidt (keyboards), with Michael Karoli (guitar), Jaki

Cockney Rebel

(Vocal group, 1973–78)

Led by singer Steve Harley, Cockney Rebel's first line-up was Jean-Paul Crocker (violin), Paul Jeffreys (bass), Milton Reame-James (keyboards) and Stuart Elliot (drums). Debut album *The Human Menagerie* (1973) was unusual for the absence of lead guitar. Harley sacked all except Elliot after *The Psychomodo* (1974). Rebel mark II emerged with the 1975 UK No. 1 'Make Me Smile (Come Up And See Me)' and made four more albums before Harley went solo.

Left

Boston's stylish soft rock was particularly popular with middle America. Their radio-friendly approach took them to the top of the charts with hits like 'More Than A Feelin'' and 'Peace Of Mind'.

Below

Can, made up of German devotees of classical *avant-garde* composer Stockhausen, successfully combined rock electronics and world music.

see The Yardbirds pp 117   see Rod Stewart pp 234   see Tina Turner pp 245

Deep Purple

(Vocal/instrumental group, 1968–present)

Deep Purple have sold over 100 million records in a 38-year career – continuous apart from a hiatus between 1976 and 1984 – so are one of the more commercially successful rock bands in history. Though classed as contemporaries of fellow early 1970s trailblazers Led Zeppelin and Black Sabbath, Purple were distinctly different, drawing on classical, jazz, R&B and (later) funk roots. They let live performance spread the word and cut one of the all time classic concert albums in 1972's *Made In Japan*, which included all time air-guitar anthem 'Smoke On the Water'.

Their classic line-up captured on 1970's *In Rock* was Ritchie Blackmore (guitar), Jon Lord (keyboards), Ian Gillan (vocals), Ian Paice (drums) and Roger Glover (bass). The latter three were still in harness in 2006 with Don Airey (keyboards) and sole American Steve Morse (guitar), and now play extensively to South American and former Iron Curtain countries where their popularity endures.

Dave Edmunds

(Guitar, vocals, b. 1944)

Multi-talented Welshman Edmunds' first exposure was as lead guitarist on Love Sculpture's 1968 hit 'Sabre Dance', followed by the UK No. 1 and US Top 5 single 'I Hear You Knocking'. After building Rockfield, a state-of-the-art studio, in south Wales his recording career took a backseat as he became an in-demand producer, working with, amongst others, Shakin' Stevens. Edmunds subsequently formed Rockpile with Nick Lowe but the band's recorded output failed to match their live shows.

Emerson, Lake and Palmer

(Vocal/instrumental group, 1970–78, 1992–98)

A British supergroup, who pioneered progressive rock in the early 1970s, comprised former Nice keyboardist Keith Emerson, Greg Lake, latterly of King Crimson (guitar, bass, vocals) and ex-Atomic Rooster drummer Carl Palmer. ELP's music was a fusion of classical music and rock, which Emerson had begun to explore in The Nice. Most of the band's lyrics were written by former King Crimson wordsmith Peter Sinfield. ELP made their first major appearance at the Isle of Wight Festival in 1970, releasing their self-titled debut album later that year. The immensely popular *Tarkus* followed in 1971 and the band's third album was a live rendition of Mussorgsky's *Pictures At An Exhibition* (1972).

Their best-known work, 1973's *Brain Salad Surgery* was dominated by the epic 'Karn Evil 9'. Notorious for their extravagant live shows, ELP fell from fashion during the punk era, disbanding in 1978 but reforming in the 1990s.

The Flying Burrito Brothers

(Vocal group, 1969–99)

Having invented country rock in The Byrds, Chris Hillman and Gram Parsons (both guitar, vocals) formed The Burritos to further explore its possibilities, recruiting pianist/bassist Chris Ethridge and guitarist 'Sneaky' Pete Kleinow. *The Gilded Palace Of Sin* (1969) featured some of Parsons' finest work but he was sacked after 1970's *Burrito Deluxe*. Bernie Leadon and former Byrds drummer Michael Clarke joined and, in 1972, Hillman departed a constantly shifting line-up.

see Introduction pp 194   *see* Sources & Sounds pp 186   *see* Key Artists pp 196

Peter Frampton

(Guitar, vocals, b. 1950)

Beginning a solo career after leaving Humble Pie, his third album *Frampton Comes Alive* (1976) was a phenomenal success in America, becoming the best-selling live album of all time. The transatlantic hit 'Show Me The Way' featured Frampton's trademark use of the talk box device. 1977's million-selling *I'm In You* was a relative failure and subsequent albums continued the downward spiral. Frampton took a four-year break from music after 1982.

Free

(Vocal/instrumental group, 1968–73)

Comprising Paul Rodgers (vocals), Simon Kirke (drums), Paul Kossoff (guitar) and Andy Fraser (bass), Free made headlines in 1970. After two respected albums, *Tons Of Sobs* (1968) and *Free* (1969), had been promoted in Britain and, via a support slot to Eric Clapton's supergroup Blind Faith, the States, their primal blues-rock power made them the stars of the year's Isle of Wight Festival. Hit single 'All Right Now' reached No. 2, and all looked set for lasting stardom.

But *Highway* (1970), a hurried follow-up to No. 2 hit album *Fire And Water* (1970), failed to break the UK Top 40, Kossoff's drug problems spiralled, songwriters Rodgers and Fraser clashed and a potentially world-beating band limped to a sorry conclusion in 1973. Rodgers and Kirke, the only originals, continued in Bad Company, who stripped out the commercial aspects of Free's raw blues and turned them into radio and stadium-friendly chest-beaters; Rodgers recently fronted a reformed Queen, while Kossoff died in 1976, one of British rock's most grievously wasted talents.

🔊 *see* Blind Faith pp 103 🔊 *see* The Byrds pp 124 🔊 *see* Atomic Rooster pp 211 🔊 *see* Black Sabbath pp 212

Genesis

(Vocal group, 1967–99)

The core of Genesis, Peter Gabriel (vocals), Tony Banks (keyboards) and Mike Rutherford (bass) met at Charterhouse School in the mid-1960s. The recruitment of Steve Hackett (guitar) and Phil Collins (drums) in 1970 completed the classic line-up, which recorded *Nursery Cryme* (1971) *Foxtrot* (1972) and *Selling England By The Pound* (1973), albums whose complex songs characterized English progressive rock.

Tensions between Gabriel and his colleagues following the ambitious concept album *The Lamb Lies Down On Broadway* (1974) saw the singer quit to be replaced at the microphone by the slightly reluctant Collins. *Trick Of The Tail* (1976) became the band's biggest US success so far. Genesis continued to prosper as a trio when Hackett departed after 1977's *Wind And Wuthering*.

In the 1980s, a more radio-friendly approach yielded the band's most commercially successful period. Collins left in 1997 and Genesis made one more album with singer Ray Wilson.

George Harrison

(Guitar, vocals, 1943–2001)

Harrison initially became the most successful solo Beatle with the blockbuster triple album *All Things Must Pass* (1971) and the transatlantic chart topper 'My Sweet Lord'. George diverted himself into raising funds for the disaster in Bangladesh with an all-star charity gig at New York's Madison Square Garden in August 1971. The event was commemorated in the triple live set *Concert For Bangladesh* (1971). He resumed his recording career with 1972's *Living In The Material World*. *Dark Horse* (1974), *Extra Texture* (1975) and *Thirty-Three And A Third* (1976) suffered from diminishing results and he took a sabbatical after 1982's poorly received *Gone Troppo*.

Harrison bounced back with *Cloud Nine* (1987) and the smash hit 'Got My Mind Set On You'. Soon afterwards, he founded the all-star outfit Travelling Wilburys. His last solo studio album would be *Brainwashed* (2002), released a year after his death from cancer in 2001.

Hawkwind

(Vocal group, 1969–present)

Purveyors of space rock since the late 1960s, when Hawkwind were formed in the hippy community of London's Ladbroke Grove. The band's line-up has rarely remained stable for long but at the time of the surprise UK No. 3 'Silver Machine' in 1972, the core members were ever-present founder Dave Brock (guitar, vocals), Nik Turner (saxophone, vocals), Del Dettmar (synthesizer), Dik Mik (audio generator),

see Introduction pp 194   see Sources & Sounds pp 186   see Key Artists pp 196

Lemmy (bass, vocals), Simon King (drums) and poet/writer Robert Calvert.

1973's double live set *Space Ritual* caught Hawkwind at their peak, and a relatively stable line-up recorded *Hall Of The Mountain Grill* (1974). Fantasy author Michael Moorcock replaced Calvert and second drummer Alan Powell and violinist Simon House were added for *Warrior On The Edge Of Time* (1975). Over the years, the band slipped into the margins but their sci-fi psychedelia and basic rhythmic throb influenced punk, heavy rock and the rave generation.

Humble Pie
(Vocal group, 1969–75)
British supergroup Humble Pie were created around former Small Face Steve Marriott (guitar, vocals) and ex-Herd man Peter Frampton (guitar, vocals), with Greg Ridley (bass) and Jerry Shirley (drums). Initially combining acoustic and hard-rocking sets, the former were abandoned shortly before Frampton left to be replaced by Colosseum's Dave Clempson. The band split in 1975 and reformed briefly in 1980. A further revival was mooted shortly before Marriott died in 1991.

Jefferson Starship
(Vocal group, 1970–84)
The successor band to Jefferson Airplane whose official debut was 1974's *Dragonfly* although the name had been used by singer/guitarist Paul Kantner on *Blows Against The Empire* (1970). Former Airplane vocalist Grace Slick joined the new band along with David Freiberg (bass), John Barbata (drums), Pete Sears (keyboards) and Craig Chaquico (guitar). Ex-Airplane singer Marty Balin signed up for 1975's *Red Octopus*, Jefferson Starship's biggest success. The band evolved into the commercially successful Starship in 1984.

Below
Hawkwind, like many of their psychedelic contemporaries went through a great many changes of personnel.

🎸 *see* The Herd pp 108 🎸 *see* The Small Faces pp 114 🎸 *see* Jefferson Airplane pp 142 🎸 *see* Phil Collins pp 292

Kraftwerk

(Vocal/instrumental group, 1970–present)

This German electronic group's pioneering use of synthesizers made them one of the all time most influential bands. Co-founders Florian Schneider and Ralf Hütter set up Kling Klang Studio in Düsseldorf in 1970 where the pair made three albums. They were augmented by electronic percussionists Wolfgang Flür and Karl Bartos on a tour to promote the band's fourth album *Autobahn* (1974), completing Kraftwerk's classic line-up. *Autobahn* brought the group to an international audience when the title track became a Top 30 hit in Britain and America in 1975.

The three albums that followed, *Radio-Activity* (1975), *Trans-Europe Express* (1977) and *The Man Machine* (1978) were to alter the course of popular music, highlighting the possibilities of the synthesizer as a lead instrument. Live performances played up the mechanical angle, using life-size robot replicas of the band members. Kraftwerk continue to release albums, albeit with increasingly long gaps.

John Lennon

(Guitar, vocals, 1940–80)

Lennon's post-Beatles solo career began with *John Lennon/Plastic Ono Band* (1970), a harrowingly honest record inspired by the Primal Scream therapy that Lennon was undergoing. *Imagine* (1971) featured his best-loved song (not released as a UK single until 1975) and was a more sugar-coated affair. The double album *Sometime In New York City* (1972) featured politically charged lyrics and received a hostile reception. The

Above

Kiss combined New York glam with heavy metal licks and became one of the biggest-selling US bands of the 1970s.

Right Middle

Lynyrd Skynyrd were an influential Florida band who suffered the loss of their lead singer, Ronnie Van Zant in a tragic air crash in 1977.

Right

Some consider John Lennon's post-Beatles output to be more sophisticated than his classic contributions to one of the greatest ever rock bands.

Kiss

(Vocal group, 1973–present)

Kiss, founded by New Yorkers Gene Simmons (bass, vocals) and Paul Stanley (guitar, vocals), combined the showmanship of glam rock and the drive of heavy metal. Recruiting Peter Criss (drums, vocals) and Paul 'Ace' Frehley (guitar, vocals) and adopting the costumes and elaborate stage make-up which they never appeared in public without, Kiss's early albums made little impact but their reputation grew via an increasingly extravagant stage show. The classic live album, 1975's *Alive* went quadruple platinum in the States.

The ambitious *Destroyer* (1976), *Rock And Roll Over* (1976) and *Love Gun* (1977) consolidated Kiss's position as America's top rock act along with a second live set *Alive II* (1977), the fourth side of which contained new studio material. All four members released solo albums simultaneously in 1978. Criss and Frehley had departed by the time Kiss unmasked in 1983 although they, and the make-up, would return.

🎙 *see* Introduction pp 194 🎙 *see* Sources & Sounds pp 186 🎙 *see* Key Artists pp 196

workmanlike *Mind Games* (1973) was recorded in the shadow of Lennon's separation from Yoko Ono. His infamous 'lost weekend' in LA produced 1974's *Walls And Bridges*, a partial return to form.

He was reunited with Yoko Ono in 1974 and, after the birth of son Sean in 1975; Lennon temporarily retired from music, becoming a house-husband. Shortly before his murder in 1980, he re-emerged with *Double Fantasy*, an album shared equally between Lennon and Ono. A second collaboration, *Milk And Honey*, was released posthumously in 1984.

Lynyrd Skynyrd
(Vocal group, 1973–present)

This southern rock band came together in Jacksonville, Florida, around the core of Ronnie Van Zant (vocals), Allen Collins (guitar) and Gary Rossington (guitar), plus Billy Powell (keyboards), Larry Junstrom (bass), and Bob Burns (drums). An air crash shortly before the release of their sixth album *Street Survivors* in 1977 claimed the lives of Van Zant and additional guitarist Steve Gaines, although the band continued. Skynyrd remain best known for the anthemic 'Freebird'.

John Martyn
(Guitar, vocals, b. 1948)

A Scottish singer/songwriter (real name Iain McGeachy) who mixed folk, blues and jazz and developed his trademark guitar sound by use of the Echoplex, a tape delay machine, Martyn made his debut with 1968's *London Conversation* and after two albums with then wife Beverly, he released the seminal *Solid Air* (1973), a prototype ambient album. On 1980's *Grace And Danger*, Martyn made the transition from solo artist to band leader. Despite health problems, he remains active.

Van Morrison
(Vocals, b. 1945)

After leaving Irish beat group Them, Van Morrison relocated to the States in 1967 to launch a solo career. His debut single 'Brown Eyed Girl' was a hit in America but not Britain. His second album *Astral Weeks* (1968) was a massively influential work, which added Celtic and jazz influences to his R&B and soul roots. Particularly prolific in the mid-1970s, Morrison has made over 30 albums in his career.

Below
Van Morrison's *Astral Weeks* remains one of rock's most interesting explorations, and Morrison himself continues to inspire new generations of musicians.

📻 *see* The Beatles pp 88 📻 *see* Them pp 115

Mott The Hoople

(Vocal group, 1969–74)

A riotous rock band comprising Ian Hunter (vocals, keyboards), Mick Ralphs (guitar), Pete 'Overend' Watts (bass), Verden Allen (organ) and Dale 'Buffin' Griffin (drums), Mott were about to split when offered 'All The Young Dudes' by David Bowie in 1972. This began a string of five hits and two successful albums *Mott* (1973) and *The Hoople* (1974). Guitarist Mick Ronson joined in 1974 but musical differences prompted the band's dissolution later that year.

Nazareth

(Vocal group, 1970–present)

Hard rockers from Dunfermline, Scotland, Nazareth comprised Dan McCafferty (vocals), Manny Charlton (guitar), Pete Agnew (bass) and Darrell Sweet (drums).

They enjoyed three UK Top 20 hits in 1973. A cover of The Everly's 'Love Hurts' went Top 10 Stateside in 1975 and the title track from *Hair Of The Dog* (1975) was a rock radio hit. Band activities were suspended in the late 1980s but Nazareth regrouped for the acclaimed *No Jive* in 1991.

Mike Oldfield

(Multi-instrumentalist, b. 1953)

A prodigiously talented musician, Oldfield played all the instruments on 1973's *Tubular Bells*. This symphonic work was a transatlantic best-seller, helped by the use of its main theme in the movie *The Exorcist* (1973). *Hergest Ridge* (1974) was a British No. 1 whilst *Ommadawn* (1975) and *Incantations* (1978) displayed African and folk influences. *Platinum* (1979) marked a change of direction to individual songs. Oldfield has since reworked *Tubular Bells* several times.

Below

The 1970s produced its fair share of rockers but Nazareth shone brighter than most with their hard-kicking rock.

see Introduction pp 194 ⏤ see Sources & Sounds pp 186 ⏤ see Key Artists pp 196

Rush

(Vocal group, 1968–present)

A Canadian power trio, Geddy Lee (bass, keyboards, vocals), Alex Lifeson (guitar) and Neil Peart (drummer, lyricist) came together in 1968, though with original drummer John Rutsey until 1974. Their blend of progressive rock and heavy metal was at its peak on the concept album *2112* (1976) and *A Farewell To Kings* (1977). *Permanent Waves* (1980) and *Moving Pictures* (1981) were punchier and new wave influenced. After the extensive use of synthesizers in the mid-1980s, Rush returned to their roots in the 1990s.

Boz Scaggs

(Guitar, vocals, b. 1944)

The smooth, sophisticated pop of the enormously successful 1976 album *Silk Degrees* remains William 'Boz' Scaggs' best-known work. Previously a member of The Steve Miller Band, Scaggs first recorded solo in 1965, but it was his seventh album which brought him widespread acclaim and spawned three hit singles, plus a cover of 'We're All Alone' by Rita Coolidge. His increasingly sporadic output since *Silk Degrees* has failed to repeat its impact.

Paul Simon

(Guitar, vocals, b. 1941)

Paul Simon (1972) was an eclectic affair followed a year later by the more straightforward *There Goes Rhymin' Simon*. His third solo album *Still Crazy After All These Years* (1975) featured a reunion with Art Garfunkel on the duet 'My Little Town'. The singer's most popular and influential work was *Graceland* (1986), which utilized African musicians, helping popularize what would be dubbed 'World Music'.

Above
Rush were proud exponents of pomp rock, with their flashy two-neck guitars and power rock sound.

see The Everly Brothers pp 46   see Simon and Garfunkel pp 147   see The Steve Miller Band pp 148   see David Bowie pp 196

Bruce Springsteen

(Guitar, vocals, b. 1949)

Hailed as the new Dylan after two albums, Springsteen fully realized his potential with the widescreen *Born To Run* (1975). Managerial problems delayed *Darkness On The Edge Of Town* (1978), a more sombre but no less compelling work. The double album *The River* appeared in 1980 followed by the stark, pessimistic *Nebraska* in 1982.

1984's *Born In The USA* catapulted Springsteen into the mainstream, selling 14 million copies worldwide, whilst an estimated two million people saw the accompanying world tour. Backed by the E Street Band, Springsteen was without equal as a live performer, with gigs often lasting over four hours, as documented on the 1986 five-record epic *Live 1977–85*. He opted for a more intimate approach for *Tunnel Of Love* (1987), which detailed the breakdown of his first marriage and was Springsteen's last work with the E Street Band until a 1999 reunion tour.

Status Quo

(Vocal group, 1967–present)

The great survivors of British rock, Quo are synonymous with three-chord boogie but first came to public attention in 1967 with the psychedelically flavoured single 'Picture Of Matchstick Men' (their only US Top 20 hit). A change of direction to their more familiar style was heralded by the single 'Down The Dustpipe' and explored more fully on the 1970 album *Ma Kelly's Greasy Spoon*. The line-up coalesced around the ever-present duo of Francis Rossi (guitar, vocals) and Rick Parfitt (guitar) with Alan Lancaster (bass) and Richard Coughlan (drums).

Bedecked in denim and plimsolls, Quo were a potent live force, consolidating their popularity with a string of consistent albums *Piledriver*, *Hello* (both 1973), *Quo* (1974), *On The Level* (1975) and *Blue For You* (1976). Their many hits include 'Caroline', their only UK singles chart topper 'Down Down' and the song that would open Live Aid, John Fogerty's 'Rocking All Over The World'.

Steely Dan

(Vocal group, 1972–81, 1993–present)

This critically acclaimed New York outfit was formed around the nucleus of songwriters of Walter Becker (bass, vocals) and Donald Fagen (keyboards, vocals). Drummer Jim Hodder and guitarists Denny Dias and Jeff 'Skunk' Baxter completed the line-up along with vocalist David Palmer, recruited because Fagen was not sufficiently confident in his own singing. Their debut *Can't Buy A Thrill* (1972) contained radio staples 'Reeling In The Years' and 'Do It Again' and displayed the band's diverse influences from jazz to pop, rock'n'roll to funk.

Palmer left before the less impressive follow-up *Countdown To Ecstasy* (1973) but the Dan were back on peak form on 1974's *Pretzel Logic*, at which point Fagen and Becker started to rely increasingly on session

Below
Springsteen has a distinctive line in gritty story-telling. His 1970s' shows though were lively, dynamic and bombastic.

🔊 *see Introduction pp 194* 🔊 *see Sources & Sounds pp 186* 🔊 *see Key Artists pp 196*

musicians, whose ranks included keyboardist/singer Michael McDonald. After an extended hiatus following 1980's *Gaucho*, Steely Dan reformed in 1993 and, surprisingly, have returned to the live arena.

Supertramp
(Vocal group, 1970–present)
Keyboard player Rick Davies assembled Supertramp under the patronage of a Dutch millionaire. His most important recruit was singer Roger Hodgson. After several line-up changes, Dougie Thomson (bass), Bob Siebenberg (drums) and John Helliwell (saxophone, keyboards) joined for the third album *Crime Of The Century* (1974), which mixed progressive rock with accessible melodies and proved their commercial breakthrough, assisted by the hit singles 'Dreamer' in Britain and 'Bloody Well Right' in America. *Crisis? What Crisis?* (1975) and *Even In The Quietest Moments* (1977) were less successful.

Supertramp relocated to the States and their material became more pop orientated. 1979's *Breakfast In America* scaled the heights worldwide, spawning hits with the title track, 'The Logical Song' and 'Take The Long Way Home'. Citing musical differences with Davies, Hodgson left after *Goodbye Stranger* (1982). Davies has kept Supertramp alive with a combination of old and new members, but without Hodgson.

Tangerine Dream
(Vocal/instrumental group, 1970–present)
A German electronic outfit founded by Edgar Froese (guitar), whose main lieutenants were Christophe Franke (drums) and Peter Baumann (organ). Operating as a keyboard trio, their experimental 1970s work fitted the progressive *zeitgeist*. Employing tape effects and synthesizer technology, Tangerine Dream's output was largely instrumental space rock, with an otherworldly ambience. They achieved an unexpected UK chart success with 1973's *Phaedra*, the first commercial album to feature the sequencer.

James Taylor
(Guitar, vocals, b. 1948)
Discovered by The Beatles' Apple label for whom he recorded his first album in 1968, Taylor moved back to America to seek a cure for heroin addiction. He signed

to Warners and unleashed the three-million selling *Sweet Baby James* in 1970. Although his early work typified the sensitive early 1970s singer/songwriter, 1977's *JT* displayed a more upbeat approach. His 1976 *Greatest Hits* collection was certified diamond for 10 million sales.

Above
Supertramp, in full flairs and white suits left the UK to become superstars in the US, with the best-selling album *Breakfast In America*.

see The Beatles pp 88   *see* The Rolling Stones pp 96   *see* Bob Dylan pp 126   *see* Kraftwerk pp 218

224

Ten Years After

(Vocal group, 1967–74)

This British blues rock outfit first found success in the States with the 1969 hit 'I'm Going Home' and an acclaimed appearance at the Woodstock Festival. Led by guitarist and singer Alvin Lee, with Leo Lyons (bass), Chick Churchill (keyboards) and Ric Lee (drums), the band reached the UK Top 10 with 'Love Like A Man' and had four Top 5 albums before disbanding in 1974. A Y2K line-up featured Joe Gooch as frontman.

Thin Lizzy

(Vocal group, 1970–84)

This Irish hard rock band were led by the charismatic Phil Lynott (bass, vocals), with Brian Downey (drums) and, for the classic line-up, the twin lead guitars of Scott Gorham and Brian Robertson. The 1976 smash 'The Boys Are Back In Town' marked the start of the band's golden period, culminating in the classic *Live And Dangerous* (1978). Thin Lizzy split in the 1980s and Lynott died in 1986.

Joe Walsh

(Guitar, vocals, b. 1947)

An American guitar hero, Walsh was in the James Gang before making his solo bow with *Barnstorm* (1972). *The Smoker You Drink, The Player You Get* (1973) contained the voice-box classic 'Rocky Mountain Way'. In 1976, Walsh joined The Eagles, replacing Bernie Leadon. Rekindling his own career with 1978's *But Seriously Folks*, featuring the self-mocking 'Life's Been Good', he has since continued to record and has participated in Eagles' reunions.

Below
Phil Lynott was a brilliant frontman for Thin Lizzy who brought them great success.

🎵 *see Introduction pp 194*   🎵 *see Sources & Sounds pp 186*   🎵 *see Key Artists pp 196*

following the sacking and subsequent death by overdose of Whitten, as reflected in *Time Fades Away* (1973), *On The Beach* (1974) and *Tonight's The Night* (1975, recorded in 1973). His next album *Zuma* (1975) featured one of Young's most celebrated songs, 'Cortez The Killer'. 1978's *Rust Never Sleeps* represented a positive reaction to punk, befitting an artist who has never allowed himself to become complacent.

Left
Yes' live shows were dominated by the rows of guitars and banks of keyboards basking in the glow of progressive rock.

Yes

(Vocal group, 1968–present)

The quintessential progressive rock outfit, Yes were formed in late-1960s London by bassist Chris Squire, singer Jon Anderson and drummer Bill Bruford. Early albums *Yes* (1969) and *Time And A Word* (1970) only hinted at their potential. *The Yes Album* (1970) featured new guitarist Steve Howe and established them as a major force with virtuoso musicianship, epic songs and Anderson's unique voice and lyrics. The classic line-up was completed when keyboard maestro Rick Wakeman joined for *Fragile* (1971). 1972's *Close To The Edge* saw Yes at the peak of their powers.

Alan White replaced Bruford on *Tales From Topographic Oceans* (1973) a double set containing four side-long compositions. Disillusioned by the band's direction, Wakeman left to be replaced by Patrick Moraz on *Relayer* (1974). He returned for 1977's *Going For The One*. Personnel changes continued to bedevil Yes through the 1980s and 1990s, with Squire the only ever-present.

Neil Young

(Guitar, vocals, b. 1945)

This highly respected Canadian musician first came to prominence in 1967 as a member of Buffalo Springfield. Young's solo career began in 1969 with *Neil Young*. For his next album, *Everybody Knows This Is Nowhere* (1969), he recruited Danny Whitten (guitar), Billy Talbot (bass) and Ralph Molina (drums), collectively known as Crazy Horse. Shortly afterwards, Young joined Crosby, Stills and Nash for an album and tour.

1972's country-tinged 'solo' album *Harvest* was a huge seller, but darkness engulfed Young's work

ZZ Top

(Vocal group, 1970–present)

A visually distinctive Texan trio comprising Billy Gibbons (vocals, guitar), Dusty Hill (bass, vocals), and Frank Beard (drums), ZZ Top honed their southern boogie through constant gigging. Supporting The Rolling Stones brought them to a wider audience and the third album *Tres Hombres* (1973) was the band's commercial breakthrough. They went on to experience million-selling success with 1983's *Eliminator* and the singles 'Gimme All Your Lovin'', 'Sharp Dressed Man' and 'Legs'.

Above
Neil Young's whining delivery and anarchic guitar style won over a generation of fans.

see Buffalo Springfield pp 138   see Crosby, Stills and Nash pp 140   see The Eagles pp 198   see Emerson, Lake and Palmer pp 214

SEVENTIES POP & DISCO

The dance culture of disco permeated the 1970s, revitalizing the career of The Bee Gees and giving Rod Stewart a nudge towards the dancefloor. 'Da Ya Think I'm Sexy?' indeed! The prevailing ethos, as *Rolling Stone* magazine put it, was 'lifeless yet sexy, campy yet populist' and disco sold in its millions. Sophisticated artists like Steely Dan and Boz Scaggs seasoned the music with a little funk, while The Average White Band proved that even Glaswegians could boogie on down with the best.

Yet there was still room in the charts and people's hearts for pop. Whether it was one woman and her piano in the case of Carole King or a bearded Brummie with string accompaniment (Jeff Lynne's Electric Light Orchestra), four clever-clogs Mancunians with a witty way with words (10cc) or a directionless blues group who hit the motherlode when they sang about their own marital problems (Fleetwood Mac), there was no shortage of radio-friendly sounds.

Though it was far from apparent at the time, the Eurovision Song Contest of 1974 defied history by throwing up a group of stature in ABBA. They transcended their origins to become pop icons – and, by not re-forming, retained their all-conquering aura.

ABBA

228

'We don't want to write political songs. We don't want to turn our records into speeches.'

Benny Andersson

The most commercially successful pop band of the 1970s, ABBA rose again in the 1990s when ABBA Gold (1992) revived their peerless singles' legacy, which has carried on ever since. ABBA were formed in 1973 in Stockholm, Sweden, by Benny Andersson (born Goran Bror Benny Andersson, 16 December 1946), Bjorn Ulvaeus (born 25 April 1945) and their girlfriends Frida Lyngstad (born Anni-Frid Lyngstad-Ruess, 15 November 1945) and Agnetha Faltskog (born 5 April 1950).

Eurovision Success

Andersson and Ulvaeus had been a songwriting partnership since 1969 after leaving their respective bands The Hep Stars (Sweden's top pop band) and The Hootenanny Singers. Their girlfriends were both singers and Faltskog – who married Ulvaeus in 1971 – had had several hits. Invited to write a song for the Swedish Eurovision Song Contest entry in 1973, Andersson and Ulvaeus submitted 'Ring Ring', which did not win the contest for Sweden's entry but was a big Swedish hit when released as a single. In 1974 ABBA tried again and this time 'Waterloo' was picked as the Swedish

Above
Behind the pianos Bjorn and Bennie wrote some of the most memorable songs of their era.

entry. The glam rock singalong won the Eurovision Song Contest convincingly and became a No. 1 single in the UK and around Europe.

'I Do I Do I Do I Do I Do' in 1975 failed to click in the UK but the girls' distinctive voices and harmonies and the boys' acute sense of pop melody and clever arrangements would not be denied for long. 'SOS' restored ABBA to the UK Top 10 and broke them into the US Top 20. And 'Mamma Mia' sent them back to the top of the UK charts at the end of 1975, although the US preferred 'I Do I Do I Do I Do I Do'.

Kings And Queens Of Pop

The next two years saw ABBA dominate the British and European charts with a string of brilliantly conceived and executed hits with sublime choruses and multi-layered voices and instruments. 'Fernando', 'Dancing Queen', 'Knowing Me Knowing You', 'The Name Of The Game' and 'Take A Chance On Me' all topped the UK charts while 'Money Money Money' made No. 3. They were all taken from No. 1 albums – *Greatest Hits* (1976), *Arrival* (1976) and *The Album* (1978).

In America, 'Dancing Queen' was their only No. 1 although 'Take A Chance On Me' got to No. 3. 'Fernando', 'Knowing Me Knowing You' and 'The Name Of The Game' made the Top 20. The rest of the world was falling under their spell, particularly Australia where the band toured in 1977, a film of which was released in 1978 as *Abba The Movie*. The band maximized their revenue by making separate licensing agreements for each country. In the Soviet Union, where the rouble was a non-convertible currency, they were paid in oil instead.

In October 1978 Andersson and Lyngstad got married, but ominously two months later Ulvaeus and Faltskog announced that they were separating. ABBA's personal relationships did not affect the songs, however. They built their own studio and the hits kept coming: 'Chiquitita' (all proceeds of which went to UNICEF), 'Does Your Mother Know', 'Voulez-Vous', 'Gimme Gimme Gimme (A Man After Midnight)'

🎙 *see Introduction pp 226* 🎙 *see Sources & Sounds pp 186* 🎙 *see A–Z of Artists pp 236*

and 'I Have A Dream' (1979), 'The Winner Takes It All' and 'Super Trouper' (1980), and 'Lay All Your Love On Me' and 'One Of Us' (1981). They played another world tour in 1979 including America where they were never as successful, although they had several big disco hits. When Andersson and Lyngstad filed for divorce in 1981 it was obvious that success was coming at a personal cost. Some of the later hits alluded to that.

The Dream Continues

The group ceased after *The Visitors* (1982). There were solo albums from Lyngstad (who had an international hit with the Phil Collins-produced 'There's Something Going On' in 1982). Andersson and Ulvaeus continued to work together, collaborating with Tim Rice for the *Chess* musical.

The release of *ABBA Gold* sparked a major ABBA revival that raised the band to iconic status. The album was a No. 1 around the world (except the US, although it still sold six million) and has continued to sell in large quantities ever since. In the UK it topped the charts three times in 1999 after the opening of Mamma Mia, the long-running musical based on ABBA songs. But despite the success of Bjorn Again, the Australian tribute band who are now an international brand name, the original ABBA have resisted all offers to reform.

Above
Abba's confident, liquid vocal style perfectly matched their intricately crafted songs.

see The Mamas and The Papas pp 143   see The Bee Gees pp 230   see Phil Collins pp 292

230

The
Bee Gees

THE SEVENTIES

POP & DISCO

Key Artists

**CLASSIC
RECORDINGS**

1967
'To Love Somebody'

1975
Main Course
'Jive Talkin''

1977
'How Deep Is Your Love'

1978
Saturday Night Fever
'Stayin' Alive'

1979
Spirits Having Flown
'Tragedy'

By adapting their songwriting and sublime harmonies to different trends over four decades, The Bee Gees have maintained a hugely successful and lucrative career. The three eldest Gibb brothers – Barry (born 1 September 1947) and twins Robin and Maurice (born 22 December 1949, died 12 January 2003) – moved to Australia with their parents in 1958. They started performing as an Everly Brothers-style harmony act in 1960 and landed a weekly spot on a TV show.

Distinctive Harmonies

Over the next five years they released two albums and a dozen singles but when they finally achieved an Australian No. 1 in 1967 they were already on a boat to the UK to re-start their career. They signed with fellow-Australian manager Robert Stigwood, an executive with Brian Epstein at NEMS Enterprises, and their first single, the distinctively high-pitched

'The black music grooves me, influences me the most. The three of us still get our inspiration from black music. It's the most innovative in terms of grooves.' Robin Gibb

narrative ballad 'New York Mining Disaster 1941', was a Top 20 hit in the UK and the US. It was the first of 10 hits over the next two years including 'To Love Somebody' and 'Massachusetts' (1967), 'Words' and 'I've Gotta Get A Message To You' (1968), and 'First Of May' and 'Don't Forget To Remember' (1969). They also had hit albums with *Bee Gees' First* (1967) and *Idea* (1968). Their clean image was at odds with the rock revolution happening around them but their quality songs were irresistible, and these were covered by Nina Simone, Frank Sinatra, Janis Joplin and Elvis Presley.

Cracks in their smiling façade had begun to show by 1969. Amid reports of fraternal strife, Robin was hospitalized with nervous exhaustion and quit after the progressive sounding *Odessa* (1969), prompting legal action from Stigwood. His first solo single, the lush 'Saved By The Bell', was a No. 2 UK hit, but then his and the remaining Bee Gees' chart career declined and Barry and Maurice both worked on solo projects.

The trio reunited in 1971 and, although their popularity had waned badly in the UK, they scored two million-selling US hits that year with 'Lonely Days' and 'How Can You Mend A Broken Heart', which was No. 1 for four weeks. But it was a brief revival and their career hit the doldrums until Stigwood paired them with producer Arif Mardin who put the funk into their falsetto on *Main Course* (1975). The result was an astonishing turnaround as they latched on to the rising disco boom with 'Jive Talkin'', which topped the US charts for two weeks, and 'Nights On Broadway'. The singles also revived their UK fortunes. More hits followed from *Children Of The World* (1976) with 'You Should Be Dancing' (another US No. 1) and 'Love So Right'.

Staying Alive

The *coup de grace* came in 1977 when Stigwood got the Bee Gees to write half a dozen songs for a film he was producing called *Saturday Night Fever*, starring the little-known John Travolta. The soundtrack (1978) topped the US charts for 24 weeks and the UK charts for 18 weeks. In addition 'How Deep Is Your Love',

 see Introduction pp 226   *see* Sources & Sounds pp 186   *see* A–Z of Artists pp 236

'Stayin' Alive' and 'Night Fever' spent a total of 15 weeks at No. 1 in the US.

The Bee Gees were even able to survive their part in Stigwood's disastrous follow-up movie, *Sgt. Pepper's Lonely Hearts Club Band*, in 1978, and *Spirits Having Flown* (1979) was again a No. 1 in the UK and US (for six weeks) with three more US No. 1 singles: 'Tragedy', 'Love You Inside Out' and 'Too Much Heaven', all proceeds from the latter going to UNICEF.

However, they failed to make the switch from disco to dance in the early 1980s and the hits tailed off, although they still managed a Top 10 US album with the *Staying Alive* soundtrack (1983) and continued to write hits for Diana Ross ('Chain Reaction') and Kenny Rogers/Dolly Parton ('Islands In The Stream').

Brotherly Love

Their own fortunes revived again with *ESP* (1987) and the worldwide hit 'You Win Again'. The title track of *One* (1989) was dedicated to fourth brother Andy who had enjoyed a successful career in the 1970s but died in 1988. In the 1990s they released the multi-million selling *Size Isn't Everything* (1993), *Still Waters* (1997) and the live *One Night Only* (1998).

After the sudden death of Maurice on 12 January 2003 from complications arising from a twisted intestine, Barry and Robin retired The Bee Gees name, although they have occasionally worked together since, most notably on the 'Grief Never Grows Old' Tsunami relief record in 2005.

Above

The disco boom of the mid-1970s turned The Bee Gees into sex symbol superstars.

Left

The Bee Gees perfected their soaring harmonies by singing and playing together from a very young age.

see The Everly Brothers pp 46   see Elvis Presley pp 52   see Janis Joplin pp 142   see ABBA pp 228

Elton John

232

'There's so much you're expected to do and you follow a pattern. You make a record, you do a video. I like to break the rules a little bit more and I did in the 1970s, I should try a little bit more now.' Elton John

Right and Far Right
Elton John burst on to the 1970s pop scene with his talent for hit songs and sheer entertainment. Although his instrument was the piano, he quickly realized that he needed to spice up his act, so the 1970s saw an impressive array of costumes and headgear.

From a shy piano player, Elton John became one of the most extrovert performers of the 1970s. He has sold over 250 million records worldwide and is now almost a national institution. Born Reginald Kenneth Dwight on 25 March 1947, he won a part-time piano scholarship to London's Royal Academy Of Music at the age of 11. By the time he left school in 1963 to work for a music publisher he was already playing in local band Bluesology who backed visiting American singers like Major Lance, Patti LaBelle, Doris Troy and Billy Stewart.

On The Road To Fame

In 1966 the group became a back-up band for Long John Baldry and Dwight changed his name, taking the Christian names of Baldry and saxophone player Elton Dean. He left in 1967 and teamed up with aspiring lyricist Bernie Taupin (born 22 May 1950). They signed to Dick James Music in 1968 and their songs were covered by Three Dog Night and Lulu. Elton's first album, *Empty Sky* (1969) showed potential but it was *Elton John* (1970) that lit the fuse, particularly in America after rave reviews for his debut at the Los Angeles Troubadour. A Top 10 single with 'Your Song' helped the album go Top 5.

Between 1971 and 1976 Elton released over a dozen albums, seven of which went to No. 1 in the US along with five No. 1 singles. While the UK chart statistics were not as impressive (four No. 1 albums, one No. 1 single) he scored just as many hits.

1971 saw four Elton albums: *Tumbleweed Connection* that reflected Taupin's fascination with the American West, the live *17-11-70*, the film soundtrack *Friends* and the lush, haunting *Madman Across The Water*.

The hits started to flow in 1972, launched by 'Rocket Man' and 'Honky Cat' from *Honky Chateau*,

followed by 'Crocodile Rock' and 'Daniel' from *Don't Shoot Me I'm Only The Piano Player* (1973), 'Goodbye Yellow Brick Road', 'Candle In The Wind' and 'Bennie And The Jets' from *Goodbye Yellow Brick Road* (1973) and 'Don't Let The Sun Go Down On Me' and 'The Bitch Is Back' from *Caribou* (1974).

Hitting The Right Note

Elton's flamboyant shows – his outrageous glasses got bigger in proportion to the venue – made him one of

see Introduction pp 226   see Sources & Sounds pp 186   see A–Z of Artists pp 236

the top live attractions. In 1974, after he had recorded a cover of The Beatles' 'Lucy In The Sky With Diamonds' with 'Dr Winston O'Boogie' on guitar, he persuaded Winston's alter ego John Lennon to join him on stage at New York's Madison Square Garden. It was to prove Lennon's last live appearance.

Elton premiered *Captain Fantastic And The Brown Dirt Cowboy* (1975) at London's Wembley Stadium and immediately followed up with *Rock Of The Westies* (1975) featuring 'Island Girl'. After his first UK No. 1 single with 'Don't Go Breaking My Heart' (a duet with Kiki Dee) and the double album *Blue Moves* (1976) Elton took a break and bought Watford Football Club.

A Single Man (1978) marked a complete career change. He disbanded his partnership with Taupin (they would work together again later), had an instrumental hit with 'Song For Guy' and generally broadened his perspectives, becoming the first pop star to tour Russia and reorganizing his career around his life rather than vice versa. The hits continued – 'Blue Eyes' (1982), 'I Guess That's Why They Call It The Blues' and 'I'm Still Standing' (1983), 'Sad Songs (Say So Much)' and 'Passengers' (1984) and 'Nikita' (1985).

No Candle In The Wind

But he was becoming almost as famous for his lifestyle as his music. He had admitted to being bisexual in the late 1970s but his marriage to Renate Blauel in 1984 surprised many. It was soon over and Elton faced up to his homosexuality, as well as his various addictions. But his popularity never waned. He continued to write major film themes ('Can You Feel The Love Tonight' from *The Lion King* in 1994) and collaborate with other singers. All proceeds from his singles go to his AIDS foundation, which also benefits from the annual 'Elton's Closet' auction.

Proof of Elton's place in the nation's affections came when he sang 'Candle In The Wind' with revised lyrics at the funeral of Princess Diana in Westminster Abbey in 1997. It became the world's biggest-selling single with sales of over 33 million. All royalties and profits went to the Diana, Princess Of Wales Memorial Fund. In 1998 he was knighted by the Queen. In 2004, Elton started a three-year Las Vegas residency, alternating with Celine Dion, and in 2005 he appeared at Live 8, 20 years after he had appeared at Band Aid.

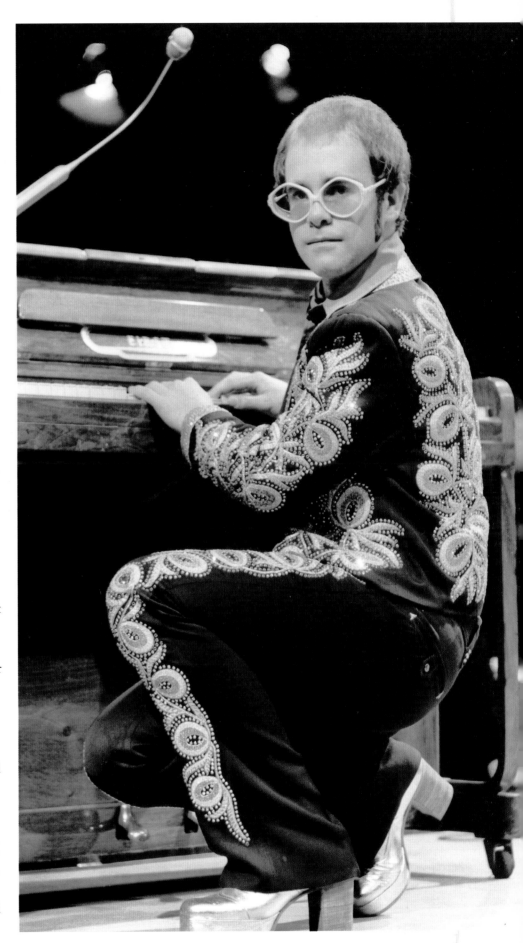

see Ray Charles pp 42   see Jerry Lee Lewis pp 66   see The Isley Brothers pp 172   see Celine Dion pp 348

Rod Stewart

THE SEVENTIES

CLASSIC RECORDINGS

1971
Every Picture Tells A Story
'Maggie May'

1972
'You Wear It Well'

1975
Atlantic Crossing
'Sailing'

1976
'The Killing Of Georgie'

1977
Footloose And Fancy Free
'You're In My Heart'

1978
'Da Ya Think I'm Sexy'

'What I do now is all my dad's fault, because he bought me a guitar as a boy, for no apparent reason.'

Rod Stewart

Above and Far Right
Rod Stewart became an international star in the 1970s, making the transition from hard rocker to smooching songster. His glamorous lifestyle became an essential and seductive part of his appeal, but he has never lost his fondness for tartan scarfs.

One of the UK's finest rock vocalists, Roderick David Stewart was born on 10 January 1945 to Scottish parents. He went to the same school as Ray and Dave Davies of The Kinks and briefly trained as an apprentice footballer before busking around Europe.

Many Faces

Back in London he started singing with The Hoochie Coochie Men in 1964 alongside Long John Baldry and followed him into Steampacket before joining the short-lived Shotgun Express. He also released a couple of unsuccessful singles.

In 1967 Stewart joined The Jeff Beck Group with bassist Ron Wood where he developed his rasping vocal style on two seminal albums: *Truth* (1968) and *Beck-Ola* (1969). He also signed a solo deal and released *An Old Raincoat Will Never Let You Down* (1969), a mixture of folk, soul and drinking songs.

When Beck disbanded his group in 1969 Stewart and Wood formed The Faces with former Small Faces Ian McLagan, Ronnie Lane and Kenney Jones. But he maintained his solo career and although the first two Faces albums – *First Step* (1970) and *Long Player* (1971) – were more successful than his own *Gasoline Alley* (1970), everything changed with the self-produced and largely self-written *Every Picture Tells A Story* (1971) and single, 'Maggie May'. For a week in October 1971 Stewart held the UK No. 1 single and album in the UK and US. Two months later The Faces' *A Nod's As Good As A Wink To A Blind Horse* (1971) got to No. 2 in the UK and No. 6 in the US. From then on the relationship between Stewart and The Faces was uneasy. Stewart's *Never A Dull Moment* (1972) and *Smiler* (1974) were major UK and US successes while The Faces' *Ooh La La* (1972) and the live *Coast To Coast (Overture and Beginners)* (1974) were decreasingly popular in the US.

see Introduction pp 226   *see* Sources & Sounds pp 186   *see* A–Z of Artists pp 236

On The Town

Stewart finally made the break, moved to Los Angeles and released *Atlantic Crossing* (1975), recorded at Muscle Shoals with most of Booker T and The MGs and veteran producer Tom Dowd. The album was another Top 10 in the US, while in the UK it was No. 1 for five weeks along with a four-week No. 1 single, the soaring ballad 'Sailing'.

A *Night On The Town* (1976) confirmed Stewart's ascension to the rock-star elite, becoming his sixth successive UK No. 1 and spending five weeks at No. 2 in the US. In addition, the lubricious 'Tonight's The Night' topped the US charts for eight weeks. He also confirmed his celebrity status with a high-profile romance and split with actress Britt Ekland. She was the first in a line of blonde wives and girlfriends. *Foot Loose And Fancy Free* (1977) featured the hit singles 'Hot Legs' and 'You're In My Heart (The Final Acclaim)'. Those who accused Stewart of unconscious self-parody felt vindicated by *Blondes Have More Fun* (1978), particularly by the butt-waggling disco single 'Da Ya Think I'm Sexy'. That didn't stop it becoming a No. 1 hit in the UK and US.

Successful Songbook

Through the 1980s and 1990s Stewart continued to fuel the fantasies of his admirers and detractors. *Foolish Behaviour* (1980), *Tonight I'm Yours* (1981), *Body Wishes* (1983), *Camouflage* (1984), *Vagabond Heart* (1991), *Unplugged … And Seated* (1993) and *If We Fall In Love Tonight* (1996) were criticized for crowd-pleasing underachievement. But they were all commercially successful and provided a string of hits including 'Baby Jane' and 'What Am I Gonna Do (I'm So In Love With You)' (1983), 'Every Beat Of My Heart' (1986), 'Downtown Train' and 'It Takes Two' (with Tina Turner) (1990), 'Rhythm Of My Heart' and 'The Motown Song' (with The Temptations) (1991), 'Tom Traubert's Blues (Waltzing Mathilda)' (1992), 'Have I Told You Lately' (1993) and 'All For Love' (with Bryan Adams and Sting, 1994). Whenever he deviated from the formula – as on *When We Were The New Boys* (1998) featuring covers of Britpop stars Blur and Oasis – the results were disappointing.

In 2002, after a successful operation for thyroid cancer, Stewart embarked on a series of albums called

The Great American Songbook featuring guest appearances by Cher, Diana Ross, Stevie Wonder and Elton John. The series revitalized Stewart's career and *Stardust … The Great American Songbook Volume III* (2004) gave him his first US No. 1 album for 25 years.

see The Small Faces pp 114   *see* Booker T and The MGs pp 166   *see* Jeff Beck pp 212   *see* Bryan Adams pp 340

Above
Chic are best remembered for their hit disco singles, including 'Le Freak', 'I Want Your Love' and 'Good Times'.

Malcolm Duncan (saxophone), Owen McIntyre (vocals, guitar), Hamish Stuart (vocals, guitar), Roger Ball (keyboards) and Robbie McIntosh (drums) topped the US charts in 1975 with the album *AWB* and single 'Pick Up The Pieces'. After dabbling in disco with 'Let's Go Round Again' a British hit in 1980, the band went on hiatus in the mid-1980s, reforming in 1989.

Chic
(Vocal group, 1976–96)
A disco outfit built around the songwriting and production team of Nile Rodgers (guitar) and Bernard Edwards (bass) who were originally part of a New York rock band but who changed direction when unable to secure a record deal. Chic evolved from demos recorded by the pair that formed the basis of their first album *Chic* (1977) for which drummer Tony Thompson and singer Norma Jean Wright were drafted in. Lead-off single 'Dance, Dance, Dance (Yowsah, Yowsah, Yowsah)' was a smash. Additional vocalist Luci Martin was added as Chic went on tour.

C'est Chic (1978) and *Risqué* (1979) were textbook examples of disco, spawning massive hit singles in 'Le Freak', 'I Want Your Love' and 'Good Times'. The latter became the rhythmic base for the early rap/hip hop song 'Rapper's Delight' by the Sugarhill Gang. Chic drifted apart in the early 1980s but reformed in 1992. Edwards died in 1996.

George Clinton
(Vocals, b. 1941)
Born in North Carolina and raised in New Jersey, Clinton became a funk legend but his first musical venture was the five-man doo-wop group The Parliaments formed in the late 1950s. After recording for various small labels, and following a spell where Clinton worked for Motown, the first flowering of his later direction appeared on The Parliaments' 1967 American Top 20 single '(I Wanna) Testify'. Contractual difficulties over the group's name prompted Clinton to record with The Parliaments' backing band, newly christened

America
(Vocal group, 1972–present)
An Anglo-American trio formed in the UK by Gerry Beckley (guitar, vocals, keyboards), Dewey Bunnell (guitar, vocals) and Dan Peek (guitar, vocals, keyboards), sons of US military personnel and British mothers. America's acoustically backed three-part harmonies were reminiscent of Crosby, Stills and Nash. Best-known for the transatlantic 1972 hit 'Horse With No Name', the band worked with Beatles producer George Martin on four albums from 1974–77, slimming to a duo when Peek departed.

Average White Band
(Vocal/instrumental group, 1973–present)
The blue-eyed soul of Scots Alan Gorrie (vocals, bass),

see Introduction pp 226 see Sources & Sounds pp 186 see Key Artists pp 228

Funkadelic to reflect their psychedelic side. Clinton then set up the collective of musicians that operated under the banner of Parliament/Funkadelic in the 1970s.

Onstage, as lead singer of Parliament, Clinton was a consummate showman indulging his penchant for bizarre costumes. Clinton's best-known song is Funkadelic's 'One Nation Under A Groove', a Top 10 UK hit in 1979. He launched a solo career in 1981.

Bootsy Collins
(Bass, vocals, b. 1951)
Formerly the bassist in James Brown's backing group the JBs of which his driving, rhythmic playing was a prominent feature, Collins joined George Clinton's musical collective in 1972, supplying bass and songwriting for Funkadelic. An outrageous showman, he founded Bootsy's Rubber Band, whose first three albums, *Stretchin' Out In Bootsy's Rubber Band* (1976), *Ahh … The Name Is Bootsy, Baby* (1977) and *Bootsy? Player Of The Year* (1978) are funk masterworks.

The Doobie Brothers
(Vocal group, 1970–present)
The Doobies were founded by Tom Johnston (guitar, vocals), Pat Simmons (guitar, vocals) and John Hartman (drums). Additional drummer Michael Hossack and Tiran Porter (bass) were recruited for the band's second album *Toulouse Street* (1972). 1973's *The*

Left

The mastermind behind Parliament and Funkadelic, George Clinton played a pivitol role in creating a new kind of funk sound influenced by jazz and psychedelic music.

Captain And Me spawned radio staples 'Long Train Running' and 'China Grove'. Steely Dan vocalist/keyboardist Michael McDonald was introduced, Johnston having temporarily quit, resulting in a move from boogie rock to the white soul of the three-million seller *Minute By Minute* (1979) and smash single 'What A Fool Believes'.

Below

The Doobie Brothers were a classic good-time band, from California.

🎵 *see* Crosby, Stills and Nash pp 140 🎵 *see* James Brown pp 154 🎵 *see* Earth, Wind and Fire pp 238 🎵 *see* Nile Rodgers pp 242

Earth, Wind and Fire

(Vocal group, 1970–83)

In 1972, Maurice White (drums) assembled a second line-up of Earth, Wind and Fire after two unsuccessful albums. This featured brother Verdine (bass), Jessica Cleaves (vocals), Ronnie Laws (saxophone), Larry Dunn (keyboards), Ralph Johnson (percussion), Roland Battista (guitar) and Philip Bailey (vocals). After further personnel changes, 'Shining Star' became the first in a string of dancefloor standards, which included 'September', 'Fantasy', 'After The Love Has Gone' and 'Boogie Wonderland'.

Electric Light Orchestra

(Vocal group, 1971–86)

Devised by Roy Wood (various instruments, vocals) to provide an alternative creative outlet to The Move, ELO consisted of that group's remaining members, Jeff Lynne (guitar, piano, vocals) and Bev Bevan (drums). The band aimed to combine rock with classical instrumentation. Bill Hunt (French horn) and Steve Woolam (violin) were brought in for *Electric Light Orchestra* (1971) (known as *No Answer* in the US) after which Wood left to form Wizzard and Lynne took over at the helm. Re-emerging in 1973, after further line-up changes, with a cover of Chuck Berry's 'Roll Over Beethoven', ELO embarked on a run of 15 consecutive UK Top 10 singles and regularly charted in America with their distinctive symphonic rock.

ELO ended when Lynne left in 1986. Drummer Bev Bevan reformed the group in 1991 as ELO Part 2 when Lynne declined to participate and objected to the use of the original name.

Below

ELO had a run of success in the early 1970s by combining great tunes with rock and classical instruments.

see Introduction pp 226   *see* Sources & Sounds pp 186   *see* Key Artists pp 228

Al Green

(Vocals, b. 1946)

An American soul and gospel singer, Reverend Al Green (he was ordained a pastor of the Full Gospel Tabernacle in Memphis in 1976) made his recording debut on *Back Up Train* (1967). His third album *Al Green Gets Next To You* (1970) was the start of a golden period when he recorded many of the songs for which he is best known – 'Tired of Being Alone', 'Let's Stay Together' and 'Take Me To The River'.

Isaac Hayes

(Saxophone, vocals, b. 1942)

This soul singer from Tennessee began his musical career as a saxophonist for Stax Records studio band The Mar-Keys. The album *Hot Buttered Soul* (1969) was his commercial breakthrough and Hayes became internationally famous with the soundtrack to the film *Shaft* (1971), the style of which anticipated disco. After leaving Stax, his records were less successful and he filed for bankruptcy in 1976. He later voiced the Chef in the cartoon series *South Park*.

Carole King

(Piano, vocals, b. 1942)

A graduate of New York's Brill Building school of songwriting, King teamed up with lyricist and future husband Gerry Goffin to compose many 1960s smashes for other artists, although 'It Might As Well Rain Until September' was a hit for King under her own name in 1962. Goffin and King split up in 1967 and she recorded one album as part of a trio, The City.

Her solo recording career began in earnest in 1970 with *Writer* but 1971's *Tapestry* proved her greatest success. The album combined re-interpretations of King's early songs, like 'Will You Love Me Tomorrow?' with new material. *Tapestry* was a benchmark in the newly popular genre of the adult-orientated singer/songwriter. Although she remained active in the 1970s, subsequent albums like *Music* (1971) and *Rhymes And Reasons* (1972) failed to live up to *Tapestry*. Her output since 1983 has been sporadic.

Above
Carole King moved on from creating great tunes for others and made a ground-breaking hit record for herself, *Tapestry*.

Kool and The Gang

(Vocal group, 1964–present)

A deep funk outfit founded in 1964 in New Jersey by brothers Ronald (saxophone) and Robert 'Kool' Bell (bass) with Robert Mickens (trumpet), Dennis Thomas (saxophone), Charles Smith (guitar) and George Brown (drums). Kool and The Gang enjoyed 13 American hits before the arrival of vocalist James 'JT' Taylor in 1979 prompted a change of style to disco for the international hits 'Ladies Night', 'Celebration' and 'Get Down On It'.

Left
Isaac Hayes was the height of cool in the 1970s, with his soundtrack to the sharpest movie of the decade, *Shaft*.

see Chuck Berry pp 38   *see* Emerson, Lake and Palmer pp 214   *see* The Bee Gees pp 230

240

Lindisfarne

(Vocal group, 1970–2003)

A folk rock group formed in Newcastle, England by Alan Hull (guitar, piano, vocals), Simon Cowe (guitar), Ray Jackson (mandolin), Rod Clements (bass, violin) and Ray Laidlaw (drums), Lindisfarne enjoyed a best-selling album with *Fog On The Tyne* in 1971 and two hit singles 'Meet Me On The Corner' and 'Lady Eleanor' the following year. After a temporary split in 1974 their 1978 reunion yielded another Top 10 entry, 'Run For Home'.

Little Feat

(Vocal group, 1971–present)

Renowned for their eclectic blend of styles, incorporating rhythm and blues, country, rock'n'roll and jazz rock, Little Feat was founded by two ex-members of Frank Zappa's Mothers of Invention, guitarist and singer Lowell George and bassist Roy Estrada. They were joined by Richard Hayward (drums) and Bill Payne (keyboards, vocals). After seven well-received albums from 1971–77, the band took a lengthy break after George died of a heart attack in 1979.

Bob Marley

(Guitar, vocals, 1945–81)

The man responsible for popularizing reggae worldwide, Bob Marley's career began in 1963 in the original Wailers, a six-piece vocal group, later slimmed to a trio, operating out of Kingston, Jamaica and enjoying great success locally. In 1969, Marley worked with producer Lee 'Scratch' Perry who introduced him to the Barrett brothers – Aston (Family Man) on bass and Carlton (drums) – who would become a vital component of the new Wailers, formed in 1974.

The previous year, Marley signed to Island Records who provided promotional clout for *Catch A Fire* (1973). Eric Clapton's 1974 version of 'I Shot The Sheriff' raised Marley's profile and 'No Woman No Cry', from *Live At*

The Lyceum (1975), proved his chart breakthrough. *Exodus* (1977) and *Kaya* (1978) were massive sellers internationally. *Uprising* (1980) was to be his last studio album. Since his death from cancer in 1981, Marley's reputation and influence has risen steadily.

Paul McCartney and Wings

(Vocal group, 1971–80)

McCartney put together Wings in the summer of 1971, featuring wife Linda (keyboards), Denny Laine (guitar) and Denny Seiwell (drums) for the debut album *Wildlife* (1971). The line-up was bolstered by the inclusion of guitarist Henry McCullough.

In 1973, Seiwell and McCullough abruptly quit, refusing to travel to Nigeria to record *Band On The Run* (1973) a commercial and artistic triumph forged in adversity. Guitarist Jimmy McCulloch and sticksman Jeff Britton joined in 1974, the latter soon replaced by Joe English. A successful world tour in 1975–76 followed but the band splintered again in 1977 when English and McCulloch departed. Undaunted, McCartney recorded 'Mull of Kintyre', which became Britain's best-selling single. Laurence Juber (guitar) and Steve Holly (drums) were added for *Back To The Egg* (1979) but the ex-Beatle's arrest for possession of cannabis in Japan in 1980 caused a cancelled tour and the end of Wings.

The O'Jays

(Vocal group, 1963–present)

A long-standing soul harmony group formed by Eddie Levert and Walter Williams, later adding William Powell, Bill Isles and Bobby Massey. The O'Jays first charted in 1963 but were considering quitting music when they came under the aegis of Philadelphia soul producers Gamble and Huff, immediately scoring a hit with 'Back Stabbers' in 1972. The remainder of the decade yielded several successful singles, including 'Love Train' and 'I Love Music'.

Below

The O'Jays scored with their ability to work the funkiest tunes around and hold the line on the smoothest of ballads from producers Gamble and Huff.

see The Beatles pp 88   *see* Cream pp 92   *see* Frank Zappa pp 151   *see* John Lennon pp 218

Nile Rodgers
(Guitar, b. 1952)

In addition to writing, producing and performing with Chic, Rodgers, along with long-time collaborator Bernard Edwards, undertook similar duties for Sister Sledge. The pair worked with Diana Ross on her 1980 *Diana* album and Deborah Harry's *Koo-Koo* (1981). Rodgers went on to helm many high-profile albums – David Bowie's *Let's Dance* (1983), Madonna's *Like A Virgin* (1985) and Duran Duran's *Notorious* (1986) – but his own solo work has failed to ignite the same interest.

Linda Ronstadt
(Vocals, b. 1946)

A former member of The Stone Poneys, Ronstadt launched a solo career in 1968 with the country-flavoured rock that would characterize her 1970s work. Her third album *Linda Ronstadt* (1972) featured the core of musicians who would go on to form The Eagles. On 1974's *Heart Like A Wheel*, Ronstadt and producer/manager Peter Asher arrived at the blueprint, which was honed to perfection on the triple-platinum *Simple Dreams* (1977).

Rose Royce
(Vocal group, 1975–88)

A soul/disco outfit originally formed as an all-purpose backing band comprising ex-Motown personnel Kenji Brown (guitar), Victor Nix (keyboards), Kenny Copeland and Freddie Dunn (both trumpets), Michael Moore (saxophone), Duke Jobe (bass) and Henry Garner and Terrai Santiel (both drums). Fronted by singer Gwen Dickey, they supplied the platinum-selling soundtrack to the movie *Car Wash* (1976) before moving to Norman Whitfield's label for the smash hits 'Wishing On A Star' and 'Love Don't Live Here Anymore'.

Roxy Music
(Vocal group, 1972–83, 1998–present)

An enduringly influential British art rock group whose combination of futuristic music and 1950s rock'n'roll emerged in 1972 with their eponymous first album and

🎸 *see* Introduction pp 226   🎸 *see* Sources & Sounds pp 186   🎸 *see* Key Artists pp 228

Left
Roxy Music, with the suarve crooning of Brian Ferry, the experimental sounds of Brian Eno and the tight guitar work of Phil Manzanera quickly made it to the top.

standalone single 'Virginia Plain'. Fronted by singer Bryan Ferry, the line-up included synthesizer player/tape operator Brian Eno, Phil Manzanera (guitar), Andy McKay (saxophone), Paul Thompson (drums) and various bassists. When Eno left after *For Your Pleasure* (1973), Roxy's music lost some of its experimental edge but continued to plough a distinctive furrow through *Stranded* (1974) and *Country Life* (1975). Eno was replaced by classically trained keyboardist Eddie Jobson.

After *Siren* (1976), which contained their only US hit 'Love Is The Drug', Roxy Music took a break, reconvening two years later for *Manifesto*. This along with *Flesh + Blood* (1980) and *Avalon* (1983) saw the band's music take on a glossy, commercial sheen. Roxy Music disbanded in 1983 and reformed in 1998.

Rufus

(Vocal group, 1973–83)
A Chicago-based funk band initially comprising Al Ciner (guitar), Charles Colbert (bass), Lee Graziano (drums), Kevin Murphy (keyboards) and Paulette McWilliams, who was quickly replaced as vocalist by Chaka Khan. Stevie Wonder wrote their first hit, 1974's 'Tell Me Something Good'. 'Ain't Nobody' was a smash in 1984, by which time Khan's parallel solo career had taken off and would peak with her signature tune 'I'm Every Woman' in 1989.

Sparks

(Vocal group, 1972–present)
This veteran group provides a vehicle for the talents of brothers Ron and Russell Mael. Anglophile Californians, the Maels came to Britain in 1973 after two failed albums, the first as Halfnelson. Recruiting Adrian Fisher (guitar), Martin Gordon (bass) and Dinky Diamond (drums) they recorded *Kimono My House* (1974) featuring the memorable hit 'This Town Ain't Big Enough For Both Of Us'. Often bracketed with glam rock, Sparks' music displayed an eclectic approach and their British success continued until late 1975 after which the hits dried up.

A very different Sparks made a comeback in 1979. Produced by Giorgio Moroder, the album *Number One In Heaven* featured extensive use of synthesizers. Moroder's familiar Euro disco beat helped the Maels back into the charts for the first time in four years with 'The Number One Song In Heaven' and 'Beat The Clock'. Sparks remain active and popular.

Below
Sparks was a hugely influential band with acerbic lyrics and a tight rocky sound.

see Stevie Wonder pp 162   see Booker T and The MGs pp 166   see Chic pp 236   see Earth, Wind and Fire pp 238

T. Rex

(Vocal group, 1970–77)

The first glam rock band evolved from acoustic duo Tyrannosaurus Rex, formed by Marc Bolan (guitar, vocals) and multi-instrumentalist Steve Peregrine-Took. Mickey Finn (bongos) replaced Took in 1969 as Bolan began to deploy electric instruments. Shortening the name to T. Rex heralded a chart breakthrough in October 1970 with the single 'Ride A White Swan'.

Steve Currie (bass) and Bill Legend (drums) were added and T. Rex achieved a further 10 Top 10 singles, including four No. 1s, as Bolan became a teen idol. The formula of speeded-up Chuck Berry riffs and Bolan's unfathomable yet hip lyrics was starting to wear thin by 1973 when T. Rex were losing ground not only to glam rivals Slade, but also to pin-up boy David Cassidy. Bolan's popularity slipped away until a new generation hailed him as one of punk's forefathers. Bolan died in a car accident in September 1977.

10CC

(Vocal group, 1972–95)

A multi-skilled foursome who operated from the self-owned Strawberry Studios, Stockport. Eric Stewart, Lol Creme, (both guitar, keyboards) Graham Gouldman, (bass) and Kevin Godley (drums) wrote, sang and produced four albums of inventive pop/rock from 1973–76. Their 1975 No. 1 'I'm Not In Love' was also a Stateside smash. 10cc split in two in 1976 with Gouldman and Stewart retaining the name whilst Godley and Creme recorded as a duo, later becoming sought-after video directors.

🔊 *see Introduction pp 226* 🔊 *see Sources & Sounds pp 186* 🔊 *see Key Artists pp 228*

Tina Turner

(Vocals, b. 1939)

An American soul/rock singer, Tina Turner was famous initially as part of a husband and wife duo with Ike Turner. The pair enjoyed several hits in the 1960s and established a formidable reputation as a live act, largely due to Tina's stage presence. The couple's last major success was 1973's 'Nutbush City Limits' a UK Top 5 hit written by Tina. Weary of Ike's mental and physical abuse, she left him, mid-tour in 1976, embarking on a solo career soon afterwards.

It was not until *Private Dancer* (1984) that Tina found the formula that would make her one of the biggest names in 1980s music. Made with the assistance of famous friends like Mark Knopfler and Jeff Beck, the album sold over 20 million copies. The successful follow-ups *Break Every Rule* (1986) and *Foreign Affair* (1989) showed that her remarkable comeback was no flash in the pan.

Barry White

(Vocals, 1944–2003)

Nicknamed the 'Walrus of Love', Barry White's image as a Lothario sometimes obscured his talents as a songwriter, producer and arranger. Working with girl group Love Unlimited, his first hit was 'Walking In The Rain With The One I Love' in 1972. White's distinctive growl was heard on 'Can't Get Enough Of Your Love Babe', a US No. 1 and 'You're The First, The Last, My Everything' a British chart topper in 1974.

Bill Withers

(Vocals, b. 1938)

This smooth-voiced performer from West Virginia broke through with 'Ain't No Sunshine' from the album *Just As I Am* (1971). His songs have been recorded by countless artists ranging from Grace Jones's version of 'Use Me' to British pop band Mud's cover of 'Lean On Me'. 'Lovely Day' has been a Top 10 hit twice for Withers in the UK, the second time, in 1988, after its use in a TV commercial.

see Chuck Berry pp 38   see The Beatles pp 88   see Marvin Gaye pp 170   see Jeff Beck pp 212

SEVENTIES PUNK & NEW WAVE

With instrumental virtuosity now becoming boring to most record buyers and rock's biggest acts heading for tax exile in an attempt to keep hold of their assets, the mid-1970s was becoming a bore – even the individual Beatles had run out of steam. Novelty hits proliferated, always a sign of a static and sluggish music scene, and *Elton John's Greatest Hits* (1974) sold in its millions.

It was against this background that punk raised two much-needed fingers. Invented in New York by The Ramones, The New York Dolls and Patti Smith but perfected by The Sex Pistols, The Clash and The Damned in the UK, it would do a good job of cleansing the stables and sending many a complacent superstar – though not Elton John – to the dole queue.

Punk's questioning attitudes were reflected in lyrics that took music back to the folk and protest arena of the 1960s. Gay rights and racial equality were among the causes championed – and if common sense sometimes gave way to shock value, that was to be forgiven. Rock'n'roll was, once again, rebel music.

There were inevitably to be bandwagon-jumpers who stole the energy and added it to good old-fashioned songwriting to create careers that are ongoing today: Elvis Costello and Sting – the latter using The Police as his springboard – had talents that clearly merited more than a brief spell in the spotlight. Others went back to their day jobs, having played their part in a guerrilla raid on complacency.

The Clash

CLASSIC RECORDINGS

1977
The Clash
'White Riot'
'London's Burning'

1978
'Tommy Gun'

1979
London Calling

1982
Combat Rock
'Should I Stay Or Should I Go'
'Rock The Casbah'

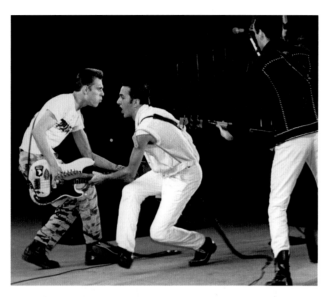

'What The Clash did was more like roots music. They were a garage band, but they were also [into] reggae, rockabilly and bluegrass. Joe just put all these different ideologies into the blender.'
Bono

Above
At their height, Joe Strummer and Mick Jones brought an unusual depth and sensitivity to the punk sound.

If The Sex Pistols were the face of UK punk, The Clash were the soul. The band was formed in the summer of 1976 by guitarist Mick Jones (born Michael Geoffrey Jones, 26 June 1955) and bassist Paul Simonon (born 15 December 1955) after their proto-punk band, London SS, broke up.

They Fought The Law

They recruited guitarist Keith Levene and drummer Terry Chimes before luring singer/guitarist Joe Strummer (John Mellors, 1952–2002) from pub rock band the 101ers. Their first gig was an unannounced support slot with The Sex Pistols in Sheffield. After five gigs Levine was fired and Terry Chimes followed early in 1977, although he had recorded their debut album on which he was credited as 'Tory Crimes'. His replacement was Topper Headon (born Nicky Headon, 30 May 1955).

The Clash (1977) was one of the definitive punk albums featuring the rallying anthem 'White Riot' and caustic rockers 'London's Burning', 'Janie Jones' and 'I'm So Bored With The USA'. CBS Records did not release the album in America although it sold an unprecedented 100,000 on import. After the 'White Riot' UK tour, which was frequently riotous, the band released a clutch of singles – 'Complete Control' (produced by Lee Perry), 'Clash City Rockers' and '(White Man) In Hammersmith Palais' – and fought the law over spraying graffiti and shooting pigeons. The law won.

The Clash picked Blue Oyster Cult producer Sandy Pearlman for their second album, *Give 'Em Enough Rope* (1978), which entered the UK charts at No. 2 and gave them their first Top 20 single with 'Tommy Gun'. But despite two successful American tours the album failed to chart in the US, as had been the aim.

London Calling The US

Switching producers again to R&B connoisseur and Mott The Hoople producer Guy Stevens, who they had worked with on their first demos, The Clash went into creative overdrive for the eclectic but stylish double album *London Calling* (1979), which they insisted on selling for the price of a single LP. This time they cracked the US Top 30 and had a hit single with 'Train In Vain'. They over-reached their creativity on the self-produced triple album *Sandinista!* (1980), which was sold at the price of double and made the US Top 30 but only scraped into the UK Top 20. Sell-out tours of Europe, North America, Japan, Hong Kong, Thailand, New Zealand and Australia were not translated into record sales either.

Combat Rock (1982), produced by veteran Glyn Johns (Rolling Stones, Who, Eagles), refocused their energy with a big rock sound. They recaptured their best songwriting on 'Rock The Casbah' (their only US Top 10 hit), 'Straight To Hell' and 'Should I Stay Or Should I Go'. But even as the album was released the band were starting to fall apart as they were pulled in different directions. Headon was fired for continued heroin use (ironically he had written 'Rock The Casbah'), the band toured stadiums with The Who with Chimes back on drums and headlined the US

see Introduction pp 246   *see* Sources & Sounds pp 186   *see* A–Z of Artists pp 256

Festival '83 in California. In September 1983 Strummer and Simonon fired Jones who had 'drifted apart from the original idea of the Clash'.

Losing Their Way

A new Clash with guitarists Vince White and Nick Sheppard toured America and Europe in 1984 but it was two and a half years before the next Clash album, *Cut The Crap* (1985). It served only to prove that the band had lost their way, although it briefly made the UK Top 20. Strummer and Simonon broke up the band early in 1986.

Jones had formed Big Audio Dynamite with film director/DJ Don Letts and Strummer reunited with him, co-producing and writing songs for their second album, *10 Upping Street* (1986), before embarking on a solo career that encompassed acting (*Mystery Train*), soundtracks (*Straight To Hell*, *Sid And Nancy*), producing The Pogues and various band projects including Latino Rockabilly War and The Mescaleros.

The posthumous legacy of The Clash continued to grow. *The Story Of The Clash Volume 1* (1988) made the UK Top 10. In 1991 the reissued 'Should I Stay Or Should I Go' gave them the UK No. 1 hit they had never come close to during their career. *From Here To Eternity: Live* (1999) was another UK Top 20 album. But, in contrast to their peers, they continued to resist lucrative offers to reform right up until the sudden death of Joe Strummer from a heart attack on 22 December 2002.

Below
Committed and powerful, The Clash's live gigs were joyful displays of perspiration and fervour.

see The Kinks pp 94   *see* Mott The Hoople pp 220   *see* Big Audio Dynamite pp 289   *see* The Pogues pp 311

The Ramones

> *'We're the only band that kept the guts, and kept the excitement, and kept the belief, you know. We never sidetracked. We never went the way of The Clash, and never wanted to get into the discotheques that bad.'*
>
> Joey Ramone

Right
The Ramones' no-nonsense two-minute songs drove the sound of punk from the mid-1970s.

The definitive American punk rock group, The Ramones, were formed in 1974 in Forest Hills, New York, by high school friends Joey Ramone (born Jeffrey Hyman, 1951–2001), Johnny Ramone (born John Cummings, 1951–2004), Dee Dee Ramone (born Douglas Colvin, 1952–2002) and Tommy Ramone (born Tom Erdelyi, 29 January 1952).

Gabba Gabba Hey

They played their first gig at CBGBs in 1974 with Joey on drums and vocals, Johnny and Dee Dee on guitars and Tommy as manager. The line-up soon changed to Joey vocals, Johnny guitar, Dee Dee bass and Tommy drums, and they quickly gained a reputation with their 20-minute sets of two-minute songs, each counted in with a rapid 'one-two-three-four'. Every show was rounded off with the slogan, 'gabba gabba hey'.

As well as adopting the same surname, 'da brudders' also wore the same uniform of torn jeans and leather jackets. The songs – a wall of guitar chords, deadpan cartoon lyrics and no solos – reflected the underbelly of the Bowery where they hung out: 'Blitzkrieg Bop', 'Beat On The Brat', 'Now I Wanna Sniff Some Glue', 'Judy Is A Punk', '53rd & 3rd'.

The band signed to Sire Records in 1975. *The Ramones* (1976), a low-budget album, created a stir in the emerging punk scene but did not make the American Top 100. Few radio stations were bold enough to give their singles airplay. But DJ John Peel and a host of punk musicians-to-be were more impressed when they toured Britain soon after the album's release. *Leave Home* (1976) was more of the same with songs like 'You're Gonna Kill That Girl', 'Pinhead' and 'Carbona Not Glue'. They toured the US and UK frequently and cracked the UK Top 30 with 'Sheena Is A Punk Rocker' from their third album, *Rocket To Russia*

(1977) that made the US Top 50 and confirmed a more bubblegum approach to their songs.

Seeking Longevity

Tommy left in 1978, worn out from touring. But he stayed on to produce *Road To Ruin* (1978) that featured new drummer Marky Ramone (born Marc Bell, 15 July 1956, New York) and songs that edged towards the three-minute mark, including the UK Top 40 'Don't Come Close'.

📼 *see Introduction pp 246*   📼 *see Sources & Sounds pp 186*   📼 *see A–Z of Artists pp 256*

After the double *It's Alive* (1979) The Ramones filmed their central role in *Rock'n'Roll High School*, directed by B-movie maestro Roger Corman. But despite being remixed by Phil Spector the title track only scraped into the UK Top 50 and failed to chart in the US. Nevertheless the band stuck with Spector for *End Of The Century* (1980), which was their most commercially successful album, going Top 20 in the UK and Top 50 in the US. They also had a Top 10 UK hit with a cover of the Spector/Ronettes classic 'Baby I Love You'.

With the punk revolution dying out The Ramones continued to seek longevity, working with 10cc's Graham Gouldman for *Pleasant Dreams* (1981) and bubblegum veteran Ritchie Cordell for *Subterranean Jungle* (1983). Even though they could not achieve a hit album they could still headline the California Festival in front of 500,000 people.

The Godfathers Of Punk

The band reached a hiatus when Marky left to be replaced by Ritchie Ramone and Joey underwent emergency brain surgery after getting into a fight over his girlfriend. But they returned with the well-received *Too Tough To Die* (1985) featuring a diatribe against President Ronald Reagan, 'Bonzo Goes To Bitburg', followed by *Animal Boy* (1986) and *Halfway To Sanity* (1986). Then there were more line-up changes as Marky returned to replace Ritchie and Dee Dee left to become a rap artist. The new bassist was CJ Ramone. The title track of *Brain Drain* (1989) was used for the Stephen King movie *Pet Sematary*, and they released *Loco Live* (1991), *Mondo Bizarro* (1992) and an album of covers, *Acid Eaters* (1994), before the appropriately titled *Adios Amigos* (1995). But they were still selling out shows right up to their last performance in Los Angeles in 1996.

The Ramones were inducted into the Rock And Roll Hall Of Fame in 2002. But by then Joey had died of cancer (15 April 2001). Soon afterwards Dee Dee died from a heroin overdose (5 June 2002) and Johnny died from cancer (15 September 2004). The band's irreverent attitude and three-minute songs will for ever see them acclaimed as Godfathers of Punk.

Above

On stage The Ramones stirred up an atmosphere of frenzy and mayhem through their tightly controlled blasts of guitar chords and neat one-liner lyrics.

see Phil Spector pp 177   *see* 10cc pp 244   *see* The Clash pp 248   *see* The Damned pp 257

The Sex Pistols

 CLASSIC RECORDINGS

1976
'Anarchy In The UK'

1977
Never Mind The Bollocks
'God Save The Queen'
'Pretty Vacant'
'EMI'

Right
After Sid Vicious joined The Pistols, replacing the more musical Glen Matlock, they became a more self-destructive force.

> '*You just pick a chord, go twang, and you've got music.*'
> Sid Vicious

Although they existed for just over two years and released only two albums, The Sex Pistols had more impact on the British music scene than any band since the 1960s. To the public they represented the face of punk.

The Sex Pistols came together in London in 1975 under the aegis of Malcolm McLaren (born 22 January 1946) who was running an 'anti-fashion' boutique called Sex in Kings Road with his partner, clothes designer Vivienne Westwood. Having unsuccessfully tried to resuscitate the ailing career of US proto-punks the New York Dolls, he turned his attention to a band featuring one of his shop assistants, bassist Glen Matlock (born 27 August 1956), guitarist Steve Jones (born 3 September 1955) and drummer Paul Cook (born 20 July 1956).

Raw, Volatile And Sneering

McLaren introduced them to singer John Lydon (born 31 January 1956) who had no previous experience but his green hair and sneering, cynical attitude was just what McLaren was looking for. He called them The Sex Pistols while the band called Lydon Johnny Rotten. Drawing on their own (and McLaren's) heroes – The Faces, The Stooges and The Who – The Sex Pistols developed a raw, volatile set, dressed in bondage clothing with safety pins and spikey hair. They attracted a small but dedicated following including the self-styled Bromley Contingent, some of who would later form Siouxsie and The Banshees and Generation X. A Manchester show inspired future members of The Buzzcocks, Joy Division and The Smiths.

In October 1976, The Sex Pistols signed to EMI and released a single 'Anarchy In The UK' that barely scraped into the Top 40. The group's notoriety was assured when they appeared on an early evening TV show presented by Bill Grundy who goaded them into swearing. In the media furore that followed EMI revoked their contract.

Matlock, who had written most of the songs, was fired in March 1977, allegedly because he 'liked The Beatles'. He was replaced by Sid Vicious (born John Beverly, 1957–79). Later that month the band signed to

A&M at a ceremony outside Buckingham Palace but that contract was rescinded within days, allegedly after pressure from the label's staff and artists.

Vicious And Rotten

In May 1977 The Sex Pistols signed to Virgin and released 'God Save The Queen', coinciding with the Silver Jubilee celebrations. It was banned by the BBC and some retailers but still sold a reported 150,000 in the first week. It reached No. 2 in the chart amid a widespread belief that it had been kept from the top.

Airplay restrictions were lifted for 'Pretty Vacant', which got to No. 6, but the band had to tour the UK under assumed names to avoid being banned. After another Top 10 single with 'Holidays In The Sun' The Sex Pistols released *Never Mind The Bollocks* (1977), which went straight to No. 1. In Nottingham, a retailer displaying the cover was arrested under the Indecent Advertising Act although magistrates 'reluctantly' dismissed the charge.

At the beginning of 1978 the band went to America and played shows in Georgia, Texas, Oklahoma, Louisiana and San Francisco's Winterland after which Rotten quit. In the ensuing chaos Vicious overdosed twice en route to New York with his girlfriend Nancy Spungen. Cook and Jones flew to Rio de Janiero and recorded with Great Train Robber Ronnie Biggs. A single, 'No One Is Innocent' backed by Vicious' version of 'My Way', made the UK Top 10 in July 1978, just as Rotten announced his new band, Public Image Ltd.

Doing Something Else

In October 1978, Vicious was arrested and charged with murder after Spungen was found dead in their hotel room. Released on bail, he died of a heroin overdose on 2 February 1979. Three weeks later his version of Eddie Cochran's 'Something Else' got to No. 3.

The Great Rock'n'Roll Swindle (1979) was the soundtrack to McLaren's film on The Sex Pistols in which Rotten was largely edited out. It yielded two more Top 10 singles – 'Silly Thing' and 'C'Mon Everybody'. By now there was no band (Cook and Jones would later form The Professionals) but there was a court-appointed receiver trying to resolve the group's financial affairs. In 1986 Rotten, Cook, Jones and Vicious' mother were awarded £1 million.

Rotten, Cook and Jones reunited for The Sex Pistols' 'Filthy Lucre' world tour in 1996 and released *Filthy Lucre Live*. They played more shows in 2002 and 2003.

Below
Johnny Rotten, never quite as rotten as his name, was the perfect frontman for the iconic figurehead band of the punk movement.

Patti Smith

254

1974
'Piss Factory'

1975
Horses
'Gloria'
'Redondo Beach'

1978
Easter
'Because The Night'

1979
'Dancing Barefoot'

Right
Smith's uncompromising delivery of her poetry and lyrics won her the approval of fans and contemporaries alike.

Unorthodox, uncompromising, Patti Smith was a seminal figure in the New York punk movement and has remained a touchstone for later generations of rock artists. Born on 30 December 1946, Smith was raised in southern New Jersey by her atheist father and Jehovah's Witness mother. Leaving school at 16 she had brief, unsatisfying stints working in a factory and studying at a teaching college before she fled to New York in 1967 and immersed herself in the underground arts scene. She was inspired by the music of The Velvet Underground, the writing of William Burroughs and Allen Ginsberg, and – after a trip to Paris in 1969 – Jean Genet, Arthur Rimbaud and Antonin Artaud.

'Dylan, he really hammered it into me that my improvisation was a gift that I had to nourish and hold sacred, and that's how he inspired me and how he pushed me.' Patti Smith

The Poetic Punk

Smith started writing poetry and in 1971 met Lenny Kaye, a walking rock and roll encyclopedia and guitarist who started accompanying her to poetry readings. She wrote several volumes of poetry, a play with Sam Shephard, articles for *Creem* Magazine, lyrics for Blue Oyster Cult, sleeve notes for Todd Rundgren and recited a Jim Morrison poem on a solo album by Ray Manzarek. In 1974 she released an independent single, 'Hey Joe'/'Piss Factory' – punk poetry set to rock music – featuring Kaye, keyboards player Richard Sohl and guitarist Tom Verlaine who had recently formed Television. She augmented the group with bassist Ivan Kral and drummer Jay Dee Daugherty and joined Television at a two-month residency at CBGBs club at the beginning of 1975.

🎧 *see* Introduction pp 246 🎧 *see* Sources & Sounds pp 186 🎧 *see* A–Z of Artists pp 256

Smith signed to Arista Records and released *Horses* (1975), produced by The Velvet Underground's John Cale. The album opened with the line 'Jesus died for somebody's sins but not mine' and included the poem 'Redondo Beach' and distinctive covers of rock classics like 'Gloria' and 'Land Of A Thousand Dances'. It was defiantly avant-garde but still made a brief appearance in the US Top 50.

The Patti Smith Group toured Britain and Europe before releasing *Radio Ethiopia* (1976), working with Aerosmith producer Jack Douglas who gave the album a harder feel with guitar solos, although the experimental spirit was never far beneath the surface and came to the fore on the 10-minute title track. However, the album was less successful than *Horses* and early in 1977 Smith's career came to a temporary halt when she fell off a stage in Tampa, Florida, while performing a whirling dervish dance and broke her neck. She spent nearly a year in a neck brace and undergoing physical therapy.

A Reluctant Star

Easter (1978) was a more commercial album (Smith preferred to call it 'communicative'), a Top 20 success in the US and UK. It was produced by Jimmy Iovine who caught the instinctive rock and roll passion in Smith's vocal style while leaving room for spontaneity and suspense. It featured the hit single (No. 5 in the UK, 13 in the US) 'Because The Night', a Bruce Springsteen song written during sessions for *Darkness On The Edge Of Town* but not released.

Wave (1979) was produced by Todd Rundgren, who again gave Smith and the group a user-friendly sound, but Smith's disenchantment with the trappings of stardom was evident on her version of The Byrds' 'So You Want To Be (A Rock And Roll Star)'. The album was dedicated to 'my clarinet teacher', Fred 'Sonic' Smith, a guitarist in seminal 1960s punk rockers The MC5 who also inspired the songs 'Frederick' and 'Dancing Barefoot'.

A Return To The Road

In 1980 Patti Smith married Fred Smith and retired from rock and roll to bring up a family in Detroit. She returned with *Dream Of Life* (1988) co-written with her husband who also co-produced with Jimmy Iovine.

It featured rallying calls ('People Have The Power'), songs of hope ('Paths That Cross') and lullabies ('The Jackson Song').

In 1994 Fred Smith died after a heart attack. A month later Patti Smith's brother Todd died from the same cause. Her response was to return to New York and start performing again, including a tour with Bob Dylan. She confronted her life as a mother, a widow and an artist on *Gone Again* (1996) and *Peace And Noise* (1997) and sang on R.E.M.'s hit single 'E-Bow The Letter'.

Smith continues to record albums – *Gung Ho* (2000), *Trampin'* (2004) – and perform. In 2005 she was the curator of London's Meltdown Festival at which she played the complete *Horses* album for the first time. The 30th anniversary edition of *Horses* (2005) included a bonus disc of live performances.

Below
Smith continues to write, record and perform today, in spite of suffering considerable personal tragedy.

see The Byrds pp 124   see Bob Dylan pp 126   see MC5 pp 143   see Aerosmith pp 210

The Adverts
(Vocal group, 1977–79)

A London punk band comprising T. V. Smith (guitar, vocals), Gaye Advert (bass), Howard Pickup (guitar) and Laurie Driver (drums), The Adverts' debut single 'One Chord Wonders', an incisive comment on punk, demonstrated Smith's lyrical skill as did the Top 20 hit 'Gary Gilmore's Eyes'. The first album *Crossing The Red Sea With The Adverts* (1978) is an unsung classic, but The Adverts split after the disastrous reception that greeted the adventurous *Cast Of Thousands* (1979).

Bauhaus
(Vocal group, 1979–83, 2005–present)

Taking their name from the German architectural movement, Bauhaus were a prototype goth outfit who made their recording debut in 1979 with the nine-minute single 'Bela Lugosi's Dead'. Peter Murphy's brooding voice was accompanied by Daniel Ash (guitar), David J. (bass) and Kevin Haskins (drums) for four albums until the singer left in 1983. Their only Top 20 hit was a faithful cover of David Bowie's 'Ziggy Stardust'. Bauhaus have since reformed.

Blondie
(Vocal group, 1976–83, 1997–present)

An internationally popular New York outfit emerging from the city's thriving new wave scene of the mid to late 1970s, Blondie's founders were Debbie Harry (vocals) and Chris Stein (guitar) with an eventual supporting cast of Clem Burke (drums), Nigel Harrison (bass), Jimmy Destri (keyboards) and Frank Infante (guitar). More pop-orientated than their contemporaries and influenced by 1960s girl groups like The Shangri-Las, Blondie had a British No. 2 hit with 'Denis', from their second album *Plastic Letters* (1978). The follow-up, *Parallel Lines* (1978), was a chart topper on both sides of the Atlantic and contained the disco-flavoured smash 'Heart of Glass', the first of six UK No. 1 singles.

Blondie dabbled in reggae ('The Tide Is High'), calypso ('Island Of Lost Souls') and can claim to have made the first white rap song, 'Rapture'. After the lacklustre *The Hunter* (1982), Blondie disbanded. The group reformed 15 years later and hit the UK No. 1 spot again with 'Maria'.

Elvis Costello
(Guitar, vocals, b. 1955)

One of the new wave's most celebrated songwriters, Costello (born Declan Patrick MacManus) initially portrayed himself as an angry, revenge-obsessed young man before steadily maturing into a genre-straddling elder statesman. His cheeky appropriation of the name 'Elvis' was in tune with the iconoclastic mood of 1977, when his debut album *My Aim Is True* was released. Temporary backing band Clover were superseded by The Attractions, Bruce Thomas (bass), Steve Nieve (real name Nason, keyboards) and Pete Thomas (drums) and their early work together, *This Year's Model* (1978) and *Armed Forces* (1979), established Costello as a major artist.

1980's *Get Happy* embraced soul music whilst an album of country covers *Almost Blue* (1981) signalled expansive musical horizons. Costello went on to work in a variety of genres and with various collaborators. These include the Brodsky (string) Quartet, songwriter Burt Bacharach, opera singer Anne-Sofie von Otter and New Orleans musician Allen Toussaint. Costello's third wife is jazz pianist Diana Krall.

see Introduction pp 246   see Sources & Sounds pp 186   see Key Artists pp 248

The Damned
(Vocal group, 1976–present)

A trailblazing outfit responsible for the first British punk single, 'New Rose' in 1976, and album *Damned, Damned, Damned* (1977). The original line-up of Dave Vanian (real name Letts, vocals), Brian James (guitar) Captain Sensible (Ray Burns, bass) and Rat Scabies (Chris Miller, drums) disintegrated after the second album *Music For Pleasure* (1978) reforming shortly afterwards, minus James, and with changing personnel since. The Damned progressed beyond punk to embrace psychedelia in the mid-1980s, their most successful period commercially.

Devo
(Vocal group, 1977–90)

This arty new wave outfit from Akron, Ohio, comprised Mark Mothersbaugh (vocals, keyboards, guitar), Bob Mothersbaugh (guitar, vocals), Bob Casale (guitar, vocals), Gerald Casale (bass, vocals) and Alan Myers (drums). Devo's influential electronic music embraced robotic and mechanical elements and is heard at its most potent on the debut album *Q: Are We Not Men? A: We Are Devo!* (1978) and at its most daring on their deconstruction of The Rolling Stones' 'Satisfaction'.

Left

Elvis Costello has battled from new wave conventions to more experimental songwriting and retains a loyal fan base.

Below

The Damned trailblazed the punk movement with their single 'New Rose' in 1976.

🔊 *see* The Rolling Stones pp 96 🔊 *see* The Shangri-Las pp 147 🔊 *see* David Bowie pp 196 🔊 *see* The Clash pp 248

Dr Feelgood
(Vocal group, 1971–present)

A London rhythm and blues band that emerged from the pub rock scene in 1974, Dr Feelgood's back to basics approach foreshadowed punk. Comprising Lee Brilleaux (Lee Collinson, vocals), Wilko Johnson (John Wilkinson, guitar), John B. Sparks (bass) and John 'The Big Figure' Martin (drums), their live album *Stupidity* was a 1976 chart topper. Brilleaux remained as the only original member until his death in 1994 when the band continued, in name only, with other musicians.

Below
The Fall's Mark E. Smith was heavily influenced by The Velvet Underground and Can.

Echo and The Bunnymen
(Vocal group, 1979–88, 1997–present)

A post-punk quartet originating in Liverpool's thriving late 1970s new wave scene, comprising Ian McCulloch (vocals), Will Sergeant (guitar), Les Pattinson (bass) and Pete DeFreitas (drums). Career highlights include the moodily atmospheric 1980 debut *Crocodiles* and the lushly epic *Ocean Rain* (1984), but mainstream acceptance eluded them and the band split up in 1988, reforming nine years later minus DeFreitas who perished in a motorcycle accident in 1989.

The Fall
(Vocal group, 1976–present)

Emerging from Manchester in 1976, The Fall are led by vocalist Mark E. Smith who has employed over 50 different musicians. The Fall's music has, however, remained largely unaltered, a basic garage band throb over which Smith half sings, half rants his frequently obscure lyrics. Apart from a brief period in the 1980s when they flirted with chart success – cover versions of The Kinks' 'Victoria' and R. Dean Taylor's 'There's A Ghost In My House' made the UK Top 40, and the album *The Frenz Experiment* (1988) went Top 20 – they have remained a cult attraction.

Championed by legendary DJ John Peel, The Fall's output has been prolific, recording some 25 studio albums, 24 live albums, five part-live, part-studio albums, 45 singles and EPs. Thirty three Fall compilations have been released, of which only *50,000 Fall Fans Can't Be Wrong* (2004) covers the band's entire career.

The Gang of Four
(Vocal group, 1978–84, 1991–95, 2005–present)

A post-punk Leeds quartet acclaimed as a major influence on twenty-first century music (e.g. Franz Ferdinand), The Gang Of Four's often jarring sound embraced funk and reggae with lyrics concerning political and social realities. Jon King (vocals), Andy Gill (guitar), Dave Allen (bass) and Hugo Burnham (drums) made two albums before Gill left in 1981. Disbanding in 1984 after two further albums, they reconvened in 1991 and, with the original line-up, in 2005. Gill produced the early Red Hot Chili Peppers.

see Introduction pp 246   see Sources & Sounds pp 186   see Key Artists pp 248

psychiatric institute, attempting to kick heroin. Bowie maintained contact which led on to the pair creating Iggy's two 1977 albums *The Idiot* and *Lust For Life* in Berlin.

The burgeoning punk movement also helped re-ignite Iggy's career. 1979's *New Values* reunited him with some former Stooges colleagues and after *Zombie Birdhouse* (1982) he took a break, returning in 1986 with *Blah Blah Blah*, which again featured Bowie. He continues to record and perform.

Left
Generation X spawned the pop rock monster that is Billy Idol.

Below
The weirdly fascinating Iggy Pop gains more attention for his bare torso than his music.

Generation X
(Vocal group, 1977–81)
A London punk band consisting of Billy Idol (William Broad, vocals), Tony James (bass), Bob Andrews (guitar) and Mark Laff (drums), Generation X were viewed with suspicion by the punk cognoscenti for their pop leanings and failure to toe the party line. They scored a Top 20 hit with 'King Rocker' in 1979 but otherwise their success was limited, and after three albums (one as Gen X) they split up.

After the split Billy Idol moved to New York and began a solo career. Working with guitarist and songwriter Steve Stevens, he recorded the album *Rebel Yell* (1984). 'White Wedding', 'Eyes Without A Face' and the title track became MTV staples, establishing him as a solo superstar in America. *Whiplash Smile* (1986) was similarly popular. Idol was involved in a serious motorcycle crash shortly before 1990's *Charmed Life*. *Cyberpunk* (1993) flopped and was his last album for 12 years.

Iggy Pop
(Vocals, b. 1947)
One of the most significant figures of the 1970s, Iggy Pop (real name James Osterberg) was hailed as the godfather of punk. But when The Stooges called it a day in 1971, he was viewed as a spent force and it was only the persistence of David Bowie that led to The Stooges reconvening for *Raw Power* (1973) and a legendary gig at London's King's Cross Cinema. The band fell apart again in 1974 and Iggy entered a

see The Stooges pp 149 ⬛ see David Bowie pp 196 ⬛ see Red Hot Chili Peppers pp 336 ⬛ see Franz Ferdinand pp 397

The Jam
(Vocal group, 1977–82)

A three-piece from Woking, Surrey The Jam comprised Paul Weller (guitar, vocals), Bruce Foxton (bass, vocals) and Rick Buckler (drums). Emerging with punk, the band embraced the movement's energy but scorned its negative aspects. After a promising debut *In The City* (1977), the follow-up *This Is The Modern World* (1977) was rushed and unconvincing. Work on a prospective third album was scrapped, prompting a serious re-think of the band's direction.

Above
The Jam burned brightly for a few short years before singer and songwriter Paul Weller pulled the plug and left their fans gasping for air.

All Mod Cons (1978) marked the start of a remarkable resurgence. 1979 saw their first Top 10 single, 'The Eton Rifles', and the quasi-concept album *Setting Sons*. The Jam swiftly became the UK's most popular group with four No. 1 singles, 'Going Underground', 'Start', 'Town Called Malice' and their final release 'Beat Surrender'. Increasingly uncomfortable with the trio's musical limitations and the demands of The Jam's huge audience, Weller disbanded the group in December 1982 to form The Style Council.

Joy Division
(Vocal group, 1977–80)

One of the UK's most important post-punk bands, Joy Division's often bleak and claustrophobic music continues to inspire and influence. Enthused by The Sex Pistols' legendary first Manchester gig in 1976, school friends Bernard Sumner (guitar) and Peter Hook (bass) formed Stiff Kittens, quickly renamed Warsaw. Recruiting Ian Curtis (vocals) and Steven Morris (drums), they became Joy Division in late 1977.

Working with maverick producer Martin Hannett for independent label Factory Records, they arrived at a unique sound that varied significantly from their live shows. *Unknown Pleasures* (1979) was immediately hailed as a classic by the British music press whilst *Closer* (1980) was richer in texture but no less austere in outlook. Standalone single 'Love Will Tear Us Apart' went Top 20 but only after Curtis, who suffered from epilepsy, hanged himself in May 1980, ending the band's career. The others went on to form New Order.

The Mekons
(Vocal group, 1978–present)

Formed at Leeds University by Jon Langford (drums – later guitar, vocals) and Tom Greenhalgh (guitar) with Andy Carrigan (vocals), Mark Lycett (vocals) and Ross Allen (bass), The Mekons' enthusiastic amateurism typified the do-it-yourself punk ideal. Their 1978 debut single, 'Never Been In A Riot', was hailed as a classic. The band went on hold after *The Quality Of Mercy Is Not Strnen* (1979). Reconvening in the mid-1980s, they embraced folk and country influences.

The New York Dolls
(Vocal group, 1971–77, 2004–present)

A trailblazing quintet whose energetic, shambolic style has been an enduring influence. The New York Dolls were formed in 1971 by David Johansen (vocals) and Johnny Thunders (guitar, died 1991), adding Sylvain Sylvain (guitar), Arthur Kane (bass, died 2004) and Billy Murcia (drums) who died in London in 1972 to be replaced by Jerry Nolan (died 1992). The 1973 debut *New York Dolls* was promoted by a legendary appearance on British television's *The Old Grey Whistle Test*.

The album was not a big seller and record company Mercury dropped The Dolls after a similar failure of the 1974 follow-up *Too Much Too Soon*.

see Introduction pp 246   *see* Sources & Sounds pp 186   *see* Key Artists pp 248

Future Sex Pistols manager Malcolm McLaren took charge of the band's final days as they flirted with communist iconography. Folding in 1977, surviving Dolls Sylvain, Johansen and Kane regrouped in 2004, the latter pair releasing a new album in 2006.

Gary Numan

(Various instruments, vocals, b. 1958)

Originally recording as Tubeway Army – the name used on his first No. 1 single 'Are Friends Electric' – Numan's electronic music was influenced by Berlin-era Bowie and set in a dystopian future of his own imagining. The hypnotic synthesizers and emotionless vocals earned him a second 1979 chart topper 'Cars', which was also a smash in America. Mainstream success proved difficult to sustain but Numan still commands a devoted cult following with a new, more industrial sound.

The Rezillos

(Vocal group, 1977–78)

Scottish cartoon punksters led by vocalists Fay Fife (real name Sheila Hynde) and Eugene Reynolds (Alan Forbes), with Jo Callis (guitar), Mark Harris (guitar), D.K. Smythe (bass), Alan Patterson (drums) and Gail Warning (backing vocals). The Rezillos released Scotland's first new wave single, 'I Can't Stand My Baby', in August 1977. Their album *Can't Stand The Rezillos* (1978) contained the hit 'Top Of The Pops'. After disbanding in 1978, Fife and Reynolds formed the similarly named Revillos.

Above

The New York Dolls brutally challenged the attitudes of pop's smart set by cross-dressing in messy drag. Platform shoes, smudged lipstick and tight Lurex kept them as proud and apart as their blasting punk sound.

see The Sex Pistols pp 252   see New Order pp 309   see The Style Council pp 318   see Paul Weller pp 370

Above
Tom Robinson's campaigning songwriting was in direct contrast to the poppy hit of his '2-4-6-8 Motorway', which gave him massive exposure in student discos throughout the English-speaking world.

Right
The Runaways' main claim to fame is the presence of Joan Jett who went on to significant solo success with a number of covers, including 'The Arrows' and 'I Love Rock'n'Roll'.

Tom Robinson
(Guitar, vocals, b. 1950)

As leader of The Tom Robinson Band, this British new wave singer/songwriter first broke through with '2-4-6-8 Motorway' a 1977 hit single that was unrepresentative of the socio-political thrust of many of his songs, such as the anthemic 'Glad To Be Gay'. After two albums, he formed Sector 27 then went solo in 1982 when 'War Baby' was a Top 10 hit. Robinson, who declared himself bisexual and became a parent, subsequently became a radio DJ.

The Runaways
(Vocal group, 1976–79)

A proto-punk all-girl outfit put together by LA producer/svengali Kim Fowley, The Runaways were influenced by heavy metal and the glam rock of The Sweet and Suzi Quatro. Initially comprising Cherie Curie (vocals), Joan Jett (guitar), Lita Ford (guitar), Jackie Fox (bass) and Sandy West (drums), the band made five

see Introduction pp 246   see Sources & Sounds pp 186   see Key Artists pp 248

albums and went through several line-up changes before splitting up in 1979. Jett and Ford went on to solo success.

Sham 69
(Vocal group, 1977–80)

A rabble-rousing punk group from Hersham, Surrey, led by the garrulous singer Jimmy Pursey with Dave Parsons (guitar), Dave Treganna (bass) and Rick Goldstein (drums). The terrace-chant choruses and suburban lyrics of singles like 'If The Kids Are United' and 'Hurry Up Harry' made Sham 69 popular but attracted a thuggish right-wing element to their gigs, many of which were disrupted by violence. After four albums, Pursey went solo in 1980.

Siouxsie and The Banshees
(Vocal group, 1976–96)

A legendary punk band, The Banshees did not release their first single, 'Hong Kong Garden', until 1978. Vocalist Siouxsie was accompanied by Steve Severin (bass), John McKay (guitar) and Kenny Morris (drums). McKay and Morris left abruptly in 1979 to be replaced by Budgie (ex-Slits) and John McGeoch, formerly of Magazine, whose more sophisticated, nimble-fingered guitar steered the band away from the punk assault of old and into their most popular phase.

Squeeze
(Vocal group, 1977–82, 1985–99)

This melodic east London quintet showcased the songwriting prowess of Chris Difford (guitar, vocals) and Glenn Tilbrook (vocals, guitar), with Jools Holland (keyboards), Harry Kakoulli (bass) and Gilson Lavis (drums). *Cool For Cats* (1979) spawned memorable hits with the title track and 'Up The Junction'. Holland left after *Argybargy* (1980). The classic *East Side Story* (1981) was followed by the disappointing *Sweets From A Stranger* (1982) after which Squeeze disbanded, reforming in 1985.

Stiff Little Fingers
(Vocal group, 1978–83, 1987–present)

The Belfast outfit, comprising Jake Burns (guitar, vocals), Henry Clunie (guitar), Ali McMordie (bass) and Brian Falloon (drums) converted to punk on seeing The Clash in 1977. With lyrics by journalist Gordon Oglivie, Fingers' early material, particularly the debut album *Inflammable Material* (1979), expressed anger at the troubles in Northern Ireland. Characterized by Burns' raw-throated vocals, the band split in 1983 and reformed four years later, remaining a popular live draw.

Below

Sham 69 deliberately incited their audiences to violence with their anthemic rallying cries and rabble-rousing live performances.

🔊 *see* The Clash pp 248   🔊 *see* The Sex Pistols pp 252

The Stranglers
(Vocal group, 1974–present)
Formed in 1974 in Guildford, Surrey, The Stranglers were relatively experienced musicians when they broke through at the same time as punk in 1977. Comprising Hugh Cornwell (guitar, vocals), Jean-Jacques Burnel (bass, vocals), Dave Greenfield (keyboards) and Jet Black (drums), the band's early sound was notable for The Doors-like keyboards and grumbling bass. The Stranglers' two 1977 albums *Rattus Norvegicus* and *No More Heroes* made them the new wave's best-selling band. *Black And White* (1978) and *The Raven* (1979) kept their profile high.

A more experimental direction was forged with 1981's *Gospel According To The Meninblack* whilst *La Folie* (1982) yielded the band's biggest hit, 'Golden Brown'. After 10 albums, Cornwell quit for a solo career in 1990. The Stranglers remain popular on the live circuit with Paul Roberts (vocalist, left 2006) and John Ellis (guitar) who was replaced by Baz Warne (now also lead vocalist) in 2000.

Below

Some regarded The Stranglers as punk poseurs for jumping on the bandwagon, but their polished, incisive performances won them a huge following.

Teardrop Explodes
(Vocal group, 1979–82)
Led by singer/bassist Julian Cope, Teardrop Explodes formed in Liverpool in 1979. Paul Simpson (keyboards), Mick Finkler (guitar) and Gary Dwyer (drums) were the first of many musicians to pass through the band's ranks. Their brassy psychedelia gained three hits, but the albums *Kilimanjaro* (1980) and *Wilder* (1981) inexplicably failed to register. Teardrop Explodes imploded whilst recording a third album in 1982. Soon afterwards, Cope began an eccentrically fascinating solo career.

Television
(Vocal group, 1973–78, 1992–present)
An art punk group formed in New York in 1973, Television originally included Richard Hell (bass), who later formed The Heartbreakers and The Voidoids, along with guitarists Tom Verlaine and Robert Lloyd and Billy Ficca (drums). Hell soon left due to friction with Verlaine. Fred Smith, briefly a member of Blondie,

see Introduction pp 246 see Sources & Sounds pp 186 see Key Artists pp 248

took over on bass. Television became part of the nascent punk scene in New York, which centred on the legendary venues Max's Kansas City and CBGBs. The interlocking guitars of Verlaine and Lloyd provided the band's trademark and set them apart from their peers.

Television's first release was a pioneering independent single, 'Little Johnny Jewel'. The debut album *Marquee Moon* (1977) was immediately hailed by critics as a classic but the band split after the disappointing follow-up, *Adventure* (1978). Television reformed in 1992 for a third, eponymous album and have performed together occasionally since.

Ultravox
(Vocal group, 1977–85)
Originally consisting of John Foxx (real name Dennis Leigh, vocals), Chris Cross (Chris Allen, bass), Billy Currie (keyboards, synthesizer), Steve Shears (guitar) and Warren Cann (drums), Ultravox were one of the first new wave bands to utilize the synthesizer. Foxx departed after three albums to be replaced in 1979 by Midge Ure, formerly of Slik and The Rich Kids, under whose influence a more accessible and commercial electro pop emerged, beginning with the single and album *Vienna* (1980).

X-Ray Spex
(Vocal group, 1977–79)
This British punk act featured Poly Styrene (Marion Elliott, vocals), Jak Airport (Jack Stafford, guitar), Paul Dean (bass), Paul 'B. P.' Hurding (drums) and Lora Logic

(Susan Whitby, saxophone). Poly's strident voice and pithy songs about consumer culture gave them minor UK hits with 'The Day The World Turned Day-Glo', 'Identity' and 'Germ Free Adolescents'. After one album, 1978's *Germ Free Adolescents*, X-Ray Spex split up and Poly Styrene joined the Hare Krishna movement.

XTC
(Vocal group, 1977–present)
Influential Swindon new-wavers, fronted by Andy Partridge (guitar, vocals) with Colin Moulding (bass, vocals), Barry Andrews (keyboards) and Terry Chambers (drums, until 1985). After two 1978 albums, *White Music* and *Go 2*, Andrews departed and the band's sound was overhauled when guitarist Dave Gregory was recruited. Critical acclaim for albums like *Skylarking* (1986) and *Oranges And Lemons* (1989) failed to translate into sales. After a seven-year lay-off, Partridge and Moulding revived XTC in 1999.

Left
Television originated from the same New York new wave scene as Blondie, gigging regularly at the influential CBGBs.

Below
Poly Styrene, the lead singer and writer of X-Ray Specs, shone briefly and brightly in the late 1970s.

🔊 *see* The Doors pp 140   🔊 *see* Blondie pp 256

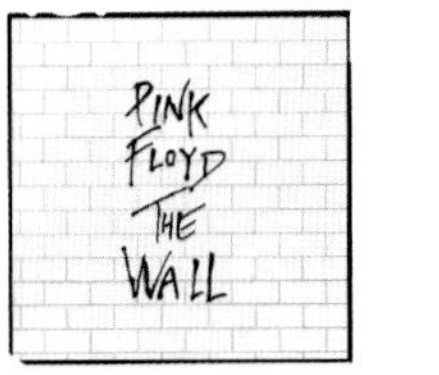

THE SEVENTIES

List of Artists

Entries appear in the following order: name, music style, year(s) of popularity, type of artist, country of origin

.38 Special, Southern Rock, 1970s-, Artist, American
101'ers, The, Pub Rock, 1970s, Artist, British
10cc, Prog Rock, 1970s-1990s, Artist, British
20/20, 1970s Pop, 1970s-1990s, Artist, American
999, British Punk, 1970s-1990s, Artist, British
Aalon, Disco, 1970s, Artist, American
ABBA, Europop, 1970s-1980s, Artist, Swedish
Abercrombie, John, Bebop, 1970s-, Artist, American
Abrahams, Mick, Blues Rock; Rhythm & Blues, 1970s-1990s, Artist, British
AC/DC, Heavy Metal, 1970s-, Artist, Australian
Accept, Heavy Metal, 1970s-1990s, Artist, German
Ace In The Hole Band, Alternative Country, 1970s-1990s, Artist, American
Ace, Pub Rock, 1970s, Artist, British
Adam and the Ants, New Wave, 1970s-1980s, Artist, British
Adams, Arthur, Modern Electric Blues, 1970s-1990s, Artist, American
Addicts, The, Hard Rock; British Punk, 1970s-, Artist, British
Adolescents, The, US Underground & Garage Rock, 1970s-1980s, Artist, American
Adverts, The, British Punk, 1970s, Artist, British
Aerosmith, Hard Rock; Arena Rock; Heavy Metal; 1970s Pop, 1970s-, Artist, American
Agitation Free, Alternative/Indie Rock, 1970s, Artist, German
Aguilar, Freddie, Folk Rock, 1970s-1990s, Artist, Filipino
Air, Free Jazz, 1970s-1980s, Artist, American
AKA, Ska, 1970s, Artist, American
Alabama, Urban Cowboys; Country Rock, 1970s-, Artist, American
Alan Parsons Project, The, Prog Rock, 1970s-1980s, Artist, British
Albion Band, The, UK Folk; Folk Rock, 1970s-, Artist, British
Alcapone, Dennis, Deejays, 1970s-1990s, Artist, Jamaican
Alexander, Willie 'Loco', American Punk, 1970s-1990s, Artist, American
Allen, Debbie, The Classic Soul Era, 1970s-1980s, Artist, American
Allen, Terry, Alternative Country; Country Rock, 1970s-1990s, Artist, American
Allman, Gregg, Southern Rock; Blues Rock, 1970s-1990s, Artist, American
Allspice, Disco, 1970s, Artist, American
Alsop, Peter, Folk Pop, 1970s-1990s, Artist, American
Alternative TV, British Punk; Alternative/Indie Rock, 1970s-1990s, Artist, British
Amazing Rhythm Aces, Country Rock, 1970s-, Artist, American
Ambrosia, Prog Rock; Melodic Rock, 1970s-1990s, Artist, American
America, Melodic Rock; 1970s Pop, 1970s-1990s, Artist, British
American Flyer, Country Rock, 1970s, Artist, American
Anderson, John, The Outlaw Movement; Honky Tonk, 1970s-, Artist, American
Anderson, Little Willie, Modern Electric Blues; Chicago Blues, 1970s-1980s, Artist, American
Angelic Upstarts, British Punk; Hard Rock, 1970s-, Artist, British
Anglo-Saxon Brown, Disco, 1970s, Artist, American
Angry Samoans, US Underground & Garage Rock, 1970s-1990s, Artist, American
Ant, Adam, New Wave, 1970s-, Artist, British
Aquarian Dream, Disco, Funk Soul, 1970s-1980s, Artist, American
Area, Prog Rock, 1970s, Artist, Italian
Armatrading, Joan, 1970s Pop Singer/Songwriters, 1970s-1990s, Artist; Songwriter, British
Arpeggio, Disco, 1970s, Artist, American
Art Bears, The, Prog Rock, 1970s-1980s, Artist, British
Ash Ra Tempel, Prog Rock; Krautrock, 1970s-, Artist, German
Ashford and Simpson, Disco; Urban Soul, 1970s-1980s, Artist, American
Asleep At The Wheel, Neo-Traditionalists, 1970s-1990s, Artist, American
Aswad, Roots, 1970s-1990s, Artist, British
Atlanta Rhythm Section, The, Southern Rock, 1970s-1980s, Artist, American
Atlantic Starr, Disco; Urban Soul; Funk Soul, 1970s-1990s, Artist, American
Avengers, The, American Punk, 1970s-1980s, Artist, American
Average White Band, Funk; Funk Metal; Funk Soul, 1970s-1980s, Artist, British
Aztec Two-Step, Folk Rock, 1970s-1990s, Artist; Songwriter, American
Azymuth, Brazilian Jazz; Fusion, 1970s-1990s, Artist, Brazilian
B-52s, The, New Wave, 1970s-1990s, Artist, American
Babys, The, Arena Rock; Hard Rock, 1970s-1980s, Artist, British
Baccara, Disco, 1970s, Artist, Spanish
Bad Company, Hard Rock; Arena Rock; Blues Rock, 1970s-1990s, Artist, British
Baker Gurvitz Army, Blues Rock, 1970s, Artist, British
Baker, Duck, Folk Rock, 1970s-1990s, Artist; Songwriter, American
Baker, George, Europop, 1970s, Artist, Dutch
Baker, Ginger, Blues Rock; Jazz Rock; Fusion, 1970s-, Artist, British
Ball, Marcia, Modern Electric Blues, 1970s-, Artist, American
Bandy, Moe, Honky Tonk; Early & Old-Time Country, 1970s-1990s, Artist, American
Barclay James Harvest, Folk Rock, 1970s-, Artist, British
Bardens, Peter, Prog Rock; Electro, 1970s-2000s, Artist, British
Barlow, Randy, Neo-Traditionalists, 1970s-1980s, Artist, American
Barnes, Roosevelt 'Booba', Modern Electric Blues, 1970s-1990s, Artist, American
Barry, Claudja, Europop; Disco, 1970s-1980s, Artist, Jamaican
Bauhaus, Goth Rock; Alternative/Indie Rock, 1970s-1990s, Artist, British
Bay City Rollers, 1970s Pop, 1970s-1980s, Artist, British
Beat, The, 1970s Pop; New Wave, 1970s-1980s, Artist, American
Bees Make Honey, Pub Rock, 1970s, Artist, British
Bell, Chris, 1970s Pop Singer/Songwriters, 1970s, Artist; Songwriter, American
Bell, Maggie, Blues Rock, 1970s-1980s, Artist, British
Bellamy Brothers, The, Country Rock, 1970s-, Artist, American
Benatar, Pat, Arena Rock; Hard Rock, 1970s-, Artist, American
Benoit, David, Fusion; Jazz Rock, 1970s-, Producer; Artist, American
Betts, Dickey, Funk Metal, 1970s-, Artist, American
Big Star, Proto-Punk; 1970s Pop, 1970s, Artist, American
Big Time Sarah, Modern Electric Blues, 1970s-, Artist, American
Big Youth, Deejays, 1970s-, Artist, Jamaican
Biggun, Ivor, Disco, 1970s-1980s, Artist, British
Birthday Party, The, Alternative/Indie Rock, 1970s-1980s, Artist, Australian
Bishop, Stephen, 1970s Pop Singer/Songwriters, 1970s-2000s, Artist, American
BIX, Ska, 1970s, Artist, British
Black Flag, US Underground & Garage Rock; American Punk, 1970s-1980s, Artist, American
Black Oak Arkansas, Southern Rock, 1970s-1990s, Artist, American
Black Uhuru, Dub; Roots, 1970s-, Artist, Jamaican
Blackbyrds, The, Funk, 1970s-1980s, Artist, American
Blackfoot, Southern Rock, 1970s-1990s, Artist, American
Blades, Ruben, Latin; Latin Jazz, 1970s-, Artist, Panamanian
Blondie, American Punk; New Wave; 1970s Pop, 1970s-1990s, Artist, American
Bloodstone, Funk; Funk Soul, 1970s-1990s, Artist, American
Blow, Kurtis, Old School; Hip Hop 1970s-1980s, Artist, American
Blue Ash, 1970s Pop, 1970s, Artist, American
Blue Magic, Urban Soul, 1970s-1990s, Artist, American
Blue Oyster Cult, Arena Rock; Hard Rock, 1970s-, Artist, American
Blues Brothers, The, Rhythm & Blues; The Classic Soul Era, 1970s-, Artist, American
Blunstone, Colin, Folk Rock, 1970s Pop, 1970s-2000s, Artist, British
Bohannon, Disco, 1970s-1980s, Artist, American
Bombers, Disco, 1970s, Artist, Australian
Boney M, Disco, 1970s-, Artist, German
Boom, Taka, Disco, 1970s-1980s, Artist, American
Boomtown Rats, The, British Punk, 1970s-1980s, Artist, British
Booth, Tony, Country Rock, 1970s, Artist, American
Bose, Michel, Latin, 1970s-, Artist, Panamanian
Boston, Arena Rock; Hard Rock, 1970s-1990s, Artist, American
Bothy Band, The, Irish Folk, 1970s, Artist, Irish
Bovell, Dennis, Dub, 1970s-1980s, Artist, British
Brady Bunch, The, 1970s Pop; Manufactured Pop, 1970s, Artist, American
Brady, Paul, Folk Rock, 1970s-, Artist, Irish
Brainticket, Krautrock, 1970s-1980s, Artist, German
Bramlett, Bonnie, Blues Rock, 1970s-, Artist, American
Bramlett, Delaney, Blues Rock, 1970s, Artist, American
Bread, Melodic Rock, 1970s; 1990s, Artist; Songwriter, American
Brennan, Máire, 1970s-1990s, UK Folk; Folk Pop, Artist, Irish
Brick, Funk; Disco, 1970s-1980s, Artist, American
Bridges, Alicia, Disco; The Classic Soul Era, 1970s-1980s, Artist, American
Brighter Side Of Darkness, The Classic Soul Era, 1970s, Artist, American
Brinsley Schwarz, Pub Rock; Country Rock; Rock'n'Roll, 1970s, Artist, British
Brooks, Elkie, Blues Rock, 1970s-, Artist, British
Brother To Brother, Funk Soul, 1970s, Artist, American
Brotherhood Of Man, 1970s Pop, 1970s-1980s, Artist, British
Brothers Johnson, The, Funk Soul, 1970s-1990s, Artist, American
Brown, Dennis, Dancehall; Ragga, 1970s-1990s, Artist, Jamaican
Brown, Peter, Disco, 1970s-1990s, Artist, American
Brown, Randy, The Classic Soul Era, 1970s-1980s, Artist, American
Brown, Shirley, Urban Soul, 1970s-, Artist, American
Bryson, Peabo, 1970s Pop; Urban Soul, 1970s-1990s, Artist, American
BT Express, Funk; Disco, 1970s-1980s, Artist, American
Buchanan, Roy, Blues Rock; Modern Electric Blues, 1970s-1980s, Artist, American
Buckingham, Lindsey, Prog Rock; British Blues; Blues Rock; Folk Pop, 1970s-1990s, Artist, American
Budgie, Heavy Metal; Hard Rock, 1970s-1980s, Artist, British
Buffet, Jimmy, Country Rock, 1970s-, Artist, American
Burch, Vernon, The Classic Soul Era, 1970s-1980s, Artist, American
Burke, Kevin, Irish Folk, 1970s-, Artist, British
Burnett, T-Bone, Folk Rock, 1970s-1990s, Artist, American
Burnette, Billy, Country Rock, 1970s-, Artist, American
Burning Spear, Dub; Roots, 1970s-1990s, Artist, Jamaican
Burrows, Tony, 1970s Pop, 1970s, Artist, British
Bush, Kate, 1980s Pop Singer/Songwriters, 1970s-, Artist; Songwriter, British
Buzzcocks, British Punk, 1970s-, Artist, British
Byles, Junior, Dub, 1970s-1990s, Artist, Jamaican
Cabaret Voltaire, Alternative/Indie Rock, 1970s-1990s, Artist, British
Caldwell, Bobby, Urban Soul, 1970s-1990s, Artist, American
Cale, J. J., Blues Rock; 1970s Pop Singer/Songwriters, 1970s-1990s, Artist; Songwriter, American
Camel, Prog Rock, 1970s-1990s, Artist, British
Cameo, Funk Soul; Urban Soul, 1970s-, Artist, American
Captain and Tennille 1970s Pop, 1970s-1980s, Artist; Songwriter, American
Captain Sensible, British Punk; Goth Rock, 1970s-1990s, Artist, British
Carlos, Don, Roots, 1970s-, Artist, Jamaican
Carmen, Eric, 1970s Pop, 1970s-1990s, Artist; Songwriter, American
Carnes, Kim, 1970s Pop, 1970s-1980s, Artist, American
Carrack, Paul, 1970s Pop; Urban Soul, 1970s-, Artist, British
Carroll, Jim, Proto-Punk; American Punk, 1970s-1990s, Artist, American
Cars, The, New Wave; 1970s Pop, 1970s-1980s, Artist, American
Carter, Carlene, Neo-Traditionalists, 1970s-1990s, Artist, American
Cash, Rosanne, 1970s Pop Singer/Songwriters; Neo-Traditionalists, 1970s-1990s, Artist; Songwriter, American
Cassidy, David, 1970s Pop, 1970s-, Artist, American
Cassidy, Shaun, 1970s Pop, 1970s-1980s, Artist, American
Cavaliere, Felix, Prog Rock, 1970s; 1990s, Artist, American
Centipede, Jazz Rock, 1970s, Artist, British
Cerrone, Disco; House, 1970s-, Producer, French
Chanson, Disco, 1970s, Artist, American
Chapin, Harry, 1970s Pop Singer/Songwriters, 1970s-1980s, Artist; Songwriter, American
Chapman, Marshall, Folk Rock, 1970s-1990s, Artist, American
Chapman, Roger, Prog Rock; Hard Rock, 1970s-, Artist, British
Chapter 8, The Classic Soul Era, 1970s-1980s, Artist, American
Charism, Disco, 1970s, Artist, American
Charles, Tina, Disco, 1970s-1980s, Artist, American
Charlie and the Wide Boys, Pub Rock, 1970s, Artist, British
Charlie Daniels Band, The, Southern Rock, 1970s-1990s, Artist, American
Cheap Trick, Hard Rock; Arena Rock; New Wave; 1970s Pop, 1970s-, Artist, American
Chic, Funk; Disco, 1970s-1990s, Artist, American
Chicano, El, The Classic Soul Era, 1970s; 1990s, Artist, American
Chicory Tip, Glam Rock & Glitter; 1970s Pop, 1970s, Artist, British
Child, Desmond, Disco, 1970s, Artist, American
Childish, Billy, Alternative/Indie Rock, 1970s-, Artist, British
Chilli Willi and the Red Hot Peppers, Pub Rock, 1970s, Artist, British
Chocolate Milk, Funk Soul, 1970s-1980s, Artist, American
Choice Four, Disco; The Classic Soul Era, 1970s, Artist, American
Christian, Meg, Folk Pop, 1970s-1980s, Artist, American
CJ and Co, Disco, 1970s, Artist, American
Clannad, UK Folk; Irish Folk, 1970s-, Artist, Irish
Clark, Guy, 1970s Pop Singer/Songwriters; Alternative Country; The Outlaw Movement; Contemporary Folk, 1970s-1990s, Artist; Songwriter, American
Clark, Mike, Funk Soul, 1970s-, Artist, American
Clarke, Johnny, Reggae Pop, 1970s-1990s, Artist, Jamaican
Clarke, Mick, British Blues; Blues Rock, 1970s-, Artist, British
Clarke, William, Modern Electric Blues, 1970s-1990s, Artist, American
Clash, The, Hard Rock; British Punk, 1970s-1980s, Artist, British
Clifford, Linda, The Classic Soul Era, 1970s-1980s, Artist, American
Clinton, George, Funk Soul; Urban Soul, 1970s-1990s, Artist, American
Clover, Country Rock, 1970s, Artist, American
Cluster, Krautrock; Ambient; Electro, 1970s-1990s, Artist, German
Cobham, Billy, Fusion, 1970s-, Artist, American
Cockney Rebel, Glam Rock & Glitter, 1970s-1990s, Artist, British
Codona, Fusion and Jazz Rock; Free Jazz, 1970s-1980s, Artist, American
Coffey, Dennis, Urban Soul, 1970s-1980s, Artist, American
Cole, Natalie, 1970s Pop,; Urban Soul, 1970s-, Artist, American
Cole, Richie, Bebop, 1970s-1990s, Artist, American
Collins, Bootsy, Disco, Funk Soul, 1970s-, Artist, American
Collins, Dave and Ansell, Rock Steady, 1970s, Artist, Jamaican
Collins, Phil, 1970s Pop, 1970s-, Artist, British
Colosseum II, Prog Rock; Hard Rock, 1970s, Artist, British
Commander Cody, Country Rock, 1970s-, Artist, American
Commodores, The, Funk; Funk Soul; Urban Soul, 1970s-1990s, Artist, American
Concord Allstars, Swing; Bebop, 1970s-1990s, Artist, American
Congos, The, Dub, 1970s; 1990s, Artist, Jamaican
Conlee, John, Neo-Traditionalists, 1970s-1990s, Artist, American
Connors, Norman, Fusion, 1970s-, Artist, American
Continental Four, The, The Classic Soul Era, 1970s, Artist, American
Controllers, The, Urban Soul, 1970s-1990s, Artist, American
Cooder, Ry, Blues Rock, 1970s-1990s, Artist, American
Coolidge, Rita, Country Rock, 1970s-1990s, Artist, American
Costa, Paulinho Da, Brazilian Jazz; Latin Jazz; Fusion and Jazz Rock, 1970s-1990s, Artist, Brazilian
Costello, Elvis, British Punk; Pub Rock; New Wave; 1970s Pop Singer/Songwriters, 1970s-, Artist; Songwriter, British
Counts, The, Funk Soul, 1970s, Artist, American
Coyne, Kevin, British Blues; Folk Rock, 1970s-, Artist; Songwriter, British
Crass, British Punk, 1970s-1980s, Artist, British
Crawford, Randy, Urban Soul, 1970s-, Artist, American
Cray, Robert, Modern Electric Blues, 1970s-, Artist, American
Creach, Papa John, Folk Rock, 1970s-1990s, Artist, American
Crosby, David, Folk Rock; 1970s Pop Singer/Songwriters, 1970s-1990s, Artist; Songwriter, American
Crowell, Rodney, Neo-Traditionalists; Country Rock, 1970s-, Artist; Songwriter, American
Crown Heights Affair, Disco; Funk Soul, 1970s-1980s, Artist, American
Culture, Roots, 1970s-, Artist, Jamaican
Cure, The, Goth Rock; Alternative/Indie Rock, 1970s-1990s, Artist, British
Curved Air, Prog Rock, 1970s; 1990s, Artist, British
Cutler, Chris, Jazz Rock; Fusion, 1970s-, Artist, American
Cymande, Funk Soul, 1970s, Artist, West Indian
Dalton, Lacy J., Neo-Traditionalists, 1970s-, Artist, American
Damned, The, British Punk; Goth Rock, 1970s-1990s, Artist, British
Danann, De, Irish Folk, 1970s-1990s, Artist, Irish
Daniels, Charlie, Urban Cowboys; Country Rock, 1970s-, Artist, American
Darts, The, Rock'n'Roll, Doo-Wop, 1970s-1980s, Artist, British
Davidson, Diane, The Classic Soul Era, 1970s-1980s, Artist; Songwriter, American
Davis, Mac, The Nashville Sound; Country Rock, 1970s-1990s, Artist, American
Dawn, 1970s Pop, 1970s, Artist, American
De Burgh, Chris, Melodic Rock; Prog Rock; 1970s Pop, 1970s-, Artist, British
Dead Boys, American Punk, 1970s-1980s, Artist, American
Dead Kennedys, US Underground & Garage Rock; American Punk, 1970s-1980s, Artist, American
DeFranco Family, The, 1970s Pop, 1970s, Artist, Canadian
Delegation, Disco; House, 1970s-1980s, Artist, British
Delgado, Junior, Dub, 1970s-1990s, Artist, Jamaican
DeMarinis, Paul, New Age; Electro, 1970s-1990s, Composer, American
Derek and the Dominoes, Hard Rock; British Blues; Blues Rock, 1970s, Artist; Songwriter, British
Destroy All Monsters, Proto-Punk; Hard Rock, 1970s-1990s, Artist, American
Deuter, Ambient; Electro; New Age, 1970s-, Artist; Composer, German
DeVaughan, William, Urban Soul, 1970s-1980s, Artist, American
DeVille, Mink, American Punk, 1970s-1990s, Artist, American
Devo, US Underground & Garage Rock; American Punk; New Wave, 1970s-1990s, Artist, American
Dhomhnaill, Triona Ni, Irish Folk, 1970s-1990s, Artist, Irish
Diamond Head, Heavy Metal, 1970s-1990s, Artist, British
Diamond Rio, Neo-Traditionalists, 1970s; 1990s-, Artist, American
Dibango, Manu, Fusion and Jazz Rock, 1970s-, Artist, African
Dickies, The, American Punk, 1970s-, Artist, American
Dictators, The, American Punk; Proto-Punk, 1970s-1980s, Artist, American
Dillinger, Dancehall, 1970s-, Artist, Jamaican
Dillon, Dean, Neo-Traditionalists, 1970s-1990s, Artist, American
Dils, American Punk, 1970s-1980s, Artist, American
DiMeola, Al, Fusion; Jazz Rock; Fusion and Jazz Rock, 1970s-, Artist, American
Dio, Heavy Metal; Hard Rock, 1970s-, Artist, American
Dire Straits, Melodic Rock, 1970s-1990s, Artist, British
Disco Tex and The Sex-O-Lettes, Disco, 1970s, Artist, American
Dissidenten, Fusion and Jazz Rock, 1970s-1990s, Artist, German
Diversions, Disco, 1970s, Artist, American
Dixie Dregs, The, Southern Rock, 1970s-1980s, Artist, American
DMZ, US Underground & Garage Rock, 1970s-1980s, Artist, American
Dobkin, Alix, Political Folk & Protest Songs, 1970s-1990s, Artist, American
Dollar Brand, Fusion and Jazz Rock, 1970s-1980s, Artist, South African
Doobie Brothers, 1970s Pop, 1970s-, Artist, American
Double Exposure, Disco, 1970s, Artist, American
Douglas, Carl, Disco, 1970s, Artist, Jamaican
Douglas, Carol, Disco, 1970s, Artist, American
Dozier, Lamont, The Classic Soul Era, 1970s-, Producer; Composer; Songwriter; Artist, American
Dr. Buzzard's Original Savannah Band, Disco, 1970s-1980s, Artist, American
Dr. Feelgood, Pub Rock, 1970s-, Artist, British
Dramatics, The, Urban Soul, 1970s-1990s, Artist, American
Dread, Mikey, Deejays, 1970s-1990s, Artist, American
Ducks Deluxe, Pub Rock, 1970s-1980s, Artist, British
Dunbar, Sly, Reggae Pop; Dancehall; Rock Steady, 1970s-1990s, Producer; Artist, Jamaican
Dunkley, Errol, Rock Steady, 1970s-, Artist, Jamaican
Duren, Van, 1970s Pop, 1970s, Artist, American
Durham, Bobby, Honky Tonk, 1970s-1980s, Artist, American
Durutti Column, The, New Wave, 1970s-, Artist, British
Dury, Ian, British Punk; Pub Rock; New Wave; Disco, 1970s-1990s, Artist, British
Dynamic Superiors, The, The Classic Soul Era, 1970s, Artist, American
Dyson, Ronnie, The Classic Soul Era, 1970s-1980s, Artist, American
Eagles, The, Melodic Rock; Country Rock; 1970s Pop, 1970s-1990s, Artist, American
Earl, Ronnie, Blues Rock; Modern Electric Blues, 1970s-, Artist, American
Earth, Wind and Fire, Disco; Funk; Funk Soul; Urban Soul, 1970s-, Artist, American
Easter, Mitch, 1970s Pop, 1970s-, Artist; Producer, American
Eastwood, Clint, Dancehall, 1970s-1980s, Artist, Jamaican
Ebonys, The, Funk Soul, 1970s, Artist, American
Echo and the Bunnymen, Alternative/Indie Rock, 1970s-, Artist, British
Eddie and the Hot Rods, British Punk; Pub Rock, 1970s-1990s, Artist, British
Edmunds, Dave, Pub Rock; Rock'n'Roll; New Wave, 1970s-, Artist, British
Edwards, Dennis, The Classic Soul Era; Urban Soul, 1970s-1980s, Artist, American
Edwards, John, Northern Soul, 1970s-1980s, Artist, American
Edwards, Jonathan, Folk Rock, 1970s-1990s, Artist; Songwriter, American
Egan, Seamus, Irish Folk, 1970s-1990s, Artist, Irish
Eggs Over Easy, Pub Rock, 1970s, Artist, American
El Coco, Disco, 1970s, Artist, American
Electric Eels, Proto-Punk, 1970s, Artist, American
Electric Light Orchestra, Prog Rock; 1970s Pop, 1970s-, Artist, British
Elliman, Yvonne, Disco, 1970s, Artist, American
Ellis, Hortense, Rock Steady, 1970s, Artist, Jamaican
Ellis, Jimmy, Disco, 1970s, Artist, American
Eloy, Prog Rock, 1970s-1990s, Artist, German
Ely, Joe, The Outlaw Movement; Country Rock, 1970s-, Artist, American
Embarrassment, The, US Underground & Garage Rock; Alternative/Indie Rock, 1970s-1990s, Artist, American
Emerson, Lake and Palmer, Prog Rock, 1970s-1990s, Artist, British
Emmanuel, Latin, 1970s-, Artist, Mexican
Emotions, The, Urban Soul, 1970s-1990s, Artist, American
Enchantment, The Classic Soul Era, 1970s-1990s, Artist, American
England Dan and John Ford Coley, 1970s Pop, 1970s-1980s, Artist, American
Enid, The, Jazz Rock; Prog Rock, 1970s-1990s, Artist, British
Eno, Brian, Prog Rock; Proto-Punk; Ambient; Electro, 1970s-, Producer; Artist, British
Eruption, Disco, 1970s-1980s, Artist, British
Essex, David, 1970s Pop, 1970s-1990s, Artist, British
Everly, Don, Folk Rock, 1970s, Artist, American
Everly, Phil, Folk Rock, 1970s-1980s, Artist, American
Exile, Urban Cowboys, 1970s-1990s, Artist, American
Fabulous Thunderbirds, The, Blues Rock, 1970s-, Artist, American
Faces, Hard Rock; Proto-Punk; Rock'n'Roll, 1970s, Artist, British
Facts Of Life, Disco, 1970s, Artist, American
Faddis, John, Bebop, 1970s-1990s, Artist, American
Fagen, Donald, Jazz Rock; 1970s Pop, 1970s-, Artist, American
Faith, Hope and Charity, The Classic Soul Era, 1970s, Artist, American
Fall, The, Alternative/Indie Rock, 1970s-, Artist, British
Fanny, Hard Rock; Rock'n'Roll, 1970s, Artist, American
Fasteau, Zusaan Kali, Fusion and Jazz Rock; Free Jazz, 1970s-, Artist, American
Faust, Prog Rock; Krautrock, 1970s-, Artist, German
Fear, US Underground & Garage Rock, 1970s-, Artist, American
Feelies, The, US Underground & Garage Rock; Alternative/Indie Rock; 1970s Pop, 1970s-1990s, Artist, American
Felt, British Punk, 1970s-1980s, Artist, British
Ferry, Bryan, Prog Rock; Glam Rock & Glitter, 1970s-, Artist, British
Finn, Neil, 1970s Pop Singer/Songwriters, 1970s-, Artist; Songwriter, New Zealander
Firefall, Country Rock, 1970s-1980s, Artist, American
First Choice, Urban Soul, 1970s-1980s, Artist, American
First Class, The, 1970s Pop, 1970s, Artist, British
Fjellgard, Gary, Young Country, 1970s-1990s, Producer, Canadian
Flaming Ember, The Classic Soul Era, 1970s, Artist, American
Flash, Prog Rock, 1970s, Artist, British
Flesh Eaters, US Underground & Garage Rock; Hard Rock, 1970s-1990s, Artist, American
Fleshtones, The, US Underground & Garage Rock; Alternative/Indie Rock, 1970s-, Artist, American
Floaters, The, The Classic Soul Era, 1970s, Artist, American
FM, Prog Rock, 1970s-, Artist, Canadian
Focus, Prog Rock, 1970s-1980s, Artist, Dutch
Fogelberg, Dan, 1970s Pop Singer/Songwriters, 1970s-, Artist; Songwriter, American
Forbert, Steve, Contemporary Folk, 1970s-, Artist; Songwriter, American
Foreigner, Hard Rock; Arena Rock, 1970s-, Artist, American
Frampton, Peter, Arena Rock; 1970s Pop, 1970s-, Artist, British
Franklin, Rodney, Urban Soul; Funk Soul, 1970s-1990s, Artist, American
Free Movement, The Classic Soul Era, 1970s, Artist, American
Frida, Europop, 1970s-1990s, Artist, Swedish
Frisell, Bill, Fusion, 1970s-, Artist, American
Froese, Edgar, Ambient; Electro, 1970s-1980s, Producer; Artist, German
Fuller and Kaz, Country Rock; Folk Rock, 1970s, Artist, American
Fureys, The, Irish Folk, 1970s-1990s, Artist, Irish
Fuzz, The, The Classic Soul Era, 1970s, Artist, American
Gabriel, Peter, Prog Rock; 1970s Pop, 1970s-, Producer; Songwriter; Artist, British
Gaines, Roy, Modern Electric Blues, 1970s-, Artist, American
Gallagher, Rory, British Blues; Blues Rock, 1970s-1980s, Artist, Irish
Gang Of Four, Alternative/Indie Rock; New Wave, 1970s-1990s, Artist, British
Gap Band, The, Funk; Funk Soul, 1970s-1990s, Artist, American
Garcia, Jerry, Folk Rock, 1970s-1990s, Artist, American
Garfunkel, Art, Folk Rock; Melodic Rock, 1970s-2000s, Artist, American
Garrett, Leif, 1970s Pop, 1970s-1980s, Artist, American
Gatlin Brothers, Urban Cowboys; Neo-Traditionalists, 1970s-, Artist, American
Gatlin, Larry, Urban Cowboys; Neo-Traditionalists, 1970s-1990s, Artist, American
Gatton, Danny, Neo-Traditionalists; Country Rock, 1970s, Artist, American
Gaughan, Dick, Political Folk & Protest Songs; UK Folk; Contemporary Folk; Irish Folk, 1970s-, Artist, British
Gayle, Crystal, Urban Cowboys, 1970s-, Artist, American
Gaynor, Gloria, Disco, 1970s-, Artist, American
Geldof, Bob, British Punk; Folk Rock; New Wave, 1970s-, Artist, Irish
Generation X, British Punk, 1970s-1980s, Artist, British
Gentle Giant, Prog Rock, 1970s-1980s, Artist,
Germs, The, US Underground & Garage Rock; American Punk, 1970s-1980s, Artist, American
Gibbons, Steve, Rock'n'Roll, 1970s-1990s, Artist, British
Gibbons, Walter, House; Disco, 1970s-1980s, Artist; Producer, American
Gibbs, Joe, Dub, 1970s, Producer, Jamaican
Gillan, Ian, Heavy Metal, 1970s-, Artist, British
Gillman, Jane, Young Country, 1970s-1980s, Artist; Songwriter, American
Gilstrap, Jim, Urban Soul, 1970s-1990s, Artist, American
Gladiators, Rock Steady; Ska, 1970s-, Artist, Jamaican
Glass House, The, The Classic Soul Era, 1970s, Artist, American
Glitter Band, Glam Rock & Glitter, 1970s-1990s, Artist, British
Goblin, Prog Rock; Hard Rock, 1970s-1980s, Artist, Italian
Godley and Crème, Prog Rock; 1970s Pop, 1970s-1980s, Artist, British
Gomm, Ian, Pub Rock, 1970s-, Artist, British
Gong, Prog Rock, 1970s-, Artist, Australian
Göttsching, Manuel, Krautrock; Ambient, 1970s-1990s, Artist, German
Graham, Ernie, Pub Rock, 1970s, Artist, British
Grammer, Reg, Folk Rock, 1970s-1990s, Artist, American
Grant, Amy, 1970s Pop, 1970s-, Artist, American
Grant, Eddy, Reggae Pop, 1970s-, Artist; Producer, African
Great Speckled Bird, Folk Rock; Contemporary Folk, 1970s, Artist, Canadian
Green, Peter, British Blues; Blues Rock, 1970s-, Artist, British
Gregson, Clive, Contemporary Folk; Folk Rock, 1970s-1990s, Artist; Songwriter, British
Griffin, Billy, The Classic Soul Era, 1970s-1980s, Artist, American
Griffith, Nanci, Contemporary Folk; Young Country, 1970s-, Artist; Songwriter, American
Grimes, Howard, The Classic Soul Era, 1970s, Artist, American
Gurtu, Trilok, Fusion and Jazz Rock; Fusion, 1970s-, Artist, Indian
Guru Guru, Krautrock, 1970s-, Artist, German
Hackett, Steve, Prog Rock, 1970s-, Artist, British
Haino, Keiji, Alternative/Indie Rock, 1970s-, Artist, Japanese
Half Japanese, US Underground & Garage Rock; Alternative/Indie Rock, 1970s-, Artist, American
Hall and Oates, 1970s Pop; The Classic Soul Era, 1970s-, Artist, American
Halpern, Steven, Ambient; Electro; New Age, 1970s-, Artist, American
Hamilton, Dirk, Folk Rock, 1970s-, Artist; Songwriter, American
Hammill, Peter, Prog Rock, 1970s-, Artist; Songwriter, British
Hammond, Beres, The Classic Soul Era; Dancehall, 1970s-, Artist, Jamaican
Hammond, Lorraine Lee, Alternative Country, 1970s-1990s, Artist, American
Hancock, Butch, Alternative Country, 1970s-, Artist, American
Harari, Funk Soul, 1970s, Artist, South African
Hargrove, Linda, Urban Cowboys; Country Rock, 1970s-1980s, Artist; Songwriter, American
Harmonia, Krautrock, 1970s, Artist, German
Harris, Major, Northern Soul, 1970s; 1990s, Artist, American
Harris, Norman, The Classic Soul Era, 1970s, Producer; Artist, American
Hartman, Don, Urban Soul, 1970s-1990s, Artist, American
Harvey, Alexander, Urban Cowboys, 1970s-1980s, Artist, American
Haskins, Clarence 'Fuzzy', Funk Soul, 1970s, Artist, American
Hassell, Jon, Tribal Dance; Techno, 1970s-, Artist; Composer, American
Hawkins, Tramaine, Urban Soul, 1970s-, Artist, American
Hawkwind, Prog Rock; Hard Rock, 1970s-, Artist, British
Heart, Hard Rock; Arena Rock, 1970s-, Artist, American
Heartbreakers, The, American Punk; Hard Rock; Proto-Punk, 1970s-1980s, Artist, American
Heatwave, Rhythm & Blues; Disco; Funk, 1970s-1990s, Artist, American
Hell, Richard, Proto-Punk, 1970s-, Artist, American
Help Yourself, Pub Rock, 1970s, Artist, British
Hendryx, Nona, Urban Soul, 1970s-1990s, Artist, American
Hiatt, John, Country Rock; 1970s Pop Singer/Songwriters, 1970s-, Artist; Songwriter, American
High Inergy, Urban Soul, 1970s-1980s, Artist, American
Hillage, Steve, Prog Rock, 1970s-1980s, Artist, British
Hinds, Justin, Ska; Rock Steady, 1970s-1990s, Artist, Jamaican
Hinton, Eddie, The Classic Soul Era, 1970s-1990s, Artist, American
Hiroshima, Fusion and Jazz Rock, 1970s-1990s, Artist, American
Hoenig, Michael, New Age; Electro, 1970s-1980s, Artist; Composer, German
Holdsworth, Allan, Jazz Rock; Fusion, 1970s-, Artist, British
Holloway, Loleatta, Northern Soul; Disco; House; US Garage, 1970s-, Artist, American
Honey Cone, Urban Soul, 1970s, Artist, American
Horslips, Folk Rock, 1970s-1980s, Artist, Irish
Hosono, Haruomi, Trance; Techno, 1970s-, Producer; Artist, Japanese
Hot Chocolate, Funk; Funk Soul, 1970s, Artist, British
Hot Tuna, Folk Rock, 1970s-, Artist, American

see Rock Key Artists pp 196 *see* Pop & Disco Key Artists pp 228 *see* Punk & New Wave Key Artists pp 248

Houston, Cissy, Urban Soul, 1970s-1990s, Artist, American
Hoyle, Linda, Folk Rock, 1970s, Artist, American
Hudson, Al, Urban Soul, 1970s-1990s, Artist, American
Hudson, Keith, Dub, 1970s-1990s, Artist; Producer, Jamaican
Hues Corporation, Northern Soul, 1970s, Artist, American
Human League, New Romantics; New Wave, 1970s-1990s, Artist, British
Humphrey, Bobbi, Soul Jazz; Fusion, 1970s-1990s, Artist, American
Hunter, Robert, Folk Rock; 1970s Pop Singer/Songwriters, 1970s-1990s, Artist; Songwriter, American
Hutson, Leroy, Northern Soul, 1970s-1990s, Artist, American
Idol, Billy, British Punk, 1970s-1990s, Artist, British
Iglesias, Julio, Latin; 1970s Pop, 1970s-, Artist, Spanish
Ijahman, Dub; Rock Steady; Ska, 1970s-1990s, Artist, Jamaican
Independents, The, The Classic Soul Era, 1970s, Artist, American
Ingram, James, Urban Soul, 1970s-1990s, Artist, American
Ingram, Luther, The Classic Soul Era, 1970s-1980s, Artist, American
Inner Circle, Reggae Pop, 1970s-, Artist, Jamaican
Instant Funk, Funk Soul, 1970s-1990s, Artist, American
Iron Maiden, Heavy Metal, 1970s-, Artist, British
I-Roy, Dancehall; Ragga, 1970s-, Artist, Jamaican
Isaacs, Gregory, Reggae Pop, 1970s-, Artist, Jamaican
J. Geils Band, Hard Rock; Rock'n'Roll; Blues Rock, 1970s-1980s, Artist, American
Jackson, Jermaine, Urban Soul, 1970s-1990s, Artist, American
Jackson, Joe, New Wave; 1970s Pop, 1970s-, Artist, British
Jackson, LaToya, Urban Soul, 1970s-, Artist, American
Jackson, Michael, 1970s Pop; Funk; The Classic Soul Era, 1970s-, Artist; Songwriter, American
Jackson, Millie, The Classic Soul Era; Urban Soul, 1970s-, Artist, American
Jackson, Paul Jr., Urban Soul, 1970s-, Artist, American
Jackson, Ronald Shannon, Fusion; Free Jazz; Hard Bop, 1970s-, Artist, American
Jah Wobble, British Punk; Dub, 1970s-1990s, Artist; Composer, British
Jam, The, British Punk; Mod; New Wave, 1970s-1980s, Artist, British
Jan Dukes de Grey, UK Folk; Folk Rock, 1970s, Artist, British
Japan, Prog Rock; New Romantics; New Wave, 1970s-1980s, Artist, British
Jarre, Jean-Michel, New Age; Electro, 1970s-, Artist; Producer; Composer, French
Jarrett, Winston, Rock Steady, 1970s-1990s, Artist, Jamaican
Jasper, Chris, Urban Soul; Funk Soul, 1970s-, Artist, American
Jefferson Starship, Arena Rock; Hard Rock, 1970s-, Artist, American
Jelly Roll Kings, The, Modern Electric Blues, 1970s-1990s, Artist, American
JetSet, The, 1970s Pop, 1970s-1990s, Artist, British
Jobriath, Glam Rock & Glitter, 1970s, Artist, American
Joel, Billy, 1970s Pop, 1970s-, Artist; Songwriter, American
Johansen, David, American Punk; Hard Rock, 1970s-, Artist, American
John, Elton, Rock'n'Roll; 1970s Pop Singer/Songwriters; 1970s Pop, 1960s-, Artist; Songwriter, British
Johnson, Linton Kwesi, Dub, 1970s-, Artist, Jamaican
Jon and Vangelis, Prog Rock, 1970s-1990s, Artist, Greek
Jones Girls, The, Urban Soul, 1970s-1990s, Artist, American
Jones, Davis Lynn, Young Country, 1970s-1990s, Artist, American
Jones, Doris, Urban Soul; Funk Soul, 1970s-1980s, Artist, American
Jones, Grace, Disco, 1970s-, Artist, American
Jones, Rickie Lee, Folk Rock, 1970s-, Artist; Songwriter, American
Jones, Thelma, The Classic Soul Era, 1970s, Artist, American
José José, Latin, 1970s-, Artist, Mexican
Joseph, Margie, Urban Soul, 1970s-1980s, Artist, American
Journey, Arena Rock; Melodic Rock; Hard Rock; 1970s Pop, 1970s-, Artist, American
Joy Division, Alternative/Indie Rock, 1970s-1980s, Artist, British
Judas Jump, Prog Rock, 1970s, Artist, British
Judas Priest, Heavy Metal; Hard Rock, 1970s-1990s, Artist, British
Junior, Funk Soul; Urban Soul, 1970s-1990s, Artist, British
K., François, House; Techno, 1970s-, Artist; Producer, French
Kaiser, Henry, Prog Rock; Alternative/Indie Rock, 1970s-, Artist, American
Kansas, Prog Rock; Arena Rock, 1970s-1990s, Artist, American
Kantner, Paul, Folk Rock, 1970s-1990s, Artist, American
Kaukonen, Jorma, Folk Rock, 1970s-, Artist, American
KC and the Sunshine Band, Disco, 1970s-1990s, Artist, American
Keane, Dolores, Irish Folk, 1970s-, Artist, Irish
Kenny, Glitter, 1970s, Artist, British
Khan, Chaka, Funk; Funk Soul; Urban Soul, 1970s-, Artist, American
Khan, Si, Contemporary Folk; Political Folk & Protest Songs, 1970s-, Artist, American
Kihn, Greg, 1980s Pop Singer/Songwriters, 1970s-, Artist; Songwriter, American
Kilburn and the High Roads, Pub Rock, 1970s, Artist, British
Killing Joke, Alternative/Indie Rock, 1970s-, Artist, British
King Fish, Folk Rock, 1970s-, Artist, American
King Jammy, Dub, 1970s-1980s, Artist, Jamaican
King, Bobby, The Classic Soul Era, 1970s-1990s, Artist, American
King, Evelyn 'Champagne', Disco; House, 1970s-1990s, Artist, American
Kiss, Hard Rock; Arena Rock, 1970s-, Artist, American
Kitaro, New Age; Electro, 1970s-, Artist; Composer, Japanese
Klaatu, 1970s Pop, 1970s-1980s, Artist, Canadian
Klugh, Earl, Fusion, 1970s-, Artist, American
Knack, The, New Wave, 1970s-, Artist, American
Knight, Frederick, The Classic Soul Era, 1970s, Artist, American
Knight, Jean, Funk Soul, 1970s-1990s, Artist, American
Kraftwerk, Electro, Krautrock, 1970s-, Artist, German
Kristofferson, Kris, The Outlaw Movement, 1970s-1990s, Artist; Songwriter, American
Krivit, Danny, US Garage, 1970s-, Artist, American
Kursaal Flyers, Pub Rock, 1970s-1980s, Artist, British
La Dusseldorf, Krautrock; Electro, 1970s-1980s, Artist, German
LaBelle, Funk; Disco, 1960s-1990s, Artist, American
Lakeside, Funk Soul, 1970s-1990s, Artist, American
Lancelot Link, 1970s Pop, 1970s, Artist, American
Larson, Nicolette, Urban Cowboys; Country Rock, 1970s-1990s, Artist, American
LaSalle, Denise, Northern Soul, 1970s-, Artist; Songwriter, American
Laswell, Bill, Ambient; Electro; Dub, 1970s-, Producer; Artist, American
Latimore, The Classic Soul Era, 1970s-, Artist, American
Lattisaw, Stacy, Urban Soul, 1970s-1990s, Artist, American
LeDoux, Chris, Urban Cowboys; Neo-Traditionalists; Cowboy Music; Young Country, 1970s-, Artist, American
Lee, Bunny, Roots; Dub, 1970s, Producer, Jamaican
Levan Larry, Disco; House; US Garage, 1970s-1990s, Producer; Artist, American
Levy, Barrington, Dancehall, 1970s-1990s, Artist, Jamaican
Levy, Ron, Modern Electric Blues, 1970s-, Artist, American
Lewis, Webster, The Classic Soul Era, 1970s-1980s, Artist, American
Linden, Colin, Modern Electric Blues, 1970s-, Artist, Canadian
Lipps Inc., Disco, 1970s-1980s, Artist, American
Little Feat, Hard Rock; Blues Rock, 1970s-, Artist, American
Little River Band, The, Hard Rock; Blues Rock, 1970s-, Artist, Australian
Little Steven, Psychedelic Rock; Prog Rock, 1970s-, Artist; Songwriter; Producer, American
Loeb, Chuck, Fusion; Hard Bop, 1970s-, Artist, American
Lofgren, Nils, Country Rock; Folk Rock; Rock'n'Roll, 1970s-, Artist, American
Loggins and Messina, Folk Rock, 1970s, Artist, American
Loggins, Kenny, Melodic Rock, 1970s-, Artist; Songwriter, American
Looking Glass, 1970s Pop, 1970s, Artist, American
Los Lobos, Alternative/Indie Rock, 1970s-, Artist, American
Lovano, Joe, Hard Bop, 1970s-, Artist, American
Love Unlimited Orchestra, Urban Soul , 1970s-1980s, Artist, American
Loverboy, Arena Rock; Hard Rock, 1970s-1990s, Artist, Canadian
Lowe, Jez, Irish Folk; UK Folk; Political Folk & Protest Songs, 1970s-, Artist, British
Lowe, Nick, Pub Rock; Country Rock; Rock'n'Roll; New Wave, 1970s-, Producer; Songwriter; Artist, British
Lunch, Lydia, US Underground & Garage Rock, 1970s-, Artist, American
Lynn, Cheryl, Urban Soul, 1970s-1980s, Artist, American
Lynyrd Skynyrd, Southern Rock; Arena Rock, 1970s-, Artist, American
Lyres, The, US Underground & Garage Rock; Alternative/Indie Rock; American Punk, 1970s-1990s, Artist, American
MacLean, Brian, Folk Rock, 1970s-1990s, Artist; Songwriter, American
Mad Professor, Dub, 1970s-, Artist; Producer, Jamaican
Madness, New Wave; 1970s Pop; Ska, 1970s-, Artist, British
Magazine, Alternative/Indie Rock, 1970s-1980s, Artist, British
Magic Slim, Modern Electric Blues, 1970s-, Artist, American
Magnum, Melodic Rock; Prog Rock; Hard Rock, 1970s-1990s, Artist, British
Magpie, Political Folk & Protest Songs; Traditional Folk, 1970s-, Artist, American
Mahavishnu Orchestra, Jazz Rock; Fusion, 1970s-1980s, Artist, American
Manchester, Melissa, 1970s Pop, 1970s-1990s, Artist, American
Mancuso, David, Disco, 1970s-, Artist, American
Manfred Mann's Earth Band, Prog Rock, 1970s-, Artist, British
Manhattan Transfer, Smooth Jazz, 1970s-, Artist, American
Manilow, Barry, 1970s Pop; Easy Listening, 1970s-, Artist, American
Mannheim Steamroller, New Age; Electro, 1970s-, Artist, American
Manuel Göttsching, Krautrock; Ambient, 1970s-1990s, Artist, German
Manzanera, Phil, Prog Rock, 1970s-, Producer; Artist, British
Marillion, Prog Rock, 1970s-, Artist, British
Marriott, Steve, Hard Rock; British Blues; Blues Rock; Mod; British Invasion, 1970s-1990s, Artist, British
Marshall Tucker Band, The, Southern Rock, 1970s-, Artist, American
Martha and the Muffins, New Wave, 1970s-1980s; 1990s, Artist, Canadian
Mason, Barbara, Urban Soul, 1960s-1980s, Artist, American
Mason, Dave, Psychedelic Rock; Prog Rock, 1970s-, Artist, British
Mason, Vaughan, Funk Soul, 1970s-1980s, Artist, American
Mass Production, Funk Soul, 1970s-1980s, Artist, American
Maze Featuring Frankie Beverly, Urban Soul; Funk Soul, 1970s-, Artist, American
Mazz, Latin, 1970s-, Artist, Mexican
McAnally, Mac, Folk Pop, 1970s-1990s, Artist; Songwriter, American
McCoo, Marilyn, Contemporary R&B, 1970s-, Artist, American
McCrae, George, Disco; Funk Soul, 1970s, Artist, American
McCrae, Gwen, Disco, 1970s-1990s, Artist, American
McCrary's, The, Urban Soul, 1970s-1980s, Artist, American
McDonald, Michael, 1970s Pop; The Classic Soul Era, 1970s-, Artist, American
McEntire, Reba, Neo-Traditionalists; Young Country, 1970s-, Artist, American
McFadden and Whitehead, The Classic Soul Era, 1970s-1980s, Artist, American
McGarrigle, Kate & Anna, Contemporary Folk, 1970s-1990s, Artist; Songwriter, Canadian
McGuinn, Clark and Hillman, Folk Rock, 1970s-1980s, Artist, American
McKenna, Joe and Antoinette, Irish Folk, 1970s, Artist, Irish
McLauchlan, Murray, Folk Rock, 1970s, Artist, British
McLean, Don, 1970s Pop Singer/Songwriters; Folk Pop, 1970s-, Artist, American
Meat Loaf, Arena Rock; Hard Rock; 1970s Pop, 1970s-, Artist, American
Mekons, The, Alternative/Indie Rock, 1970s-, Artist, British
Mellencamp, John Cougar, Hard Rock; 1970s Pop, 1970s-, Artist, American
Menudo, Latin, 1970s-, Artist, Puerto Rican
Metheny, Pat, Fusion, 1970s-, Artist; Composer, American
MFSB, Urban Soul; Disco, 1970s-1980s, Artist, American
Michaels, Lee, 1970s Pop, 1970s, Artist, American
Midnight Oil, Alternative/Indie Rock, 1970s-, Artist, Australian
Midnight Star, Urban Soul, 1970s-1990s, Artist, American
Miller, Frankie, Pub Rock; The Classic Soul Era, 1970s-1990s, Artist, British
Mills, Stephanie, The Classic Soul Era, 1970s-1990s, Artist, American
Minott, Sugar, Dancehall; Ragga, 1970s-1990s, Artist, Jamaican
Misfits, The, US Underground & Garage Rock, 1970s-1990s, Artist, American
Mitchell, Prince Phillip, The Classic Soul Era, 1970s, Composer; Artist, American
Modern Lovers, The, American Punk; Proto-Punk; Rock'n'Roll, 1970s, Artist, American
Moebius, Krautrock; Ambient; Electro, 1970s-, Artist, German
Moffatt, Katy, Alternative Country, 1970s; 1990s-, Artist, American
Molly Hatchet Band, The, Southern Rock, 1970s-, Artist, American
Montclairs, The, Northern Soul, 1970s, Artist, American
Montrose, Hard Rock; Arena Rock, 1970s, Artist, American
Moore, Dorothy, Urban Soul, 1970s-1990s, Artist, American
Moore, Gary, Heavy metal; Hard Rock; Blues Rock, 1970s-, Artist, Irish
Moore, Jackie, The Classic Soul Era, 1970s, Artist, American
Motels, The, American Punk; New Wave, 1970s-1980s, Artist, American
Mother's Finest, Funk Soul, 1970s-1990s, Artist, American
Motörhead, Heavy Metal, 1970s-, Artist, British
Motors, 1970s Pop; New Wave, 1970s-1980s, Artist, British
Mtume, Urban Soul, 1970s-1980s, Artist, American
Mumps, The, American Punk, 1970s, Artist, American
Murphey, Michael Martin, Neo-Traditionalists; Country Rock; Cowboy Music, 1970s-, Artist; Songwriter, American
Murphy, Elliott, Folk Rock, 1970s-, Artist, American
Musical Youth, Reggae Pop; Ska, 1970s-1990s, Artist, British
Nash, Graham, Folk Rock, 1970s-1980s, Artist; Songwriter, British
National Health, Prog Rock, 1970s-1980s, Artist, British
Nazareth, Hard Rock, 1970s-, Artist, British
Near, Holly, Political Folk & Protest Songs; Folk Rock; Folk Pop, 1970s-, Artist; Songwriter, American
Nelson, Bill, Prog Rock; Electro, 1970s-2000s, Artist, British
Nerves, The, 1970s Pop, 1970s-1980s, Artist, American
Neu!, Krautrock, 1970s-1990s, Artist, German
New Seekers, The, 1970s Pop, 1970s, Artist, Australian
New York City, Northern Soul; Urban Soul, 1970s, Artist, American
New York Dolls, The, Proto-Punk, 1970s, Artist, American
Newton-John, Olivia, 1970s Pop; Young Country, 1970s-, Artist, British
Nicks, Stevie, Prog Rock; British Blues; Blues Rock; 1980s Pop, 1970s-, Artist; Songwriter, British
Nightingale, Maxine, Urban Soul, 1970s-1980s, Artist, British
Ninjaman, Dancehall; Ragga, 1970s-1990s, Artist, Jamaican
NoMeansNo, US Undeground & Garage Rock; Alternative/Indie Rock, 1970s-, Artist, Canadian
Nucleus, Jazz Rock, 1970s-1980s, Artist, British
Numan, Gary, New Wave; New Romantics, 1970s-, Artist, British
O'Hara, Mary, Irish Folk, 1970s-1990s, Artist, Irish
O'Hearn, Patrick, New Age; Electro, 1970s-, Artist; Producer; Composer, American
O'Sullivan, Gilbert, 1970s Pop; 1970s Pop Singer/Songwriters, 1970s-, Artist; Songwriter, Irish
Ocean, Billy, 1970s Pop; Urban Soul, 1970s-1990s, Artist, West Indian
Ocean, The Classic Soul Era, 1970s, Artist, Canadian
Odyssey, Urban Soul, 1970s-1980s, Artist, American
Off Broadway, 1970s Pop, 1970s-1990s, Artist, American
Oldfield, Mike, Prog Rock; New Age, 1970s-, Artist, British
Olson, Carla, Country Rock, 1970s-, Artist, American
Only Ones, The, New Wave, 1970s-1980s, Artist, British
Orange Juice, New Wave, 1970s-1980s, Artist, British
Oregon, Fusion; Fusion and Jazz Rock, 1970s-1990s, Artist, American
Osborne, Jeffrey, Urban Soul; Funk Soul, 1970s-, Artist, American
Oskar, Lee, Contemporary R&B, 1970s-1990s, Artist, Danish
Osmond, Donny, 1970s Pop, 1970s-, Artist, American
Ottowan, Disco, Artist, 1970s-1980s, French
Otway, John, British Punk, 1970s-1990s, Artist; Songwriter, British
Outlaws, The, Southern Rock, 1970s-1980s, Artist, American
Pablo, Augustus, Dub, 1970s-1990s, Artist; Producer, Jamaican
Palmer, Robert, Arena Rock; 1970s Pop; The Classic Soul Era, 1970s-, Artist, British
Paper Lace, 1970s Pop, 1970s, Artist, British
Parker, Graham, Pub Rock; New Wave; 1970s Pop Singer/Songwriters, 1970s-, Artist; Songwriter, British
Parker, Maceo, Funk Soul, 1970s-, Artist, American
Parker, Ray Jr., Urban Soul, 1970s-1990s, Artist, American
Parliament, Funk; Funk Soul; Urban Soul, 1970s-, Artist, American
Parsons, Alan, Prog Rock, 1970s-1990s, Artist; Producer, British
Parsons, Gene, Folk Rock, 1970s-1990s, Artist, American
Passport, Fusion, 1970s-, Artist, American
Pastorius, Jaco, Fusion, 1970s-1980s, Artist, American
Pat Travers Band, The, Hard Rock; Blues Rock, 1970s-1990s, Artist, Canadian
Paul, Billy, Urban Soul, 1970s-, Artist, American
Pena, Paul, Rhythm & Blues, 1970s; 1990s, Artist, American
Pendergrass, Teddy, Urban Soul, 1970s-, Artist, American
Pentagram, Doom Metal; Heavy Metal, 1970s-, Artist, British
Pere Ubu, US Underground & Garage Rock; American Punk, 1970s-, Artist, American
Peterson, Colleen, Folk Rock, 1970s-1990s, Artist; Songwriter, Canadian
Petty, Tom, Hard Rock; Rock'n'Roll, 1970s-, Artist, American
Pezband, New Wave, 1970s-1980s, Artist, American
Plainsong, Folk Rock, 1970s; 1990s, Artist, British
Planxty, Irish Folk; Contemporary Folk, 1970s-1980s, Artist, Irish
Pleasure, Funk Soul, 1970s-1980s, Artist, American
Pointer Sisters, Urban Soul, 1970s-1990s, Artist, American
Police, The, New Wave, 1970s-1980s, Artist, British
Pop Group, The, Alternative/Indie Rock, 1970s-1980s, Artist, British
Pop, Iggy, Proto-Punk; Hard Rock, 1970s-, Artist, American
Porter, George Jr., Funk Soul, 1970s-1990s, Artist, American
Pretenders, The, Hard Rock; New Wave; 1970s Pop, 1970s-1990s, Artist, British
Pride, Lou, The Classic Soul Era, 1970s-, Artist, American
Primer, John, Modern Electric Blues, 1970s-, Artist, American
Prince Fari, Dub; Deejays, 1970s-1980s, Artist, Jamaican
Prince Jazzbo, Dancehall; Ragga; Deejays, 1970s; 1990s-, Producer; Artist, American
Prince, Funk; 1970s Pop; Funk; Funk Soul, 1970s-, Artist, American
Princess, Urban Soul, 1970s-1980s, Artist, American
Prine, John, Contemporary Folk; Folk Rock; Country Rock, 1970s-, Artist; Songwriter, American
Public Image Limited, British Punk; Alternative/Indie Rock, 1970s-1990s, Artist, British
Pure Prairie League, Country Rock, 1970s-1980s, Artist, American
Quatro, Suzi, Glam Rock & Glitter, 1970s-1990s, Artist, American
Queen, Arena Rock; Glam Rock & Glitter; Prog Rock; Hard Rock; 1970s Pop, 1970s-1990s, Artist, British
Radio Birdman, Hard Rock, 1970s-1980s, Artist, Australian
Rafferty, Gerry, Folk Pop, 1970s-, Artist; Songwriter, British
Rainbow, Hard Rock; Progressive Metal; Heavy Metal, 1970s-1980s; 1990s, Artist, British
Raincoats, The, Folk Rock; British Punk; Alternative/Indie Rock, 1970s-1980s; 1990s, Artist, British
Raitt, Bonnie, Blues Rock; 1970s Pop Singer/Songwriters, 1970s-, Artist, American
Ramones, The, American Punk, 1970s-1990s, Artist, American
Ramzy, Hossam, Fusion and Jazz Rock, 1970s-, Artist, Egyptian
Ranking Joe, Trip Hop, 1970s-1990s, Artist, Jamaican
Ras Michael, Roots; Dub, 1970s-1990s, Artist, Jamaican
Raspberries, The, 1970s Pop, 1970s, Artist, American
Raye, Susan, Country Rock, 1970s, Artist, American
Rea, Chris, Rock'n'Roll, 1970s-2000s, Artist; Songwriter, British
Real Kids, The, American Punk, 1970s-1980s, Artist, American
Real Thing, The, Northern Soul; Funk Soul, 1970s-1990s, Artist, American
Record, Eugene, Urban Soul, 1970s-1980s, Artist, American
Records, The, 1970s Pop; New Wave, 1970s-1980s, Artist, British
Redd, Sharon, Urban Soul; US Garage, 1970s-1990s, Artist, American
Reddy, Helen, 1970s Pop, 1970s, Artist, Australian
Reed, Lou, Proto-Punk; Hard Rock, 1970s-, Artist; Songwriter, American
Reflections, The, The Classic Soul Era, 1970s-1980s, Artist, American
REO Speedwagon, Arena Rock, 1970s-, Artist, American
Residents, The, Alternative/Indie Rock, 1970s-, Artist, American
Rezillos, The, British Punk, 1970s, Artist, British
Rhodes, Emitt, 1970s Pop Singer/Songwriters; Wall of Sound; 1970s Pop, 1970s, Artist, American
Richman, Jonathan, Proto-Punk; US Underground & Garage Rock, 1970s-, Artist, American
Riley, Jimmy, UK Reggae, 1970s-1990s, Artist, British
Ripple, Funk Soul, 1970s, Artist, American
Ritenour, Lee, Fusion, 1970s-1990s, Artist, American
Roach, Steve, Ambient; Electro; New Age; Tribal Dance; Techno, 1970s-, Artist; Producer, American
Robbins, Rockie, Urban Soul, 1970s-1980s, Artist, American
Roberts, Bruce, The Classic Soul Era, 1970s-1990s, Artist, American
Robinson, Tom, British Punk; Hard Rock, 1970s-, Artist, British
Robinson, Vicky Sue, Disco, 1970s-1990s, Artist, American
Roches, The, Contemporary Folk, 1970s-1990s, Artist; Songwriter, American
Rocket From The Tombs, Proto-Punk, 1970s, Artist, American
Rockpile, Pub Rock; Rock'n'Roll; New Wave, 1970s-1980s, Artist, British
Rodgers, Nile, Disco; Urban Soul, 1970s-1980s, Producer; Songwriter; Artist, American
Roedelius, Krautrock; Ambient, 1970s-, Artist, German
Rogers, Roy, Blues Rock, 1970s-, Artist; Producer, American
Romao, Dom Um, Latin Jazz; Brazilian Jazz; Fusion and Jazz Rock, 1970s-, Artist, Brazilian
Ronson, Mick, Glam Rock & Glitter; Proto-Punk; Hard Rock, 1970s-1990s, Artist, British
Roogalator, Pub Rock, 1970s, Artist, American
Roomful Of Blues, Jump Blues; Modern Electric Blues, 1970s-, Artist, American
Rose Royce, Disco; Urban Soul; Funk Soul, 1970s-1980s, Artist, American
Roxy Music, Prog Rock; Glam Rock & Glitter, 1970s-1980s, Artist, British
Rubettes, The, 1970s Pop; Glam Rock & Glitter, 1970s-1980s; 1990s, Artist, British
Rubinoos, The, 1970s Pop; New Wave, 1970s-1990s, Artist, American
Rufus, Funk Soul, 1970s-1980s, Artist, American
Ruiz, Hilton, Latin Jazz; Bebop, 1970s-1990s, Artist, Cuban
Runaways, The, Proto-Punk; American Punk; Heavy Metal, 1970s, Artist, American
Rundgren, Todd, Prog Rock; Proto-Punk; Hard Rock 1970s Pop; The Classic Soul Era, 1970s-, Artist, American
Runrig, Contemporary Folk; Folk Rock, 1970s-, Artist, British
Rush, Prog Rock; Arena Rock; Hard Rock, 1970s-, Artist, Canadian
Rushen, Patrice, Urban Soul , 1970s-, Artist, American
Rypdal, Terje, Fusion, 1970s-1990s, Artist, Norwegian
Sad Café, Melodic Rock; 1970s Pop, 1970s-1990s, Artist, British
Saints, The, Alternative/Indie Rock, 1970s-1990s, Artist, Australian
Salsoul Orchestra, The, Disco, 1970s-1980s, Artist, American
Santos, Larry, Urban Soul, 1970s; 1990s, Artist, American
Saxon, Heavy Metal, 1970s-, Artist, British
Sayer, Leo, 1970s Pop, 1970s-, Artist, British
Schnitzler, Conrad, Krautrock; Electro, 1970s-1990s, Artist, German
Scientist, Dub, 1970s-, Artist; Producer, Jamaican
Scientists, Alternative/Indie Rock, 1970s-1990s, Artist, Australian
Scofield, John, Fusion, 1970s-, Artist, American
Scorpions, Heavy Metal; Hard Rock, 1970s-, Artist, German
Scott, Millie, Funk Soul, 1970s-1980s, Artist, American
Scruffs, 1970s Pop, 1970s-1980s, Artist, American
Sea Level, Southern Rock, 1970s, Artist, American
Seals, Son, Modern Electric Blues, 1970s-, Artist, American
Sebastian, John, Contemporary Folk; Folk Rock, 1970s-, Artist; Songwriter, American
Secret Affair, New Wave, 1970s-1980s, Artist, British
Selecter, New Wave, 1970s-1980s; 1990s-, Artist, British
Sensational Alex Harvey Band, The, Glam Rock & Glitter, 1970s, Artist, British
Sex Pistols, The, British Punk, 1970s; 1990s, Artist, British
Seymour, Phil, New Wave, 1970s-1980s, Artist, American
Shakers, The, UK Folk; Folk Rock, 1970s-1980s, Artist, British
Shakti, Fusion and Jazz Rock; Fusion, 1970s, Artist, American
Shalamar, Urban Soul, 1970s-1990s, Artist, American
Sham 69, British Punk, 1970s-, Artist, British
Shankar, Lakshminarayana, Fusion and Jazz Rock; Fusion, 1970s-1990s, Artist, Indian
Shaver, Billy Joe, The Outlaw Movement; Honky Tonk, 1970s-, Artist; Songwriter, American
Shoes, New Wave; 1970s Pop, 1970s-1990s, Artist, American
Shotgun, Funk Soul, 1970s-1980s, Artist, American
Showaddywaddy, Glam Rock & Glitter, 1970s-1980s, Artist, British
Sibbles, Leroy, Rock Steady; Roots, 1970s-1990s, Artist, Jamaican
Siebel, Paul, Contemporary Folk; Folk Rock, 1970s-1990s, Artist; Songwriter, American
Siffre, Labi, Urban Soul, 1970s-1990s, Artist, British
Sigler, Bunny, The Classic Soul Era, 1970s-1980s, Producer; Artist, American
Silver Convention, The Classic Soul Era, 1970s-1980s, Artist, German
Silvertones, Rock Steady, 1970s-1990s, Artist, Jamaican
Simon, Carly, 1970s Pop Singer/Songwriters, 1970s-, Artist; Songwriter, American
Simpson, Valerie, Urban Soul, 1970s-1980s, Artist; Songwriter, American
Siouxsie and The Banshees, British Punk; Goth Rock, 1970s-1990s, Artist, British
Sister Sledge, Disco, 1970s-, Artist, American
Sister Sledge, Disco; Urban Soul, 1970s-, Artist, American
Skaggs, Ricky, Bluegrass; Young Country, 1970s-, Artist, American
Slave, Funk; Funk Soul; Disco, 1970s-1990s, Artist, American
Slits, The, British Punk, 1970s-1980s, Artist, British
Sly and Robbie, Dub; Roots; Dancehall, 1970s-, Artist, Jamaican
Smart, Leroy, Dancehall; Ragga, 1970s-1990s, Artist, Jamaican
Smith, Lonnie Liston, Fusion, 1970s-1990s, Artist, American
Sneakers, The, 1970s Pop, 1970s, Artist, American
Snow, Phoebe, 1970s Pop Singer/Songwriters; Contemporary Folk, 1970s-1990s, Artist; Songwriter, American
Soft Boys, The, British Punk; New Wave, 1970s-1980s, Artist, British
Sonnier, Jo-El, Alternative Country, 1970s-, Artist, American
Soul Train Gang, Urban Soul, 1970s, Artist, American
Sound Experience, Funk Soul, 1970s, Artist, American
Souther, J. D., 1970s Pop Singer/Songwriters; Country Rock; Urban Cowboys, 1970s-1990s, Artist; Songwriter, American
Southside Johnny and the Asbury Jukes, Rhythm & Blues; Rock'n'Roll, 1970s-, Artist, American
Sparks, 1970s Pop, 1970s-, Artist, American
Special Delivery, Urban Soul, 1970s-1980s, Artist, American
Specials, The, New Wave, 1970s-, Artist, British
Spencer, Jeremy, British Blues; Blues Rock, 1970s, Artist, British
Spillane, Davy, Irish Folk; Contemporary Folk, 1970s-, Artist, Irish
Split Endz, New Wave; 1970s Pop, 1970s-1980s, Artist, New Zealander
Spoonie Gee, Old School; Hip Hop, 1970s-1980s, Artist, British
Springsteen, Bruce, Arena Rock; Rock'n'Roll; 1970s Pop Singer/Songwriters, 1970s-, Artist; Songwriter, American
Spyro Gyra, Smooth Jazz; Fusion, 1970s-, Artist, American
Squeeze, New Wave; 1970s Pop, 1970s-1990s, Artist, British
Squire, New Wave, 1970s-1980s, Artist, British
Stamey, Chris, 1970s Pop, 1970s-1990s, Producer; Artist, American
Steagal, Red, The Nashville Sound; Honky Tonk; Cowboy Music, 1970s-1990s, Artist, American
Stealers Wheel, Folk Rock; 1970s Pop, 1970s, Artist, British
Steel Pulse, Reggae Pop; Roots, 1970s-1990s, Artist, British
Steeleye Span, UK Folk; Folk Rock, 1970s-, Artist, British
Steely Dan, Jazz Rock; 1970s Pop, 1970s-, Artist, American
Stevens, Mike, The Classic Soul Era, 1970s-1990s, Artist, British
Stevenson, B. W., 1970s Pop, 1970s-1980s, Artist, American
Stiff Little Fingers, British Punk, 1970s-1990s, Artist, British
Sting, Alternative/Indie Rock, 1970s-, Artist, British
Strait, George, Western Swing; Neo-Traditionalists, 1970s-, Artist, American
Stranglers, The, British Punk, 1970s-1990s, Artist, British
Stylistics, The, Urban Soul, 1970s-1990s, Artist, American
Styx, Prog Rock; Arena Rock; Hard Rock, 1970s-, Artist, American
Sugar Blue, Modern Electric Blues, 1970s-1990s, Artist, American
Suicide, American Punk; Electro, 1970s-1990s, Artist, American
Summer, Donna, Disco, 1970s-, Artist, American
Suns Of Arca, Dub, 1970s-, Artist, British
Supertramp, Prog Rock; Arena Rock; 1970s Pop, 1970s-, Artist, British
Sutherland Brothers, The, Folk Rock, 1970s, Artist, British
Swan, Billy, Rockabilly; Country Rock; Rock'n'Roll, 1970s-1980s, Artist, American
Sweet Sensation, Urban Soul, 1970s, Artist, British
Sweet, Glam Rock & Glitter, 1970s-1990s, Artist, British
Swell Maps, British Punk, 1970s-1980s, Artist, British
Switch, Funk Soul, 1970s-1990s, Artist, American
Sylvers, Leon F. III, The Classic Soul Era, 1970s-1980s, Artist, American
Sylvester, Disco, 1970s-1980s, Artist, American
Syreeta, The Classic Soul Era, 1970s-1980s, Artist; Songwriter, American
Tabor, June, Folk Rock; Contemporary Folk; UK Folk, 1970s-, Artist, British
Talking Heads, US Underground & Garage Rock; New Wave; 1970s Pop, 1970s-1980s, Artist, American
Talley, James, Delta/Country Blues; Modern Electric Blues, 1970s-, Artist; Songwriter, American
Tate, Tommy, The Classic Soul Era; Urban Soul, 1970s-1990s, Artist, American
Tawatha, Urban Soul, 1970s-1990s, Artist, American
Taylor, Alex, Folk Rock, 1970s-1980s, Artist; Songwriter, American
Taylor, James 'J.T.', Urban Soul, 1970s-, Artist; Producer, American
Taylor, Kate, Traditional Folk; Folk Rock, 1970s, Artist; Songwriter, American
Tchaikovsky, Bram, New Wave, 1970s-1980s, Artist, British
T-Connection, Funk Soul, 1970s-1980s, Artist, American
Teardrop Explodes, The, British Punk, 1970s-1990s, Artist, British
Television, American Punk; Proto-Punk, 1970s; 1990s, Artist, American
Tempress, The, The Classic Soul Era, 1970s, Artist, American
Terry, Tony, The Classic Soul Era, 1970s-, Artist, American
Thin Lizzy, Heavy Metal; Hard Rock, 1970s-1990s, Artist, Irish
Third World, Reggae Pop, 1970s-, Artist, Jamaican
Thomas, Ruddy, UK Reggae, 1970s-1990s, Artist, British
Thomas, Timmy, Funk Soul, 1970s, Artist, American
Thompson, Barbara, Free Jazz; Fusion, 1970s-1990s, Artist, British
Thompson, Linval, Dancehall; Dub, 1970s-1990s, Artist, American
Thompson, Ron, Modern Electric Blues, 1970s-1980s, Artist, American
Thorogood, George, Blues Rock, 1970s-1990s, Artist, American
Throbbing Gristle, Alternative/Indie Rock, 1970s-1980s, Artist, British
Thunders, Johnny, Hard Rock; American Punk, 1970s-1990s, Artist, American
Tibbetts, Steve, Fusion, 1970s-, Artist, American
Tiger, Dancehall, 1970s-1990s, Artist, Jamaican
Tigres del Norte, Los, Latin, 1970s-, Artist, Mexican
Toms, 1970s Pop, 1970s, Artist, American
Toto, Melodic Rock; 1970s Pop, 1970s-1990s, Artist, American
Touchstone, Irish Folk, 1970s-1980s, Artist, Irish
Tourists, The, 1970s Pop; Folk Pop, 1970s-1980s, Artist, British
Tower Of Power, Funk Soul, 1970s-1990s, Artist, American
Trader Horne, Folk Rock, 1970s, Artist, British
Trapeze, Prog Rock; Hard Rock, 1970s-1990s, Artist, British
Trees, UK Folk; Folk Rock, 1970s, Artist, British
True, Andrea, Disco, 1970s, Artist, American
Tubes, The, Arena Rock; Hard Rock, 1970s-, Artist, American
Tucker, Tanya, Young Country, 1970s-1990s, Artist, American
Turre, Steve, Latin Jazz; Hard Bop; Bebop, 1970s-, Artist, American
Twilley, Dwight, 1970s Pop, 1970s-, Artist, American
Twisted Sister, Heavy Metal, 1970s-1980s; 1990s-, Artist, American
Tyler, Bonnie, 1980s Pop, 1970s-, Artist, British
U2, Alternative/Indie Rock, 1970s-, Artist, Irish
U-Brown, Dancehall, 1970s-, Artist, Jamaican
UFO, Arena Rock; Hard Rock, 1970s-, Artist, British
UK Subs, British Punk, 1970s-, Artist, British
UK, Prog Rock, 1970s, Artist, British
Undertones, The, British Punk; New Wave, 1970s-1980s, Artist, Irish
Undisputed Truth, The Classic Soul Era; Funk Soul, 1970s, Artist, American
Urbaniak, Michal, Fusion, 1970s-, Artist, Polish
Uriah Heep, Prog Rock; Heavy Metal, 1970s-1990s, Artist, British
Utopia, Prog Rock; Arena Rock; 1970s Pop; New Wave, 1970s-1990s, Artist, American
Valentine Brothers, The, The Classic Soul Era, 1970s-1980s, Artist, American
Van Halen, Hard Rock; Arena Rock; Heavy Metal, 1970s-1990s, Artist, American
Vangelis, Ambient; Electro, 1970s-, Artist; Producer, Greek
Vapors, The, New Wave, 1970s-1980s, Artist, American
Vega, Tata, The Classic Soul Era; Urban Soul, 1970s-1990s, Artist, American
Verlaine, Tom, American Punk; Proto-Punk, 1970s-, Artist; Songwriter, American
Vibrators, The, British Punk, 1970s-, Artist, British
Village People, Disco, 1970s-1990s, Artist, American
Wailer, Bunny, Roots, 1970s-, Artist, Jamaican
Wailing Souls, The, Dub; Roots, 1970s-, Artist, Jamaican
Wainwright, Loudon III, Contemporary Folk, 1970s-, Artist; Songwriter, American
Waits, Tom, Alternative/Indie Rock, 1970s-, Artist, American
Wakeman, Rick, Prog Rock, 1970s-, Artist, British
Walcott, Colin, Fusion and Jazz Rock, 1970s-1980s, Artist, American
Walden, Narada Michael, Urban Soul, 1970s-1990s, Producer; Artist, American
Walker, Philip, Modern Electric Blues, 1970s-1990s, Artist, American
Walsh, Joe, Arena Rock; Melodic Rock; Hard Rock, 1970s-1990s, Artist, American
Wansel, Dexter, Urban Soul, 1970s-1990s, Producer; Artist, American
War, Funk; Funk Soul, 1970s-1990s, Artist, American
Ward, Anita, Disco; Urban Soul, 1970s; 1990s-, Artist, American
Wasserman, Rob, Fusion, 1970s-, Artist, American
Weather Girls, The, Urban Soul, 1970s-1980s, Artist, American
Weather Report, Fusion, 1970s-1980s, Artist, American
Weirdos, The, American Punk, 1970s-1980s, Artist, American
Whispering Smith, Rhythm & Blues, 1970s, Artist, American
White, Barry, Disco; Urban Soul, 1970s-, Artist; Songwriter, American
White, Maurice, Funk Soul, 1970s-1990s, Artist, American
Whitesnake, Heavy Metal; Hard Rock, 1970s-1990s, Artist, British
Wild Cherry, Funk; Funk Soul, 1970s-1980s, Artist, American
Wilder, Johnny, Funk Soul, 1970s-1980s, Artist, American
William St James, Folk Rock, 1970s, Artist, American
Williams Brothers, The, Folk Rock, 1970s-, Artist, American
Williams, Deniece, Urban Soul, 1970s-1990s, Artist, American
Williams, Lenny, Urban Soul, 1970s-, Artist, American
Williams, Lucinda, Alternative Country, 1970s-, Artist, American
Winbush, Angela, Urban Soul, 1970s-1990s, Artist, American
Winchester, Jesse, Contemporary Folk; Folk Rock, 1970s-, Artist; Songwriter, American
Wings, Melodic Rock; 1970s Pop, 1970s, Artist, British
Winwood, Steve, The Classic Soul Era, 1970s-1990s, Artist, British
Wipers, US Underground & Garage Rock; Alternative/Indie Rock, 1970s-, Artist, American
Wire, British Punk; Alternative/Indie Rock, 1970s-1990s, Artist, British
Wishbone Ash, Prog Rock; Hard Rock, 1970s-, Artist, British
Withers, Bill, Urban Soul, 1970s-1990s, Artist, American
Wizzard, Glam Rock & Glitter; 1970s Pop, 1970s, Artist, British
Worrell, Bernie, Funk Soul, 1970s-, Artist, American
Wright, Betty, The Classic Soul Era, 1970s-, Artist, American
Wright, Gary, Prog Rock, 1970s-1990s, Artist, American
X-Ray Spex, British Punk, 1970s-1990s, Artist, British
XTC, Alternative/Indie Rock; 1970s Pop; New Wave, 1970s-, Artist, British
Yellow Magic Orchestra, 1970s Pop, 1970s-1990s, Artist, Japanese
Zorn, John, Fusion & Jazz Rock, 1970s-, Artist; Composer, American
Zukie, Tapper, Dub, 1970s-1990s, Artist, Jamaica
Zwingenberger, Axel, Boogie Woogie, 1970s-1980s, Artist, German
ZZ Top, Hard Rock; Arena Rock; Blues Rock, 1970s-1990s, Artist, American

see David Bowie pp 196 see Led Zeppelin pp 200 see Pink Floyd pp 204 see ABBA pp 228 see The Clash pp 248

THE EIGHTIES

This was a decade when the impact of dance culture on rock and vice versa sometimes led to exciting results: it opened with 'Thriller' and closed with the Madchester scene of Happy Mondays.

Punk had subsided to become the less threatening new wave movement, which, along with the new romantics, dominated the early days of the decade. As with the 1960s, producers emerged with their own distinctive sound – none more so than Trevor Horn, whose work with Frankie Goes To Hollywood was particularly influential.

The synthesizer was the decade's dominant sound, with many groups replacing guitars with synths. One exception was Dublin's U2, which started the 1980s supporting Talking Heads and ended it a supergroup. With live rock thin on the ground, a new wave of heavy metal swept Britain before the rise of 'hair-band' rock from the States later in the decade redressed the transatlantic balance.

Hip-hop was beginning to be heard via the likes of Afrika Bambaataa, while disco kings Chic would become the decade's hottest writing and production property (though Britain's Stock, Aiken and Waterman might dispute that).

The descent of the Berlin Wall in 1989 threatened to open new markets to rock, both live and via the new compact disc medium, while even China had allowed western bands to penetrate the Bamboo Curtain. Popular music was now truly an international language.

270

Sources & Sounds

KEY ARTISTS

Bon Jovi

Michael Jackson

Madonna

The Police

Prince

U2

Above

1985's 'Like A Virgin' was Madonna's biggest hit. One of the top sellers of the decade, it stayed at No. 1 on the *Billboard* Hot 100 for six consecutive weeks.

'I came here to play music, and I didn't really realize the full extent and magnitude of what it is all about. Now I'm here. It's the greatest event ever.'

Ozzy Osbourne on Live Aid

Right

Ozzy Osbourne was one of many aging rockers who revived their reputation at Live Aid, one of the 1980s' most memorable and impactive events.

Just as the 1970s will be recalled for punk's anti-fashion statements, so the decade that followed will be remembered as much for artists' return to the dressing-up box as much as the music they made. Duran Duran, Adam and The Ants, Visage, Spandau Ballet, Soft Cell, Simple Minds, The Human League, Thompson Twins and Depeche Mode were just some of the bands to spring from so-called new romantic roots.

Fun And Fashion

David Bowie was the single main influence on the movement, his 1980 hit 'Fashion' becoming something of an anthem. London clubs such as Billy's (which became the Blitz) gave the likes of doorman Steve Strange (Visage) and cloakroom attendant Boy George (Culture Club) their first leg-up to fame.

Instead of guitars, these new bands for the most part preferred synthesizers and rhythm machines. The synth was now considerably less expensive and, inspired by Gary Numan's late-1970s hits, British youth was favouring the instrument over the previously ubiquitous six-string. And their exploits were chronicled in a new magazine for teens, *Smash Hits*.

America's Talking Heads would attempt to forge a link between new wave and black music, more than doubling their quartet with an influx of funk musicians. New Order, who sprang from the ruins of Joy Division after Ian Curtis's 1980 suicide, had a greater impact with their dance-oriented 'Blue Monday' which, available exclusively in extended 12-inch, rather than 7-inch single form, proved one of the most influential dance tracks of the era.

A New Attitude

The previous decade had gone out with a bang in the spitting, snarling shape of punk. But while The Sex Pistols played their final gig in San Francisco, the impact of punk and its nihilistic attitude had not really been felt in the land of the greenback. So US musicians and producers took the energy and lost the attitude, resulting in 'new wave', a highly marketable proposition.

The biggest single promoter of 1980s music was MTV (Music Television), which first broadcast its mix of videos in the States in 1981. It would take until the end of the decade for satellite television to reach Britain, but by that time it and sister channel VH1 (Video Hits 1, launched in 1985) had proved themselves starmakers of the highest order. Their VMAs (Video Music Awards) would become as important as the Grammies in reflecting public taste, which the channel itself had helped shape.

see Introduction pp 268   see Key Artists pp 274   see A–Z of Artists pp 286   see List of Artists pp 324

Poptastic

Former Jackson Five singer Michael Jackson created the soundtrack for the 1980s dancefloor in the shape of the 1982 50 million-selling *Thriller*. 'Jacko' was also the first black artist to break big on MTV, thanks in no small part to his ground-breaking videos and also the shrewd device of inviting guitar god Eddie Van Halen to contribute to 'Beat It' – one of an unprecedented seven US Top 10 hit singles to be mined from this mega-successful album. The echoes of *Thriller* were still being felt two decades later via artists such as Justin Timberlake.

Jackson's female counterpart was Madonna Veronica Louise Ciccone, whose certainty was such that she could afford to jettison all but the first of her names in her successful quest for fame. She made an indelible mark on both sides of the Atlantic, and no female performer, with the exception of the resurgent Tina Turner, would remain untouched by her influence. Her fashions, attitude, willingness to mock religion and sell her sexuality put her on top of the charts and on the cover of *Time* magazine. And though there was a deliberate element of disposability in everything she did, she would reinvent herself to remain relevant in the current millennium.

Britain's biggest pop-dance star in the making was George Michael of Wham!. He emerged from his

group to find solo fame with a more adult brand of music, as did Sting when the three egos that comprised The Police could co-exist no more. The brand of intelligent adult rock Sting offered found a similar audience to that which allowed Phil Collins to split his time between progressive rockers Genesis and a multi-platinum solo career.

Prince emerged from left field to become first a 'more credible Jacko' and then something intangibly more. His edgy songs and liberal obscenities/profanities kept him deliberately on the fringes of popular acceptability, but by donating songs to the likes of Sheena Easton, Chaka Khan, The Bangles and Sinead O'Connor he could lay claim to being the decade's Stevie Wonder figure. He also courted Hollywood with the autobiographical *Purple Rain* (1984), *Under The Cherry Moon* (1986) and, later in the decade, the soundtrack for a big-screen adaptation of *Batman* (1989).

Political Awareness

America's Bruce Springsteen finally took the last step to global superstardom in 1984 with 'Born In The USA' and its attendant album. The song, musing on post-Vietnam America, became unintentionally ironic when taken up (without prior permission) by Ronald Reagan, a heavy-handed president who was rapidly becoming the most unpopular with the younger generation since Nixon.

📻 **CLASSIC RECORDINGS**

1982
Michael Jackson: *Thriller*

1983
The Police: 'Every Breath You Take'

1984
Prince: *Purple Rain*

1986
Bon Jovi: *Slippery When Wet*

1987
U2: *The Joshua Tree*

1989
Madonna: *Like A Prayer*

Above

At the beginning of the decade punk rockers still hung around but their music had already turned into the more friendly new wave, which soon turned its back on them.

Left

Madonna constantly reinvented herself throughout the decade, shaping the sounds and the moves the 1980s dance floors.

📻 *see David Bowie pp 196* 📻 *see Gary Numan pp 261* 📻 *see Michael Jackson pp 276* 📻 *see Madonna pp 278*

Above

The follow-up to Live Aid was a Christmas single, 'Do They Know It's Christmas', which brought together the might and majesty of modern pop royalty in an uncharacteristic burst of altruism.

Paul Simon, long amicably divorced from Art Garfunkel, had yet to approach the success that duo had obtained, but his *Graceland* album (1986), recorded in defiance of the cultural boycott of South Africa with black musicians of that country, would see him reinvent himself to register one of the first best-sellers of the infant compact-disc era. More importantly, it put world music well and truly on the map.

The 1980s was arguably the decade when rock rediscovered its conscience. Boomtown Rat Bob Geldof followed up 1984's charity single 'Do They Know It's Christmas?', inspired by watching BBC news reports of the famine in Africa, with simultaneous all-star concerts at Wembley Stadium and JFK Stadium, Philadelphia, in 1985. Fifteen-minute mini-sets were the order of the day, even supergroups like Queen, U2 and the re-formed Led Zeppelin bowing to Geldof's iron will.

Of the bands that featured, Ireland's U2 would prove to display the most lasting political awareness. Bono, the Edge Larry Mullen and Adam Clayton appeared calculatedly controversial with songs like 'Sunday Bloody Sunday' (titled after a 1972 incident between troops and protesters in Belfast), yet were always at the forefront when it came to promoting good causes. This would continue in the current millennium when Bono, along with Geldof, was instrumental in the G8 countries affording Africa a debt relief two decades after Live Aid.

As the decade rolled on, 'conscience rock' did its bit for Farm Aid, Red Wedge, Amnesty International and Ferry Aid. The Nelson Mandela 70th Birthday Tribute Concert in 1988 was an awareness-raiding exercise that both hastened the release of the future South African president and made

see **Introduction pp 268** *see* **Key Artists pp 274** *see* **A–Z of Artists pp 286** *see* **List of Artists pp 324**

an overnight star of Tracy Chapman, who happily busked as a backstage hunt unfolded for Stevie Wonder's keyboard software. Even charity had its commercial kickbacks....

In With The New

The compact disc arrived in Europe in 1983 and, by the end of the decade, the traditional vinyl record was on the way out. Initially derided as a 'yuppie' status symbol, more and more people turned over to the handy five-inch format as the decade continued. The system developed by Philips in Holland saw the information stored on the disc read by a laser, resulting in pristine sound. While players were prohibitively expensive when the first CD album, Billy Joel's 52nd Street, was launched (in Japan only) in 1982, the sales of Dire Straits' album Brothers In Arms three years later showed the compact disc was indeed here to stay.

Black music regrouped to make a new mark in the post-disco world when Kurtis Blow became the first rap act to be signed by a major label. The likes of Grandmaster Flash and Afrika Bambaataa (who jointly headlined the first rap festival in Britain in 1986), would follow, but it would take three middle-class white Jewish boys from New York – The Beastie Boys – to make the biggest commercial impact this decade with their tongue-in-cheek take on the genre, summed up by the 1987 hit single 'Fight For Your Right (To Party)'.

Heavy rock enjoyed boosts at the beginning and the end of the decade. The first flowering came in the shape of the so-called New Wave of British Heavy Metal (NWOBHM), which spawned the long-running likes of Saxon, Iron Maiden and Def Leppard. Metallica were big fans of this grass-roots movement based around live performance, the big bands of the 1970s (Purple, Zeppelin, Judas Priest) having now split up or entered tax exile.

Above

The 1980s audience was more manicured and self-conscious with their fashion than in the late 1970s, reacting against the brutal torn shirt and jeans look of the punks.

Big Hair And Big Sellers

By the end of the decade the US answer to NWOBHM had materialized in the shape of 'hair' bands, so-called because of the preposterous bouffants sported by some of the (universally good-looking) participants. These bands cleverly allied rock power with MTV-friendly image and videos, resulting in mammoth sales for the likes of Bon Jovi whose 1986 Slippery When Wet album was the Thriller of its genre. It sold 10 million copies in the US alone and spawned two No. 1 singles. From Britain, Def Leppard managed to catch the coat-tails of the movement to enjoy Stateside success that continues today.

Maybe the slowest-burning success story of the 1980s was R.E.M., who entered the recording world with the indie single 'Radio Free Europe' (1981) and closed the decade signed for major label Warner Brothers. The four-piece from Athens, Georgia, were the visible part of an 'iceberg' known as US college radio. Britain's equivalent was The Smiths, fronted by a similarly androgynous figure to Michael Stipe in Morrissey. However, they failed to see out the decade in a welter of recrimination between 'Moz' and guitarist/songwriting partner Johnny Marr.

With legwarmers, kilts, 'Frankie Says' T-shirts and Spandau Ballet's kilts, the 1980s could claim to be the decade popular music dressed to impress. It was also the decade when video killed the radio star: from now on, you would have to look the part as well as sound it.

Left

And still the girls cried and screamed, continuing the by now well-worn tradition created by The Beatles in the 1960s.

see U2 pp 284   see Tracy Chapman pp 290   see Metallica pp 332   see R.E.M. pp 338

Bon Jovi

274

CLASSIC RECORDINGS

1986
Slippery When Wet
'Livin' On A Prayer'

1987
'Wanted Dead Or Alive'

1988
New Jersey
'Bad Medicine'

1992
'Keep The Faith'

1994
'Always'

1995
These Days

2000
'It's My Life'

'If you wanted to torture me, you'd tie me down and force me to watch our first five videos.'

Jon Bon Jovi

Right

Though now more a happy-clappy stadium soft rock band, Bon Jovi's pop-metal had some edge in the mid-1980s, allowing the group to enter the 1990s with their fan base still intact.

America's leading hard rock band in the 1980s, Bon Jovi have broadened their appeal still further by combining their musical aggression with catchy pop songs to achieve a universal appeal.

The band was formed in 1983 in New Jersey by singer Jon Bon Jovi (b. John Francis Bongiovi, 2 March 1962), guitarist Richie Sambora (b. 11 July 1969), keyboard player David Bryan (b. David Bryan Rashbaum, 7 February 1962), bassist Alec John Such (b. 14 November 1956) and drummer Tico Torres (b. Hector Torres, 7 October 1953).

Runaway Success

As teenagers, Jon Bon Jovi and Bryan played in various local bands. After leaving high school Jon went to work with his cousin, noted record producer Tony Bongiovi, at New York's Power Plant where he wrote and recorded a demo of 'Runaway' that picked up radio play in New Jersey. He signed a deal with Mercury Records and recruited the other band members.

Bon Jovi (1984) stalled just outside the US Top 40 and 'Runaway' was a minor hit. *7800 Fahrenheit* (1985) peaked just inside the Top 40 and made the UK Top 30 following a British tour. Recruiting songwriter Desmond Child (of Aerosmith and Kiss) and producer Bruce Fairburn (of Blue Oyster Cult) they recorded their make-or-break

album, *Slippery When Wet* (1986). It stormed to the top of the US charts, propelled by two No. 1 singles – 'You Give Love A Bad Name' and 'Livin' On A Prayer' (both co-written by Child). In the UK it reached No. 6 and stayed in the charts for two years.

🎧 *see* Introduction pp 268　🎧 *see* Sources & Sounds pp 270　🎧 *see* A–Z of Artists pp 286

They repeated the formula with even greater success on *New Jersey* (1988). It was a No. 1 album in the UK and the US where it topped the charts for four weeks, providing five Top 10 singles, including two No. 1s: 'Bad Medicine' (co-written by Child) and 'I'll Be There For You'.

The band capitalized with a gruelling American and international touring schedule that included headlining the UK Monsters of Rock Festival at Castle Donington in 1987 and the Moscow Music Peace Festival in 1989. In 1990, the band took a break that turned into an extended hiatus. Jon Bon Jovi wrote the soundtrack to the *Young Guns II* movie. The album *Blaze Of Glory* (1990) reached No. 3 in the US while the title track went to No. 1. With Sambora also recording a solo album, *Stranger In This Town* (1991), rumours grew that the band had split up.

Keeping The Faith

But in 1992 they reassembled to record their first album for four years. *Keep The Faith* (1992) updated their sound with producer Bob Rock (of Metallica, Motley Crüe and Dave Lee Roth) while the band kept faith with Child who co-wrote the title track. While there were no major hit singles, the album reached No. 5 in the US and No. 1 in the UK where it stayed in the charts for more than a year.

Crossroads (1994) was a greatest hits collection that was a worldwide No. 1, except in America where it peaked at No. 8. It featured two new songs that became hits as well: 'Always' and 'Someday I'll Be Saturday Night'. Soon afterwards Such decided to leave the band. His replacement was Huey McDonald who had played with the band back in New Jersey.

For *These Days* (1995) Bon Jovi turned to producer Peter Collins (of Queensryche) who gave them a leaner sound that kept them in touch with the new generation of rock fans. Even though there were no major hits it spent four weeks at No. 1 in the UK, although it peaked at No. 9 in the US.

International Popularity

After a world tour that included three nights at London's Wembley Stadium the band took another extended break. Jon Bon Jovi recorded a second solo album, *Destination Anywhere* (1997), and pursued an

acting career while Sambora recorded his second solo album, *Undiscovered Soul* (1998).

Crush (2000) showed that a four-year lay-off had not damaged Bon Jovi's status. It was a worldwide No. 1, helped by the smash hit 'It's My Life'. Such was their international popularity that the *Crush* world tour was extended from six months to a year.

Bounce (2002) restored their popularity in America, reaching No. 2 in the US and UK. They then reinterpreted their hits on *This Left Feels Right* (2003). The title track of *Have A Nice Day* (2005) was previewed at Live 8 and the band followed up with another world tour in 2006. No longer innovators, they nevertheless retain their enormous popularity with pop and rock fans, male and female.

Above

In 1985, Bon Jovi released their *7800 Fahrenheit* LP. They had yet to reach the all-pervasive success that came with the following year's *Slippery When Wet*, but it paved the way, becoming their first album to go gold.

see Aerosmith pp 210   see Kiss pp 218   see Elton John pp 232   see Gins N'Roses pp 298

Michael Jackson   Key Artists

Right
Michael Jackson's solo career
gave him a worldwide
popularity that would eclipse
all other 1980s pop acts.

'He was like a sponge. Michael showed a curiosity for everything. It was unbelievable in someone so young. I appreciated watching it work.' Quincy Jones

Far Right
Though *Bad* may be seen as
Jackson's first commercial
misstep, Jackson was still
filling stadiums worldwide,
and in 1987 also enjoyed
the success of his feature
film, *Moonwalker*.

The self-proclaimed 'King of Pop', Michael Jackson (born 29 August 1958 was the biggest star of the 1980s following the success of Thriller (1982), which remains the world's best-selling album with sales of more than 48 million.

The King Of Pop

The youngest member of The Jackson Five, Jackson signed a solo deal in 1971 with Motown Records, aged 13. Within a year he had overtaken the Jackson Five on the strength of two US Top 5 singles – 'Got To Be There' and 'Rockin' Robin' – followed by a No. 1 with 'Ben'. But after that his career stalled, due to the sub-standard material he was given.

In 1975, The Jacksons (as they were now known) and Michael switched to Epic but his career continued to stagnate until 1977 when he landed a part in *The Wiz* movie and teamed up with producer Quincy Jones. Their first album together, *Off The Wall* (1979), reached No. 3 in the US charts and Jackson became the first solo artist to have four US Top 10 singles from one album. Two of them – 'Don't Stop 'Til You Get Enough' and 'Rock With You' – went to No. 1 In the UK the album also went Top 5. More significantly, *Off The Wall* stayed in the US charts for a year (more than three years in the UK). It encompassed the dance floor and pop radio with outstanding songs, quality arrangements and high-definition production. It also won Jackson two Grammy Awards in 1981.

Thrilling Success

Thriller eclipsed the high standards of *Off The Wall* with seven US Top 10 singles including two No. 1s – 'Billie Jean' and 'Beat It' – and three more that went Top 5. Jackson also won an unprecedented eight Grammy Awards in 1983. The album, which stayed at No. 1 in America for 37 weeks and was still in the charts 21 months later, again straddled different genres of mass appeal with consummate skill. But the album was also visually choreographed by videos, including a mini-epic for 'Thriller'. As a result Jackson became the first black artist to get regular exposure on MTV and his dancing (the moonwalk) and fashion quirks (one gloved hand) became as iconic as his music. His megastar status was confirmed in 1985 when he co-wrote (with Lionel Richie) the all-star USA For Africa single 'We Are The World', which got to No. 1.

see Introduction pp 268   *see* Sources & Sounds pp 270   *see* A–Z of Artists pp 286

In the UK *Thriller* topped the charts on three separate occasions and it also went to No. 1 in every Western country. It was an impossible album to follow and while *Bad* (1987) could not compete in chart terms it still sold 22 million copies and produced a record five US No. 1 singles: 'I Just Can't Stop Loving You', 'Bad', 'The Way You Make Me Feel', 'Man In The Mirror' and 'Dirty Diana'. The year-long *Bad* world tour was the biggest-grossing rock tour of the 1980s. *Bad* was the last album Jackson made with Jones.

A Troubled Star

Dangerous (1991) was co-produced by Teddy Riley who kept Jackson abreast of R&B and hip-hop trends. It topped the US charts for four weeks and 'Black Or White' was No. 1 for seven weeks. The *Dangerous* world tour was his biggest yet but it ended prematurely in 1993 when he was engulfed in scandal. Fans had been tolerant of his eccentricities (cosmetic surgery, Bubbles the chimpanzee and the children's sleepovers at his Neverland ranch) but allegations of child abuse – settled out of court – caused lasting damage to his reputation that all his trusts and foundations (mostly for children) and subsequent marriage to Lisa Marie Presley could not repair.

HIStory (1995) was a double CD of greatest hits and new songs, which was backed by a massive marketing campaign and was another US and UK No. 1, along with the single 'You Are Not Alone'. But Jackson was now more popular in the rest of the world than the US; a fact that became obvious when his *HIStory* world tour included no American shows, apart from Hawaii. Even outside America his shows attracted criticism for their messianic overtones.

Blood On The Dancefloor (1997) featured remixes from *HIStory* and new songs, including the title track that was a UK No. 1, although it failed to make the US Top 40. *Invincible* (2001) was Jackson's first album of all-new material since *Dangerous* and debuted at No. 1 in the US, selling over 11 million worldwide.

But controversy was never far away. He inexplicably dangled his child over a hotel balcony in Berlin; an image-restoring TV documentary, *Living With Michael Jackson*, had the opposite effect; and in 2005 he faced more child abuse allegations, this time in court. He was acquitted of all charges. Afterwards he relocated to Bahrain, his musical future uncertain.

see The Jackson Five pp 172   see Lionel Richie pp 312

Madonna

Key Artists

278

'Madonna is the speedboat, and the rest of us are just the Go-Gos on water skis.'
Liz Phair

The most successful female recording artist of all time, Madonna also reigns supreme as top female producer and songwriter. Madonna Louise Ciccone (b. 16 August 1958) spent her formative years in Detroit. After graduating from high school in 1976, she won a dance scholarship to the University of Michigan but dropped out after two years to seek a career in dance in New York. She sang and played guitar and drums in two rock groups before recording the demos that brought her to the attention of Sire Records, who initially offered her a singles-only contract.

Singled Out For Success

The first fruits of this, 'Everybody' and 'Burning Up', made little impact on the mainstream American charts but were dance hits and proved sufficient to convince Sire to sanction an album. *Madonna* (1983) (subtitled 'The First Album' on re-issue in 1985) was a collection of disco/pop songs remixed by John 'Jellybean' Benitez as the singer was unhappy with the initial outcome. The album was not a major success on original release, although it received good reviews and 'Holiday' was a British Top 20 hit.

Like A Virgin (1984) established Madonna as an international star, its title track becoming her first worldwide smash. Her material was given a commercial sheen by producer Nile Rodgers (of Chic fame) and the album featured another massive hit in 'Material Girl'. Madonna's first UK No. 1 single 'Into The Groove' (from the movie *Desperately Seeking Susan*) was added to the re-release in 1985, the year when she truly became a phenomenon with the runaway success of the album and her domination of the singles charts.

On *True Blue* (1986), the newly crowned 'Queen of Pop' took full control of her music, writing or co-writing all the songs and acting as co-producer. The album, featuring 'Papa Don't Preach', 'Open Your Heart' and 'La Isla Bonita', displayed a new maturity and, predictably, was another blockbuster.

In Vogue

Next, Madonna starred in the film *Who's That Girl* (1987) and the soundtrack album featured four of her

Right

Though these days Madonna's image and lifestyle have overshadowed her earlier pop success, in 1987, she enjoyed her fifth No. 1 single with 'Open Your Heart' – the third from that year's *True Blue* album to top the charts.

Far Right

1990 was arguably Madonna's biggest year. Her hugely theatrical *Blonde Ambition* tour, in support of *Like A Prayer*, lasted the whole year, and she would also star in the *Dick Tracy* film alongside Warren Beatty.

🔊 *see* Introduction pp 268 🔊 *see* Sources & Sounds pp 270 🔊 *see* A–Z of Artists pp 286

songs. Her next album proper, *Like a Prayer* (1989), was an adventurous project, incorporating elements of rock, dance, pop, soul and funk into a multi-platinum package. The video for the title track invited controversy over its use of religious imagery, providing Madonna with priceless publicity.

1990 was another busy year, as Madonna appeared in the movie *Dick Tracy* and released *I'm Breathless*. Described as 'music from and inspired by' the film, the album contains the singles 'Vogue' and 'Hanky Panky'. *The Immaculate Collection* (1990), her first greatest hits album, featured two new songs, 'Justify My Love' and 'Rescue Me', whilst other tracks were remixed and edited. It became one of the best-selling greatest hits compilations ever.

Erotica (1992), an album themed around sexuality, was largely overshadowed by the furore over *Sex* an ill-judged coffee table book, featuring soft-core photography and Madonna's explicit prose. On *Bedtime Stories* (1994) she reacted with a more mainstream work, which was less controversial lyrically. The album included 'Secret' and 'Take A Bow'.

In 1996, she played the title role in the film adaptation of the Andrew Lloyd Webber/Tim Rice musical *Evita*, appearing on the soundtrack album, which contained the specially written single 'You Must Love Me'.

Into Orbit

Returning to her own music, Madonna worked with British musician/producer William Orbit on the ambitious *Ray Of Light* (1998), which restored her commercial pre-eminence. The album expertly blended pop with electronica, ambient trance and quasi-psychedelia whilst the lyrics were largely personal, with Madonna reflecting on her recent motherhood. Further collaborations with Orbit followed on *Music* (2000), which developed its predecessor's shift towards European dance music. The non-north American version featured the hit cover of Don McLean's 'American Pie'.

2003's *American Life* was mired in controversy when, during the prelude to the second Iraq war, the video for the title track was criticized for being unpatriotic, leading Madonna, uncharacteristically, to withdraw it. As a result of the row, the album, a blend of acoustic and techno, suffered commercially.

Confessions On A Dance Floor (2005) returned Madonna to straightforward dance music. A continuous mix of songs, the album was issued in multiple formats, demonstrating her ability to exploit downloading technology as adroitly as she has used the pop video and the mass media throughout her career.

see Aretha Franklin pp 156   see Blondie pp 256   see The Pretenders pp 311   see Lenny Kravitz pp 353

The Police

CLASSIC RECORDINGS

1978
Outlandos D'Amour
'Roxanne'
'Can't Stand Losing You'

1979
Reggatta De Blanc
'Message In A Bottle'

1980
'Don't Stand So Close To Me'

1982
'Invisible Sun'

1983
Synchronicity
'Every Breath You Take'

'The contemporary hit radio format – they don't like jazz, they don't like hip-hop. It is against their formula. But because it is my record they have to take it seriously.'
Sting

Above
Though contemporaries of the UK's new wave scene, The Police's technical abilities far outstripped any of the punks', and their pop nous, coupled with experiments in jazz and world music, made them one of the most popular bands of the 1980s.

One of the 1980s' most successful British bands, The Police were founded in London at the height of the punk boom in 1977 by former Curved Air drummer Stewart Copeland (b. 16 July 1952) with singer/bassist Sting (b. Gordon Sumner, 2 October 1951) and original guitarist Henry Padovani. After one independent single 'Fall Out', they were joined by veteran guitarist Andy Summers (b. Andrew Somers, 31 December 1942) formerly of Dantalian's Chariot and Eric Burdon's New Animals.

Popular Newcomers

Padovani soon departed and the remaining threesome developed a unique, almost minimalist sound in the blend of Summers' crisp guitar, Sting's distinctive voice and Copeland's clattering drums. Heavily influenced by reggae, their first two singles 'Roxanne' and 'Can't Stand Losing You' did not chart when first released in

1978 as the BBC took a dim view of the subject matter, prostitution and suicide respectively. Reason prevailed the following year when the belated success of the reactivated singles ('Roxanne' also became a Top 30 hit in America) launched the debut album *Outlandos D'Amour* (1978) into the UK chart for a two-year residency.

Reggatta De Blanc (1979) quickly followed. As the title suggests, the album was in the same light reggae groove as its predecessor with several of Sting's songs touching on familiar themes of loneliness and alienation. It went to No. 1 in Britain, along with the first two singles lifted from it, 'Message In A Bottle' and 'Walking On The Moon', confirming The Police as the country's most popular new group.

Political Messages

Mainstream success in America arrived when *Zenyatta Mondatta* (1980) went Top 5 and spawned two US Top 10 singles, 'Don't Stand So Close To Me' (another UK chart topper) and 'De Do Do Do, De Da Da Da'.

see Introduction pp 268   *see* Sources & Sounds pp 270   *see* A–Z of Artists pp 286

Recorded quickly in the midst of touring commitments, the band were dissatisfied with the album and the critical reception was lukewarm, although *Zenyatta...* has since been favourably reassessed. It was the last Police album to rely heavily on reggae rhythms and to use only the three main instruments almost exclusively. It was also notable for Sting's first politically inspired lyric, 'Driven To Tears'.

This theme continued on the lead single from *Ghost In The Machine* (1981), 'Invisible Sun', which referred to Northern Ireland and, sonically, was a brave departure for the band. The album featured a more expansive sound, utilizing saxophones and synthesizer, with more thoughtful lyrics to match, something not necessarily reflected in the second single, the infectious No. 1 'Every Little Thing She Does Is Magic'.

Summers, Copeland and Sting took a year out for solo projects in 1982, reconvening the following year to record *Synchronicity* (1983). By this time, tensions, particularly between Sting and Copeland were threatening to tear the band apart. Nevertheless, The Police managed to produce their most crafted and diverse album which would go on to become the biggest seller in their catalogue, spending 17 weeks on top of the American chart. The first of four singles to be taken from it was the classic, subtly sinister 'Every Breath You Take', an international chart topper. 'Wrapped Around Your Finger' followed it into the Top 10 but both 'Synchronicity II' and 'King Of Pain', the final Police single in the band's lifetime, could only reach No. 17 in the UK.

Going Solos

The Police played their final shows in Melbourne, Australia in March 1984 at the end of the *Synchronicity* world tour. There was no official announcement that the band had split up, although Sting was quick to launch his solo career. The Police have reconvened occasionally since, playing three dates on the Amnesty International Conspiracy of Hope tour in 1986, which led to re-recordings of 'De Do Do Do, De Da Da Da' and 'Don't Stand So Close To Me'. In 1992, they played together at Sting's wedding and, in March 2003, performed three numbers to celebrate their induction into the Rock And Roll Hall Of Fame.

One of rock's highest profile stars, Sting's solo work, comprising eight studio albums, has been predictably successful if less adventurous, starting with the jazzy *Dream Of The Blue Turtles* (1985) through the loose concept album *Ten Summoner's Tales* (1993) to *Sacred Love* (2003) an ambitious, twenty-first century affair. He has also been a high-profile campaigner for the Rainforest Foundation.

Above
Despite being at the height of their worldwide fame in 1983, lead singer and bassist Sting dissolved the band the following year, and embarked upon an almost equally successful solo career.

see **The Who** pp 100   see **Bob Marley** pp 240   see **The Clash** pp 248   see **UB40** pp 319

Prince

'I got to think of myself as music. It's really hard to go to sleep at night, I'm always hearing music.'

Prince

Right

Dirty Mind saw Prince's take on new wave funk come into its own, as he crafted complex, lascivious, yet danceable pop.

Far Right

Prince was the first artist since The Beatles to simultaneously have a film, album and single at No. 1 after the release of *Purple Rain*.

The most innovative, mercurial and controversial black rock star since Jimi Hendrix, Prince is also one of the most mysterious. He was born Prince Rogers Nelson, 7 June 1958. His father was the leader of a local jazz band, his mother was a singer. He formed his first band at 14 and signed a self-production deal with Warner Brothers in 1977.

Controversial Star

His debut, *For You* (1978), was almost entirely self-written and self-played, a formative blend of R&B, rock and pop with titles like 'Soft And Wet' creating an early notoriety. *Prince* (1979) peaked just outside the US Top 20 with the R&B hits 'I Wanna Be Your Lover' and 'Why You Wanna Treat Me So Bad' extending his range. Another track, 'I Feel For You', would later be a major hit for Chaka Khan.

Prince toured America, supporting and outshining Rick James. *Dirty Mind* (1980) was loosely conceptual with provocative songs like 'Head' and 'Sister' but was less successful. *Controversy* (1981) refined his adult-oriented funk and revived his fortunes, again narrowly missing the US Top 20. His breakthrough came with the harder rocking double album *1999* (1982) that hit the US Top 10 six months after its release on the back of three Top 10 singles: 'Little Red Corvette', 'Delirious' and the title track.

Purple Rain (1984) vaulted Prince to superstardom, topping the US charts for 24 weeks. The soundtrack to an autobiographical movie, it featured two US No. 1 hits – 'When Doves Cry' and 'Let's Go Crazy'. The album also made the UK Top 10.

Soundtrack Of The Times

Eschewing media interviews and promotion, Prince's image rested on his albums, videos and dynamic live shows. He was prolific too. In 1985, he won two Grammies and an Oscar, wrote Sheena Easton's US Top 10 hit 'Sugar Walls' and donated '4 The Tears In Your Eyes' to the *USA For Africa* benefit album. He also released the spiritually inclined *Around The World In A Day* (1985) that topped the US charts for three weeks (along with the No. 2 single 'Raspberry Beret') and made the UK Top 5.

Parade (1986), his eighth album in as many years, went Top 5 in the US and UK and featured songs from his second movie, *Under The Cherry Moon*,

🔊 *see* Introduction pp 268   🔊 *see* Sources & Sounds pp 270   🔊 *see* A–Z of Artists pp 286

including the US No. 1 (and UK No. 4) 'Kiss'. The critically acclaimed double album *Sign 'O' The Times* (1987) was similarly successful and *Lovesexy* (1988) was the first of three consecutive UK No. 1 albums, although it only reached No. 11 in the US.

Batman (1989), the soundtrack to the year's movie blockbuster, was a US and UK No. 1 with 'Batdance' also topping the US charts (UK No. 2). *Graffiti Bridge* (1990) was another soundtrack, this time to Prince's sequel to *Purple Rain*. It was a US Top 10, along with the single 'Thieves In The Temple'. But a version of the Prince-penned 'Nothing Compares 2 U' by Sinead O'Connor topped the US and UK charts in 1990. Prince scored another US No. 1 with 'Cream' from *Diamonds And Pearls* (1991), which reached No. 3 (No. 2 in the UK).

Highly Independent

For *Symbol* (1992), Prince created his own hieroglyph out of combining the male and female symbols and scored his fourth UK No. 1 (US No. 6). In a rare public pronouncement Prince then changed his name to the unpronounceable symbol and became embroiled in a contractual dispute with Warners over his next album and painting the word 'Slave' on his cheek. The independently released 'The Most Beautiful Girl In The World' was a No. 1 hit around much of the world in 1994 (US No. 3).

The Warners-released *Come* (1994) was another UK No. 1 although it peaked at US No. 15. But the much-bootlegged *Black Album* (1994), recorded in 1987, failed to make the Top 30. However, *The Gold Experience* (1995) featuring 'The Most Beautiful Girl In The World' restored Prince to the Top 10 in the UK and US.

Prince's contract with Warners ended with *Chaos And Disorder* (1996), a US Top 30 and UK Top 20 album. He celebrated his release with the triple CD *Emancipation* (1996) which went Top 20 in the US and UK. But once independent he made little effort to court commercial success. *Rave Un2 The Joy Fantastic* (1999) made the US Top 20 but subsequent albums were increasingly self-indulgent until the focused *Musicology* (2004) made No. 3 in the UK and US.

3121 (2006) gave Prince his first US No. 1 since *Batman* and made the UK Top 10, proving that he still has huge commercial potential if he chooses to use it.

see Jimi Hendrix pp 132   see Madonna pp 278   see Lenny Kravitz pp 353   see Sinead O'Connor pp 360

'*Pop music often tells you everything is OK, while rock music tells you that it's not OK, but you can change it.*'

Bono

Above

On stage in 1983, around the time of their Steve Lillywhite-produced breakthrough album, 1983's *War*. It would see U2 start to become the stadium-filling act they were destined to be.

One of the world's most successful rock groups, U2 are unique in having kept a stable line-up throughout a lengthy career. Singer Bono (b. Paul Hewson, 10 May 1960), guitarist The Edge (b. David Evans, 8 August 1961), bassist Adam Clayton (b. 13 March 1960) and drummer Larry Mullen Jr. (b. 31 October 1961) formed a band at school in Dublin in 1977. Settling on the name U2 in 1978, they came to England in 1980 after two Irish chart-topping singles.

Gathering Momentum

Three flop singles preceded their debut album *Boy* (1980), a well-received work concerning adolescence. Constant gigging, including a first visit to America, helped establish their formidable reputation as live performers. Minor hits 'Fire' and 'Gloria' were taken from the religiously themed *October* (1981), regarded one of U2's least satisfying albums. The long-awaited chart breakthrough came with the typically passionate 'New Year's Day' from 1983's *War*, an album about conflict. The live mini-album *Under A Blood Red Sky* (1984) was a largely successful attempt to capture U2's live act, its version of 'Sunday Bloody Sunday' eclipsing the original on *War*. The album earned them their first US Top 30 placing.

U2 continued to gather momentum with *The Unforgettable Fire* (1984), featuring 'Pride (In The Name Of Love)'. The band's anthemic music acquired a new depth via the atmospheric production by Daniel Lanois and Brian Eno. It cracked the Top 20 in America, fittingly for an album which revealed U2's growing fascination with the United States.

Adding A Touch Of Irony

Live Aid proved a pivotal moment in the band's ascension into the major leagues. An unforgettable performance at Wembley Stadium was capped by

📻 *see* Introduction pp 268 📻 *see* Sources & Sounds pp 270 📻 *see* A–Z of Artists pp 286

Bono's unscripted foray over the lip of the stage and towards the crowd to the bemusement of his colleagues. U2's next album, the eagerly anticipated *The Joshua Tree* (1987) did not diappoint. Again produced by Lanois and Eno, a widescreen element was added to the band's stirring rock music. The first three tracks were all hit singles – 'Where The Streets Have No Name', 'I Still Haven't Found What I'm Looking For' and 'With Or Without You' – all encapsulating the album's themes of spirituality and soul-searching. *The Joshua Tree* went on to sell 25 million copies worldwide.

It was quickly followed by *Rattle And Hum* (1988), a part-live/part-studio double set which also served as the soundtrack to U2's documentary film of the same name, a memento of the *Joshua Tree* tour. Although it sold well and gave the band their first UK No. 1 single, 'Desire', *Rattle And Hum*'s apparently haphazard sequencing resulted in a lack of cohesion.

Achtung Baby (1991) was a deliberate attempt to forge a new direction, incorporating elements of dance and electronica, which caused much conflict within U2's ranks. Containing 'The Fly' and 'One', *Achtung Baby* was lyrically darker than its predecssors but a touch of irony was beginning to temper the earnestness. The result rivals *The Joshua Tree* as U2's finest album.

Even more ambitious was *Zooropa* (1993), recorded between legs of the extravagantly staged *Zoo TV* tour and influenced by its theme of media overkill. U2 began to reinvent themselves, producing an ambient-leaning album, featuring sampling and treated sounds, which was totally unlike their previous work. Further experimentation followed on *Original Soundtracks 1* (1995), recorded by U2 and Brian Eno but released under the pseudonym Passengers.

The ironically entitled *Pop* (1997) completed U2's transformation into a post-modern rock band on an album which featured familiar themes of love, desire and faith in crisis. It was one of the band's lesser-selling albums, although 'Discotheque' was a British No. 1 single. The accompanying *Popmart* tour was another spectacular visual extravaganza.

Making A Better World

The gap between new albums was filled by *The Best Of 1980–90* (1998), which featured one 'new' song, 'Sweetest Thing', a re-worked B-side. This heralded the back to basics approach of *All That You Can't Leave Behind* (2000), which reunited the band with producers Lanois and Eno. The album yielded a UK chart topper in 'Beautiful Day'.

Parallel to his music, Bono has been increasingly involved in economic/humanitarian concerns but returned to participate in *How To Dismantle An Atomic Bomb* (2004), spawning yet more UK No. 1s in 'Vertigo' and 'Sometimes You Can't Make It On Your Own'.

Below
Touring in support of *Rattle & Hum* in 1989 – a ramshackle album that soundtracked their failed feature film project. It seemed that U2 needed some time to get used to being one of the world's biggest rock'n'roll bands.

see The Beatles pp 88   *see* The Rolling Stones pp 96   *see* Simple Minds pp 314   *see* Coldplay pp 380

ABC

(Vocal/instrumental group, 1980–91, 1996–present)
Sheffield's ABC essentially rewrote classic 1960s soul
and pop for the new romantic 1980s. Their golden era
began in 1981 with 'Tears Are Not Enough'. 'Poison
Arrow', 'The Look Of Love' and 'All Of My Heart'
followed. The perfect pop of Trevor Horn-produced
debut *The Lexicon of Love* (1982) was a UK No. 1.
'When Smokey Sings' was the band's last big-seller.
Singer Martin Fry still flies the ABC flag, but their
well-crafted chartbusters of the 1980s mark their zenith.

Adam and The Ants

(Vocal/instrumental group, 1977–82)
The charismatic Adam Ant (b. Stuart Goddard) was
a prominent figure in the boutiques and clubs of the
punk scene, appearing in Derek Jarman's film *Jubilee*,
and releasing *Dirk Wears White Sox* in 1979. After his
backing band became Bow Wow Wow, he started from
scratch, gaining huge fame with his follow-up – 1980's
Kings Of The Wild Frontier. Powered by African-style
drumming, courtesy of Merrick and Terry Lee Miall,
and Marco Pirroni's emphatic, Link Wray-influenced

Below
One of the more flamboyant
performers of the 1980s,
Adam Ant had a late 1970s
post-punk/new wave
background that gave even
his hit singles an edge.

guitar, the hits streamed out. 'Dog Eat Dog', 'Ant
Music', (both 1980), and tracks from third album
Prince Charming (1981) – 'Stand And Deliver', 'Prince
Charming' (both No. 1s in 1981) and 'Ant Rap' – were
all boosted by videos which emphasized flamboyance
and a good-time ethic, and helped define the new
romantic movement. It was exciting pop music, which
continued in Adam's solo career, including the chart-
topper 'Goody Two Shoes', which became his first US
smash in 1982.

Afrika Bambaataa

(DJ/rap artist, b. 1960)
As a DJ, Bambaataa (b. Kevin Donovan) was at the
forefront of the rise of hip-hop in the late 1970s. In
1982, he released 'Planet Rock', which borrowed from
Kraftwerk's 'Trans-Europe Express', and essentially
invented electro. In the mid-1980s he collaborated
with both John Lydon *and* James Brown. His debut
album, *Beware (The Funk Is Everywhere)* arrived in
1986. His immeasurable influence on progressive black
music continued as he nurtured the likes of De La Soul
and A Tribe Called Quest.

🔊 *see* Introduction pp 268 🔊 *see* Sources & Sounds pp 270 🔊 *see* Key Artists pp 274

Left
One of the key progenitors of thrash metal, Anthrax fused heavy metal proficiency and punk energy to create their influential sound.

Anthrax
(Vocal/instrumental group, 1981–present)
Formed in New York with Dan Spitz (guitar), Scott Ian (guitar), Dan Lilker (bass) and Charlie Benante (drums). After adding Joey Belladonna (vocals) they hit paydirt, recording *Spreading The Disease* for Island in 1986. They gained an awesome live reputation, while issuing blistering records (*State Of Euphoria*, 1988 and *Sound Of White Noise*, 1993), including a team-up with rapper Chuck D, 'Bring The Noise'. They remain one of the most interesting and charismatic modern metal bands.

Aztec Camera
(Vocal/instrumental group, 1980–95)
Roddy Frame was 19 when his band's debut *High Land Hard Rain* appeared in 1983. His quirky brand of tuneful pop, spiced with clever lyrics, was a breath of fresh air at the time. Two fellow Scots, Craig Gannon (bass) and Malcolm Ross (guitar), joined him for 1984's *Knife*. The superb soul pop of 1988's 'Somewhere In My Heart' remains Aztec Camera's biggest hit, but Frame continues to ply his trade as one of the UK's most talented songsmiths.

The B52s
(Vocal/instrumental group, 1976–present)
The band's kitsch dress sense and spiky, surreal updating of 1960s dance music won a huge college following during the punk/new wave years. Guitarist Ricky Wilson died from AIDS in 1985. In 1986, an updated version of 1978's 'Rock Lobster' became a UK Top 20 smash. 'Love Shack', 'Roam' and 'Meet The Flintstones' followed it up the charts. Original members Kate Pierson (organ, vocals), Cindy Wilson (guitar, vocals), Fred Schneider (keyboards, vocals) and Keith Strickland (drums) can still claim to be the best party band around.

Bad Brains
(Vocal/instrumental group, 1978–present)
This dreadlocked crew – Dr Know (guitar), Darryl Jenifer (bass) and Earl Hudson (drums) – ditched jazz-fusion for thrash-punk. They wowed New York's hip CBGB club, and released the excellent *Rock The Light* (1983). The volatile H.R. ('throat', not vocals) left and rejoined, as they incorporated reggae and funk on the likes of *I Against I* (1986) and *God Of Love* (1995). Worshipped by Henry Rollins, they also influenced The Beastie Boys and Red Hot Chili Peppers.

Below
Despite only releasing a few records during their early 1980s heyday, Bad Brains' hardcore US punk has been an influence upon many over the decades.

see Kraftwerk pp 218   *see* The Sex Pistols pp 252   *see* The Beastie Boys pp 288   *see* Red Hot Chili Peppers pp 336

The Beastie Boys

(Vocal/rap/instrumental group, 1981–present)

The Beastie Boys – Michael 'Mike D' Diamond, Adam 'MCA' Yauch and Adam 'King Ad-Rock' Horovitz – began life as a New York hardcore punk band, but under the auspices of producer Rick Rubin, became the first important white rap act. Debut *Licensed To Ill* (1986) was a good-time rap-metal crossover, which spawned the hit singles 'Fight For Your Right To Party', 'No Sleep Till Brooklyn' and 'She's On It'. These bratty anthems and the band's over-the-top stage show caused as much controversy as first-wave punk. *Licensed…* was the first No. 1 rap album in the US. Disputes with Rubin led to a hiatus. The unexpectedly diverse and even thoughtful *Paul's Boutique* arrived in 1989. Equally interesting collections arrived at fairly lengthy intervals; the funky *Check Your Head* (1992), *Ill Communication* (1994), and double Grammy-winning *Hello Nasty* (1998). Over 25 years, they stretched rap's boundaries and produced some of the wittiest music around.

Pat Benatar

(Vocals, b. 1953)

Brooklyn-born Benatar established herself as queen of arena rock with a trio of fine albums. Her poppier debut *In The Heat Of The Night* (1979) was followed by heavier, Grammy-winning *Crimes Of Passion* (1980) and her only No. 1 *Precious Time* (1981). Her expressive tones powered several hit singles including 'Hit Me With Your Best Shot', 'Love Is A Battlefield' and 'We Belong'. Husband Neil Giraldo provided guitar support while Benatar blazed a trail for women rockers.

George Benson

(Guitar, vocals, b. 1943)

A child jazz guitar prodigy, Benson later recorded with giants of the genre Miles Davis and Herbie Hancock. In his mid-30s he followed in the crossover footsteps of Nat 'King' Cole and Louis Armstrong, reinventing himself as a honey-toned, R&B singer. 1976's *Breezin'* set him on his way, and he consolidated his pop star

🎵 *see Introduction pp 268* 🎵 *see Sources & Sounds pp 270* 🎵 *see Key Artists pp 274*

status with *In Flight* (1977) and 1980's *Give Me The Night*, the title track of the latter his biggest US hit single at No. 4.

Big Audio Dynamite
(Vocal/instrumental group, 1984–95)
Mick Jones followed his stint as a founder member of The Clash with the genre-hopping BAD. He enlisted filmmaker Don Letts on 'effects' and adventurously married punk, hip-hop and electronica on 1985's *This Is BAD*. The album's single, 'E=MC^2' scored highly in the UK. Jones recruited old chum Joe Strummer for the similar *No. 10 Upping Street* (1986). An excitingly innovative outfit at the outset, BAD succumbed to the law of diminishing returns.

Big Country
(Vocal/instrumental group, 1981–2001)
Stuart Adamson began with Scottish punk band The Skids. His Caledonian heritage came to the fore with Big Country, as he employed guitar gizmos to create a choral 'bagpipe' sound. The epic, yearning songs of debut album *The Crossing* (1983) played well in America. The follow-up, the more political *Steeltown* (1984), was a UK No. 1, and singles such as 'Wonderland' and 'Look Away' fared well for Scotland's equivalent to U2. Adamson committed suicide in 2001.

Black Uhuru
(Vocal/instrumental group, 1973–present)
Derrick 'Ducky' Simpson co-founded this mighty Jamaican reggae outfit in the early 1970s. The line-up settled with Michael Rose on lead vocals, Puma Jones and Simpson harmonizing, and the legendary Sly and Robbie acting as rhythm section. A deal with Island

paved the way for the group's international reputation. The Grammy-grabbing *Anthem* (1984) established them in America, and though they never quite attained superstar status, their atmospheric, melodic sound combined accessibility with authenticity.

The Blues Brothers
(Vocal/instrumental group, 1978–present)
Jake and Elwood Blues began life in a 1976 *Saturday Night Live* sketch featuring John Belushi and Dan Aykroyd singing 'I'm A King Bee' dressed as giant bees. The show's musical director, Paul Shaffer helped assemble a band to support comedian Steve Martin in 1978. They recruited legendary Booker T. and The MGs guitarist Steve Cropper, his bassist bandmate Donald 'Duck' Dunn, alongside Chicago blues sideman extraordinaire, Matt 'Guitar' Murphy, and a wealth of session talent. The show was released as *Briefcase Full Of Blues* and became a huge hit. The film directed by John Landis followed in 1980, featuring cameo appearances from James Brown, Aretha Franklin, Cab Calloway and Ray Charles. *Best Of The Blues Brothers* was released in 1981. Belushi died in 1982. Steve Cropper recorded a follow-up album in 1988, *Red White and Blues. Blues Brothers 2000* furthered the film franchise, again helping reintroduce America to its black musical heritage.

Above
One of the most successful reggae acts since Bob Marley, Black Uhuru became the first reggae group to win a Grammy Award in 1983.

Below
A *Saturday Night Live* creation of Dan Aykroyd and John Belushi, the phenomenal success of the movie, *The Blues Brothers*, made the duo a household name in 1980.

🎙 *see* Ray Charles pp 42 🎙 *see* James Brown pp 154 🎙 *see* The Clash pp 248 🎙 *see* Eminem pp 382

290

Michael Bolton
(Vocals, b. 1953)

Blue-eyed soul singer, Bolton (or Bolotin as he was born), spent the early part of his career as a much heavier proposition singing for rock band Blackjack, before making his name with powerful renditions of soul classics intermingled with classy AOR ballads, often co-written with Dianne Warren. His change in style came with 1987's *The Hunger* on Columbia, which yielded his first Top 20 hit, 'That's What Love Is All About'. *Soul Provider* (1989) and *Time, Love And Tenderness* (1991) followed with Bolton earning Grammys for 'How Am I Supposed to Live Without You' (1990) – which he had originally co-written for Laura Branigan – and Percy Sledge's 'When A Man Loves A Woman' (1991). A surprising songwriting collaboration with Bob Dylan, 'Steel Bars' (1992) was also a hit, as was 'Can I Touch You … There' (1995). Golden-throated Bolton is still a fine interpreter and songwriter.

Above

A best-selling soft rock artist of the 1980s, Michael Bolton actually began by fronting hard rockers Blackjack, under his real name Michael Bolotin.

Right

Emerging from Australia's new wave, Nick Cave formed The Birthday Party, before becoming one of the most respected solo artists of the past two decades.

Far Right

In the 1980s, Cher ran her successful adult pop career alongside her arguably more successful acting career, starting with 1983's *Silkwood*.

Cabaret Voltaire
(Experimental vocal/instrumental group, 1973–94)

Founded in Sheffield by Krautrock fans Chris Watson, Richard H. Kirk and Stephen Mallinder. The trio manipulated tapes and played conventional instruments against and over them. Signed to Rough Trade in 1978, an underground hit 'Nag Nag Nag' emerged. The group became more interested in danceable beats, but still retained an experimental edge. 1984's 'Sensoria' and 1985's 'James Brown' are seen as precursors of house music. Many 'industrial' acts also cite The Cabs as an influence.

The Cars
(Vocal/instrumental group, 1976–88)

Songwriter Ric Ocasek (vocals, guitar) joined original members Benjamin Orr (bass), Elliot Easton (guitar) and Greg Hawkes (keyboards) to form a powerful unit. They drove The Cars up the charts on both sides of the Atlantic with their self-titled 1978 debut. The band cleverly mixed classic rock melody with a smattering of new-wave edge. The deliciously catchy 'My Best Friend's Girl' from the first LP was a No. 3 hit in the UK. Follow-up collection *Candy-O* (1979) repeated the formula, but *Panorama* (1980) and *Shake It Up* (1981) were a little less immediate, the latter going for a more synth-oriented sound. 1984's *Heartbeat City* was quintessential American AOR; radio-friendly, big tunes and polished production. The evocative 'Drive', the big single from the album, was used on a Live Aid documentary soundtrack on the Ethiopian famine. It went Top 5 in both the US and UK.

Nick Cave and The Birthday Party
(Vocal/instrumental group, 1980–83)

Nick Cave (vocals) began his fascinating career in Boys Next Door, who became The Birthday Party; Mick Harvey (guitar), Tracy Pew (bass), Phil Calvert (drums). A gothic, blues punk band of fearsome intensity, showcasing Cave's brutal, Captain Beefheart-style lyrics, they released three albums, 1981's *Prayers*

On Fire being the pick. 1982's *Junkyard* is the sound of the band falling apart.

Cave regrouped, retaining Mick Harvey and adding guitarist Blixa Bargeld to form the slightly less deranged Bad Seeds. Their highly influential mixture of corrupted lounge music, gothic gospel and misanthropic post-punk balladry is displayed on many fine albums, including *From Her To Eternity* (1984), *Henry's Dream* (1992), *Murder Ballads* (1996; Kylie Minogue and P.J. Harvey guest), and the very witty *Abattoir Blues/Lyre Of Orpheus* (2004). Cave is an important figure, a Leonard Cohen for Generation X.

Tracy Chapman
(Singer/songwriter, b. 1964)
Cleveland, Ohio-born Chapman became an overnight success with her expressive self-titled debut in 1988 after appearing at a Nelson Mandela benefit gig at Wembley Stadium. Her emotive voice and politicized pop folk chimed with the opposition to the Thatcher/Reagan axis, and it went to No. 1 on both sides of the Atlantic, with 'Fast Car' hitting the singles charts. Chapman continued the sterling work, albeit with less commercial success, on *Crossroads* (1989), *New Beginning* (1995) – which included the huge US hit 'Give Me One Reason' – and 2000's *Telling Stories*.

Cher
(Vocals, b. 1946)
Born Cherilyn Sarkasian La Pier in California, her early career yielded hits such as 'All I Really Want To Do' (1965) and 'Gypsys, Tramps And Thieves' (1971), alongside successes with husband, Sonny Bono ('I Got You Babe', 'All I Ever Need Is You'). She emphasized her Native American heritage on 'Half-Breed' (1973) and 'Dark Lady' (1974); but apart from 1979's 'Take Me Home' the next decade was a musical blank. She acted in successful movies, however – *Moonstruck* (winning an Oscar), *Silkwood*, *Mask* – which catalyzed her chart revival with the soft metal of 'I Found Someone' (1987), the classy power-ballad, 'Just Like Jesse James' (1990) and 'Love And Understanding' (1991). She continued to chart in the UK, but it was not until 1998's transatlantic No. 1 'Believe', with its treated vocal and heavy dance beat, that she had another US smash. Cher's career is a testament to talent combined with perseverance.

see Bob Dylan pp 126   see Leonard Cohen pp 139   see Sonny and Cher pp 148   see Kylie Minogue pp 356

China Crisis

(Vocal/instrumental group, 1979–95)
Liverpudlians Eddie Lundon (guitar, vocals) and Gary Daly (keyboards) shared a mutual love for Eno and Bowie, with a dash of Steely Dan thrown in. Walter Becker from The Dan actually produced their third album *Flaunt The Imperfection* (1985). The band had hits with 'Christian' (1983), 'Wishful Thinking' (1984) and 'Black Man Ray' (1985). Their technical ability and almost jazzy musical imagination set them apart from most new romantic and post-punk contemporaries.

The Cocteau Twins

(Vocal/instrumental group, 1980–98)
The otherworldly tones of albums such as *Treasure* (1983) and *Victorialand* (1986) helped define ambient music. The Cocteaus comprised Robin Guthrie's layered soundscapes and Liz Fraser's spectral voice (also used by Massive Attack), plus bassist Will Heggie (replaced by Simon Raymonde). None of their lyrics could be discerned, but the atmospheric 'Pearly Dewdrops Drop' (1984) charted, and is still used by TV producers. *Heaven Or Las Vegas* (1990) and the more conventional *Four Calendar Cafe* (1993) went US Top 100. 1996's *Milk And Kisses* closed their career.

Phil Collins

(Vocals, b. 1951)
The London-born drummer and vocalist from Genesis established himself as an unlikely pop star in the early 1980s, alternating between atmospheric ballads such as 'In The Air Tonight' and 'One More Night', and up-tempo, soul-based numbers and covers, including 'Easy Lover', 'Sussidio' and 'You Can't Hurry Love'. Enormous selling albums *Face Value* (1981), *No Jacket Required* (1985) and *... But Seriously* (1989) made him one of the most successful artists of the decade.

Robert Cray

(Guitar, vocals, b. 1953)
By the 1970s the blues was a debased currency amongst Afro-Americans. Robert Cray was the first major black artist to rehabilitate the genre. Born in Columbus, Georgia, Cray paid a lot of dues before eventually releasing *Who's Been Talkin'* in 1980. Several hundred gigs down the road, *Bad Influence* emerged in late 1983 (1984 in the UK) with Eric Clapton sitting in (Cray still works with 'Slowhand').

Showdown (1985), an album shared with two of Cray's heroes, Albert Collins and Johnny Copeland, displayed the tradition Robert was coming from. Where he was going to was pointed out on his soul-tinged breakthrough, *Strong Persuader* in 1986. This married Cray's full-toned, economic guitar style and his beautiful, gospelly voice, reaching No. 13 in the US. Cray continues to renew the blues with his strong songwriting skills and interesting arrangements, on the likes of *Sweet Potato Pie* (1997) and *Shoulda Been Home* (2001).

The Cult

(Vocal/instrumental group, 1984–95, 2001–02, 2006–present)
Centred on singer Ian Astbury and Billy Duffy (guitar), The Cult (initially Southern Death Cult), released the goth/psychedelic *Dreamtime* in 1984. An alliance with producer Rick Rubin in 1987 resulted in third album *Electric*, influential on many nu-metal bands and Guns

Below

Robert Cray's technical guitar skills helped ensure that a 1980s revival in the blues would be sustained over the decades and across 15 albums.

🎵 *see Sources & Sounds pp 270* 🎵 *see Key Artists pp 274*

N' Roses (who stole drummer Matt Sorum). *Sonic Temple*
(1989) was more mainstream rock and made the US Top
10; after that the band trod water. Astbury 'played' Jim
Morrison when The Doors reunited in 2002.

Culture Club

(Vocal/instrumental group, 1982–86, 1998–99)
The larger-than-life George O'Dowd is better known as
Boy George. His smooth pop tenor, his outlandish get-
up and the band's catchy tunes made them unmissable.
Roy Hay (guitar), Mikey Craig (bass) and Jon Moss
(drums) provided the music for the lilting 'Do You
Really Want To Hurt Me' which topped the UK chart
in late 1982, and six smash hits ensued, including
'Church Of The Poison Mind', 'Karma Chameleon' (a
transatlantic No. 1) and 'The War Song'. *Kissing To Be
Clever* (1982) was a good debut and 1983's *Colour By
Numbers* – a collage of pop styles – even better. But,
as George's relationship with Moss deteriorated and his
drug habit grew, their next three outings sounded
increasingly thin. They returned in 1998 with big hit
'I Just Wanna Be Loved' but this reunion was a one-off.
Their time in the 'new pop' vanguard of the 1980s is
their legacy.

The Cure

(Vocal/instrumental group, 1976–present)
This influential post-punk outfit, led by Robert Smith
(vocals, guitar) with Lol Tolhurst (drums) and Michael
Dempsey (bass), debuted in 1978 on the Albert Camus-
inspired 'Killing An Arab'. Simon Gallup (bass,
keyboards) replaced Dempsey and the tone got even

darker with *Seventeen Seconds* (1980), *Faith* (1981) and
Pornography (1982). Yet in the same year, 'Let's Go To
Bed' showed Smith's quirky pop sensibility, which would
resurface on hits such as the jazzy 'Lovecats' and the
mutant soul of 'Close To Me.' In 1987, the ambitious
double album *Kiss Me, Kiss Me, Kiss Me* broke into the
American Top 40 and 1989's 'Lovesong' was a US No. 2.
Smith's writing still hinted at deep depression, but his
music displayed great eclecticism on offerings such as
Disintegration (1989), *Wish* (1992) and *Wild Mood Swings*
(1996). Often hailed as fathers of goth, they inspired
many on the alternative music scene.

🎵 **see The Doors pp 140**   🎵 **see David Bowie pp 196**   🎵 **see Guns N' Roses pp 298**   🎵 **see Massive Attack pp 356**

The Dead Kennedys
(Vocal/instrumental group, 1978–86)

This controversial bunch of San Franciscans were one of the truly great punk bands. Debut 1979 single 'California Uber Alles' set the template, with Jello Biafra (Eric Boucher) trashing the American dream, voice quavering with menace; East Bay Ray Glasser's guitar, Klaus Flouride (Geoffrey Lyall)'s bass and Bruce Slesinger's drums in thunderous support. Debut album *Fresh Fruit For Rotting Vegetables* (1980) became a cult classic. *Plastic Surgery Disasters* (1982) furthered their reputation, but the band fell out. Biafra now pursues a spoken word career.

Def Leppard
(Vocal/instrumental group, 1977–present)

The band appropriately formed in Sheffield, erstwhile home of the British steel industry. Their fresh brand of poppy heavy metal, led by Joe Elliott (vocals) and Pete Willis (lead guitar), soon won them fans. An early B-side 'Hello America' hinted at their ambitions. Debut album *On Through The Night* (1980) just missed the US Top 50; but with 1983's *Pyromania* they became giants of the genre, hitting the stateside No. 2. Drummer Rick Allen lost an arm in a car accident, but adapted his kit, and 1987's *Hysteria* made US No. 1, and UK No. 2.

Guitarist Steve Clark died from drink and drugs in 1991, but once again the band returned, topping the charts with *Adrenalize* (1992). Since these heady days – replete with smashes such as 'Love Bites' and 'Let's Get Rocked' – they have modernized successfully on *Slang* (1996), *Euphoria* (1999) and X (2002). Their pioneering, catchy, pop rock still draws crowds.

Depeche Mode
(Vocal/instrumental group, 1976–present)

Formed by Essex schoolboys Vince Clarke (keyboards), Martin Gore (vocals, guitar, keyboards), Andy Fletcher (keyboards) and singer Dave Gahan. New label Mute took a punt on their melancholic but hooky synth-pop and were rewarded with the Top 10 album *Speak And Spell* (1981) and classic dance track 'Just Can't Get Enough'. Clarke departed to create Erasure, and Gore assumed songwriting duties, racking up hits that combined Gahan's world-weary delivery with a riffy, industrial-lite appeal – 'Everything Counts', 'People Are People' (their first US hit) and 'Master And Servant'. Deeply depressive collections such as *Some Great Reward* (1984), *Black Celebration* (1986) and *Music For The Masses* (1987) cemented their US reputation, while 1990's *Violator* and its premier single

Below

Famously playing with a one-armed drummer since 1985, Sheffield-based Def Leppard evolved from the New Wave of British Heavy Metal to become one of the 1980s' heaviest rock groups.

see Introduction pp 268   *see* Sources & Sounds pp 270   *see* Key Artists pp 274

'Personal Jesus' marked a move to a more guitar-oriented sound. Bands such as Nine Inch Nails paid homage. Gahan suffered drug-related problems in the 1990s, but varied outings such as *Ultra* (1997) and *Exciter* (2001) proved the band had plenty of life left.

Dexy's Midnight Runners
(Vocal/instrumental group, 1978–86)
The brainchild of Kevin Rowland, Dexy's bagged a UK No. 1 with the punky, singalong soul of 'Geno' (1980). The manifesto album *Searching For The Young Soul Rebels* (1980) backed it up. After internal disruptions, a Celtic element was added, and the stomping anthem 'Come On Eileen' from the 1982 album *Too-Rye-Ay* became a global No. 1. 'Jackie Wilson Said' charted in 1982, but a disappointing 1985 album, *Don't Stand Me Down* preceded Rowland's patchy solo career.

Dire Straits
(Vocal/instrumental group, 1977–95)
Led by guitarist Mark Knopfler with brother David (guitar), John Illsley (bass) and Pick Withers (drums), Dire Straits went from playing the London pub circuit to a US hit album. Knopfler's inventive, plectrum-free guitar playing, street-poet lyrics and fine pop rock tunesmithery combined to launch their huge career. Debut single, 'Sultans Of Swing' was a punchy, likeable helping of Dylanesque roots rock. *Communique* (1979) and *Love Over Gold* (1982), paved the way for the multiple-platinum *Brothers In Arms* (1985). 'Money For Nothing' from that selection satirized the very business they were in. Only one studio album, 1991's slightly disappointing *On Every Street* followed, and Knopfler

embarked on a solo career that included soundtrack composition. Dire Straits will be remembered as an intelligent but accessible band who could run the gamut from the borderline experimental (the intro to 'Private Investigations', 1982) to the chug-a-long pop rock of 'Walk Of Life' (1985).

Duran Duran
(Vocal/instrumental group, 1978–present)
The most glamorous of the new romantic bands, Birmingham's Duran Duran (named after the evil scientist in the movie *Barbarella*), looked very good in the ambitious videos that accompanied their many Top 10 hits. These included 'Girls On Film' (1981), 'Hungry Like A Wolf', 'Save A Prayer' and 'Rio' (all 1982), 'The Reflex' and 'Wild Boys' (1984): a mixture of sexually charged, up-tempo pop and beguiling ballads, which played perfectly to the hedonism of the decade. The albums combined these approaches to varying effect, with 1982's *Rio* (which broke the band in America in 1983), probably the best of the bunch. In 1985, Simon Le Bon (vocals), Nick Rhodes (keyboards) and Roger Taylor (drums) worked on side project Arcadia, while the Taylors, Andy (guitar) and John (bass), joined The Power Station. After these excursions some of the magic seemed to have gone, excepting 1993's *The Wedding Album*, which yielded the smash 'Ordinary World'.

Above
Their big-budget video productions and good looks made them famous, but Duran Duran ruled the charts through part of the 1980s with singles like 'Girls On Film' and 'Rio'.

Left
1985's *Brothers In Arms* made Dire Straits global superstars, and was also one of the very first albums to be released on CD.

see Bob Dylan pp 126   see The Ramones pp 250   see Bon Jovi pp 274   see U2 pp 284

Enya
(Vocals, b. 1961)
Born Eithne Patricia Brennan in County Donegal, into the Clannad musical dynasty, Enya trained as a classical pianist, and remains a major innovator in ambient music. Her first solo endeavour was a 1986 BBC soundtrack, *The Celts*. Her trademark luxuriant soundscapes and melodic mysticism are present and correct. These elements washed through her follow-up, *Watermark* (1988) – which produced the UK No. 1 'Orinoco Flow' – and all subsequent albums, including US No. 2 *A Day Without Rain* (2000).

Below
One of the most enigmatic electro-pop groups of the 1980s, Dave Stewart's songwriting and production, coupled with Annie Lennox's image, voice and charisma allowed Eurythmics to become one of the most enduring duos of the 1980s.

Eurythmics
(Vocal/instrumental group, 1980–90, 1999–2000)
Dave Stewart (keyboards, guitars) and Annie Lennox (vocals) were Eurythmics. In 1983, the title track of *Sweet Dreams (Are Made Of This)* went to No. 1 in America. The synth-powered pop noir of 'Who's That Girl' was followed by the joyous, tropical-tinged 'Right By Your Side', proving their adaptability and intelligence. (Lennox's versatile, soulful voice is almost unparalleled in modern pop.) Another 1983 album, *Touch*, yielded the yearning 'Here Comes The Rain Again'. On *Be Yourself Tonight* (1985) their

Right
Alongside the likes of Journey, Foreigner had a 1970s pedigree that, in the 1980s, saw them enjoy stadium-filling AOR success with MTV-dominating hits such as 'I Want To Know What Love Is'.

bluesier side emerged, with hit singles such as 'Would I Lie To You?' and the wonderful 'Sisters Are Doin' It For Themselves' with Aretha Franklin. The album's beautiful 'There Must Be An Angel' became their only UK No. 1. Their truly great albums behind them, they still released great singles in 'Missionary Man' (1986) and 'I Need A Man' (1988) before solo careers beckoned.

Everything But The Girl
(Vocal/instrumental group, 1982–present)
Ben Watt (guitar) and Tracey Thorn (vocals, bass) travelled a fascinating road, from the jazz-inflected indie of their self-titled debut in 1984 to the trip-hop and drum'n'bass of *Walking Wounded* in 1996. This crossover was catalyzed by Thorn's guest appearance on Massive Attack's *Protection* in 1994, and DJ Todd Terry's remix of 'Missing', from the mainly acoustic *Amplified Heart* (1994), which hit No. 2 in the US. The common denominator in both styles is Tracey's pure, wistful voice.

Foreigner
(Vocal/instrumental group, 1976–present)
These AOR giants established themselves in 1977 with their eponymous debut album and single 'Feels Like The First Time', which both reached No. 4 in the US.

📻 *see* Introduction pp 268   📻   *see* Sources & Sounds pp 270   📻   *see* Key Artists pp 274

The band were founded by Englishman Mick Jones (guitar) with Lou Gramm's dramatic tenor vocals to the fore. The original line-up was completed by Ian McDonald (guitar, keyboards), Al Greenwood (keyboards, replaced by Rick Wills, 1979), Ed Gagliardi (bass) and Dennis Elliott (drums). Further hits such as 'Cold As Ice' and 'Double Vision' piled up in America, then 1981's 4 attained the UK Top 5. Their monster smash, the mother of all power ballads 'I Want To Know What Love Is' arrived in 1984. But Gramm was getting restless; he cut a solo album and then left officially. Johnny Edwards filled his shoes, but it was clear that the band's days as the US's top melodic rock outfit were over, even when Gramm returned in the mid-1990s.

Frankie Goes To Hollywood

(Vocal/instrumental group, 1980–87)

Fronted by the charismatic Holly Johnson, FGTH – Paul Rutherford (vocals), Peter Gill (drums), Mark O'Toole (bass) and Brian Nash (guitar) – hit Britain with three consecutive No. 1s: the exciting, synthesized funk pop of 1983's 'Relax' (banned by the BBC) and 'Two Tribes' – both precursors of house music – and the huge ballad 'The Power Of Love', all inventively produced by Trevor Horn. The title track of *Welcome To The Pleasure Dome* (1984) only reached No. 2. After a second album, named after their hometown, *Liverpool* (1986), Johnson went solo.

Peter Gabriel

(Singer/songwriter, b. 1950)

Gabriel left Genesis in 1975. His first solo album produced the intriguing hit 'Solsbury Hill' telling of that exit. In 1980, the avant-pop of 'Games Without Frontiers' began a run of accessible art rock albums and singles including the political 'Biko', 1982's *Peter Gabriel* (*Security* in the US), and 1986's triumphant world-music influenced *So* and its mega-hit 'Sledgehammer'. Gabriel now spends much of his time on his influential world-music label, Real World.

The Go-Betweens

(Vocal/instrumental group, 1978–89, 2000–6)

One of Australia's greatest and most underrated bands. Built round the complementary songwriting skills of Robert Forster and Grant McLennan (with Lindy Morrison, drums and Robert Vickers, bass), the band's thoughtful but powerful indie rock obviously owes a certain debt to Dylan, but with a punky feel; best showcased on 1983's *Before Hollywood* and 1986's *Liberty Belle And The Black Diamond Express*. After solo careers, their twenty-first century reunion was cut short by Grant McLennan's untimely death.

Below
1984 was Frankie's year, as the group enjoyed brief chart dominance helped by their controversial videos.

see Bob Dylan pp 126   see Aretha Franklin pp 156   see Genesis pp 216   see Massive Attack pp 356

Grandmaster Flash

(DJ/turntablist, b. 1958)

Born Joseph Saddler in Barbados, Flash was the inventor of turntablism – the use of a DJ's equipment as a musical instrument. He started out in the Bronx in the early 1970s becoming the first DJ to manipulate records by hand, cutting and mixing songs into each other. Blondie's 'Rapture' opines 'Flash is fast, Flash is cool'; Flash returned the favour in 1981's ground-breaking 'The Adventures Of Grandmaster Flash On The Wheels Of Steel', which sampled 'Rapture' as well as Chic and Queen. 'The Message' was the track that broke Flash and The Furious Five, the team of rappers he had assembled in the late 1970s: Melle Mel (Melvin Glover), Cowboy (Keith Wiggins), Raheim (Guy Williams), Mr Ness (Eddie Morris) and Kid Creole (Nathaniel Glover). 'White Lines (Don't Don't Do It)' credited to Flash and Mel, followed in 1983. The two fell out and continued solo careers, reuniting for 1988's *On The Strength*.

Guns N'Roses

(Vocal/instrumental group, 1985–present)

Axl Rose (b. William Bailey, vocals) and Izzy Stradlin (b. Jeffrey Isbell, guitar) were joined by Slash (b. Saul Hudson, guitar), Duff McKagan (bass) and Steve Adler (drums) to form a band that gave the heavy rock scene a mighty shaking. Signed to Geffen – after the 1986 EP *Live ?1*@ Like A Suicide* had attracted industry interest – their debut album *Appetite For Destruction* (1987) combined the attack of AC/DC with a punk aesthetic and powerful lyrics about the underbelly of LA. It went to the US No. 1 spot, as did 'Sweet Child O' Mine'. The next few years saw much debauchery; the departure of Adler; the US Top 5 ballad 'Patience'; and the releases of the massive-selling *Use Your Illusion I* and *II* (1991). Stradlin also jumped ship; as, in 1995, did Slash, to form Slash's Snakepit and then Velvet Revolver. Rose keeps the name of the band alive.

The Happy Mondays

(Vocal/instrumental group, 1985–92)

Led by vocalist Shaun Ryder, the band were at the forefront of the 'Madchester' scene. They appropriated licks from psychedelia, soul and hip-hop to come up with a danceable brand of rock that reached its apotheosis on 1990's *Pills 'n' Thrills And Bellyaches*, which included UK Top 5s 'Step On' and 'Kinky Afro'. The chaotic, drug-addled nature of the band meant the hits diminished, and when the Factory label subsided, Ryder moved on to form Black Grape.

Emmylou Harris

(Singer/songwriter, b. 1947)

Possessing the voice of an angel, Harris is one of the most adventurous country artists of the past four decades. Born in Birmingham, Alabama, she released a folk album in 1969; but it was her duets with Gram Parsons in the early 1970s that set her on the road.

🎵 *see Introduction pp 268* 🎵 *see Sources & Sounds pp 270* 🎵 *see Key Artists pp 274*

Fine solo sets with Parsons' backing musicians, including the legendary James Burton (guitar) and Glen D. Hardin (piano) followed.

In 1977 *Luxury Liner* became her best-selling album, and she worked with Dylan, Little Feat and The Band. Estimable albums ensued in the 1980s, more in the straight country vein including the concept album *The Ballad Of Sally Rose* (1985) and *Trio* (1987) with Linda Ronstadt and Dolly Parton. The 1990s saw a reappraisal of her direction. With producer Daniel Lanois and Steve Earle guesting, she delivered the atmospheric, rockier *Wrecking Ball* (1995), and followed it in 2000 with the equally impressive *Red Dirt Girl*.

The Housemartins
(Vocal/instrumental group, 1983–88)
Formed in Hull by Paul Heaton (vocals), Stan Cullimore (guitar, vocals), Ted Key (bass) and Hugh Whitaker (drums), the band were the epitome of unassuming British indie pop. Their up-tempo, melodic songs belied some abrasive, politically charged lyrics on the likes of 'Sheep' and their first big hit 'Happy Hour', from 1986's all-conquering debut *London 0 Hull 4*. They scored a UK No. 1 with the gospelly 'Caravan Of Love'. Heaton went on to form The Beautiful South, while latter-day bassist Norman Cook became Fatboy Slim.

Whitney Houston
(Vocals, b. 1963)
Houston has good genes; her mother is soul singer Cissy Houston and her cousin, Dionne Warwick. After working as a model and actress she plunged into her destined career. Her debut album, *Whitney* rose to No. 1 in 1985, with the ballad 'Saving All My Love For You', the first of many chart-topping singles. These included disco-floorfiller 'I Wanna Dance With Somebody', 'Didn't We Almost Have It All' (both 1987) and 'One Moment In Time' (1988). She actually broke The Beatles' record run of seven consecutive US No. 1s. More records fell with the Dolly Parton-penned 'I Will Always Love You' (1992) from the soundtrack to *The Bodyguard*. Her third album *I'm Your Baby Tonight* (1990) was her last until 1998's *My Love Is Your Love*, which featured Lauryn Hill from The Fugees and rapper Missy Elliott. One of R&B's greatest voices, she has been dogged by rumours of drug abuse and her strife-filled marriage to Bobby Brown.

see Blondie pp 256   *see* The Beautiful South pp 341   *see* Fatboy Slim pp 349   *see* The Fugees pp 349

Human League
(Vocal/instrumental group, 1977–present)
The original line-up of this Sheffield band produced the Top 20 UK album *Travelogue* (1980). Martyn Ware and Ian Craig-Marsh then left, later forming Heaven 17. Singer Phil Oakley enlisted Joanne Catherall and Susanne Sulley (vocals) and Jo Callis, ex-Rezillos (guitar). Adrian Wright (synthesizers, visuals) and Ian Burden (bass, synthesizers) completed the personnel who made *Dare* in 1981. This superb album combined the arty, Krautrock beginnings of the band with an irresistible pop feel. The group had already charted big with 'The Sound Of The Crowd' and 'Love Action', but *Dare* unleashed the transatlantic No. 1 'Don't You Want Me'. *Hysteria* (1984) was a disappointment but the group delivered another US chart-topper with 'Human' from *Crash* (1986), made with hip American producers Jimmy Jam and Terry Lewis. Further albums and a good mid-1990s revival did not quite live up to a heyday that had produced synth-pop perfection.

Right

Promising late 1970s experimental new wavers, Human League became a hugely successful synth-pop group when two of its founding experimentalists left, and Phil Oakey replaced them with a more radio-friendly female duo.

Below

Merging rock and dance influences, Australian group INXS became one of the late 1980s' biggest success stories with their sixth album, 1987's Kick.

Hüsker Dü
(Vocal/instrumental group, 1978–87)
Bob Mould (vocals, guitar), Grant Hart (drums, vocals) and Greg Norton (bass) were forefathers of emo, and an immensely important bridge between hardcore and alternative rock. The Minneapolis trio are cited by the likes of The Pixies and Nirvana as a massive influence. Their third album *Zen Arcade* (1984) is an exemplary collection of punk pop. They made a dignified transition to a major label with *Candy Apple Grey* (1986). After the band's demise, Mould formed Sugar and Hart, Nova Mob.

INXS
(Vocal/instrumental group, 1977–present)
Michael Hutchence (vocals), Tim Farriss (guitar), Andrew Farriss (keyboards, guitar), Garry Gary Beers (bass), Kirk Pengilly (guitar, saxophone, vocals) and John Farriss (drums) paid their dues on the Australian pub circuit. Taking elements of The Stones, Doors and funk rock, the band broke into the American market with *Shabooh Shoobah* (1982). 1985's *Listen Like Thieves* consolidated their position, while *Kick* (1987) and the excitingly sleazy 'I Need You Tonight' – No. 1 in America and No. 2 in the UK – deservedly confirmed them as global superstars. 1990's 'Suicide Blonde' from their highest charting album *X*, had a prophetic ring. Hutchence, a genuine rock god, was dating petite blonde Kylie Minogue; he later partnered peroxide blonde Paula Yates, and his death in 1997 came by his own hand. The band had been slightly on the wane since 1993's *Full Moon, Dirty Hearts*. A posthumous solo album was released. Hutchence has since been replaced with a *Pop Idol*-style talent-contest winner.

see Introduction pp 268 *see* Sources & Sounds pp 270 *see* Key Artists pp 274

Iron Maiden

(Vocal/instrumental group, 1976–present)

Original lead vocalist Paul Di'Anno led this East London heavy metal outfit to No. 4 on the UK chart in 1980 with their self-titled debut. New singer Bruce Dickinson went three places better with 1982's *The Number Of The Beast*. The band soon became Britain's top metal group, with their hard rocking, if slightly tongue-in-cheek, approach. Steve Harris (bass, vocals), Dave Murray (guitar), Adrian Smith (guitar) and Nicko McBrain (drums) are the most enduring members, though both Dickinson and Smith left and returned. Between 1985 and 1995 the band's singles and albums were rarely out of the Top 10 in the UK, or Top 20 in the US. Particular highlights include the 1988 concept album *Seventh Son Of A Seventh Son*, and the bullet-spitting rock of 1990's *No Prayer For The Dying*, which spawned the band's only UK No. 1 single 'Bring Your Daughter To The Slaughter'.

Gregory Isaacs

(Vocals, b. 1951)

Born in Kingston, Jamaica, Isaacs is one of the top reggae artists of the last four decades. After a handful of records for smaller labels he started his own African Museum label with fellow singer Errol Dunkley. He also recorded for myriad other producers, and discs with Lee 'Scratch' Perry and Sly and Robbie began to make his reputation. He signed to Virgin's Front Line label and released *Cool Ruler* in 1978, the title becoming his most common nickname. His unhurried, sweet-toned brand of lover's rock found favour with the public and 1982's *Night Nurse* was a big hit, as was the title track. The mid-1980s proved difficult, but after drug and legal problems, he returned with 1988's 'Rumours', a hi-tech precursor to ragga. In 1989 he teamed up with Dennis Brown, a reggae star of similar stature, for *No Contest*. Isaacs continues to record.

Janet Jackson

(Vocals, b. 1966)

Jackson's music career started slowly, though she performed with the family firm aged seven. The youngest of The Jacksons of Michael etc. fame, she was also a child actor but it was her third collection *Control* (1986), which gained her musical recognition. Produced by ace production duo Jimmy Jam and Terry Lewis – as all her albums have been – it offered hits such as the feisty 'What Have You Done For Me Lately'. Follow-up *Rhythm Nation 1814* (1989) was surprisingly political, and the video for the hit title track proved that Michael was not the family's only dancer. 'Miss You Much' was another chartbuster from the set. On *Velvet Rope* (1997) and *All For You* (2001) Janet exploited her sexuality, as on raunchy No. 1 'All For You' and the most famous moment of her career, her 'wardrobe malfunction' at Super Bowl XXXVIII, 2004.

Above

One of the most enduring and endearing bands to emerge from the 1970s NWOBHM, Iron Maiden's career has been typified by change, and one of rock's greatest vocalists (and fencers), Bruce Dickinson.

see The Doors pp 140   see The Rezillos pp 261   see The Pixies pp 310   see Nirvana pp 334

Joe Jackson
(Vocals, b. 1954)

Sharp-suited keyboardist and singer Jackson, from Portsmouth, rode the new wave with quirky love songs such as 'Is She Really Going Out With Him', and a varied US Top 20 album *Look Sharp* (1979). He then reverted to his musical background in jazz. With 1981's *Joe Jackson's Jumpin' Jive* he updated big band swing. More eclectic albums, *Night And Day* (1982) and *Body And Soul* (1984) and a Top 10 smash 'Steppin' Out' followed from this always-interesting songsmith.

Japan
(Vocal/instrumental group, 1974–82, 1991)

This South-East London band led by singer David Sylvian (real name Batt) traced an odd career trajectory.

Starting out playing guitar-based glam, they tried to fit in with punk, but found their forte in the new romantic era. Mick Karn (bass, saxophone), Rob Dean (guitar), Richard Barbieri (synthesizers), and Steve Jansen (b. Stephen Batt, drums) completed the personnel who finally made inroads with their third album *Quiet Life* (1980). This relied on the band's conversion to intricate, intelligent synth-based pop, and after *Gentlemen Take Polaroids* in late 1980, Dean left. Their next album *Tin Drum* (1981) seemed to point towards greatness. It reached No. 12 in the UK and produced one of the most captivating Top 5 singles of the time, the ethereal 'Ghosts'. Internal tensions, however, precluded any further releases. Sylvian then pursued a successful solo career. Strangely, the band reconvened under the name Rain Tree Crow for one final album in 1991.

Below

Heavily style-conscious, and with a mix of influences including glam, ambience, funk and world music, Japan were one of the decade's most successful and critically acclaimed synth-led art rockers.

🎵 *see* Introduction pp 268   🎵 *see* Sources & Sounds pp 270   🎵 *see* Key Artists pp 274

Jean-Michel Jarre

(Composer, b. 1948)

Frenchman Jarre is best known for his 1977 hit 'Oxygene' taken from the album of the same name, which reached No. 2 in the UK. He was one of the first rock musicians to employ synthesizers. A series of instrumental albums in the 1970s and 1980s repeated the pattern, including *Equinoxe* (1978), *Magnetic Fields* (1981) and the 1982 *Concerts In China* live album. His gigs, such as his 1989 show in London's Docklands, are huge *son et lumiere* spectacles.

The Jesus and Mary Chain

(Vocal/instrumental group, 1983–98)

This irascible, much-lauded Scottish crew featured the Reid brothers, William and Jim (both vocals, guitar) and, for a while, Bobby Gillespie of Primal Scream (drums). They took The Velvet Underground's art rock and overlaid surprisingly poppy melodies. Their early gigs turned into riots, but 1985's *Psychocandy* was a very good debut album that never quite matched. They had several Top 20 UK singles including the classic 'Some Candy Talking'. Ultimately, the siblings launched interesting solo ventures.

Billy Joel

(Singer/songwriter, b. 1949)

New Yorker William Martin Joel released his first solo album in 1972, and broke the US Top 30 with his second set, *Piano Man*, in 1975. The quality of his classic pop rock songwriting and equal skill with a ballad was obvious, and 'Just The Way You Are' became his first major hit in 1977. 1980's chart-topping *Glass Houses* also furnished his first No. 1, the infectious 'It's Still Rock'n'Roll To Me'. The apex of his career came with 1983's *Innocent Man*, which generated three US Top 10 singles – the title track, the ubiquitous 'Uptown Girl' and 'Tell Her About It'. Joel's output began to slow in the latter half of the decade, though 1989 produced the splendid list-song 'We Didn't Start The Fire'. Joel will be remembered for his engaging stage shows and a large portfolio of some the best songs of the 1970s and 1980s.

Judas Priest

(Vocal/instrumental group, 1969–present)

This Birmingham heavy metal outfit, led by vocalist Rob Halford, first charted with *Sin After Sin* in 1977. *British Steel* (1980) consolidated their position as one of the leading bands in the New Wave of British Heavy Metal. Their lyrics littered with Satanic imagery, the band were unsuccessfully sued in 1985 by parents of two of the band's fans who committed suicide. Storming albums such as *Screaming For Vengeance* (1982) were an acknowledged influence on Metallica and others.

Below left

Despite worldwide success with overly slick pop, Joel remains one of the most enduring and respected singer/songwriters to rise to prominence in the 1980s.

Below

Judas Priest are best known for their twin lead guitar sound and complex duets of ever-present guitarists K.K. Downing and Glenn Tipton (right).

see Mike Oldfield pp 220   see Elton John pp 232   see Duran Duran pp 295   see Metallica pp 332

Despite becoming more a melodic indie group in the 1990s, the 1980s saw The Lemonheads enter the world as a hardcore post-punk trio closer to The Replacements.

post-punk bands. They are now considered forefathers of American nu-punk. Their compulsive, tribal blasts on debut *Killing Joke* (1980) and *Revelations* (1982) created a legion of rabid fans and a handful of hit singles, including 1985's 'Love Like Blood'. The band still crop up with strong albums. Youth is also an in-demand producer and Coleman a modern classical composer.

The Lemonheads
(Vocal/instrumental group, 1983–96, 2005–present)
Evan Dando (vocals, guitar, drums) and Ben Deily (guitar, drums) were the main movers behind the indie rock of Boston's Lemonheads. *Hate Your Friends* and *Creator* (both 1988) and *Lick* (1989) got them a deal with Atlantic. An acrimonious split with Deily eventually brought Dando's girlfriend, Juliana Hatfield, into the fold for the melodic grunge and Americana of *It's A Shame About Ray* (1992). A version of Simon and Garfunkel's 'Mrs Robinson' saw British chart action, though the US – apart from the indie and college crowd – remained fairly indifferent to the handsome Mr Dando. 1993's *Come On Feel The Lemonheads* was a UK Top 5 entry, but did not even make the American Top 50. Dando's drug problems mounted and it was not until 1996 that the meandering, melancholic beauty of *Car Button Cloth* emerged. Nevertheless, Dando is a major figure on the alternative scene and a talented songwriter, though his solo career has not been prolific. The Lemonheads reformed in 2005.

Level 42
(Vocal/instrumental group, 1980–95)
Driven by Mark King's virtuoso funk-style bass playing, Mark Lindup (keyboards), Boon Gould (guitar) and Phil Gould (drums) comprised the outfit that started as a purely instrumental concern. When King's earnest vocals were added, their eponymous debut album went UK Top 20 in 1981. It was not until 1984, however, that their decade-long string of soul pop hits began with 'The Sun Goes Down (Living It Up)'. 'Something About You' became their first big US hit, bringing credibility to British soul music.

Killing Joke
(Vocal/instrumental group, 1979–present)
Jeremy 'Jaz' Coleman (vocals), Geordie Walker (guitar, synthesizers), Youth (b. Martin Glover, bass, vocals) and Paul Ferguson (drums) formed one of the most alluring

Huey Lewis and The News
(Vocal/instrumental group, 1979–present)
Huey Lewis (b. Hugh Cregg III, vocals, guitar) and

🎙 *see* Introduction pp 268   🎙 *see* Sources & Sounds pp 270   🎙 *see* Key Artists pp 274

Sean Hopper (vocals, guitar) were refugees from country rock band Clover. They found global success with the pop-inflected blue-collar rock of their next incarnation. Their third album *Sports* (1983) became an American No. 1, and bore three Top 10 US tracks including 'Heart And Soul'. 'The Power Of Love' established the band in the UK, and 1986 outing *Fore!* also sold big. The 1980s succumbed to the honest charm of Lewis.

Living Colour
(Vocal/instrumental group, 1984–95)
Taking a leaf out of the books of Hendrix and Bad Brains, Living Colour – Vernon Reid (guitar), Corey Glover (vocals), Muzz Skillings (bass, replaced by Doug Wimbish) and William Calhoun (drums) – were a black rock band formed in New York. Three albums, *Vivid* (1988), *Time's Up* (1990) and *Stain* (1993), all charted well and they even entered the UK Top 20 singles chart with 'Love Rears Its Ugly Head'. Their politicized rock/funk was a welcome addition to the era.

Kirsty MacColl
(Vocals, 1959–2000)
The daughter of folk singer Ewan MacColl, her appealing, wry voice brought her hits with 'There's A Guy Works Down The Chip Shop Swears He's Elvis' (1981), 'A New England' (1985) and 'Days' (1989). She duetted on The Pogues' 1987 Christmas smash 'Fairytale Of New York'. She released warm, witty albums in *Electric Landlady* (1991) and *Tropical Brainstorm* (2000), and had developed an interest in Latin music when she was tragically killed in a holiday accident.

Madness
(Vocal/instrumental group, 1979–present)
This London band – Graham 'Suggs' McPherson and Chas Smash (both vocals), Dan Woodgate (drums), Mark Bedford (bass), Mike Barson (keyboards), Chris Foreman (guitar) and Lee Thompson (saxophone) only managed one US hit, 1983's 'Our House', but inspired the American ska-punkers of the 1990s. 1979's *One Step Beyond* was a cornerstone of the ska revival, but Madness soon developed a broader pop-oriented sensibility. An influence on the likes of Blur and Supergrass, their use of videos was trailblazing.

Highlights include 'Embarrassment' (1979), 'House Of Fun' (1982) and 'The Sun And The Rain' (1983).

Marillion
(Vocal/instrumental group, 1978–present)
Fish (b. Derek Dick) was the band's charismatic vocalist until 1988, writing the lyrics to their complicated but engaging neo-prog rock: *Script For A Jester's Tear* (1983) and *Fugazi* (1984). They also landed UK hits with 'Kayleigh', 'Lavender' and 'Incommunicado'. Since Steve Hogarth took over they have kept the unfashionable banner of prog flying with aplomb on *Brave* (1994) and *Anoraknophobia* (2001), and have pioneered the use of the internet as a sales tool.

Below
Named after J.R.R. Tolkien's *Silmarillon*, Marillion were perhaps the biggest of the new wave of prog rock artists in the 1980s, though lead singer Fish would leave for a solo career in 1987.

see Bad Brains pp 287 🎸 see The Pogues pp 311 🎸 see Blur pp 343 🎸 see Supergrass pp 368

Meat Loaf

(Vocals, b. 1947)

Born Marvin Lee Aday in Dallas, Texas, Meat Loaf had a musical theatre (he starred in *The Rocky Horror Picture Show*) as well as a rock'n'roll background. This was apparent on the camp but hugely appealing excess of breakthrough album *Bat Out Of Hell* in 1977, written by Jim Steinman and produced by Todd Rundgren. The live shows supporting the album have attained mythic status; with Meat Loaf's good-naturedly melodramatic delivery and massive stature making him an unlikely rock icon. Its successor, *Dead Ringer* (1981), did even better in the UK, topping the charts, with 'Dead Ringer For Love' – featuring Cher as co-vocalist – also a hit. Meat Loaf released several pot-boiling collections before reuniting with Steinman for *Bat Out Of Hell II: Back Into Hell* (1993), which was a transatlantic No. 1, as was its main single 'I'd Do Anything For Love (But I Won't Do That)'.

Megadeth

(Vocal/instrumental group, 1983–present)

Ex-Metallica guitarist Dave Mustaine hardened and sped up his erstwhile band's already ferocious thrash metal. His pessimistic, politicized lyrics drive the likes of *Peace Sells … But Who's Buying?* (1986), and his best album so far *Rust In Peace* (1990) matching his former employers' impact in the process. After an attempt to go more mainstream the band – essentially Mustaine with hired hands – returned to form with *The System Has Failed* (2004), featuring original guitarist Chris Poland.

John (Cougar) Mellencamp

(Vocals, b. 1951)

Indiana-born Mellencamp endured several years of hard apprenticeship and some unsuccessful recordings for MCA before he was rechristened John Cougar by

see Introduction pp 268   *see* Sources & Sounds pp 270   *see* Key Artists pp 274

Bowie's manager Tony DeFries. His 1979 debut album charted in the US, and a handful of minor hits followed. In 1982, *American Fool* made him a big star in the States, and delivered a No. 1 in 'Jack And Diane'. His style of mildly gritty Stones-influenced pop rock was also showcased on *Uh-Huh* (1984), the first collection to bear his real surname. 1985 saw an interesting reinvention, drawing on Springsteen's stories of struggling blue-collar Americans. The sparser roots rock of *Scarecrow* (1985) and *Lonesome Jubilee* (1987) still achieved huge sales, and the latter gave Mellencamp his first British Top 40 entry. After a heart attack he collaborated with dance producer Junior Vasquez on the funkier *Mr Happy Go Lucky* (1996), but still retained the more traditional elements that had brought him success.

George Michael
(Singer/songwriter, b. 1963)
Born Giorgios Panayiotou of North London, Greek-Cypriot heritage, Michael served a very public initiation with teeny-boppers Wham! In the mid-1980s, he released a pair of solo singles 'Careless Whisper' and 'A Different Corner', dissolving Wham! in 1986. He re-emerged in 1987 with the pristine adult pop of *Faith*, which hooked the American market. A series of singles, including 'Father Figure', 'One More Try' and 'Monkey', performed better in the US than the UK. 1990's *Listen Without Prejudice Vol 1* was an altogether darker affair, which heralded a battle with record label Sony. The dispute was resolved in 1995, clearing the way for the introspective *Older* (1986), which nevertheless furnished several hit singles, including 'Fastlove' and 'Jesus To A Child'. Michael is a superb songwriter, inveterate duetter (Aretha Franklin, Mary J. Blige, and a No. 1 with Elton John), and a genuine star. Yet 2004's *Patience* was only his fourth studio album.

Midnight Oil
(Vocal/instrumental group, 1978–present)
Fronted by the striking, bald, six and a half footer Peter Garrett, this 1960s-influenced, politically committed Australian band still have plenty to say. They played hundreds of gigs before making their US and UK album debut with *10,9,8,7,6,5,4,3,2,1* in 1983. It was not until 'Beds Are Burning' from the superb *Diesel And Dust* (1988) made the world aware of the Aborigines'

plight, that they became internationally renowned. *Blue Sky Mining* (1990) was another palatable helping of tuneful, intelligent rock.

The Mission
(Vocal/instrumental group, 1985–96)
Ex-Sister of Mercy Wayne Hussey (guitar, vocals) employed Simon Hinkler (guitar), Craig Adams (bass) and Mick Brown (drums) to form another charismatic goth rock band renowned for their dramatic live shows. The powerful *God's Own Medicine* emerged in 1986 and 'Wasteland' went No. 11 in the UK charts. The John Paul Jones-produced *Children* (1988) reached No. 2. Their best set, *Carved In Sand* (1990), was the last with their original personnel and their last Top 20.

Above
One half of Wham!, George Michael's songwriting and lead singer position would lead him to become bigger than the duo partnership with Andrew Ridgeley, and in 1987 he would find solo success with the *Faith* LP.

see The Rolling Stones pp 96   see David Bowie pp 196   see Bruce Springsteen pp 222   see Elton John pp 232

308

Motley Crüe
(Vocal/instrumental group, 1980–present)
Vince Neil (vocals), Mick Mars (guitar), Nikki Sixx (bass) and Tommy Lee (drums) became the world's most notorious heavy metal band, as much for their off-record excesses as for their music. They released their crude but effective glam metal debut *Too Fast For Love* in 1981. Over the years, they became technically more adept, and the production got slicker, but their lyrical subject matter (sex and drugs and rock'n'roll) remained the same. *Shout At The Devil* (1983) became

their American Top 20 debut. *Theatre Of Pain* (1985) and *Girls Girls Girls* (1987) kept the ball rolling and *Dr Feelgood* (1989) registered their first No. 1 (No. 4 in the UK). Guns N'Roses, who had obviously been influenced by The Crüe, had emerged by this time, and a feud erupted between the two bands. Neil left in 1992, returning in 1996 for more ever so slightly toned-down mayhem.

Below

The most iconic of the hair metal bands, Motley Crüe's sex, drugs and rock'n'roll lifestyle ultimately overshadowed any musical merit, leaving them to become rock'n'roll tabloid heroes.

Motörhead
(Vocal/instrumental group, 1975–present)
The seemingly indestructible Lemmy Kilmister (vocals, bass) was a former member of Hawkwind, and a vicar's son. Motörhead are named after a Hawkwind song he penned. The line-up settled in the late 1970s with 'Fast' Eddie Clarke (guitar) and Phil 'Filthy Animal' Taylor (drums). The title track of 1980's *Ace Of Spades* was a UK hit, and became the blueprint for the band's sound for the next quarter of a century: ear-shatteringly loud guitar, chordal bass and Kilmister's gruff vocals shouted over the top. Their gigs are legendary, often featuring a life-size replica of a German bomber. The live experience was captured on a UK No. 1 from 1981 *No Sleep 'Til Hammersmith* (book-ended in 1988 by *No Sleep At All*). Personnel changes in bass and drum departments did not much alter their sound, which was highly influential on the thrash and nu-metal scenes.

My Bloody Valentine
(Vocal/instrumental group, 1984–present)
MBV began as a thrashy 1960s garage band and ended up redefining the sound of rock guitar on the swirling, distorting but lambently beautiful *Loveless* (1991). *Isn't Anything* from 1988, features slightly more recognizable tunes and song forms. Vocalist/guitarist Bilinda Butcher

see Introduction pp 268   *see* Sources & Sounds pp 270   *see* Key Artists pp 274

contributed lyrics and (guitarist/vocalist) Kevin Shields the revolutionary sounds. Deb Googe (bass) and Colm O'Ciosoig (drums) contributed the rhythm. The next album has been promised for many years. Shields also works with Primal Scream.

New Model Army
(Vocal/instrumental group, 1980–present)
Alongside The Levellers and Chumbawumba, this long-lived punk folk band from Bradford have kept alive the tradition of rock protest songs married to listenable music. Justin 'Slade The Leveller' Sullivan (vocals, guitar), Stuart Morrow (bass, guitar) and Robb Heaton (drums) first launched their sonic assault on Margaret Thatcher with 1984's *Vengeance*. An expedient alliance with EMI started a steady flow of Top 50 albums from *No Rest For The Wicked* (1985) to *The Love Of Hopeless Causes* (1993).

New Order
(Vocal/instrumental group, 1980–present)
Formed by the remaining members of Joy Division after Ian Curtis's suicide. Bernard Sumner (guitar, vocals), Peter Hook (bass) and Stephen Morris (drums) with Gillian Gilbert (keyboards, synthesizers) added extra groove and technology to the angular post-punk beats of their former band, thus heavily influencing the 'Madchester' and dance music scenes of the late 1980s and 1990s. The darkly throbbing anthem 'Blue Monday' came from 1983's essential *Power, Corruption And Lies* album. The electro-dominated *Technique* went to No. 1 in 1989.

NWA
(Rap group, 1985–91)
Founders of gangsta rap, NWA stands for Niggaz With Attitude; their visceral debut *Straight Outta Compton* (1989) featured controversial tracks such as 'Fuck Tha Police', a reaction to the unprovoked beating the LA cops gave Rodney King. However, many tracks – despite their exciting delivery – were mindlessly violent and sexist, as on their 1991 No. 1 album *Efil4zaggin* (try it backwards). They imploded acrimoniously, Ice Cube, Eazy-E and Dr Dre going on to solo careers.

Above
One of the more endearing post-punkers, New Model Army were politically charged, anthemic rockers that could stand alongside Billy Bragg with their mix of anti-Thatcherism sloganeering and accessible introspection.

Left Middle
Motörhead's load'n'fast style made them one of the most ground-breaking metallists of the 1970s, solidifying all further success with 1980's *Ace Of Spades* LP and hit single of the same name.

see Joy Division pp 260   *see* Guns N'Roses pp 298   *see* The Happy Mondays pp 298   *see* Dr. Dre pp 348

Orchestral Manoeuvres In The Dark
(Vocal/instrumental group, 1978–96)
A Liverpudlian duo formed by a pair of Eno and
Kraftwerk fans, Andy McCluskey (bass, vocals) and

Paul Humphreys (keyboards). Their supporting cast
varied as they produced a series of fine electro pop
albums, including *Architecture And Morality* (1981)
and *Dazzle Ships* (1983), and a string of brooding hits
which married intelligence and innovation: 'Enola
Gay' (1980), 'Souvenir' and 'Joan Of Arc' (both 1981)
and 'Locomotion' (1985). McCluskey revived OMD as
a solo project in the early 1990s.

Tom Petty
(Singer/songwriter, b. 1952)
Petty, born in Gainsville, Florida, formed his long-time
backing band The Heartbreakers from Mike Campbell
(guitar), Benmont Tench (keyboards), Ron Blair (bass)
and Stan Lynch (drums). An eponymous album in
1977 was a hard-hitting brand of country rock, with
plenty of modern attack, rootsy authenticity and good
tunes. The UK was impressed, but it was not until
1979's *Damn The Torpedoes* that the US took a native
son (and another 'new Dylan') to its breast. Alongside
Springsteen, Petty helped revitalize the reputation of
intelligent blue-collar rock, while tapping into its
folkier heritage. They scored a couple of big US singles
in 'Refugee' (1979) and 'Don't Do Me Like That'
(1980). In 1988, Petty wound-up the band, working
with Dylan, Orbison and George Harrison in The
Travelling Wilburys. An excellent solo album *Full
Moon Fever* resulted in 1989, before The Heartbreakers
reformed; still one of America's most consistent bands
behind a consistently good songwriter.

The Pixies
(Vocal/instrumental group, 1986–92, 2004–present)
One of the most important alternative rock bands ever
came together in Boston with Charles Thompson IV,
who styled himself Black Francis (vocals, guitar), Joey
Santiago (guitar), Kim Deal (bass, vocals), and Dave
Lovering (drums). Lyrically, Thompson explored
religion, weird sex and sci-fi, singing with a
preternaturally forceful yelp. The words were fitted to
an eclectic array of styles. Punk, surf, pop, hardcore
and Spanish elements all collided on a succession of
superb albums: the raging *Surfer Rosa* (1988), 1989's
Doolittle (by far the poppiest), *Bossanova* (1990) and
Trompe Le Monde (1991). Their stop-start dynamics
were a strong influence on Nirvana. Their combination
of melody and abrasiveness, and Santiago's skewed
guitar heroics were also adopted by many indie rockers.
Ultimately, Deal wanted more of her songs used. Frank
Black, as he soon became in his solo career, refused.

 see Introduction pp 268 *see* Sources & Sounds pp 270 *see* Key Artists pp 274

She formed The Breeders. The Pixies reunited to play ecstatically received gigs in 2004.

The Pogues

(Vocal/instrumental group, 1982–present)
Formed in North London around gifted songwriter Shane MacGowan (vocals). Other long-term members include Spider Stacey (tin whistle, vocals), Jem Finer (banjo, guitar), Phil Chevron (guitar) and Andrew Ranken (drums). They breathed fresh, punky life into Irish music on excellent albums *Rum, Sodomy And The Lash* (1985) and *If I Should Fall From Grace With God* (1988), and big hit 'Fairytale Of New York' (duet with Kirsty MacColl). MacGowan's wild lifestyle led to his departure, though band and singer reunited sporadically.

Prefab Sprout

(Vocal/instrumental group, 1982–present)
Durham-born songwriter Paddy McAloon crafts credible, intelligent pop music, drawing on a treasury of past styles. Brother Martin (bass), Wendy Smith (vocals, guitar) and Neal Conti (drums) played on 1985's *Steve McQueen*, their breakthrough album. *From Langley Park To Memphis* (1988) made the Top 5, and 'The King Of Rock'n'Roll' went to the UK No. 7 spot. Paddy's obsession with Elvis and Americana in general, resurfaced on *Jordan: The Comeback* (1990) and *The Gunman And Other Stories* (2001).

The Pretenders

(Vocal/instrumental group, 1978–present)
Ohio-born Chrissie Hynde's tough, tuneful voice has established her as an iconic female rocker. Drawing on punk and 1960s pop (she had a daughter with The

Kinks' Ray Davies and had hits with two of his songs, 'Stop Your Sobbing' and 'I Go To Sleep'), The Pretenders produced an exhilarating, melodic hybrid with broad appeal. 'Brass In Pocket' was a 1979 UK No. 1, and a hit in 1980 in her native US, which had already sent the band's self-titled debut to the Top 10. Hynde and drummer Martin Chambers overcame the loss of original members James Honeyman-Scott (guitar, keyboards) and Pete Farndon (bass) to drugs in 1982 and 1983, and *Pretenders II* (1981) and *Learning To Crawl* (1984) also charted highly. In 1986, 'Don't Get Me Wrong' went Top 10. Further albums have been successful, if released at increasing intervals. Hynde spends much of her time campaigning for animals, her place in modern pop assured.

Left
With 1988's *Surfa Rosa*, The Pixes arguably became one of the most influential groups since The Beatles.

Below
Fusing punk with traditional Irish folk, The Pogues have become one of Ireland's most successful exports, and lead singer Shane MacGowan one of the country's most celebrated lyricists.

see The Kinks pp 94   see Kraftwerk pp 218   see Patti Smith pp 254   see Kirsty MacColl pp 305

Public Image Limited

(Vocal/instrumental group, 1978–92)

To the surprise of many, Johnny Rotten reinvented himself after The Sex Pistols as John Lydon. He enlisted Keith Levene (guitar, drums), Jah Wobble (b. John Wardle, bass) and a variety of other transient contributors. The punky thunder of 'Public Image' stormed the UK Top 10 and a good self-titled debut album followed. Their second collection, 1979's *Metal Box 1* (packaged in a metal box) was extraordinary: a beguiling mix of dub, Krautrock and Eastern-inflected weirdness and Lydon's inspired, spooky rants, it was released as *Second Edition* (1980) in the US, and amazingly made the UK Top 20. Two more masterpieces ensued before PIL's output got a little muddy: the powerful UK hit 'This Is Not A Love Song' in 1985 and 1986's 'Rise', with unlikely collaborators such as Steve Vai, Ravi Shankar and Ginger Baker. With PIL Lydon proved he was no one-trick pony but a major player and innovator.

The Replacements

(Vocal/instrumental group, 1980–91)

The talented Paul Westerberg (vocals, guitar) was the main songwriter of this highly influential alternative rock outfit. Brothers Bob and Tommy Stinson (guitar and bass) and Chris Mars (drums) completed this initially shambolic punk band. After three albums on local Minneapolis label Twin-Tone, Tommy Ramone produced *Tim* (1985). Westerberg's hooky garage rock songs pointed forward to punk's acceptance into the mainstream. Despite the excellent *Pleased To Meet Me* (1987), the band did not make it there themselves.

Lionel Richie

(Vocals, b. 1949)

Alabama-born Richie was in several R&B bands before he signed to Motown with The Commodores. He penned and sang most of their biggest hits like 'Easy', 'Three Times A Lady' and 'Still', all massive smashes during the 1970s. He branched out with Diana Ross on 1981's 'Endless Love'. He then went solo and his skill as a balladeer served him well. His first, self-titled album yielded a trio of hits, including the American chart-topper 'Truly'. But that was as nothing to 1983's *Can't Slow Down*, which poured forth five US Top 10s, including the Latin-flavoured dancefloor favourite 'All Night Long', and Richie's only UK No. 1, the tear-jerking ballad 'Hello'. In 1985, he won an Oscar for 'Say You, Say Me', but after 1986's *Dancing On The Ceiling* he released very little. Nevertheless, he will always be remembered for his timeless slowies.

Run DMC

(Rap group, 1982–2002)

Pioneers of hip-hop, Run was born Joseph Simmons; DMC was Darryl McDaniel; with Jam Master Jay (b. Jason Mizell) on the decks. Their big, simple beats were heard on the eponymous debut (1983) and *King Of Rock* (1985), and as part of the first and best rock-rap crossover 'Walk This Way' with Aerosmith. Run eventually translated his socially conscious raps into a Christian ministry. 'It's Like That' topped the UK chart in 1998, but their story ended in tragedy with the shooting of Jay in 2002.

Joe Satriani

(Guitar, b. 1956)

Satriani was an influential teacher – students include Steve Vai, Kirk Hammett of Metallica and Primus's Larry LaLonde – before becoming a recording artist in his late 20s. He is not simply a stunt-guitarist, even though some of his playing on his debut *Surfing With*

see Introduction pp 268   *see* Sources & Sounds pp 270   *see* Key Artists pp 274

They released six albums in four years, including 1980's *Wheels Of Steel* – the title track of which gave them their first of four UK Top 20 hits – and 1981's *Denim And Leather*. Their honest, hard-rocking style brought new life to a weary genre and, despite many personnel changes behind Byford, still does.

The Alien (1987) is jaw dropping. It reached the US Top 30 and inspired a generation of players. He mixes a plethora of styles from rock'n'roll workouts to lyrical ballads via jazz and funk odysseys. He added passable vocals to *Flying In A Blue Dream* (1989). 1992's *The Extremist* went to a surprising No. 13 in the UK, after nu-metal guitarists started to sing his praises. After a short spell with Deep Purple he released an entertaining live set with former pupil Vai and fellow axe-man Eric Johnson, entitled *G3 In Concert* (1997). Ever open-minded, he even experimented with electronica on *Engines Of Creation* (2001).

Saxon
(Vocal/instrumental group, 1978–present)
The older generation of British heavy metal was sounding tired when out of Yorkshire came Peter 'Biff' Byford (vocals), Paul Quinn and Graham Oliver (both guitar), Steve Dawson (bass) and Pete Gill (drums).

see Aerosmith pp 210   *see* Deep Purple pp 214   *see* Metallica pp 332   *see* Primus pp 363

Shakin' Stevens
(Vocals, b. 1948)

The former Michael Barratt worked the clubs for many years with his superb backing band The Sunsets, delivering old-fashioned rock'n'roll based on his convincing Elvis-isms. Success came late to the Welshman when he signed to Epic and delivered a seemingly endless stream of professionally reworked 1950s classics, including the No. 1s 'This Ole House' and 'Green Door' (1981), and 'Oh Julie' (1982). His run dried up, but he ended the decade its most successful UK singles artist.

Below
Starting off as post-punk art rockers, thanks to the likes of hit single 'Don't You (Forget About Me'), by 1985 Simple Minds had become a Live Aid-playing stadium pop group.

Simple Minds
(Vocal/instrumental group, 1978–present)

Formerly known as Johnny and The Self-Abusers, Glaswegians Jim Kerr (vocals), Charlie Burchill (guitar), Derek Forbes (bass), Mick McNeil (keyboards) and Brian McGee (drums) took on board the experimentations of Krautrock and Eno for their second album *Real To Real Cacophony* (1979). They gently sloughed off their weirder tendencies over their next two albums, before 1982's *New Gold Dream (81-82-83-84)* chimed with the era's love of melodic, but mildly arty synth-pop. The album went to No. 3 and housed their first hits 'Promised You A Miracle' and 'Glittering Prize'. It also gained them a foothold in America, which they exploited with 1984's *Sparkle In The Rain* and US chart-topper 'Don't You (Forget About Me)'. *Once Upon A Time* (1985) kept up the momentum, as they vied with U2 as the world's No. 1 stadium rock band; but by the early 1990s Jim Kerr's anthemic pop was beginning to date.

Slayer
(Vocal/instrumental group, 1981–present)

The most extreme of the major thrash metal bands, lyrically and sonically, Tom Araya (bass, vocals), Kerry King and Jeff Hanneman (both guitar) and Dave Lombardo (drums) rejoice in album titles such as *Show No Mercy* (1984) and 1987's breakthrough *Reign In Blood* replete with a song about Nazi butcher 'Dr' Mengele. 1994's US Top 10 *Divine Intervention* was a return to the high-decibel speedcore at which they excel, after a flirtation with slightly more mainstream metal.

Sly and Robbie
(Production team/rhythm section, 1975–present)

Sly Dunbar (drums) and Robbie Shakespeare (bass) both worked for various reggae artists, including Lee 'Scratch' Perry, before coming together at Kingston's Channel One Studio in the mid-1970s, where their innovative, but funky combination powered the new 'rockers' sound. They backed practically every Jamaican artist of note, from Peter Tosh to Gregory Isaacs, forming their own label Taxi. They toured with Black Uhuru and played sessions and/or produced for Grace Jones (on her 1981 *Nightclubbing* album), Bob Dylan, Ian Dury and Serge Gainsbourg! Dunbar in particular was interested in new technologies, adopting 'syndrums'

🔊 *see Introduction pp 268* 🔊 *see Sources & Sounds pp 270* 🔊 *see Key Artists pp 274*

early. In 1987 the pair had a UK Top 20 with 'Boops (Here To Go)', sampled by Robbie Williams in 2006, and in 1997 teamed up with Mick Hucknall for a hit version of 'Night Nurse'. They also played a large part in the dancehall and ragga movements of the late 1980s and 1990s, working with the likes of Chaka Demus and Pliers, and Shabba Ranks.

The Smiths

(Vocal/instrumental group, 1982–87)

Manchester's finest coalesced around the songwriting pair of former journalist Stephen Patrick Morrissey (vocals) and Johnny Marr (guitar). Andy Rourke (bass) and Mike Joyce (drums) completed a team who became the darlings of bed-sit melancholics everywhere, and exerted a huge influence on indie rock over the following decades. Their mesmerizing blend of 1960s beat music and new wave artiness was driven by Marr's ringing, inventive guitar, topped off by Morrissey's idiosyncratic wail and clever, often drily humorous lyrics. In 1984, 'What Difference Does It Make?' went Top 20 and their self-titled debut waltzed to No. 2. 1985's *Meat Is Murder* went one better, while *The Queen Is Dead* from the following year, broke America. The shimmering power of 'How Soon Is Now' represents one of the best singles of the decade. Tensions between Morrissey and Marr grew and a split in 1987 became inevitable. Both went on to strong solo careers.

Soft Cell

(Vocal/instrumental group, 1980–84)

Marc Almond (vocals) and Dave Ball (keyboards) created a charismatic art pop act, landing a huge hit with 'Tainted Love' (1981). Several other dark disco tracks followed: 'Say Hello, Wave Goodbye', 'Torch' and 'What!'. Their debut *Non-Stop Erotic Cabaret* (1981, 1982 in the US) explored the steamier side of life. Almond's solo career followed a varied route as a camp divo, while Ball expanded on his pioneering musical approach with dance acts such as The Grid.

Left

One of Jamaica's greatest production teams, Sly and Robbie have not only had a string of successes under their own name, but have also helped others inject a reggae sound into their work.

Below

One of Britain's most enduring bands, The Smiths typified life in Thatcher's Britain, with lead singer Morrissey's lyrics perfectly framed by the pop sensibilities and musical ambition of his bandmates, most notably, guitarist Johnny Marr.

Sonic Youth
(Vocal/instrumental group, 1981–present)
Starting life as avant-garde noise merchants, Thurston Moore (vocals, guitar), Kim Gordon (bass, vocals), Lee Ranaldo (guitar, vocals) and a variety of drummers, including Steve Shelley have been at the centre of New York's alternative music scene ever since, influencing indie rock immeasurably. Highlights include the striking art rock of 1987's *Sister*; the almost conventional *Goo* (1990); their Madonna covers side project, Ciccone Youth; and a typically genre-defying collaboration with Chuck D of Public Enemy.

Spandau Ballet
(Vocal/instrumental group, 1979–90)
Tony Hadley (vocals), Gary Kemp (guitar), Steve Norman (saxophone), Martin Kemp (bass) and John Keeble (drums) enjoyed success with their amalgam of late 1960s orchestral pop and 1980s technology. Firmly at the forefront of new romantics, their hits included 'Chant No 1 (Don't Need This Pressure On)', 'Gold' and 'True'. The latter brought them a US Top 5

breakthrough in 1983. Their star faded rapidly in the late 1980s, the Kemps finding further fame as actors.

Spear Of Destiny
(Vocal/instrumental group, 1980–present)
Born out of singer Kirk Brandon's previous project, Theatre of Hate, this outfit married post-punk beats with an epic rock vibe; regular accomplice Stan Stammers played bass. They developed a strong live reputation and toured constantly in support of albums such as *One Eyed Jacks* (1984) and *World Service* (1985). As various problems dogged the band, their sole Top 20 hit arrived in 1987 with 'Never Take Me Alive'. Brandon tours to this day.

The Specials
(Vocal/instrumental group, 1978–81)
As frontrunners of the ska revival, this superb Coventry band released the genre's finest single, 'Ghost Town' (1981), on their own 2Tone label. Terry Hall and Neville Staples (both vocals), Lynval Golding and Roddy Radiation (both guitar), Jerry Dammers

Below

One of the leading lights of new romanticism, Spandau Ballet scaled the charts with the likes of 'Gold' and 'True', while Martin Kemp would later find huge success as an actor in UK TV's *Eastenders*.

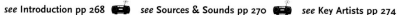 *see* Introduction pp 268   *see* Sources & Sounds pp 270   *see* Key Artists pp 274

(keyboards), Horace 'Gentleman' Panter (bass) and John Bradbury (drums) also had hits with 'Rat Race' and 'Do Nothing', and released two excellent albums. Hall, Staples and Golding became Fun Boy Three, and Dammers had a huge smash as The Special AKA with 'Free Nelson Mandela'.

Stock, Aitken and Waterman
(Musicians, producers, writers, 1984–91)
Mike Stock, Pete Waterman and Matt Aitken joined forces in 1984 to manufacture pop gold. Waterman had already produced hits for Nik Kershaw and Tracey Ullman. The team's first chart-topper was Dead or Alive's 'You Spin Me Round (Like A Record)'. They then updated classic girl-group pop with Bananarama, Mel and Kim (including the 1987 No. 1 'Respectable'), Pepsi and Shirlie, and Sinitta. 1987 also saw the soul stylings of Rick Astley joining the stable, with smash 'Never Gonna Give You Up'. They also scored under their own names

with 'Roadblock', and 'Mr Sleaze'. In 1988, they hooked up with Kylie Minogue ('I Should Be So Lucky') and Jason Donovan, leading to an *annus mirabilis* in 1989 when they logged 20 Top 20 hits from the Aussies, plus Sonia and Donna Summer. Mick Stock's departure in 1991 halted the conveyor belt. Waterman now enjoys even greater fame as a *Pop Idol* TV judge.

The Stray Cats
(Vocal/instrumental group, 1979–92)
This east coast American trio revitalized rockabilly with a fusillade of scorching singles and an incendiary live show centred on Brian Setzer's astonishing guitar playing. Setzer, with Lee Rocker (bass) and Slim Jim Phantom (drums) burst forth with 'Runaway Boys' (1980), 'Rock This Town' and the sleazy 'Stray Cat Strut'. Their eponymous 1981 debut and that year's bluesier *Gonna Ball* are must-haves. Setzer now plays with a full big band, while The Stray Cats occasionally reunite.

Above
Crafting slick, dance-pop tunes for almost every British 1980s pop artist, the production/writing trio Stock, Aitken and Waterman masterminded some of the most successful hits of the decade.

see Madonna pp 278   *see* Duran Duran pp 295   *see* Madness pp 305   *see* Public Enemy pp 363

The Style Council
(Vocal/instrumental group, 1983–90)
After The Jam, Paul Weller was seeking a smoother
sound; with Mick Talbot (keyboards), Steve White
(drums) and Dee C. Lee (vocals) he came up with the
modern soul of Top 5 UK hits 'Speak Like A Child',
'Long Hot Summer' and 'My Ever Changing Moods'.
Café Bleu (1984) was a fine showcase of his new
direction, and classics 'Shout It To The Top' and *Our
Favourite Shop* (1985) emerged before the band
stagnated, and Weller plotted anew.

The Sugarcubes
(Vocal/instrumental group, 1987–92)
Centred on the magnetic persona and ethereal vocals

of Björk Gudmunsdottir, this Icelandic crew captivated
the UK indie world with the avant-garde, alternative
pop of whooping debut single 'Birthday'. 1988's *Life's
Too Good*, a riveting debut – half commercial, half
crazy – reached the UK No.14, No. 54 in the US.
Einar Orn Benediktsson's mad rapped vocals and Thor
Jonson's fine guitar added to the unique sound. *Hit* was
a UK hit in 1991, before Björk's solo career soared.

Talk Talk
(Vocal/instrumental group, 1981–91)
Mark Hollis (vocals, keyboards, guitar), Paul Webb
(bass, vocals) and Lee Harris (drums) were initially
packaged as new romantics. They developed into a
well-respected group in the mould of Roxy Music with
It's My Life (1984) and *The Colour Of Spring* (1986);
venturing into jazz territory on *Spirit Of Eden* (1988)
and *Laughing Stock* (1991). They had hits on the way,
including 'Talk Talk' and 'It's My Life'. Their
significance is cited by the likes of Spiritualized.

Talking Heads
(Vocal/instrumental group, 1975–91)
David Byrne (vocals), Tina Weymouth (vocals) and
Chris Frantz (drums) formed Talking Heads at art
school and were signed after performances at New
York's famed CBGBs. Jerry Harrison (guitar, keyboards)
joined soon after. Their 1977 debut album *Talking
Heads '77* established their nervy, funky style, with
Byrne's cryptic lyrics. Brian Eno became their producer
with *More Songs About Buildings And Food* (1978). *Fear
Of Music* (1979) broadened their palate with African
sounds, while *Remain In Light* (1980) yielded the UK
hit 'Once In A Lifetime'. Live album *Stop Making Sense*
(1984), with its wonderful Jonathan Demme-directed
film, set new standards in the field. After 1985's *Little
Creatures*, the band, particularly Byrne, seemed
distracted by solo projects (Frantz and Weymouth with
Tom Tom Club, Byrne with his world music label
Luaka Bop) and the end was inevitable. Giants of new
wave, and immeasurably influential, they made art rock
palatable to the mainstream.

Tears For Fears
(Vocal/instrumental group, 1981–96, 2005–present)
Masters of a well-made song, Roland Orzabal (vocals,

guitar, synthesizers) and Curt Smith (vocals, synthesizers, bass) began their chart-busting career in electro-pop mode with the sombre but enthralling 'Mad World', 'Pale Shelter' and 'Shout' (the latter a US No. 1), and debut album *The Hurting* (1983). But the release of 1985's *Songs From The Big Chair* saw a more expansive approach incorporating classic styles from the past. The positively jaunty 'Everybody Wants To Rule The World' (1985) gave them another US No. 1, and was reissued as a charity single. Their next

album was a long time coming. The superb Beatles-pastiche 'Sowing The Seeds Of Love', another global smash, was a misnomer. *The Seeds Of Love* (1989) was the band's final collection, as the duo argued over Smith's contribution, or lack thereof. A surprise reunion for 2005's *Everybody Loves A Happy Ending* was prompted by the 2003 smash cover of their 'Mad World' by Gary Jules.

UB40

(Vocal/instrumental group, 1979–present)
Innovative Birmingham pop reggae band who helped popularize the genre with early albums *Signing Off* (1980) and *Present Arms* (1981) fronted by the Campbell brothers Robin and Ali (both guitar, vocals). They were UK chart regulars with their gently skanking but political singles 'The Earth Dies Screaming' and 'One In Ten', punctuated by Brian Travers plaintive sax. Their 1993 version of 'Can't Help Falling In Love' gave them a US No. 1. They still record and tour.

Left
More ambitious than many 1980s pop acts, Tears For Fears tried to meld jazz, pop, rock and psych, and the soulful *Songs From The Big Chair* led them to major US successes as well.

Below
Taking their name from an unemployment benefit form, mixed-race Birmingham reggaeists UB40 became one of the 1980s' biggest chart successes with songs such as the politically charged 'One In Ten' and their cover of 'Red Red Wine'.

see The Velvet Underground pp 134   *see* Roxy Music pp 242   *see* The Jam pp 260   *see* The Police pp 280

Above

Ridiculously over the top, Van Halen's finger tapping-derived style graced heavy metal and pop tunes throughout the 1980s, with 'Jump' becoming an undying rock behemoth of a song.

Right

New romantic pioneers mixing Bowie, Kraftwerk and Roxy Music, Visage were led by the movement's ultimate scenester, Steve Strange, who had appeared in Bowie's 1980 video for 'Ashes To Ashes'.

Steve Vai

(Guitar, b. 1960)

After learning many of his chops from Joe Satriani, New Yorker Vai became Frank Zappa's 'stunt guitarist' on his albums between 1981 and 1986. He was also a hired axe for John Lydon's PIL, Dave Lee Roth and Whitesnake. His own work shows a compositional maturity. Rather than just 'shredding' on *Passion And Warfare* (1990), *Fire Garden* (1996) and *The Ultra Zone* (1999) he experiments and develops moods. And he shreds.

Van Halen

(Vocal/instrumental group, 1974–99, 2004)

Van Halen stepped out of California to define the US heavy metal scene for a decade. They boasted a dashing, tuneful frontman, Dave Lee Roth (vocals), a wizard guitarist in Eddie Van Halen and poppy but rocking tunes, as 1978's debut *Van Halen I* proved. Eddie's brother Alex (drums) and Michael Anthony

(bass) completed this golden gang. *Van Halen II* (1979) consolidated their position, entering the US Top 10, and in 1983 Eddie provided the dazzling solo to Michael Jackson's 'Beat It'. But it was 1984's *1984* and its attendant pop metal smash 'Jump' which promoted the band to the superstar stratum. Roth soon left for a solo career, and Sammy Hagar took over with no effect on chart placings, but a diminution in charisma. When Hagar left in 1996, Roth returned to record two new songs before Extreme's Gary Cherone briefly filled the berth. A reunion of the original line-up is regularly mooted despite Eddie's battle with cancer, but it was Hagar who helped them promote their second *Greatest Hits* album in 2004.

Luther Vandross

(Vocals, 1951–2005)

One of the US's premier soul balladeers of the 1980s and 1990s, Vandross first sang backing vocals on

Bowie's *Young Americans* (1975) and charted as a guest vocalist with Change. His smooth baritone amassed R&B hits, until his 1989 crossover hit 'Here And Now'. He won his first of eight Grammys for 'Power Of Love – Love Power'. Collaborations with Janet Jackson and Mariah Carey were also successful. He died in 2005 aged 54.

Vangelis
(Musician, b. 1943)
Greece-born Evanghelos Odyssey Papathanassiou played keyboards behind Demis Roussos in Aphrodite's Child before going solo with various jazzy, prog rock excursions. In the course of these he hooked up with vocalist Jon Anderson from Yes. Their 1980 Top 5 album *Short Stories* produced the hit 'I Hear You Now'. In 1981 he released his seminal synth-driven soundtrack to the film *Chariots Of Fire*, which became a US No. 1. Further soundtracks, and Anderson and Vangelis albums followed.

Stevie Ray Vaughan
(Guitar, vocals, 1954–90)
Born in Dallas, Vaughan distilled Albert King, Jimi Hendrix and Lonnie Mack's blues and rock stylings on his superb US Top 40 album *Texas Flood* (1983). Tommy Shannon (bass) and Chris Layton (drums) formed his trusted Double Trouble back-up team. His ferocious but lyrical playing on *Couldn't Stand The Weather* (1984) and live showmanship confirmed him as the new king of the blues guitar. After a 1990 show with Eric Clapton, Vaughan died in a helicopter crash, but SRV music lives on.

Visage
(Vocal/instrumental group, 1978–84)
A synth-pop 'side project' which featured members of other electronica and post-punk bands, including Midge Ure, Billy Currie of Ultravox, Gary Numan's entourage, and Barry Adamson (bass) and John McKeogh (guitar) of Magazine. Steve Strange, a key new romantic catalyst, sang. Several evocative, groundbreaking hits followed, including 'Fade To Grey' (1980), 'Damned Don't Cry' and 'Night Train' (both 1982). The band were important to the Ibiza trance movement of the late 1980s.

📻 *see* Ultravox pp 265　📻 *see* Public Image Ltd pp 312　📻 *see* Joe Satriani pp 312　📻 *see* Mariah Carey pp 345

(1973). On *Blue Valentine* (1979) and the US Top 100 *Heartattack And Vine* (1980) he introduced a rockier sound. Then came his move into the trailblazing, percussive sounds of *Swordfishtrombones* (1983) and the UK Top 30 *Rain Dogs* (1985), with superb cult musicians such as Victor Feldman (marimba), Marc Ribot (guitar) and Ralph Carney (saxophone). Waits developed a career in soundtracks, including Francis Ford Coppola's *One From The Heart* (1981) with Crystal Gayle, and Jim Jarmusch's *Night On Earth* (1992), and also acted in the likes of *Rumblefish*, *Short Cuts* and *The Fisher King*. His 1999 album *Mule Variations* was a US Top 30 and Rod Stewart made big hits of 'Downtown Train' and 'Tom Traubert's Blues'. His legacy continues to grow.

The Waterboys
(Vocal/instrumental group 1982–93, 1999–present)
Created by singer/guitarist Mike Scott who enlisted Anthony Thistlethwaite (saxophone, mandolin), Karl Wallinger (keyboards), Kevin Wilkinson (drums) and Steve Wickham (violin) and re-established folk rock as a medium. 1985's *This Is The Sea* first delivered 'The Whole Of The Moon', which went to No. 3 when reissued in 1991. 1988's *Fisherman's Blues* scored in the US, where Scott's Celtic manner was a live draw. Scott went solo, then reformed the band for the new century.

Above

Having left his 1970s wino-balladeer persona behind, with 1983's *Swordfishtrombones* Tom Waits forged a path that would lead to him being one of the most consistently interesting artists of the century.

Tom Waits
(Singer/songwriter, b. 1949)
Born in Pomona, California, Waits has built an extremely well-regarded career as a gravel-voiced documentator of American low-life. The Eagles covered 'Ol '55' from his jazzy debut *Closing Time*

The Wedding Present
(Vocal/instrumental group, 1984–97)
Pioneers of British indie rock, the band's fizzing post-punk guitars and homely, oddball lyrics took them to the UK Top 50 with *George Best* (1987). David Gedge (vocals, guitar), Pete Solowka (guitar), Keith Gregory

see Introduction pp 268   *see Sources & Sounds pp 270*   *see Key Artists pp 274*

(bass) and Shaun Charman (drums) filled their debut major label outing with Ukrainian songs from Solowka's heritage. After 1991's Steve Albini-produced *Seamonsters*, they released a single a month throughout 1992, which all reached the Top 30! Solowka formed The Ukrainians and Gedge Cinerama.

Womack and Womack
(Vocal duo, 1983–94)

Cecil Womack began as part of The Womacks, with brother Bobby. Linda was Sam Cooke's daughter. They both had good track records as soul songwriters before they married and released *Love Wars* in 1983, the title track becoming their first hit. In 1985, *Radio M.U.S.I.C. Man* featured unfinished Cooke songs the pair completed. In 1988, 'Teardrops' was a massive smash for the sugar-voiced couple who helped reclaim soul as a well-crafted, song-based medium.

Robert Wyatt
(Drums, singer/songwriter, b. 1945)

Wyatt became drummer and vocalist with jazz-rockers Soft Machine. Forming Matching Mole in 1971, he overcame being wheelchair-bound after a 1973 accident to record solo eclectic classics such as *Rock Bottom* (1975), and had an unlikely hit single with The Monkees' 'I'm A Believer'. In 1983, he charted again with Elvis Costello's 'Shipbuilding'. 2003's *Cuckooland* proved his continuing creativity. His expressive vocals can be heard guesting with many artists, including Björk and Dave Gilmour. He is an icon of the leftfield in British music.

Left Middle
Based around singer-songwriter Mike Scott, The Waterboys have had a revolving door line-up that has seen them take in traditional Irish music, pop ambition and straight ahead rock over two decades.

Below
The Wedding Present became a hugely successful indie rock outfit, notably releasing a single on the first Monday of every month in 1992.

see Sam Cooke pp 168   see The Eagles pp 198   see The Pogues pp 311   see Simply Red pp 365

List of Artists

THE EIGHTIES

Entries appear in the following order: name, music style, year(s) of popularity, type of artist, country of origin

10,000 Maniacs, Alternative/Indie Rock, 1980s-1990s, Artist, American
2 Live Crew, Hip Hop, 1980s-, Artist, American
3 Mustaphas 3, Fusion and Jazz Rock, 1980s-, Artist, Balkan
52nd Street, Urban Soul, 1980s, Artist, British
808 State, House; Acid, 1980s-, Artist, British
A Flock of Seagulls, New Romantics; 1980s Pop, 1980s; 1990s-2000s, Artist, British
A Tribe Called Quest, Hip Hop; Alternative, 1980s-1990s, Artist, American
Abbott, Gregory, Urban Soul, 1980s-, Artist, American
ABC, New Wave; 1980s Pop, 1980s-1990s, Artist, British
Abdul, Paula, 1980s Pop; Urban Soul, 1980s-1990s, Artist, American
A-Bones, The, US Underground & Garage Rock, 1980s-1990s, Artist, American
Abou-Khalil, Rabih, World Fusion, 1980s-, Artist; Composer, Lebanese
Abrams, Colonel, US Garage; House, 1980s-1990s, Artist, American
Adams, Brian, 1980s Pop, 1980s-, Artist; Songwriter, American
Adamson, Barry, Alternative/Indie Rock, 1980s-, Artist, British
Admiral Bailey, Dancehall, 1980s-1990s, Artist, Jamaican
Admiral Tibbet, Ragga; Dancehall, 1980s-, Artist, Jamaican
Adrenalin OD, US Underground & Garage Rock; Thrash & Speed Metal, 1980s-1990s, Artist, American
Afghan Whigs, Alternative/Indie Rock, 1980s-, Artist, American
African Disciples, Ragga, 1980s, Artist, Jamaican
African Head Charge, Dub, 1980s-1990s, Artist, British
Afrika Bambaataa, Electro; Hip Hop; Old School, 1980s-, Artist; Producer, American
Agent Orange, US Underground & Garage Rock, 1980s-1990s, Artist, American
Agnostic Front, US Underground & Garage Rock, 1980s-, Artist, American
A-Ha, 1980s Pop, 1980s-, Artist, Norwegian
Alger, Pat, Young Country, 1980s-1990s, Artist, American
Alien Sex Fiend, Goth Rock, 1980s-, Artist, British
All About Eve, Goth Rock, 1980s-1990s, Artist, British
Allen, Donna, Urban Soul, 1980s-1990s, Artist, American
Almond, Marc, New Wave; New Romantics, 1980s-, Artist, British
Alpha and Omega, Trip Hop; Ambient; Dub, 1980s-, Artist, British
Alpha Blondy, Reggae Pop, 1980s-, Artist, African
Alter Ego, Techno, 1980s-1990s, Artist, German
Altered Images, New Wave, 1980s, Artist, British
Alvin, Dave, Alternative Country, 1980s-, Artist; Songwriter, American
Ambel, Eric, Alternative Country; Country Rock, 1980s-, Artist, American
Ambitious Lovers, US Underground & Garage Rock; Alternative/Indie Rock, 1980s-1990s, Artist, American
American Music Club, Alternative/Indie Rock, 1980s-1990s, Artist, American
Amos, Tori, 1980s Pop, 1980s-, Artist, American
Anacrusis, Thrash & Speed Metal, 1980s-1990s, Artist, American
Anderson, Carl, The Classic Soul Era; Urban Soul, 1980s-1990s, Artist, American
Anderson, Jamie, Folk Pop, 1980s-, Artist; Songwriter, American
Anderson, Pete, Alternative Country, 1980s-1990s, Producer; Artist, American
Anderson, Roshell, Urban Soul, 1980s-1990s, Artist, American
Annihilator, Thrash & Speed Metal, 1980s-, Artist, Canadian
Anthrax, Thrash & Speed Metal, 1980s-, Artist, American
Arkenstone, David, New Age; Electro, 1980s-, Artist, American
Armstrong, Vanessa Bell, Urban Soul, 1980s-, Artist, American
Arrington, Steve, The Classic Soul Era, 1980s, Artist, American
Art Of Noise, The, Electro, 1980s-, Artist, British
Asia, Prog Rock; Arena Rock, 1980s-, Artist, British
Associates, The, New Romantics, 1980s-1990s, Artist, British
Astley, Rick, 1980s Pop, 1980s, Artist, British
Atheist, Death Metal & Grindcore, 1980s-1990s, Artist, American
Atkins, Juan, Techno, 1980s-, Artist; Producer, American
Au Pairs, The, British Punk, 1980s, Artist, British
Aurra, Disco; Urban Soul, 1980s, Artist, American
Aztec Camera, New Wave, 1980s-1990s, Artist, British
B., Stevie, Urban Soul, 1980s-, Artist, American
Babes In Toyland, Riot Grrrl; Alternative/Indie Rock; Grunge, 1980s-1990s, Artist, American
Babyface, Contemporary R&B, 1980s-, Producer, American
Bad Brains, US Underground & Garage Rock; Alternative/Indie Rock, 1980s-1990s, Artist, American
Bad Manners, Ska, 1980s-, Artist, British
Bad Religion, US Underground & Garage Rock; Alternative/Indie Rock, 1980s-, Artist, American
Bailey, Philip, Urban Soul, 1980s-, Artist, American
Baillie and the Boys, Young Country, 1980s-, Artist, American
Baker, Anita, Urban Soul, 1980s-1990s, Artist, American
Baker, Arthur, US Garage; Electro, 1980s-, Producer; Artist, American
Baker, Butch, Young Country, 1980s-1990s, Artist, American
Balancing Act, The, Folk Rock, 1980s, Artist, American
Ball, David, Young Country, 1980s-, Artist, American
Ball, Patrick, Irish Folk, 1980s-, Artist, Irish
Ball, Tom, Young Country; Bluegrass, 1980s, Artist, American
Bananarama, New Wave; 1980s Pop, 1980s-1990s, Artist, British
Bangles, The, New Wave; 1980s Pop, 1980s, Artist, American
Banton, Pato, Ragga, 1980s-, Artist; Producer, British
Barmby, Shane, Young Country, 1980s-1990s, Artist, American
Barnes, Max D., Young Country; Neo-Traditionalists, 1980s-, Artist, American
Barracudas, The, US Underground & Garage Rock, 1980s; 2000s, Artist, Anglo-American
Barton, Lou Ann, Texas Blues; Blues Rock, 1980s-, Artist, American
Base, Rob, Hip Hop, 1980s-, Artist, American
Basement 5, Dub, 1980s, Artist, British
Basia, 1980s Pop, 1980s-1990s, Artist, Polish
Bathory, Death Metal & Grindcore, 1980s-, Artist, Swedish
Batish, Ashwin, Fusion and Jazz Rock; Fusion, 1980s-1990s, Artist, Indian
Beastie Boys, The Alternative/Indie Rock; Funk Metal; Old School; Golden Age; Alternative Hip Hop; Hip Hop, 1980s-, Artist, American
Beasts Of Bourbon, Alternative/Indie Rock; Pub Rock, 1980s-1990s, Artist, Australian
Beat Happening, Alternative/Indie Rock; 1980s Pop, 1980s-1990s, Artist, American
Beautiful South, The, 1980s Pop, 1980s-, Artist, British
Beck, Robin, Disco, 1980s, Artist, American
Beenie Man, Dancehall; Ragga, 1980s-, Artist, Jamaican
Beethoven, Camper Van, 1980s Pop, 1980s, Artist, American
Belew, Adrian, Prog Rock; Alternative/Indie Rock, 1980s-, Artist, American
Believer, Thrash & Speed Metal, 1980s-1990s, Artist, American
Bell Biv Devoe, Urban Soul, 1980s-, Artist, American
Belle, Regina, Urban Soul, 1980s-, Artist, American
Beltram, Joey, Techno, 1980s-, Artist; Producer, American
Berlin, New Wave, 1980s-, Artist, American
Berry, Heidi, Folk Rock; 1980s Pop Singer/Songwriters, 1980s-1990s, Artist, American
Berryhill, Cindy Lee, Folk Rock, 1980s-1990s, Artist; Songwriter, American
Bevis Frond, The, Alternative/Indie Rock, 1980s-, Artist, British
Bhatt, Vishwa Mohan, Fusion and Jazz Rock, 1980s-1990s, Artist, Indian
Biff Bang Pow!, 1980s Pop, 1980s-1990s, Artist, British
Big Audio Dynamite, Alternative/Indie Rock; Hip Hop, 1980s-1990s, Artist, British
Big Black, US Underground & Garage Rock; Alternative/Indie Rock, 1980s, Artist, American
Big Boys, The, US Underground & Garage Rock; Alternative/Indie Rock, 1980s-1990s, Artist, American
Big Country, New Wave; 1980s Pop, 1980s-1990s, Artist, British
Big Daddy Kane, Hip Hop; Golden Age; Gangsta, 1980s-1990s, Artist, American
Big Drill Car, 1980s Pop, 1980s-1990s, Artist, American
Big Head Todd and The Monsters, Jam Rock, 1980s-, Artist, American
Bim Skala Bim, Ska, 1980s-, Artist, American
Biohazard, Hard Rock; Heavy Metal; Hip Hop, 1980s-, Artist, American
Bitch Magnet, Alternative/Indie Rock, 1980s-1990s, Artist, American
Black Britain, Disco, 1980s, Artist, British
Black Dog, The, Techno, 1980s-, Artist, British
Black, Clint, Neo-Traditionalists; Young Country, 1980s-1990s, Artist, American
Black, Mary, Contemporary Folk; Irish Folk, 1980s-, Artist, Irish
Blackgirls, Folk Rock; Folk Pop, 1980s-1990s, Artist; Songwriter, American
Blanchard, Terence, Hard Bop, 1980s-, Artist, American
Blast, C. L., The Classic Soul Era, 1980s, Artist, American
Blasters, The, Rock'n'Roll, 1980s, Artist, American
Blaze, House; US Garage, 1980s-, Artist, American
Blind Guardian, Heavy Metal, 1980s-, Artist, German
Blow Monkeys, The, New Romantics; New Wave, 1980s-1990s, Artist, British
Blue Aeroplanes, The, Alternative/Indie Rock, 1980s-2000s, Artist, British
Blue Mercedes, Disco, 1980s, Artist, British
Blue Nile, The, 1980s Pop, 1980s-1990s, Artist, British
Blue Rodeo, Folk Rock; Alternative Country, 1980s-, Artist, American
Bluesbusters, The, Blues Rock, 1980s, Artist, American
Blundell, James, Young Country, 1980s, Artist, American
BMX Bandits, Alternative/Indie Rock; 1980s Pop, 1980s-1990s, Artist, British
Bogguss, Suzy, Neo-Traditionalists, 1980s-1990s, Artist, American
Bolt Thrower, Death Metal & Grindcore, 1980s-, Artist, British
Bon Jovi, Arena Rock; Melodic Rock, 1980s-, Artist, American
Bongwater, US Underground & Garage Rock; Alternative/Indie Rock, 1980s-1990s, Artist, American
Boogie Down Productions, Golden Age; Political Rap; Gangsta, Hip Hop 1980s-1990s, Artist, American
Boom Shaka, US Reggae, 1980s-1990s, Artist, American
Boone, Larry, Young Country; Neo-Traditionalists, 1980s-1990s, Artist, American
Boredoms, Alternative/Indie Rock, 1980s-, Artist, Japanese
Boss Hog, Alternative/Indie Rock, 1980s-, Artist, American
Bourbon Tabernacle Choir, The, Contemporary R&B, 1980s-1990s, Artist, American
Bourelli, Jean-Paul, Blues Rock , 1980s-, Artist, American
Bow Wow Wow, New Wave, 1980s-1990s, Artist, British
Box Of Frogs, Blues Rock, 1980s, Artist, British
Boy George, New Romantics; 1990s Pop, 1980s-, Artist; Songwriter, British
Boyz II Men, 1980s Pop; Contemporary R&B; Urban Soul, 1980s-, Artist, American
Bragg, Billy, 1980s Pop Singer/Songwriters; UK Folk; Alternative Folk, 1980s-, Artist; Songwriter, British
Bramhall, Doyle, Texas Blues; Modern Electric Blues, 1980s-1990s, Artist, American
Brickell, Edie, Folk Rock, 1980s-1990s, Artist, American
Bridges, Calvin, Contemporary R&B, 1980s-1990s, Artist, American
Broggs, Peter, US Reggae, 1980s-, Artist, American
Bronski Beat, 1980s Pop; New Wave, 1980s-1990s, Artist, British
Brook, Michael, Tribal Dance; Techno, 1980s-1990s, Composer; Artist, Canadian
Brooks, Garth, Neo-Traditionalists, 1980s-, Artist, American
Brooks, Karen, Young Country, 1980s-1990s, Artist, American
Bros, 1980s Pop; Boy Bands, 1980s-1990s, Artist, British
Brothers Figaro, Folk Rock; Folk Pop, 1980s, Artist, American
Broudie, Ian, 1980s Pop, Alternative/Indie Rock, 1980s-, Artist; Producer, British
Brown, Bobby, 1980s Pop; Urban Soul, 1980s-, Artist, American
Brown, Ian, Alternative/Indie Rock, Madchester, 1980s-, Artist, British
Brown, Jocelyn, Disco; House; Contemporary R&B, 1980s-, Artist, American
Brown, T. Graham, Urban Cowboys; Country Rock, 1980s-, Artist, American
Brownmark, The Classic Soul Era, 1980s, Artist, American
Bruce Hornsby and the Range, Jazz Rock, 1980s-1990s, Artist, American
Bryant, Leon, The Classic Soul Era, 1980s-1990s, Artist, American
Bryant, Sharon, The Classic Soul Era, 1980s, Artist, American
Buffalo Tom, Melodic Rock, 1980s-1990s, Artist, American
Buggles, The, 1980s Pop; New Wave, 1980s, Artist, British
Burch Sisters, Young Country, 1980s, Artist, American
Burmer, Richard, New Age; Ambient; Electro, 1980s-1990s, Artist, American
Burns Sisters, The, Contemporary Folk; Folk Rock, 1980s-, Artist, American
Burton, Jenny, Disco, 1980s, Artist, American
Butthole Surfers, The, US Underground & Garage Rock; Alternative/Indie Rock, 1980s-1990s, Artist, American
By All Means, The Classic Soul Era, 1980s-1990s, Artist, American
Byrne, David, Alternative/Indie Rock, 1980s-, Producer; Artist, British
Camouflage, Disco, 1980s-, Artist, German
Campbell, Cornell, The Classic Soul Era; Ska; Rock Steady, 1980s-, Artist, Jamaican
Camper Van Beethoven, US Underground & Garage Rock; Alternative/Indie Rock, 1980s, Artist, American
Cancer, Death Metal & Grindcore, 1980s-1990s, Artist, American
Candlemass, Doom Metal, 1980s-1990s, Artist, Swedish
Cannibal Corpse, Death Metal & Grindcore, 1980s-, Artist, American
Capleton The Prophet, Bobo Dread Deejays; Dancehall; Roots; Ragga; Rock Steady, 1980s-, Artist, Jamaican
Carcass, Death Metal & Grindcore, 1980s-1990s, Artist, British
Carlisle, Belinda, 1980s Pop, 1980s-1990s, Artist, American
Carne, Jean, The Classic Soul Era, 1980s-1990s, Artist, American
Carpenter, Mary Chapin, Contemporary Folk; Young Country, 1980s-, Artist; Songwriter, American
Carter USM, Alternative/Indie Rock, 1980s-1990s, Artist, British
Cartwright, Lionel, Young Country, 1980s-1990s, Artist, American
Cave, Nick, Alternative/Indie Rock, 1980s-, Artist; Songwriter, Australian
Celibate Rifles, Alternative/Indie Rock, 1980s-1990s, Artist, Australian
Celtic Frost, Thrash & Speed Metal, 1980s-1990s, Artist, Swiss
Cervenka, Exene, Folk Rock, 1980s-1990s, Artist, American
Chameleons, The, Alternative/Indie Rock, 1980s-, Artist, British
Champaign, Urban Soul, 1980s-1990s, Artist, American
Chaplin, Charlie, Ragga, 1980s-1990s, Composer, British
Chapman, Beth Nielson, Young Country, 1980s-, Artist, American
Chapman, Ce Ce, Young Country, 1980s-1990s, Artist, American
Chapman, Tracy, 1980s Pop Singer/Songwriters; 1980s Pop; Alternative Folk; Contemporary Folk, 1980s-, Artist; Songwriter, American
Chapterhouse, Alternative/Indie Rock; Shoegazing, 1980s-1990s, Artist, British
Charlatans, The, Madchester; Alternative/Indie Rock; Britpop, 1980s-, Artist, British
Cherelle, Contemporary R&B; Urban Soul, 1980s-1990s, Artist, American
Cherry, Neneh, 1980s Pop; Urban Soul, 1980s-1990s, Artist, Swedish
Chesterfield Kings, US Underground & Garage Rock, 1980s-1990s, Artist, American
Chicken Chokers, The, Alternative Country, 1980s, Artist, American
Childers, Bob, Young Country, 1980s-1990s, Artist, American
China Crisis, New Romantics; 1980s Pop, 1980s-, Artist, British
Christians, The, Urban Soul, 1980s-1990s, Artist, British
Chuck D., Hip Hop; Gangsta, 1980s-1990s, Artist, American
Chumbawamba, 1990s Pop; Alternative/Indie Rock, 1980s-, Artist, British
Church, The, Alternative/Indie Rock, 1980s-, Artist, Australian
Cinderella, Heavy Metal; Hard Rock, 1980s-1990s, Artist, American
Circle Jerks, The, American Punk, 1980s-1990s, Artist, American
Clail, Gary, Dub, 1980s-1990s, Artist, British
Clan Of Xymox, Goth Rock, 1980s-, Artist, Dutch
Clark, W. C., Texas Blues; Modern Electric Blues, 1980s-1990s, Artist, American
Clarke, Vince, 1980s Pop, 1980s-, Artist, British
Clay, Joe, Rockabilly, 1980s, Artist, American
Club Nouveau, Disco; Urban Soul, 1980s-1990s, Artist, American
Cobra, Ragga, 1980s-1990s, Artist, Jamaican
Cockney Rejects, British Punk, 1980s-1990s, Artist, British
Cocoa Tea, Dancehall; Ragga, 1980s-, Artist, Jamaican
Cocteau Twins, 1980s Pop, 1980s-1990s, Artist, British
Coffee, Disco, 1980s, Artist, American
Coldcut, Trip Hop; Electro, 1980s-, Artist, British
Cole, Lloyd, Alternative/Indie Rock, 1980s-, Artist; Songwriter, British
Coleman, Durrell, The Classic Soul Era, 1980s, Artist, American
Collie, Mark, Neo-Traditionalists, 1980s-1990s, Artist, American
Collins, Edwyn, 1980s Pop, 1980s-1990s, Artist, British
Colvin, Shawn, 1980s Pop Singer/Songwriters; Contemporary Folk, 1980s-, Artist; Songwriter, American
Communards, The, 1980s Pop, 1980s, Artist, British
Concrete Blonde, Alternative/Indie Rock, 1980s-1990s; 2000s, Artist, American
Conflict, British Punk, 1980s-, Artist, British
Conley, Earl Thomas, Urban Cowboys; Neo-Traditionalists, 1980s-1990s, Artist, American
Connors, Loren MazzaCane, Alternative/Indie Rock, 1980s-, Artist, American
Cool Notes, The, The Classic Soul Era, 1980s, Artist, British
Cooper, Michael, Urban Soul, 1980s-, Artist, American
Cope, Julian, British Punk; 1980s Pop, 1980s-, Artist, British
Coroner, Thrash & Speed Metal, 1980s-1990s, Artist, Swiss
Corrosion Of Conformity, Thrash & Speed Metal, 1980s-, Artist, American
Cover Girls, The, Urban Soul, 1980s-1990s, Artist, American
Cowboy Junkies, Alternative/Indie Rock; Alternative Country, 1980s-, Artist, Canadian
Cows, The, US Underground & Garage Rock; Alternative/Indie Rock, 1980s-1990s, Artist, American
Craig, Carl, Techno, 1980s-, Producer, American
Cramps, The, US Underground & Garage Rock, 1980s-1990s, Artist, American
Crash Test Dummies, The, Folk Rock; Alternative/Indie Rock, 1980s-, Artist, Canadian
Crazy Bugs, The, Folk Rock, 1980s, Artist, Italian
Creation Rebel, Dub, 1980s-1990s, Artist, British
Creatures, The, Goth Rock, 1980s-1990s, Artist, British
Crenshaw, Marshall, New Wave; 1980s Pop, 1980s-, Artist, American
Crimson Glory, Heavy Metal, 1980s-1990s, Artist, American
Cristina, Disco, 1980s, Artist, American
Cro-Mags, US Underground & Garage Rock; Thrash & Speed Metal, 1980s-, Artist, American
Cross, Christopher, 1980s Pop, 1980s-, Artist; Songwriter, American
Crowded House, Alternative/Indie Rock; 1980s Pop, 1980s-1990s, Artist, New Zealander
Cult, The, Goth Rock; Hard Rock, 1980s-, Artist, British
Culture Club, New Wave; 1980s Pop; The Classic Soul Era, 1980s-1990s, Artist, British
Cybotron, Electro; Techno, 1980s-, Artist, American
Cynics, US Underground & Garage Rock; Alternative/Indie Rock, 1980s-1990s, Artist, American
D Train, US Garage; House, 1980s-1990s, Artist, American
D'Arby, Terence Trent, Contemporary R&B, 1980s-1990s, Artist, American
Dag Nasty, US Underground & Garage Rock, 1980s-, Artist, American
Damien Youth, Folk Rock, 1980s-1990s, Artist, British
Damier, Chez, House; US Garage, 1980s-1990s, Producer, American
Dan Reed Netwrok, Funk Metal, 1980s-, Artist, American
Daniel, Jeffrey, Disco, 1980s, Artist, American
Danzig, Heavy Metal, 1980s-, Artist, American
Das Damen, US Underground & Garage Rock; Alternative/Indie Rock, 1980s-1990s, Artist, American
Dash Rip Rock, Alternative Country, 1980s-, Artist, American
Davis, Roy Jr. House; US Garage, 1980s-, Artist; Producer, American
Dawson, Julian, Alternative Country, 1980s-1990s, Artist, American
Day, Otis, and The Knights, Contemporary R&B, 1980s, Artist, American
Dazz Band, Funk Soul, 1980s-, Artist, American
DBs, The, 1980s Pop, 1980s-1990s, Artist, American
De La Soul, Alternative Hip Hop; Golden Age, 1980s-, Artist, American
Deacon Blue, 1980s Pop, 1980s-1990s, Artist; Songwriter, British
Dead Can Dance, Shoegazing; 1980s Pop, 1980s-, Artist, Australian
Dead Or Alive, Disco, 1980s-, Artist, British
Dean, Hazell, Disco, 1980s-1990s, Artist; Songwriter, American
Death Angel, Thrash & Speed Metal, 1980s-1990s, Artist, American
Death, Christian, Goth Rock; Thrash & Speed Metal, 1980s-1990s, Artist, American
Death, Death Metal & Grindcore, 1980s-, Artist, American
DeBarge, Urban Soul, 1980s, Artist, American
Deee-Lite, 1980s Pop; House, 1980s-1990s, Artist, American
Def Leppard, Hard Rock; Heavy Metal; 1980s Pop, 1980s-, Artist, British
Def Squad, Gangsta, 1980s-, Artist, American
DeFrancesco, Joey, Soul Jazz; Hard Bop, 1980s-, Artist, American
Defunkt, Funk Soul, 1980s-1990s, Artist, American
Déja, The Classic Soul Era, 1980s-1990s, Artist, American
Del Amitri, Folk Rock, 1980s-1990s, Artist, British
Depeche Mode, Alternative/Indie Rock; 1980s Pop, 1980s-, Artist, British
Depth Charge, Techno; Acid; House, 1980s-, Producer, British
Descendents, US Underground & Garage Rock; 1980s Pop, 1980s-1990s, Artist, American
Desert Rose Band, Country Rock, 1980s-1990s, Artist, American
Deus, Alternative/Indie Rock, 1980s-, Artist, Belgian
Dexy's Midnight Runners, New Wave, 1980s, Artist, British
Dicks, US Underground & Garage Rock, 1980s, Artist, American
Die Kreuzen, US Underground & Garage Rock, 1980s-1990s, Artist, American
Died Pretty, Alternative/Indie Rock, 1980s-, Artist, Australian
DiFranco, Ani, 1980s Pop Singer/Songwriters; Alternative Folk, 1980s-, Artist; Songwriter, American
Digital Underground, Alternative Hip Hop; Hip Hop, 1980s-1990s, Artist, American
Dinosaur Jr., US Underground & Garage Rock; Alternative/Indie Rock, 1980s-1990s, Artist, American
DJ Jazzy Jeff and The Fresh Prince, Hip Hop, 1980s-1990s, Artist, American
DJ Pooh, Gangsta, 1980s-, Producer, American
DJ Red Alert, Old School; Hip Hop, 1980s-, Artist, American
DOC, The Gangsta, 1980s-1990s, Artist, American
Dolby, Thomas, New Wave, 1980s-1990s, Artist, British
Dr. Dre, Gangsta, 1980s-, Producer; Artist, American
Dream Syndicate, US Underground & Garage Rock; Alternative/Indie Rock; 1980s Pop, 1980s, Artist, American
Dream Theater, Heavy Metal; Hard Rock, 1980s-, Artist, American
DRI, US Underground & Garage Rock; Thrash & Speed Metal, 1980s-, Artist, American
Dub Syndicate, Dub, 1980s-, Artist, British
Dukes Of Stratosphear, The, Psychedelic Rock; Alternative/Indie Rock, 1980s, Artist, British
Duncan, Daryll, Urban Soul, 1980s, Artist, American
Dunn, Holly, Young Country, 1980s-1990s, Artist, American
Duran Duran, New Wave; New Romantics; 1980s Pop, 1980s-1990s, Artist, British
Dust Brothers, The, Hip Hop, 1980s-, Artist, American
Dyer, Ada, Urban Soul, 1980s-1990s, Artist, American
Dynamix II, Electro, 1980s-, Artist, American
E., Sheila, 1980s Pop, 1980s-, Artist, American
Eaglesmith, Fred, Alternative Country, 1980s-, Artist; Songwriter, Canadian
Earle, Steve, 1980s Pop Singer/Songwriters; Alternative Country; Neo-Traditionalists, 1980s-, Artist; Songwriter, American
Easton, Sheena, 1980s Pop, 1980s-, Artist, British
Eazy-E, Gangsta, 1980s-1990s, Artist, American
E-Dancer, Techno, 1980s-1990s, Producer, American
Eden Burning, Folk Rock, 1980s-1990s, Artist, British
Edwards, Archie, Modern Electric Blues, 1980s, Artist, American
Edwards, Rupie, Ska, 1980s, Artist, Jamaican
Eek-A-Mouse, Dancehall; Ragga, 1980s-, Artist, Jamaican
Egyptian Lover, The, Electro, 1980s-1990s, Producer, American
Eight-Eyed Spy, US Underground & Garage Rock, 1980s, Artist, American
Eitzel, Mark, 1990s Pop Singer/Songwriters, 1980s-, Artist, American
Electronic, Electro, 1980s-, Artist, British
Eleventh Dream Day, Alternative/Indie Rock, 1980s-, Artist, American
Ellis, Tinsley, Modern Electric Blues, 1980s-, Artist, American
En Vogue, Urban Soul, 1980s-, Artist, American
English Beat, The, New Wave, 1980s, Artist, British
Eno, Roger, Ambient; Electro, 1980s-, Composer; Artist, British
Entombed, Death Metal & Grindcore, 1980s-, Artist, Swedish
Enuff Znuff, Hard Rock; 1980s Pop, 1980s-, Artist, American
Enya, Irish Folk; Contemporary Folk, 1980s-, Artist, Irish
EPMD, Golden Age; Gangsta, 1980s-1990s, Artist, American
Erasure, 1980s Pop, 1980s-, Artist, British
Eric B and Rakim, Golden Age; Hip Hop, 1980s-1990s, Artist, American
Estefan, Gloria, 1980s Pop; Latin, 1980s-, Artist, American
Etheridge, Melissa, 1980s Pop Singer/Songwriters, 1980s-, Artist; Songwriter, American
Eurythmics, New Wave; 1980s Pop, 1980s-1990s, Artist, British
Everlast, Alternative Hip Hop; Gangsta, 1980s-, Artist, American
Everything But The Girl, 1980s Pop, 1980s-, Artist, British
Ewing, Skip, Neo-Traditionalists, 1980s-1990s, Artist; Songwriter, American
Ex, The, Alternative/Indie Rock, 1980s-, Artist, Dutch
Exodus, Thrash & Speed Metal, 1980s-1990s, Artist, American
Exploited, The, British Punk, 1980s-, Artist, British
Extreme Noise Terror, Death Metal & Grindcore, 1980s-, Artist, British
Extreme, Heavy Metal; Hard Rock, 1980s-1990s, Artist, American
Fabio, Jungle; Drum'n'Bass, 1980s-1990s, Artist; Producer, British
Fair, Jad, US Underground & Garage Rock; Alternative/Indie Rock, 1980s-, Artist, American
Fairground Attraction, 1980s Pop, 1980s, Artist, British
Faith No More, Funk Metal, 1980s-1990s, Artist, American
Falco, Tav, Alternative/Indie Rock, 1980s-, Artist, American
Farm, The, Madchester, 1980s-1990s, Artist, British
Farmer, Mylene, Europop, 1980s-, Artist, French
Fastbacks, Alternative/Indie Rock; 1980s Pop, 1980s-1990s, Artist, American
Faster Pussycat, Heavy Metal; Hard Rock, 1980s-1990s, Artist, American
Fat Boys, Old School; Hip Hop 1980s-1990s, Artist, American
Fate's Warning, Heavy Metal, 1980s-, Artist, American
Fatima Mansions, Jazz Rock; Alternative/Indie Rock, 1980s-1990s, Artist, Irish
Field Mice, The, 1980s Pop, 1980s-1990s, Artist, British
Fields Of The Nephilim, Goth Rock, 1980s-1990s, Artist, British
Fine Young Cannibals, Contemporary R&B, 1980s-1990s, Artist, British
Firehouse, Heavy Metal, 1980s-, Artist, American
Fish, Prog Rock, 1980s-2000s, Artist, British
Fishbone, Funk Metal, 1980s-, Artist, American
Five Star, Urban Soul, 1980s, Artist, British
Flaming Lips, The, US Underground & Garage Rock; Alternative/Indie Rock, 1980s-, Artist, American
Flatmates, 1980s Pop, 1980s-1990s, Artist, British
Flesh For Lulu, Goth Rock, 1980s-1990s, Artist, British
Fleshcrawl, Death Metal & Grindcore, 1980s-, Artist, American
Flipper, US Underground & Garage Rock; Alternative/Indie Rock, 1980s-1990s, Artist, American
Flock of Seagulls, A, New Romantics; New Wave, 1980s-1990s, Artist, British
Flotsam and Jetsam, Thrash & Speed Metal, 1980s-, Artist, American
Force MD's, Urban Soul, 1980s-, Artist, American
Forester Sisters, The, Neo-Traditionalists, 1980s-1990s, Artist, American
Foster and Lloyd, Neo-Traditionalists; Young Country, 1980s-1990s, Artist, American
Fowlkes, Eddie 'Flashin', Techno, 1980s-, Artist; Producer, American
Fox, George, Young Country, 1980s-1990s, Artist, Canadian
Foxworthy, Jeff, Young Country, 1980s-, Artist, American
Frankie Goes to Hollywood, New Wave; 1980s Pop, 1980s, Artist, British
Fraser, Dean, Dancehall, 1980s-, Artist, Jamaican
Freakwater, Alternative Country, 1980s-1990s, Artist, American
Freddy Fresh, Trip Hop; Electro, 1980s-, Artist; Producer, American
Freestyle, Electro, 1980s-1990s, Producer, American
Fresh, Doug E., Old School; Golden Age; Hip Hop 1980s-1990s, Artist, American
Fugazi, US Underground & Garage Rock; Alternative/Indie Rock, 1980s-, Artist, American
Fun Boy Three, New Wave, 1980s, Artist, British
Funderburgh, Anson, Modern Electric Blues, 1980s-, Artist, American
Fushitsusha, Alternative/Indie Rock, 1980s-1990s, Artist, Japanese
Fuzztones, The, US Underground & Garage Rock; Alternative/Indie Rock, 1980s-1990s, Artist, American
G., Kenny, 1980s Pop; Smooth Jazz, 1980s-, Artist, American
Galaxie 500, Alternative/Indie Rock; Shoegazing; 1980s Pop, 1980s-1990s, Artist, American
Game Theory, 1980s Pop, 1980s, Artist, American
Gang Starr, Golden Age; Political Rap; Hip Hop, 1980s-1990s, Artist, American
Garnier, Laurent, House; Acid; Techno, 1980s-, Artist; Producer, French
Garrett, Siedah, Urban Soul, 1980s-1990s, Artist, American
Gene Loves Jezebel, Goth Rock, 1980s-, Artist, British
General Kane, Urban Soul, 1980s, Artist, American
General Public, New Wave, 1980s-1990s, Artist, British
General Saint, Dancehall, 1980s, Artist, Jamaican
General Trees, Dancehall; Ragga; Deejays, 1980s-1990s, Artist, American
Georgia Satellites, The, Southern Rock, 1980s-1990s, Artist, American
Georgio, Urban Soul, 1980s-1990s, Artist, American
Geto Boys, Gangsta, 1980s-1990s, Artist, American
Gibson, Debbie, 1980s Pop, 1980s-1990s, Artist, American
Gill, Vince, Neo-Traditionalists; Bluegrass; Young Country, 1980s-, Artist, American
Gilmore, Jimmie Dale, Alternative Country, 1980s-, Artist; Songwriter, American
Girls Next Door, Young Country, 1980s-1990s, Artist, American
Girlschool, Heavy Metal, 1980s-, Artist, British
Glenn, Garry, The Classic Soul Era, 1980s, Artist, American
Go West, 1980s Pop, 1980s-1990s, Artist, British
Go-Betweens, The, 1980s Pop; New Wave, 1980s-, Artist, Australian
Godflesh, Death Metal & Grindcore, 1980s-, Artist, British
Go-Gos, The, New Wave; 1980s Pop, 1980s; 2000s, Artist, American
Gold, Brian and Tony, Ragga, 1980s-1990s, Artist, Jamaican
Golden Palominos, The, American Punk; Funk, 1980s-1990s, Artist, American
Goldens, The, Young Country, 1980s-1990s, Artist, American
Gone, US Underground & Garage Rock; Alternative/Indie Rock, 1980s-, Artist, American
Goo Goo Dolls, Alternative/Indie Rock; Hard Rock, 1980s-, Artist, American
Gorefest, Death Metal & Grindcore, 1980s-1990s, Artist, Dutch
Government Issue, US Underground & Garage Rock, 1980s-1990s, Artist, American
Grace Pool, Folk Rock, 1980s-1990s, Artist, American
Grandmaster Flash, Electro; Old School; Hip Hop, 1980s-, Artist; Producer, West Indian
Grant, David, Urban Soul, 1980s-1990s, Artist, British
Great White, Heavy Metal; Hard Rock, 1980s-, Artist, American
Green Day, 1980s Pop, 1980s-, Artist, American
Green On Red, 1980s Pop, 1980s-1990s, Artist, American
Green River, Grunge; Alternative/Indie Rock, 1980s, Artist, American
Grissom, Rich, Young Country, 1980s-1990s, Artist, American
Grooverider, Jungle; Drum'n'Bass, 1980s-1990s, Artist; Producer, British
Guadalcanal Diary, 1980s Pop, 1980s-1990s, Artist, American
Guided By Voices, Alternative/Indie Rock, 1980s-, Artist, American
Gun Club, US Underground & Garage Rock; Hard Rock; Alternative/Indie Rock, 1980s-1990s, Artist, American
Guns 'n' Roses, Hard Rock, 1980s-, Artist, American
Guy, Urban Soul, 1980s-, Artist, American
Haircut 100, New Wave; 1980s Pop, 1980s, Artist, British
Half Man Half Biscuit, Alternative/Indie Rock, 1980s-, Artist, British
Half Pint, Dancehall; Roots; Reggae Pop, 1980s-, Artist; Composer, Jamaican
Hangman's Beautiful Daughters, US Underground & Garage Rock, 1980s, Artist, American
Hanoi Rocks, Heavy Metal, 1980s, Artist, Finish
Hanrahan, Kip, Fusion and Jazz Rock; Fusion, 1980s-1990s, Producer; Artist, American
Happy Mondays, Madchester; Alternative/Indie Rock, 1980s-1990s, Artist, British
Hardcastle, Paul, Electro, 1980s-, Artist; Producer, British
Harriss, Don, New Age; Electro, 1980s-1990s, Artist; Composer, American
Hartnoll, Phil and Paul, Techno, 1980s-, Artist, British
Hawkins, Ted, Rhythm & Blues, 1980s-1990s, Artist, American
Head Of David, Death Metal & Grindcore, 1980s-1990s, Artist, British
Healey, Jeff, Blues Rock, 1980s-1990s, Artist, Canadian
Heart Of Gold Band, Folk Rock, 1980s, Artist, American
Heaven and Earth, Urban Soul, 1980s-, Artist, American
Heaven 17, New Romantics; New Wave, 1980s-1990s, Artist, British
Heavy D and The Boyz, Hip Hop, 1980s-1990s, Artist, American
Helloween, Thrash & Speed Metal, 1980s-, Artist, German
Henley, Don, 1980s Pop; 1980s Pop Singer/Songwriters, 1980s-, Artist; Songwriter, American
Henry, Joe, Alternative Country, 1980s-, Artist, American
Hewett, Howard, Urban Soul, 1980s-, Artist, American
Heyman, Richard X., 1980s Pop, 1980s-, Artist, American
Heyward, Nick, New Wave; 1980s Pop, 1980s-2000s, Artist, British
Hickman, Sara, Folk Pop; Alternative Country, 1980s-, Artist; Songwriter, American
Hidalgo, Giovanni, Latin Jazz; Fusion and Jazz Rock, 1980s-1990s, Artist, Puerto Rican
High Country, Young Country, 1980s-1990s, Artist, American
Highway 101, Young Country, 1980s-, Artist, American
Hill, Kim, Folk Rock, 1980s-1990s, Artist, American
Hines, Gregory, Urban Soul, 1980s, Artist, American
Hitchcock, Robyn, Alternative/Indie Rock; Folk Rock; 1980s Pop, 1980s-, Artist, British
Ho, Fred, Fusion and Jazz Rock, 1980s-, Artist, American
Holland, Jools, Boogie-Woogie, 1980s-, Artist, British
Holmes Brothers, The, The Classic Soul Era; Modern Electric Blues, 1980s-, Artist, American
Honeybunch, 1980s Pop, 1980s-1990s, Artist, American
Hoodoo Gurus, Alternative/Indie Rock, 1980s-1990s, Artist, Australian
Hornsby, Bruce, Alternative/Indie Rock; 1980s Pop, 1980s-, Artist, American
Hothouse Flowers, Irish Folk; Folk Rock, 1980s-1990s, Artist, Irish
House Band, The, Irish Folk, 1980s-1990s, Artist, British
House Of Love, The, Alternative/Indie Rock, 1980s-1990s, Artist, British
Housemartins, The, 1980s Pop, 1980s, Artist, British
Houston, Whitney, 1980s Pop; Urban Soul, 1980s-, Artist, American
Howard, Miki, Urban Soul, 1980s-, Artist, American
Huey Lewis and the News, Blues Rock; Soul, 1980s-1990s, Artist, American
Hugh, Grayson, Urban Soul, 1980s-1990s, Artist, American
Humphries, Tony, House; US Garage, 1980s-, Artist; Producer, American
Hüsker Dü, US Underground & Garage Rock; American Punk, 1980s, Artist, American
Ice Cube, Golden Age; Gangsta, 1980s-, Artist, American
Iced Earth, Heavy Metal, 1980s-, Artist, American
Ice-T, Golden Age; Gangsta, 1980s-, Artist, American
Icicle Works, 1980s Pop, 1980s, Artist, British
Imagination, Urban Soul, 1980s-1990s, Artist, British
Incognito, Acid Jazz, 1980s-, Artist, British
Indigo Girls, Folk Rock; 1980s Pop Singer/Songwriters, 1980s-, Artist; Songwriter, American
Innocence Mission, Folk Rock, 1980s-, Artist, American
Insane Clown Posse, Heavy metal; Gangsta, 1980s-1990s, Artist, American
Inspiral Carpets, Madchester, 1980s-1990s, Artist, British
INXS, New Wave, 1980s-2000s, Artist, Australian
Irie, Tippa, Ragga; Dancehall, 1980s-, Artist, Jamaican-British
Isaak, Chris, Rockabilly; Rock'n'Roll, 1980s-, Artist; Songwriter, American
It Bites, Prog Rock; Hard Rock, 1980s-1990s, Artist, British
Itals, The, Roots, 1980s-1990s, Artist, Jamaican
Jackson, Freddie, Urban Soul, 1980s-, Artist, American
Jackson, Janet, 1980s Pop; Contemporary R&B, 1980s-, Artist, American
Jackson, Rebbie, Urban Soul, 1980s-1990s, Artist, American
Jacksons, The, 1980s Pop; The Classic Soul Era, 1980s, Artist, American
Jamaica Boys, The, Urban Soul, 1980s-1990s, Artist, Jamaican
James, Madchester; Alternative/Indie Rock, 1980s-2000s, Artist, British
Jane's Addiction, Alternative/Indie Rock, 1980s-1990s, Artist, American
Jarreau, Al, Rhythm & Blues; 1980s Pop; Jazz, 1970s-, Artist, American
Jason and the Scorchers, Country Rock; Rock'n'Roll, 1980s-1990s, Artist, American
Jawbreaker, Grunge; Alternative/Indie Rock, 1980s-1990s, Artist, American
Jaye, Miles, Urban Soul, 1980s-1990s, Artist, American
Jayhawks, The, Alternative Country, 1980s-, Artist, American

see Introduction pp 268 see Sources & Sounds pp 270 see Key Artists pp 274 see A–Z of Artists pp 286

Jazz Warriors, The, Acid Jazz, 1980s, Artist, British
Jellybean, House; US Garage, 1980s-1990s, Artist; Producer, American
Jenkins, Tomi, The Classic Soul Era, 1980s, Artist, American
Jesus and Mary Chain, The, Alternative/Indie Rock; 1980s Pop, 1980s-1990s, Artist, British
Jesus Jones, 1980s Pop, 1980s-, Artist, British
Jesus Lizard, The, US Underground & Garage Rock; Alternative/Indie Rock, 1980s-1990s, Artist, American
Jett, Joan, Hard Rock; Arena Rock, 1980s-, Artist, American
Joan Jett and the Blackhearts, Hard Rock; Rock'n'Roll, 1980s-1990s, Artist, American
Jobson, Eddie, New Age; Electro, 1980s, Artist, British
Johnson, Jesse, Funk Soul, 1980s-1990s, Artist, American
Johnson, Paul, Trance; Techno, 1980s-, Artist, British
Jolly Boys, Ska, 1980s-1990s, Artist, Jamaican
Jones, Glenn, Urban Soul, 1980s-1990s, Artist, American
Jones, Howard, 1980s Pop; New Wave, 1980s-, Artist, British
Jones, Jill, Urban Soul, 1980s-, Artist; Songwriter, American
Jones, Marti, 1980s Pop, 1980s-, Artist, American
Jones, Oran 'Juice', Urban Soul, 1980s, Artist, American
Jonzun Crew, The, Electro, 1980s-1990s, Artist, American
Joss, Scott, Neo-Traditionalists, 1980s-, Artist, American
Judds, The, Young Country, 1980s-1990s, Artist, American
Jungle Brothers, Golden Age; Political Rap; Alternative Hip Hop; Hip Hop, 1980s-, Artist, American
Kamoze, Ini, Ragga, 1980s-1990s, Artist, American
Karet, Djam, Tribal Dance; Techno, 1980s-, Producer; Artist, American
Kashif, Funk Soul, 1980s-1990s, Artist, American
Katrina and the Waves, 1980s Pop, 1980s-1990s, Artist, British
Keen, Robert Earl Jr., Alternative Country, 1980s-, Artist; Songwriter, American
Keene, Tommy, 1980s Pop, 1980s-, Artist, American
Kelly, Jeff, Folk Rock, 1980s-, Artist, American
Kelly, Paul, Folk Rock, 1980s-, Artist, Australian
Kemp, Jack, Urban Soul, 1980s, Artist, American
Kennedy Rose, Country Rock, 1980s-1990s, Artist, American
Kentucky Headhunters, Young Country, 1980s-, Artist, American
Kershaw, Nik, 1980s Pop, 1980s-, Artist; Songwriter, British
Kershaw, Sammy, Young Country; Neo-Traditionalists, 1980s-, Artist, American
Ketchum, Hal, Neo-Traditionalists, 1980s-,Artist, American
Kid Creole and the Coconuts, 1980s Pop, 1980s-, Artist, American
Kidjo, Angelique, The Classic Soul Era, 1980s-, Artist, African
Killdozer, US Underground & Garage Rock; Alternative/Indie Rock, 1980s-1990s, Artist, American
King Diamond, Thrash & Speed Metal, 1980s-, Artist, American
King, Will, The Classic Soul Era, 1980s, Artist, American
King's X, Prog Rock; Hard Rock, 1980s-, Artist, American
KLF, The, House; Acid, 1980s-1990s, Artist, British
Klymaxx, Urban Soul, 1980s-1990s, Artist, American
KMFDM, Alternative/Indie Rock, 1980s-1990s, Artist, German
Knitters, The, Alternative Country, 1980s, Artist, American
Knopfler, Mark, Melodic Rock, Folk Rock, 1980s-, Artist; Songwriter, British
Koller, Fred, Young Country, 1980s-, Artist; Songwriter, American
Kool G. Rap and DJ Polo, Golden Age; Gangsta, 1980s-1990s, Artist, American
Krauss, Alison, Bluegrass; Neo-Traditionalists, 1980s-, Artist, American
Kravitz, Lenny, Psychedelic Rock, 1980s-, Artist, American
Kreator, Thrash & Speed Metal, 1980s-, Artist, German
Kuepper, Ed, Alternative/Indie Rock, 1980s-1990s, Artist, German
LA Guns, Heavy Metal; Hard Rock, 1980s-, Artist, American
La India, Latin, 1980s-, Artist, Puerto Rican
La's, The, Alternative/Indie Rock; Britpop, 1980s-, Artist, British
LaFave, Jimmy, Alternative Country, 1980s-, Artist; Songwriter, American
Laing, Shona, Folk Rock, 1980s-1990s, Artist, New Zealander
Lambert, Michael, Bebop, 1980s-1990s, Artist, American
Lambrettas, The, 1980s Pop; New Wave, 1980s, Artist, British
Lang, k. d. 1990s Pop Singer/Songwriters; Neo-Traditionalists; Alternative Country, 1980s-, Artist; Songwriter, Candian
Last Fair Deal, Folk Pop, 1980s, Artist, American
Lauper, Cyndi, 1980s Pop; New Wave, 1980s-1990s, Artist, American
Leaving Trains, US Underground & Garage Rock; Alternative/Indie Rock, 1980s-1990s, Artist, American
LeBlanc, Keith, Dub, 1980s-1990s, Artist, British
LeBlanc, Will, Young Country, 1980s-1990s, Artist; Songwriter, American
Lemonheads, The, Alternative/Indie Rock; US Underground & Garage Rock; 1980s Pop, 1980s-1990s, Artist, American
Lennon, Julian, 1980s Pop, 1980s-1990s, Artist; Songwriter, British
Lennox, Annie, 1980s Pop, 1980s-, Artist, British
Let's Active, 1980s Pop, 1980s, Artist, American
Level 42, 1980s Pop; 1980s Pop Singer/Songwriters, 1980s, Artist; Songwriter, British
LeVert, Urban Soul, 1980s-1990s, Artist, American
Lewis, Huey, Arena Rock; 1980s Pop, 1980s-, Artist, American
LFO, House; Techno; Acid, 1980s-1990s, Artist, British
Lieutenant Stitchie, Dancehall; Ragga, 1980s-1990s, Artist, Jamaican
Lightening Seeds, The 1990s Pop; Alternative/Indie Rock, 1980s-2000s, Artist, British
Lil' Ed and The Blues Imperials, Modern Electric Blues, 1980s-, Artist, American
Lime Spiders, Alternative/Indie Rock, 1980s-1990s, Artist, Australian
Liquid Liquid, Electro, 1980s, Artist, American
Lisa Lisa, 1980s Pop, 1980s-1990s, Artist, American
Little Charlie and the Nightcats, Modern Electric Blues, 1980s-1990s, Artist, American
Live Skull, US Underground & Garage Rock, 1980s-1990s, Artist, American
Live, Alternative/Indie Rock, 1980s-, Artist, American
Living Colour, Funk Metal, 1980s-1990s, Artist, Anglo-American
LL Cool J, Golden Age; Hip Hop, 1980s-, Artist; Songwriter, American
Lodge, J. C., Dancehall; Reggae Pop, 1980s-1990s, Artist, American
Logan, Josh, Young Country, 1980s, Artist, American
Lone Justice, Country Rock, 1980s-1990s, Artist, American
Lonesome Strangers, Alternative Country; Country Rock, 1980s-1990s, Artist, American
Long Ryders, The, 1980s Pop, 1980s, Artist, American
Loop, Alternative/Indie Rock; Shoegazing, 1980s-1990s, Artist, British
Loose Ends, Urban Soul, 1980s-1990s, Artist, British
Love and Rockets, Goth Rock, 1980s-1990s, Artist, British
Loveless, Patty, Neo-Traditionalists, 1980s-, Artist, American
Lovesmith, Michael, Urban Soul, 1980s, Artist; Songwriter, American
Lovett, Lyle, Alternative Country, 1980s-, Artist; Songwriter, American
Lush, Shoegazing; Alternative/Indie Rock; Britpop; 1980s Pop, 1980s-1990s, Artist, British
Lynne, Shelby, Alternative Country, 1980s-, Artist; Songwriter, American
Lynott, Phil, Heavy Metal; Hard Rock, 1980s, Artist, British
Mac Band, Urban Soul, 1980s-1990s, Artist, American
MacColl, Kirsty, Alternative/Indie Rock; Folk Rock, 1980s-1990s, Artist, British
Macka B, Dancehall, 1980s-, Artist, British
MacMaster, Natalie, Irish Folk, 1980s-, Artist, Irish
Madonna, 1980s Pop, 1980s-, Artist, American
Main Source, Golden Age; Alternative Hip Hop; Hip Hop, 1980s-1990s, Artist, American
Major, Charlie, Young Country, 1980s-, Artist; Songwriter, Canadian
Malmsteen, Yngwie, Heavy Metal; Hard Rock, 1980s-, Artist, Swedish
Man Called Adam, A, Acid Jazz, 1980s-1990s, Artist, British
Mann, Aimee, 1980s Pop Singer/Songwriters, 1980s-, Artist, American
Manning, Roger, Contemporary Folk; Folk Rock, 1980s-, Artist; Songwriter, American
Mantronix, Electro; Golden Age; Old School; Hip Hop, 1980s-1990s, Artist, American
Marley Marl, Golden Age; Old School; Hip Hop, 1980s-, Artist, American
Marley, Ziggy, Reggae Pop, 1980s-, Artist, Jamaican
Marsalis, Branford, New Orleans Jazz; Hard Bop, 1980s-, Artist, American
Marx, Richard, 1980s Pop, 1980s-, Artist, American
Material Issue, 1980s Pop, 1980s-1990s, Artist, American
Material, Prog Rock; Alternative/Indie Rock; Ambient, 1980s-1990s, Artist, American
Mattea, Kathy, Young Country, 1980s-, Artist, American
May, Derrick, Techno, 1980s-1990s, Artist; Producer, American
Mayhem, Black Metal, 1980s-, Artist, Norwegian
Mazzy Star, 1980s Pop, 1980s-1990s, Artist, American
MC Hammer, Hip Hop, 1980s-, Artist, American
McCarthy, Alternative/Indie Rock, 1980s-1990s, Artist, British
McDowell, Carrie, Urban Soul; Contemporary R&B, 1980s, Artist, American
McKee, Maria, Country Rock, 1980s-, Artist, American
McLachlan, Sarah, 1980s Pop Singer/Songwriters; Folk Pop, 1980s-, Artist; Songwriter, Canadian
Meat Puppets, US Underground & Garage Rock; American Punk; Alternative/Indie Rock, 1980s-, Artist, American
Meatmen, US Underground & Garage Rock; American Punk, 1980s-1990s, Artist, American
Megadeth, Thrash & Speed Metal, 1980s-, Artist, American
Mekong Delta, Thrash & Speed Metal, 1980s-, Artist, American
Melvins, Grunge; Alternative/Indie Rock, 1980s-, Artist, American
Men at Work, New Wave; 1980s Pop, 1980s-1990s, Artist, Australian
Mercyful Fate, Thrash & Speed Metal, 1980s-1990s, Artist, Danish
Metal Church, Thrash & Speed Metal, 1980s-1990s, Artist, American
Metallica, Thrash & Speed Metal, 1980s-, Artist, American
Michael, George, 1980s Pop; Urban Soul, 1980s-, Artist, British
Michigan and Smiley, Dancehall, 1980s-1990s, Artist, Jamaican
Microdisney, 1980s Pop; Alternative/Indie Rock, 1980s, Artist, British
Mighty Lemon Drops, The, Alternative/Indie Rock, 1980s-1990s, Artist, British
Mighty Mighty Bosstones, The, Ska, 1980s-, Artist, American
Miguel, Luis, Latin, 1980s-, Artist, Mexican
Mike and the Mechanics, 1980s Pop; Prog Rock, 1980s-1990s; 2000s, Artist, British
Milira, Contemporary R&B, 1980s-1990s, Artist, American
Milkshakes, The, Alternative/Indie Rock, 1980s-1990s, Artist, British
Milli Vanilli, 1980s Pop; Europop, 1980s-1990s, Artist, German
Mills, Jeff, Techno, 1980s-, Artist, American
Ministry, Alternative/Indie Rock, 1980s-, Artist, American
Minogue, Kylie, 1980s Pop; Manufactured Pop, 1980s-, Artist, Australian
Minor Threat, US Underground & Garage Rock; American Punk, 1980s, Artist, American
Minutemen, US Underground & Garage Rock, 1980s, Artist, American
Miracle Legion, 1980s Pop, 1980s-1990s, Artist, American
Miracle Workers, The, US Underground & Garage Rock; Hard Rock, 1980s-1990s, Artist American
Mission Of Burma, American Punk, 1980s-1990s, Artist, American
Mission, The, Goth Rock, 1980s-, Artist, British
Moby, House; Trance; Techno, 1980s-, Artist; Producer, American
Model 500, Techno; House, 1980s-, Producer, American
Momus, 1980s Pop, 1980s-, Artist, British
Monks Of Doom, US Underground & Garage Rock; Alternative/Indie Rock, 1980s-1990s, Artist, American
Mono Men, US Underground & Garage Rock; Alternative/Indie Rock, 1980s-1990s, Artist, American
Monochrome Set, The, Alternative/Indie Rock, 1980s-1990s, Artist, British
Moore, Chanté, Urban Soul, 1980s-, Artist, American
Moore, Thurston, US Underground & Garage Rock; Alternative/Indie Rock, 1980s-, Artist, American
Morbid Angel, Death Metal & Grindcore, 1980s-, Artist, American
Morgan, Lorrie, Neo-Traditionalists, 1980s-, Artist, American
Morphine, Alternative/Indie Rock, 1980s-1990s, Artist, American
Morrissey, Alternative/Indie Rock, 1980s-, Artist, British
Mother Love Bone, Grunge; Hard Rock, 1980s-1990s, Artist, American
Mötley Crüe, Heavy Metal; Hard Rock, 1980s-, Artist, American
Mould, Bob, Alternative/Indie Rock, 1980s-, Artist, American
Moving Cloud, Irish Folk, 1980s-1990s, Artist, Irish
Moving Targets, US Underground & Garage Rock; Alternative/Indie Rock, 1980s-1990s, Artist, American
Mr Big, Heavy Metal; Hard Rock, 1980s-, Artist, American
Mudhoney, US Underground & Garage Rock; Grunge, 1980s-, Artist, American
Murdock, Shirley, Urban Soul, 1980s-1990s, Artist, American
Murphy, Mic, Contemporary R&B, 1980s-1990s, Artist, American
Murphy, Peter, Goth Rock, 1980s-, Artist, British
Mutabaruka, Dub, 1980s-, Artist, Jamaican
My Bloody Valentine, Shoegazing; Alternative/Indie Rock; 1980s Pop, 1980s-1990s, Artist, Irish
My Dad Is Dead, US Underground & Garage Rock; Alternative/Indie Rock, 1980s-, Artist, American
Naked Eyes, New Romantics; New Wave, 1980s, Artist, British
Naked Raygun, US Underground & Garage Rock; 1980s Pop, 1980s-1990s, Artist, American
Napalm Death, Death Metal & Grindcore, 1980s-, Artist, British
Necros, The, US Underground & Garage Rock; Thrash & Speed Metal, 1980s, Artist, American
Ned's Atomic Dustbin, Alternative/Indie Rock, 1980s-1990s, Artist, British
Negative Approach, US Underground & Garage Rock, 1980s, Artist, American
Neville, Ivan, Urban Soul, 1980s-1990s, Artist, American
New Age Steppers, The, Dub, 1980s-1990s, Artist, British
New Edition, 1980s Pop; Urban Soul, 1980s-1990s, Artist, American
New Kids on the Block, 1980s Pop, 1980s-1990s, Artist, American
New Model Army, Alternative/Indie Rock; Folk Rock, 1980s-, Artist, British
New Order, Alternative/Indie Rock; 1980s Pop, 1980s-, Artist, British
Newcleus, Electro, 1980s, Artist, American
Nice and Smooth, Hip Hop; Golden Age, 1980s-1990s, Artist, American
Nicole, Urban Soul, 1980s-, Artist, American
Nine Inch Nails, Alternative/Indie Rock; Nu Metal, 1980s-, Artist, American
Nirvana, Grunge; Alternative/Indie Rock, 1980s-1990s, Artist, American
No Doubt, Funk Metal; Ska, 1990s-, Artist, American
Nomads, The, Alternative/Indie Rock, 1980s-, Artist, Swedish
Nomi, Klaus, Pop; New Wave, 1980s, Artist, German
Nu Shooz, Urban Soul, 1980s-1990s, Artist, American
Nuclear Assault, Thrash & Speed Metal, 1980s-1990s, Artist, American
NWA, Golden Age; Gangsta, 1980s-1990s, Artist, American
O'Connor, Sinéad, 1980s Pop, 1980s-, Artist, Irish
O'Kanes, The, Neo-Traditionalists; Country Rock; Bluegrass, 1980s-1990s, Artist, American
O'Neal, Alexander, Urban Soul, 1980s-, Artist, American
O'Rourke, Jim, Alternative/Indie Rock, 1980s-, Artist, American
Obituary, Death Metal & Grindcore, 1980s-1990s, Artist, American
Offspring, The, 1980s Pop, 1980s-, Artist, American
Omar and the Howlers, Modern Electric Blues; Blues Rock, 1980s-, Artist, American
Omar and the Howlers, Modern Electric Blues; Blues Rock, 1980s-, Artist, American
OMD, New Romantics; 1980s Pop; New Wave, 1980s-1990s, Artist, British
One Way, Urban Soul, 1980s-1990s, Artist, American
Operation Ivy, Ska, 1980s, Artist, American
Optic Nerve, The, US Underground & Garage Rock, 1980s, Artist, American
Orb, The, House; Acid; Ambient; Electro, 1980s-, Artist, British
Orbit, William, Tribal/Progressive Dance, 1980s-, Artist; Producer, British
Orbital, Techno, 1980s-, Artist, British
Orchestral Manoeuvres in the Dark, New Wave; New Romantics, 1980s-1990s, Artist, British
Orchids, The, 1980s Pop, 1980s-1990s, Artist, British
Osbourne, Johnny, Dancehall, 1980s-1990s, Artist, Jamaican
Osbourne, Ozzy, Hard Rock; Heavy Metal, 1980s-, Artist, British
Oslin, K. T., Young Country, 1980s-, Artist, American
Overkill, Thrash & Speed Metal, 1980s-, Artist, American
Overstreet, Paul, Young Country, 1980s-, Artist, American
Page, Jimmy, British Blues, 1980s-, Artist; Composer; Producer, British
Pale Saints, Shoegazing; Alternative/Indie Rock; 1980s Pop, 1980s-1990s, Artist, British
Pantera, Thrash & Speed Metal; 1980s-, Artist, American
Panzer, Jag, Heavy metal; Hard Rock, 1980s-, Artist, American
Paradise Lost, Doom Metal; Death Metal & Grindcore, 1980s-, Artist, British
Paradise, Ska, 1980s, Artist, American
Paris, Mica, Urban Soul; Rhythm & Blues, 1980s-1990s, Artist, British
Paris, Political Rap; Gangsta, 1980s-1990s, Artist, American
Parrish, Man, Electro, 1980s-1990s, Producer, American
Partridge, Andy, Dub, 1980s-, Artist; Composer; Songwriter, British
Pasadenas, The, Contemporary R&B, 1980s-1990s, Artist, American
Pastels, The, Alternative/Indie Rock; 1980s Pop, 1980s-, Artist, British
Patitucci, John, Fusion, 1980s-, Artist, American
Paul, Frankie, Dancehall, 1980s-, Artist, American
Pebbles, 1980s Pop, 1980s-1990s, Artist, American
Peech Boys, The, House; US Garage, 1980s-, Producer, American
Penn, Michael, 1980s Pop; 1980s Pop Singer/Songwriters, 1980s-, Artist, American
Perry, Phil, Urban Soul, 1980s-, Artist, American
Pet Shop Boys, 1980s Pop; House, 1980s-, Artist, British
Phillinganes, Greg, Urban Soul, 1980s-1990s, Artist, American
Phillips, Sam, Alternative/Indie Rock; 1980s Pop, 1980s-, Artist, American
Phish, Jam Rock, 1980s-, Artist, American
Phranc, Folk Rock; Alternative Folk, 1980s-1990s, Artist, American
Pierce, Jo Carol, Alternative Country, 1980s-1990s, Artist; Songwriter, American
Pinchers, Dancehall; Ragga, 1980s-, Artist, American
Pixies, Alternative/Indie Rock, 1980s-1990s, Artist, American
Pizzicato Five, 1980s Pop, 1980s-, Artist, Japanese
Planet Patrol, Electro, 1980s-1990s, Artist, American
Plasticland, US Underground & Garage Rock, 1980s-, Artist, American
Plimsouls, The, New Wave, 1980s-1990s, Artist, British
Pogues, The, Alternative/Indie Rock; UK Folk, 1980s-1990s, Artist, British
Poison, Heavy Metal, 1980s-, Artist, American
Pooh Sticks, The, 1980s Pop, 1980s-1990s, Artist, British
Pop Will Eat Itself, Alternative/Indie Rock, 1980s-1990s, Artist, British
Posies, The, 1980s Pop, 1980s-, Artist, American
Possessed, Thrash & Speed Metal, 1980s, Artist, American
Prefab Sprout, 1980s Pop, 1980s-, Artist, British
Pretty Poison, Urban Soul, 1980s-1990s, Artist, American
Pretty Tony, Electro, 1980s-1990s, Producer, American
Price, Louis, Contemporary R&B, 1980s-1990s, Artist, American
Priest, Maxi, Dancehall; Reggae Pop; UK Reggae, 1980s-1990s, Artist, British
Primal Scream, Alternative/Indie Rock, 1980s-, Artist, British
Prisoners, The, Alternative/Indie Rock, 1980s-1990s, Artist, British
Proclaimers, The, Folk Rock; 1980s Pop, 1980s-, Artist, British
Psychedelic Furs, Alternative/Indie Rock; New Wave, 1980s-, Artist, British
Public Enemy, Golden Age; Political Rap; Hip Hop, 1980s-, Artist, American
Pulp, Alternative/Indie Rock; Britpop, 1980s-, Artist, British
Pussy Galore, US Underground & Garage Rock; Alternative/Indie Rock, 1980s-, Artist, American
Queen Latifah, Golden Age; Alternative Hip Hop; Hip Hop, 1980s-1990s, Artist, American
Queensrÿche, Melodic Rock, 1980s-, Artist, American
Rain Parade, 1980s Pop, 1980s, Artist, American
Rainy Day, 1980s Pop, 1980s, Artist, American
Ramazzotti, Eros, Latin, 1980s-, Artist, Italian
Ranaldo, Lee, US Underground & Garage Rock; Alternative/Indie Rock, 1980s-1990s, Artist, American
Ranks, Shabba, Dancehall; Ragga, 1980s-1990s, Artist, Jamaican
Rapeman, US Underground & Garage Rock, 1980s, Artist, American
Rare Air, Irish Folk, 1980s-1990s, Artist, Canadian
Ratt, Heavy Metal; Hard Rock, 1980s-1990s, Artist, American
Rave-Ups, The, Folk Rock, 1980s-1990s, Artist, American
Razorcuts, The, 1980s Pop, 1980s-1990s, Artist, British
Reader, Eddi, 1980s Pop; Folk Rock; Folk Pop, 1980s-, Artist, British
Reagan Youth, American Punk; US Underground & Garage Rock, 1980s, Artist, American
Rebel MC, Drum'n'Bass; Jungle, 1980s-1990s, Artist; Producer, British
Red Hot Chili Peppers, Funk Metal, 1980s-, Artist, American
Redd Kross, US Underground & Garage Rock; 1980s Pop, 1980s-1990s, Artist, American
Reid, Junior, Bobo Dread Deejays, 1980s-, Artist, Jamaican
Reid, Mike, Young Country, 1980s-1990s, Artist; Songwriter, American
REM, US Underground & Garage Rock; Alternative/Indie Rock; 1980s Pop, 1980s-, Artist, American
Renegade Soundwave, Dub, 1980s-, Artist, British
Replacements, The, Hard Rock; Alternative/Indie Rock; 1980s Pop, 1980s-1990s, Artist, American
Restless Heart, Young Country, 1980s-1990s, Artist, American
Reyes, Jorge, Tribal Dance; Techno, 1980s-1990s, Artist, Mexican
Rhianna, Funk Soul, 1980s-1990s, Artist, American
Rhodes, Kimmie, Alternative Country, 1980s-, Artist; Songwriter, American
Rich, Robert, Ambient; Electro; Tribal Dance; Techno, 1980s-, Artist; Producer; Composer, American
Richie, Lionel, 1980s Pop; Urban Soul, 1980s-, Artist, American
Ride, Shoegazing; Alternative/Indie Rock; 1980s Pop, 1980s-, Artist, British
Roachford, Contemporary R&B, 1980s-1990s, Artist, British
Robbins, Dennis, Young Country, 1980s-1990s, Artist; Songwriter, American
Rockwell, Urban Soul, 1980s, Artist, American
Rodgers, Paul, Hard Rock; Blues Rock, 1980s-, Artist; Songwriter, British
Rodman, Judy, Young Country, 1980s, Artist, American
Rollins, Henry, Alternative/Indie Rock; US Underground & Garage Rock, 1980s-, Artist, American
Romantics, The, 1980s Pop, 1980s-, Artist, American
Roots Radics, Dub, 1980s-, Artist, Jamaican
Rose Brothers, The, The Classic Soul Era, 1980s-1990s, Artist, American
Roth, Gabrielle, Tribal Dance; Techno, 1980s-, Artist, American
Roxette, Europop; 1980s Pop, 1980s-, Artist, Swedish
Royal Trux, Alternative/Indie Rock, 1980s-, Artist, American
Rubin, Rick, Hip Hop; Heavy Metal; Nu Metal, 1980s-, Producer, American
Run DMC, Golden Age; Hip Hop, 1980s-, Artist, American
Russell, Tom, Young Country, 1980s-, Artist; Songwriter, American
S.O.S. Band, The, Urban Soul; Funk Soul, 1980s-1990s, Artist, American
Saadiq, Raphael, Contemporary R&B, 1980s-, Artist, American
Saccharine Trust, US Underground & Garage Rock, 1980s, Artist, American
Sade, 1980s Pop; Urban Soul, 1980s-, Artist, British
Saint Vitus, Doom Metal; Alternative/Indie Rock, 1980s-1990s, Artist, American
Salem 66, Folk Rock, 1980s-1990s, Artist, American
Salt-N-Pepa, Urban Soul; Golden Age; Hip Hop, 1980s-1990s, Artist, American
Samples, The, Folk Rock, 1980s-, Artist, American
Sanchez, Reggae Pop; Ragga, 1980s-, Artist, Jamaican
Santa Rosa, Gilberto, Latin, 1980s-, Artist, Puerto Rican
Satriani, Joe, Hard Rock, 1980s-, Artist, American
Saunderson, Kevin, House; Techno, 1980s-, Artist; Producer, American
Savatage, Heavy Metal, 1980s-, Artist, American
Saw Doctors, The, Folk Rock, 1980s-1990s, Artist, Irish
Sawyer Brown, Young Country, 1980s-, Artist, American
Scared Reich, Thrash & Speed Metal, 1980s-1990s, Artist, American
Schoolly D, Golden Age; Gangsta, 1980s-, Artist, American
Scratch Acid, US Underground & Garage Rock; Alternative/Indie Rock, 1980s, Artist, American
Scrawl, Alternative/Indie Rock, 1980s-1990s, Artist, American
Screaming Trees, US Underground & Garage Rock; Grunge, 1980s-1990s, Artist, American
Screeching Weasel, Alternative/Indie Rock; 1980s Pop, 1980s-, Artist, American
Scritti Politti, 1980s Pop; New Wave, 1980s-1990s, Artist, British
Sebadoh, Alternative/Indie Rock, 1980s-1990s, Artist, American
Sepultura, Thrash & Speed Metal; Death Metal & Grindcore, 1980s-, Artist, Brazilian
Sevelle, Taja, Urban Soul, 1980s-1990s, Artist, American
Sex Gang Children, Goth Rock, 1980s-, Artist, British
Shack, Britpop, 1980s-1990s, Artist, British
Shakatak, 1980s Pop; Smooth Jazz, 1980s-, Artist, British
Shakespear's Sister, Alternative/Indie Rock; 1980s Pop, 1980s-1990s, Artist, British
Shamen, The, Acid; Techno, 1980s-1990s, Artist, British
Shanice, Funk Soul, 1980s-, Artist, American
Shea, Rick, Honky Tonk, 1980s-, Artist, American
Shear, Jules, 1980s Pop Singer/Songwriters, 1980s-, Artist; Songwriter, American
Shelton, Ricky van, Young Country, 1980s-, Artist, American
Shenandoah, Young Country, 1980s-, Artist, American
Sherrick, The Classic Soul Era, 1980s, Artist, American
Sherwood, Adrian, Dub, 1980s-, Producer, British
Shinehead, Dancehall; Ragga, 1980s-1990s, Artist, British
Shocked, Michelle, 1980s Pop Singer/Songwriters; Alternative Folk, 1980s-1990s, Artist; Songwriter, American
Shonen Knife, 1980s Pop, 1980s-, Artist, Japanese
Shop Assistants, 1980s Pop, 1980s-1990s, Artist, British
Siberry, Jane, New Wave; Alternative/Indie Rock, 1980s-, Artist; Songwriter, Canadian
Silk, Garnett, Roots; Ragga; Dancehall, 1980s-1990s,Artist, Jamaican
Silkworm, Alternative/Indie Rock, 1980s-, Artist, American
Silos, The, Folk Rock, 1980s-, Artist, American
Simmons, Patrick, The Classic Soul Era, 1980s, Artist, American
Simple Minds, New Wave; 1980s Pop, 1980s-, Artist, British
Simply Red, 1980s Pop; Urban Soul, 1980s-, Artist, British
Sinitta, Urban Soul, 1980s, Artist, American
Sisters Of Mercy, The, Goth Rock, 1980s-1990s, Artist, British
Skid Row, Heavy Metal, 1980s-, Artist, American
Slaughter, Heavy Metal; Hard Rock, 1980s-1990s, Artist, American
Slayer, Thrash & Speed Metal, 1980s-, Artist, American
Slick Rick, Golden Age; Gangsta; Hip Hop, 1980s-1990s, Artist, British
Slint, US Underground & Garage Rock; Alternative/Indie Rock, 1980s-1990s, Artist, American
Slowdive, Shoegazing; Alternative/Indie Rock, 1980s-1990s, Artist, British
Smiley Culture, Dancehall, 1980s, Artist, British
Smith, Darden, Young Country, 1980s-, Artist, American
Smith, Patti, Proto-Punk; Hard Rock, 1980s-, Artist, American
Smithereens, The, Folk Rock; 1980s Pop, 1980s-1990s, Artist, American
Smiths, The, Alternative/Indie Rock, 1980s-1990s, Artist, British
Smog, Alternative/Indie Rock, 1980s-, Artist, British
Soda Stereo, Latin, 1980s-, Artist, Spanish
Soft Cell, New Wave; New Romantics, 1980s-1990s, Artist, British
Software, New Age; Electro, 1980s-1990s, Artist, German
Sonic Boom, Alternative/Indie Rock, 1980s-1990s, Artist, British
Sonic Youth, Alternative/Indie Rock; US Underground & Garage Rock, 1980s-, Artist, American
Soul Asylum, US Underground & Garage Rock; Hard Rock, 1980s-1990s, Artist, American
Soul II Soul, 1980s Pop; Urban Soul; House; Acid, 1980s-1990s, Artist, British
Soundgarden, Grunge; Alternative/Indie Rock, 1980s-1990s, Artist, American
Soup Dragons, The, Alternative/Indie Rock, 1980s-1990s, Artist, British
Southern Culture On The Skids, Alternative/Indie Rock, 1980s-, Artist, American
Southern Death Cult, Goth Rock; Hard Rock, 1980s, Artist, British
Spacemen 3, Alternative/Indie Rock, 1980s-1990s, Artist, British
Spandau Ballet, New Romantics; New Wave; 1980s Pop, 1980s, Artist, British
Spear Of Destiny, Alternative/Indie Rock, 1980s-, Artist, British
Spencer, Tracie, Urban Soul, 1980s-, Artist, American
Spheeris, Chris, Folk Pop, 1980s-, Artist; Composer, Greek
Spice 1, Gangsta, 1980s, Artist, American
Spongetones, The, 1980s Pop; New Wave, 1980s-, Artist, American
Squirrel Bait, US Underground & Garage Rock; Alternative/Indie Rock, 1980s, Artist, American
Stansfield, Lisa, 1980s Pop, 1980s-, Artist, British
Steelie and Cleevie, Dancehall; Roots, 1980s-1990s, Artist, Jamaican
Stephenson, Van, Urban Soul, 1980s, Artist, American
Stereo MCs, Acid Jazz; House, 1980s-, Artist, British
Stetsasonic, Hip Hop; Golden Age, 1980s-1990s, Artist, American
Steven, Jeff, Young Country, 1980s-1990s, Artist, American
Stock/Aitken/Waterman, 1980s Pop, 1980s-1990s, Producer; Songwriter, British
Stone Roses, The, Madchester; Alternative/Indie Rock; Britpop, 1980s-1990s, Artist, British
Stone, Doug, Young Country; Neo-Traditionalists, 1980s-1990s, Artist, American
Stormtroopers Of Death, Thrash & Speed Metal, 1980s-, Artist, American
Stratovarius, Heavy Metal, 1980s-, Artist, Finnish
Straw, Syd, 1980s Pop, 1980s-1990s, Artist; Songwriter, American
Stray Cats, Rockabilly; New Wave, 1980s-1990s, Artist, American
Street, Patrick, Irish Folk, 1980s-1990s, Artist, Irish
Stuart, Marty, Neo-Traditionalists; Bluegrass; Country Rock, 1980s-, Artist, American
Style Council, 1980s Pop, 1980s-, Artist, British
Sublime, Ska, 1980s-, Artist, American
Sugarcubes, Alternative/Indie Rock, 1980s-1990s, Artist, Icelandic
Suicidal Tendencies, US Underground & Garage Rock; Thrash & Speed Metal, 1980s-, Artist, American
Super Cat, Dancehall; Ragga, 1980s-1990s, Artist, Jamaican
Superchunk, Alternative/Indie Rock, 1980s-, Artist, American
Sure, Al B., Urban Soul, 1980s-1990s, Artist, American
Surface, Urban Soul, 1980s-, Artist, American
Swamp Rats, US Underground & Garage Rock, 1980s, Artist, American
Swans, US Underground & Garage Rock, 1980s-1990s, Artist, American
Sweat, Keith, Urban Soul, 1980s-, Artist, American
Sweet, Matthew, 1980s Pop, 1980s-1990s, Artist, American
Sweethearts Of The Rodeo, Young Country, 1980s-1990s, Artist, American
Swing Out Sister, 1980s Pop, 1980s-, Artist, British
Sylvian, David, Prog Rock, 1980s-, Artist, British
Tad, Grunge; Alternative/Indie Rock, 1980s-1990s, Artist, American
Talk Talk, New Romantics; New Wave, 1980s-1990s, Artist, British
Talulah Gosh, 1980s Pop, 1980s-1990s, Artist, British
Tamplin, Ken, The Classic Soul Era, 1980s-1990s, Artist; Songwriter, American
Tashan, Urban Soul, 1980s-1990s, Artist, American
Taylor, Gary, Urban Soul, 1980s-, Artist, American
Taylor, James, Acid Jazz; Soul Jazz, 1980s-, Artist, British
Tears For Fears, New Wave, 1980s Pop, 1980s-, Artist, British
Teenage Fanclub, 1980s Pop, 1980s-, Artist, British
Tell-Tale Hearts, US Underground & Garage Rock, 1980s, Artist, American
Tenaglia, Danny, House; US Garage, 1980s-, Artist, American
Terrorvision, Heavy Metal, 1980s-1990s, Artist, British
Terry, Todd, House; US Garage, 1980s-1990s, Artist; Producer, American
Tesla, Heavy Metal; Hard Rock, 1980s-, Artist, American
Testament, Thrash & Speed Metal, 1980s-, Artist, American
Tetes Noires, Folk Rock, 1980s, Artist, American
Texas, Britpop; 1980s Pop, 1980s-, Artist, British
That Petrol Emotion, Alternative/Indie Rock, 1980s-1990s, Artist, Irish
The The, Alternative/Indie Rock, 1980s-, Artist, British
Therapy?, Hard Rock; Heavy Metal, 1980s-, Artist, Irish
They Might Be Giants, Alternative/Indie Rock; 1980s Pop, 1980s-, Artist, American
Thin White Rope, US Underground & Garage Rock; Alternative/Indie Rock; 1980s Pop, 1980s-1990s, Artist, American
Thomas, Lillo, Urban Soul, 1980s-1990s, Artist; Songwriter, American
Thompson Twins, New Wave; 1980s Pop, 1980s-1990s, Artist, British
Three Fourgiven, US Underground & Garage Rock; Alternative/Indie Rock, 1980s-1990s, Artist, American
Three Headcoats, Alternative/Indie Rock, 1980s-, Artist, British
Three O'Clock, The, US Underground & Garage Rock; Alternative/Indie Rock; 1980s Pop, 1980s, Artist, American
Throwing Muses, Alternative/Indie Rock, 1980s-1990s, Artist, American
Thunder, Shelley, Dancehall, 1980s-1990s, Artist, Jamaican
Tiamat, Death Metal & Grindcore, 1980s-1990s, Artist, Swedish
Tian, Funk Soul, 1980s-1990s, Artist, Japanese
Tickell, Kathryn, UK Folk; Irish Folk, 1980s-, Artist, British
Tieghem, David van, Tribal Dance; Techno, 1980s-1990s, Artist, American
Til Tuesday, 1980s Pop; New Wave, 1980s, Artist, British
Tillis, Pam, Young Country; Urban Cowboys, 1980s-, Artist, American
Time, The, Funk Metal, 1980s-1990s, Artist, American
Times Two, Urban Soul, 1980s-1990s, Artist, American
Tin Star, Alternative Country, 1980s, Artist, American
Tiny Lights, Folk Rock, 1980s-1990s, Artist, American
Toad the Wet Sprocket, Alternative/Indie Rock, 1980s-1990s, Artist, American
Today, Urban Soul, 1980s-1990s, Artist, American
Tone-Loc, Hip Hop, 1980s-1990s, Artist, American
Tones on Tail, Goth Rock, 1980s, Artist, British
Tony Toni Tone, Contemporary R&B, 1980s-1990s, Artist, American
Too Short, Golden Age; Gangsta, 1980s-, Artist, American
Traveling Wilburys, Folk Rock, 1980s-1990s, Artist, American
Travis, Randy, Neo-Traditionalists, 1980s-, Artist, American
Treepeople, Grunge; Alternative/Indie Rock, 1980s-1990s, Artist, American
Tribe Called Quest, A, Alternative Hip Hop; Hip Hop, 1980s-1990s, Artist, American
Triffids, The, Folk Pop, 1980s, Artist, Australian
Trouble, Doom Metal, 1980s-1990s, Artist, American
True West, 1980s Pop, 1980s, Artist, American
Tuff, Tony, UK Reggae, 1980s; 2000s-, Artist, British
Tupelo, Uncle, Alternative Country, 1980s-1990s, Artist, American
Turner, Ruby, Urban Soul, 1980s-1990s, Artist, British
Tutone, Tommy, New Wave, 1980s-1990s, Artist, American
UB40, Reggae Pop, 1980s-, Artists, British
Ugly Kid Joe, Hard Rock; Heavy Metal, 1980s-1990s, Artist, American
Ultra Naté, Tribal Dance; House; US Garage, 1980s-, Artist, American
Ultramagnetic MCs, Golden Age; Hip Hop, 1980s-1990s, Artist, American
Ultravox, New Romantics; New Wave, 1980s-1990s, Artist, British
Uncle Jamm's Army, Electro, 1980s, Artist, American
Uncle Tupelo, Country Rock; Alternative Country; Contemporary Folk, 1980s-1990s, Artist, American
Underworld, House; Progressive Dance; Techno, 1980s-, Artist, British
Unity 2, Dancehall; Ragga, 1980s-1990s, Artist, Jamaican
Unrest, Alternative/Indie Rock; US Underground & Garage Rock, 1980s-1990s, Artist, American
Unsane, US Underground & Garage Rock; Alternative/Indie Rock, 1980s-1990s, Artist, American
Ure, Midge, New Romantics; New Wave; British Punk, 1980s-, Artist, British
Urge Overkill, Hard Rock; Alternative/Indie Rock, 1980s-1990s, Artist, American
Vai, Steve, Heavy Metal; Hard Rock, 1980s-, Artist, American
Van Shelton, Ricky, Young Country, 1980s-, Artist, American
Vandross, Luther, Urban Soul, 1980s-, Artist, American
Varttina, Folk Pop, 1980s-, Artist, Finnish
Vaselines, The, 1980s Pop, 1980s, Artist, British
Vasquez, Junior, House; US Garage, 1980s-, Artist, American
Vaughan, Jimmie, Modern Electric Blues; Blues Rock, 1980s-, Artist, American
Vaughan, Stevie Ray, Texas Blues; Modern Electric Blues; Blues Rock, 1980s-1990s, Artist, American
Vega, Suzanne, 1980s Pop Singer/Songwriters; Alternative Folk; Contemporary Folk, 1980s-, Artist; Songwriter, American
Venom, Black Metal, 1980s, Artist, British
Vesta, Urban Soul, 1980s-1990s, Artist, American
Violent Femmes, Alternative/Indie Rock; New Wave, 1980s-, Artist, American
Vipers, The, US Underground & Garage Rock Revival, 1980s-1990s, Artist, American
Virgin Prunes, The, New Wave, Alternative/Indie Rock, 1980s, Artist, Irish
Visage, New Romantics; New Wave, 1980s, Artist, British
Vixen, Heavy Metal; Hard Rock, 1980s-1990s, Artist, American
Vogl, Nancy, Folk Rock, 1980s-1990s, Artist; Songwriter, American
Voice Of The Beehive, 1990s Pop, 1980s-1990s; 2000s, Artist, British
Voivod, Thrash & Speed Metal, 1980s-, Artist, Canadian
Volebeats, The, Alternative Country, 1980s-, Artist, American
W.A.S.P., Heavy Metal, 1980s-, Artist, American
Wagoners, The, Alternative Country, 1980s, Artist, American
Wah!, 1980s Pop, 1980s-, Artist, British
Waite, John, Arena Rock; Melodic Rock; Psychedelic Rock, 1980s-, Artist, British
Wakeman, Dusty, Alternative Country, 1980s-1990s, Artist, American
Wales, Josey, Ragga, 1980s-, Artist, Jamaican
Walkabouts, The , Alternative Country, 1980s-, Artist, American
Walker, Joe Louis, Modern Electric Blues, 1980s-, Artist, American
Wariner, Steve, Neo-Traditional, 1980s-, Artist, American
Warrant, Heavy Metal; Hard Rock, 1980s-, Artist, American
Warren, Jamie, Young Country, 1980s-1990s, Artist; Producer, American
Watchtower, Thrash & Speed Metal, 1980s, Artist, American
Waterboys, The, Folk Rock, 1980s-1990s, Artist, British
Waterman, Pete, 1980s Pop; Manufactured Pop, 1980s-, Producer, British
Watkins, Kit, New Age; Electro, 1980s-1990s, Artist, American
Watley, Jody, Urban Soul, 1980s-, Artist, American
Weatherall, Andrew, Techno; Acid; House, 1980s-, Producer, British
Weathers, Barbara, Urban Soul, 1980s-1990s, Artist, American
Wedding Present, The, Alternative/Indie Rock, 1980s-1990s, Artist, British
Wellington, Valerie, Modern Electric Blues, 1980s-1990s, Artist, American
WestBam, Acid; Techno, 1980s-, Artist, German
Wet Wet Wet, 1990s Pop, 1980s-, Artist, British
Wham!, Britpop; 1980s Pop, 1980s-1990s, Artist, British
Wheeler, Caron, Urban Soul, 1980s-1990s, Artist, British
Whelan, John, Irish Folk, 1980s-, Artist, Irish
White Lion, Hard Rock; Glam Rock & Glitter, 1980s-1990s, Artist, American
White Zombie; Heavy Metal, 1980s-1990s, Artist, American
White, Karyn, Urban Soul, 1980s-1990s, Artist, American
White, Lynn, The Classic Soul Era, 1980s-1990s, Artist, American
Whitley, Keith, Neo-Traditionalists; Bluegrass, 1980s-1990s, Artist, American
Whodini, Golden Age; Old School; Hip Hop 1980s-1990s, Artist, American
Wilde, Eugene, Urban Soul, 1980s-1990s, Artist, American
Wilde, Kim, 1980s Pop, 1980s-1990s, Artist, British
Williams, Vanessa, Urban Soul, 1980s-, Artist, American
Williams, Victoria, Alternative Country, 1980s-, Artist; Songwriter, American
Willson-Piper, Marty, Folk Rock, 1980s-, Artist; Songwriter, Australian
Wilson, Cassandra, Fusion and Jazz Rock, 1980s-, Artist, American
Winans, CeCe, Urban Soul, 1980s-, Artist, American
Winger, Heavy Metal; Hard Rock, 1980s-1990s, Artist, American
Winter Hours, Folk Rock, 1980s-1990s, Artist, American
Wolfhounds, The, Alternative/Indie Rock, 1980s-1990s, Artist, British
Womack and Womack; Urban Soul, Contemporary R&B, 1980s-1990s, Artist, American
Wonder Stuff, Alternative/Indie Rock, 1980s-, Artist, British
Woods, Mitch, Boogie Woogie; Jump Blues, 1980s-, Artist, American
Wopat, Tom, Young Country, 1980s-, Artist, American
World Party, Alternative/Indie Rock, 1980s-, Artist, British
Wright, Michelle, Young Country, 1980s-1990s, Artist, Canadian
Wurm, US Underground & Garage Rock, 1980s, Artist, American
X, US Underground & Garage Rock; American Punk, 1980s-, Artist, American
Yanni, New Age; Electro, 1980s-, Artist, Greek
Yaz, 1980s Pop; New Wave, 1980s, Artist, British
Yazoo, 1980s Pop; Electro, 1980s, Artist, American
Yello, 1980s Pop, 1980s-, Artist, Swiss
Yellowjackets, The, Smooth Jazz; Fusion, 1980s-1990s, Artist, American
Yellowman, Dancehall; Ragga, 1980s-, Artist, Jamaican
Yo La Tengo, Alternative/Indie Rock; 1980s Pop, 1980s-, Artist, American
Yoakam, Dwight, Neo-Traditionalists; Alternative Country; Country Rock, 1980s-, Artist, American
Yonics, Los, Latin, 1980s-, Artist, Mexican
You Am I, Grunge; Alternative/Indie Rock, 1980s-1990s, Artist, Australian
Young, Paul, 1980s Pop; Urban Soul, 1980s-1990s, Artist, British
Youth Of Today, US Underground & Garage Rock, 1980s-1990s, Artist, American
Yturbe, Victor, Latin, 1980s-1990s, Artist, Mexican
Zapp, Urban Soul; Funk Soul, 1980s-1990s, Artist, American
Zeni Geva, Alternative/Indie Rock, 1980s-, Artist, Japanese
Zephaniah, Benjamin, Trip Hop; Dub, 1980s-1990s, Artist, Jamaican
Zombie, Rob, Hard Rock; Heavy Metal, 1980s-, Artist, American

see Bon Jovi pp 274 *see* Michael Jackson pp 276 *see* Madonna pp 278 *see* Prince pp 282 *see* U2 pp 284

THE NINETIES

West-coast city Seattle was the unanticipated epicentre as grunge, the biggest 'back to basics' movement since punk, shook traditional American rock; Nirvana enjoyed iconic status for a spell until Kurt Cobain's death. The dance-rock of The Stone Roses, a holdover from the late 1980s, put Manchester briefly in the picture, but it was American bands like Metallica, The Red Hot Chili Peppers and R.E.M. who had put in nearly a decade of hard graft apiece, whose influential but very different rock sounds gained commercial acceptance at last.

The now dominant influence of MTV made sure the emphasis remained on the visual, while the Brit-pop 'war' in the mid-1990s saw Blur and Oasis deliver a much-needed kiss of life to a British music business already in a torpor. After that excitement came The Spice Girls, whose Shangri-Las meets The Monkees act appealed to both sexes and proved you could still manufacture a pop phenomenon. They were, perhaps, the ultimate extension of the karaoke craze.

1990s acts were not known for their staying power, but the sheer variety of sounds and styles on offer reflected a society where diversity and tolerance were the buzzwords.

Sources & Sounds

KEY ARTISTS

Metallica

Nirvana

Red Hot Chili Peppers

R.E.M.

Above

Oasis burst onto the UK's music scene as a healthy dose of guitar pop. *What's the Story Morning Glory* remains one of the best and most effective albums.

> '*Americans want grungy people, stabbing themselves in the head on stage. They get a bright bunch like us, with deodorant on, they don't get it.*'
>
> Liam Gallagher, Oasis

Right

With 'Nothing Compares 2U' Sinead O'Connor maintained rock and pop's long tradition of sending an artist to the top of the charts while singing someone else's song. From Elvis, through the Rolling Stones, it's the performance that seems to count the most.

The 1990s was a decade of rapid change – few of the names that dominated the early part of the decade would be conspicuous at its end. One such was Sinead O'Connor whose take on the Prince classic 'Nothing Compares 2U' was the UK chart-topper for the whole of February 1990 and, however briefly, one of the fastest-selling singles in worldwide chart history.

Equally, a pair of rap artists, one black (MC Hammer) and one white (Vanilla Ice) took the first year of the decade by storm only to subside as rapidly – no pun intended – as they had risen. Both 'U Can't Touch This' and 'Ice Ice Baby' (both 1990) purloined riffs from Rick James and Queen respectively for their hits, and sampling would now become an ever-growing ingredient of music due to advanced and ever more affordable studio technology.

Keeping It Real

But technology was about to spawn a powerful rival to music in the affection of the younger generation. The first popular handheld console was launched by Nintendo in 1989, and computer games quickly became the status symbol for anyone under 20. New initiatives were necessary to prevent music from becoming just another teen lifestyle choice like Gameboys, Sega Megadrive and their ilk.

These came in many shapes and from many sources. The Lollapalooza travelling festival kicked off in July 1991 and, staged annually thereafter, would launch many an alt-rocker's career – Nine Inch Nails the first beneficiary. Unusually it was the idea of a musician, Perry Farrell of Jane's Addiction.

MTV, keen to capture the 'mature' rock audience, kicked the *Unplugged* series into gear in January 1990, inviting established acts to bring their acoustic guitars and present their hits in stripped-down form. As well as a TV show, a best-selling album often resulted (Eric Clapton's winning an unbelievable six

Grammies), but this 'exercise in creative recycling' eventually became a cliché itself. It took Bruce Springsteen – who insisted on performing plugged – to underline the fact.

Out With The Old

At street level, grunge ruled, raucous Seattle three-piece Nirvana inspiring a host of soundalikes with their multi-platinum *Nevermind* and attendant anthemic single, 'Smells Like Teen Spirit' (both 1991). Eventually grunge met unplugged as Cobain and co. indulged MTV in one of their last shows before the troubled singer blew his brains out.

🎙 *see* Introduction pp 326   🎙 *see* Key Artists pp 332   🎙 *see* A–Z of Artists pp 340   🎙 *see* List of Artists pp 372

American bands tended to dominate the decade as a whole. Guns N'Roses, whose brand of bad-boy rock had hit big in the last years of the 1980s were losing momentum, the tactic of releasing two albums simultaneously rebounding on them. 1992 saw them tour in partnership with Metallica whose self-titled album had topped both the UK and US charts – the passing of the torch?

R.E.M., on the other hand, reaped the reward of continuity that had seen them capitalize on a decade's apprenticeship away from the spotlight in the indie hinterland. They swept the board at MTV's Video Music Awards in 1991. The Red Hot Chili Peppers had similarly built gradually through the previous decade and, just like R.E.M., hit paydirt after pacting with the Warners label. Their fifth album *Blood Sugar Sex Magik* (1991) went multi-platinum and contained the ballad 'Under The Bridge', which remains their signature track today.

In both cases adding polish to a promising product reaped immense rewards, even if some originality was inevitably sacrificed. Elsewhere, the trend seemed to be updating previous decades' stereotypes for a new audience: shock-rocker Marilyn Manson was the 1990s' Alice Cooper, Hanson were a cross between The Osmonds and The Jackson Five; and white funk hope Jamiroquai was a Stevie Wonder soundalike.

The alt. Scene

Country music was hitting the mainstream, in the US at least, with the likes of Garth Brooks selling in millions and leading a posse of 'hat acts' – Alan Jackson, Clint Black, Dwight Yoakam and Kenny Chesney among them – to multi-platinum glory. Interestingly, it was young performers taking the pioneering spirit of The Byrds and The Flying Burrito Brothers and producing what became known as alt.country – Wilco, Son Volt, The Jayhawks and Whiskeytown among them – that came up with more exciting, if lesser-selling results.

The post-Nirvana alt.rock scene was increasingly attacked by British acts as the pendulum swung. The Manic Street Preachers, Primal Scream, Pulp and Supergrass were among those creating genuinely

CLASSIC RECORDINGS

1991
Metallica: *Metallica*
Nirvana: 'Smells Like Teen Spirit', *Nevermind*
The Red Hot Chili Peppers: *BloodSugarSexMagik*

1992
R.E.M.: *Automatic For The People*

1995
Oasis: (*What's The Story*) *Morning Glory?*

Above
The Lollapalooza Festival became an annual highlight for alternative rock.

Left
MTV's *Unplugged* shows attracted big names like Eric Clapton and the power of television created a huge demand for spare, unembellished music.

see The Byrds pp 124   *see The Flying Burrito Brothers pp 214*   *see Jamiroquai pp 352*   *see Sinead O'Connor pp 360*

innovative music, while former Jam mainman Paul Weller was undergoing a creative renaissance. The Stone Roses bloomed briefly but influentially as a hangover from the Madchester scene of the late 1980s, trading on the excellence of their 1989 debut album.

The so-called Brit-pop war of 1995 that set Oasis and Blur against each other and made the national television news bulletins in saw Blur's 'Country House' (with sales of 274,000) beat 'Roll With It' (a mere 216,000) to pole position. The Mancunians would have their revenge when their album (*What's The Story*) *Morning Glory* (1995) debuted at No. 1.

The Shape Of Things To Come

This stage-managed 'battle' was also, in retrospect, the last hurrah of the singles chart. This had long been the case in the States, where rankings were now based

Below

With effortless cool Wyclef Jean and other members of The Fugees collective, indulged in an orgy of popular hip-hop and rock.

see Introduction pp 326   see Key Artists pp 332   see A–Z of Artists pp 340   see List of Artists pp 372

the stars to lose their lives in violent fashion. The Fugees were the first hip-hop supergroup, spawning Lauryn Hill, Pras Michel and Wyclef Jean as solo performers.

Boys And Girls

Solo acts Alanis Morissette, Robbie Williams, Björk, Beck and Sheryl Crow emerged to challenge the dominance of the groups – reinforced by the biggest crop of boy bands since The Osmonds and Jackson Five in the 1970s. Take That, Boyzone, Backstreet Boys, New Kids … all seemed more or less interchangeable. The same, however, could not be said of the Spice Girls, whose 'Girl Power' arrived in timely fashion to fill the tabloid newspaper gap created by Princess Diana's sad demise.

But pop's true princess was Kylie Minogue, the former soap star who became first a teenybop idol, then tried indie pop for size before wisely rejecting it and, as the decade ended, becoming a hot-panted, dance-music diva. Madame Tussauds, the legendary London waxworks, took the near unprecedented step in 1998 of updating her mannequin to reflect the change. As the music business faced yet another bout of unwelcome challenges with the arrival of file-sharing on the internet (Napster launched in 1999), Kylie was somehow an unthreatening, much-loved constant.

Left

Kylie Minogue, everybody's girl next door, was the perfect pop pixie for the 1990s. Her success was driven by her soap-stardom but she eventually created a unique cutsie appeal all of her own.

Below

For a short period Britpop made it respectable to accessorize with the Union Jack. Even in inflatable form.

more on radio airplay than sales, the result being that some hits never actually sold to the public in singles form, being offered to radio only. In Britain, sales would decline year on year until revived by the download-based charts of the 2000s.

For now, it took 'oldies' acts Aerosmith and The Rolling Stones to cotton on to the potential of the internet. In 1994, Steven Tyler and friends released an unissued single for download, while The Stones authorized a 20-minute concert webcast. Comparatively few fans had access to the world wide web at that time, but within a decade these things would be commonplace.

In the States, the often overlooked Hispanic population were coming into their own as record-buyers. Puerto Rico-born Ricky Martin emerged from their midst to top the chart in 1999 with his first English-language album. (Only Gloria Estefan had hitherto captured a significant slice of the pop market.) His success would open the door for Marc Anthony, Christina Aguilera, Enrique Iglesias and others, not to mention a revival for Carlos Santana. The foundation of the Latin Grammies in 2000 was soon to follow.

Hip-hop and rap was on the upswing, even if some of its practitioners seemed intent on destroying each other: Tupac Shakur and the Notorious BIG were among

🎸 see Blur pp 343 🎸 see Kylie Minogue pp 356 🎸 see Oasis pp 360 🎸 see The Spice Girls pp 366

Metallica

Key Artists

'Guitar players in the Nineties seem to be reacting against the technique-oriented Eighties.'

Kirk Hammett

Above

The self-titled album *Metallica* (commonly referred to as the *Black Album*) enabled the group to reach out to a wider audience, although they were criticized by some for selling out.

Formed in California 1981 by drummer Lars Ulrich (born in Denmark, 26 December 1963) and James Hetfield (born 3 August 1963, vocals, guitar) who shared a mutual love of British new-wave heavy metal. Dave Mustaine (lead guitar) and Ron McGovney (bass) were recruited for early live work but due to personal and musical issues the pair were quickly replaced by Kirk Hammett (born 10 November 1962, lead guitar) and Cliff Burton (born 10 February 1962, bass). Burton wore bell-bottoms at all times and insisted that, if the band wanted to work with him, they relocate to San Francisco – they did.

This classic line-up recorded the poorly produced but seminal debut *Kill 'Em All* (1983) funded and released by their first manager Johnny Zazula on his Megaforce label. Fast interlocking instrumentals and brutal loud speed on tracks like 'Search And Destroy'

and 'No Remorse' laid the foundation stone of thrash metal. Hard touring and a second album *Ride The Lightning* (1984) cemented a growing international cult status achieved with little radio play.

Puppet Life

By this time the band had parted with Zazula and Megaforce, signing an eight-album deal with Elektra Records. Instrumental prowess on complex extended tracks like 'Orion' and the anti-war message of 'Disposable Heroes' – played at blistering speed – saw *Master Of Puppets* (1986) become Metallica'a first fully-fledged masterpiece. Along with Slayer's *Reign In Blood* (1986) it remains one of the best extreme metal albums ever recorded.

Tragedy struck during a 1986 European tour when Burton was killed when the band's bus turned over. After a decent interval, Jason Newsted (born 4 March 1963), formerly of Flotsam and Jetsam, was drafted in as a replacement and slotted into the live and studio machine. On the *Garage Days Re-Visited* EP (1987) tribute was loudly paid to influences like Diamond Head and Budgie. *And Justice For All* (1988) showed that there was musical chemistry after Burton with trademark speed, hard riffing and quality control. Lyrically the confident vocals of Hetfield were turning away from hell, damnation, war and suffering to more mature and social lyrical concerns. The single 'One' became an international hit and the first of many Metallica videos.

Black Masterpiece

Bands like Slayer, Anthrax and Megadeth (formed by Mustaine) had followed in the wake of Metallica to turn thrash into a defined genre that reinvigorated heavy metal as a musical form. Metallica cemented their status as tribal leaders on the aptly named *Metallica* (1991) by adding orchestral backing and shorter, more melodic songs to the trademark hard-edged sound. Seen as a sell-out by some long-term fans used to extended tracks, this 'Black Album' became a

▣ *see Introduction pp 326*　　▣ *see Sources & Sounds pp 328*　　▣ *see A–Z of Artists pp 340*

metal *Thriller*, selling 15 million copies worldwide and spawning five hit singles including 'Enter Sandman' and 'Nothing Else Matters'.

Whilst touring this set around the world for over two years grunge changed the points on the American music railroad. It was not until 1996 that a new Metallica album *Load* was released. As equally commercial and compelling as *Metallica*, some fans reacted against the band's new 'indie' look although this did not hurt album or ticket sales for the subsequent world tour, which included headlining the sixth Lollapalooza. *Reload* (1997) came hot on its heels and *Garage Inc.* (1998) expanded on the *Re-Visited* EP by offering a full set of covers.

Always musically sure-footed – to the extent of collaborating with the San Francisco Symphony Orchestra to retool classics for live album *S&M*

(1999) – the band made the wrong headlines in 2000 by taking Napster and file sharers to court. Whilst defending the distribution of their music was a legitimate aim, bad publicity saw Metallica eventually withdraw their case.

In 2001, Newsted left the band and Metallica recorded *St Anger* (2003) with Bob Rock before drafting in ex-Ozzy Osborne bassist Rob Trujillo. Critically mauled, the album was something of a throwback to the early Metallica sound with the crunching majesty of 'Some Kind Of Monster' clocking in at nine-minutes long. The traumatic process of recording the album was captured on the DVD *Some Kind Of Monster* (2005). Today, Metallica remain revered by metal heads around the world and culturally significant enough to warrant an appearance in *The Simpsons* (2006).

Below

Metallica, pictured here on tour in 1991 to support the *Black Album*.

see Black Sabbath pp 212   see Anthrax pp 287   see Megadeath pp 306   see Slayer pp 314

Nirvana

◙ CLASSIC RECORDINGS

1988
'Love Buzz'

1989
Bleach, 'About A Girl'

1991
Nevermind, 'Smells Like Teen Spirit', 'Come As You Are' 'Lithium' 'In Bloom' 'Here She Comes Now'

1992
Incesticide, 'Big Long Now', 'Aneurysm'

1993
In Utero, 'Heart Shaped Box' *MTV Unplugged In New York*, 'The Man Who Sold The World', 'Where Did You Sleep Last Night'

Above
'Smells Like Teen Spirit' of 1991 brought Nirvana success around the world – the single was voted by *Rolling Stone* magazine 9th in the list of its 500 Greatest Songs of All Time in 1994.

'We proved that alternative music is a viable commodity.'
Krist Novoselic

One of the most influential acts of the 1990s, Nirvana formed in Aberdeen, Washington, in 1988 when Kurdt Kobain (1967–94, guitar, vocals), Krist Novoselic (born 16 May 1965, bass) and Chad Channing cemented the line-up of Nirvana. Signed by Seattle's growing Sub Pop label their first single was a cover version of The Shocking Blue's 'Love Bug' with the renamed Kurt Cobain penning 'Big Cheese' on the B-side. The initial pressing was limited to 1,000 copies.

Over the next year, Nirvana appeared on various compilations and briefly became a four-piece when Jason Everman (guitar) was drafted in for live work. Everman's $600 paid for the recording of Nirvana's first Sub Pop album *Bleach* (1989). Although pictured on the cover he did not play on the record. Released in

June 1989 the bedrock of the Nirvana sound was evident, the melodic beauty of 'About A Girl' contrasting with the loud, aggressive punk metal of 'Swap Meet' and 'Paper Cuts'. With hand-to-mouth American and European touring, Nirvana began to receive critical acclaim with Cobain keen to stress the influence of The Pixies on the Nirvana sound. A second UK tour planned for the spring of 1990 was cancelled when Channing departed.

Nirvana's second Sub Pop single – 'Sliver'/'Dive' – was followed by the recruitment of experienced drummer David Grohl (born 14 January 1969) who had toured and recorded with hardcore act Scream. Courted and signed by Geffen, Nirvana set about recording a second album with producer Butch Vig. Geffen were taken by surprise when initial pressing of 50,000 copies of *Nevermind* sold out in two days upon release in October 1991. By now, generational anthem

🎞 *see Introduction pp 326* 🎞 *see Sources & Sounds pp 328* 🎞 *see A–Z of Artists pp 340*

'Smells Like Teen Spirit' had been released and became Nirvana's first Top 10 single in America and the UK. The follow up 'Come As You Are' cemented Nirvana as the most celebrated new band in the world and the multi-platinum *Nevermind* became one of the most important and influential albums of the decade.

In Utero

For Cobain, success was a double-edged sword as, like Bob Dylan before him, he was now perceived as the spokesman of a generation – and the entire Seattle-inspired 'grunge' movement. Touring *Nevermind* around the world Cobain tired of 'Teen Spirit', improvising new lyrics and appeared on UK TV's *Top of The Pops* delivering the vocal as if sung by former Smiths lead singer Morrissey. Reacting against the commercial sheen of *Nevermind*, sessions for the next album were recorded mostly live in two weeks with producer Steve Albini, formerly of the thunderous Big Black.

Despite record company objection to the raw sound and pressure that led to the remixing of two tracks, 'Pennyroyal Tea' and 'Dumb', by R.E.M. producer Scott Litt, *In Utero* was released as the band intended and topped the charts on both sides of the Atlantic in 1993. Away from music, Cobain married Hole singer Courtney Love in February 1992 who gave birth to their daughter Frances Bean six months later. By 1993, Cobain and Love were addicted to heroin, a chemical romance that was, in part, played out in public with state threats to remove the child from their care.

The End

In November 1993, Nirvana demonstrated on a live MTV *Unplugged* session that their loud guitar-based songs could be distilled into acoustic beauty. Cobain's state of mind grew darker and, after failing with one suicide attempt in March 1994 during a European tour, he blew his brains out with a rifle at his Seattle home a month later on 8 April 1994. Like Joy Division lead singer Ian Curtis before him it was only after his suicide that songs like 'I Hate Myself And Want To Die' were judged to be Cobain's state of mind rather than mere lyrics.

He left a wife, a daughter and a personal legacy that, today, has expanded into iconic proportions. The publication of portions of his journals, a slew of biographies, films, albums, documentaries and even a comic-book graphic novel continue to stoke and expand the legend. Now singing and playing guitar, Grohl formed the successful Foo Fighters. Novoselic has chosen to keep a lower profile and turn to politics.

Above
Kurt Cobain, 'the leader of a generation'.

see Joy Division pp 260   *see* The Smiths pp 315   *see* Hole pp 350   *see* Foo Fighters pp 396

Red Hot Chili Peppers

> 'Once you start playing, the sort of chemicals and spirits that get released inspire you to become even more creative.'
>
> Anthony Kiedis

Above

The phenomenal success of the Chili Peppers' fifth album *BloodSugarSexMagik*, released in September 1991, launched the band into superstardom.

International fame seemed far away when, in 1983, upstaged by strippers The Red Hot Chili Peppers resorted to playing a cover version of Jimi Hendrix's 'Fire' naked with socks covering their genitalia. This routine was to become a trademark.

Anthony Kiedis (born 1 November 1962, vocals), Michael 'Flea' Balzary (born 16 October 1962, bass), Jack Irons (born 13 April 1962, drums) and Israeli-born Hillel Slovak (31 March 1962, guitar) met at Fairfax High School in Hollywood, around 1980. Active in various bands, they first played Los Angeles clubs under The Chili Peppers banner in 1983. Influenced by funk, rap, jazz and punk rock, their frenetic intensity won a local following.

Getting Going

Signed by EMI America only Flea and Kiedis appeared on the self-titled debut (1984) as Irons and Slovak were contractually tied to Mercury Records with another band, What Is Is?. Both returned when George

Clinton produced *Freaky Styley* (1985) a more spirited affair showcasing The Peppers' unique funk rock on tracks like 'Sex Rap' and 'Lovin' And Touchin''. Sales were low and only long, grinding tours kept tattoo parlours in business.

The critical tide turned with *The Uplift Mofo Party Plan* (1987). Featuring cult single 'Fight Like A Brave' as well as an assault upon Bob Dylan's 'Subterranean Homesick Blues' this strong set was well marshalled by producer Michael Beinhorn. Further momentum came with the *Abbey Road* EP (1988) featuring The Peppers' version of 'Fire' and a cover showing them walking across the famed Abbey Road crossing naked apart from their now trademark socks.

Too Much Too Young?

The Peppers embraced the vices as well as pleasures of the road and Slovak died of a heroin overdose on 25 June 1988. When Irons quit shortly afterwards to seek psychiatric treatment the end seemed nigh. After various auditions The Peppers regrouped with 18-year-old fan John Frusciante (born 5 March 1972) on guitar – who had to strip naked and show Flea an erect penis as part of the audition process – and former Toby Redd drummer Chad Smith (born 25 October 1962).

Although recorded in mourning, *Mother's Milk* (1989) was a commercial breakthrough, spawning their first US hit single 'Knock Me Down'. Switching labels to Warners for a reputed $7 million advance, Def Jam founder Rick Rubin produced the next Peppers album in a deserted house. As well as familiar fare like 'Funky Monks' and 'Suck My Kiss', Rubin coaxed the ballad 'Under The Bridge' out of The Peppers, which was another hit single. The album *BloodSugarSexMagik* (1991) went multi-platinum and the band was now international arena headliners.

In May 1992, a Far East tour was cancelled when Frusciante left the band citing stress and battle fatigue. The revolving guitar seat was filled twice in quick succession with Arik Marshall making his debut in front of 60,000 fans in Belgium before the band

see Introduction pp 326   *see* Sources & Sounds pp 328   *see* A–Z of Artists pp 340

headlined the highly successful Lollapalooza II tour (1992). The Peppers were now public property even appearing in an episode of *The Simpsons*, although Marshall was soon out of the band.

Musical And Spiritual Renewal

After Flea spent some months recovering from a debilitating illness, former Jane's Addiction guitarist Dave Navarro (born 7 June 1967) settled in as Frusciante's long-term replacement. Navarro played his debut gig at Woodstock '94 where The Peppers opened their set in silver suits with lightbulbs on their heads. *One Hot Minute* (1995) was a more rock-edged affair and met with indifferent reviews. With the band getting involved in various side projects – Flea and

Navarro joining the 1997 Jane's Addiction reunion – The Peppers appeared to be winding down. In fact, after jam sessions in Flea's garage, Frusciante rejoined, leading to a musical and spiritual renewal.

With Rick Rubin back in the producer's chair the resulting album *Californication* (1999) – exploring American influence on the world – was their most mature statement and spawned four hit singles. The Peppers were now one of the biggest international live draws, a position confirmed with *By The Way* (2003). Kiedis published his autobiography *Scar Tissue* in 2005 and 2006 saw the two-CD whammy of *Stadium Arcadium* recorded with Rubin in the same house where *BloodSugarSexMagik* was laid down in 1991 – with the same wonderful results.

Below
The Peppers' 'Johnny Kick A Hole In The Sky' dealt with the plight of native Americans in the US, influenced in no small way by part native-American vocalist Anthony Kiedis.

see **Bob Dylan** pp 126   see **Jimi Hendrix** pp 132   see **George Clinton** pp 236   see **Jane's Addiction** pp 352

338

R.E.M.

'Rock'n'roll is a joke, people who take it seriously are the butt of the joke.'

Michael Stipe

Above

R.E.M., touring in 1995, were at the peak of their success, with a string of Top 40 hits under their belt, including 'Losing My Religion'.

Right

In the late 1990s, R.E.M. became more electronica-influenced, providing inspiration to later bands like Radiohead.

Michael Stipe (born 4 January 1960, vocals) met Peter Buck (born 6 December 1956, guitar) in the Wuxtry record store in Athens, Georgia, in 1978. Two years later they met Bill Berry (born 31 July 1958, drums) and Mike Mills (born 17 December 1958, bass) at a party and Rapid Eye Movement – R.E.M. – was formed.

A demo secured the release of 'Radio Free Europe'/'Sitting Still' on the Hib-Tone label, which, in turn, led a long-term deal with Miles Copelands IRS label. Mini-album *Chronic Town* (1982) was critically received. On debut album *Murmur* (1983) Stipe's sometimes slurred, allusive vocals were a texture of the rich melodic music rather than a dominant force. Fans were not helped by song titles deliberately listed in the wrong order on the Stipe-designed album sleeve; a habit continued on early IRS albums like *Fables Of The Reconstruction* (1985) recorded in London with legendary 1960s producer Joe Boyd.

By *Document* (1987) – their fifth album – R.E.M. were the biggest and most imitated band on the American alternative college circuit receiving critical acclaim for their intelligent mixture of rock, pop and harmony drawing on influences as diverse as British new wave, The Byrds, The Velvet Underground and Stipe's extensive reading material. The mountain moved to them in 1987 when 'The One I Love' became their first US hit single. The frantic 'It's The End Of The World As We Know It (And I Feel Fine)' also entered the US and UK charts.

Out Of Time

Outgrowing IRS, R.E.M. signed to Warners in 1987. Produced by Scott Litt, *Green* (1988) retained artistic integrity, a commercial edge on singles like 'Stand' and the first wielding of Buck's mandolin on 'You Are The Everything'. After a globe-trotting tour the band took time out before returning with *Out Of Time* (1991). Adding strings to a startling set of folk, rock and country-tinged songs this watershed album sounded like a modern *Forever Changes* and catapulted R.E.M. to the very top of the big league.

📼 *see* Introduction pp 326   📼 *see* Sources & Sounds pp 328   📼 *see* A–Z of Artists pp 340

As well as topping the US and UK album charts, addictive singles like 'Losing My Religion', 'Shiny Happy People' and 'Near Wild Heaven' became anthems at the height of the Nirvana-led grunge boom. With Stipe refusing all promotional interviews the eagerly awaited follow-up *Automatic For The People* (1992) was another classic yielding an astonishing five hit singles, including 'The Sidewinder Sleeps Tonight', 'Nightswimming', 'Everybody Hurts' and a tribute to comedian Andy Kaufman, 'Man On The Moon'. Even with the band not touring the album went multi-platinum.

Monster

The shaven-headed, erudite and sexually ambiguous Stipe stamped out a new template of the aware, enigmatic, literate lead singer and generational spokesman on political and social matters. Musically, *Monster* (1994) returned to the guitar-heavy early days and kicked off R.E.M.'s first international tour for five years. Recorded during sound checks and stolen moments on a grinding 132-date schedule, *New Adventures In Hi Fi* (1996) was a brave departure, although apart from 'E Bow The Letter' – a collaboration with Patti Smith – it did not yield the usual quota of hits or hit previous sales figures. Shortly after re-signing to Warners for a reputed $80 million, Berry left the band in October 1997. During the Monster tour he had suffered a brain aneurysm that required surgery and, after recovery, retired to spend time at home with his family.

Buck, Mills and Stipe threw the rule-book out of the window to experiment on the radical set of *Up* (1998) that veered from the drum machine Krautrock of 'Hope' to the poignant ballad 'At My Most Beautiful'. R.E.M. returned to festivals, stadiums and venues as unique as London's Trafalgar Square for a South Africa Freedom Day Concert in front of Nelson Mandela. *Reveal* (2001) was a return to the *Automatic* harmony formula, yielding strong singles like 'Daysleeper'. *Around The Sun* (2004) sounded like a band painting by numbers for the first time with 'Bad Day' literally repainting 'It's The End Of The World As We Know It'. Buck's 2002 arrest for alleged air rage and a bizarre appearance on *The Muppet Show* aside, even as they play out their coda, R.E.M. remain as essential to the 2000s as they did to the 1980s and 1990s.

see The Byrds pp 124   see The Velvet Underground pp 134   see Patti Smith pp 254   see Nirvana pp 334

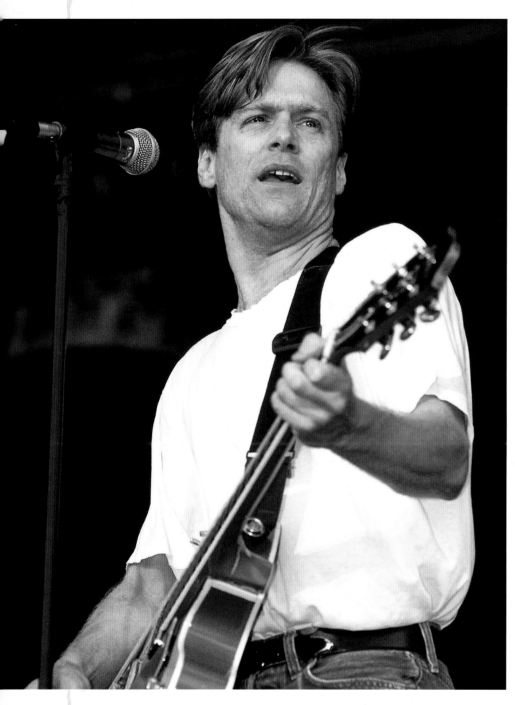

Above

Despite Bryan Adam's other successes, he will always be remembered for 'Everything I Do (I Do It For You)', which spent 16 consecutive weeks at the UK No. 1 and a mammoth 32 weeks in his native Canada.

Bryan Adams
(Singer/songwriter, b. 1959)

This Canadian singer/songwriter first found US success with his third album *Cuts Like A Knife* (1984). With material ranging from pleasing orthodox rock to lung-sucking ballads, the rest of the 1980s were fertile soil especially for rousing singles like 'Summer Of '69'. Adams began the 1990s with the theme song from *Robin Hood Prince Of Thieves*, '(Everything I Do) I Do It For You', which topped the UK charts for a record 16 weeks in 1991. *Waking Up The Neighbours* (1991) and *So Far So Good* (1993) both went multi-platinum and spawned more singles. Although ballads always seem to predominate – on singles and MTV rotation – Adams' roots were never hidden and *18 Till I Die* (1996) was a rousing collection of radio-friendly rock. Adams ended the 1990s where he began with 'When You're Gone', a UK Top 3 duet with Mel C from The Spice Girls. He has concentrated on photography in the new millennium.

Alice In Chains
(Vocal/instrumental group, 1987–2002)

This Seattle group, Layne Staley (vocals), Jerry Cantrell (guitar), Mike Starr (bass) and Sean Kinney (drums), cut their teeth on a winning blend of metal and acoustic numbers before being remarketed as a 'grunge' act after Nirvana's huge success. Their second album *Dirt* (1992) won acclaim and huge sales, a position cemented by *Jar Of Flies* EP (1994) and an eponymous third album (1995). Despite spawning imitators, they never realized full potential. Staley died in 2002 of a drug overdose.

Tori Amos
(Singer/songwriter, b. 1963)

Originally compared to Joni Mitchell, North Carolina-born Amos has an ability to blend crafted confessional and confident songwriting with pop and rock hooks. Subject matter included rape – 'Me And A Gun' – as well as miscarriage, marriage and the celebration of her own

sexuality. As well as singles like 'Cornflake Girl' and 'Pretty Good Year', strong albums from *Little Earthquakes* (1991), *Strange Little Girls* (2001) and recent *The Beekeeper* (2006) demonstrate mature talent and no little staying power.

Arrested Development
(Vocal group, 1990–94)
Formed in Georgia, and based around Todd 'Speech' Thomas and Timothy 'DJ Headliner' Barnwell. Taking a pastoral rather than city attitude, Arrested Development fused articulate social concerns, black pride and education on to music that blended hip-hop, funk and heavy doses of Sly. *3 Years, 5 Months And Two Days In The Life Of…* (1992) featured vital hits 'People Everyday' and 'Mr Wendel'. After *Zingalamadni* (1994) the band split. Speech went on to a solo career.

Ash
(Vocal/instrumental group, 1992–present)
Hailing from Northern Ireland, Ash comprise Tim Wheeler, (vocals, guitar), Mark Hamilton (bass) and Rick McMurray (drums). Initially trading as teenagers, their infectious blend of indie rock was captured on their debut album *1977* (1996). They had expanded to a wider palette on *Nu-Clear Sound* (1998) by which time they had added Charlotte Hatherley on additional

guitar. Fourth album *Meltdown* (2005) was a mature rock album. In 2006, Hatherley left the band.

Backstreet Boys
(Vocal group, 1992–present)
Nick Carter, Howie Dorough, AJ McLean, Brian Littrell and Kevin Richardson (left 2006). An American boy band, their first taste of success came in Europe in 1996 with soft-focus ballads like 'Get Down (You're The One For Me)'. They conquered the US in 1998, and albums like *Millennium* (1999) – the obligatory Christmas album – and *Black & Blue* (2000) sold in their millions. 'Quit Playing Games (With My Heart)' and *Now Or Never* (2002) kept them on the main chart freeway.

The Beautiful South
(Vocal group, 1989–present)
Paul Heaton formed The Beautiful South with drummer Dave Hemingway after the demise of The Housemartins as a vehicle for finely crafted, ironic and honest pop songs (co-written with guitarist Dave Rotheray). *Welcome To The Beautiful South* (1989) spawned three hits that set the tone for the entire 1990s. Singing alone or in duet with Briana Corrigan and later Jacqueline Abbott, Heaton's sugar-coated melodies were radio-friendly Trojan horses for bittersweet stories of love, romance and Rotterdam.

Above
Having sold almost 80 million albums worldwide, The Backstreet Boys are credited as being the most successful boy band of all time.

Left
Tori Amos is one of the few modern artists that use the piano as their main musical instrument.

see Joni Mitchell pp 144   see The Housemartins pp 299   see Nirvana pp 334   see The Spice Girls pp 366

Beck

(Vocals, b. 1970)

By making music that incorporates eclectic influences from folk, hip-hop, rock, electronica and studio prowess, Beck Hansen has become one of the most influential American solo artists. Early EPs, albums and singles like the classic 'Loser' were released on a variety of labels. When Beck signed to Geffen he retained the unheard-of right to release material on other labels. *Odelay* (1996) delivered every promise. *Mutations* (1998) was more acoustic and *Midnite Vultures* (1999) equally assured.

Below

The highly individual and immensely creative Björk has had three Top 10 and seven Top 20 hits in the UK.

Björk

(Vocals, b. 1965)

Lead singer with native Icelandic band The Sugarcubes, Björk Gudmundsdóttir went solo in 1991. *Debut* (1993) was a starting collection of songs yielding hits like the dance entrancing 'Human Behaviour' and 'Venus As A Boy' complete with Indian soundtrack string arrangements. Björk's unique keening and infectiously enthusiastic singing style was a refreshing change and *Debut* charted internationally. Always with an ear to the UK club scene – and a savvy video star – the driving beats of 'Big Time Sensuality', 'Violently Happy' and 'Army Of Me' helped to drive the success of *Post* (1995). A lush orchestral cover version of 1948 hit ''It's Oh So Quiet' demonstrated the eclectic nature of her music. Despite media intrusion into her personal life – Tricky and Goldie had both been lovers – Björk began producing her own albums and success continued. Following her own muse at all times, she even recorded a vocals only-album, *Medulla* (2004).

The Black Crowes

(Vocal/instrumental group, 1984–present)

Musically, The Crowes were a throwback to the classic rock swagger of The Rolling Stones. Formed in Atlanta, Chris Robinson (vocals), Richard Robinson (guitar), Jeff Cease (guitar), Johnny Colt (bass) and Steve Gorman (drums) combined hard touring and compelling albums like *Shake Your Money Maker* (1990) and *The Southern Harmony And Musical Companion* (1992). These laid the foundations for a long-term career and extensive chart success, despite a 2002–05 sabbatical. Chris married actress Kate Hudson in 2000.

Right

The Black Crowes' best-selling album *Shake Your Money* (1990) sold over 5 million copies and was certified five-times platinum by 1995.

Far Right

Blur's massive success in the UK with *Parklife* (1994) gave birth to a whole new Britpop scene that dominated British popular culture from the mid- to late 1990s.

Bikini Kill

(Vocal/instrumental group, 1990–98)

Named after a feminist magazine of the same name, Seattle's Bikini Kill spearheaded the riot grrrl movement. Kathleen Hanna (vocals), Tobi Vail (drums) and Kathi Wilcox (bass) published the magazine and roped in Billy Boredom on guitar. Musically a mixture of punk and feminist lyrics, the band built up a no-compromise reputation as a live act. EPs, singles and first album *Pussy Whipped* (1994) documented the musical and polemical prowess of the entire riot grrrl movement.

see Introduction pp 326   see Sources & Sounds pp 328   see Key Artists pp 332

Blues Traveler

(Vocal/instrumental group, 1988–present)
This New York jam band initially favoured the
extended blues rock format made popular by The
Grateful Dead. John Popper (vocals, harmonium),
Chan Kinchla (guitar), Bobby Sheehan (bass) and
Brendan Hills (drums) built a solid following that was
vastly amplified when aptly named fourth album – *Four*
(1995) – sold four million copies on the back of the hit
single 'Run-Around'. Although Sheean died in 1999 –
at 31 – the band continue to record and tour with great
success.

Blur

(Vocal/instrumental group, 1989–present)
Formed at London's Goldsmiths College, Damon
Albarn (vocals), Graham Coxon (guitar), Alex James
(bass) and Dave Rowntree (drums) tuned into vibe
generated by The Stone Roses with baggy anthems
'She's So High' and 'There's No Other Way'. Although
Leisure (1991) showed a band adept at updating 1960s
pop *Modern Life Is Rubbish* (1993) revealed depth
beneath the iceberg of Albarn's pretty face.

  With the release of infectious electro single 'Boys
And Girls' and cockney swagger of 'Parklife' Blur found
themselves the leaders of the 'Britpop' movement.
Albums *Parklife* (1994) and *The Great Escape* (1995)
cemented their reputation. Rivalry with Oasis was ill
timed, although taking a more loud and experimental
approach on *Blur* (1997) and *13* (1999) displayed
greater musical maturity without losing sales or fans.
Coxon departed to concentrate upon a solo career in
2002. Albarn's desire for wider experimentation and
collaboration found full flower in the Gorillaz project.

The Boo Radleys

(Vocal/instrumental group, 1988–99)
Best remembered for the 1995 UK hit single 'Wake
Up Boo!', The Radleys had been a previously struggling
indie band. Formed in 1988 by Simon 'Sice' Rowbottom
(guitar, vocals), Martin Carr (guitar), Timothy Brown,
(bass) and Steve Drewitt (drums) they were second-
generation shoegazers with ideas. Third album *Giant
Steps* (1993) traded blows with memorable melody and
hooks before *Wake Up* (1995) became a must-own
album for everyone in the UK. The band split in 1999.

see The Grateful Dead pp 130   see The Sugarcubes pp 318   see The Stone Roses pp 367   see Gorillaz pp 398

Boyz II Men
(Vocal group, 1988–present)

The sound of Motown in the early 1990s *was* the harmonies of this R&B vocal group. Wanya 'Squirt' Morris, Michael 'Bass' McCary, Shawn 'Slim' Stockman and Nathan 'Alex-Vanderpool' Morris formed when students at a Philadelphia High School. Their first two albums *Cooleyhighharmony* (1991) and *II* (1994) spawned monster hit singles like 'One Sweet Day' and 'On Bended Knee'. By *Full Circle* (2000) the romantic boys were men with families and thus less popular to girls….

Boyzone
(Vocal group, 1993–2000)

This Irish answer to Take That racked up seven Top 10 singles and spawned an equally successful solo star in Ronan Keating. Mikey Graham, Keith Duffy, Shane Lynch, Stephen Gately and Keating were mustered by future *X-Factor* svengali Louis Walsh in 1993. Their first UK hit was a cover version of The Osmonds' 'Love Me For A Reason'. After that, hits and photo-shoots came thick and fast including a delightful version of Tracy Chapman's 'Baby, Can I Hold You?'

Toni Braxton
(Vocals, b. 1968)

Initially singing with her sisters as The Braxtons, she was signed as a solo artist to La Face productions (L.A. Reid and Babyface) in 1991. This production/writing team crafted her eponymous debut (1993). At ease with soul vocals and the rhythms of R&B, the attractive Braxton was soon scoring hits with emotive ballads like 'Breathe Again'. 'Un-Break My Heart' was a massive international strike in 1996 and all subsequent albums confirm her mainstream chart credentials. She has since dropped her last name in diva-esque style.

Garth Brooks
(Singer/songwriter, b. 1962)

Brooks was pivotal in bringing country music into the mainstream. His warm honky-tonk style and trademark cowboy hat ensured his early material found an audience. The aptly titled *No Fences* (1990) and *Ropin' The Wind* (1991) crossed into the pop charts on the strength of the material and Brooks' canny employment of theatrical rock devices on his arena tours. By the bizarre concept album *In The Life Of Chris Gaines* (1999) he was an established platinum act, though he took a step back from fame in the 2000s.

Jeff Buckley
(Guitar, singer/songwriter, 1966–97)

Son of singer/songwriter Tim, Jeff Buckley possessed an astonishing vocal range, emotional capacity and genuine songwriting talent. His mini album *Live At Sin-e* (1992) was the signpost to the classic debut *Grace* (1994). As well as stellar original material like 'Last Goodbye', Buckley delivered the definitive cover of

see Introduction pp 326   *see* Sources & Sounds pp 328   *see* Key Artists pp 332

Switching to Virgin for $80 million in 2001, Carey experienced a breakdown due to exhaustion, and sales of the *Glitter* soundtrack (2001) were so poor, that Virgin paid her $28 million to leave. The *Emancipation Of Mimi* (2005) returned her to chart ways.

Leonard Cohen's 'Hallelujah'. Sessions for an eagerly awaited second album ended in May 1997 when Buckley drowned in the Mississippi River. Posthumous releases and acclaim followed.

Bush
(Vocal/instrumental group, 1992–present)
Formed in 1992 by Gavin Rossdale, (guitar, vocals), Dave Parsons (bass), Nigel Pulsford (guitar) and Robin Goodridge (drums), Bush were playing UK dives when signed by American label Interscope. The grunge-powered sound of their debut album *Sixteen Stones* (1994) received heavy rotation on American radio – with equally healthy sales – after the breakthrough 'Everything Zen' single. Hard touring and hard sounding *Razorblade Suitcase* (1996) produced by Steve Albini cemented their reputation – for a few years anyway. Rossdale is now Mr Gwen Stefani.

Mariah Carey
(Singer/songwriter, b. 1970)
Along with Whitney Houston, Carey (New York-born of Irish/African-American/Venezuelan descent) is one of the most successful female singers in American pop history. Her eponymous debut (1990) showcased her five-octave range and songwriting talent. Gorgeously sexy promotional videos meant songs like 'Vision Of Love' and 'Love Takes Time' were soon topping the charts. *Emotions* (1991) and *Music Box* (1993) spawned more hits and Carey began to tour. Equally at home singing romantic ballads, R&B and hip-hop fare with tracks like 'Hero' and 'Fantasy', her 'Endless Love' duet with Luther Vandross was particularly memorable.

see Tracy Chapman pp 291   *see* Luther Vandross pp 320   *see* Take That pp 368   *see* Gwen Stefani pp 412

The Charlatans
(Vocal/instrumental group, 1989–present)
Emerging out of the 'Madchester' scene, The Charlatans' initial organ-led groove music was soon embraced by the charts. Outgrowing this sound, Tim Burgess (vocals), Jon Baker (guitar), Martin Blunt (bass), John Brookes (drums) and Rob Collins (keyboards) matured into a rock band with a devoted fanbase. Collins' death in 1996 was a massive blow but subsequent albums like *Tellin' Stories* (1997) and *Up At The Lake* (2004) confirmed longevity. Burgess has released solo material.

The Chemical Brothers
(Electronic group, 1989–present)
Initially working under the name The Dust Brothers, Tom Rowlands and Edward Simons began their career as DJ's and remixers. After threats of litigation from US Dust Brothers they began recording under the name The Chemical Brothers. Their eclectic, analogue beat-driven dance tracks won a huge following. Live work and collaborations with John Lydon, Noel Gallagher and Beth Orton also displayed their versatility. Albums *Dig Your Own Hole* (1997) and *Surrender* (1999) remain classics.

Collective Soul
(Vocal/instrumental group, 1992–present)
Formed in Georgia, USA by Ed Rowland (guitar, vocals), brother Dean Rowland (guitar), Ross Childress (guitar), Will Turpin (bass) and Shane Evans (drums). Helped by the ripple effect of the Seattle grunge movement, their hook-laden 1994 single 'Shine' became an American hit securing a willing audience for the band's intense but melodic rock. *Hints, Allegations And Things Best Left Unsaid* (1993) and eponymous second album (1995) are the best representations of their sound. The band is still active.

The Cranberries
(Vocal/instrumental group, 1991–present)
Formed in Limerick, Eire in 1991, Dolores O'Riordan (vocals), Noel Hogan (guitar), Mike Hogan (bass) and Feargal Lawler (drums) soon became a UK and US chart staple. O'Riordan's unique and keening vocal style made chiming melodic singles like 'Linger', 'Dreams' and 'Zombie' into compelling pop. *Everybody Else Is Doing It, So Why Can't We?* (1993) and *No Need To Argue* (1994) both produced by Stephen Street best showcase their radio-friendly sound. On hiatus since 2004.

Creed
(Vocal/instrumental group, 1995–2004)
One of the biggest post-grunge rock acts formed in Tallahassee, Florida, in 1995. Scott Stapps (vocals), Mark Tremonti (guitar, vocals), Brian Marshall (bass) and Scott Phillips (drums) self-financed their debut album *My Own Prison* (1998). This collection of powerful rock tunes and genuinely spiritual lyrics went

Below

The protest song 'Zombie' (1994) by The Cranberries is the band's most memorable hit to date, winning the MTV Music Award for best song in 1995.

see Introduction pp 326   *see* Sources & Sounds pp 328   *see* Key Artists pp 332

Remember Two Things (1993) on their own label.

Signed to a major, *Under The Table And Dreaming* (1994) and *Crash* (1996) greatly expanded their US following and led to chart albums. As well as launching a campaign against the bootleggers Matthews released the *Live At Red Rocks 8.15.95* (1997), which showcased the band's compelling stage sound. *Before These Crowded Streets* (1998) was a chart topper and hit single 'Don't Drink The Water' featured Alanis Morissette. On recent albums like *Everyday* (2001) and *Stand Up* (2006) Matthews' winning compositional ability and band interplay remain undimmed.

Left

Creed's *Human Clay* (1999) is one of the Top 100 best-selling albums of all time in the US.

Below

A former music teacher and session singer, Sheryl Crow hit the big time in 1993 with the multi-platinum *Tuesday Night Music Club* album.

on to spawn a record four US No. 1 singles including 'One' and 'What's This Life For'. *Human Clay* (1999) and *Weathered* (2001) followed but troubled Stapps, and the band (now renamed Alter Bridge) agreed to go their separate ways in 2004.

Sheryl Crow
(Singer/songwriter, b. 1962)

This former jingle and session singer – a backing vocalist on Michael Jackson's *Bad* tour – was already having her songs recorded by the likes of Eric Clapton when she finally secured a solo deal. *Tuesday Night Music Club* (1993) showcased her rootsy compositional and vocal style to great effect and was dragged up the charts by the eventual success of the lyrically idiosyncratic 'All I Wanna Do' single. Her eponymous second self-produced album (1996) showcased her wonderfully observant lyrical prowess and ability to make throwaway lines memorable. Her finest effort, it spawned hits in 'A Change Would Do You Good' and the angular pop of 'Every Day Is A Winding Road'. With Grammys on the shelf and songs recorded for soundtracks, *The Globe Sessions* (1998) was solid commercial fare. There was a pause before later albums *C'mon C'mon* (2002) and *Wildflower* (2005). Briefly romanced cyclist Lance Armstrong.

The Dave Matthews Band
(Vocal/instrumental group, 1991–present)

South African-born Matthews (guitar, vocals) formed his band in Virginia, recruiting Stefan Lessard (bass) Leroi Moore (saxophone) Boyd Tinsley (violin) and Carter Beauford (drums) into the ranks. Fusing elements of world music on to a sound that celebrated folk, funk and rock in equal parts they built an audience by undertaking constant touring releasing their debut

see Cream pp 92   see Michael Jackson pp 276   see Alanis Morissette pp 357   see Oasis pp 360

Dr. Dre
(Producer, rapper, songwriter, b. 1964)
Adopting the name Dr. Dre, Andre Young is colossally influential in rap. A creative force behind Niggaz With Attitude, he pioneered gangsta rap and has a vast number of production credits, including Snoop Dogg and Blackstreet's 'No Diggity' to his name. Dre also created the more laid back G-funk musical style. Classic debut solo album *The Chronic* (1992) was released on his own label Death Row Records (1992–96). Dre also discovered and produced Eminem.

Steve Earle
(Vocals, b. 1955)
Earle is an artist whose heartfelt songwriting and passionate vocals straddle both rock and country music. Despite several marriages and periods of drug and alcohol abuse Earle's music was a vital part of the 1990s, especially the acoustic prisms of *Train A Comin'* (1995) and *El Corazon* (1997). Bluegrass album *Mountain* (1999) recorded with the Del McCoury Band is particularly impressive. Recent political albums like *Jerusalem* (2001) and *The Revolution Starts… Now* (2004) are essential.

Above

'My Heart Will Go On', the theme tune to the blockbuster movie *Titanic*, was a huge international success for Celine Dion, reaching No. 1 in several countries around the world.

Celine Dion
(Vocals, b. 1968)
Dion had already released a handful of French-language albums in her native Canada before her English-singing debut *Unison* (1990). Hit ballads like 'Where Does My Heart Beat Now' revealed a potent singer. Her emotional duet with Peabo Bryson on *The Beauty And The Beast* movie theme (1992) was a monster hit and the first of many successful soundtrack songs including 'My Heart Must Go On' (*Titanic*, 1997).

    Albums like *The Colour Of My Love* (1994) and *Falling For You* (1998) generated a constant flow of hit singles and award after award. Although taking a child-bearing career break in 2001 Dion remains a significant artist, especially after agreeing in 2002 to undertake 600 concerts at Caesar's Palace, Las Vegas over a three-year period, which suitably began with the release of new album *One Heart* (2003). *Miracles* followed in 2004.

Right

Having spent two years in prison and recovering from drug addiction in the early 1990s, Steve Earle made a comeback with his album *Train A Comin'*, which was nominated for a Grammy in 1996.

East 17
(Vocal group, 1992–97, 2006–present)
Named after their Walthamstow postal district, Tony Mortimer, Brian Harvey, John Hendy and Terry

see Introduction pp 326   see Sources & Sounds pp 328   see Key Artists pp 332

Coldwell were a 'bad' boy vocal band who took style and attitude from America. Musically they racked up an impressive number of Top 40 hits between 1992 and 1997 – mostly penned by Mortimer – ranging from dance rap to balladry. Harvey was thrown out in 1997 for comments about drugs. When Mortimer went solo the same year East 17 soon folded, but re-formed in the wake of clean-cut 'rivals' Take That.

Gloria Estefan
(Vocals, b. 1957)
Originally scoring hits as part of the Latin-powered Miami Sound Machine in the late 1980s with husband Emilio, Cuban-born Estefan soon went solo with hugely successful pop albums like *Into The Light* (1991) and *Destiny* (1996). Always keeping a foot firmly in the Latin market with Spanish-language albums like *Abriendo Puertas* (1995), she was ideally placed when the Latin boom of Ricky Martin and Enrique Iglesias ignited in 1999. *Alma Caribena* (2000) typically sold worldwide.

Fatboy Slim
(Producer, b. 1963)
Norman Cook, former bassist with The Housemartins, has since operated under a number of guises with huge success. As Fatboy Slim he managed to combine the engine room of dance with great rock sounds – including The Who – to create some of the greatest

anthems of the 1990s. *You've Come A Long Way, Baby* (1998) remains the best shop window to his addictive sound. Subsequent Fatboy albums – who else would sample Jim Morrison? – also deserve attention.

The Fugees
(Vocal group, 1987–1997, 2004–present)
Although Wyclef Jean and cousin Prakazrel 'Pras' Michel had Haitian backgrounds, The Fugees came together in New York, with Lauryn Hill completing this multi-instrumental compositional singing and production trio. *Blunted On Reality* (1994), released as Fugees Tranzlator Crew, contained most of the components of their sound blending in acoustic guitars and reggae along with traditional beats and hip-hop musical motifs. *The Score* (1996) was perfection, blending samples from sources as diverse as Enya's 'Song For Bodecia' and generating masterful hits including a magnificent modern day retooling of Bob Marley's 'No Woman No Cry'. Hill's compelling and emotional delivery of 'Killing Me Softly' was offset beautifully by the casual trademark interjections – 'one time' – of her partners. The album became a deserved international hit. Whilst fans awaited a follow-up, *The Bootleg Versions* (1996) was released featuring remixed tracks from both albums. Pras, Wyclef and Hill then went solo, the latter releasing *The Miseducation Of Lauryn Hill* (1998), which sold internationally.

Below

The phenomenal success of The Fugees in the mid-1990s with the release of the innovative and intelligent album *The Score* marked a turning point in rap music, offering an alternative to the violent and often misogynistic lyrics of gangsta rap.

Fun Lovin' Criminals
(Vocal/instrumental group, 1993–present)
Forming in New York, Huey Morgan (vocals, guitar), Steve Borovini (drums, programming) and Brian 'Fast' Leisler (bass, keyboards) blended hip-hop, funk and soundtrack references on early releases with some success. Debut album *Come Find Yourself* (1996) was a fine work spawning the addictive single 'Scooby Snacks'. Barry White tribute single 'Love Unlimited' became a huge UK hit as did the soulful *100% Columbian* (1998). More albums followed, although why Criminals were never huge in America remains a mystery.

Below

The Fun Lovin' Criminals are perhaps best known for their hit single 'Scooby Snacks' (1996), which featured samples from Quentin Tarantino films.

Garbage
(Vocal/instrumental group, 1994–present)
Butch Vig, Steve Marker and Duke Erikson were already successful producers and musicians – Vig producing Nirvana's *Nevermind* (1991) – before they recruited Scottish singer Shirley Manson to form Garbage.

Below

'Stupid Girl' was Garbage's biggest hit. Lead singer Shirley Manson said: 'It became an anthem for a girl settling for less than what she wants or deserves.'

Pristine intelligent rock of eponymous solo album (1995) spawned monster international single 'Stupid Girl'. Follow up *Version 2.0* (1998) was more electronic but an equally compelling set. *Beautiful Garbage* (2001) and subsequent *Bleed Like Me* (2005) shows that, as producers and musicians, Garbage still retain their edge.

Goldie
(Producer, vocals, b. 1965)
Clifford Price aka Goldie was the most significant and visual exponent of the dance style known as jungle that emerged out of drum'n'bass in the UK in 1993. Early *Angel* EP (1993) and 'Inner City Life' single (1995) were masterful and his major label debut album *Timeless* (1995) confirmed his talent. A highly collaborative artist, the two-CD set of *Saturnz Return* (1998) divided critics and the faithful. As a celebrity and remixer Goldie remains very much in demand.

The Goo Goo Dolls
(Vocal/instrumental group, 1986–present)
Johnny Rzeznik (guitar, vocals), Robby Takec (bass, vocals) and George Tutuska (drums) formed The Goo Goo Dolls in Buffalo, New York, in 1986. Their first two albums took inspiration from the new wave although there were endless comparisons to the pop-punk sound of The Replacements. By *Superstar Car Wash* (1993) and *A Boy Named Goo* (1996) The Dolls discovered their own melodic rock sound, which reaped American chart rewards until the end of the decade.

Hanson
(Vocal/instrumental group, 1992–present)
Like The Cowsills and The Jacksons, Hanson was a band of brothers. Based in Tulsa, Isaac, Taylor and Zac began playing together as children and by 1992 tried to break into the music business. It was not until 1997 they began to score hits with refreshing and sophisticated pop songs like 'MMMBop', 'Where's The Love' and 'Thinking Of You', which also went international. *Middle Of Nowhere* (1997) and *This Time Around* (2000) still refresh.

Hole
(Vocal/instrumental group, 1989–2002)
Hole formed in LA with Eric Erlandson (guitar), Jill Emery (bass) and Caroline Rue (drums). As lead singer, Courtney Love was an arresting presence delivering lyrics whose concerns raged from sleaze to sex. Early singles and debut album *Pretty On The Inside* (1991) won UK and US followings. By *Live Through This* (1994) Love's husband, Nirvana frontman Kurt Cobain, was dead and a media circus in full swing. *Celebrity Skin* (1998) was aptly named.

see **Introduction pp 326**   *see* **Sources & Sounds pp 328**   *see* **Key Artists pp 332**

Hootie and The Blowfish

(Vocal/instrumental group, 1989–present)
Formed in South Carolina, Darius Rucker
(vocals), Mark Bryan (guitar), Dean Felber
(bass) and Jim 'Soni' Sonefeld (drums) played
pleasing blues rock with a hint of folk and a pop
edge. That Rucker, nicknamed Hootie, was an
Afro-American also gave their material an
unconscious soulful element. Constant touring
built a dedicated following that helped sell an
initial self-financed EP *Kootchypop* (1992).

Debut album *Cracked Rear Mirror* (1994)
was a sleeper, building sales slowly. US chart
success of compulsive ecological single 'Hold
My Hand' (featuring former Byrd Davis Crosby)
and 'Let Her Cry' turned the album into a
multi-platinum success eventually selling 13
million copies in America alone. *Fairweather
Johnson* (1996) was another pleasing set,
although not as commercially successful at three
million. The band continued to tour and
showcased their feelgood style on albums like
Musical Chairs (1998) and, after leaving
Atlantic, *Looking For Lucky* (2005). A *Best
Of* collection was issued in 2004.

Above

Hootie and The Blowfish's
debut album, *Cracked Rear
View* (1994), sold over 16
million copies in the US,
making it the best-selling
album of the year.

Left

Hole, fronted by Courtney
Love, were voted No. 77 in
Vh1's 100 Greatest Hard
Rock Bands.

see The Byrds pp 124   see Barry White pp 245   see The Replacements pp 312   see Nirvana pp 334

Right

Lenny Kravitz's highest chart climber is the single 'It Ain't Over Til It's Over', released in 1991, which was written for his ex-wife Lisa Bonet.

Below

The most successful acid jazz group of the 1990s, Jamiroquai have sold over 70 million albums to date.

Ice T

(Vocals, b. 1958)

Tracy Marrow took his well-known name from pimp Iceberg Slim who wrote and published novels and poetry. Growing up wild in California, the release of a handful of singles on a variety of labels in the 1980s showed promise. Securing a solo deal, early albums like *Rhyme Pays* (1987) *Power Power* (1988) and the classic *OG* (1991) showcased his articulate lyrical style dealing with themes of good times, drugs, guns, girls and incisive social comment on what it was like to be young and black in America.

As well as building a film career Ice-T stretched himself musically with a Lollapalooza-touring thrash metal band Body Count whose track 'Cop Killer' (which appeared on OG) made Ice-T Public Enemy No. 1 to right-wing America in 1992. Riding the storm – which included being dropped by his record label – Ice-T continued to release albums, although his highly successful Hollywood career took priority.

Jamiroquai

(Vocal/instrumental group, 1992–present)

Emerging out of London's crucial acid jazz scene, Jay (Jason) Kay patented a brand of urban retro-funk with ecological lyrics on debut album *Emergency On Planet Earth* (1993). 'Too Young To Die' and 'Blow Your Mind' were chart hits as big as his trademark hats. *The Return Of The Space Cowboy* (1994) mined the same musical seam and did equal business. *Travelling Without Moving* (1996) was a modern masterpiece that subsequent albums have not matched.

Jane's Addiction

(Vocal/instrumental group, 1986–1991, 1997, 2002–04)

The charismatic Perry Farrell formed Jane's Addiction in Los Angeles in 1986, Dave Navarro (guitar), Eric Avery (bass) and Stephen Perkins (drums) completing the line-up. Musically the band compacted punk, rock and elements of funk and jazz best showcased on *Ritual De Lo Habitual* (1991). Although Farrell instigated the Lollapalooza travelling festival, the band fractured just as they were hitting the big time in 1991, though re-formations in 1997 and 2002 were followed by albums and tours.

R. Kelly

(Producer, singer/songwriter, b. 1969)

With his roots firmly planted in R&B, pop and balladry Robert Kelly is one of America's most successful male artists. Early albums like *12 Play* (1993) and *R. Kelly* (1995) showcased his booty grabbing smooth vocal style over self-written and produced sensual music. 'Sex Me Pts 1 & 2', 'She's Got That Vibe' and 'Bump 'N' Grind' were massive hit singles.

Apparently finding God, Kelly cemented mainstream success with ballad 'I Believe I Can Fly' from the movie *Space Jam* (1997), which paved the

see Introduction pp 326   see Sources & Sounds pp 328   see Key Artists pp 332

way for subsequent albums like *R* (1998) and *TP-2.com* (2000). Kelly has written and produced for many other artists including Michael Jackson, Whitney Houston, Boyz II Men and the late Aaliyah (to whom he was briefly married). He has even recorded two albums with rapper Jay-Z. Although Kelly's armour was tarnished by under-age sex allegations, he continues to write, record and produce.

Lenny Kravitz
(Multi-instrumentalist, producer, singer/songwriter, b. 1964)
Accused of being 'retro' when first emerging in 1989, Lenny Kravitz proved a trendsetter. Inspired by 1960s icons like Led Zeppelin, The Who and Jimi Hendrix, Kravitz developed a similarly warm, guitar-led sound that became hugely popular. *Mama Said* (1991) and *Are You Gonna Go My Way?* (1993) are prime examples. As well as his own resonant material, Kravitz wrote for other artists, including the sultry 'Justify My Love' for Madonna. He uses a multi-racial/sexual backing band, like Sly and Prince.

Kula Shaker
(Vocal/instrumental group, 1995–99, 2005–present)
Crispin Mills (vocals), Jay Darlington (keyboards), Alonzo Bevan (bass) and Paul Winter-Hart (drums) formed with the sole intention of making music that sounded as if it had been recorded in the 1960s. Their debut album *K* (1996) delivered this vision in spades and hits included a cover version of Deep Purple's 'Hush'. By second album – *Peasants Pigs & Astronauts* (1999) – the air had been let out of their retro tyres and they split shortly after, reforming in 2005.

The Lightning Seeds
(Vocal/instrumental group, 1989–present)
Ian Broudie produced bands as diverse as Echo And The Bunnymen and Icicle Works before his own success. The electronic hook of 'Pure' was recorded alone, becoming an unexpected hit in 1989. From here The Lightning Seeds then became a studio and touring act in support of a string of immaculate hit pop songs including 'Three Lions' for the England Football team in 1996. Like the Jules Rimet trophy, Broudie still gleams as a solo artist and producer.

see Michael Jackson pp 276   see Madonna pp 278

Early singles mixed the beat power of Run-DMC with his pioneering and infectious bad-boy rap style. Canny enough to have a pop edge to his music as well as work in TV and film *Mama Said Knock You Out* (1990) and compilation *All World* (1996) are fine career showcases. The name means Ladies Love Cool James.

Jennifer Lopez
(Vocals, b. 1969)
The attention paid to Lopez's backside by tabloids probably reflects the amount of light that shines from it. An accomplished actress with a successful Hollywood career she released a debut album in 1999 that spawned hits 'If You Had My Love' and 'Waiting For Tonight'. *J Lo* (2001) generated more of the same for this immaculate Latin diva. A remix album went down well and *Rebirth* (2005) revealed no sign of flagging talent or interest.

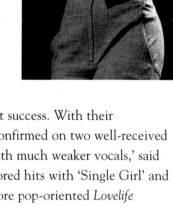

Lush
(Vocal group, 1988–96)
Formed in 1988, Miki Berenyi (guitar, vocals) Emma Anderson (guitar, vocals) Chris Acland (drums) and Steve Rippon (bass) were a classic 4AD label band whose early EPs won cult success. With their 'shoegazers' reputation confirmed on two well-received albums – 'loud guitars with much weaker vocals,' said Anderson – the band scored hits with 'Single Girl' and 'Lady Killer' from the more pop-oriented *Lovelife* (1995). Acland committed suicide in 1996 and – understandably – the band split shortly after.

M People
(Vocal/instrumental group, 1990–present)
The brainchild of Manchester DJ and scene-maker Mike 'M' Pickering who recruited Heather Small (vocals) and Paul Heard (keyboards, electronics) to form the band. Mixing impeccable melody with beats and influences ranging from Northern soul to pop the band were soon

Above
Throwing Copper launched Live into the commercial spotlight in 1994, reaching No. 1 in the US; it is their best-selling and most highly regarded album to date.

Right
Singer, actress and dancer Jennifer Lopez achieved success in 1999 with her debut album *On The 6*, which featured the No. 1 single 'If You Had My Love'. She went on to achieve superstardom in the 2000s.

Live
(Vocal/instrumental group, 1989–present)
Formed in Pennsylvania, Live – who pulled their name out of a hat – comprise Chad Taylor (guitar), Patrick Dahlheimer (bass), Chad Gracey (drums) and Ed Kowalczyk (vocals). Local shows soon won a following for their blend of rock with a spiritual message that suggested a 40-watt U2. Their debut album *Metal Jewelry* (1991) won a wider indie fanbase whilst *Throwing Copper* (1994) saw them enjoy US chart success. The band continue to tour and record.

LL Cool J
(Vocals, b. 1969)
James Todd Smith was one of the first and most astute signings Rick Rubin made for his Def Jam Label.

🔊 *see* **Introduction pp 326** 🔊 *see* **Sources & Sounds pp 328** 🔊 *see* **Key Artists pp 332**

Zombie, Manson is articulate in his own defence and is simply an updated version of the Kiss/Alice Cooper formula of character rock.

Ricky Martin
(Vocals, b. 1971)

Born in Puerto Rico, Enrique Martin Morales, was a member of the Latin boy-band Menudo in the 1980s. As an actor he also enjoyed TV work in Mexico and America, notably as a singing bartender in *General Hospital*. Martin made his Spanish-language solo debut in 1991 and a string of albums like *A Medio Vivur* (1995) won him a devoted following in Latin music circles. These firm foundations were built upon when the Latin pop craze swept America in the late 1990s and his single 'Livin' La Vida Loca' became an international No. 1 hit. His debut eponymous English-singing album was a huge success although by follow-up *Sound Loaded* (2000) the star of Latin pop was falling out of favour. Returning to his core audience with the Spanish language *Almas Del Silencio* (2003) he was simply trying too hard to remake/remodel himself on the English language album *Life* (2005).

Left
Welsh Britpop band Manic Street Preachers were at their peak in Britain in the late 1990s, and earned a reputation for intelligent political lyricism and lively stage performances.

Below
The highly individual and somewhat scary Marilyn Manson, pictured here performing in 1996.

scoring UK hits like 'How Can I Love You More?' and 'One Night In Heaven'. Small's powerful emotive vocals were as essential as their sound and *Elegant Slumming* (1993) and *Bizarre Fruit* (1994) remain evergreen.

Manic Street Preachers
(Vocal/instrumental group, 1990–present)

When guitarist Richey Edwards disappeared/committed suicide in 1995 the end of the line seemed in sight for this band of Welsh Generational Terrorists. James Dean Bradfield (vocals, guitar), Nicky Wire (bass) and Sean Moore (drums) soldiered on delivering *Everything Must Go* (1996). Retaining the artistic integrity which was one of their punk-inspired founding principles it yielded hit anthem after hit anthem. Subsequent albums were equally compelling as is *The Holy Bible* (1994) recorded before Edwards' presumed death.

Marilyn Manson
(Vocals, b. 1969)

Setting out to shock everyone, Brian Warner certainly succeeded. After assuming the name Marilyn Manson all members of his Florida-based band were required to adopt the names of female divas and serial killers. Industrially functional music grew increasingly melodic as time wore on, culminating in *Antichrist Superstar* (1996) and *Mechanical Animals* (1998). Like Rob

see Alice Cooper pp 211   see Kiss pp 218

Above
Massive Attack's trip-hop or 'Bristol Sound' has a timeless appeal; their debut album *Blue Lines* (1991) is considered to be one of the most influential albums of the decade.

Below
Moby's big breakthrough came in 1999 with the critically acclaimed album *Play*.

Massive Attack
(Dance/vocal group, 1987–present)
Founders and exponents of a downtempo groove of trip hop, 3D (Robert Del Naja), Daddy G (Grant Marshall) and Mushroom (Andrew Vowles) began working together in Bristol in the late 1980s in a loose collective under the name of The Wild Bunch. Named after a line in a comic book, their debut album *Blue Lines* (1991) introduced this new sound, and with vocal contributions from Shara Nelson and Tricky, spawned three hit singles including the masterful 'Unfinished Symphony'.

Sought after as remixers, by *Protection* (1994) their sound had matured to a deep dub-laden perfection made even more compelling with guest vocals from Tracy Thorn (Everything But The Girl) on the title track as well as Tricky and Horace Andy. *Mezzanine* (1998) was another masterpiece, which along with trademark soundscapes, featured vocals from Liz Fraser (Cocteau Twins) on 'Teardrop'. By *100th Window* (2003) only 3D remained of the original trio.

The Mighty Mighty Bosstones
(Vocal/instrumental group, 1985–2003)
This Boston band was instrumental in mixing together ska and punk with metal stylings for a wider American audience. Tim Bridewell (vocals), Dicky Barrett (vocals), Nate Albert (guitar), Joe Gittleman (bass), Josh Dalsimer (drums), Tom 'Johnny Vegas' Burton (saxophone) was a classic line-up that enjoyed cult success with albums like *Don't Know How To Party* (1993) and *Let's Face It* (1997). The single 'The Impression That I Get' charted in 1997. No Doubt took extensive musical notes.

Kylie Minogue
(Vocals, b. 1968)
This star of Australian TV soap *Neighbours* scored her first UK hit with 'I Should Be So Lucky' in 1988. Since then she has built a career that rivals Madonna in image changes and fusing pop songs with ever-changing contemporary dance beats. 'Can't Get You Out Of My Head' (2002) – underpinned by New Order's 'Blue Monday' – was a massive UK and US hit. Recovering from breast cancer, more hits are expected.

Missy Elliot
(Singer/songwriter, b. 1971)
One of rap's most iconic and important female stars, Melissa Elliot began writing for artists like Aaliyah before securing her own record deal. *Supa Dupa Fly* (1997) was a startling debut showcasing Elliot's witty female empowering lyrics and masterful songwriting talent. Subsequent albums delivered hit after hit as well as featuring guest appearances from a male rap aristocracy eager to lyrically spar with 'Misdemeanor'. *Da Real World* (1999) and *Miss E … So Addictive* (2001) are classics.

Moby
(Instrumentals, producer, vocals, b. 1965)
New Yorker Richard Melville Hall started his career in punk Vatican Commandos before becoming fascinated by the sound and possibilities of dance music when it emerged during the 1980s. Ambient and techno works won him club reputation with tracks like 'Go' and 'I Feel It' seeping into the lower branches of UK charts. His abilities continued to develop throughout the 1990s reflected in chart success of his reworked James

see Introduction pp 326   see Sources & Sounds pp 328   see Key Artists pp 332

Bond theme and album *Animal Rights* (1996). All styles were fair game in his musical brew and masterful incorporation of Alan Lomax's field recordings of blues singers was fused into the far ranging landscapes of *Play* (1999). 'Why Does My Heart Feel So Bad' was the spearhead single from this album that made him an international Christian vegan superstar. There was a break before *18* (2002), which mined a similar seam and *Hotel* (2005), which showed familiar adept signs of his musical creativity.

Alanis Morissette
(Singer/songwriter, b. 1974)
This Canadian singer recorded two teen-oriented albums that went nowhere in 1990 and 1992. Signed to Madonna's Maverick label, major debut *Jagged Little Pill* (1995) was a multi-platinum success. Music aside, it was Morissette's abrasive, honest, sharp lyrical concerns ranging from anger at being jilted to confessional that captivated. Singles like 'Ironic' and the Chilis-esque rock power of 'You Oughta Know' were huge hits. Second album *Supposed Former Infatuation Junkie* (1998) spawned 'Thank U' but little else. Drummer Taylor Hawkins joined Foo Fighters.

Morrissey
(Singer/songwriter, b. 1959)
Adored by fans almost as much as he adores himself, Morrissey's post-Smiths career has been nothing less than stellar. Writing mainly with guitarist Boz Boorer,

Morrissey delivered a number of hit albums and singles. With North and Latin America eventually falling for him, he could even afford to lose his way on *Maladjusted* (1997). Recent albums *You Are The Quarry* (2004) and *Ringleader Of The Tormentors* (2006) have returned Suedehead's former glory – and then some.

Above
Morrissey's lyrics of lost love and alienation appealed to angst-ridden youths.

Left
Alanis Morissette's album *Jagged Little Pill* (1995) sold over 30 million copies.

 see Madonna pp 278   *see* New Order pp 309   *see* No Doubt pp 359   *see* Foo Fighters pp 396

Mudhoney

(Vocal/instrumental group, 1988–present)

Mark Arm (vocals), Steve Turner (guitar), Matt Lukin (bass) and Dan Peters (drums) were the band that put the Seattle Sub Pop label on the map. Now seen as the Godfathers of grunge, their loud, guitar-driven rock was encapsulated by the 'Touch Me I'm Sick' single (1988). Tours and mini LP *Superfuzz Bigmuff* (1988) cemented their reputation. Although overtaken by Nirvana, Mudhoney were significant. *Under A Billion Suns* (2006) was issued by a re-formed band.

My Dying Bride

(Vocal/instrumental group, 1990–present)

Fronted by Aaron Stainthorpe (vocals), this goth metal outfit formed in 1990 and released their first EP, *Symponiare Infernus Et Spera Empyrium* (1991). With dark lyrical concerns and matching music, they spent the 1990s building up a strong loyal following. *Like Gods Of Sun* (1996) aptly showcase this period sound. In recent years albums like *Turn Loose The Swan* (2003) and *Songs Of Darkness Words Of Light* (2006) reveal growing lyrical depth and musical maturity.

Napalm Death

(Vocal/instrumental group, 1982–present)

As their name suggests, this UK band dealt in burning extremes of sound and volume. The original exponents of grindcore, their songs were brutally short – 'You Suffer' was exactly one second long – but played with maximum intensity and speed. Numerous personnel changes occurred between cult days of *Scum* (1986) and the metal-pounding of *Fear, Emptiness And Despair* (1994). As recently as 2001, a line-up delivered the aptly-titled *Enemy Of The Music Business*.

New Kids On The Block

(Vocal group, 1986–94)

Manufactured by producer Maurice Starr, this white vocal group of Donnie Wahlberg, Jordan Knight, Jon Knight, Danny Wood and Joey McIntyre were one of the most successful American teen bands. Formed in 1986 they hit their peak between 1988 and 1990, scoring hit single after hit single with safe pop/rap/ballad numbers. There was the obligatory Christmas album as well as a line of New Kids comic books. Hit records slowed in 1990 and they split in 1994. Wahlberg found movie fame.

📻 *see Introduction pp 326*   📻 *see Sources & Sounds pp 328*   📻 *see Key Artists pp 332*

became a classic. As well as cultivating career of Lil' Kim, B.I.G. was involved in the East Coast-West Coast feud with Tupac which eventually lead to the murder of both. *Life After Death* (1997), named before but released after his demise, is another rap classic.

*NSYNC
(Vocal group, 1996–2001)
The launch point for the career of Justin Timberlake, *NSYNC formed in Florida in 1996. J.C. Chasez, Chris Kilpatrick, Joey Fatone and James Lance Bass scored their first hits in Europe with 'I Want You Back' and 'Tearing Up My Heart'. America fell for their good looks and vocal charms in 1998 and by *No Strings Attached* (2000) they were platinum-selling artists. Timberlake and Kilpatrick even enjoyed a cameo in a Wolverine comic book.

Left
'Don't Speak' was No Doubt's biggest hit, making it to No. 1 in the US, UK, Canada and Australia.

Below
Since his death in 1997, the Notorious B.I.G. is considered to be one of the best rappers of his time.

No Doubt
(Vocal/instrumental group, 1987–present)
Gwen Stefani (vocals), Tom Dumont (guitar), Tony Kanal (bass) and Adrian Young (drums) began life as a ska/punk band from California. Their eponymous debut album (1992) went against the grain of grunge and they were dropped by their label. Success followed after their self-financed *Tragic Kingdom* (1995) crashed into US charts on the back of the 'Just A Girl' single. A typical ballad 'Don't Speak' made UK No. 1. The charismatic Stefani later launched a very successful solo career.

Notorious B.I.G.
(Vocals, 1972–97)
Born Christopher Wallace in New York, he sold crack to make ends meet which ended up in a jail term. Because of his large size he began rapping under the name of Biggie Smalls and an early demo eventually found its way to Sean Combs, aka Puff Daddy, who signed him to his Bad Boy label. Early singles as the Notorious B.I.G., created a buzz and *Ready To Die* (1994) sealed his position as the Big Poppa of Rap. These lyrically adroit and highly detailed accounts of street life created by some of the best studio talent

see Nirvana pp 334   see Puff Daddy pp 363   see Gwen Stefani pp 412   see Justin Timberlake pp 414

360

Paul Oakenfold

(DJ, remixer, b. 1963)

Training as a chef, Oakenfold found his calling as a DJ and scenemaker during the acid house, Ibiza club and the later trance boom. As an in-demand club DJ he also opened for a number of rock bands including The Stone Roses and U2. He began remixing and producing under the Perfecto banner in collaboration with Steve Osbourne with great success. Oakenfold remains one of the most visibly successful DJs in the world.

Oasis

(Vocal/instrumental group, 1993–present)

Mancunian brothers Liam (vocals) and Noel (guitar) Gallagher, Paul 'Bonehead' Arthurs (guitar), Paul 'Guigsy' McGuigan (bass) and Tony McCarroll (drums) signed to Creation Records in 1993. Debut single 'Supersonic' (1994) was a melodic, guitar-driven tune over which Liam snarled out lyrics. By the end of the year another four singles – all instant classics – had graced the charts. *Definitely Maybe* (1994) began a run

of 174 weeks in the album charts. Aside from Noel's perfectly constructed pop songs dominated by memorable Beatle-esque choruses, the fights and feuding between the two brothers delighted tabloid editors. This friction did not affect the music with *(What's The Story) Morning Glory?* (1995) going on to become the second biggest-selling UK album of all time. Although America never fell stadium tours of the UK became obligatory and *Be Here Now* (1997) kept the hits coming. Despite personnel changes Liam and Noel are still together.

Sinéad O'Connor

(Singer/songwriter, b. 1966)

A woman apt to speak her mind and sing her heart out, O'Connor's strong sense of personal feminism has informed all of her work. Her cover version of Prince's 'Nothing Compares 2 U' propelled her second album *I Do Not Want What I Haven't Got* (1990) into the international waters of multi-platinum success. More hit singles like 'Haunted' – with Shane MacGowan – followed, as did controversy, but although in self-imposed exile fans eagerly await her return.

The Offspring

(Vocal/instrumental group, 1985–present)

Coming together in California, Bryan 'Dexter' Holland (vocals, guitar), Greg Kriesel (bass), Kevin 'Noodles' Wasserman (guitar) and Ron Welty (drums) began delivering a compelling punk buzz that won cult success. Their third album *Smash* (1994) spawned the Nirvana-sounding hit 'Come Out And Play' and paved the way for extensive American success. 'Pretty Fly (For A White) Guy' and resulting album *Americana* (1998) were deserved international hits. Their loud brand of catchy guitar tunes remains popular.

The Orb

(Electronic group, 1989–present)

The main fountainhead of creativity was the highly collaborative Dr. Alex Patterson. The Orb redefined ambient music taking listeners on journeys irrespective of genre-fusing elements of dub and even progressive music into long extended pieces. Singles 'A Huge Ever Growing Pulsating Brain That Rules From The Centre Of The Ultraworld' (sampling Minnie Riperton's

see Introduction pp 326   *see* Sources & Sounds pp 328   *see* Key Artists pp 332

'Loving You') and 'Little Fluffy Clouds' are essential. *The Orb's Adventures Beyond The Underworld* (1991) remains their seminal work.

Paradise Lost
(Vocal/instrumental group, 1988–present)
Taking their name from the famed John Milton poem, it was only fitting that Nick Holmes (vocals), Gregor Mackintosh (guitar), Aaron Aedy (guitar), Stephen Edmonson (bass) and Matthew Archer (drums) delivered a slower brand of dark thrash metal. Early EPs and albums enjoyed a noisy cult success although by *Shades Of God* (1992) and *Icon* (1993) they had gained a more extensive international following. Tours and albums flowed regularly until the end of the decade.

Pearl Jam
(Vocal/instrumental group, 1990–present)
Emerging out of former Seattle band Mother Love Bone, the classic line-up consisted of Eddie Vedder (vocals), Stone Gossard (guitar), Mike McCready (guitar), Jeff Ament (bass) and Dave Abbruzzese (drums). The spiky hook-laden rock of *Ten* (1991) sold in large numbers after Nirvana made Seattle alternative

bands popular. Touring with the Lollapalooza II circus cemented their position as major players. A refusal to record promotional videos, release singles or tour, this did not prevent their second album *Vs* (1993) going platinum. *Vitalogy* (1994) confirmed their position as one of the biggest bands in America. Rather than plough one musical furrow, on subsequent albums like *No Code* (1996) Pearl Jam vastly expanded their musical references to include folk and even world music. In an effort to defeat bootleggers they also released 25 double live albums in 2002 of which five clambered into the US charts, confirming longevity and long-term appeal.

see Prince pp 282   see U2 pp 284   see Nirvana pp 334   see The Stone Roses pp 367

Phish
(Vocal/instrumental group, 1983–present)

Formed in New England, Phish are a jam band comprising Trey Anastasio (vocals, guitar), Page McConnell (keyboards, vocals), Mike Gordon (bass) and Jon Fishman (drums, vocals). Musically an eclectic mix of rock, jazz, blues, folk and whatever took their improvisational fancy, they became a word-of-mouth touring phenomenon, building up a devoted American following. Perceived like Widespread Panic as a modern Grateful Dead, Phish showcased their concert chops on *A Live One* (1995) whilst *Billy Breathes* (1996) remains their best studio offering.

Portishead
(Electronica group, 1995–98)

Like fellow Bristolians Massive Attack, Portishead were pioneers of the trip-hop sound. Although the band – Geoff Barrow (keyboards), Beth Gibbons (vocals), Adrian Utley (guitar) and Dave MacDonald (drums) – kept a low media profile, their debut album *Dummy* (1996) with its laid-back, almost trance-like beats over which Gibbons sang was voted record of the year by a diverse number of music magazines. 'Sour Times' remains the classic single. *Portishead* (1997) was more of the same.

Primal Scream
(Vocal/instrumental group, 1984–present)

Bobby Gillespie was the drummer in The Jesus And Mary Chain before forming Primal Scream. Early releases paid tribute to the 1960s sound of The Byrds and Love before beginning to steer towards Cult-like rock territory on second album *Primal Scream* (1989). Discovering the acid-house scene was a revelation to the now stable line-up of Gillespie (vocals), Andrew Innes (guitar), Robert Young (guitar), Martin Duffy (keyboards), Henry Olsen (bass) and Philip 'Toby' Tomanov (drums). Crafting material with and for remixers, singles like 'Loaded' and 'Come Together' were 1990 club and chart anthems. *Screamadelica*

see Introduction pp 326   *see* Sources & Sounds pp 328   *see* Key Artists pp 332

(1991) was as compelling a classic as The Stone Roses' debut (their Mani soon joined the band on bass). The band returned to rock with *Give Out, But Don't Give Up* (1994) and further dub-like sonic explorations on *Vanishing Point* (1997). Restless explorations yielded techo guitar fuzz of *XTRMTR* (2000) and reversion to rock fare on *Riot City Blues* (2006).

Primus
(Vocal/instrumental group, 1986–present)
A wilfully avant-garde Californian trio of Les Claypool (bass, vocals), Larry Lalonde (guitar) and Tim 'Herb' Alexander (drums) whose left-field instrumental prowess and Claypool's emphatic vocals pleased themselves. As their sound, humour and greater prowess developed so did a larger audience with albums like *Pork Soda* (1993) and *Tales From The Punch Bowl* (1996) winning acclaim and generating sales. Always stretching, *Antipop* (1999) employed a different producer for each track. Claypool also recorded solo albums under various guises.

The Prodigy
(Dance/vocal group, 1990–present)
After releasing the infectious 'Charley', Prodigy mainman Liam Howlett secured acid-house credentials with a series of singles, recruiting dancers Keith Flint, Leeroy Thornhill and singer MC Maxim to distract live fans from his knob-twiddling. *Music For The Jilted Generation* (1994) displayed wide-ranging styles fused on to the frenetic beats. *The Fat Of The Land* (1997) broke the band worldwide on the back of 'Breathe' and the punk-beat of Flint-sung 'Firestarter', a UK No. 1.

Public Enemy
(Rap group, 1982–present)
Although Public Enemy began trading pioneering hip-hop in the late 1980s the resonance of their music and message of black empowerment resonated through the entire 1990s. Chuck D, Hank Shocklee, Flavor Flav and the informational Professor Griff delivered seminal third and fourth albums *Fear Of A Black Planet* (1990) and *Apocalypse 91 … The Enemy Strikes Back* (1991). 'Elvis was a hero to most, but he didn't mean shit to me' summed up everything they stood for.

Puff Daddy
(Producer, vocals, b. 1970)
Sean Combs, also known as Puff Daddy, was the most important hip-hop and rap impresario of the 1990s who remains a major player today. Starting in the A&R department of Uptown Records for artists like Mary J. Blige he formed the Bad Boy label in 1983. Breakthrough artists Craig Mack and the Notorious B.I.G. and then the R&B of Faith Evans and Total established the label. Combs also kept busy as a producer although his debut as a recording artist was delayed by a feud with Death Row Records which – indirectly – led to the death of Tupac Shakur and B.I.G.. *No Way Out* finally arrived in 1997 and laid the foundations for a slick mainstream style which may have its detractors but every subsequent album has been a platinum carpet-ride. With media attention fixated on his personal life and court cases Combs showed diversity recording – but not releasing – a gospel album.

Above

The Prodigy appeared on the rave scene in the early 1990s and went on to achieve popularity throughout the world, with hits including 'Firestarter' and 'Breathe'.

Above top

In 1992, Primal Scream won the Mercury Music Prize on the strength of the success of their album *Screamadelic*. They celebrated so much, however, that they lost the actual award.

see The Byrds pp 124   see Love pp 142   see The Jesus and Mary Chain pp 303   see Massive Attack pp 356

Pulp

(Vocal/instrumental group, 1981–99)

This Sheffield band secured their first John Peel session when still at school (1981). Pulp then enjoyed/endured over a decade of cult success. Albums and singles pulsed out occasional sounds of potency with Jarvis Cocker's droll observational lyrics fitting snugly over indie guitars that brushed occasional electronica on tracks like 'My Legendary Girlfriend'. By the time of *His 'N' Hers* (1994) Russell Senior (guitar), Candida Doyle (keyboards), Steve Mackey (bass), Mark Webber (guitar) and Nick Banks (drums) had found a patch of four-leaf clovers and the beginning of chart success. Replacing The Stone Roses at Glastonbury (1995) Pulp's 'Common People' and 'Sorted For E's And Wizz' became anthems. *Different Class* (1995) was just that, spawning hits and turning Cocker into a media darling – especially after his bottom-waving protest at Michael Jackson's 1996 Brit awards performance. *This is Hardcore* (1998) was a pretty soft farewell, however.

Rage Against The Machine

(Vocal/instrumental group, 1991–2000)

Formed in Los Angeles by Zack De La Rocha (vocals), Tom Morello (guitar), Tim Commerford, (bass) and Brad Wilk (drums), their left-wing lyrics were as polemical as their metallic rhythmic music. Their eponymous debut album (1992) bottled their live sound and frank social commentary. The rock-hop of *Evil Empire* (1993) where La Rocha (who left in 2000) really got the bit between his teeth on songs like 'Bulls On Parade' and 'Vietnow', which remain their finest moments both commercially and critically.

Ride

(Vocal/instrumental group, 1988–96)

Formed in Oxford in 1988 by Mark Gardner (vocals, guitar), Andy Bell (guitar) and Stephen Overalt (bass), Ride revelled in a loud guitar sound that won favour with critics and fans alike. With more than a nod in the direction of The Who's 'Won't Get Fooled Again', 'Leave Them All Behind' was their biggest hit single and *Going Blank Again* (1992) their most memorable album. After going through a Hurricane, Bell dropped guitar anchor with Oasis.

Below

Although Ride received plenty of critical acclaim, they failed to gain the commercial success they had aspired to.

Below Right

Country starlet LeAnn Rimes.

LeAnn Rimes

(Vocals, b. 1982)

Country singer Rimes scored her first hit single 'Blue' (1995) – originally written for Patsy Cline – at the tender age of 13. Her subsequent album *Blue* (1996) – amazingly, her *second* – sold vastly.

see Introduction pp 326   *see Sources & Sounds pp 328*   *see Key Artists pp 332*

The Smashing Pumpkins

(Vocal/instrumental group, 1988–2000, 2005–present)
Formed in Chicago, Billy Corgan (guitar, vocals),
James Iha (guitar), D'Arcy Wretzky (bass) and Jimmy
Chamberlin (drums) are, along with Nirvana, one of
the most important alternative bands of the 1990s.
Corgan fused metal, punk and melody over which he
delivered compelling lyrical narratives. *Siamese Dream*
(1993), *Mellon Collie And The Infinite Sadness* (1995)
and *Adore* (1998) are essential. After they split in
2000, Corgan recorded *Mary Star Of The Sea* (2003)
as Zwan, but re-formed The Pumpkins two years later.

Left

Swedish pop rock band
Roxette were at the height of
their fame in the early 1990s,
with hits including 'Listen To
Your Heart'.

Below

The Smashing Pumpkins
have sold more than 40
million albums.

Her career gained momentum via *Sittin' On Top Of The
World* (1998), which spawned the international hit 'How
Do I Live'. Despite the sexy image portrayed on the pop
confection of *Twisted Angel* (2002), her roots remain
down-home. Appeared in chick-flick *Coyote Ugly*, 2000.

Roxette

(Vocal duo, 1984–present)
As Sweden spawned ABBA, it should come as no
surprise that the country's biggest pop export of the
1990s were also masters of melodic, hook-laden pop
songs. Per Gessle and the striking-looking Marie
Fredriksson announced themselves with *Look Sharp!*
(1989), which spawned hit singles like the aptly named
'Dressed For Success'. Over the next five years they
scored over a dozen more as well as delivering fine-
sounding pop albums. Hit 'Must Have Been Love'
was used in 1990's *Pretty Woman* movie.

Simply Red

(Vocal/instrumental group, 1985–present)
Fronted by ginger-haired Mick Hucknall, this
Manchester band remain the finest exponents of blue-
eyed soul, even though no other original members
remain. By 1990, they already had 12 sophisticated hits
to their name and spent the decade adding another
dozen to the locker. *Stars* (1991) was a *tour de force* and
Life (1995) was not shabby either. Despite his celebrity,
Hucknall's emotional delivery makes self-penned ditties
like 'For Your Babies' and covers like Gregory Isaacs'
'Night Nurse' a pleasure.

see The Who pp 100　　see Patsy Cline pp 139　　see Michael Jackson pp 276　　see Oasis pp 360

Snoop Dogg

(Rapper, b. 1972)

Raised in Long Beach, California, his teenage years often found Calvin Broadus – aka Snoop Dogg – in trouble with the law. He was fortunate that Warren G., his collaborator in early rap explorations, was stepbrother of Dr. Dre of N.W.A.. Dre gave Snoop's laconic style a break on early solo material notably the classic *The Chronic* (1992).

Above

Snoop Dog's *Doggystyle*, released in November 1991, is the first album to ever debut straight in at No. 1. Although surrounded by controversy because of its violent and sexist lyrics, to many it remains his best work.

A solo career began with *Doggystyle*'s (1993) tough sexist verbose sex-girls-ganja-gangsta rap over Dre's soulful G-funk vibe. Tracks like 'Murder Was The Case' appeared to be based on personal experience when Snoop was arrested in connection with a drive-by shooting. He was cleared, although *Dogfather* (1996) suffered from media backlash in the wake of Tupac and B.I.G.'s murders. Further albums – guests aplenty –

peddling similar themes turned Snoop into rap royalty, yielding film appearances and an autobiography (2001). Whilst others fell wayside Snoop's invention remains strong, especially on *R&G (Rhythm & Gangsta) The Masterpiece* (2004).

Soundgarden

(Vocal/instrumental group, 1984–97)

Like Mudhoney, Soundgarden were another early signing to the Seattle based Sub Pop label. Chris Cornell (vocals, guitar), Kim Thayil (guitar), Hiro Yamamoto (bass) and Matt Cameron (drums) came on like Led Zeppelin and Sabbath chewing metal on early releases like *Badmotorfinger* (1991) and gained success. When Nirvana broke into the big league, the Seattle connection saw the riff-heavy melodic sound of Soundgarden re-marketed as 'grunge'. *Superunknown* (1994) was their finest hour and 10 minutes.

The Spice Girls

(Vocal group, 1993–2000)

If Bikini Kill were one extreme of Grrrl Power then The Spice Girls were the most successful. With each girl adopting a defined image – Posh Spice (Victoria Adams), Scary Spice (Melanie Brown), Baby Spice (Emma Bunton), Sporty Spice (Melanie Chisholm) and Ginger Spice (Geri Halliwell, went solo 1998) – they were unstoppable after debut single 'Wannabe' topped the UK charts in July 1996. They added European and American chart rule to their portfolio, relishing the attention and rewards thrown their way. Feature film *Spiceworld* (1997) was made before the bubble burst.

The Spin Doctors

(Vocal/instrumental group, 1988–present)

This American band formed in New York, comprising Chris Barron (vocals), Eric Schenkman (guitar), Mark White (bass) and Aaron Comess (drums). Their good-time blend of blues rock in Phish/Blues Traveler vein was pleasant without appearing to threaten the charts. Debut album *Pocket Full Of Kryptonite* (1991) sold steadily due to hard touring, although when MTV picked up on 'Little Miss Can't Be Wrong' sales went through the roof. Subsequent albums proved inessential.

see Introduction pp 326   *see* Sources & Sounds pp 328   *see* Key Artists pp 332

Stereolab

(Vocal/instrumental group, 1991–present)

Fronted by French-speaking Laetitia Sadler, Stereolab actually formed in London with boyfriend Tim Gane, Mary Hansen and Andy Ramsay being the other essential core members. Delighting in limited-edition vinyl releases their fascination with 1960s music, bossa nova, lounge, ambience, John Cage and even dance resulted in startling music and cult success that rippled outwards. *Mars Audio Quintet* (1994) and compilation *Refried Ectoplasm (Switched On Volume 2)* (1995) are good places to start.

The Stereophonics

(Vocal/instrumental group, 1996–present)

Kelly Jones (guitar, vocals), Richard Jones (bass) and Stuart Cable (drums) were friends who formed the band in the Welsh village of Cwmaman. Their obvious chemistry delivered loud, passionate melodic rock dominated by Jones' observational lyrics and full-on delivery. *Word Gets Around* (1997) was a mature set delivering UK chart hits like 'A Thousand Trees' as did the follow-up *Performance And Cocktails* (1999). By *Language. Sex. Violence. Other?* (2005) they were on their third drummer but were established rock stars.

The Stone Roses

(Vocal/instrumental group, 1985–96)

This Manchester band – Ian Brown (vocals), John Squire (guitar), Gary 'Mani' Mounfield (bass) and Alan

'Reni' Wren (drums) – announced their jangling guitar pop with second single 'Sally Cinnamon'. An eponymous debut album (1989) fused the vibe of acid house on to hook-laden melodic hypnotic pop songs. Funk groove of 'Fool's Gold' and anthemic 'One Love' remain untouchable singles. *Second Coming* (1994) fell short of their debut, which is now considered one of the greatest albums of all time.

Above

The Stone Roses are often considered to be the founders of Britpop.

Left

In 1998, The Stereophonics won a Brit Award for Best New Group and their first album went gold in the UK.

see Bikini Kill pp 342   see Dr. Dre pp 348   see Mudhoney pp 358   see Phish pp 362

Stone Temple Pilots

(Vocal/instrumental group, 1992–2001)
Scott Weiland (vocals) met Robert DeLeo (bass) at a Black Flag gig, then recruited Dean DeLeo (guitar) and Eric Kretz (drums). *Core* (1992) and *Purple* (1994) made an impact as well as spawning accusations that their thunderous style was purloined from Pearl Jam. With Weiland in and out of rehab, the band stalled when promoting their third album but continued to release records until 2001. A clean Weiland now fronts Velvet Revolver.

Below

Super Furry Animals had their first Top 10 hit in July 1996 with 'Something For The Weekend'.

Suede

(Vocal/instrumental group, 1989–2002)
With lead singer Brett Anderson stating 'I'm a bisexual who has never had a homosexual experience', Suede were one of the most exciting bands to emerge in the UK for years. After a startling eponymous debut (1993) and overblown – but masterful – follow-up *Dead Man Star* (1994) guitarist Bernard Butler departed. After recruiting another guitarist and keyboard player *Coming Up* (1996) and *Head Music* (1999) kept the faithful happy without ever fully delivering upon initial promise. Butler and Anderson reunited as The Tears in 2005.

Super Furry Animals

(Vocal/instrumental group, 1993–present)
Proud enough of their heritage to record a Welsh language LP – *Mwng* (2000) – at the height of their powers this is a band who enjoyed success of their own terms. Gruff Rhys (vocals, guitar), Cian Ciaran (electronics), Huw Bunford (guitar, vocals) Guto Pryce (bass) and Dafydd Ieuan (drums) signed to Alan McGee's Creation label crafting fine albums *Fuzzy Logic* (1996) and *Guerilla* (1999). As well as pushing video to collaborative limits, *Phantom Power* (2003) is a masterpiece.

Supergrass

(Vocal/instrumental group, 1993–present)
This Oxford group – Gary 'Gaz' Coombes (vocals, guitar), Mickey Quinn (bass) and Danny Goffey (drums) – delivered some of the finest and most chirpy pop to come out of the UK in the 1990s. Although 'Caught By The Fuzz' dealt with being busted for carrying cannabis, 'Alright', 'Going Out', 'Richard III', 'Pumping On Your Stereo' and 'Moving' were less controversial feel-good anthems. *I Should Coco* (1995) and *In It For The Money* (1997) remain essential albums.

Take That

(Vocal group, 1990–96, 2006–present)
Formed in Manchester around vocalist and songwriter Gary Barlow with Jason Orange, Howard Donald, Mark Owen and Robbie Williams providing totty appeal. Debut single 'Do What U Like' was released

see Introduction pp 326   *see* Sources & Sounds pp 328   *see* Key Artists pp 332

on their own label in 1991 leading to a deal with RCA.
From that point Take That dominated the charts and
teen magazines generating devotion amongst their fans
not seen since the heyday of The Beatles and Bay City
Rollers. Barlow penned hits like 'Pray' and 'Everything
Changes', while the dance routines, videos and
hysterical tours kept the ball rolling year after year. The
down-to-earth nature – and Northern accents – of the
band kept a critical backlash at bay. Williams departed
for a solo career in 1995 and the band folded in 1996.
Greatest Hits (1996) was exceptional and the band
reformed without Williams in 2006.

Texas

*(Vocal/instrumental
group, 1986–present)*
Although this Scottish
act never did become
big in Texas they did
enjoy massive chart
success in the UK and
Europe. Original line-
up Sharleen Spiteri
(vocals), Ally McErlaine (guitar), Johnny McElhone
(bass) and Stuart Kerr (drums) hit chart paydirt early
in 1989 with the country-tinged 'I Don't Want A
Lover'. Spiteri's good looks and their later soulful
melodic pop songs took care of the rent with *White
On Blonde* (1997) their best album.

Richard Thompson

(Guitar, singer/songwriter, b. 1949)
The career of this brilliant guitarist and songwriter
began in the 1960s with Fairport Convention. Solo
releases throughout the 1970s and 1980s – especially *I
Want To See The Bright Lights Tonight* (1974), with then-
wife Linda – cemented a reputation for an influential
guitar style equally at home in folky acoustic and
electric settings. During the 1990s, retrospectives like
Watching The Dark (1993) and new albums like *Mirror
Blue* (1994) more than kept him in the public eye.

🎸 *see* The Beatles pp 88 🎸 *see* Fairport Convention pp 105 🎸 *see* Pearl Jam pp 361 🎸 *see* Robbie Williams pp 371

370

TLC
(Vocal group, 1991–present)
Atlanta trio of Lisa 'Left Eye' Lopes, Rozanda 'Chilli' Thomas and Tionna 'T –Boz' Watkins combined a sexy strident image with infectious new jack swing, yielding early hits 'Ain't 2 Proud To Beg' and 'Baby Baby Baby'. Funky R&B-led second album *Crazysexycool* (1995) yielded more hits revealing their staying power. The soap drama of their personal and business lives kept them in the news between chart hits and sultry MTV videos. Lopes died in a car crash in 2002, but the remaining duo persisted.

Above
Come On Over (1997), Shania Twain's third album, is the biggest-selling female artist's album ever.

Tupac Shakur
(Rapper, 1971–96)
New York-born rapper who has assumed near sainthood since his murder in 1996. Debut *2Pacalypse* (1991) revealed talent, with Shakur mixing normal male bravado with more lyrical insight than his peers. Along with a successful acting career, he lived out the bad boy image – being shot, found guilty of assault – and was in jail when *Me Against The World* (1995) topped the US album charts. *All Eyez On Me* (1996) is essential.

Shania Twain
(Vocals, b. 1965)
Canadian Twain (real name Eileen Regina Edwards) really was born dirt-poor and thus was ideally placed to become a country star. Her first two albums were typically slick affairs with singles like 'Any Man Of Mine' crossing with ease into the US pop charts. With *Come On Over* (1997) she broke worldwide, scoring monster singles like 'Man! I Feel Like A Woman' whose promotional video parodied Robert Palmer's 'Addicted To Love' concept. She is married to record producer Robert 'Mutt' Lange.

Vanilla Ice
(Rapper, b. 1968)
As one-hit wonders go Vanilla Ice is the exception – as he had two! Born Robert Van Winkle in Florida, this white rapper was crafty enough to transform the Queen/Bowie collaboration 'Under Pressure' into the self-advertising rap-pop of 'Ice Ice Baby', a UK/US chart-topper in 1990. Despised by the rap hardcore for daring to have another hit, 'Play That Funky Music' was at least ironic. *To The Extreme* (1990) sold well but his chart career had ended by 1991. He dated Madonna in 1992, and became a motocross racer under his real name.

The Verve
(Vocal/instrumental group, 1989–99)
Founded in Wigan, Richard Ashcroft (vocals), Nick McCabe (guitar), Simon Jones (bass) and Peter Salisbury (drums) enjoyed critical indie success after the masterfully arranged *A Northern Soul* (1995). After a brief split they re-formed for *Urban Hymns* (1997) which, propelled by the hit single 'Bittersweet Symphony', transformed them into international stars. Ashcroft's charisma and passionate vocal style also turned 'The Drugs Don't Work' into an anthem. The band split in 1999 and Ashcroft went solo.

Paul Weller
(Guitar, singer/songwriter, b. 1958)
Weller had already written himself into pop history with the feisty guitar pop of The Jam and soulfully commercial groove of The Style Council when he went solo in 1990. Musically and spiritually renewed by live work, *Paul Weller* (1992) laid strong acoustic foundations for the masterful *Wild Wood* (1994). This mature collection of songs showcased Weller's emotional depth and confirmed a songwriting genius not afraid to explore confessional and pastoral themes. Hit singles as diverse as the tender 'You Do Something

might be slipping away due to Williams' passion for late nights, drugs and alcohol. In fact co-writing material with collaborator Guy Chambers *Life Thru A Lens* (1997) was an excellent collection of songs and when 'Angels' became an anthem Williams was no longer written off.

Embracing success with both hands Williams' *I've Been Expecting You* (1998), *Sing When You're Winning* (2000) and *Escapology* (2003) revelled in rock powerchords and pop nous as singles like 'Rock DJ' and the wide-angled beauty of Bond-inspired 'Millennium' confirmed. *Intensive Care* (2006) showed mature exploration with co-songwriter Stephen Duffy. As the No. 1 male artist in the UK Williams could afford to ignore the 2006 Take That reunion.

Left
One of British music's major influences of the 1990s, Paul Weller became a somewhat reluctant leader of the mod revival.

Below
Robbie Williams has the reputation of being the best live performer and showman in the industry.

To Me' and the rocky 'The Changingman' confirmed his appeal. Although prickly with an adoring media, a strong relationship with adoring younger 'Britpop' musicians from Oasis to Ocean Colour Scene confirmed his influential 'Modfather' status. Always a well-dressed style icon, albums like *Stanley Road* (1995), *Heavy Soul* (1997) and *Studio 150* (2004), on which he tackled a daring array of cover versions, are essential.

Wet Wet Wet
(Vocal/instrumental group, 1982–99, 2004–present)
Scottish group Marti Pellow (vocals), Neil Mitchell (keyboards), Graeme Clark (bass) and Tom Cunningham (drums) were exponents of blue-eyed soul with a pleasing pop edge. Chart success was immediate in 1987 with 'Wishing I Was Lucky' and continued for a decade. Cover version of The Troggs' 'Love Is All Around' from film *Four Weddings And A Funeral* (1994) spent 15 weeks at UK No. 1. Pellow went solo in 1999 after the hits had dried up, beat a heroin addiction, starred in *Chicago* and in 2004 re-formed the band.

Robbie Williams
(Vocals, b. 1974)
Typically, the first single issued in 1996 by this former Take That member was a cover version of George Michael's 'Freedom'. Although 'Old Before I Die' was another hit in 1997, there was a perception that things

see The Jam pp 260   see George Michael pp 307

List of Artists

Entries appear in the following order: name, music style, year(s) of popularity, type of artist, country of origin.

112, Urban Soul, 1990s-, Artist, American
2LW, Contemporary R&B, 1990s-, Artist, American
3 Colours Red, Hard Rock, 1990s, Artist, British
3T, Urban Soul, 1990s, Artist, American
4 Non Blondes, Alternative/Indie Rock, 1990s, Artist, American
5ive, Boy Bands; 1990s Pop, 1990s-2000s, Artist, British
7 Year Bitch, Riot Grrrl; Alternative/Indie Rock; Hard Rock, 1990s, Artist, American
Aaliyah, Contemporary R&B; Urban Soul, 1990s-, Artist, American
AC, Death Metal & Grindcore, 1990s-, Artist, American
Ace Of Base, Europop, 1990s-, Artist, Swedish
Aces, Rock Steady, 1990s, Artist, American
Adams, Oleta, Urban Soul, 1990s-, Artist, American
Addison's Walk, Folk Rock, 1990s, Artist, American
Adventures in Stereo, 1990s Pop, 1990s-, Artist, British
Agnelli & Rave, Folk Rock; Folk Pop, 1990s, Artist, American
Air Miami, Alternative/Indie Rock, 1990s, Artist, American
Alastis, Death Metal & Grindcore, 1990s, Artist, Swiss
Ali, Tatayana, Urban Soul; Contemporary R&B, 1990s-, Artist, American
Alice In Chains, Grunge; Alternative/Indie Rock, 1990s-, Artist, American
All Saints, 1990s Pop, 1990s-, Artist, British
All-4-One, Contemporary R&B, 1990s-, Artist, American
Allan, Gary, Young Country; Neo-Traditionalists, 1990s-, Artist, American
Allure, Urban Soul, 1990s-, Artist, American
ALT, Folk Rock, 1990s, Artist, Irish
Aluminum Group, 1990s Pop, 1990s-, Artist, American
America's Most Wanted, Gangsta, 1990s, Artist, American
Anam, Irish Folk, 1990s-, Artist, Irish
Anathema, Doom Metal; Death Metal & Grindcore, 1990s-, Artist, British
André, Peter, Contemporary R&B, 1990s, Artist, Australian
Answered Questions, Urban Soul, 1990s, Artist, American
Ant Banks, Gangsta, 1990s-, Artist, American
Anthony, Marc, Latin, 1990s-, Artist, Puerto Rican
Aphex Twin, Acid; Techno; Trance, 1990s-, Producer, British
Apple, Fiona, 1990s Pop Singer/Songwriters, 1990s, Artist; Songwriter, American
Apples in Stereo, The, 1990s Pop, 1990s-, Artist, American
Appliance, Krautrock, 1990s-, Artist, British
Aqua, Europop, 1990s-, Artist, Danish
Arc Angels, The, Blues Rock, 1990s, Artist, American
Arch Enemy, Death Metal & Grindcore, 1990s-, Artist, British
Archers Of Loaf, Alternative/Indie Rock; 1990s Pop, 1990s-, Artist, American
Arcon 2, Jungle; Drum'n'Bass, 1990s-, Producer, British
Arranmore, Folk Pop, 1990s-, Artist, American
Arrested Development, Political Rap; Alternative Hip Hop; Hip Hop, 1990s, Artist, American
Art Institute, The, Folk Pop, 1990s, Artist, American
Artful Dodger, The, UK Garage, 1990s-, Artist, British
Ash, Britpop; 1990s Pop, 1990s-, Artist, British
Asian Dub Foundation, Dub; Dancehall; Ragga, 1990s-, Artist, British
Assorted Phlavors, Gangsta, 1990s, Artist, American
At The Drive-In, Alternative/Indie Rock, 1990s-2000s, Artist, American
At The Gates, Death Metal & Grindcore, 1990s, Artist, Swedish
Atari Teenage Riot, Gabba; Techno, 1990s-2000s, Artist, German
Auteurs, The, Britpop, 1990s, Artist, British
Avail, Alternative/Indie Rock, 1990s-, Artist, American
AZ, Hip Hop; Gangsta, 1990s-, Artist, American
B*Witched, 1990s Pop; Manufactured Pop, 1990s-2000s, Artist, British
Babybird, Alternative/Indie Rock, 1990s-, Artist, British
Backsliders, The, Alternative Country; Country Rock, 1990s, Artist, American
Backstreet Boys, Boy Bands; 1990s Pop, 1990s-, Artist, American
Badu, Erykah, Alternative Hip Hop; Hip Hop; Contemporary R&B, 1990s, Artist, American
Ballard, Roger, Young Country, 1990s, Artist, American
Banach, Karen, Young Country, 1990s, Artist, American
Banda Machos, Latin, 1990s-, Artist, Mexican
Bantam Rooster, US Underground & Garage Rock; Alternative/Indie Rock, 1990s-, Artist, American
Banton, Mega, Dancehall; Ragga, 1990s, Artist, Jamaican
Barenaked Ladies, Alternative/Indie Rock, 1990s-, Artist, Canadian
Barnett, Mandy, Young Country; Neo-Traditionalists, 1990s, Artist, American
Basement Jaxx, House; UK Garage, 1990s-, Artist, British
Baylor, Helen, Urban Soul, 1990s-, Artist, American
Beatnuts, The, Hip Hop, 1990s-, Artist, American
Beck, Alternative/Indie Rock, 1990s-, Artist; Songwriter, American
Bedard, George, Blues Rock, 1990s, Artist, American
Bee, Celi, Disco, 1990s, Artist, Puerto Rican
Bega, Lou, Latin, 1990s-, Artist, German
Bell, T. D. , Texas Blues; Modern Electric Blues, 1990s, Artist, American
Belle & Sebastian, Folk Rock; 1990s Pop, 1990s-, Artist, British
Beltran, Graciela, Latin, 1990s-, Artist, Mexican
Benet, Eric, Contemporary R&B; Urban Soul, 1990s-, Artist, American
Benoit, Tab, Modern Electric Blues, 1990s-, Artist, American
Bentley Rhythm Ace, Trip Hop, 1990s-, Artist, British
Berg, Matraca, Young Country, 1990s, Artist, American
Bernard, Crystal, Young Country, 1990s, Artist, American
Berry, John, Young Country, 1990s-, Artist, American
Beta Band, The, Trip Hop, 1990s-, Artist, British
Bettii Serveert, Alternative/Indie Rock, 1990s-, Artist, Dutch
Big Dave and the Ultrasonics, Blues Rock; Modern Electric Blues, 1990s, Artist, American
Big Fish Ensemble, Folk Rock, 1990s-, Artist, American
Big House, Young Country, 1990s-, Artist, American
Big Mountain, Reggae Pop, 1990s-, Artist, American
Big Punisher, Gangsta, 1990s, Artist, American
Big Sandy and his Fly-Rite Boys, Country Rock; Bluegrass; Western Swing, 1990s-, Artist, American
Bikini Kill, Riot Grrrl; Alternative/Indie Rock, 1990s, Artist, American
Bilal, Contemporary R&B; Urban Soul, 1990s-, Artist, American
Binder, Milo, Folk Pop; Contemporary Folk, 1990s, Artist; Composer, American
Björk, Alternative/Indie Rock; Trip Hop; Electro, 1990s-, Artist, Icelandic
Blac Monks, Gangsta, 1990s, Artist, American
Black Crowes, The, Southern Rock; Jam Rock, 1990s-, Artist, American
Black Grape, Britpop, 1990s, Artist, British
Black Rebel Motorcycle Club, Psychedelic Rock; American Punk, 1990s-, Artist, American
Black Sheep, Alternative Hip Hop; Golden Age; Hip Hop, 1990s, Artist, American
Black, Frank, 1990s Pop; Alternative/Indie Rock, 1990s-, Artist, American
Blackstreet, Urban Soul; Hip Hop, 1990s, Artist, American
Blaque, Contemporary R&B, 1990s-, Artist, American
B-Legit, Gangsta, 1990s-, Artist, American
Blige, Mary J., Contemporary R&B; Hip Hop, 1990s-, Artist, American
Blind Melon, Rock'n'Roll; Alternative/Indie Rock, 1990s, Artist, American
Blink-182, 1990s Pop, 1990s-, Artist, American
Blonde Redhead, Alternative/Indie Rock, 1990s-, Artist, American
Blood and Cripps, Gangsta, 1990s, Artist, American
Blood Oranges, The, Alternative Country; Country Rock, 1990s, Artist, American
Bloodhound Gang, The, Alternative/Indie Rock, 1990s-, Artist, American
Bloque, Latin, 1990s, Artist, Columbian
Blue Mountain, Alternative Country, 1990s-, Artist, American
Bluebirds, The, Blues Rock, 1990s-, Artist, American
Blueboy, 1990s Pop, 1990s, Artist, British
Blues Traveler, Jam Rock; Blues Rock, 1990s-, Artist, American
Blur, Britpop, 1990s-, Artist, British
Bog Noyd, Gangsta, 1990s, Artist, American
Bolo, Yami, Dancehall, 1990s-, Artist, Jamaican
Bonamy, James, Young Country, 1990s, Artist, American
Bone Thugs N Harmony, Gangsta; Hip Hop 1990s-, Artist, American
Boneshakers, The, Urban Soul, 1990s, Artist, American
Bonti, Michael, Folk Pop, 1990s, Artist, American
Boo Radleys, The, Shoegazing; Alternative/Indie Rock; Britpop, 1990s, Artist, British
Boo, Gangsta, 1990s, Artist, American
Bosworth, Libbi, Alternative Country, 1990s-, Artist; Songwriter, American
Bottle Rockets, The, Alternative Country, 1990s-, Artist, American
Bounty Killer, Dancehall; Ragga, 1990s-, Artist, Jamaican
Bowery Electric, 1990s Pop; Trip Hop; Ambient, 1990s-, Artist, American
Boy Howdy, Young Country; Country Rock, 1990s, Artist, American
Boyzone, Boy Bands; Manufactured Pop; 1990s Pop, 1990s-2000s, Artist, Irish
BR5-49, Neo-Traditionalists; Alternative Country, 1990s-, Artist, American
Brainiac, Alternative/Indie Rock, 1990s, Artist, American
Bran Van 3000, Electro; Techno; Alternative/Indie Rock; 1990s Pop, 1990s-2000s, Artist, Canadian
Brand New Heavies, Acid Jazz, 1990s-, Artist, British
Brandt, Paul, Young Country, 1990s, Artist, Canadian
Brandy, Urban Soul, 1990s-, Artist, American
Branson Brothers, Young Country, 1990s, Artist, American
Bratmobile, Riot Grrrl; Alternative/Indie Rock, 1990s-, Artist, American
Braxton, Toni, 1990s Pop; Contemporary R&B; Urban Soul, 1990s-, Artist, American
Braxtons, The, Urban Soul, 1990s, Artist, American
Brazton, Tamar, Contemporary R&B, 1990s-, Artist, American
Breeders, The, Alternative/Indie Rock, 1990s-, Artist, American
Brevette, Lloyd, Ska, 1990s, Artist, American
Brissett, Bunny, UK Reggae, 1990s-, Artist, British
Brooks & Dunn, Neo-Traditionalists; Young Country, 1990s-, Artist, American
Brooks, Kix, Young Country, 1990s, Artist, American
Brotha Lynch Hung, Gangsta, 1990s-, Artist, American
Brown, Foxy, Hip Hop; Gangsta, 1990s-, Artist, American
Brown, Junior, Neo-Traditionalists; Alternative Country, 1990s-, Artist, American
Brown, Marty, Young Country, 1990s, Artist, American
Brown, Roger, Young Country, 1990s-, Artist, American
Browne, Jann, Young Country, 1990s-, Artist; Songwriter, American
Brownstone, Urban Soul, 1990s-, Artist, American
Brutal Truth, Death Metal & Grindcore, 1990s-, Artist, American
Bucaneer, Ragga, 1990s, Artist, Jamaican
Buckcherry, Hard Rock, 1990s-2000s, Artist, American
Bucklew, Wendy, Folk Rock, 1990s, Artist; Songwriter, American
Buckley, Jeff, Folk Rock; 1990s Pop Singer/Songwriters, 1990s, Artist; Songwriter, American
Buckner, Richard, Alternative Country, 1990s-, Artist, American
Buckshot LeFonque, Contemporary R&B, 1990s, Artist, American
Buffalo Club, Young Country, 1990s, Artist, American
Built To Spill, Alternative/Indie Rock, 1990s-, Artist, American
Bums, The, Gangsta, 1990s, Artist, American
Bunnygrunt, 1990s Pop, 1990s, Artist, American
Burlison, Paul, Rockabilly; Rock'n'Roll, 1990s, Artist, American
Burnin' Daylight, Young Country, 1990s, Artist, American
Burzum, Black Metal, 1990s-, Artist, Norwegian
Bush, Grunge; Alternative/Indie Rock, 1990s-, Artist, British
Busta Rhymes, Gangsta; Alternative Hip Hop; Hip Hop, 1990s-, Artist, American
Butch Quick, Disco; House, 1990s, Artist, American
Butchies, The, Riot Grrrl; Alternative/Indie Rock, 1990s-, Artist, American
Butterglory, Alternative/Indie Rock, 1990s, Artist, American
C+C Music Factory, 1990s Pop; House, 1990s, Artist, American
Cactus Brothers, The, Alternative Country, 1990s, Artist, American
Caedmon's Call, Folk Rock, 1990s-, Artist, American
Campbell, Al, Reggae Pop; UK Reggae, 1990s-, Artist, British
Campbell, Tevin, Urban Soul, 1990s-, Artist, American
Candlebox, Grunge; Alternative/Indie Rock, 1990s, Artist, American
Canibus, Gangsta, 1990s-, Artist, Jamaican
Cannanes, 1990s Pop, 1990s-, Artist, Australian
Capone-N-Noriega, Gangsta, 1990s-, Artist, American
Cardigans, The, 1990s Pop, 1990s-, Artist, Swedish
Cardinal, 1990s Pop, 1990s, Artist, American
Carey, Mariah, 1990s Pop; Contemporary R&B, 1990s-, Artist, American
Carlson, Paulette, Young Country, 1990s, Artist, American
Carpetbaggers, The, Alternative Country, 1990s, Artist, American
Carson, Jeff, Young Country, 1990s-, Artist, American
Carter, Aaron, 1990s Pop, 1990s, Artist, American
Carter, Deana, Young Country; Neo-Traditionalists, 1990s-, Artist, American
Carter, James, Hard Bop, 1990s-, Artist, American
Cartouche, Urban Soul, 1990s, Artist, American
Case, Ed, UK Garage, 1990s-, Artist; Producer, British
Case, Neko, Alternative Country, 1990s-, Artist, American
Cassidy, Eva, Easy Listening, 1990s, Artist, American
Cast, Britpop, 1990s-, Artist, British
Castro, Cristian, Latin, 1990s-, Artist, Mexican
Cat's Miaow, The, 1990s Pop, 1990s, Artist, Australian
Catatonia, Britpop, 1990s-2000s, Artist, British
Cathedral, Doom Metal; Heavy Metal, 1990s-, Artist, British
Catherine Wheel, Shoegazing; Alternative/Indie Rock, 1990s-, Artist, British
Caustic Resin, Alternative/Indie Rock, 1990s-, Artist, American
C-Bo, Gangsta, 1990s-, Artist, American
Celly Cell, Gangsta, 1990s-, Artist, American
Cemetary, Doom Metal; Death Metal & Grindcore, 1990s, Artist, Swedish
Ceolbeg, Irish Folk, 1990s-, Artist, Irish
Chambers, Kasey, Young Country, 1990s-, Artist, Australian
Chance, Dean, Young Country, 1990s, Artist, American
Chance, Jeff, Young Country, 1990s, Artist, American
Channel Live, Gangsta, 1990s-, Artist, American
Charles & Eddie, 1990s Pop, 1990s, Artist, American
Chase, Charlie, Young Country, 1990s, Artist, American
Chavez, Alternative/Indie Rock, 1990s, Artist, American
Chemical Brothers, The, Big Beat; Trip Hop; Electro, 1990s-, Artist, British
Cherry Poppin' Daddies, Ska, 1990s-, Artist, American
Cherubs, Alternative/Indie Rock, 1990s, Artist, American
Chesney, Kenny, Neo-Traditionalists, 1990s-, Artist, American
Chesnutt, Mark, Young Country, 1990s-, Artist, American
Chesterman, Charlie, Alternative Country, 1990s, Artist, American
Chimera, Folk Rock, 1990s, Artist, British
Chino XL, Gangsta, 1990s, Artist, American
Chokebore, Alternative/Indie Rock, 1990s, Artist, American
Chuckleberry, Dancehall; Ragga; Deejays, 1990s, Artist, Jamaican
CIN, Gangsta, 1990s, Artist, American
City High, Contemporary R&B; Hip Hop, 1990s-2000s, Artist, American
Clarendonians, Rock Steady; Ska, 1990s-, Artist, Jamaican
Clark, Terri, Young Country; Neo-Traditionalists, 1990s-, Artist, Canadian
Cleopatra, 1990s Pop; Urban Soul, 1990s-, Artist, British
Cochran, Anita, Young Country; Neo-Traditionalists, 1990s-, Artist, American
Coctails, The, Alternative/Indie Rock, 1990s, Artist, American
Cohn, Marc, 1990s Pop; 1990s Pop Singer/Songwriters, 1990s, Artist; Songwriter, American
Coko, Contemporary R&B, 1990s, Artist, American
Cole, Paula, 1990s Pop Singer/Songwriters, 1990s, Artist; Songwriter, American
Coleman, Deborah, Modern Electric Blues, 1990s-, Artist, American
Collective Soul; Alternative/Indie Rock, 1990s-, Artist, American
Come, Alternative/Indie Rock, 1990s, Artist, American
Compton's Most Wanted, Gangsta, 1990s-, Artist, American
Compulsion, 1990s Pop, 1990s, Artist, Irish
Confederate Railroad, Young Country; Neo-Traditionalists, 1990s-, Artist, American
Conscious Daughters, Gangsta, 1990s, Artist, American
Cook, Norman, Trip Hop, 1990s-, Producer, British
Cool Nutz, Gangsta, 1990s-, Artist, American
Coolbone Brass Band, Acid Jazz, 1990s-, Artist, American
Coolio, Hip Hop, 1990s, Artist, American
Copeland, Shemekia, Modern Electric Blues, 1990s-, Artist, American
Copley, Jeff, Young Country, 1990s, Artist, American
Cordelia's Dad, Folk Rock; Neo-Traditional Folk, 1990s-, Artist, American
Corduroy, Acid Jazz, 1990s-, Artist, British
Corrs, The, 1990s Pop, 1990s-, Artist, Irish
Count Basic, Acid Jazz, 1990s-, Artist, American
Counting Crows, Alternative/Indie Rock, 1990s-, Artist, American
Cox, Carl, House; Techno; Acid, 1990s-, Artist; Producer, British
Cox, Deborah, Contemporary R&B, 1990s-, Artist, American
Cox, Ronnie, Young Country, 1990s-, Artist, American
Cracker, Alternative/Indie Rock; Country Rock; American Punk, 1990s-, Artist, American
Cradle Of Filth, Black Metal, 1990s-, Artist, British
Craig, Cathryn, Young Country, 1990s, Artist, American
Cranberries, The, 1990s Pop, 1990s-, Artist, British
Creed, Hard Rock, 1990s-2000s, Artist, American
Creedence Clearwater Revisited, Rock'n'Roll, 1990s, Artist, American
Crime Boss, Gangsta, 1990s-, Artist, American
Croisette, Disco, 1990s, Artist, American
Crow, Sheryl, Alternative/Indie Rock; 1990s Pop Singer/Songwriters, 1990s-, Artist, America
Cru, Gangsta, 1990s, Artist, American
Crutchfield, Captain Sam, Neo-Traditionalists, 1990s, Artist, American
Cryner, Bobby, Young Country, 1990s, Artist, American
Crystal, Conrad, UK Reggae, 1990s, Artist, British
Cub, Alternative/Indie Rock; 1990s Pop, 1990s, Artist, American
Cul de Sac, Alternative/Indie Rock, 1990s-, Artist, American
Curtis, Tony, Ragga, 1990s-, Artist, Jamaican
Curve, Alternative/Indie Rock, 1990s-2000s, Artist, British
Cutty Ranks, Ragga; Dancehall, 1990s-, Producer, Jamaican
Cynic, Death Metal & Grindcore, 1990s, Artist, American
Cypress Hill, Gangsta; Alternative Hip Hop, 1990s-, Artist, American
Cyrus, Billy Ray, Young Country, 1990s-, Artist, American
D Of Trinity Garden Cartel, Gangsta, 1990s, Artist, American
D'Angelo, Contemporary R&B, 1990s-, Artist, American
Da Bush Babees, Ragga; Gangsta, 1990s, Artist, Jamaican
Da Lench Mob, Gangsta, 1990s, Artist, American
Daft Punk, House, 1990s-, Artist, French
Dallas County Line, Young Country, 1990s, Artist, American
Damon and Naomi, 1990s Pop, 1990s-, Artist, American
Dan The Automator, Trip Hop; Electro; Hip Hop; Alternative Hip Hop, 1990s-, Artist; Producer, American
Dance Hall Crashers, Ska, 1990s-, Artist, American
Daniel, Dale, Young Country, 1990s, Artist, American
Daniel, Davis, Young Country, 1990s, Artist; Songwriter, American
Dark Tranquillity, Death Metal & Grindcore, 1990s-, Artist, Swedish
Darkroom Familia, Gangsta, 1990s-, Artist, American
Darkthrone, Black Metal, 1990s-, Artist, Norwegian
Das EFX, Golden Age; Hip Hop, 1990s, Artist, American
Dat Nigga Daz, Gangsta, 1990s, Artist, American
Dave and Deke Combo, The, Alternative Country, 1990s, Artist, American
Dave Matthews Band, Southern Rock; Jam Rock, 1990s-, Artist, American
Davies, Richard, 1990s Pop, 1990s-, Artist, Australian
Davis, Ronnie, Reggae Pop, 1990s, Artist, Jamaican
Day, Curtis, Young Country, 1990s-, Artist, American
Days Like These, Folk Pop, 1990s, Artist, American
Days Of The New, Hard Rock, 1990s, Artist, American
Dayton, Jesse, Alternative Country, 1990s-, Artist, American
De Paul, Lynsey, Disco, 1990s, Artist, American
Dead Ringas, Gangsta, 1990s, Artist, American
Dean, Billy, Neo-Traditionalists, 1990s, Artist, American
Death In Vegas, Trip Hop; Electro; Big Beat, 1990s, Artist, British
Defectors, The, Alternative/Indie Rock, 1990s-, Artist, Danish
Deftones, Nu Metal, 1990s-, Artist, American
Deicide, Death Metal & Grindcore, 1990s-, Artist, American
Del Tha Funkee Homosapien, Alternative Hip Hop; Hip Hop, 1990s-, Artist, American
Delinquent Habits, Gangsta, 1990s-, Artist, American
Delray, Martin, Neo-Traditionalists, 1990s, Artist, American
Dement, Iris, Neo-Traditionalists; Alternative Country, 1990s, Artist; Songwriter, American
Dennis, Wesley, Young Country, 1990s, Artist, American
Derailers, Alternative Country; Honky Tonk; Country Rock, 1990s-, Artist, American
Destiny's Child, 1990s Pop; Urban Soul, 1990s-, Artist, American
Detroit's Most Wanted, Gangsta, 1990s, Artist, American
Diamond, Davis, Young Country, 1990s, Artist, American
Diffie, Joe, Young Country, 1990s-, Artist, American
Dimmu Borgir, Black Metal, 1990s-, Artist, Norwegian
Dion, Celine, 1990s Pop, 1990s-, Artist, French-Canadian
Disco Biscuits, The, Jam Rock, 1990s-, Artist, American
Disco Circus, Disco, 1990s, Artist, American
Disposable Heroes Of Hiphoprisy, The, Political Rap; Alternative Hip Hop, 1990s, Artist, American
Dissection, Death Metal & Grindcore, 1990s-, Artist, Swedish
Disturbed, Nu Metal; Hard Rock; Heavy Metal, 1990s-, Artist, American
Divine Comedy, New Wave; Britpop, 1990s-2000s, Artist; Songwriter, British
Dixie Chicks, Young Country, 1990s-, Artist, American
Dixon, Willie Dee, Chicago Blues; Modern Electric Blues, 1990s, Artist, American
DJ Clue, Hip Hop, 1990s, Producer, American
DJ Faust, Deejays; US Reggae, 1990s, Artist; Producer, American
DJ MT, Gangsta, 1990s-, Producer, American
DJ Muggs, Gangsta; Alternative Hip Hop, 1990s-, Artist; Producer, American
DJ Quik, Gangsta, 1990s-, Artist, American
DJ Shadow, Hip Hop; Trip Hop; Electro, 1990s-, Artist; Producer, American
DMX, Gangsta, 1990s-, Artist, American
Do Or Die, Gangsta, 1990s-, Artist, American
Dodd, Deryl, Neo-Traditionalists; Honky Tonk, 1990s-, Artist, American
Dodgy, Britpop, 1990s-, Artist, British
Dog House Posse, Gangsta, 1990s, Artist, American
Doky Brothers, Hard Bop, 1990s, Artist, American
Donatello, Joe, Disco; House, 1990s, Producer, American
Donnas, The, Alternative/Indie Rock; Hard Rock, 1990s-, Artist, American
Doomsday Productions, Gangsta, 1990s-, Artist, American
Doucet, Camey, Young Country, 1990s-, Artist, American
Dowd, Johnny, Alternative Country, 1990s-, Artist, American
Dread Flimstone, Acid Jazz, 1990s, Artist, American
Drive Like Jehu, Alternative/Indie Rock, 1990s, Artist, American
Drovers, The, Folk Rock, 1990s, Artist, American
Dru Hill, Urban Soul; Hip Hop, 1990s, Artist, American
D-Shot, Gangsta, 1990s, Artist, American
Duarte, Chris, Blues Rock, 1990s-, Artist, American
Dubee, Gangsta, 1990s-, Artist, American
Duncan, Steve, Alternative Country, 1990s, Artist, American
Dupri, Jermaine, Hip Hop, 1990s-, Producer, American
E-40, Gangsta, 1990s-, Artist, American
East 17, Boy Bands; 1990s Pop, 1990s-, Artist, British
East River Pipe, 1990s Pop Singer/Songwriters; 1990s Pop, 1990s-, Artist; Songwriter, American
East Village, 1990s Pop, 1990s, Artist, British
Eatman, Heather, Folk Rock, 1990s-, Artist; Songwriter, American
Ebo, Vince, Urban Soul, 1990s, Artist, American
Echobelly, Britpop; Alternative/Indie Rock, 1990s-2000s, Artist; British/Swedish
Ed OG and Da Bulldogs, Gangsta, 1990s, Artist, American
Edge Of Sanity, Death Metal & Grindcore, 1990s, Artist, Swedish
Edwards, Daniel, Young Country, 1990s, Artist, American
Eels, Alternative/Indie Rock, 1990s-, Artist, American
Eggs, Alternative/Indie Rock, 1990s, Artist, American
Elastica, Britpop, 1990s-, Artist, British
Ellis, Darryl and Don, Young Country, 1990s, Artist, American
EMF, Techno; Alternative/Indie Rock, 1990s-2000s, Artist, British
Emmet Swimming, Folk Rock, 1990s, Artist, American
Emperor, Black Metal, 1990s-, Artist, Norwegian
England, Ty, Young Country, 1990s, Artist, American
Eric's Trip, Alternative/Indie Rock, 1990s, Artist, Canadian
Erickson, Craig, Modern Electric Blues, 1990s-, Artist, American
Escovedo, Alejandro, Alternative Country, 1990s-, Artist; Songwriter, American
Eternal, Urban Soul, 1990s-, Artist, British
Evans, Faith, Urban Soul, 1990s-, Artist, American
Evans, Sara, Young Country; Neo-Traditionalists, 1990s-, Artist, American
Everclear, Grunge; Hard Rock; Alternative/Indie Rock, 1990s-, Artist, American
Facemob, Gangsta, 1990s-, Artist, American
Faith Healers, The, Shoegazing; Alternative/Indie Rock, 1990s, Artist, British
Faithless, House; Progressive Dance; Trance, 1990s-, Artist, British
Falkner, Jason, 1990s Pop, 1990s-, Artist, American
Farrell, Perry, American Punk; Goth Rock; Alternative/Indie Rock, 1990s-2000s, Artist, American
Fat Joe, Gangsta, 1990s-, Artist, American
Fatboy Slim, Big Beat; Trip Hop; Electro, 1990s-, Artist; Producer, British
Fear Factory, Heavy Metal, 1990s-, Artist, American
Fifth Ward Boyz, Gangsta, 1990s-, Artist, American
Figgs, The, 1990s Pop, 1990s-, Artist, American
Filthy Rich, Gangsta, 1990s, Artist, American
Finitribe, Krautrock, 1990s, Artist, British
Fisher, Toni, 1990s Pop, 1990s, Artist, American
Flaming Lips, The, Alternative/Indie Rock, 1990s-, Artist, American
Flowered Up, Madchester, 1990s, Artist, British
Flying Saucer Attack, Alternative/Indie Rock, 1990s-, Artist, British
Fo' Clips Eclipse, Gangsta, 1990s, Artist, American
Foe, Gangsta, 1990s, Artist, American
Folds, Ben, 1990s Pop, 1990s-, Artist, American
Folk Implosion, Alternative/Indie Rock, 1990s-, Artist, American
Foo Fighters, Grunge; Alternative/Indie Rock, 1990s-, Artist, American
Foster, Radney, Neo-Traditionalists, 1990s-, Artist, American
Fourplay, Smooth Jazz, 1990s-, Artist, American
Fox, Ted, Folk Pop, 1990s, Artist, American
Frank and Walters, Britpop, 1990s, Artist, Irish
Frazier River, Young Country; Country Rock, 1990s, Artist, American
Freestyle Fellowship, Hip Hop; Political Rap, 1990s-, Artist, American
Freight Hoppers, The, Early & Old-Time Country; Neo-Traditionalists, 1990s, Artist, American
Frumpies, Riot Grrrl; Alternative/Indie Rock, 1990s, Artist, American
Fruvous, Moxy, Contemporary Folk; Folk Rock, 1990s-, Artist, Canadian
Fuck, Alternative/Indie Rock, 1990s-, Artist, American
Fugees, The, Alternative Hip Hop; Hip Hop, 1990s, Artist, American
Fulks, Robbie, Alternative Country; Neo-Traditionalists, 1990s-, Artist; Songwriter, American
Fun Lovin' Criminals, The, Hip Hop; Blues Rock, 1990s-, Artist, American
Funkmaster Flex, Hip Hop; Old School, 1990s-, Artist, American
Further, 1990s Pop, 1990s, Artist, American
Future Sound Of London, Trip Hop; Ambient; Techno, 1990s-, Artist, British
Gabrielle, Contemporary R&B, 1990s-, Artist, British
Gaines, Rosie, Urban Soul; US Garage, 1990s-, Artist, American
Galactic Cowboys, The, Heavy Metal; Hard Rock, 1990s-, Artist, American
Galactic, Funk Soul, 1990s-, Artist, American
Galliano, Acid Jazz, 1990s, Artist, British
Gamma Ray, Heavy Metal, 1990s-, Artist, American
Garbage, Alternative/Indie Rock, 1990s-2000s, Artist, American
Gastr del Sol, Alternative/Indie Rock, 1990s, Artist, American
Gathering, The, Death Metal & Grindcore, 1990s-, Artist, Dutch
Gaye, Nona, Urban Soul, 1990s, Artist, American
Gaza Strippers, US Underground & Garage Rock; Alternative/Indie Rock, 1990s-, Artist, American
G-Clefs, Contemporary R&B, 1990s, Artist, American
Gemrino, Mark, Country Rock, 1990s, Artist; Songwriter, American
Gene, Britpop, 1990s-, Artist, British
Germano, Lisa, 1990s Pop, 1990s-, Artist, American
Gilmour, Amanda, Young Country, 1990s, Artist, American
Gin Blossoms, 1990s Pop, 1990s, Artist, American
Ginn, Greg, US Underground & Garage Rock; Alternative/Indie Rock, 1990s, Artist, American
Ginuwine, Contemporary R&B, 1990s-, Artist, American
Girls Against Boys, Alternative/Indie Rock, 1990s-, Artist, American
Glory Fountain, Alternative Country, 1990s-, Artist, American
Godspeed You Black Emperor, Alternative/Indie Rock, 1990s-, Artist, Canadian
Golden Smog, Alternative Country, 1990s, Artist, American
Goldfinger, Ska, 1990s-, Artist, American
Goldie, Jungle, Drum'n'Bass, 1990s-, Artist; Producer, British
Gomez, Britpop, 1990s, Artist, British
Gordon, Noah, Young Country; Bluegrass, 1990s, Artist, American
Gorky's Zygotic Mynci, Britpop, 1990s-, Artist, British
Grandaddy, Alternative/Indie Rock, 1990s-2000s, Artist, American
Grant Lee Buffalo, Alternative/Indie Rock, 1990s, Artist, American
Grassy Knoll, The, Acid Jazz, 1990s, Artist, American
Gravediggaz, Gangsta, 1990s-, Artist, American
Grays, The, 1990s Pop, 1990s, Artist, American
Great Big Sea, Irish Folk, 1990s-, Artist, Canadian
Great Divide, The, Neo-Traditionalists; Honky Tonk, 1990s-, Artist, American
Great Plains, The, Young Country; Country Rock, 1990s, Artist, American
Gregory, Clinton, Young Country, 1990s-, Artist, American
Greyboy Allstars, The, Funk Soul; Urban Soul; Acid Jazz, 1990s, Artist, American
Griffin, Mary, Contemporary R&B, 1990s-, Artist, American
Griffin, Patty, Contemporary Folk; Folk Pop, 1990s-, Artist; Songwriter, American
Grifters, Alternative/Indie Rock, 1990s, Artist, American
Grindcrusher, Death Metal & Grindcore, 1990s, Artist, British
Groove Armada, House, 1990s-, Artist, British
Groove Collective, Acid Jazz, 1990s-, Artist, American
Groove Theory, Urban Soul, 1990s-, Artist, American
Grubbs, David, Alternative/Indie Rock, 1990s-, Artist, American
Gumball, Grunge; Alternative/Indie Rock, 1990s, Artist, American
Guy, Jasmine, Urban Soul, 1990s, Artist, American
Haggard, Marty, Neo-Traditionalists, 1990s, Artist, American
Halliwell, Geri, 1990s Pop, 1990s-, Artist, British
Hamilton Pool, Folk Rock, 1990s, Artist, American
Hammerfall, Heavy Metal, 1990s-, Artist, Swedish
Hancock, Wayne, Neo-Traditionalists; Alternative Country, 1990s-, Artist, American
Hanson, 1990s Pop, 1990s-, Artist, American
Harbour Voices, Young Country, 1990s, Artist, American
Hardwick, Billy Jr., Neo-Traditionalists, 1990s, Artist, American
Harlow, Camp, Young Country, 1990s, Artist, American
Harper, Ben, Folk Rock; 1990s Pop Singer/Songwriters, 1990s-, Artist; Songwriter, American
Harris, Corey, Delta/Country Blues; Modern Electric Blues, 1990s-, Artist, American
Harvey, P. J., Alternative/Indie Rock, 1990s-, Artist, British
Hatfield, Juliana, 1990s Pop; Alternative/Indie Rock, 1990s-, Artist, American
Haunted, The, Death Metal & Grindcore, 1990s-, Artist, Swedish
Hayes, Martin, Irish Folk, 1990s, Artist, Irish
Hayes, Wade, Honky Tonk; Neo-Traditionalists, 1990s-, Artist, American
Health and Happiness Show, Alternative Country; Country Rock, 1990s, Artist, American
Heartbeats Rhythm Quartet, The, Irish Folk, 1990s, Artist, Irish
Heat, Reverend Horton, Alternative/Indie Rock, 1990s-, Artist, American
Heavenly, 1990s Pop, 1990s-, Artist, British
Heavens To Betsy, Riot Grrrl, 1990s, Artist, American
Helium, Alternative/Indie Rock, 1990s, Artist, American
Hellecasters, The, Alternative Country, 1990s-, Artist, American
Henderson, Michael, Young Country, 1990s, Artist, American
Hennen, Joe Pat, Neo-Traditionalists, 1990s, Artist, American
Henry, Don, Young Country, 1990s-, Artist; Songwriter, American
Hentchmen, US Underground & Garage Rock; Alternative/Indie Rock, 1990s-, Artist, American
Hersh, Kristin, 1990s Pop Singer/Songwriters, 1990s-, Artist; Songwriter, American
Hi-Five, Urban Soul, 1990s, Artist, American
High Llamas, The, 1990s Pop, 1990s-, Artist, British
Hill, Faith, Young Country, 1990s-, Artist, American
Hill, Lauryn, Alternative Hip Hop; Hip Hop; Contemporary R&B, 1990s-, Artist, American
His Name Is Alive, Alternative/Indie Rock; 1990s Pop, 1990s-, Artist, American
Hoax, The, British Blues; Blues Rock, 1990s-, Artist, British
Hole, Grunge; Alternative/Indie Rock, 1990s-, Artist, American
Hollister, Dave, Urban Soul, 1990s-, Artist, American
Holloway, Contemporary R&B, 1990s, Artist, American
Honeyz, Urban Soul, 1990s-, Artist, British
Hood, Bobby, Young Country, 1990s, Artist, American
Hood, Ray, Young Country, 1990s-, Artist, American
Hootie and the Blowfish, Alternative/Indie Rock, 1990s-, Artist, American
Hornbuckle, Linda, Modern Electric Blues, 1990s-, Artist, American
House Of Pain, Hip Hop; Gangsta, 1990s-, Artist, Irish

see Introduction pp 326 *see* Sources & Sounds pp 328 *see* Key Artists pp 332 *see* A–Z of Artists pp 340

Howard, Adina, Urban Soul, 1990s, Artist, American
Huggy Bear, Riot Grrrl; Alternative/Indie Rock, 1990s, Artist, British
Hummon, Marcus, Alternative Country, 1990s, Artist; Songwriter, American
Hunter, Alfonzo, Urban Soul, 1990s, Artist, American
Hunter, Jesse, Young Country, 1990s, Artist, American
Hyatt, Walter, Alternative Country, 1990s, Artist; Songwriter, American
Idha, Folk Rock; 1990s Pop Singer/Songwriters, 1990s, Artist; Songwriter, Swedish
Imajin, Contemporary R&B, 1990s, Artist, American
Imbruglia, Natalie, 1990s Pop; 1990s Pop Singer/Songwriters, 1990s-, Artist; Songwriter, Australian
Immortal, Black Metal, 1990s, Artist, Norwegian
Impala, US Underground & Garage Rock, 1990s, Artist, American
IMX, Urban Soul, 1990s-, Artist, American
In Flames, Death Metal & Grindcore, 1990s-, Artist, Swedish
Incubus, Alternative/Indie Rock, 1990s-, Artist, American
Indians, The, Folk Rock, 1990s, Artist, American
Ingram, Jack, Neo-Traditionalists, 1990s-, Artist, American
Intveld, James, Neo-Traditionalists; Country Rock, 1990s-, Artist, American
Ishtar, Death Metal & Grindcore, 1990s-, Artist, Danish
Jackopierce, Folk Rock, 1990s, Artist; Songwriter, American
Jackson, Alan, Neo-Traditionalists; Young Country, 1990s-, Artist, American
Jagged Edge, Contemporary R&B; Urban Soul, 1990s-, Artist, American
Jale, Alternative/Indie Rock, 1990s, Artist, Canadian
James, Brett, Neo-Traditionalists, 1990s, Artist, American
Jamiroquai, Acid Lazz; Trip Hop, 1990s-, Artist, British
Jason, Alternative Country, 1990s, Artist, American
Jawbox, Alternative/Indie Rock, 1990s-, Artist, American
Jayo Felony, Gangsta, 1990s-, Artist, American
Jay-Z, Hip Hop; Gangsta, 1990s-, Artist; Producer, American
Jean, Wyclef, Contemporary R&B; Hip Hop; Alternative Hip Hop, 1990s-, Artist; Producer, American
Jefferson, Paul, Young Country, 1990s, Artist; Songwriter, American
Jellyfish, 1990s Pop, 1990s , Artist, American
Jeru The Damaja, Gangsta; Hip Hop 1990s, Producer; Songwriter; Artist, American
Jetz, Jennifer Y los, Latin, 1990s-, Artist, American
Jewel, 1990s Pop Singer/ Songwriters, 1990s-, Artist; Songwriter, American
Jigsy King, Dancehall; Ragga, 1990s, Artist, Jamaican
Jimmy Eat World, Alternative/Indie Rock, 1990s-, Artist, American
Jimmy Jam and Terry Lewis, Contemporary R&B; Urban Soul, 1990s-, Artist; Producer, American
Jodeci, Urban Soul, 1990s, Artist, American
Joe, Urban Soul, 1990s-, Artist, American
Johnson, Jack, 2000s Pop Singer/Songwriters, 1990s-, Artist; Songwriter, American
Johnson, Luther, Modern Electric Blues, 1990s, Artist, American
Johnston, Freedy, 1990s Pop Singer/Songwriters; Folk Rock; Alternative Country, 1990s-, Artist; Songwriter, American
Johnstone, Jimmy, Irish Folk, 1990s, Artist, Irish
Joi, Dub, 1990s, Artist, American
Jon B., Contemporary R&B; Urban Soul, 1990s-, Artist; Producer, American
Jon Spencer Blues Explosion, Alternative/Indie Rock, 1990s, Artist, American
Jones, Floyd, Chicago Blues, 1960s, Artist; Songwriter, American
Jones, Larry Lee, Young Country, 1990s, Artist, American
Jones, Tuta, Modern Electric Blues, 1990s-, Artist, American
Jordan, Montell, Contemporary R&B, 1990s-, Artist, American
Judd, Wynonna, Neo-Traditionalists; Young Country, 1990s-, Artist, American
Juggling Suns, Folk Rock, 1990s, Artist, American
Jump In The Water, Folk Rock, 1990s, Artist, American
Junior MAFIA, Gangsta, 1990s, Artist, American
Jurassic 5, Alternative Hip Hop; Hip Hop, 1990s-, Artist, American
Kahn, Brenda, Contemporary Folk; Folk Rock, 1990s, Artist; Songwriter, American
Kane, Kieran, Young Country, 1990s, Artist, American
K-Ci and JoJo, Urban Soul; Contemporary R&B, 1990s-, Artist, American
Keb' Mo', Blues Rock, 1990s-, Artist, American
Keith, Toby, Young Country, 1990s-, Artist, American
Kelly, Matt, Folk Rock, 1990s, Artist, American
Kelly, R., Urban Soul, 1990s-, Artist; Producer; Songwriter, British
Kennedy, Bap, Irish Folk, 1990s-, Artist, Irish
Kersh, David, Young Country; Neo-Traditionalists, 1990s, Artist, American
Khan, Brenda, Folk Rock, 1990s, Artist, American
Kid Rock, Heavy Metal; Hard Rock, 1990s-, Artist, American
Killbilly, Alternative Country, 1990s, Artist, American
Kimes, Royal Wade, Neo-Traditionalists, 1990s, Artist, American
King, Diana, Dancehall; Ragga; US Reggae, 1990s-, Artist, American
King, Grant, Folk Pop, 1990s, Artist, American
King, Shirley, Modern Electric Blues, 1990s, Artist, American
Kinney, Kevin, Folk Rock, 1990s-, Artist, American
Kirchen, Bill, Alternative Country; Country Rock, 1990s-, Artist, American
Kitten, Young Country, 1990s, Artist, American
Knight, Beverley, Contemporary R&B; Urban Soul, 1990s-, Artist, American
Knight, Jeff, Young Country, 1990s, Artist; Songwriter, American
Kool Keith, Hip Hop, 1990s-, Artist; Producer, American
Korn, Nu Metal, 1990s-, Artist, American
Krikorian, Rob, Folk Pop, 1990s, Artist, American
KRS-One, Political Rap; Gangsta; Hip Hop, 1990s-, Artist, American
Kubek, Smokin' Joe, Modern Electric Blues, 1990s-, Artist, American
Kula Shaker, Britpop, 1990s, Artist, British
Kurupt, Gangsta, 1990s-, Artist; Producer, American
Kyuss, Heavy Metal; Hard Rock, 1990s, Artist, American
L7, Riot Grrrl; Grunge; Alternative/Indie Rock, 1990s, Artist, American
La La, Urban Soul, 1990s, Artist, American
La Ley, Latin, 1990s-, Artist, Chilean
Ladybug Transistor, 1990s Pop, 1990s-, Artist, American
Lagwagon, 1990s Pop, 1990s, Artist, American
Lake Of Tears, Doom Metal; Heavy Metal, 1990s-, Artist, Sweden
Lambchop, Alternative/Indie Rock; Alternative Country, 1990s-, Artist, American
Land, Gene, Young Country, 1990s-, Artist, American
Lang, Jonny, Blues Rock; Modern Electric Blues; 1990s-, Artist, American
Lansdowne, Jerry, Young Country, 1990s, Artist, American
Lara, Nils, Latin, 1990s, Artist, Cuban-American
Last Round, Alternative Country; Neo-Traditionalists, 1990s, Artist, American
Latin Breed, Latin, 1990s, Artist, American
Lattimore, Kenny, Contemporary R&B; Urban Soul, 1990s-, Artist, American
Lauderdale, Jim, Young Country, 1990s-, Artist, American
Lawrence, Tracy, Young Country, 1990s-, Artist, American
Lee, Rory, Young Country, 1990s, Artist, American
Lee, Woody, Young Country, 1990s, Artist, American
Leftfield, House; Progressive Dance, 1990s-, Artist, British
Leftover Salmon, Jam Rock; Folk Rock, 1990s-, Artist, American
Les Nubians, Urban Soul, 1990s-, Artist, French
Leslie Spit Treeo, Folk Pop, 1990s, Artist, Canadian
Levellers, Folk Rock; Alternative/Indie Rock, 1990s-, Artist, British
Levert, Gerald, Urban Soul, 1990s-, Artist, American
LFO, 1990s Pop; Boy Bands, 1990s-, Artist, American
Lighthouse Family, Contemporary R&B, 1990s-, Artist, British
Lil' Blunt, Gangsta, 1990s-, Artist, American
Lil' Kim, Gangsta; Hip Hop, 1990s-, Artist, American
Lilac Time, Folk Rock, 1980s-, Artist, British
Lilys, Shoegazing; Alternative/Indie Rock, 1990s-, Artist, American
Limp Bizkit, Nu Metal, 1990s-, Artist, American
Lo Fidelity Allstars, Trip Hop; Electro, 1990s-, Artist, British
Loeb, Lisa, 1990s Pop Singer/Songwriters, 1990s-, Artist; Songwriter, American
Lois, 1990s Pop Singer/Songwriters, 1990s-, Artist; Songwriter, American
London, Eddie, Young Country, 1990s, Artist, American
Lonestar, Neo-Traditionalists, 1990s-, Artist, American
Longpigs, Britpop, 1990s, Artist, British
López, Jennifer, 1990s Latin Pop, 1990s-, Artist, American
Lords Of The Underground, Hardcore; Golden Age; Gangsta, 1990s, Artist, American
Lorenzo, Urban Soul; Contemporary R&B, 1990s, Artist, American
Loud Family, 1990s Pop, 1990s-, Artist, American
Louis, Big Joe, and his Blues Kin, British Blues, 1990s, Artist, British
Louise, 1990s Pop, 1990s-, Artist, British
Louisiana Boys, Alternative Country, 1990s, Artist, American
Love Battery, Grunge; Alternative/Indie Rock, 1990s, Artist, American
Luciano, Dancehall; Roots, 1990s-, Artist, Jamaican
Ludacris, Gangsta; Hip Hop, 1990s-, Artist, American
Luna, 1990s Pop, 1990s-, Artist, American
M People, 1990s Pop; House, 1990s-, Artist, British
Machine Head, Heavy Metal, 1990s-, Artist, American
Mack 10, Gangsta, 1990s-, Artist, American
Mack, Craig, Hip Hop, 1990s-, Artist, American
Mad Cobra, Ragga; Dancehall, 1990s-, Artist, Jamaican
Mad Season, Grunge; Alternative/Indie Rock, 1990s, Artist, American
Madcat and Kane, Rhythm & Blues, 1990s, Artist, American
Magic Dick, Blues Rock; Modern Electric Blues, 1990s, Artist, American
Magic Hour, 1990s Pop, 1990s, Artist, American
Magnetic Fields, Alternative/Indie Rock; 1990s Pop, 1990s, Artist, American
Make-Up, The, Alternative/Indie Rock, 1990s-, Artist, American
Malevolent Creation, Death Metal & Grindcore, 1990s-, Artist, American
Mana, Latin, 1990s-, Artist, Spanish
Mandators, Dancehall, 1990s, Artist, Nigerian
Manders, Mark David, Young Country, 1990s-, Artist, American
Manfreds, The, Blues Rock; Rhythm & Blues, 1990s-, Artist, British
Manic Street Preachers, Alternative/Indie Rock; Britpop, 1990s-, Artist, British
Mansun, Alternative/Indie Rock, 1990s-2000s, Artist, British
Marcy Brothers, Young Country, 1990s, Artist, American
Margana Lefay, Heavy Metal, 1990s, Artist, Swedish
Marilyn Manson, Nu Metal, Goth Rock, 1990s-, Artist, American
Martin, Paul, Folk Rock, 1990s, Artist, American
Martin, Ricky, Latin; 1990s Pop, 1990s-, Artist, Puerto Rican
Marvin, Alternative Country, 1990s, Artist; Songwriter, American
Masen, Sarah, Folk Pop, 1990s-, Artist, American
Massive Attack, Alternative/Indie Rock; Trip Hop; Electro, 1990s-, Artist, British
Masta Ace Incorporated, Gangsta, 1990s, Artist, American
Master P, Gangsta; Hip Hop, 1990s-, Artist; Producer, American
Matchbox 20, Alternative/Indie Rock, 1990s-, Artist, American
Matt, Jim, Young Country, 1990s, Artist; Songwriter, Canadian
Matthews, Eric, 1990s Pop Singer/Songwriters, 1990s, Artist; Songwriter, American
Matthews, Wright and King, Country Rock, 1990s, Artist, American
Maule, Brad, Young Country, 1990s, Artist, American
Mavericks, The, Neo-Traditionalists, 1990s, Artist, American
Maxwell, Contemporary R&B, 1990s-, Artist, American
Mazzy Star, 1990s Pop, Alternative/Indie Rock, 1990s, Artist, American
MC Breed, Gangsta, 1990s-, Artist, American
MC Ren, Gangsta, 1990s-, Artist, American
McBride and the Ride, Young Country, 1990s-, Artist, American
McBride, Martina, Young Country, 1990s, Artist, American
McCarter, Jennifer, Young Country, 1990s, Artist, American
McCarty, Fred, Young Country, 1990s, Artist, American
McCoy, Neal, Young Country; Neo-Traditionalists, 1990s-, Artist, American
McGee, Kieran, Folk Rock, 1990s, Artist, American
McGraw, Tim, Young Country; Neo-Traditionalists, 1990s-, Artist, American
McKnight, Brian, Contemporary R&B, 1990s-, Artist, American
McLennan, Grant, Folk Rock, 1990s, Artist, Australian
McNabb, Ian, Hard Rock; Arena Rock, 1990s-, Artist, British
Me'Shell NdegéOcello, Contemporary R&B, 1990s-, Artist; Songwriter, American
Medaski, Martin and Wood, Jam Rock, 1990s-, Artist, American
Medicine, Alternative/Indie Rock; 1990s Pop, 1990s, Artist, American
Mee, Michie, Dancehall; Ragga, 1990s, Artist, Canadian
Mellons, Ken, Young Country, 1990s, Artist, American
Mellotones, Rock Steady, 1990s-, Artist, American
Melody Makers, Reggae Pop, 1990s, Artist, Jamaican
Memento Mori, Doom Metal, 1990s, Artist, American
Memphis Exchange, Alternative Country, 1990s, Artist, American
Menswear, Britpop, 1990s, Artist, British
Merchant, Natalie, Folk Rock; Alternative/Indie Rock; 1990s Pop, 1990s-, Artist; Songwriter, American
Mercury Rev, Alternative/Indie Rock; 1990s Pop, 1990s-, Artist, American
Meshuggah, Death Metal & Grindcore, 1990s-, Artist, Swedish
Messina, Jo Dee, Neo-Traditionalists, 1990s-, Artist, American
Method Man, Gangsta; Hip Hop, 1990s-, Artist, American
Mia X, Gangsta, 1990s, Artist, American
Miller, Buddy, Alternative Country; Neo-Traditionalists, 1990s-, Artist, American
Miller, Dean, Young Country, 1990s, Artist, American
Miller, Julie, Folk Pop, 1990s, Artist; Songwriter, American
Miller, Lisa, Alternative Country, 1990s-, Artist, American
Minogue, Aine, Irish Folk, 1990s, Artist, Irish
Miranda Sex Garden, Goth Rock, 1990s-, Artist, British
Missy 'Misdemeanor' Elliot, Urban Soul; Alternative Hip Hop; Hip Hop, 1990s-, Artist, American
Mix Master Mike, Hip Hop; Alternative Hip Hop, 1990s-, Artist, American
Mobb Deep, Gangsta; Hip Hop, 1990s-, Artist, American
Mock Turtles, The, Alternative/Indie Rock, 1990s-2000s, Artist, British
Modest Mouse, Alternative/Indie Rock; 1990s Pop, 1990s-, Artist, American
Moe, Jam Rock, 1990s-, Artist, American
Mogwai, Alternative/Indie Rock, 1990s-, Artist, British
Mojave 3, 1990s Pop, 1990s-, Artist, British
Mollys, The, Irish Folk, 1990s-, Artist, Irish
Moloko, Trip Hop; Electro, 1990s-, Artist, British
Monch, Pharaoh, Hip Hop; Alternative Hip Hop, 1990s-, Artist, American
Mondo Grosso, Acid Jazz, 1990s-, Artist, Japanese
Monica, Urban Soul, 1990s-, Artist, American
Monster Magnet, Heavy Metal; Hard Rock, 1990s-, Artist, American
Montgomery, John Michael, Young Country, 1990s-, Artist, American
Moonshine Willie, Alternative Country, 1990s, Artist, American
Moore, Hamish, Irish Folk; UK Folk, 1990s-, Artist, British
Moose, Shoegazing; Alternative/Indie Rock; 1990s Pop, 1990s-, Artist, British
Morcheeba, Electro; Trip Hop, 1990s-, Artist, British
Morgan, Debelah, Contemporary R&B; Urban Soul, 1990s-, Artist, American
Morgan, Mike, Modern Electric Blues; Texas Blues, 1990s-, Artist, American
Morissette, Alanis, 1990s Pop Singer/Songwriters, 1990s-, Artist; Songwriter, Canadian
Morris, Joni, Neo-Traditionalists, 1990s, Artist, American
Mos Def, Political Rap; Hip Hop, 1990s-, Artist, American
Mount McKinleys, US Underground & Garage Rock; Alternative/Indie Rock, 1990s, Artist, American
Mr Quikk, Gangsta, 1990s-, Artist, American
Mudvayne, Nu Metal, 1990s-, Artist, American
Muffs, The, 1990s Pop, 1990s-, Artist, American
Mummies, The, US Underground & Garage Rock; Alternative/Indie Rock, 1990s, Artist, American
Murphy, David Lee, Neo-Traditional Country, 1990s, Artist, American
MXPX, 1990s Pop, 1990s-, Artist, American
My Dying Bride, Doom Metal; Death Metal & Grindcore, 1990s-, Artist, American
Mya, Contemporary R&B; Urban Soul, 1990s-, Artist, American
Mystic Eyes, US Underground & Garage Rock; Alternative/Indie Rock, 1990s-, Artist, American
Mystikal, Hip Hop; Gangsta, 1990s-, Artist, American
Nas, Hip Hop; Gangsta, 1990s-, Artist, American
Natalie Merchant, 1990s Pop Singer/Songwriters, 1990s-, Artist; Songwriter, American
Nation Of Ulysses, US Underground & Garage Rock; Alternative/Indie Rock, 1990s, Artist, American
Naughty By Nature, Golden Age; Gangsta, 1990s-, Artist, American
Nayobe, Urban Soul, 1980s-1990s, Artist, American
Ndegeocello, Me'Shell, Contemporary R&B, 1990s-, Artist, American
Nelson, Shara, Urban Soul, 1990s, Artist, British
Neptunes, The, Hip Hop; 1990s Pop, 1990s-, Producer, American
Nevermore, Heavy Metal, 1990s-, Artist, American
New Bomb Turks, US Underground & Garage Rock; Alternative/Indie Rock, 1990s-, Artist, American
New Radicals, The, 1990s Pop, 1990s, Artist, American
Newcomer, Carrie, Contemporary Folk; Folk Rock, 1990s-, Artist, American
Next, Contemporary R&B, 1990s-, Artist, American
Nichols, Joe, Neo-Traditionalists, 1990s-, Artist, American
Nichols, Roy, Honky Tonk, 1990s, Artist, American
Nightmares On Wax, Trip Hop; Electro, 1990s-, Artist, British
Noriega, Gangsta, 1990s-, Artist, American
Norwood, Daron, Young Country, 1990s, Artist, American
Notorious B.I.G., Gansta; Hip Hop, 1990s, Artist, American
*NSYNC, 1990s Pop, 1990s-, Artist, American
N-Toon, Urban Soul, 1990s-, Artist, American
O'Hara, Jamie, Neo-Traditionalists, 1990s-, Artist; Songwriter, American
Oakenfold, Paul, House; Trance; Progressive Dance; Acid, 1990s-, Producer; Artist, British
Oasis, Hard Rock; Alternative/Indie Rock; Britpop, 1990s-, Artist, British
Oblivians, US Underground & Garage Rock; Alternative/Indie Rock, 1990s, Artist, American
Ocean Colour Scene, Britpop, 1990s-, Artist, British
October Project, The, Folk Rock, 1990s, Artist, American
Of Montreal, 1990s Pop, 1990s-, Artist, American
Old 97's, Alternative Country, 1990s-, Artist, American
Olson, Kim, Young Country, 1990s, Artist, American
Omar, Urban Soul, 1990s-, Artist, American
Onyx, Gangsta, 1990s-, Artist, American
Opeth, Death Metal & Grindcore, 1990s-, Artist, Swedish
Original River Road Boys, Neo-Traditionalists, 1990s, Artist, American
Orozco, Rick, Young Country, 1990s, Artist, Mexican
Orrall and Wright, Young Country, 1990s, Artist, American
Orton, Beth, 1990s Pop Singer/Songwriters; Alternative Folk; Trip Hop, 1990s-, Artist; Songwriter, British
Osborne, Joan, Alternative/Indie Rock, 1990s-, Artist, American
Out Of Eden, Urban Soul, 1990s-, Artist, American
Outback, Fusion and Jazz Rock, 1990s, Artist, British
Outkast, Alternative Hip Hop; Hip Hop, 1990s-, Artist, American
Palace, Alternative/Indie Rock; Alternative Country, 1990s, Artist, American
Paleface, Folk Rock, 1990s, Artist, American
Palm Skin Productions, Trip Hop; Electro; Acid Jazz, 1990s-, Producer, American
Palmer, Joe, Irish Folk, 1990s, Producer, Irish
Palomino Road, Young Country, 1990s, Artist, American
Papa San, Dancehall; Ragga, 1990s, Artist, American
Parker, Caryl Mack, Young Country, 1990s, Producer, American
Parks, John Andrew, Young Country, 1990s, Artist, American
Patra, Dancehall; Ragga, 1990s, Artist, Jamaican
Patterson, Rahsaan, Contemporary R&B, 1990s-, Artist, American
Patton, Wayland, Young Country, 1990s, Artist, American
Pavement, Alternative/Indie Rock, 1990s, Artist, American
Paw, Grunge; Alternative/Indie Rock, 1990s-, Artist, American
Pawtuckets, Alternative Country, 1990s-, Artist, American
Pearl Jam, Grunge; Hard Rock; Alternative/Indie Rock, 1990s-, Artist, American
Pearl River, Young Country, 1990s, Artist, American
Penn, Dan, Alternative Country, 1990s, Artist; Songwriter, American
Penn, Dawn, Dancehall; Rock Steady, 1990s-, Artist, Jamaican
Pennington, J. P., Young Country, 1990s, Artist, American
Perfect Stranger, Neo-Traditionalists, 1990s-, Artist, American
Pernice Brothers, The, 1990s Pop, 1990s-, Artist, American
Peters, Gretchen, Young Country, 1990s-, Artist; Songwriter, American
Peterson, Gilles, Trip Hop; Acid Jazz, 1990s-, Artist, British
Peterson, Michael, Neo-Traditionalists; Honky Tonk, 1990s-, Artist, American
Phair, Liz, Alternative/Indie Rock, 1990s-, Artist, American
Pharcyde, The, Political Rap; Alternative Hip Hop; Hip Hop, 1990s-, Artist, American
Philosopher Kings, The, Funk Soul, 1990s, Artist, Canadian
Photek, Jungle; Drum'n'Bass, 1990s-, Producer, British
Placebo, Alternative/Indie Rock; Britpop, 1990s-, Artist, British
Planet BEN, Trance; Techno, 1990s, Artist, British
Playford, Rob, Jungle; Drum'n'Bass, 1990s, Artist; Producer, British
PM Dawn, Urban Soul; Alternative Hip Hop, 1990s, Artist, American
Porno For Pyros, Alternative/Indie Rock, 1990s, Artist, American
Portishead, Alternative/Indie Rock; Trip Hop; Electro, 1990s, Artist, British
Prairie Oyster, Young Country, 1990s, Artist, American
Presidents Of The United States Of America, Grunge; Alternative/Indie Rock; 1990s Pop, 1990s-, Artist, American
Prewitt, Archer, 1990s Pop, 1990s-, Artist, American
Price, Kelly, Contemporary R&B; Urban Soul, 1990s-, Artist, American
Primus, Funk Metal, 1990s, Artist, American
Prince Paul, Alternative Hip Hop; Hip Hop, 1990s, Producer, American
Prodigy, The, Big Beat; Techno, 1990s-, Artist, British
Propellerheads, Trip Hop; Electro, 1990s, Artist, British
Prophet, Chuck, Folk Rock, 1990s-, Artist, American
Psyclone Rangers, The, US Underground & Garage Rock; Alternative/Indie Rock, 1990s, Artist, American
Puff Daddy/P. Diddy, Hip Hop; Urban Soul, 1990s-, Artist; Producer, American
Puya, Latin, 1990s-, Artist, Spanish
Qualls, Henry, Texas Blues; Modern Electric Blues, 1990s, Artist, American
Quasi, Alternative/Indie Rock, 1990s-, Artist, American
Quickspace, Alternative/Indie Rock; 1990s Pop, 1990s-, Artist, British
Rachel's, Alternative/Indie Rock, 1990s , Artist, American
Radics, Jack, Dancehall; Ragga, 1990s, Artist, American
Radiohead, Britpop; Alternative/Indie Rock, 1990s-, Artist, British
Rage Against The Machine, Funk Metal, 1990s-, Artist, American
Rakim, Hip Hop; Gangsta, 1990s, Artist, American
Rammstein, Progressive Metal, 1990s-, Artist, German
Ranch Romance, Alternative Country; Western Swing, 1990s, Artist, American
Rancid, Alternative/Indie Rock; 1990s Pop; Ska, 1990s-, Artist, American
Ranks, Cutty, Dancehall; Ragga, 1990s-, Producer, Jamaican
Ranks, Nardo, Dancehall; Ragga, 1990s, Artist, Jamaican
Rappin' 4-Tay, Gangsta, 1990s, Artist, American
Raye, Collin, Young Country; Neo-Traditionalists, 1990s-, Artist, American
Ray-J, Funk Soul, 1990s-, Artist, American
Rayvon, Dancehall, 1990s-, Artist, American
Rebel, Tony, Dancehall; Ragga, 1990s-, Artist, American
Red House Painters, 1990s Pop; 1990s Pop Singer/Songwriters, 1990s-, Artist; Songwriter, American
Red Meat, Alternative Country; Neo-Traditionalists, 1990s-, Artist, American
Red Rivers, Neo-Traditionalists, 1990s, Artist, American
Redman, Hip Hop; Gangsta, 1990s-, Artist; Producer, American
Reef, Alternative/Indie Rock; Britpop, 1990s Artist, British
Reel Big Fish, Ska, 1990s-, Artist, American
Reeves, Ronna, Young Country, 1990s, Artist, American
Rembrandts, The, 1990s Pop, 1990s-, Artist, American
Remingtons, The, Young Country, 1990s, Artist, American
Republica, Alternative/Indie Rock; 1990s Pop, 1990s-2000s, Artist, British
Rex, 1990s Pop, 1990s, Artist, American
Rice, Gene, Contemporary R&B; Urban Soul, 1990s, Artist, American
Rich, Tony, Contemporary R&B; Urban Soul, 1990s, Artist; Songwriter, American
Ricochet, Young Country, 1990s-, Artist, American
Riddle, Bo, Young Country, 1990s, Artist, American
Rigby, Amy, Alternative Country, 1990s-, Artist; Songwriter, American
Right Said Fred, 1990s Pop, 1990s-, Artist, British
Riley, Thomas Michael, Young Country, 1990s, Artist, American
Rimes, LeAnn, Young Country, 1990s-, Artist, American
Riptones, Alternative Country, 1990s-, Artist, American
Road Music, Honky Tonk, 1990s, Artist, American
Robison, Bruce, Alternative Country; Young Country, 1990s-, Artist; Songwriter, American
Robison, Charlie, Alternative Country; Young Country, 1990s-, Artist; Songwriter, American
Robyn, Europop, 1990s-, Artist, Swedish
Rock, Pete, and CL Smooth, Golden Age; Hip Hop, 1990s, Artist, American
Rocket From The Crypt, Alternative/Indie Rock, 1990s-, Artist, American
Rodan, Alternative/Indie Rock, 1990s, Artist, American
Roddy, Ted, Alternative Country, 1990s-, Artist; Songwriter, American
Rodriguez, Rico, Ska, 1990s, Artist, Jamaican
Rogers, Ron, Young Country, 1990s, Artist; Songwriter, American
Rogers, Wayne, 1990s Pop, 1990s, Artist, American
Rooks, The, 1990s Pop, 1990s, Artist, American
Roots, The, Alternative Hip Hop; Hip Hop, 1990s-, Artist, American
Rotting Christ, Death Metal & Grindcore, 1990s-, Artist, Greek
Runaway Express, Young Country, 1990s-, Artist, American
RZA, Gangsta, Alternative Hip Hop, 1990s-, Artist, American
S Club 7, 1990s Pop; Manufactured Pop, 1990s-2000s, Artist, British
S*M*A*S*H, New Wave, 1990s, Artist, British
Saint Etienne, Britpop, 1990s-, Artist, British
Samael, Death Metal & Grindcore, 1990s, Artist, Swiss
Sammie, Contemporary R&B, 1990s-, Artist, American
Sandals, Acid Jazz, 1990s, Artist, British
Sarge, Alternative/Indie Rock, 1990s, Artist, American
Satyricon, Black Metal, 1990s-, Artist, Norwegian
Savage Garden, 1990s Pop, 1990s-2000s, Artist, Australian
Scarface, Gangsta, 1990s-, Artist, American
Schneider, Mimi, Folk Pop, 1990s, Artist; Songwriter, American
Schramms, Alternative Country, 1990s-, Artist, American
Scott, Jill, Contemporary R&B, 1990s-, Artist, American
Scud Mountain Boys, Alternative Country, 1990s, Artist, American
Seahorses, Alternative/Indie Rock, 1990s, Artist, British
Seal, 1990s Pop; Urban Soul, 1990s-, Artist, British
Sears, Dawn, Alternative Country; Young Country, 1990s, Artist, American
Secada, Jon, Latin; Urban Soul, 1990s-, Artist, Cuban
Seely, 1990s Pop, 1990s-, Artist, American
Selena, Latin, 1980s-1990s, Artist, American
Sexsmith, Ron, 1990s Pop Singer/Songwriters, 1990s-, Artist; Songwriter, Canadian
Shaggy, Dancehall; Ragga, 1990s-, Artist, American
Shakira, Latin; 1990s Pop, Artist, Colombian
Shakur, Tupac, Gangsta, 1990s, Artist, American
Shankin's Pickle, Ska, 1990s, Artist, American
Shanks and Bigfoot, UK Garage, 1990s-, Artist; Producer, British
Sharp, Kevin, Young Country, 1990s, Artist, American
Sharpe, B. J., Blues Rock, 1990s, Artist, American
Shaw, Victoria, Young Country, 1990s, Artist, American
Shed Seven, Britpop, 1990s-, Artist, British
Shivers, Alternative Country, 1990s, Artist, American
Shoestrings, 1990s Pop, 1990s, Artist, American
Shy FX, Jungle; Drum'n'Bass, 1990s, Artist; Producer, British
Sigur Ros, Alternative/Indie Rock, 1990s-, Artist, Iceland
Silkk The Shocker, Gangsta, 1990s-, Artist, American
Silver Jews, The, Alternative/Indie Rock, 1990s-, Artist, American
Silverchair, Grunge; Alternative/Indie Rock, 1990s-, Artist, Australian
Sister Carol, Dancehall; Ragga, 1990s-, Artist, Jamaican
Sister Souljah, Political Rap; Gangsta, 1990s, Artist, American
Six Shooter, Young Country, 1990s, Artist, American
Six String Drag, Alternative Country, 1990s, Artist, American
Size, Roni, Jungle; Drum'n'Bass, 1990s-, Producer, British
Skinner, Tom, Alternative Country, 1990s, Artist, American
Skinyele, Gangsta, 1990s-, Artist, American
Skunk Anansie, Alternative/Indie Rock; Heavy Metal, 1990s-2000s, Artist, British
Skyclad, Thrash & Speed Metal, 1990s-, Artist, British
Sleater-Kinney, Riot Grrrl; Alternative/Indie Rock, 1990s-, Artist, American
Sleeper, Britpop, 1990s, Artist, British
Slide Five, Acid Jazz, 1990s, Artist, American
Sloan, 1990s Pop, 1990s-, Artist, Canadian
Small Factory, Alternative/Indie Rock, 1990s, Artist, American
Smash Mouth, Alternative/Indie Rock, 1990s-, Artist, American
Smashing Pumpkins, The, Alternative/Indie Rock, 1990s-, Artist, American
Smith, Elliott, Alternative/Indie Rock, 1990s-2000s, Artist; Songwriter, American
Smith, Will, Hip Hop, 1990s-, Artist, American
Smith, Willie 'Big Eyes', Modern Electric Blues, 1990s-, Artist, American
Smokin' Armadillos, Alternative Country, 1990s, Artist, American
Sneaker Pimps, Trip Hop; Electro, 1990s-, Artist, British
Snoop Dogg, Gangsta, 1990s-, Artist, American
Snow, Dancehall; Reggae Pop; Ragga, 1990s, Artist, Canadian
Softies, 1990s Pop, 1990s-, Artist, American
Solitude Aeternus, Doom Metal, 1990s, Artist, American
Some Velvet Sidewalk, US Underground & Garage Rock; Alternative/Indie Rock, 1990s, Artist, American
Sordid Humor, Folk Rock, 1990s, Artist, American
Soul Assassins, Gangsta, 1990s, Artist, American
Soulfly, Heavy Metal, 1990s-, Artist, Brazilian
Soulwax, Alternative/Indie Rock, 1990s-, Artist, Belgian
South Mountain, Young Country, 1990s, Artist, American
Space, Alternative/Indie Rock, 1990s-, Artist, British
Sparklehorse, 1990s Pop, 1990s-, Artist, American
Spears, Britney, 1990s Pop; Manufactured Pop, 1990s-, Artist, American
Spice Girls, Europop; 1990s Pop, 1990s-, Artist, British
Spice, Mikey, Ragga, 1990s-, Artist, Jamaican
Spin Doctors, The, Jam Rock, 1990s, Artist, American
Spinanes, The, Alternative/Indie Rock; 1990s Pop, 1990s, Artist, American
Spiritualized, Alternative/Indie Rock; 1990s Pop, 1990s-, Artist, British
Spoozys, Alternative/Indie Rock, 1990s-, Artist, Japanese
Spragga Benz, Dancehall; Ragga, 1990s-, Artist, Jamaican
St Christopher, 1990s Pop, 1990s-, Artist, British
Stackabones, Folk Rock, 1990s, Artist, American
Staind, Nu Metal, 1990s-, Artist, American
Sta-Prest, Riot Grrrl; Alternative/Indie Rock, 1990s, Artist, American
Starsailor, Alternative/Indie Rock, 1990s-, Artist, British
Steele, Jeffrey, Alternative Country, 1990s-, Artist, American
Steps, 1990s Pop, 1990s-2000s, Artist, British
Stereolab, Alternative/Indie Rock; 1990s Pop; Easy Listening, 1990s-, Artist, British
Stereophonics, Alternative/Indie Rock, 1990s-, Artist, British
Stone Temple Pilots, Grunge; Hard Rock; Alternative/Indie Rock, 1990s-, Artist, American
Stone, Angie, Contemporary R&B; Urban Soul, 1990s-, Artist; Songwriter, American
Strapping Fieldhands, Alternative/Indie Rock, 1990s-, Artist, American
Suede, Britpop, 1990s-, Artist, British
Sugar Ray, Funk Metal, 1990s-, Artist, American
Sugar Shack, US Underground & Garage Rock, 1990s-, Artist, American
Sugar, Alternative/Indie Rock, 1990s, Artist, American
Suicide Machines, The, Ska, 1990s-, Artist, American
Sundays, The, 1990s Pop, 1990s, Artist, British
Sunny Day Real Estate, Alternative/Indie Rock, 1990s-, Artist, American
Super Friendz, The, 1990s Pop, 1990s, Artist, Canadian
Super Furry Animals, Britpop, 1990s-, Artist, British
Supergrass, Britpop; 1990s Pop, 1990s-, Artist, British
Sutton, Shane, Young Country, 1990s, Artist, American
Swervedriver, Shoegazing; Alternative/Indie Rock, 1990s, Artist, British
Swirlies, The, Shoegazing; Alternative/Indie Rock, 1990s-, Artist, American
SWV, Urban Soul, 1990s, Artist, American
Symphony X, Heavy Metal, 1990s-, Artist, American
System Of A Down, Nu Metal, 1990s-, Artist, American
Tad Morose, Heavy Metal, 1990s-, Artist, Swedish
Take That, Boy Bands; Europop, 1990s, Artist, British
Tamlins, The, UK Reggae, 1990s, Artist, British
Tarnation, Alternative Country, 1990s, Artist, American
Taylor, Melvin, and the Slack Band, Modern Electric Blues, 1990s, Artist, American
Team Dresch, Riot Grrrl; Alternative/Indie Rock, 1990s, Artist, American
Temple Of The Dog, Grunge; Alternative/Indie Rock; Hard Rock, 1990s, Artist, American
Terror Fabulous, Dancehall; Ragga, 1990s, Artist, Jamaican
Terrorizer, Death Metal & Grindcore, 1990s, Artist, American
Texas Kellys, Young Country, 1990s, Artist, American
Texas Tornados, The, Alternative Country, 1990s, Artist, American
Therion, Death Metal & Grindcore, 1990s-, Artist, Swedish
Third Eye Blind, Alternative/Indie Rock, 1990s-, Artist, American
Thornton, Marsha, Young Country, 1990s, Artist, American
Threadgill Troubadors, Alternative Country, 1990s, Artist, American
Thrush Hermit, Alternative/Indie Rock, 1990s, Artist, American
Tiger Trap, Alternative/Indie Rock; 1990s Pop, 1990s, Artist, American
Timbaland, Urban Soul; Hip Hop, 1990s-, Artist; Producer, American
Tindersticks, 1990s Pop, 1990s-, Artist, British
TLC, 1990s Pop; Hip Hop; Urban Soul, 1990s-, Artist, American
Toliver, Tony, Young Country, 1990s, Artist, American
Tool, Heavy Metal, 1990s-, Artist, American
Tortoise, Alternative/Indie Rock, 1990s-, Artist, American
Tractors, The, Neo-Traditionalists, 1990s-, Artist, American
Trailer Bride, Alternative Country, 1990s-, Artist, American
Trailer Park Rangers, Alternative Country, 1990s, Artist, American
Transambient Communication, Alternative/Indie Rock, 1990s-, Artist, British
Travis, Britpop, 1990s-, Artist, British
Trembling Blue Stars, 1990s Pop, 1990s-, Artist, British
Trevino, Geronimo, Alternative Country, 1990s, Artist, American
Trevino, Rick, Young Country, 1990s-, Artist, American
Tricky, Alternative/Indie Rock; Trip Hop; Electro, 1990s-, Artist; Producer, British
Tritt, Travis, Neo-Traditionalists, 1990s-, Artist, American
Tsunami, Alternative/Indie Rock, 1990s, Artist, American
Twain, Shania, 1990s Pop; Young Country, 1990s-, Artist, American
Twister Alley, Young Country, 1990s, Artist, American
Two Dollar Pistols, Alternative Country, 1990s-, Artist, American
Type O Negative, Heavy Metal, 1990s-, Artist, American
Tyree and Company, Young Country, 1990s, Artist, American
Tyrese, Contemporary R&B; Urban Soul, 1990s-, Artist, American
Ugly Americans, The, Folk Rock, 1990s, Artist, American
Union Wireless, Krautrock, 1990s, Artist, British
UNKLE, Trip Hop; Ambient; Electro, 1990s, Artist, British
Unwound, Alternative/Indie Rock, 1990s-, Artist, American
Usher, Urban Soul; 1990s-, Artist, American
Vanilla Ice, Hip Hop, 1990s-, Artist, American
Velocity Girl, Alternative/Indie Rock; 1990s Pop, 1990s, Artist, American
Venice, Folk Rock, 1990s, Artist, American
Veronica, Riot Grrrl; Alternative/Indie Rock, 1990s, Artist, American
Versus, Alternative/Indie Rock, 1990s-, Artist, American
Vertical Horizon, Alternative/Indie Rock, 1990s-, Artist, American
Veruca Salt, Grunge; Alternative/Indie Rock, 1990s-, Artist, American
Verve, The, Shoegazing; Alternative/Indie Rock; Britpop, 1990s, Artist, British
Vezner, Jon, Young Country, 1990s, Artist, American
Vidalias, The, Alternative Country, 1990s, Artist, American
Vigilantes Of Love, Folk Rock, 1990s-, Artist, American
Vitamin C, 1990s Pop, 1990s-, Artist, American
Vives, Carlos, Latin, 1990s-, Artist, Colombian
Voice Squad, The, Irish Folk, 1990s, Artist, Irish
Waco Brothers, The, Alternative Country, 1990s-, Artist, American
Wainright, Rufus, 1990s Pop Singer/Songwriters, 1990s-, Artist; Songwriter, American
Waiters, Mel, Contemporary R&B, 1990s-, Artist, American
Walker, Clay, Young Country, 1990s-, Artist, American
Wall, Chris, Alternative Country, 1990s, Artist; Songwriter, American
Waller, Juliana, Young Country, 1990s, Artist, American
Wallflowers, The, Alternative/Indie Rock, 1990s-, Artist, American
Walser, Don, Alternative Country; Western Swing, 1990s, Artist, American
Warden, Monte, Alternative Country, 1990s, Artist, American
Warped, Alternative/Indie Rock, 1990s, Artist, American
Washington, Bobby, Contemporary R&B, 1990s-, Artist, American
Waters, Crystal, 1990s Pop, 1990s-, Artist, American
Weathersby, Carl, Modern Electric Blues, 1990s-, Artist, American
Ween, Alternative/Indie Rock, 1990s-, Artist, American
Weezer, 1990s Pop, 1990s-, Artist, American
Weissman, Shari, Young Country, 1990s, Artist, American
Weller, Paul, Alternative/Indie Rock; Britpop, 1990s-, Artist; Songwriter, British
Westside Connection, Gangsta, 1990s, Artist, American
Whigfield, Europop, 1990s-, Artist, Danish
White Winged Moth, Alternative/Indie Rock, 1990s, Artist, American
White, Andy, Folk Rock, 1990s-, Artist; Songwriter, American
Whitley, Chris, Alternative Country, 1990s-, Artist; Songwriter, American
Whitley, Dwight, Alternative Country, 1990s, Artist, American
Why Store, The, Folk Rock, 1990s, Artist, American
Widespread Panic, Southern Rock; Jam Rock, 1990s, Artist, American
Wilco, Alternative Country, 1990s-, Artist, American
Wild Rose, Neo-Traditionalists, 1990s, Artist, American
Williams, Jett, Alternative Country; Hony Tonk; Neo-Traditionalists, 1990s, Artist, American
Williams, Robbie, 1990s Pop; Britpop, 1990s-, Artist, British
Williams, Tene, Contemporary R&B, 1990s, Artist, American
Willis, Kelly, Young Country, 1990s-, Artist, American
Wills, Mark, Young Country, 1990s-, Artist, American
Wilson, Slim, Young Country, 1990s, Artist, American
Windy and Carl, Alternative/Indie Rock, 1990s-, Artist, American
Witness, Alternative/Indie Rock; Britpop, 1990s-, Artist, British
Wolfie, 1990s Pop, 1990s-, Artist, American
Womack, LeeAnn, Young Country, 1990s-, Artist, American
Wondermints, The, 1990s Pop, 1990s-, Artist, American
Wright, Curtis, Young Country, 1990s, Artist, American
Wu-Tang Clan, Hip Hop; Gangsta, 1990s-, Artist, American
Wylie and the Wild West Show, Alternative Country; Western Swing, 1990s-, Artist, American
X-Ecutioners, The, Hip Hop, 1990s-, Artist, American
Xscape, Urban Soul, 1990s, Artist, American
Young, Harvey Thomas, Young Country, 1990s, Artist, American
Zumpano, 1990s Pop, 1990s, Artist, Canadian

see Metallica pp 332 *see* Nirvana pp 334 *see* Red Hot Chili Peppers pp 336 *see* R.E.M. pp 338

THE NOUGHTIES

The impact of rap on the rock market was everywhere to be seen in the first years of the new millennium. White artists, black artists and rock bands attempting to incorporate the style made this area the biggest musical melting pot since the 1950s.

The means by which music is accessed switched from CD to downloading from the Internet, requiring a shift in thinking from a record business already in recession. Yet some of the world's biggest acts remained guitar/bass/drums orientated. The success of British art rockers Radiohead and Coldplay was probably unsurprising, given the publicity surrounding the re-formation of Pink Floyd for 2005's G8 concert. Add the popularity of Black Sabbath veteran Ozzy Osbourne and it was clear that conservatism still existed.

A smattering of punk outrage was supplied by the likes of The Libertines, with original lead singer Pete Doherty, and, more profitably, by Americans Green Day. But even though the world was in turmoil with the events of 9/11 and the terror war that followed, music was now more an escape from reality than a way to make feelings known. Lighting a cigarette at a gig was as rebellious as it got – unless you were Keith Richards, who fell out of a tree when inebriated. Though he survived, the spirit of rock'n'roll was looking distinctly peaky.

Sources & Sounds

KEY ARTISTS

Coldplay

Eminem

Green Day

Radiohead

Above

Eminem's 'Lose Yourself' went to No. 1 in the US, UK, Australia and New Zealand and was the first rap song to win an Academy Award.

Right

Carlos Santana came back with a bang by combining sheer musical brilliance with modern marketing tools.

'I rap in such a way where the hood can respect it but I can sit right in front of a white executive and spit the exact same verse and he'll understand at least 80 per cent of it.'

Kanye West

Opposite top

Korn pioneered a new sub-genre of rock, nu-metal, by combining rap and hard rock.

Opposite Right

TV's influence on musical trends took an excrutiating turn as reality TV and star maker Simon Cowell took a firm grip on modern music.

Never since the arrival of the black vinyl record had there been a quantum shift in how music was consumed than in the 2000s. While computer games had rivalled music for fans' attention in the 1990s, the new decade saw the personal computer (PC) become the new way to obtain music via downloading. Further to this, the internet was making new stars via its Myspace platform, 2006 UK chart-toppers The Arctic Monkeys and Sandi Thom to name but two.

Hearing It All Over Again

In purely musical terms, the decade opened with a look back to the future – the biggest-selling album of 2000–01 was *1*, The Beatles first bona fide greatest hits collection. This sold 3.6 million units in its first week and more than 12 million worldwide in three weeks, becoming the fastest-selling album of all time.

When American duo Steely Dan returned with their first LP for two decades and venerable guitarist Carlos Santana (aged 53) bagged eight Grammies, many were glancing at the calendar in disbelief. Santana, in particular, was the beneficiary of some great marketing, recruiting such hip names as Dave Matthews, Lauryn Hill, Eagle-Eye Cherry and Rob Thomas to make cameo appearances. His Grammy haul equalled Michael Jackson's in 1983.

As Seen On TV

Another return to the 1960s came in the form of manufactured pop groups, a recurring theme of this decade. Yet while The Monkees had been the brainchild of music-biz mogul Al Kirshner, the public were (theoretically at least) to blame for the likes of Hear'say, a five-piece group that emerged from 2001's *Popstars* programme. Inspired by the format of MTV's *Making The Band* a couple of years earlier, the concept of voting off inferior candidates was eagerly embraced by the UK public. Sadly, the result was generic and when a chart-topping album was followed by a No. 24 before the end of the year they surrendered to the inevitable.

Further manufactured bands like Eden's Crush, Scene 23 (both US) and Sugar Jones (Canada) made even less of a mark, Britain's Girls Aloud from 2002 the exception that proved the rule. Yet some critics said reality TV was a more honest way of creating entertainment than either The Monkees or the many Motown groups Berry Gordy shoehorned together. In the karaoke era, the competition for 15 minutes of fame was keener than ever.

see Introduction pp 374 • see Key Artists pp 380 • see A–Z of Artists pp 390 • see List of Artists pp 418

More influential in producing something like 'real' stars were the solo starmaking machines *Pop Idol* (UK) and *American Idol*. The latter's Kelly Clarkson became its first winner in 2002 and was still around four years later, while UK runner-up Will Young proved equally durable. A less expected beneficiary of reality TV was Ozzy Osbourne, the befuddled former Black Sabbath singer, whose household endured the MTV fly-on-the-wall documentary treatment and emerged with superstar status – a kind of heavy metal *Simpsons*.

Nu Directions

The last months of 2000 saw the two leading bands in the nu-metal category unveil best-selling albums. Linkin Park, whose line-up contained one singing and one rapping frontman plus a 'turntablist', released *Hybrid Theory*, which would go on to become a top-selling album in 2001. Limp Bizkit's 12 million-selling *Chocolate Starfish And the Hot Dog Flavoured Water* (2000) spawned the UK No. 1 single 'Rollin'', while

📼 CLASSIC RECORDINGS

2000
Eminem: *The Marshall Mathers LP*
Limp Bizkit: *Chocolate Starfish And The Hotdog Flavored Water*
Radiohead: *Kid A*

2001
The White Stripes: *White Blood Cells*

2005
Coldplay: *X&Y*
Green Day: *American Idiot*

📼 *see* Arctic Monkeys pp 391 📼 *see* Kelly Clarkson pp 393 📼 *see* Limp Bizkit pp 404 📼 *see* Will Young pp 417

Above

Hip-hop's move from street scene and underground to extravagant chart success was finally completed in early 2000.

Below

Live 8 was a headline-grabbing showcase for new and old rock to reaffirm their commitment to the 'Make History Poverty' movement.

their link with the WWE wrestling franchise was an interesting tactic that attracted fans as their success eclipsed Korn, the outfit that had originally discovered them. Nu-metal was an undeniably new strain of music that won bands like Crazy Town brief acclaim, but appeared to have burned out by the middle of the decade.

The first decade of the new millennium was inspiring comparison with past times. The best-selling music of female vocalist Dido paralleled the yuppie music of Sade 20 years on while Norah Jones, daughter of India's Ravi Shankar, continued the undemanding listening theme by topping the 2002 charts with debut album *Come Away With Me*. Political comment seemed out of fashion, America's Dixie Chicks receiving widespread flak for anti-George Bush remarks made on stage in London in 2003. With the so-called 'war on terror' that followed the 9/11 atrocity, it seemed a conspiracy of silence existed that was broken at the artist's peril.

The British art-rock banner once carried by Pink Floyd had been re-hoisted by Coldplay and Radiohead. While the later had built through the 1990s to achieve their pre-eminent position, Coldplay – four London University students – were relative newcomers on the scene whose stock soared when singer Chris Martin (whom few would have picked out in a crowd) met and married Hollywood star Gwyneth Paltrow. His band now attracted the attention of 'serious' fans and tabloid readers alike.

The Video Generation

With the video revolution still evolving, *Smash Hits*, the teen magazine that had helped a generation of bands to find fame for two decades, closed in 2006. It was the same story with BBC-TV's *Top of the Pops*, which ended its 42-year history, swamped by music on demand from innumerable channels. The days of waiting all week to watch your favourite band were long gone, with TV and the net now offering 24-hour access.

Moby was quick to cash in on TV commercials. Though technically released in 1999, his album *Play* became one of the major hits of the early 2000s when every track on it was licensed for use in an ad. One of

see Introduction pp 374   see Key Artists pp 380   see A–Z of Artists pp 390   see List of Artists pp 418

the most notable was for Nike where Tiger Woods plays golf across downtown Manhattan to the strains of 'Find My Baby'.

Former Nirvana drummer Dave Grohl seemed to have captured the post-grunge *zeitgeist* with his new band Foo Fighters, for which he played guitar and sang. A great favourite at festivals, which were enjoying a renaissance in the new millennium, his songs – each accompanied by a clever video that could be enjoyed at more than one level – demanded little yet satisfied for a while. Rock as fast Foo(d)?

The rave culture that had flourished in the 1990s was fading, hip-hop now very much the dance music of choice. The steady stream of rappers showing off to scantily-clad 'hoes' on specialist channels such as MTV Base was, however, somewhat depressing.

Sisters Are Doing For Themselves

Black music monopolized the US charts as the 2000s got into gear. In the 2001 singles listings, only nu-metallists Crazy Town and Canadians Nickelback registered in the top spot from outside the R&B/soul genre, names like Janet Jackson, Destiny's Child, Alicia Keys and Mary J. Blige also correctly suggesting a female bias.

Talking of females, the Britney v Christina 'battle of the blondes' was gatecrashed by an edgier performer in Pink. The former Alecia Moore appeared to mix a little controversy and punk attitude into her pop songs, which Ms Spears and Aguilera lacked.

But when it came to controversy, Eminem was the man. Raised on the seamy side of Detroit by his teenage mother, Debbie, he never knew his father but became one himself at 22. His inability to relate to his wife, mother, indeed any female but his daughter fuelled his muse and, like The Beastie Boys in the 1980s, the biggest rapper of the noughties was ironically destined to be white. Yet the former Marshall Mathers gained a much appreciated seal of approval when Missy Elliot, the much-respected female rapper, invited him to record with her.

A Change For The Better?

Downloading music not only changed the basis of the pop charts but created a teen status symbol in the shape of the iPod, Apple computers' take on the MP3 player. Apple were among those to start an online

music buying service, iTunes, which sold tracks for as little as 99 cents apiece.

Unlike the internet, the DVD (Digital Versatile Disc) failed to make the impact many had predicted. While concerts and collections of promo clips sold respectably, consumers seemed unwilling to pay the price such releases were initially pitched at. They appeared more a way of clawing back money after mammoth tours, as with Madonna's *I'm Going To Tell You A Secret*, or to satisfy demand for now non-existent bands, as with Pink Floyd's *Pulse*.

The Floyd had re-formed for 2005's Live 8, a re-run of Live Aid 20 years on, which suggested that the cyclical nature of popular music would continue for the foreseeable future.

Above

At the beginning of the decade Soul and R&B divas such as Mary J. Blige were stealing the limelight from guitar rock.

see Dido pp 395   see Foo Fighters pp 396   see Nickelback pp 407   see Pink pp 409

Coldplay

Key Artists

> *'Coldplay are just four friends trying to make great music.'*
>
> Will Champion

Coldplay were formed in London in 1996 by four college friends – Chris Martin (born 2 March 1977, vocals), Jonny Buckland (born 11 September 1977, guitar), Will Champion (born 31 July 1978, drums) and Guy Berryman (born 12 April 1978, bass). Their early years were similar to thousands of other struggling young bands in the UK's capital, with continued gigging at venues in the Camden area and numerous support slots to bands they would later go on to shadow and supercede.

Indie Roots

A popular route into the 'recorded world' that Coldplay soon followed was the self-funded single – in this case the *Safety EP* CD (1998). It is rumored that less than 20 per cent of the 500 copies made found their way to actual gig-goers, and that most ended up in the hands of record-company executives. But a concert in north London attracted the head of the cool Fierce Panda label, Simon Williams, and a single was quickly slated for release on the strength of that night's performance ('Brothers And Sisters').

After their responsibilities at university were fulfilled, the band signed a then massive five-album deal with UK label Parlophone, also home to 'Britpop' bands like Blur and Supergrass that many claim Coldplay were influenced by. After initial internal squabbles that were soon resolved, the band decided to act as a democracy whereby each member received the same amount of money from their burgeoning career. On top of such equality, the four claimed to live a comparatively clean lifestyle, and from very early on Coldplay found themselves dogged by accusations of being dull or 'not rock'n'roll enough'.

A Rush Of Sales

Parachutes, Coldplay's debut album from 2000, found the band and Martin in good voice, but shadows of influences from college days still hung over the work – for example, 'Shiver' was almost colour-by-numbers Jeff Buckley. However, later single smashes from the album, 'Yellow' and 'Trouble' – both emotionally fraught and plaintively played (particularly by Buckland), and accompanied by dramatically simple videos – gained them exposure on a worldwide scale.

Returning in 2002 with the thoroughly impressive 'In My Place', an epic, haunting track with a guitar motif to die for, Coldplay found their position in world music to have swelled enormously. This was largely as a result of the intense touring to promote *Parachutes*, but also because of a growing confidence among the band and Martin. (His profile soared due to a relationship with movie star Gwyneth Paltrow; they married in 2003.)

A Rush Of Blood To The Head, which arrived in 2002, was full of much the same balladry and sly musicianship that its predecessor had been, but here the band had stretched their wings and had honed their live show to one that could fill the largest of

stadiums. 'The Scientist' and 'Clocks' were more explicitly piano-driven, and the latter was used as music for a BBC TV station ident, pushing the band further into the mainstream.

Keeping Momentum

Coldplay's musical influences were apparently shifting by 2003–04. The band began to cite Kraftwerk and the more electronic side of Radiohead as influences as work for the follow-up to *A Rush...* progressed. Expectation was high, and when *X&Y* was finally delivered in 2005, fans seemed pleased that the album was not in fact a techno record – although elements of Kraftwerk were slightly evident on single 'Talk'.

The tours got bigger still, culminating in a busy week in June 2005, when the band headlined the prestigious Glastonbury festival on a Saturday night and then duetted with their hero Richard Ashcroft (on his Verve track, 'Bittersweet Symphony') at the London leg of the Live 8 concerts the following weekend. The performances revealed a Coldplay far removed from the struggling band in Camden of just five years prior, but one capable of handling even the biggest gigs the world could throw at them (the audience at the Hyde Park gig alone numbered well over 120,000, millions more watched on TV).

Seemingly with every album that Coldplay release, talk of a split seems to surface, but these rumours are continually rebuffed by the band. One thing was made clear by Martin at the Brit Awards in 2006 however – namely that the group may well take time out to consider their next move. If the anticipation before *X&Y* was anything to go by, there will be a lot of people waiting for that next announcement.

Above

Coldplay singer Chris Martin on stage in support of *A Rush Of Blood To The Head*. Proving that they were no one-album-wonders, if anything, 2002's follow up to *Parachutes* took its predecessor's success even further.

see Kraftwerk pp 218   see Jeff Buckley pp 344   see Supergrass pp 368   see Radiohead pp 386

Eminem

*'Anybody with a sense
of humour is going to put
on my album and laugh
from beginning to end.'*
Eminem

Above

Courting controversy from the
start with a nothing-is-taboo
lyrical content, Eminem has
become one of the most
successful rap artists ever.

Right

Eminem on stage during a
tour for 2000's *The Marshall
Mathers LP*.

**Marshall Bruce Mathers III was born on
17 October 1972 in Detroit, Michigan. The
exact details of his upbringing there and in
nearby Warren are unknown, suffice to say
he was raised solely by his mother Debbie,
and the upbringing, reputedly poverty-
stricken, provided ample subject matter for
much of the rapper's lyrical material.**

8 Mile And Detroit

Marshall Mathers was introduced to hip-hop music,
which he soon came to adore, by his uncle Ronald
Polkingham. A high school drop-out, Mathers entered
the hip-hop world with gusto. Taking the name
Eminem (after his initials), he performed from the
age of 13, and quickly built a reputation as a skilled
wordsmith (in the local scene at least). Early work
with the group Soul Intent was popular but relatively
unknown, but increasingly the young Mathers found

himself ranking highly as a solo performer in verbal
battles with other local rappers.

The period is covered in the 2002 film *8 Mile*
(named after an area of Detroit), in which Eminem
played himself in a story based on his life. The film
would earn him an Academy Award and Grammy for
the accompanying soundtrack.

A debut album *Infinite* (1996), which Eminem
recorded while still living with friends and family, was
sold from the boot of his car – although few sold. The
aim had been to raise enough money to support his
girlfriend (Kim Scott) through her recent pregnancy.
Hailie Scott was born in late 1995, with Kim's threat
of refused access pushing Mathers to a suicide attempt.

Long-Awaited Success

Rap entrepreneur/producer Dr. Dre, of seminal outfit
N.W.A. – himself a mean rapper – somehow found
Eminem's demo cassette in 1997, although the exact

📻 *see* Introduction pp 374   📻 *see* Sources & Sounds pp 376   📻 *see* A–Z of Artists pp 390

details of how remain sketchy. *Infinite* therefore paved the way for Eminem's *Slim Shady LP* (1999). Slim Shady was an alias for Eminem, and a character who represented the more damaged side of the rapper. Here was a narrator who would urge men to kill cheating wives and then dispose of the body in a lake. Unsurprisingly, the album caused a storm of controversy, but for every detractor there would be a voice championing the white star – one increasingly ruling a traditionally black genre.

The album sold triple platinum in its first year – but music fans were not surprised. Debut single 'My Name Is' was a comedic romp with a lazy, addictive sample. 'Stan', a chillingly self-aware tale of a man driven to murder, supposedly inspired by Eminem, saw its sampling of Dido project her to new levels of fame, such was the growing magnitude of the rapper.

The next step for Eminem seemed to be to self-reference, to verbalize the strains that came with superstardom. Fans liked this just as much, and *The Marshall Mathers LP* (2000) sold three times as well as its predecessor. Later albums, although still selling extremely well, were perhaps too infused with Mathers' increasing mental instability to cross over as well as they had previously. Perhaps to counter this, Eminem diversified his talents, through his own label (Shady), producing other artists and guesting in the group D-12 – six Detroit rappers and their six alter-egos.

At the time of writing, the future of Eminem the rapper remains unclear – with nothing since 2004's *Encore*. He is typically vague, claiming that he will remain in a more production-based role, calling his 2005 hits collection *Curtain Call* yet proclaiming onstage there would be more chance of the moon exploding than him retiring.

Personal Issues

Many of Eminem's lyrics, although strikingly amusing at times in their absurdity, stem from real events in the rapper's life. And, such events have had adverse effects on his state of mind. Legal battles with his mother (for alleged defamation), two divorces from Kim and a constant battle with alcohol and drugs have seen a volatile performer emerge from the cocoon of a prodigiously talented artist. At times these twists and turns have been what has made Eminem great, but when it was mooted in 2005 that the singer might be retiring, many felt it might just be the best option, lest the rollercoaster career end in tears.

see Dr. Dre pp 348   see Dido pp 395

384

Green Day

📻 **CLASSIC RECORDINGS**

1993
Dookie, 'Welcome To Paradise', 'When I Come Around'

1997
Nimrod, 'Good Riddance (Time Of Your Life)'

2000
Warning, 'Warning'

2005
American Idiot, 'Boulevard Of Broken Dreams', 'Wake Me Up When September Ends'

Billie Joe Armstrong (born 17 February 1972, vocals, guitar), Tré Cool (born Frank Edwin Wright III, 9 December 1972, drums) and Mike Dirnt (born 4 May 1972, bass) first started working together as a trio in California in the late 1980s when Armstrong and Dirnt needed a drummer to complete their already fledgling Green Day project (which had been renamed from Sweet Children). Cool joined after his band The Lookouts disbanded. At this point all members were still under 18.

'Punk has always been about doing things your own way. What it represents for me is ultimate freedom and a sense of individuality.'

Billie Joe Armstrong

Right
Since the 1990s Green Day have evolved from being slightly mindless punkers for teens, to becoming one of the most influential bands of their generation.

Far Right
Green Day's overtly poppy *Warning* album saw them continue to break free from the shackles of regenerative punk, and by 2002, singer and lyricist Billy Joe Armstrong was able to simply revel in the love of making music for music's sake.

Punk Origins

Green Day began a recording career with EPs on local labels such as Lookout! and Skene!. There was major label interest at this time, but the band, headstrong then and now, refused to ink a deal that they saw as a 'sellout'. Rather, they were content with the sales of their debut, *Kerplunk!* (1992), and expressed little desire to move outside of the independent punk scene at the time. However, within a year the trio had signed a deal with Reprise, and *Dookie* (1993) was a global success. It was a big, dumb pop record, dressed up as noisy punk. The trio, still young of course, found success with the sinewy 'When I Come Around' and the moronic, if memorable, 'Basket Case'. Here was a band not afraid to mess around, to play their

instruments as loud as they could, and, it seemed, to have fun. Punk rock, or the spirit of it, seemed to have crossed over to the mainstream in a fashion Nirvana could never ape.

Shifting position again, 1995 saw the release of *Insomniac* and a marked decision to 'get serious'. 1997s *Nimrod* was bleaker still, and the acoustic gem

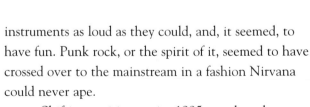

📻 see Introduction pp 374   📻 see Sources & Sounds pp 376   📻 see A–Z of Artists pp 390

that was 'Good Riddance (Time Of Your Life)' – just Armstrong and an acoustic guitar, backed by cello – remains a firm fan favourite to this day.

2000's *Warning* was a further trek down the road of seriousness that the band had craved since they stopped dying their hair after *Dookie*. A mixed critical reception did nothing to stop the band, however, and indeed, The Kinks' sound of the title track was a melodic highpoint Green Day had not reached previously. Those who cared to look could see that things were in place for something important.

The American Idiot Phenomenon

After a *Greatest Hits* compilation in 2001 (usually a sign a band is on the ropes), Green Day took three years to produce what is easily their finest work – one of such staggering political significance, beautifully crafted yet simple power pop and sly objectivity that *American Idiot* (2004) is often considered one of the greatest punk albums ever made – no mean feat for a record released some 30 years after the movement first arose.

A concept album in a loose sense, the album gained a respect for these ever-young punks from a new generation of critics – and some older ones too. From the melancholy of single 'Wake Me Up When September Ends' to the more traditional Green Day rock of the title track (another single), the record gave the finger to those who said the band were no longer relevant. Here they were more significant in directing the youth of the world's largest nation toward political opinion than any amount of governmental campaigning or advertising.

And the *American Idiot* phenomenon continued apace. The tour that the album inevitably triggered took in some of the biggest arenas the world had to offer, often with triple or quadruple nights at certain venues. Keen to maintain a kind of momentum, and of course capitalize on the rush of (justified) interest in the group, Reprise saw fit to release a deluxe live album and DVD package, provocatively titled *Bullet In A Bible* (2005) – worth viewing for the scale of the concerts alone, and the inverse proportionality to the intimacy Armstrong, Dirnt and Cool seem to bring to the massive shows.

Talks of a screenplay based on the album 'storyline' were started in late 2005, further proving that

American Idiot, and Green Day as a whole, are now innovators, and not the scene-hogging bandwagon-jumpers of the late 1980s many assumed they would be remembered as.

🎸 *see* The Kinks pp 94   🎸 *see* The Offspring pp 360   🎸 *see* Good Charlotte pp 398   🎸 *see* Sum 41 pp 414

Radiohead

CLASSIC RECORDINGS

1993
Pablo Honey, 'Creep'

1995
The Bends, 'Street Spirit', 'My Iron Lung'

1997
OK Computer, 'Paranoid Android', 'Let Down', 'No Surprises'

2000
Kid A, 'The National Anthem', 'How To Disappear Completely'

2001
Amnesiac, 'Packt Like Sardines In A Crushd Tin Box', 'Pyramid Song', Life In A Glass House'

2003
Hail To The Thief, '2+2=5', 'There There'

2005
'I Want None Of This'

'It's a fine line between writing something with genuine emotional impact and turning into little idiots feeling sorry for ourselves and playing stadium rock.'
Thom Yorke

Above
Radiohead have consistently pushed boundaries in music without ever losing their fanbase. Singer Thom Yorke has become one of the most singular minds in music.

Right
Radiohead at the Hammersmith Apollo, London, May 2006 as part of a sold-out European and US tour.

The five members of Radiohead are the same today as they were on the day they formed. Thom Yorke (born 7 October 1968, vocals, guitar, piano), Jonny Greenwood (born 5 November 1971, lead guitar, effects), Ed O'Brien (born 15 April 1968, guitar, vocals), Phil Selway (born 23 May 1967, drums) and Colin Greenwood (born 26 June 1969, bass) met at school in Oxfordshire and started jamming in around 1986. **Initially called On A Friday, after the day of the week they were permitted to rehearse, the band somehow, inexplicably, managed to stay together while each member went off to study a degree. On returning to Oxford and its environs after places at various other UK universities, the band picked up where they had left off and began to take gigs around their home city more seriously.**

Oxford

At venues like the Jericho Tavern, a small upstairs room at a pub with a PA, On A Friday began to learn their craft. Oxford was by no means a musical backwater, as the band went to great lengths to point out (to this day, whenever possible, the band conduct interviews in hotels there). Bands such as Ride had already made quite a name for the city, spearheading a new 'shoegazing' movement in the early 1990s.

Local music papers took more interest as the groups gigging circuit grew and grew – spreading south, occasionally to London, and other venues in the Thames Valley area. EMI, impressed with what they saw, signed the band on a six-album deal, providing they change their name. Radiohead came from a track on the Talking Heads album, *True Stories*.

Creeping Up

The debut album, *Pablo Honey* (1993), is most Radiohead fans' least favourite. But tucked away in the middle was a song called 'Creep', a slab of neo-12-bar blues, which was thrillingly 'messed up' by Jonny Greenwood with his now trademark double-guitar crunch before each chorus. The song was released to little hoorah, but it was not until a second release, in the US this time, that radio stations started to pick up on the song. Tours followed, and slowly but surely the band made a name in these new territories. But, cruelly, the track seemed to suffocate them, and the band began to resent it – touring a foreign land also lost favour. *The Bends* (1995) was written very much in this frame of mind ('My Iron Lung' even obliquely references 'Creep').

Ironically, the album became Radiohead's most American-sounding, awash with guitars and high-pitched guitar/vocal histrionics. However, lyrically, it was perhaps their meanest, a sarcastic repost to the lifestyle unfolding before them. One positive thing that stemmed from the recording was initial work with producer Nigel Godrich (then an engineer), who the band described working with as similar to school when the teacher was absent.

see Introduction pp 374   *see* Sources & Sounds pp 376   *see* A–Z of Artists pp 390

The OK Computer Effect

With high worldwide sales figures for *The Bends*, the band found themselves in a comparatively luxurious position whereby their label was actually happy to wait for the follow-up. With the pressure off, the band asked Godrich to fashion a portable studio that they could take with them to record where they chose. They settled on a country retreat once owned by Jane Seymour, and set to work on a follow-up using ideas that were forming at an alarming rate.

The first the public got to hear of their new work was a track called 'Lucky', which appeared on the Warchild charity's *Help* album (1995). The track was produced in just seven days (as the album dictated), and was a clear signifier that Radiohead had moved on from formulaic rock.

OK Computer (1997) was released at a time when the public were anticipating a possible end of the world with the encroaching end of the millennium. The album somehow encapsulated these fears, along with other, more general themes of escaping, of being trapped and of travel. It remains Radiohead's most acclaimed work, and saw influences from artists as diverse as DJ Shadow (on the rhythm of 'Airbag') and classical, avant-garde composers such as Penderecki (on the drowsy 'Climbing Up The Walls'). The band set out on tour, and by the end of 1997 *OK Computer* was lauded as the greatest album of the year in many publications. Over the decade since it was released, its status as one of rock music's greatest achievements has grown steadily, and the album frequently ranks alongside The Beatles and Elvis in magazine reader polls.

Electronic Change

Radiohead, ever-forward thinking, saw no point in replicating what they had achieved with *OK Computer*. Instead, they took the music that they had been listening to towards the end of the 1990s and tried to work that into their songwriting and performing. Artists on dance labels like Warp and Mo' Wax such as Autechre and Boards Of Canada replaced guitar music, and this filtered into the sound of the 'new' Radiohead. Advances in technology meant Yorke could summarize his ideas for songs on computer, and the word quickly spread that his band might be making a 'techno' record. In fact, they were making two.

🎸 *see* Joy Division pp 260 🎸 *see* The Smiths pp 315 🎸 *see* Talking Heads pp 318 🎸 *see* Ride pp 364

Above

Jonny Greenwood's pyrotechnical guitar rock is essential to the soaring appeal of the Radiohead sound.

Kid A (2000) and *Amnesiac* (2001) were made up of works from the same sessions, but released as two separate albums. These sessions had not been easy for the band (as anyone charting their internet-only performances over the three years' gestation would testify), but much of the material remains as interesting as anything from *OK Computer*. 'The National Anthem' saw Yorke playing bass, drunk, while 'Pyramid Song' was a Top 3 UK single with no chorus, haunting piano and an impassioned vocal.

Under The Influence

Bands started to fall over themselves to claim Radiohead as an influence. Even giant globetrotting bands like R.E.M. and U2 claimed them to be among the greatest in the world, and Coldplay's Chris Martin deemed himself unworthy of comparison to Yorke. Muse, however, in a strange about-face and after many years of touring under comparisons to the band, decided they did not like the band after *OK Computer*. The feeling among fans was that Radiohead, never necessarily crushed by label pressure, were finally doing exactly what they wanted. If that meant 'going electronic', then so be it – enough of the Radiohead that people loved remained in whatever they did. They somehow did right, even when they were trying to do wrong, such was their status. Thankfully, acclaim was nearly always justified.

2003 brought the release of *Hail To The Thief*, a provocatively-titled collection that almost saw a return to the rock of the mid-1990s, but not quite. '2+2=5', a rock blast supposedly written on the spot, showed the

see Introduction pp 374   *see* Sources & Sounds pp 376   *see* A–Z of Artists pp 390

raft of imitators that had followed after *OK Computer* that the Oxford quintet were still the bosses when it came to blow outs. But there was still a well-tempered love of synthetic sound evident throughout.

Having fulfilled their initial contract, Radiohead found themselves in 2006 the biggest unsigned band in the world. They have expressed an interest in internet-only releases, or possibly a string of EPs as their next move. On a short world tour of 2006, the band 'demoed' over 15 new, as-yet unrecorded songs to appreciative crowds – many of which hinted at a return to a style of songwriting not heard since *The Bends* days.

Dreaded 'Solo' Albums

Both Thom Yorke and Jonny Greenwood have released solo albums in their time as Radiohead members. Greenwood released the sublime soundtrack *Bodysong* in 2003, and Yorke saw his glitchy *The Eraser* released to general surprise in 2006 (he had been working on it for two years or more, but only industry insiders and Radiohead knew).

Politics

Over the years, Radiohead, and Yorke especially, have campaigned tirelessly for many causes. At their own concerts they promote the work of Greenpeace, and, increasingly, charities that look to alternative energy methods. Yorke was invited to Downing Street to discuss his concerns about climate change with the Prime Minister Tony Blair, but declined.

Radiohead are also staunchly anti-sponsorship, choosing companies to cater their own events that bear no advertising on products given to the public, and forbidding the use of their music in adverts. Aside from the 'Lucky' track for the original 'Help' album, they also contributed the excellent unreleased piano ballad, 'I Want None Of This', to the album sequel, *Help: A Day In The Life*, in 2005.

Below

Thom Yorke in 2000, just as *Kid A* was being released, and redefining what it meant to make pop music an artistic statement in the new millennium.

see U2 pp 284 see R.E.M. pp 338 see Coldplay pp 380 see Muse pp 406

Christina Aguilera

(Vocals, b. 1980)

NYC native Aguilera has been making records since 1999, but singing since her very earliest years, inspired by the talents of the likes of Whitney Houston and Madonna. Her own vocal ability has long been the selling point of her talent, but her 'blonde bombshell' looks have not hindered her progress.

Breaking on to the scene with the single 'Genie In A Bottle', Aguilera's overt sexuality was always evident. By the time of 2002's 'Dirrty', a track that saw the singer virtually naked in the video, wrestling while covered in oil and/or sweat, there was little left to the public's imagination. Subsequent magazine interviews even hinted at bisexuality, but many thought these comments to be a mere marketing ploy (she married music executive Jordan Bratman in 2005). She even went so far as to kiss Madonna onstage at the 2003 MTV awards. Such controversy aside, Aguilera has a powerful vocal range and a domineering style of delivery similar to and as high as Mariah Carey.

Antony and The Johnsons

(Vocal group, 2000–present)

New Yorker Antony Hegarty (vocals) and his fluid supporting cast are an act that affect everyone who hears them. Lou Reed liked them so much he recruited Hegarty to his band, and provided vocals, along with Boy George, on the Mercury Award-winning *I Am A Bird Now* (2005). What captivates fans is undoubtedly Hegarty's voice, a successor to Nina Simone but also one clearly indebted to the 1980s acts he loved as a youth, such as Alison Moyet and Marc Almond.

Arcade Fire

(Vocal/instrumental group, 2003–present)

Canadian performers Arcade Fire – Win Butler (vocals), Regine Chassagne, Richard Reed Parry, William Butler, Tim Kingsbury, Sarah Neufeld and Jeremy Gara (all multi-instrumentalists) – gave the public what they did not think they would like with

see Introduction pp 374   *see Sources & Sounds pp 376*   *see Key Artists pp 380*

the 2004 *Funeral* debut. Essentially a modern gothic masterpiece, the record covered dance, folk, baroque, dancehall, ragtime and lashings of melancholy in a way no other band were at the time. David Bowie and David Byrne admired them, the former even performing onstage with them in New York in 2006.

Arctic Monkeys

(Vocal/instrumental group, 2005–present)

After a story that the band had formed through Myspace (they had in fact just put their demos online, and never had a presence on the site), Sheffield's Arctic Monkeys – Alex Turner (vocals), Jamie Turner (guitar), Matt Helders (drums) and Andy Nicholson (bass) – saw their wryly accurate take on northern English life consumed by the public. Their debut album *Whatever People Say I Am, That's What I'm Not* was released in January 2006 and became the fastest-selling album ever in the country, and their breakneck indie soon became a template through which all A&R men looked for new talent.

Audioslave

(Vocal/instrumental group, 2001–present)

Formed from various seminal rock groups of the heaviest ilk, Audioslave – Chris Cornell (vocals), Tom Morello (guitar), Brad Wilk (drums) and Tim Commerford (bass) – make a racket honed through experience gained in the likes of influential acts Rage Against The Machine and Soundgarden. Perhaps too dry to be taken in one sitting, their eponymous debut still served up 'Cochise' (2002), a track so immediately energizing that the band could well have formed for that alone.

Babyshambles

(Vocal/instrumental group, 2004–present)

In every way a vehicle for ex-Libertine Pete Doherty (vocals), Babyshambles – Adam Ficek (drums) and Drew McConnell (bass) – continually teeter on the edge of greatness but more often than not fail dismally, often as a result of their singer's criminal misdemeanours. A shame, as debut *Down In Albion* (2005) had some fine moments – most notably the track 'Pentonville', a stirring reggae melody sung by an ex-inmate of Doherty's from his time in the London prison of the same name.

Badly Drawn Boy

(Vocals, b. 1970)

Damon Gough's charming Badly Drawn Boy alter ego found initial (if cult) success on the roster of the UK's DIY Twisted Nerve label. A folk singer with allusions of grandeur, Gough sidestepped the tag of troubadour by soundtracking the *About A Boy* film (2002) and steadily learning to incorporate string sections and orchestras into his sound. He leapt from alternative oddball to daytime radio staple with ease, losing none of his songwriting skill, lightness of touch or allure in the process.

Far Left

A one-time rival for Britney Spears' Queen of Pop crown, Christina Aguilera's image changes have been as frequent as Madonna's, and allowed her to remain an evolving pop singer for the Noughties.

Far Left

If anyone in 2005 was still sceptical over internet downloading providing a viable way of selling and promoting music, Arctic Monkeys would prove its worth. Their 'I Bet You Look Good On The Dancefloor' was a hit out of nowhere, thanks to online support.

Below

Often painted as the English Bruce Springsteen, Badly Drawn Boy emerged, with trademark tea-cosy hat, to become one of Britain's most talented (and collectable) modern singer-songwriters.

see David Bowie pp 196   *see* Whitney Houston pp 299   *see* Rage Against The Machine pp 364   *see* The Libertines pp 404

The Black Eyed Peas

(Vocal group, 1998–present)

The four main players in The Black Eyed Peas – Will.I.Am (Will Adams), Apl.de.Ap (Allen Pineda), Taboo (Jaime Gomez) and Fergie (Stacy Ferguson) – came to the wider public attention in 2003 on the back of the success of their 'Where Is The Love?' single, which topped the charts for a record six weeks in the UK alone. But the group's origins can be traced back to 1989 and rap competitions in LA. Their individual style, very much removed from the gangsta look of the time, and performances with a live band set them apart from the majority of hip-hop crews in the charts in the 1990s.

Naturally fame beckoned, and on the strength of *that* Justin Timberlake-featuring hit in 2003, the group became something of a force. Will.I.Am is a producer every artist seems to lust after, the band perform countless charity benefits, and certain members are already mooting solo careers.

Above

Since the 1990s, Basement Jaxx had been a respected dance act, pushing British house music forward. By the Noughties, they'd become equally successful in the charts, with each release pleasing hardcore dance fans as much as mainstream music lovers.

Basement Jaxx

(Dance group, 1994–present)

Producers, DJs and remixers Basement Jaxx (duo Felix Buxton and Simon Ratcliffe) rose to prominence in the mid-1990s, on the back of initial success at various south London club nights – most notably their highly eclectic but always uplifting Rooty evenings. On record, their sound lies somewhere between a carnival sound system and more conventional house music, but all with a telling urban bite.

Debut album *Remedy* (1999) found flamenco guitars, pounding beats and cheeky female MCs boiled down into a collection of irresistible party anthems for the new century. The follow-up, 2001's *Rooty*, contained the duo's best-known hit 'Where's Your Head At?', perhaps a reference to the state of mind of many clubbers who were now listening in their masses. The album won a Grammy, but rather than rest on their laurels, Basement Jaxx continued with *Kish Kash* (2003), a more complex work which saw guest vocal appearances from Siouxsie Sioux and grime star Dizzee Rascal.

Right

Once a moderately well respected hip-hop act, during the early Noughties, Black Eyed Peas eschewed all pretensions to artistic growth, and began churning out the hits to an ever-growing youth-dominated audience.

Blink-182

(Vocal/instrumental group, 1992–2005)

Kings of the snotty, toilet humoured nu-punk genre, Blink-182 – Travis Barker (drums), Tom DeLonge (vocals) and Mark Hoppus (bass) – formed while at school, recording in their then-drummer Scott Raynor's bedroom. Since then, they have grown older but not matured, with 2001's 'Rock Show' a fine

see Introduction pp 374   see Sources & Sounds pp 376   see Key Artists pp 380

example of the band's awareness of its target audience. They may yet return from their 'indefinite hiatus' and one day make a fun punk record of lasting significance.

Bloc Party
(Vocal/instrumental group, 2002–present)

Bloc Party – Kele Okereke (vocals), Matt Tong (drums), Russell Lissack (guitar) and Gordon Moakes (bass) – achieved massive critical acclaim for their debut, *Silent Alarm* (2005). The record managed to appeal to a cross section of music lovers (Okereke even guested on a Chemical Brothers' track), but is largely remembered for its stop-start guitar anthems, such as 'Helicopter' and 'Banquet'. Very much indebted to the likes of Gang of Four and Franz Ferdinand after them, Bloc Party have nevertheless found such imitation highly profitable.

James Blunt
(Vocals, b. 1974)

A former member of the British army, Blunt (real name James Blount) served until 2003 (once at the Queen Mother's funeral) and took songs he had written on duty in Kosovo into the studio. The piano balladry of 'You're Beautiful' (2005) received so much airplay in the UK it moved *up* the charts (a rare occurrence), then remained at No. 1 for six weeks. A backlash then developed against the high-pitched singer, a sign that the public needed a follow-up to an album, *Back To Bedlam*, which was mined for singles.

Kelly Clarkson
(Vocals, b. 1982)

2002's *American Idol* victor, Clarkson has, like many, tried hard to escape the show's shadow. Indeed, it is her later material that the general public will remember if asked – singles 'Because Of You' (2005) and 'Since You Been Gone' (2004) are rockier, a direct result of the star trying to break away from the pop which made her name. They remain far more memorable than 'A Moment Like This' (2002), her first US No. 1 – a typically schmaltzy show-winning ballad.

The Coral
(Vocal/instrumental group, 1996–present)

The Wirral's most innovative and carefree band, The Coral – James Skelly (vocals), Ian Skelly (drums), Bill

Ryder-Jones (trumpet), Nick Power (keyboards), Lee Southall (guitar), Paul Duffy (bass) and John Duffy (drums) – have become something of the market leaders in the ramshackle if wholly enjoyable modern folk scene. Hugely prolific, any one of their seven albums and EPs (from just five years) can house rock, blues, skiffle, punk and more besides – they are something like the successors to Captain Beefheart's strange throne.

Below
2002 *American Idol* winner, Kelly Clarkson has had a surprising longevity for a Noughties reality TV show competition winner, having toured as recently as 2006.

see The Gang Of Four pp 258   see Dizzee Rascal pp 395   see Franz Ferdinand pp 397   see Girls Aloud pp 398

The Darkness
(Vocal/instrumental group, 2000–present)

The Darkness – Justin Hawkins (vocals), Dan Hawkins (guitar), Ed Graham (drums) and Richie Edwards (bass) – are the most unlikely rock stars. Good looks and credibility take second place to stadiums full of fans and steely rock riffs transplanted straight from their heroes, Queen. After witty singles titles and Christmas offerings, debut *Permission To Land* (2003) sold well. Critics were initially baffled, unsure whether to party or remain aloof. The group retain a hardcore fan base despite a water-treading second album without iconic original bass player Frankie Poullain.

Craig David
(Vocals, b. 1981)

Initially inspired by a musical father (a reggae bass guitarist), Craig David's first appearance on the music scene to those outside the Southampton club circuit was his vocal for Artful Dodger's 'Rewind' (1999). Subsequently signing to Telstar, David made his name with melodic, often acoustically laced R&B that reflected his casanova lifestyle in a down-to-earth fashion. 'Fill Me In' (2000) detailed suspicion over a girlfriend's monogamy, while 'Walking Away' (2001) showed a desire to live a less stressful lifestyle.

The timeless '7 Days' (2000) became something of a joke among detractors, who lampooned the singer for 'chilling on Sundays' after a week of lovemaking. David took such jibes, along with a highly amusing puppet version of himself on UK comedy program *Bo' Selecta* (itself named after his early catchphrase), with grace. Two further albums, *Slicker Than Your Average* (2005) and *The Story Goes …* (2005) fared less well chartwise, but the fact remains that Craig David is an exceptional soul singer.

Destiny's Child
(Vocal group, 1997–2005)

In the most famous incarnation, the trio of Destiny's Child (Beyoncé Knowles, Kelly Roland and Michelle Williams) were an extremely successful and hardworking vocal group that formed in Texas in 1990 as a quartet. After numerous line-up changes the group found their stride in 2000 with the soulful 'Say My Name' and the party-rocking 'Jumpin' Jumpin''. A tie-in single with the film *Charlie's Angels* the same year ('Independent Women Pt. 1') saw mass chart domination. Later singles such as 'Bootylicious' and 'Survivor' (both 2001) raised the band's cool factor further, leading to a fourth album, *Destiny Fulfilled* (2004) – and by 2005 they were even able to release a convincing best of album.

Managed by Knowles' father Mathew, the trio eventually split that year (albeit perhaps temporarily), with each member already pursuing a solo career. Knowles' was the most successful after work with boyfriend/rapper Jay-Z resulted in the infectious smash hit 'Crazy In Love' (2003).

Dido

(Singer/songwriter, b. 1981)

The daughter of a French poet mother, this singer was born Dido Florian Cloud de Bounevialle Armstrong on Christmas Day. She waited on the sidelines while her musician brother, Rollo Armstrong (of the band Faithless), achieved pop success in the mid-1990s. But encouraged after providing vocals for some of his tracks, her own songwriting came to the fore. When 1998's serene 'Thank You' was sampled in part by rapper Eminem for his own 'Stan' single, music lovers around the globe clamoured to find the source.

The profile provided by the sample provided fresh interest in her *No Angel* album (1999), a collection of smooth, sultry ballads and slightly rockier numbers that struck a chord with a middle-aged, often middle-class audience keen to identify with this new 'everywoman'. It has sold in excess of 13 million copies worldwide, and the follow-up, 2003's *Life For Rent*, although unconnected to any rap artist, sold equally strongly and was very much a continuation of the same themes.

Dizzee Rascal

(Rapper, b. 1985)

Dizzee Rascal (real name Dylan Mills) has become known as something of a young godfather of the emergent 'grime' music scene, swiftly delivering a new kind of rap, quickly spoken and aggressive, over synthetic, staccato rhythms. His critical acclaim stems from a wide understanding of music (he cites Nirvana's *In Utero* as his favourite) and a deft sociological wordplay. *Boy In Da Corner* (2003) won the Mercury Music Prize, and he even lectured at Oxford University in 2006.

Embrace

(Vocal/instrumental group, 1997–present)

Embrace – Danny McNamara (vocals), Richard McNamara (guitar), Steven Firth (bass), Mike Heaton (drums) and Mickey Dale (keyboards) – have had numerous career resuscitations in their decade-long existence. But the band started life as press-darlings after a number of singles on the fiercely independent Fierce Panda label. It was these early, near-demo quality recordings that caught the Hut label's attention. After three albums of diminishing returns the group signed to Independiente, and saw a track donated to

Above

Dido's success was helped by her 'Thank You' being sampled by Eminem for his single 'Stan', leading to her being the perfect artist for an audience more likely to buy their music in supermarkets.

them by Coldplay's Chris Martin, 'Gravity' (2004), reach the UK Top 10.

By now Oasis' star was on the wane, and fans of earnest singalong rock found comfort with Embrace, and their *Out Of Nothing* (2004) and *This New Day* (2006) albums topped the UK charts. In 2006, the band were chosen to record the officially sanctioned anthem for their country's World Cup football squad, offering a track called 'World At Your Feet'.

Feeder

(Vocal/instrumental group, 1992–present)

Feeder – Grant Nicholas (guitar, vocals), Taka Hirose (bass) and Mark Richardson (drums) – formed in London, but are a Welsh/Japanese/English hybrid. It was not until third album *Echo Park* (2001) that their brand of bombastic, yelping yet highly singalong rock was noticed by the masses. The suicide of first drummer Jon Lee in early 2002 cast a grim light on subsequent material, but by 2005's *Pushing The Senses* the group were selling more records than ever, even releasing a greatest hits package.

see The Fugees pp 349   see Oasis pp 360   see Coldplay pp 380   see Eminem pp 382

50 Cent
(Rapper, b. 1975)

Curtis James Jackson II was born in New York, and has come to symbolize a brand of rap/actor that somehow manages to place circumstance over actual style. 50 Cent's main claim to infamy is the fact he has been shot numerous times. Understandably brash in his delivery, his thug attitude towards many aspects of life, a psychiatrist might add, is really a self-defence mechanism.

Either way, after writing for Run DMC in the mid-1990s, 50 Cent found himself without a deal until Eminem and Dr Dre signed him to their label/ publishing company, after hearing him on mixtapes. He is now six albums into his career, the best of which is *Get Rich Or Die Tryin'* (2003), which also titled a film of his life. Produced by Dre, it featured the blunt, syncopated chart hit 'In Da Club' (co-produced by Eminem), a *Billboard* single of the year.

Flaming Lips
(Vocal/instrumental group, 1983–present)

A longstanding antithesis to manufactured pop, the current incarnation of Oklahoma's Flaming Lips – Wayne Coyne (vocals), Michael Ivins (bass) and Steven Drozd (drums) – plough a decidedly odd furrow, at odds with their more 'traditional' alternative rock past. Now famed for their live performances, which can feature aliens, giant animals, fireworks and prosthetic

hands, the music is also innovative, with show tunes, contemporary covers, political rants and beautifully childlike melodies in abundance.

Foo Fighters
(Vocal/instrumental group, 1995–present)

Foo Fighters, the post-Nirvana project of Dave Grohl with Taylor Hawkins (drums), Nate Mendel (bass) and Chris Shiflett (guitar) saw the drummer turned singer storm the charts again and again with an honest, workaday approach to rock that was, more often that not, humorously handled. Thankfully too, Grohl could write a melody, and this meant his new band made countless radio hits rather than initiating the obscure punk that had influenced them.

'This Is A Call', 'I'll Stick Around' (both 1995), 'My Hero', 'Walking After You' (both 1997) – the list went on and on, each single more radio-friendly than the last. Often the singles would come backed with hammy promotional films – but while critics accused Grohl of selling out, the likeability of the singer and the quality of his songwriting won through. The band now find themselves five albums into their career, and more popular than ever.

see Introduction pp 374   see Sources & Sounds pp 376   see Key Artists pp 380

Fountains Of Wayne

(Vocal/instrumental group, 1995–present)
Chris Collingwood (guitar), Adam Schlesinger (bass), Jody Porter (guitar) and Brian Young (drums) formed their band in New Jersey. The early single 'That Thing You Do' (1996), used in the film of the same name, broke the band to mainstream audiences (and brought an Oscar nomination), but even that could not stop a four-year hiatus. 2001 saw the band high in the charts once more, with the tongue-in-cheek 'Stacy's Mom' single, an insistent, Weezer-esque romp lyrically concerned with having designs on friends' parents.

Franz Ferdinand

(Vocal/instrumental group, 2001–present)
Glasgow's Franz Ferdinand – Alex Kapranos (vocals), Robert Hardy (bass), Nicholas McCarthy (guitar) and Paul Thomson (drums) – formed from the scene around the city's college of art, but only drummer Thomson actually attended. Many wrongly consider their tightly suggestive brand of 'art rock' to be a result of years spent studying the visual arts, but it more likely stems from their obsession with music's history.

Fans of bands such as The Gang of Four and Fire Engines (even going so far as to release a split single with the latter), the band added in their own twist via slants on the showmen of rock – bands like Queen and Roxy Music. Their winning melodies took them outside of the cult circuit to mainstream acclaim, with their eponymous debut winning the Mercury Music award in 2004 and follow-up *You Could Have It So Much Better* (2005) debuting at No. 1 in the UK charts.

Nelly Furtado

(Vocals, b. 1978)
Portuguese/Canadian singer and sometime actress, Furtado is a shining exponent of feelgood modern pop. After a musical youth spent with DJs and rappers instead of musicians per se, her debut album from 2000, *Whoa, Nelly!*, accordingly fused the more palatable ingredients of music of the streets with an upbeat pop approach that garnered success for singles like 'I'm Like A Bird'. Later albums, *Folklore* (2003) and *Loose* (2006), the latter including the UK chart-topping 'Maneater', have seen Furtado further explore the fruits of cross-genre pollination.

The Futureheads

(Vocal/instrumental group, 2004–present)
The Futureheads – Ross Millard, Barry Hyde (both vocals), Dave Hyde (drums) and David Craig (bass) – came to the public's attention with their cover of Kate Bush's 'Hounds Of Love', delivered in fine northern accents (they hail from Sunderland). Yet the single was the band's fifth, thankfully acting as a pointer for many towards the energetic, intelligent guitar pop they could produce. Signed to dance imprint 679, they enjoy a rare freedom that is reflected in their output.

Below
Thanks to her Portuguese background, Nelly Furtado has been able to mix her own brand of R&B with a myriad of sounds and influences, making 2000's 'I'm Like A Bird' an all-pervasive 2000s pop single.

see Roxy Music pp 242   see Run-DMC pp 312   see Dr. Dre pp 348   see Eminem pp 382

worldwide, and went Top 5 in a further 10. A smooth blend of soul (courtesy of Callaway's booming vocal) and treated, dancefloor-friendly beats, the song proved irresistible enough to become the first ever download-only chart-topper in the UK.

Goldfrapp
(Dance/vocal group, 1999–present)

Like Blondie before them, Goldfrapp are often mistaken for a mere solo artist. They are in fact a duo – captivating vocalist Alison Goldfrapp certainly steals the limelight, while Will Gregory dwells in the shadows on stage. Something of a mix between electro, burlesque, the surreal and good old-fashioned pop, their sound has evolved from the minimal neo-opera of debut *Felt Mountain* (2000) into a more seductive, synthetic hybrid – best exemplified by the chart friendly, and highly catchy 'Ooh La La' (2005).

Good Charlotte
(Vocal/instrumental group, 1996–present)

Maryland's Good Charlotte – Joel Madden (vocals), Benji Madden (guitar), Billy Martin (keyboards) and Paul Thomas (bass) – exist in much the same sphere as rockers such as Sum 41 and Blink-182, pop rock bands formed startlingly young, signed to majors and then reaping successes normally attributed to older bands. 2002's *The Young And The Hopeless*, for example, has reached triple platinum sales. Despite losing drummer Chris Wilson in 2005, the band were set to release their fourth album in 2006.

Girls Aloud
(Vocal group, 2002–present)

Girls Aloud have managed to sustain a career after forming on a UK TV talent show (*Popstars: The Rivals*) where many have faltered before. The five girls (Nadine Coyle, Cheryl Tweedy, Nicola Roberts, Kimberley Walsh and Sarah Harding) rarely sing live at concerts, despite having had to win their places in the band, but strong singles such as 'Sound Of The Underground' and canny covers like The Pointer Sisters' 'Jump (For My Love)' somehow keep them burning bright in the pop world.

Gnarls Barkley
(Dance/vocal group, 2006–present)

The main brains behind the modern soul spectacular that is Gnarls Barkley are Brian Burton (aka producer Danger Mouse) and hip-hop underdog Thomas Callaway (aka Cee-Lo). Their debut single 'Crazy' reached No. 1 in no less than eight countries

Gorillaz
(Animated vocal group, 2001–present)

Gorillaz, a virtual band created as an antidote to the bland pop its creators (Blur's Damon Albarn and cartoonist Jamie Hewlett) saw dominating the charts, have, through stunning choice of guest vocalists and Albarn's gift for melody, made some of the most memorable pop music of recent years. Their self-titled debut (2001) was comparatively low key in comparison to its follow-up, but nevertheless held the breezy UK Top 10 hit 'Clint Eastwood'.

2005's *Demon Days* took the four animated characters in the band and coupled them with real-life musical legends, in a glittering ensemble cast that

see Introduction pp 374   *see* Sources & Sounds pp 376   *see* Key Artists pp 380

Left
Masterminded by Damon
Albarn, Gorillaz mixed hip-
hop with a more traditional
British songwriting, and a
cartoon-band-as-real-group
concept that made them a
more globally successful
group than Albarn's first
band, Blur.

included De La Soul, Ike Turner, Bootie Brown, Neneh Cherry and Shaun Ryder. Singles 'Feel Good Inc' and 'Dirty Harry' saw child choirs, rap artists and Albarn's insightful harmonizing employed to near universal acclaim. The band are also pioneering in their sadly infrequent live performances, utilizing everything from computer graphics to simple shadows to convey the characters without actually revealing the masterminds behind them.

David Gray
(Singer/songwriter, b. 1968)

Born near Manchester, the Dylanesque Gray toiled throughout the 1990s, while seemingly only Irish audiences listened. But mainstream success would not escape a songwriter with Gray's talent, and soon chart hit after chart hit ('Please Forgive Me', 'Babylon') snatched mass radio airplay, bolstered by a middle-aged fan base and anyone who liked a tune they could whistle underpinned by danceable rhythms, a winning formula perfected in his home studio. 2005's *Life In Slow Motion* found Gray in a darker but no less successful place.

Macy Gray
(Vocals, b. 1970)

Born Natalie McIntyre in Ohio, Macy Gray is a modern soul singer whose voice is distinctive and demeanor often startlingly original. In 1998, early hits 'Why Didn't You Call Me?' and 'I've Committed Murder' started to cause minor ripples in her home country, but by the following year her star was well in ascent. The 'I Try' single, equally as impressive as the same year's 'Still', was nominated for three Grammy's and won best vocal performance, while the debut album it came from (*On How Life Is*) sold over five million copies worldwide.

Later years saw Gray try to diversify with acting, and unfortunate scheduling saw her *The Id* (2001) sell poorly after the 9/11 tragedy. 'Demons', a vocal contribution to Fatboy Slim's 2001 album, proved the singer was as adept at dance as she was soul, and she also tried hip-hop on tracks by Common and The Black Eyed Peas.

Below
Steeped in the soulful funk of Marvin Gaye and Aretha Franklin, Macy Gray's voice was so unique that it would either endear or irritate, and in the early 2000s, hers was a chart success that has seen her collaborate with many artists since, as well as continue her solo career.

see Blondie pp 256   see Van Halen pp 320   see Blur pp 343   see Fatboy Slim pp 349

Hard Fi

(Vocal/instrumental group, 2004–present)

True suburban boys, Hard-Fi – Richard Archer (vocals), Ross Phillips (guitar), Kai Stephens (bass) and Steven Kemp (drums) – claim to have recorded their debut, *Stars Of CCTV* (2005) in a local taxi office in Staines, east London. A heady mix of social observation and steely dance rhythms, the four-piece play on their 'everyman' status with increasing charm. Recently, The Jam's Paul Weller has taken Hard-Fi under his wing, doubtless aware of the similarities between the two bands.

P.J. Harvey

(Vocals, b. 1969)

Hailing from the UK's 'west country', P. J. Harvey is now eight albums into her career. Trading in a primeval, highly feminine strain of blues rock, Polly Jean Harvey has moved from stripped-down rock to sophisticated acoustic ballads before a stomping brand of indie that is incendiary when caught live. She has influenced many female acts since the mid- 1990s, and has guested and duetted with artists as diverse as Thom Yorke, Nick Cave, Josh Homme and Tricky.

The Hives

(Vocal/instrumental group, 1993–present)

Sweden's Hives – Pelle Almqvist (vocals), Niklas Almqvist (guitar), Mikael Karlsson Åström (guitar), Mattias Bernval (bass) and Christian Grahn (drums) – suffered relative obscurity in their home country until the UK's garage rock obsession in 2000, after signing to the Poptones label. Immaculately attired and only slightly serious, the band excelled at an almost pantomime ability to wow an audience, often leaving them uncertain if the mock arrogance, particularly from vocalist Almqvist, was genuine or not.

Hundred Reasons

(Vocal/instrumental group, 1999–present)

Hundred Reasons – Colin Doran (vocals), Paul Townsend (guitar), Larry Hibbitt (keyboards), Andy Gilmour (bass) and Andy Bews (drums) – are a UK hard rock band just three albums into their career. A change from Columbia to V2 in September 2005 saw Hibbitt take production duties for the excellent *Kill Your Own* album of 2006. Outside of the metal genre the band have covered The Smiths' classic 'How Soon Is Now?' for a 2004 tribute album.

see Introduction pp 374   *see* Sources & Sounds pp 376   *see* Key Artists pp 380

Jack Johnson
(Vocals, b. 1975)

The acoustic musings of Jack Johnson have a laid-back feel that betray a lifetime dedicated to surfing and skateboarding. Indeed, until an accident Johnson was a professional surfer himself, but subsequently became a musician. Unsurprisingly, this Hawaii-born surfer was a hit in Australia before the rest of the world, but his third album *In Between Dreams* (2005) saw him achieve a No. 1 placing in the UK charts, with Top 3 positions in the US and Canada.

Norah Jones
(Vocals, b. 1979)

Despite being the daughter of superstar Ravi Shankar, Geetali Norah Jones Shankar is more jazz than world musician. Her debut *Come Away With Me* (2002) fuses elements of folk and soul into the genre, topped off with her sultry vocals, sounding as if they were beamed in from a smoky cellar bar. Her ability on the piano is equally as impressive, and her skills have been called on by artists including Andre 3000 and The Foo Fighters.

The Kaiser Chiefs
(Vocal/instrumental group, 2003–present)

Formerly known as Parva, Leeds' Kaiser Chiefs – Ricky Wilson (vocals), Andrew White (guitar), Simon Rix (bass), Nick Hodgson (drums) and Nick Baines (keyboards) – plough the same indie furrow that fellow Brit-poppers Blur did during their *Parklife* era. Wilson, something of an everyman, elicits playful singalong choruses from the most unexpected places while his band behind him churn out the building, shuddering riffs of singles such as 'I Predict A Riot' and, even more momentously 'Oh My God'.

Above

In some ways reminiscent of an early Blur, Kaiser Chiefs made 2005 their year when they released hit power-pop singles 'I Predict A Riot', 'Oh My God', and their debut LP *Employment*.

see The Beach Boys pp 120   see The Jam pp 260   see Nick Cave pp 290   see Foo Fighters pp 396

Kasabian

(Vocal/instrumental group, 1999–present)

From the same school as proletariat rockers Oasis, Kasabian – Tom Meighan (vocals), Serge Pizzorno (guitar), Chris Karloff (guitar) and Christopher Edwards (bass) – hail from Leicester. There is more to the four-piece than a simple rock template, however, with much of the band's sound augmented by multiple vocal sections and a chatter of electronica in the same vein as Primal Scream's mid-period albums. Self-assured, arrogant and growing in stature by the day, Kasabian might well have won over even the harshest detractor.

Keane

(Vocal/instrumental group, 1997–present)

Ever since guitarist Dominic Scott left the band in 1999, Keane – Tom Chaplin (vocals), Tom Rice-Oxley (piano, bass) and Richard Hughes (drums) – have taken the unusual route of not replacing him, supplementing their sound instead with piano. The move proved to be a wise one, as the comparatively unique sound they created has produced two albums of idiosyncratic pop music, a brand which has come to represent a well-mannered, measured yet sizeable corner of the UK market.

Formed, like many indie bands, as friends in their home town (Battle, Sussex), the group were lucky enough to score a single deal with Fierce Panda, a label synonymous with tipping major talent for the future. Island Records soon snapped them up, and new material and re-recorded older numbers soon littered the charts. The best example of their work is 'Everybody's Changing', a chiming slice of whimsy that reached No. 4 on its UK re-release in 2004.

Kelis

(Vocals, b. 1979)

New York native Kelis Rogers has somehow retained her position at the forefront of chart R&B for over seven years – from the sharp burst of debut single 'Caught Out There' through to the exquisitely provocative 'Milkshake' and 'Trick Me' from 2003's aptly named *Tasty*. Other notable appearances include the risqué 1999 collaboration with Ol' Dirty Bastard, 'Got Your Money', and 'Honey' on Moby's *Play* (2000). Kelis is currently rumoured to be working on a cookbook.

Alicia Keys

(Vocals, b. 1980)

Born Alicia Cook in New York, Keys has that most rare of talents – a vocal range matched by a musical ability. She has played piano from the age of seven and retains classical ambitions to this day. Her 2001 debut *Songs In A Minor* contained her first US No. 1, modern soul epic

see Introduction pp 374   *see* Sources & Sounds pp 376   *see* Key Artists pp 380

'Fallin'', which showcased her vocal range dramatically. In 2005, Keys joined an elite rank of artists who have released their own *MTV Unplugged* albums.

The Killers

(Vocal/instrumental group, 2002–present)
Vegas' Killers – Brandon Flowers (vocals), Dave Keuning (guitar), Mark August Stoermer (bass) and Ronnie Vannucci Jr. (drums) – were formed from a variety of wanted adverts after Flowers was thrown out of his first band. Influenced by the mass singalongs of Oasis, the technological edge of New Order (their name even came from a fictional band in one of their videos) and the introspection of The Smiths and The Cure, the band found mass acclaim in 2004 with their *Hot Fuss* album. 'All These Things That I've Done' was a fine mixture of all the influences, and the other four singles from the debut album fared equally well. 'Somebody Told Me' was a cheeky slight to an ex-lover, and 'Mr Brightside', a firm fan favourite, even reached the Top 10 in the UK, a country where listeners seemed to latch on to the band's slightly sleazy side quicker than they had at home.

The Kooks

(Vocal/instrumental group, 2004–present)
Brighton's Kooks – Luke Pritchard (vocals), Hugh Harris (guitar), Max Rafferty (bass) and Paul Garred

(drums) – are the next in a long line of British acts that can be traced as far back as The Kinks, taking in the likes of Supergrass, Blur and even The Coral on their list of influences. Formed and signed by Virgin on the same night at a gig at a pub in their hometown, they have already graced the cover of the *NME* despite their tender age.

Korn

(Vocal/instrumental group, 1993–present)
Californians Korn – often typeset with the 'r' reversed, Jonathon Houseman Davis (vocals), Reginald Arvizu (bass), David Silveria (drums) and James Shaffer (guitar) – are part of the nu-metal school of rock, although their music is often more horror-themed and straight-edge rock than the genre they supposedly spawned. Their eponymous 1994 debut is often credited as the point where this brash, moody new style of music started – although the band deny any involvement with such a 'scene'.

Like Radiohead in the UK, Korn were pioneering in the utilization of the internet in promoting themselves and their upcoming releases. In 1999, the band founded the *Family Values* tour package, which grouped artists from the rock genre together on a traveling stage, much like the famed Lollapalooza. Such a move prompted exposure for the likes of Limp Bizkit, Incubus and even rapper Ice Cube. Now nine albums into their career and showing no signs of stopping, Korn have sold over 25 million records.

Left
Fusing hip-hop, jazz and soul, Alicia Keys became one of the greatest soul voices of the 2000s, and so well respected that she inducted Prince into the Rock And Roll Hall Of Fame in 2004.

Below
Part 1980s throwback, part 2000s pop, The Killers emerged as one of the most stylish bands of the decade, with an interesting lyrical bent that made them, by 2005, the proverbial 'ones to watch'.

see The Kinks pp 94   see The Cure pp 293   see The Coral pp 393   see Limp Bizkit pp 404

Avril Lavigne

(Vocals, b. 1984)

Something of a mass of contradictions, Canada's Lavigne has latterly been trying to shed the skater-pop image of her debut album *Let Go* (2002), which contained the massive single 'Sk8er Boi', in favour of a more mature, feminine approach. This was clear from her second album *Under My Skin* (2004), which displayed patently darker themes than the debut, but also through her decision to become the face of Chanel fragrances in 2006 – the year she wed Sum 41 frontman Deryck Whibley.

The Libertines

(Vocal/instrumental group, 2001–04)

The Libertines – Pete Doherty (vocals, guitar), Carl Barat (vocals, guitar), John Hassall (bass) and Gary Powell (drums) – hailed from the east end of London. Across their short lifespan they made two albums (*Up The Bracket*, 2002 and *The Libertines*, 2004) of exceptionally idiosyncratic indie, with The Clash's Mick Jones at the production desk and one-time Suede guitarist Bernard Butler occasionally behind the axe.

In Doherty and Barat lay a raucous and compelling songwriting team, capable of bouncing ideas off one another, and presenting them in a ramshackle yet intoxicating way. When the band eventually spluttered out in 2004 (with Doherty sacked for his drug problems, later forming the group Babyshambles, Barat would form Dirty Pretty Things) the music world became a sadder place. Bands quickly sprang up to replace them, but many would deem The Libertines the true originators of post-millennial, post-punk chaos, and their influence is already well felt.

Limp Bizkit

(Vocal/instrumental group, 1994–present)

Limp Bizkit – Fred Durst (vocals), Mike Smith (guitar), DJ Lethal (turntables), Sam Rivers (bass) and John Otto (drums) – are something of a global phenomenon, and the benchmark against which all nu-metal and rapcore bands are judged. Since their earliest recordings, their fusion of the direct vocal delivery of rap with the sledgehammer riffing of metal has found a fan base with disaffected youths the world over.

Second album *Significant Other* (1999) broke the band small-scale, and the single 'Break Stuff' remains a firm fan favourite. At this point in their career the group were still receiving good reviews from critics, and Durst even formed his own label – Flip. After founding guitarist Wes Borland left in 2000, a nationwide search for a replacement was launched. However, Borland returned in 2004. Singles from the third album *Chocolate Starfish And The Hotdog Flavored Water* (2000) such as 'My Way' and the UK chart-topping 'Rollin'' remain the band's best-remembered legacy. The current status of the band is tantalizingly uncertain.

Linkin Park

(Vocal/instrumental group, 1996–present)

Other bands in the genre may be more acclaimed, and some more stylistically diverse, but Linkin Park – Chester Bennington (vocals), Mike Shinoda (MC), Brad Delson (guitar), Dave Farrell (bass), Joseph Hahn (DJ) and Rob Bourdon (drums) – are certainly the most successful in the nu-metal sphere. Formed from the remains of various Californian college bands, the five-piece (initially called Hybrid Theory) signed to Warners on the back of a demo of the same name.

see Introduction pp 374   see Sources & Sounds pp 376   see Key Artists pp 380

Left

Ostensibly a rap-metal act, Linkin Park would be embraced by the like-minded Limp Bizkit, but would also be traditionally metal enough to receive praise from the likes of Metallica.

As their line-up suggests, the band incorporate hip-hop approaches to music into their heavy rock sound – and the formula works well. Each of their four studio albums since 2000 has reached the Top 3 in the US, and their collaboration with rapper Jay-Z, *Collision Course* (2004), topped the chart while fusing their twin loves of hip-hop and rock. In 2005, the band founded a charity for victims of Hurricane Katrina and played the ground-breaking Live 8 concert.

Maroon 5
(Vocal/instrumental group, 2001–present)
Maroon 5 – Adam Levine (vocals), James Valentine (guitar), Jesse Carmichael (keyboards), Mickey Maddon (bass) and Ryan Dussick (drums) – came to be in 2001 when Valentine joined flop band Kara's Flowers. The release of 2002's *Songs About Jane* (an album recorded entirely during the break-up of Levine from girlfriend Jane) was well received, but it was not until singles 'This Love' and 'She Will Be Loved' dominated charts for months at a time that the band became a household name, winning two Grammys.

Maximo Park
(Vocal/instrumental group, 2003–present)
Signed to Sheffield's Warp Records, a label more synonymous with ambient dance acts like Boards of Canada, Newcastle's Maximo Park – Paul Smith (vocals), Duncan Lloyd (guitar), Archis Tiku (bass), Lucas Wooller (keyboards) and Tom English (drums) – deliver a view of the north-east of England that is refreshingly different to the sterilized slants on London. Like Pulp

before them, they somehow undermine pop stardom, dissecting it and revealing it as a sham. At the same time, there is an abstraction in lines like 'I'll do graffiti if you sing to me in French' that is irresistibly mysterious. Their label of choice also offers a freedom from normal expectations imposed on up and coming bands.

Debut album *A Certain Trigger* (2005) was a brash statement of intent. It portrayed a band happy to highlight their personal misgivings (largely through Smith's pithy lyrics) over the top of sometimes frenetic, often asymmetrical indie rock that remains head and shoulders above any of their contemporaries.

Below

Essentially a boy band writing their own songs with guitars, Maroon 5 won a Grammy for Best New Artist in 2005, despite having released two more albums since their 2002 debut, *Songs About Jane*.

🔊 *see* Pulp pp 364   🔊 *see* Suede pp 368   🔊 *see* Green Day pp 384   🔊 *see* Babyshambles pp 391

Katie Melua

(Vocals, b. 1984)

Ketevan Melua had a roving childhood that took in Ajaria, Georgia (where she was born) and Belfast, and her music falls somewhere between the categories of jazz, blues and radio-friendly pop. Debut single 'The Closest Thing To Crazy' (2003) found Melua in mournful mood, and one that has largely continued throughout her two-album career. 'Nine Million Bicycles', from 2005's *Piece By Piece*, was equally sombre, inspired by a visit to the city of Beijing, and featured ocarinas and bamboo flutes.

Mis-Teeq

(Vocal group, 2001–05)

Although starting life as a quartet, Sabrina Washington, Alesha Dixon and Su-Elise Nash are how Londoners Mis-Teeq are more commonly remembered. Releasing just two albums and a greatest hits in their short career, the group found fame through a suggestive stage presence and tight harmonies. 'One Night Stand' (2001) is perhaps the best example of their work, a cross between 1960s girl groups, the rhythms of club culture at the time and odd, almost operatic vocal samples, all with a cool street savvy.

Ms Dynamite

(Vocals, b. 1981)

Born Niomi McLean-Daley, Ms Dynamite emerged in 2002 with her debut *A Little Deeper*. The record won the prestigious Mercury Award the following year. A rapper who worked with So Solid Crew, Ms Dynamite sang about issues facing young women, with backing tracks often beautifully produced instrumentals in their own right. Subsequent legal troubles in 2006 surrounding a nightclub altercation seemed to put her career on hold, but Ms Dynamite assures fans she will return in 2007.

Muse

(Vocal/instrumental group, 1997–present)

Matthew Bellamy (vocals), Chris Wolstenholme (bass) and Dominic Howard (drums) provide such an enlivening take on the classic power trio formation in rock that it is sometimes easy to forget they are just a trio. Even their earliest singles ('Cave' and 'Muscle Museum', both 1999) were delivered with ferocity and an understanding of what makes a heavy guitar riff exciting – and radio-friendly.

Formed in Cornwall, but building their sound through American influences such as Soundgarden and Nirvana rather than the British ones bands of the time jumped on, Muse were very much outsiders from the start. The American Maverick label took an interest, though, and constant worldwide touring saw a fan base grow steadily. Albums *Showbiz* (1999) and *Origin Of Symmetry* (2001) saw them stretch rock's confines further, and 2006's UK chart-topping *Black Holes And Revelations* was so outrageous, so bombastic in its scope and blatant in its nods to rock's past, that critics found it hard to criticize the project.

Nelly

(Rapper, b. 1974)

Nelly's first album *Country Grammar* was released in 2000 and went platinum nine times over. Although housing four hit singles, he is best remembered today for his sublime, smoothly produced and utterly sexy

Below

Muse's prog-metal ambitions, and slight self-obsession of lead Matt Bellamy, has given them a certain crossover appeal within a mainstream youth market looking to oust their demons.

see Introduction pp 374   see Sources & Sounds pp 376   see Key Artists pp 380

'Hot In Herre' single (2002), a track that began a run of 17 weeks at the top of the US *Billboard* Hot 100 chart (along with follow-up 'Dilemma'). This remains an unbeaten record, which Nelly (real name Cornell Hayes) shares with Elton John.

Nickelback
(Vocal/instrumental group, 1995–present)
Canadians Nickelback – Chad Kroeger (vocals), Ryan Peake (guitar), Mike Kroeger (bass) and Daniel Adair (drums) – came to prominence in their home country via a law that stated a certain percentage of the radio play must be homegrown. This coupled with Kroeger's distinctively gravelly vocal style lead to massive exposure and a snowballing interest in the post-grunge rockers. 2001 single 'How You Remind Me' took the swagger of grunge imbibed with an arena mentality and proved irresistible to the rock masses.

Nine Inch Nails
(Vocal/instrumental group, 1988–present)
Nine Inch Nails – Trent Reznor (vocals), Aaron North (guitar), Jeordie White (bass), Alessandro Cortini (keyboards) and Josh Freese (drums) – are the latest line-up of Reznor's ever popular band. Somehow walking the thin line between electro and metal,

mainstream yet eternally credible, they are one of America's least deified rock bands, but a five-album, double Grammy-winning career shows they are not totally forgotten. Rap superstar Eminem, on debut single 'My Name Is', opted for a closeted reference to the band in the lyrics.

Largely a showcase for Reznor's prodigious multi-instrumental talent, NIN (as it is often abbreviated) found their music reaching the most unexpected of ears when a certain Johnny Cash recorded their 'Hurt' epic in 2004 on the fourth of his hugely appreciated *American Recordings* albums. The death of the country giant less than a year later, and the emotionally draining video, brought legions of new appreciators of Reznor's work.

Above

Essentially the work of Trent Reznor, NIN were solely responsible for bringing industrial metal into the mainstream, and successfully doing so without compromising an artistic vision.

Left

With their 2001 single 'How You Remind Me', post-grunge metallists Nickelback became only the second Canadian band to simultaneously top the US and Canadian charts since The Guess Who's 'American Woman'.

see Johnny Cash pp 59   see Soundgarden pp 366   see Eminem pp 382   see Norah Jones pp 401

Orson
(Vocal/instrumental group, 2000–present)
Hollywood's Orson – Jason Pebworth (vocals), George Astasio (guitar), Kevin Roentgen (guitar), Johnny Lonely (bass) and Chris Cano (drums) – slaved away at the club gig circuit for five years before an appearance at the UK's In The City festival scored a Universal deal. Pebworth hails from a theatrical background, clearly evidenced by his non-rock vocal delivery. The band claim to always wear hats as a nod to the forgotten film history of their hometown. Their name is also a tribute to cinematography, via Orson Welles.

Outkast
(Rap duo, 1992–present)
Smooth dressing, slick talking and devastatingly cool, Outkast – the duo of Antwan 'Big Boi' Patton and Andre 'Andre 3000' Benjamin – rapped their way out of Georgia in the mid-1990s. Their first four collaborative album efforts (released between 1995 and 2000) contained everything from straight Snoop Dogg gangsta rap, albeit with more brains, to near-George Clinton parody, and plenty of attitude.

But it was not until 2003's *Speakerboxxx/The Love Below*, a double album divided equally between the two, that the duo found hitherto unknown adoration – largely thanks to, it must be noted, the Andre 3000 single 'Hey Ya'. The track was a fast-paced, goodtime practically R&B tune, with Benjamin's infectious southern drawl laced on top. It reached No. 1 in the US and Austria, and hung around the charts for months. To this day, Andre 3000 (now also an actor and clothes designer) reluctantly admits he will probably never better it.

Papa Roach
(Vocal/instrumental group, 1993–present)
Stars of the nu-metal era at the turn of the century, Californians Papa Roach – Jacoby Shaddix (vocals), Jerry Horton (guitar), Tobin Esperance (bass) and David Buckner (drums) – had to wait until *Infest* (2000) to break through, alongside the likes of Limp Bizkit. 2002's *lovehatetragedy* saw increased sales, but by 2003's *Getting Away With Murder* many fans felt the band had softened their sound for the sake of radio airplay. Despite such grudges, the record sold well, seeing the band reach platinum status.

Below
OutKast are a rare beast in the Noughties, being not only a revolutionary hip-hop group, but also one that is adored by the mainstream.

Pink
(Vocals, b. 1979)

Alecia Beth Moore, aka Pink or P!nk, has risen to prominence through her refreshing dissimilarity to more conventional pop starlets – happy to wear her hair cropped pink and wear leather when others were long blondes in dresses. A protégé of Linda Perry, the songwriter who also took Christina Aguilera and Gwen Stefani into the charts, her career is best summarized by excellent singles from her four albums, such as 'Get The Party Started', 'Feel Good Time' and 'Trouble'.

Daniel Powter
(Singer/songwriter, b. 1976)

Mainstream in every sense of the word, be-hatted Canadian Powter has really made a career from the success of one, admittedly enormous, single. 'Bad Day' (2005) was initially supposed to soundtrack a Coca Cola advert, but was subsequently a test for *American Idol* entrants – as big a fast-track to recognition as is possible. A traditional piano singer/songwriter, it remains to be seen if Powter can maintain the hysterical level of interest in his one big single.

The Pussycat Dolls
(Vocal group, 2003–present)

Here are a fine example of style over substance, a mid-1990s dance collective originating from burlesque shows that eventually wound up with a record contract in 2003. The current six-girl line-up (headed by singer Nicole Scherzinger) struck big with their 2005 single 'Don't Cha' sounding as infectious as anything in the charts, and the 'visual appeal' of the group assisted them further. Collaborations with Snoop Dogg, Will.I.Am and Busta Rhymes added a certain cachet to the music, which might have otherwise been passed over.

Left

Not just another pop singer in the mould of Spears, Aguilera, *et al*, Pink has constantly reinvented her image while also challenging the notions of what it means/costs to be a female pop singer in the 2000s.

Queens Of The Stone Age
(Vocal/instrumental group, 1997–present)

Godfathers of the Californian desert rock scene, QOTSA – Troy van Leeuwen (guitar), Joey Castillo (drums), Alain Johannes (bass) and Natasha Schneider (keyboards) – were formed from the ashes of Kyuss by Josh Homme (vocals, guitar), and are one of the heaviest bands on the planet. Sometimes counting Dave Grohl and Mark Lanegan in their ranks (most notably on 2002's *Songs For The Deaf*), their breakthrough came with 2000's *Rated 'R'* featuring the sarcastic anthem 'Feel Good Hit Of The Summer'.

Above

Formed following the dissolution of Kyuss, QOTSA became one of the most successful and interesting new metallists of the decade, with a latent pop nous that equalled big radio hits.

see Christina Aguilera pp 390   see The Black Eyed Peas pp 392   see Limp Bizkit pp 404   see Gwen Stefani pp 412

Right

Right

The camp glamour of The Scissor Sisters is as distinctive as their fusion of glam rock, disco and alternative music.

Below

The biggest Latin-pop crossover since Jennifer Lopez, Shakira is the epitome of an artist stuck together from something old, new and borrowed, resulting in pop hits and an image of cultivated sex appeal.

The Raconteurs

(Vocal/instrumental group, 2005–present)
Formed by The White Stripes' Jack White and friend/songwriter Brendan Benson (along with Jack Lawrence and Patrick Keeler from Detroit's Greenhornes), The Raconteurs fuse White's guitar know-how with Benson's songwriting panache. The concoctions are heady, if openly throwback, and those recorded for debut *Broken Boy Soldiers* (2006) are interesting in the way they were recorded between the main men's projects – and not premeditated, heralded as the work of a supergroup or overly produced.

Razorlight

(Vocal/instrumental group, 2002–present)
Very much a vehicle for precociously talented singer Johnny Borrell, four-piece Razorlight – with Bjorn Agren (guitar), Carl Dalemo (bass) and Andy Burrows (drums) – trade in modern indie rock, so appealing that their performance at Live 8 in 2005 saw sales of their debut album *Up All Night* (2004) rocket. Often accused of speaking only in soundbites and self-aggrandizing, Borrell remains an intriguing frontman who clearly has a melodic skill. His band, perhaps bolstered by such attentions, now sit proudly atop a pile of Razorlight impostors.

Scissor Sisters

(Vocal/instrumental group, 2003–present)
Another example of a band who have gained exposure in the UK (their *Scissor Sisters* debut was the highest-selling album there in 2004), the glam of Scissor Sisters – Jake Shears (Jason Sellards, vocals), Babbydaddy (Scott Hoffman, keyboards), Ana Matronic (Ana Lynch, vocals), Del Marquis (Derek Gruen, guitar) and Paddy Boom (Patrick Secord, drums) – is as indebted to the New York gay club scene that spawned them as the traditional pop of the likes of Elton John that influenced it. The group mix cabaret and performance in a gaudy, alluring fashion.

Shakira

(Vocals, b. 1977)
Shakira's debut album *Magia* was actually released in 1991, when Ms Ripoll was just 15. Singing in Spanish for her first four albums, it was not until 2001's *Laundry Service* that the singer 'crossed over' to the English language, a move which prompted hit after hit, most

📻 *see Introduction pp 374* 📻 *see Sources & Sounds pp 376* 📻 *see Key Artists pp 380*

notably 'Whenever, Wherever'. Her Colombian ancestry and flamenco themes remained, and more importantly, appealed, and she has gone on to win numerous MTV awards.

Sigur Rós
(Vocal/instrumental group, 1994–present)

Sigur Rós could only come from Iceland. Formed by Jón Þór (Jónsi) Birgisson (vocals), Georg Hólm (bass) and Ágúst Ævar Gunnarsson (drums) in Reykjavik, their wholly unique sound, perhaps most successfully achieved on third album *Ágætis Byrjun* (1999), is a lulling, lurching blend of classical music and ambient, of rock with something from far outside the genres' confines. Orri Páll Dyrason has since joined on drums, while Kjartan 'Kjarri' Sveinsson now adds smooth keyboard sounds.

Simple Plan
(Vocal/instrumental group, 1999–present)

Formed by school friends Jeff Stinco (guitar), Chuck Corneau (drums) and Pierre Bouvier (vocals) after the demise of their Reset project in Quebec, Simple Plan trade in a similar brand of punk to fellow countrymen Sum 41. Ever at loggerheads with their critics on charges of immaturity or 'selling out', the band referenced this in the title of their second album *Still Not Getting Any …* (2004) – a cool sideswipe at the absence of any good reviews.

Slipknot
(Vocal/instrumental group, 1995–present)

Iowa-based metallers Slipknot – Corey Taylor (vocals), James Root (guitar), Nathan Jordison (drums), Sean Crahan, Chris Fehn (both percussion), Sid Wilson (DJ), Mick Thompson (guitar), Paul Gray (bass) and Craig Jones (samples) – are literally unrecognizable. When playing or posing for photographs, this nu-metal band (very much in the vein of bands like Limp Bizkit but far heavier and less rap-oriented) wear a selection of masks and boiler suits, giving them a menacing anonymity.

Word-of-mouth meant their debut album *Slipknot* (1996) sold close to a million copies and is widely considered their best. Follow-up *Iowa* (2001) saw an almost commercial (for Slipknot) approach to marketing; with the group even appearing as a cameo in the 2002 film *Rollerball*. After a two-year break, the band returned in 2004 with the excellent, Rick Rubin-produced *Volume 3: The Subliminal Verses*, which debuted at No. 2 in the *Billboard* chart.

Below

Mask-wearing rap-metallers, Slipknot's early success was built on shock tactics, technical proficiency and good old fashioned theatrics. They have become one of the most enduring bands of the rap-metal world.

🔊 *see* Queen pp 208   🔊 *see* Elton John pp 232   🔊 *see* Jennifer Lopez pp 354   🔊 *see* The White Stripes pp 416

Snow Patrol
(Vocal/instrumental group, 1994–present)

Gary Lightbody (vocals) is the sole remaining member from the mid-1990s line-up of Snow Patrol – now Paul Wilson (bass), Johnny Quinn (drums), Nathan Connolly (guitar) and Tom Simpson (keyboards) – from college days in Dundee. He has since released four albums of indie rock that can stun a listener with its simplicity or multi-layered walls of sound. More recent Snow Patrol music has graced TV's *Grey's Anatomy* and *ER*, but many fans claim early albums from 1998 and 2001 to be their best.

So Solid Crew
(Vocal group, 2001–04)

A staggeringly expansive outlet for a collective of south London MCs, DJs, producers and singers trading in an early incarnation of grime music, So Solid Crew were formed from the popular Sunday afternoon pirate radio shows on Delight FM. Debut album *They Don't Know* (2001) has achieved platinum status, although the fortunes of certain members of the 40+ group have been less attractive, with both Asher D. and G-Man serving prison sentences in recent years.

Britney Spears
(Vocals, b. 1981)

Britney Spears started life, after a short stage career, on American TV's *New Mickey Mouse Club* from 1993 onwards. Her debut single 'Hit Me Baby One More Time' (1998) was a masterly slice of melancholy pop that topped the charts – due in no small part to its suggestive video featuring the singer/actress in a school uniform.

A year later, and the star's level of fame was enormous, with a relationship with fellow popster Justin Timberlake prime fodder for newspapers and magazines. Her career since has been one of reinvention, much like Madonna. She has sexed herself up, flirted with various religions and even found time to have children. Singles such as 'Oops … I Did It Again' (2000) and 'Toxic' (2004) proved there was still plenty of marketable ability in the singer, and in 2004 she went so far as to release a greatest hits package, entitled *My Prerogative*.

Gwen Stefani
(Vocals, b. 1969)

After finding success with the ska-punk/balladry of band No Doubt, Californian Stefani went out on her own to attempt a solo career away from the genre. After a 2001 smash single

see Introduction pp 374   see Sources & Sounds pp 376   see Key Artists pp 380

Albert Hammond Jr. (both guitar), Nikolai Fraiture (bass) and Fabrizio Moretti (drums) – have come to signify the mass appeal revivalist bands from the US can achieve. After a bidding war, the band signed to RCA in 2001, releasing *Is This It?*, a short burst of well-trimmed songs and lean riffs. Three albums on, their formula may be familiar, but the excitement remains.

The Sugababes

(Vocal group, 1998–present)

The Sugababes' current position as perhaps the best but certainly the *coolest* UK girl band is a given. Their body of work contains countless memorable singles – even their debut 'Overload' was a masterpiece of construction with sultry hooks. Several line-up changes have provided the trio with continued fresh life, and the latest Keisha Buchanan/Heidi Range/Amelle Berrabah formation, coupled with a subtle understanding (if not direct acknowledgement) of club culture, sees them continue to dominate the UK charts.

Far Left
Her breakthrough hit 'Oops!... I Did It Again' marked Britney Spears out as a singularly designed teen pop icon.

Left
Former frontwoman for No Doubt, Gwen Stefani's image and experimental-pop bent framed her as one of the most exciting independent pop artists of the mid-00s.

Below
A case of right place, right time allowed New York's The Strokes to spearhead a garage rock'n'roll revival of the early 2000s.

with Eve, 'Let Me Blow Ya Mind', she worked with dance and hip-hop producers such as Dr Dre and the ever-popular Neptunes, and the plan worked. Her debut, 2004's *Love Angel Music Baby*, initially outsold any No Doubt album and contained the US No. 1 single 'Hollaback Girl'. The band were back in the studio in 2006, with Stefani (now a mother, having married Bush's Gavin Rossdale) on board.

The Streets

(Vocals, b. 1978)

Mike Skinner sings the sound of honesty, set to a music that stems from the clubs of his beloved south London. Early singles like 'Let's Push Things Forward' set the template well, with minimal beats and piano snippets topped with observations on modern life. At times too acute to be a wholly comfortable listen (particularly on 2006's 'rehab' album *The Hardest Way To Make An Easy Living*), Skinner's music remains, at the very least, totally unique.

The Strokes

(Vocal/instrumental group, 2001–present)

Formed after a complicated network of Swiss schooling and gigging frenzy in New York's lower east side, The Strokes – Julian Casablancas (vocals), Nick Valensi,

🔊 *see No Doubt pp 359* 🔊 *see Arctic Monkeys pp 391* 🔊 *see Dizzee Rascal pp 395* 🔊 *see Justin Timberlake 414*

high jinks, but lately the trio have displayed a more mature, often political side, and seem keen to progress to the second phase of their career, playing benefit concerts and covering John Lennon for charity.

Justin Timberlake
(Vocals, b. 1981)
Timberlake, once liberated from the confines of former band *NSYNC, managed to appeal to critics and fans alike after the release of his Michael Jackson-influenced *Justified* album in 2002, and in particular the stunningly modern single 'Like I Love You'. Helped in no small part by the crisp work of The Neptunes' production team, the single signposted a pop icon in the making. 2006's follow-up album *Sexyback* had much to live up to.

KT Tunstall
(Vocals, b. 1975)
'One-woman band' Kate Tunstall started out busking the streets of Edinburgh and playing to students. Her break came with a UK TV appearance on Jools Holland's *Later* …, hastily scheduled to replace rapper Nas. Her mix of folk sensibilities with a more boisterous, bawdy yet gentle delivery (doubtless honed on Scottish streets), combined with her striking good looks have seen her find mass acceptance, and resulted in vast sales of debut album *Eye To The Telescope* (2004).

Turin Brakes
(Vocal duo, 1999–present)
The smooth sounds of London duo Olly Knights and Gale Paridjanian found them initial fame though the emerging 'nu-folk' scene of the late 1990s. The fact that their records were released by market leaders in that genre, Source Records, certainly helped, but acts such as Elbow and Kings of Convenience also crested a buzz around the new scene. The pair have toured the US for the first time in 2006 on the strength of their third album *Jackinabox* (2005).

Usher
(Vocals, b. 1978)
Usher Raymond IV, often called the 'prince of pop' after his 2004 *Confessions* album sold 1.1 million copies in the first week, is the perfect blend of pop and R&B.

Above

With production help from The Neptunes, Timberlake was able to appeal to an adult male market that Britney Spears perhaps was not.

Right

The Vines have a punkiness that have found them fans in the post-Nirvana grunge camp.

Sum 41
(Vocal/instrumental group, 1996–present)
Canadian rockers Sum 41 – Deryck Whibley (vocals), Jason McCaslin (guitar) and Steve Jocz (drums) – have struggled to shed the lightweight or 'novelty act' tag that often latched on to them. Certainly earlier albums, *All Killer No Filler* (2001) and *Does This Look Infected?* (2002), were high on infantile, skate-punk

see Introduction pp 374   *see* Sources & Sounds pp 376   *see* Key Artists pp 380

A singer since the age of 13, Usher made his name via singles such as 'You Make Me Wanna' (1997), which topped charts on both sides of the Atlantic. He has sung on albums by artists as diverse as Mariah Carey, Phil Collins, P. Diddy and Alicia Keys.

The Vines
(Vocal/instrumental group, 2002–present)
Although recent years have seen the group's future thrown into question as a direct result of singer Craig Nicholls being diagnosed with Asperger's Syndrome, Australia's Vines – Nicholls, Ryan Griffiths (guitar) and Hamish Rosser (drums) – continue to make their neat fusion of Nirvana-style noise and 1960s melodicism. Despite no longer touring as a result, the trio, now on their third album (2006's *Vision Valley*) possess a ferocity and snarl that is offset by their blatant understanding of just what makes music catchy and memorable.

Kanye West
(Producer, rapper, b. 1977)
Often dubbed the 'Vuitton Don' because of his costly clothing, the story of this US rapper is fraught with controversy. Never one to hide his political or religious views, the star claims to be a born-again Christian, and publicly denounced George W. Bush on television. Thankfully, West's music is worthy of the headlines, as some of today's most creative hip-hop is to be found on his second album, 2005's *Late Registration*.

Above
Kanye West has not only proven an amazing producer for himself and others, but with his choice of hook-laden samples, he has revitalized the crate-digging aspect of hip-hop.

see John Lennon pp 218   *see* Nirvana pp 334   *see* No Doubt pp 359   *see* Alicia Keys pp 402

Above

The most influential, talented and consistently amazing group to come out of the early-00s garage explosion, 2002 saw The White Stripes achieve mainstream success, after years of working as a garage band out of Detroit.

Westlife

(Vocal group, 1998–present)

Thirteen UK No. 1s and albums sales of over 40 million perhaps say more about the obsessive (and young) nature of Westlife's fan base than their actual music. A clean-cut Irish boy band – Shane Filan, Nicky Byrne, Mark Feehily, Kian Egan and (originally) Brian McFadden – formed in the image of Boyzone and Take That before them, they produce radio-friendly, often ballad-driven pop that does little to trouble critics. Their appeal lies in a canny and highly choreographed knowledge of what will sell to the young pop fan.

The White Stripes

(Vocal/instrumental duo, 1997–present)

Divorcées Jack (vocals, guitar) and Meg White (percussion) formed The White Stripes with the mission statement of keeping a childlike simplicity in their music and imagery. Dressing only in red, white and black and playing a thrilling version of blues and rock (owing as much to Led Zeppelin as pioneers like Son House and Lead Belly), the pair found mass international acclaim with third album *White Blood Cells* (2001), which married Jack's jackhammer riffing with a more tender, acoustic side (most notably on single 'Hotel Yorba').

But the duo are far from one-trick ponies. Next album *Elephant* (2003, recorded in a fortnight on a shoestring budget, then receiving massive sales figures) explored multi-tracked vocals, and the follow-up *Get Behind Me Satan* (2005) saw an even darker approach employed, often incorporating marimbas and xylophones. Through their attention to detail and refusal to compromise, The White Stripes remain unchallengeable. Few have tried, none have succeeded.

Wilco

(Vocal/instrumental group, 1994–present)

Frontman and principal songwriter Jeff Tweedy formed Wilco – John Stirratt (bass), Nels Cline (guitar), Glenn Kotche (drums), Pat Sansone (various instruments) and Mikael Jorgensen (keyboards) – after disbanding country heroes Uncle Tupelo. Throughout countless personnel 'changes' and label squabbles they made a series of five albums (culminating in 2005's *A Ghost Is Born*) that moved further and further away from Americana. In 1995, the group reinterpreted a

batch of lyrics donated by Woody Guthrie (donated by his daughter) with Billy Bragg.

Will Young
(Vocals, b. 1979)

Will Young is perhaps most famously remembered as the winner of UK TV talent show *Pop Idol* in 2002 over favourite Gareth Gates. Since then he has achieved the rare privilege of sustaining a chart career. After secrecy surrounding his homosexuality during the competition, the singer/actor went on to chart highly several times and sustain his career. Very much a pure pop artist, Young manages to overcome novelty via a crack team of songwriters.

Zero 7
(Dance group, 1998–present)

The group that initially started life as a remixing duo (Sam Hardaker and Henry Binns) has since flourished into a downtempo collective of sorts, with guest vocalists adding their talents to the group's three albums and bringing the pair a huge fan base among 'coffee table' listeners. Their music is all at once ambient, soulful and commercial, best evidenced by collaborations and remixes with and for artists including Radiohead, Mozez, Terry Callier and Sophie Barker.

The Zutons
(Vocal/instrumental group, 2001–present)

Liverpool's Zutons – Dave McCabe (vocals), Boyan Chowdhury (guitar), Abi Harding (saxophone), Sean Payne (drums) and Russell Pritchard (bass) – found their initial press coverage through a songwriting style indebted to their city's 1960s musical ancestry. McCabe possesses a vocal snarl and lyrical deftness that has seen both the bands' albums – *Who Killed … The Zutons?* (2004) and *Tired Of Hanging Around* (2006) – chart highly, and outlive idle comparisons to fellow Liverpudlian acts such as The Coral.

Above

Mining a seam of jazz-tinged electro-fusion, Zero 7 have partially spearheaded an ambient renaissance of the 2000s that has appealed to fans of 'chill out' music.

Below

Emerging at a similar time to The Coral, The Zutons' 2003 debut, *Who Killed...... The Zutons* marked them out as exemplary songwriters with a singular vision.

see **Led Zeppelin** pp 200   *see* **Take That** pp 368   *see* **Radiohead** pp 386   *see* **The Coral** pp 393

List of Artists

Entries appear in the following order: name, music style, year(s) of popularity, type of artist, country of origin.

50 Cent, Gangsta; Hip Hop, 2000s-, Artist, American
98 Degrees, 2000s Pop, 2000s-, Artist, American
A1, Boy Bands; 2000s Pop, 2000s, Artist, British
Aceyalone, Hip Hop; Alternative Hip Hop, 2000s-, Artist, American
Acoustic Ladyland, Experimental, 2000s Jazz, 2000s-, Artist, American
Adams, Ryan, Alternative Country; Country Rock, 2000s-, Artist; Songwriter, American
Adem, Singer-Songwriter; Folktronica, 2000s-, Artist, American
Agnostic Mountain Gospel Choir, The Alternative Country, 2000s, Artist, American
Aguilera, Christina, 2000s Pop, 2000s-, Artist, American
Alabama 3, Alternative Rock, 2000s-, Artist, American
Alien Ant Farm, Nu Metal, 2000s-, Artist, American
Allen, Lily, Alternative Pop, 2000s-, Artist, British
Amen, Nu Metal, 2000s-, Artist, American
Anastacia, Contemporary R&B; Urban Soul, 2000s-, Artist, American
Anastacia, 2000s Pop; Urban Soul, 2000s-, Artist, American
And You Will Know Us By The Trail Of Dead, Alternative/Indie Rock, 2000s-, Artist, American
Anderson, Sunshine, Contemporary R&B; Urban Soul, 2000s-, Artist, American
Antony and the Johnsons, 2000s Pop, 2000s-, Artist, American
Arcade Fire, Alternative/Indie Rock, 2000s-, Artist, Canaadian
Arctic Monkeys, The, Alternative/Indie Rock, 2000s-, Artist, British
Ashanti, Contemporary R&B; Urban Soul, 2000s-, Artist, American
Athlete, Alternative/Indie Rock; Britpop, 2000s-, Artist, British
Atomic Kitten, Manufactured Pop; 2000s Pop, 2000s-, Artist, British
Audioslave, Hard Rock; Alternative/Indie Rock, 2000s-, Artist, American
Autechre, Techno; Dance; Ambient; Electronica; Post-Rock, 2000s-, Artist, British
Avant, Contemporary R&B, 2000s-, Artist, American
B2K, Contemporary R&B, 2000s-, Artist, American
Babyshambles, Alternative/Indie Rock, 2000s-, Artist, British
Badly Drawn Boy, 2000s Pop Singer/Songwriters, 2000s-, Artist; Songwriter, British
Banner, David, Hip Hop; Crunk, 2000s-, Artist; Producer, American
Banhart, Devendra, Singer-Songwriter; Contemporary Folk, 2000s-, Artist, American
Bedingfield, Daniel, Dance Pop, 2000s-, Artist, British
Bedingfield, Natasha, Conemporary Pop, 2000s-, Artist, British
Bees, The, Indie Rock, 2000s-, Artist, British
Bell, Ricky, Urban Soul, 2000s-, Artist, American
BellRays, The, Funk, Indie Rock, 2000s-, Artist, American
Benson, Brendan, Pop, Singer-Songwriter, 2000s-, Artist, American
Big Browaz, Urban; UK Garage; Rap, 2000s-, Artist, American
Billy, Bonnie 'Prince', Alt-Country, Singer-Songwriter, 2000s-, Artist, American
Black Eyed Peas, The, Alternative Hip Hop; Hip Hop, 2000s-, Artist, American

Black Keys, The, Contemporary Blues Rock; Indie Rock, 2000s-, Artist, American
Blacknificent Seven, The, Hip-Hop, 2000s-, Artist, British
Blind Boys Of Alabama, The, Gospel, 2000s-, Artist, American
Blink 182, Pop Punk; Alternative Rock, 2000s-, Artist, American
Bloc Party, Alternative/Indie Rock, 2000s-, Artist, British
Blue, Boy Bands 2000s Pop, 2000s-, Artist, British
Blunt, James, 2000s Pop, 2000s-, Artist, British
Boy Kill Boy, Indie Rock, 2000s-, Artist, British
Brakes, Indie Rock, 2000s-, Artist, British
Brian Jonestown Massacre, The, Indie Rock, 2000s-, Artist, American
Bright Eyes, Singer-Songwriter, 2000s-, Artist, American
British Sea Power, Indie Rock, 2000s-, Artist, British
Bullet For My Valentine, Metal, Thrash, Punk, 2000s-, Artist, British
Bunton, Emma, Contemporary Pop, 2000s-, Artist, British
Busted, Contemporary Pop-Rock, 2000, Artist, British
Calexico, Indie Rock, Alternative Country, 2000s-, Artist, American
Callum, Jamie, 2000s Jazz; Pop, 2000s-, Artist, British
Cam'ron, Contemporary Hip-Hop, 2000s-, Artist, American
Cannibal Ox, Underground Rap; Left-Field Hip Hop, 2000s-, Artist, American
Cantrell, Blu, Contemporary R&B; Urban Soul, 2000s-, Artist, American
Cee-Lo, Hip-Hop, Nu-Soul, R&B, 2000s-, Artist, American
Chamillionaire, Contemporary Rap, 2000s-, Artist, American
Cheeky Girls, The, Manufactured Pop, 2000s-, Artist, Transylvanian
Chestnutt, Cody, Contemporary R&B, 2000s-, Artist, American
Church, Charlotte, Indie Pop, 2000s-, Artist, British
Circulus, Neo-Prog; Neo-Psych, 2000s-, Artist, British
Clap Your Hands Say Yeah, Indie Rock, 2000s-, Artist, American
Clarkson, Kelly, 2000s Pop, 2000s-, Artist, American
Claypool, Les, Funk Metal; Alternative Rock, 2000s-, Artist, American
Clor, Indie/Art Rock, 2000s, Artist, American
Coldplay, Alternative/Indie Rock; Britpop, 2000s-, Artist, British
Common, Contemporary Rap, 2000s-, Artist, American
Cooper Temple Clause, Experimental; Indie-Rock, 2000s-, Artist, British
Coral, The, Alternative/Indie Rock, 2000s-, Artist, British
Crazy Town, Hip Hop; Alternative/Indie Rock, 2000s-, Artist, American
D12, Hip-Hop, 2000s-, Artist, American
DJ Yoda, Hip-Hop, Turntablism, 2000s-, Artist, British
Dandy Warhols, The, Alternative/Indie Rock; US Underground & Garage Rock, 2000s-, Artist, American
Darkness, The, Hard Rock; Glam Rock & Glitter, 2000s-, Artist, British
Dashboard Confessional, Alternative; Emo, 2000s-, Artist, British
Datsuns, The, Garage Rock, 2000s-, Artist, Kiwi
David, Craig, Contemporary R&B; UK Garage, 2000s-, Artist, British
Death From Above 1979, Indie Rock, 2000s, Artist, American
Deerhoof, Experimental Indie-Rock, 2000s-, Artist, American
Demons and Wizards, Heavy Metal, 2000s-, Artist, American
Destiny's Child, Contemporary R&B, 2000s-, Artist, American
Dido, 2000s Pop Singer/Songwriters, 2000s-, Artist; Songwriter, British
Dilated Peoples, Underground Rap, Left-Field Hip Hop, 2000s-, Artist; Producer, American
Dirty Pretty Things, Indie Rock, 2000s-, Artist, British
Dizzee Rascal, UK Garage, 2000s-, Artist, British
Doves, The, Britpop; Alternative/Indie Rock, 2000s-, Artist, British
Duke Spirit, The, Indie Rock, 2000s-, Artist, British
Eagles Of Death Metal, Hard Rock, 2000s-, Artist, British

Eden's Crush, 2000s Pop, 2000s, Artist, American
Editors, The, Indie Rock, 2000s-, Artist, British
Elbow, Alternative/Indie Rock, 2000s-, Artist, British
Electrelane, Indie Rock; Experimental, 2000s-, Artist, British
Electric Six, Indie Rock, 2000s-, Artist, American
Electric Soft Parade, Indie Rock; Pop, 2000s-, Artist, British
Embrace, 2000s Pop; Britpop, 2000s-, Artist, British
Eminem, Gangsta; Hip Hop, 2000s-, Artist, American
Euros Child, Experimental Pop, Indie, 2000s-, Artist, British
Evanescence, Metal; Goth Rock, 2000s-, Artist, American
Fall Out Boy, Emo; Alternative Rock, 2000s-, Artist, American
Feeder, Alternative/Indie Rock, 2000s-, Artist, British
Feeling, The, Pop Rock, 2000s-, Artist, British
Flickerstick, Alternative/Indie Rock, 2000s-, Artist, American
Floetry, Contemporary R&B, 2000s-, Artist, British
;Forward, Russia!, Indie Rock, 2000s-, Artist, British
Fountains Of Wayne, 2000s Pop, 2000s-, Artist, American
Four Tet, Experimental; Dance; Techno; Electronica; Post-Rock, 2000s-, Artist; Producer, British
Frank, Manufactured Pop, 2000s-, Artist, American
Franz Ferdinand, Alternative/Indie Rock, 2000s-, Artist, British
Funeral For A Friend, Metal; Rock; Emo, 2000s-, Artist, British
Furtado, Nelly, 2000s Pop Singer/Songwriters; Hip Hop; Contemporary R&B, 2000s-, Artist, Canadian
Futureheads, The, Alternative/Indie Rock, 2000s-, Artist, British
Game, The, Contemporary Rap, 2000s-, Artist, British
Gates, Gareth, Manufactured Pop; 2000s Pop, 2000s-, Artist, British
Girls Aloud, 2000s Pop, 2000s-, Artist, British
Gnarls Barkley, Urban Soul; Hip Hop; Electro, 2000s-, Artist; Producer, American
Go! Team, The, Experimental Indie Rock, 2000s, Artist, British
Godspeed You! Black Emperor, Experimental post-rock, 2000s-,
Goldfrapp, Electro, 2000s-, Artist, British
Goldie Lookin' Chain, Hip-Hop; Pop, 2000s-, Artist, British
González, José, Singer-Songwriter, 2000s-, Swedish
Good Charlotte, 2000s Pop, 2000s-, Artist, American
Goodrem, Delta, Singer Songwriter, 2000s-, Artist, Australian
Gorillaz, Hip Hop; Trip Hop; Dub, Ska, 2000s-, Artist, British
Gray, David, 2000s Pop Singer/Songwriters; 2000s Pop, 2000s-, Artist; Songwriter, British
Gray, Macy, 2000s Pop Singer/Songwriters; Contemporary R&B, 2000s-, Artist; Songwriter, American
Green Day, Punk; Indie Rock; Pop, 2000s-, Artist, American
Greenhornes, The, Garage Rock, 2000s-, Artist, American
Guillemots, The, Indie Rock, 2000s-, Artist, American
Har Mar Superstar, Pop/R&B, 2000s-, Artist, British
Hard-Fi, Alternative/Indie Rock, 2000s-, Artist, British
Harper, Ben, Singer Songwriter; Alternative Pop, 2000s-, Artist, American
Hawley, Richard, Singer-Songwriter, 2000s-, Artist, British
Hear'Say, 2000s Pop, 2000s-, Artist, British
Hilton, Paris, Contemporary Pop, 2000s-, Artist, American
Hives, The, Alternative/Indie Rock, 2000s-, Artist, Swedish
Hot Chip, 2000s, Indie Rock, 2000s-, Artist, British
Hot Hot Heat, Indie Rock, 2000s-, Artist, American
Hundred Reasons, Alternative/Indie Rock, 2000s-, Artist, British
Iglesias, Enrique, Latin; 2000s Pop; 1990s-, Artist, Spanish
Ima Robot, Experimental; Indie-Rock; Pop
India, Arie, Contemporary R&B; Urban Soul, 2000s-, Artist, American
J Dilla, Underground Rap, Left-Field Hip Hop, 2000s, Artist; Producer, American
Ja Rule, Golden Age; Hip Hop, 2000s-, Artist, American
Jaheim, Contemporary R&B; Urban Soul, 2000s-, Artist, American
Jamelia, Contemporary R&B, 2000s-, Artist, American
Jenkins, Katherine, Contemporary Opera, 2000s-, Artist, British
Jet, Garage Rock; Indie Rock, 2000s-, Artist, Australian
Jhene, Urban Soul, 2000s-, Artist, America
Johnson, Jack, Pop Singer-Songwriter, 2000s-, Artist, American
Jones, Norah, 2000s Pop; Contemporary Folk, 2000s-, Artist, American
Juliette And The Licks, Indie Rock, 2000s-, Artist, American
Kaiser Chiefs, The, Britpop; Alternative/Indie Rock, 2000s-, Artist, British
Kano, Grime, UK Garage, Underground Hip-Hop, 2000s-, Artist, British
Kasabian, Alternative/Indie Rock; Britpop, 2000s-, Artist, British
Keak Da Sneak, Hip-Hop, Hyphy, 2000s-, Artist, American
Keane, Alternative/Indie Rock; Britpop, 2000s-, Artist, British
Kelis, Contemporary R&B, 2000s-, Artist; Songwriter, American
Kelis, Alicia, Contemporary R&B; Urban Soul, 2000s-, Artist, American
Kid Koala, Turntablism, 2000s-, Artist, Canadian
Killers, The, Alternative/Indie Rock, 2000s-, Artist, American
Kina, Contemporary R&B; Urban Soul, 2000s-, Artist, American
Klaxons, Indie-Rock, 2000s-, Artist, British
Knowles, Beyoncé, 2000s Pop; Urban Soul, 2000s-, Artist, American
Kooks, The, Alternative/Indie Rock, 2000s-, Artist, British
Kubb, Alternative Pop, 2000s-, Artist, British
Lacuna Coil, Metal; Neo-Prog; Goth Rock, 2000s-, Artist, Italian
Lakeman, Seth, Contemporary Folk, 2000s-, Artist, British
Lavigne, Avril, 2000s Pop, 2000s-, Artist; Songwriter, Canadian
Legend, John, Contemporary R&B; Soul, 2000s-, Artist, American
Lewis, Glenn, Contemporary R&B; Urban Soul, 2000s-, Artist, Canadian
Libertines, The, Alternative/Indie Rock, 2000s, Artist, British
Lidell, Jamie, Electronica; Experimental Pop; Dance, 2000s-, Artist, American
Lil Jon, Crunk; Hip-Hop, 2000s-, Artist; Producer, American
Lina, Contemporary R&B, 2000s-, Artist, French
Linkin Park, Nu Metal, 2000s-, Artist, American
Lohan, Lindsay, Contemporary Teen Pop, 2000s-, Artist, American
Lone Pigeon, Indie Rock, 2000s-, Artist, British
Longview, Indie Rock, 2000s-, Artist, British
Lopez, Jennifer, Contemporary Pop; Contemporary R&B, 2000s-, Artist, American
Lostprophets, Metal; Contemporary Grunge, 2000s-, Artist, British
Low, Indie Rock; Experimental, 2000s-, Artist, American
Lowgold, Indie Rock; Experimental, 2000s-, Artist, British
Lucy Pearl, Contemporary R&B; Urban Soul, 2000s-, Artist, American
MF Doom, Underground Rap; Left-Field Hip-Hop, 2000s, Artist; Producer, American
Madlib, Underground Rap; Left-Field Hip-Hop, 2000s, Artist; Producer, American
Magic Numbers, The, Alternative Pop; Indie Rock, 2000s, Artist, American
Mario, Contemporary R&B, 2000s-, Artist, American
Maroon 5, 2000s Pop; Alternative/Indie Rock, 2000s-, Artist, American
Mars Volta, The, Alternative Rock; Contemporary Prog, 2000s-, Artist, American
Mason, Willie, Singer-Songwriter, 2000s-, Artist, American
Matisyahu, Contemporary Reggae; Jewish Reggae, 2000s-, Artist, American
Matthews, Cerys, Singer-Songwriter, Indie Rock, 2000s-, Artist, British
Maximo Park, Alternative/Indie Rock, 2000s-, Artist, British
McFly, Contemporary Pop Rock, 2000s-, Artist, British
Melua, Katie, 2000s Pop; Jazz Pop, 2000s-, Artist, British
Mis-Teeq, Urban Soul, 2000s-, Artist, British
Monet, Jerzee, Contemporary R&B, 2000s-, Artist, American
Moore, Mandy, 2000s Pop, 2000s-, Artist, American
Morrison, James, Pop, 2000s-, Artist, British
Mr Lif, Left-Field Hip-Hop, 2000s, Artist, British
Ms Dynamite, Contemporary R&B; Urban Soul; UK Garage, 2000s-, Artist, British
Mull Historical Society, Indie Rock, 2000s-, Artist, British
Múm, Electronica, 2000s-, Artist, Icelandic
Mumba, Samantha, 2000s Pop; Contemporary R&B, 2000s, Artist, Irish
Muse, Alternative/Indie Rock, 2000s-, Artist, British
My Chemical Romance, Pop-Metal; Emo, 2000s-, Artist, American
My Morning Jacket, Country-Rock; Alternative Rock, 2000s-, Artist, American
Mystery Jets, Experimental Pop; Indie Rock, 2000s-, Artist, British

N*E*R*D, Hip Hop, 2000s, Artist, American
Nelly, Hip Hop, 2000s Pop, 2000s-, Artist; Producer, American
Neptunes, The, Hip-Hop; Contemporary R&B; Pop, 2000s-, Producer, American
New York Trio Project, The, Jazz; 2000s-, Artist, American
Newsom, Joanna, Contemporary Folk; Singer-Songwriter, 2000s-, Artist, American
Nickelback, Melodic Rock; Hard Rock, 2000s-, Artist, Canadian
Nine Inch Nails, Metal; Industrial Rock, 2000s-, Artist, American
Nivea, Contemporary R&B; Urban Soul, 2000s-, Artist, American
Nizlopi, Contemporary R&B, 2000s-, Artist, British
Non Phixion, Underground Rap; Left-Field Hip Hop, 2000s-, Artist, American
O.P.M., Rap-Rock; Alt-Pop, 2000s-, Artist, American
Oneida, Experimental Pop, Indie Rock, 2000s-, Artist, American
Ordinary Boys, The, Indie Rock, 2000s-, Artist, British
Orson, 2000s Pop; Alternative/Indie Rock, 2000s-, Artist, American
Osbourne, Kelly, Alternative; Pop, 2000s-, Artist, American
Ozomatli, Latin; Hip-Hop; Funk; Rock, 2000s-, Artist, American
P.O.D., Christian Rock, Heavy Metal, 2000s-, Artist, American
Panic! At The Disco, Punk-Pop, Emo, 2000s-, Artist, American
Papa Roach, Nu Metal, 2000s-, Artist, American
Parks, Alex, Manufactured Pop, 2000s-, Artist, British
Paul, Sean, Reggae, Contemporary Pop, 2000s-, Artist, Jamaican
Peaches, Electronica, 2000s-, Artist, American
Perez, Amanda, Contemporary R&B, 2000s-, Artist, American
Pernice Brothers, The, Pop-rock/Indie-rock, 2000s-, Artist, American
Pharoahe Monch, Hip-Hop; Rap, 2000s-, Artist, American
Pharrel, Hip-Hop; Contemporary R&B, 2000s-, Artist, Producer, American
Pink, 2000s Pop, 2000s-, Artist, American
Pipettes, The, 2000s Pop/Girl Group, 2000s-, Artist, British
Plan B, Urban; UK Underground, 2000s-, Artist, British
Polwart, Karine, Contemporary Folk; Singer-Songwriter, 2000s-, Artist, British
Polyphonic Spree, The, Gospel Pop; Experimental Pop, 2000s-, Artist, American
Powter, Daniel, 2000s Pop Singer/Songwriters, 2000s-, Artist; Songwriter, Canadian
Pretty Girls Make Graves, Indie Rock, 2000s-, Artist, American
Pussycat Dolls, The, 2000s Pop; Contemporary R&B, 2000s-, Artist, American
Quasimoto, Underground Rap, Left-Field Hip Hop, 2000s-, Artist, American
Queens Of The Stone Age, Hand Rock; Heavy Metal, 2000s-, Artist, American
Raconteurs, The, Alternative/Indie Rock, 2000s-, Artist, American
Rakes, The, Indie Rock, 2000s-, Artist, British
Ravonettes, Garage Indie-Rock, 2000s-, Artist, Scandanavian
Razorlight, Alternative/Indie Rock, 2000s-, Artist, British
Relaxed Muscle, Electro, 2000s, Artist, British
Remy Shand, Contemporary R&B, 2000s-, Artist, American
RES, Contemporary R&B, 2000s-, Artist, American
Rooster, Indie Rock, 2000s-, Artist, British
Roots Manuva, R&B, UK Garage, Hip-Hop, 2000s-, Artist, British
Rowland, Kelly, Contemporary R&B; Urban Soul, 2000s-, Artist, American
Ruff Endz, Contemporary R&B; Urban Soul, 2000s-, Artist, American
Scissor Sisters, Glam Rock & Glitter, 2000s Pop, 2000s-, Artist, American
Sergeant Buzfuz, Singer Songwriter, 2000s-, Artist, British
Shakira, Latin; Contemporary Pop, 2000s-, Artist
Sigur Rós, Experimental Indie Rock, Post-Rock, 2000s-, Icelandic
Simple Kid, Singer-Songwriter, 2000s-, Irish
Simple Plan, 2000s Pop, 2000s-, Artist, Canadian
Simpson, Ashlee, 2000s Pop, 2000s-, Artist, American
Simpson, Jessica, 2000s Pop, 2000s-, Artist, American
Sisqo, Urban Soul, 2000s-, Artist, American
Sleepy Jackson, The, Indie Rock, 2000s-, American
Slipknot, Nu Metal, 2000s-, Artist, American
Snow Patrol, Alternative/Indie Rock, 2000s-, Artist, Irish
Sparklehorse, Alternative Country; Indie Rock, 2000s-, Artist, American
Spektor, Regina, Singer-Songwriter; Contemporary Folk, 2000s-, Artist, American
So Solid Crew, UK Garage, 2000s-, Artist, British
Song Of Dork, Indie Pop, 2000s-, Artist, British
Soundtrack Of Our Lives, The, Indie Rock, 2000s-, Artist, American
Spank Rock, UK Hip-Hop; Electro; Underground, 2000s-, Artist, British
Stefani, Gwen, 2000s Pop, 2000s-, Artist, American
Stevens, Rachel, Contemporary Pop, 2000s-, Artist, British
Stone, Joss, Contemporary Soul, 2000s-, Artist, British
Streets, The, UK Garage; Electro, 2000s-, Artist, British
Strokes, The, Alternative/Indie Rock, 2000s-, Artist, American
Subways, The, Indie/Rock, 2000s-, Artist, British
Sugababes, 2000s Pop; Contemporary R&B; UK Garage, 2000s-, Artist, British
Sum 41, 2000s Pop, 2000s-, Artist, Canadian
Thompson, Teddy, Contemporary Folk, 2000s-, Artist, British
Thrills, The, Indie Pop, 2000s-, Irish
Timberlake, Justin, 2000s Pop, 2000s-, Artist, American
Tindersticks, Indie Rock, 2000s-, Artist, American
Toploader, Alternative/Indie Rock, 2000s-, Artist, British
Toya, Contemporary R&B; Urban Soul, 2000s-, Artist, American
Tragedi Khadafi, UK Hip-Hop, 2000s-, Artist, British
Train, Alternative/Indie Rock; Jam Bands, 2000s-, Artist, American
Trice, Obie, Contemporary Rap, 2000s-, Artist, American
Trivium, Metal, 2000s-, Artist, American
Truth Hurts, Contemporary R&B; Urban Soul, 2000s-, Artist, American
Tunng, Folktronica; Experimental Folk, 2000s-, Artist, British
Tunstall, KT, 2000s Pop Singer/Songwriters, 2000s-, Artist; Songwriter, British
Turin Brakes, Folk Pop, 2000s-, Artist, British
TV On The Radio, Indie Rock; Experimental, 2000s-, Artist, American
Tweet, Contemporary R&B; Urban Soul, 2000s-, Artist, American
Ty, Hip-Hop, 2000s-, Artist, British
Uncle Kracker, Hip Hop; Alternative/Indie Rock, 2000s-, Artist, American
Valance, Holly, Manufactured Pop, 2000s-, Artist, Australian
Velvet Revolver, Hard Rock; Heavy Metal, 2000s-, Artist, American
Vines, The, Alternative/Indie Rock, 2000s-, Artist, Australian
Viva Voce, Indie Rock; Alternative Rock, 2000s-, Artist, American
W. K., Andrew, Rock; Heavy Metal, 2000s-, Artist, American
Wainwright, Martha, Singer-Songwriter, 2000s-, Artist, American
Wainwright, Rufus, Singer-Songwriter, Alt-Pop, 2000s-, Artist, American
Ward, Shayne, Manufactured Pop, 2000s-, Artist, British
Warlocks, The, Garage Indie-Rock, 2000s-, Artist, American
We Are Scientists, Indie Rock, 2000s-, British
Welch, Gillian, Alt-Country, Singer-Songwriter, 2000s-, Artist, American
West, Kanye, Hip Hop, 2000s-, Artist; Producer, American
Westlife, Boy Bands; Manufactured Pop; 2000s Pop, 2000s-, Artist, Irish
Wheatus, 2000s Pop, 2000s-, Artist, American
White Stripes, The, Blues Rock; Alternative/Indie Rock, 2000s-, Artist, American
Wilco, Indie Rock, Alternative Country, 2000s-, Artist, American
Williams, Michelle, The Classic Soul Era, 2000s-, Artist, American
Winehouse, Amy, Contemporay Jazz, 2000s-, Artist, British
Whirlwind Heat, Indie-Rock, 2000s', Artist, American
Wolfmother, Heavy Metal; Hard Rock, 2000s-, Artist, Australian
Wyatt, Keke, Urban Soul, 2000s-, Artist, American
Yeah Yeah Yeahs, Indie Rock, 2000s-, Artist, American
Yo La Tengo, Indie Rock; Experimental Rock, 2000s-, Artist, American
Yorkston, James, Alternative Country; Singer-Songwriter, 2000s-, Artist, British
Young Knives, The, Indie Rock, 2000s-, Artist, British
Young, Will, Manufactured Pop; 2000s Pop, 2000s-, Artist, British
Zero 7, 2000s-, Artist; Producer, British
Zutons, The, Alternative/Indie Rock, 2000s-, Artist, British

see **Coldplay** pp 380   see **Eminem** pp 382   see **Green Day** pp 384   see **Radiohead** pp 386

ONE-HIT WONDERS

The history of rock music tells us that there are great artists and great songs. The two, however, do not always go together. As if to prove that the magic of the music cannot be summoned at will, some of the most memorable three-minute symphonies have been created by singers or groups whose subsequent achievements have signally failed to trouble either chart compilers or book writers.

This section attempts, however symbolically, to right that wrong by identifying some of the one-hit wonders to have made their mark over the decades. Not all, however, are examples of great songwriting or musicianship. Some have been elevated to an artificial chart-placing by a TV show, commercial or film tie-in, catching on to a craze or simply a shocking lack of taste by the general public, but all, for one reason or another, very much overshadow anything else their makers ever achieved.

From 'Cry Me A River' to 'Living In A Box', we present a hit parade with a difference. You will not find an album that contains all these tracks – and it probably would not sell if you could – but they each individually qualify as entertaining footnotes in rock history. And if you want to find out where their makers are now, start Googling….

THE FIFTIES

Julie London
'Cry Me A River', 1955

'Cry Me A River' was a US No. 2 hit single for Julie London, thanks in part to her involvement in the movie, *The Girl Can't Help It*. In the film, London appears during a fantasy scene in press agent Tom Miller's apartment and sings the song to him. Despite an extensive movie career and recording 32 albums, London will always be remembered as the sultry singer of this hit.

Sheb Wooley
'Purple People Eater', 1958

Sheb Wooley's 'Purple People Eater' stayed at No. 1 in the US charts for six weeks. Despite being a serious country musician since 1945, Wooley's hit was a comedy song that parodied popular culture's horror-movie craze.

Below
Country singer turned TV comedy actor Sheb Wooley.

Wooley had to fight with his record label to get the song released, and despite its success, he would not get to see another hit until 1962's country song, 'That's My Dad'. Wooley continued to record under both his own name, and the pseudonym Ben Colder, well into the 1980s. He died of leukaemia in 2003.

Phil Phillips
'Sea Of Love', 1959

Phillips has always remained a mysterious figure, despite having an almost accidental hit with his self-penned 'Sea Of Love'. A bellhop, he had written it after the dissolution of his vocal group, The Gateway Quartet, and it reached No. 2 in the US. It was subsequently kept alive, thanks to covers by the likes of Del Shannon (1984), and being the title song to the 1985 Al Pacino film of the same name. Phillips has kept a low profile ever since, though he worked as a DJ into the 1990s, and made a rare live performance at the Ponderosa Stomp, New Orleans, in 2003.

THE SIXTIES

Arthur Alexander
'You Better Move On', 1962

Co-founder of the famed Muscle Shoals recording studio, Arthur Alexander's 'You Better Move On' was a No. 24 US hit that showcased his country-soul roots. Despite being covered by The Rolling Stones (and having other songs covered by Elvis Presley and The Beatles – the latter covering his biggest hit, 'Anna (Go To Him)', Alexander remained largely unknown, and retired in the 1970s. He died while promoting his 1993 return, *Lonely Just Like Me*.

The Cascades
'Rhythm Of The Rain', 1963

The Cascades were a white R&B/vocal group that, despite never matching the success of their first hit, 'Rhythm Of The Rain', continued recording until the early 1970s. It reached No. 1 in many countries, but was anchored at the No. 2 spot in the US by Frankie Valli and The Four Seasons' 'Walk Like A Man'. 'Rhythm''s songwriter, John Gummoe, continues as a jobbing musician today.

see The Fifties pp 32   see The Sixties pp 76   see The Seventies pp 184

The Honeycombs
'Have I The Right?', 1964

A vehicle for legendary British producer Joe Meek, The Honeycombs' 'Have I The Right?' was a UK No. 1 in 1964. Plenty of other singles followed, as well as two full-length LPs, but Meek and The Honeycombs were unable to re-create this debut's chart-topping magic. After Meek passed away in 1967, The Honeycombs had no one to write for, produce or mould them, and they dissolved.

The Lemon Pipers
'Green Tambourine', 1967

The Lemon Pipers did not write much of their material, and are alleged never to have liked 'Green Tambourine'. Recorded as a contractual obligation to Buddah, it was a UK bubblegum pop No. 1. The Lemon Pipers always wanted to explore a more psychedelic direction, however, and by the time they were finally allowed to self-produce 1968's *Jungle Marmalade*, they had lost all commercial appeal, and disbanded the following year.

Thunderclap Newman
'Something In The Air', 1969

Named – partially – after pianist Andy Newman, Thunderclap were a three-piece group that drummer John 'Speedy' Keen assembled with the aid of Pete Townshend. The Who guitarist's involvement was a favour for Keen, who wrote 'Armenia City In The Sky' for *The Who Sell Out* (1967). 'Something In The Air' was a UK No. 1 smash, but Thunderclap were unable to capitalize on its success, taking over a year to follow it up. Never a touring success, Newman himself left the group in the middle of a tour; Keen returned to drumming in the stage production *Hair*; and the group split in 1971, leaving no remaining original members.

THE SEVENTIES

Norman Greenbaum
'Spirit In The Sky', 1970

A UK and US No. 1, 'Spirit In The Sky' was Greenbaum's first solo hit after performing in some short-lived groups, and a number of singles from the *Spirit In The Sky* LP came to very little. Intended as a commentary on contemporary religious beliefs, it was to be his only hit. Further singles, and 1972's *Petaluma* LP, were failures, though Greenbaum would become a manager and promoter in the 1980s, and at the time of writing, appears to spend much of his time maintaining the *Spirit In The Sky* website.

Ashton, Gardner and Dyke
'Resurrection Shuffle', 1971

Keyboardist/vocalist Tony Ashton and drummer Roy Dyke were seasoned 1960s beat group musicians who had played behind George Harrison on his *Wonderwall Music* LP. In 1969, they met bassist Kim Gardner to form AG&D, and had a No. 3 hit with 'Resurrection Shuffle'. Having recorded three LPs by 1972, nothing else matched 'Shuffle''s hit appeal, and the trio – augmented by guitarist Mick Liber – finally split that year.

Above
The artistically shackled Lemon Pipers.

see Elvis Presley pp 52   *see* The Rolling Stones pp 96   *see* The Who pp 100   *see* The Four Seasons pp 141

Maria Muldaur
'Midnight At The Oasis', 1974

Muldaur began her career as a folk singer, performing in New York's early 1960s Greenwich Village folk scene, famed by the likes of Bob Dylan and Dave Van Ronk. 'Midnight At The Oasis' was a seductive Top 10 pop hit, however, which sticks out in her wildly varying *oeuvre*. Never achieving such mass commercial appeal again, Muldaur is now more well known for exploring American roots and blues music.

Carl Douglas
'Kung Fu Fighting', 1974

Jamaican-born Carl Douglas had his finger on the pulse when he recorded 'King Fu Fighting', a mid-1970s novelty disco hit that reflected that era's fascination with king fu movies and the martial arts. It reached No. 1 on both sides of the Atlantic, and is said to have been recorded in just 10 minutes, and to have sold over nine million copies worldwide. Douglas' follow-up, 'Dance The Kung Fu', was a US flop and UK Top 20 hit,

Above
Seductive songstress Maria Muldaur.

Right
Carl Douglas, strutting his kung fu stuff.

Manu Dibango
'Soul Makossa', 1973

Fusing jazz and *makossa*, the traditional Cameroonian music, Dibango is possibly Africa's best-known jazz musician. However, anything 'world' in music finds it hard to sustain longevity in the pop world, so despite having a hit with 'Soul Mokossa', Dibango's international fame was short lived. He remains a respected jazz musician, having played with, among others, Sly and Robbie and Fela Kuti.

see The Seventies pp 184   *see* The Eighties pp 268

making sure he would only be remembered for his novelty songs, despite releasing a couple of albums into the 1980s. He now owns a production company in Hamburg, producing music for films and commercials.

Minnie Riperton
'Lovin' You', 1975

Having virtually retired in the early 1970s, Epic Records slowly restarted Riperton's career in 1973, having her record backing vocals for Stevie Wonder, followed by recording her own solo album, *Perfect Angel* (which featured Wonder as co-writer and musician), and releasing a string of singles, which culminated in 1975's No. 1 hit, 'Lovin' You'. Despite a respected recording career that started with Rotary Connection in the late 1960s, and a tragic death from breast cancer in 1979, she will always be remembered for this hit, and her five-octave vocal range. Since her death, the song has been covered, sampled and used on soundtracks countless times.

Randy Vanwarmer
'Just When I Needed You Most', 1979

Written when Vanwarmer was only 18, 'Just When I Needed You The Most' was a surprising UK No. 8 and US No. 4 hit, and a pop ballad that also appealed to the disco market. Unable to recreate his pop success in 1980, Vanwarmer embarked upon a country music career that he sustained, on and off, until the mid-1990s. He died from leukaemia in 2004.

THE EIGHTIES

Lipps, Inc.
'Funkytown', 1980

Possibly the last *bona fide* disco hit in the US, Lipps, Inc.'s 'Funkytown' was a worldwide hit that reached No. 1 (and went platinum) in America, and also reached No. 2 in the UK. Its sparse production was not dissimilar to Prince's early work of the time (interestingly, both came from Minneapolis), and was actually at odds with disco's bloated, overproduced excesses. Though subsequent singles were not as popular, they did manage to dent the US dance chart, before the group split up.

Musical Youth
'Pass The Dutchie', 1982

Based on The Mighty Diamonds' reggae hit, 'Pass The Kouchie', Birmingham-based Musical Youth's 'Pass The Dutchie' was a pro-cannabis hit that reached No. 1 in the UK. One of the fastest-selling singles of the year, they could not capitalize on its success, and had disbanded within two years. A reunion was mooted in 1993, but it ultimately came to nothing after band member Patrick Waite died of natural causes while in police custody, aged just 30.

Below
Britain's Musical Youth.

Falco
'Rock Me Amadeus', 1986

Perhaps Austria's great pop export, Falco (born Johann Hölzl) was a classically trained child prodigy who later fronted a jazz rock combo. His early career mixed a lot of techno-synths with German rap, and he even had a single, 'Jenny', banned. 'Rock Me Amadeus' played on his classical background, fusing synths with classical strings, and it reached No. 1 on both sides of the Atlantic. Falco's subsequent releases

see Bob Dylan pp 126   see Stevie Wonder pp 162   see Prince pp 282   see Sly and Robbie pp 314

yielded diminishing returns, and his career had all but ended by 1988. He died in 1998, in a car accident, aged 40.

Swing Out Sister
'Breakout', 1987

A Top 10 hit in the UK, and the group's only US Top 10 hit, 'Breakout' also went so far as to earn the group two Grammy Awards – for Best New Artist and Best New Pop Vocal Performance By A Group Or Duo. Subsequent album and single releases were acclaimed hits in some circles, though time has erased Swing Out Sister from the memories of many. They now enjoy a cult fan base in the US and UK, and a continued success in Japan, where they recorded their latest offering, 2005's *Live In Japan*.

Living In A Box
'Living In A Box', 1987

This self-titled single was Living In A Box's only Top 40 hit in the US. In the UK, however, the group enjoyed much more success, with a short run of Top

Below

Swing Out Sister swung in with just one great hit.

10 singles. They disbanded before their third album was released, and vocalist/guitarist, Richard Derbyshire, included several songs slated for that album on his solo debut, 1994's *How Many Angels*.

Climie Fisher
'Love Changes (Everything)', 1988

A duo, vocalist Simon Climie and keyboardist Rob Fisher co-wrote their best-known song with Dennis Morgan. It hit No. 2 in the UK charts, and featured on their debut album, *Everything*. They split up after their follow-up LP, however, 1989's *Coming In For The Kill*. Fisher died in 1999, while undergoing surgery for bowel cancer, whereas Climie has since done production work for Louise (Redknapp), and co-written and played on much of Eric Clapton's latterday albums.

M/A/R/R/S
'Pump Up The Volume', 1988

If you are going to release only one song, make sure it is a good one. 'Pump Up The Volume' is one of the most influential one-hit wonders of all time. A major milestone in British house music and sampling culture, it marked many people's first point of contact with the underground dance scene. It also attracted a lawsuit from Stock Aitken Waterman, who detected seven seconds' worth of their 'Roadblock' in the track. Though it reached No. 1 in the UK and was an overseas hit, the group split over financial disputes.

Edie Brickell and The New Bohemians
'What I Am', 1989

Late 1980s folk rockers, Edie Brickell and The Bohemians were really riding on the talent of chief songwriter Edie Brickell. 'What I Am' was a Top 10 hit from their debut LP, *Shooting Rubberbands At The Stars*, though the group disbanded after its 1990 follow-up, *Ghost Of A Dog*, failed to perform to expectations. Edie kick-started a solo career in 2003, with longtime Dylan sideman Charlie Sexton producing her debut solo album, *Volcano*. In 2006, she reunited with some of The New Bohemians for a new LP, *Stranger Things*.

see The Eighties pp 268   *see* The Nineties pp 326

THE NINETIES

Deee-Lite
'Groove Is In The Heart', 1990

With the legendary P-Funk bassist Bootsy Collins on bass, the equally legendary Maceo Parker (of James Brown fame – as, incidentally, so was Bootsy) on saxophone, and A Tribe Called Quest's Q-Tip as a guest vocalist, all the elements were in place for a modern funk anthem. 'Groove Is In The Heart' *was* pop-funk perfection that reached No. 4 in the States, and No. 2 in the UK. Deee-Lite were a slightly psych/mod-influenced US dance group that, despite releasing three albums and one remix compilation, were never as popular as when this song was on the turntables. Despite disbanding in 1996, 'Groove Is In The Heart' packs dancefloors to this day.

Chesney Hawkes
'The One And Only', 1991

Born to famous parents, Len 'Chip' Hawkes of 1960s group The Tremeloes, and TV host Carol Hawkes, Chesney is perhaps the greatest definition of a one-hit wonder. Although Hawkes continues to try and restart his career (he is currently writing songs with British comedian Tony Hawks), everyone will remember him for his brief stint singing the Nik Kershaw-penned 'The One And Only'. A Top 10 hit in the US, and UK No. 1 for five weeks, it has become more a nostalgic song most suited for student-union parties, as opposed to the lasting anthem of individuality it wanted to be.

Monty Python
'Always Look On The Bright Side Of Life', 1991

Despite releasing nine albums, changing the face of British comedy, creating (both as a group, and as individual members) some of the most memorable television comedy, and enjoying a string of hit movies, most people remember Monty Python for this one song. Sung by Eric Idle at the end of *Monty Python & The Life Of Brian* (1979 – the song was reissued in 1991), it was a chirpy little ditty about looking at every cloud's silver lining. Its sentiment was all the more admirable, considering that Idle's character was leading a singalong of criminals that were, at that moment in the film, being crucified. A hit at the time, the song has yet to die, thanks to its annoyingly catchy whistled tune.

Above
King of the one-hit wonders, Chesney Hawkes.

see The Tremeloes pp 117   *see* James Brown pp 154   *see* Bootsy Collins pp 237   *see* Stock, Aitken and Waterman pp 316

Above

Country crooner Billy
Ray Cyrus.

Billy Ray Cyrus
'Achy Breaky Heart', 1992

Known as much for this song as he was for his mullet
hairstyle, Billy Ray Cyrus has never been able to
escape – nor replicate – the success of this lightweight
country pop tune. About as genuine as The Eagles and
Garth Brooks combined, it spent 17 weeks at the top
of the US country chart, marking a depressing moment
when insincere country was more popular than the real
deal. Having forged a more serious career over nine
albums (his most recent, *Wanna Be Your Joe*, came out
in 2006), he has never set the charts alight as he did
with this plea for a lady not to break his heart.

Tasmin Archer
'Sleeping Satellite', 1993

Some described her style as a more pop-orientated Seal,
and Archer's first single, 'Sleeping Satellite', knocked
The Shamen's all-pervasive 'Ebenezer Good' off of the
UK No. 1 spot, staying there for two weeks. In 1993,
she won a Brit Award for Best Breakthrough Act. A
one-hit wonder to many, Archer has released albums as
recently as 2006's *On*, though only an extremely niche
fan base continues to keep up with her work.

Stiltskin
'Inside', 1994

'Inside' made Stiltskin a worldwide name after it
featured in an extremely successful advertising campaign
for Levi's jeans. Written by Peter Lawlor, who believed
he had a hit song on his hands, he convinced the
clothing company to use it to soundtrack one of their
adverts. Auditions were then held to assemble the band
that would front the song, and the successful candidates
became Stiltskin. They released a debut album, *The
Mind's Eye* (1995), before splitting two years later during
the recording of their second. One of the original
members now leads a new line-up under the same name,
and has recorded a new album, *She* (2006).

Edwyn Collins
'A Girl Like You', 1995

When 'A Girl Like You' became a hit on both sides
of the Atlantic, not many remembered that Edwyn
Collins used to be part of the talented Scottish pop
group Orange Juice. The song was Collins' biggest hit
since Orange Juice's 'Rip It Up' in 1983, and it is a
standout pop tune that has allowed Collins to remain a
household name. His recording career has been sporadic
since, and in February 2005, Collins suffered a brain
hemorrhage, but thankfully survived the operation.

Joan Osborne
'One Of Us', 1995

'One Of Us' was a popular radio-friendly hit that
Osbourne followed with a few minor singles, though she
has never replicated its popularity. Questioning what
would happen if God were 'one of us', it earned
Osbourne a mid-1990s supporting slot for Bob Dylan,
while Prince would later take to covering the song in

concert. It took until 2000 for Osbourne to release the follow up to *Relish* (the album from which 'One Of Us' came), by which time her popularity had worn off.

The Rembrandts
'I'll Be There For You', 1995

Thanks to its use as the theme tune to the mid-1990s (and then some) hit US comedy TV show *Friends*, 'I'll Be There For You' is probably known to everyone on the planet over the age of 10. Initially, the song was written to fill the TV show's opening credits, but as demand for a hit single grew, The Rembrandts – who had enjoyed moderate success before penning the song – had to create a full-length single out of it. Their last album, *Lost Together*, came out in 2001, though most are content with the couple of minutes it takes for the *Friends*' opening credits to end.

Babylon Zoo
'Spaceman', 1996

Another case of Levi's jeans popularizing a song into a hit single – something they had done, not only with new songs, but also with reissues of classic soul songs in the 1980s – Babylon Zoo's 'Spaceman' was an electro-pop hit that appealed instantly to a mid-1990s crowd, but would seem dated and clumsy today. Jas Mann (pronounced 'jazz man') was the group's driving force, and he/they were pretentious enough (and lacking in a talent that allows for longevity) for their 1996 debut album, *The Boy With The X-Ray Eyes*, to sell disappointingly, and for Babylon Zoo to never be heard from again.

see Bob Dylan pp 126   see The Eagles pp 198   see Prince pp 282

430

White Town
'Your Woman', 1997

White Town (really one-man-show Jyoti Mishra) found hit success in the US and UK with 'Your Woman', a song that partially recounted his youthful obsession with a lesbian. Despite EMI signing him to their Chrysalis subsidiary, no amount of backing could conjure interest in his subsequent releases, and so White Town quickly went to recording for indie labels, with a new album allegedly scheduled for 2006.

New Radicals
'You Get What You Give', 1999

Garnering most of its attention from its celebrity-baiting outro, 'You Get What You Give' was a UK Top 5 hit for retroactive funk/soul/rock group New Radicals – a collective that revolved around the only *bona fide* member, Gregg Alexander. After releasing the New Radicals' album, *Maybe You've Been Brainwashed Too* (1998), Alexander disbanded the group to concentrate more on production work.

Below

Jimmy Eat World

see The Nineties pp 326   *see* The Noughties pp 374

THE NOUGHTIES

Spiller
'Groovejet (If This Ain't Love)', 2000

Italian DJ Cristiano Spiller's 'Groovejet (If This Ain't Love)' was helped in no small part by vocalist Sophie Ellis-Bextor, who herself would have something of a one-hit wonder two years later with 'Murder On The Dancefloor'. Initially an instrumental, Spiller invited Ellis-Bexter to guest on the track, giving it more commercial appeal and securing a No. 1 in the UK. 'Groovejet' was ultimately one of the biggest club hits of the year, but like with others of the time (Modjo's 'Lady (Hear Me Tonight)'), the British public at large were not about to indulge a full-blown career by the artist, and Spiller never enjoyed such popularity again.

LeAnn Womack
'I Hope You Dance', 2001

Despite having recorded since 1997, and continuing to record as a country artist today, duetting with the likes of Willie Nelson, Womack will for ever be associated with country-pop hit, 'I Hope You Dance', and the album of the same name. A dedication to her daughters, both the song and album saw Womack become the first female country-pop artist to make any major impact since Shania Twain.

M&S Presents Girl Next Door
'Salsoul Nugget (If You Wanna)', 2001

A seemingly faceless group with a knack for a club hit, M&S/Girl Next Door were well aware of their club-music lineage when they gave this song the title 'Salsoul Nugget'. Salsoul is one of the most collectable 1970s disco/dance labels of all time, and an inspiration to similar labels since. Mostly now to be found on Ibiza compilations, the song was a hit, and then its creators disappeared from mainstream ears. The song contains samples of Double Exposure's 'Everyman', and Loleatta Holloway's 'Hit & Run'.

Jimmy Eat World
'The Middle', 2002

Where many bands imploded, or just did not have the legs for it, Jimmy Eat World survived the mid-1990s grunge scene. 'The Middle' was the second single from their 2001 *Bleed American* album, and it proved to be a worldwide smash, and their biggest single to date. Once linked with grunge, now linked – in the media at least – to emo, Jimmy Eat World still continue to ply their trade.

Gary Jules
'Mad World', 2003

Gary Jules had recorded as a solo artist since 1998, but in 2001 he collaborated with Michael Andrews to cover Tears For Fears' 'Mad World'. The sombre remake was featured in 2003's hit film *Donnie Darko*, and the appeal of the film, coupled with the song's popularity and Jules' strange choice of cover, made 'Mad World' 2003's UK Christmas No. 1 single. Never quite hitting a nerve the same way since, Jules continues to record as a solo artist.

Room 5, Feat Oliver Cheetham
'Make Luv', 2003

Masterminded by Belgium-based producer Vito Lucente (aka Junior Jack), Room 5 was a Daft Punk-styled funk-dance creation. Based around Oliver Cheetham's 1980s hit, 'Get Down Saturday Night', 'Make Luv' became a UK No. 1 in 2003, though the Room 5 concept was dropped the following year, after Lucente/Room 5 released a full-length album, *Music & You: The Album*.

Below
Gary Jules – mad world, mad hat.

see Tears For Fears pp 318   see Shania Twain pp 370

THE INSTRUMENTS

In the late 1950s and early 1960s, the 'beat combo' was established: drum kit, electric bass guitar and two electric guitars (lead and rhythm guitars). The development of more advanced recording techniques in the 1960s, especially that of multi-tracking, meant that groups could create very rich, multi-layered textures. In styles such as rhythm and blues, funk and disco, extra musicians were often included to add richness: string sections (violins), horn sections (trumpet, saxophone and trombone) and backing singers.

Electronic instruments such as the Fender organ, the Minimoog synthesizer and the clavinet were incorporated in the 1960s and 1970s by groups keen to create a new 'sound'. The availability of programmable drum machines and synthesizers from the late 1970s meant that live musicians could be dispensed with for the first time.

In the late 1980s and 1990s, music technology took a further hold on popular music, as dance music took off. Sequencers enabled musical patterns to be continually 'looped' and other sounds manipulated and rhythms tightened up. Rap and hip-hop also exploits music technology, using rhythmical speaking over drum loops and samples. As the influence of pop music has spread across the globe, countless new ensembles have been created from the fusion of world music styles and rock influences, including Bhangra (Punjabi and Jamaican influences) and Salsa (Cuban and Puerto Rican influences).

The Rock Band

electric guitar's mass appeal. Rock'n'rollers like Chuck Berry exploited the chugging rhythmic capability of semi-acoustic instruments from the late 1950s into the 1960s. From the early 1960s, countless groups, led by The Beatles and The Rolling Stones, based their music around the electric guitar.

The advent in the late 1960s of very loud blues-influenced rock music saw the flowering of the solid electric guitar, led by the hugely influential Jimi Hendrix playing a Fender Stratocaster. The popularity of electric guitars was renewed in the 1990s and into the 2000s with the success of groups like Nirvana, Oasis and Radiohead.

Bass Guitar

In 1951, guitar maker Leo Fender launched the first commercially available electric bass guitar, the Fender Precision. Compared to the cumbersome and often difficult-to-hear acoustic double bass, Fender offered an instrument that had many advantages. Not only was it louder because it was amplified – and more portable – it allowed for more precise intonation because the neck was fretted. Country-and-western players were among the first to adopt the Precision, and during the 1950s and 1960s the bass guitar became established as a mainstay of all styles of modern music making. Four strings tuned E, A, D and G are usual, although a few models with five or more strings are made.

The design principles of the Fender bass guitars have stood the test of time remarkably well: a solid body, larger machine-heads to cope with heavier strings, one or two electro-magnetic pickups, and a bolt-on neck. Fender went on to introduce the Jazz Bass in 1960 and other less successful models. Apart from notable exceptions such as the Rickenbacker 4001S (1964) and the Gibson Thunderbird IV (1964), the electric basses of other big guitar companies never gained the broad acceptance of the Fenders. From the 1970s' specialist bass makers such as Ampeg, Alembic and Wal began to cater for more discerning players.

The Fender-based style of construction went unchallenged until Ned Steinberger brought out his radical innovation in the early 1980s: a bass guitar with no headstock and a tiny body. He did this by using reinforced epoxy resin (claimed to be stronger and lighter than steel) instead of wood, and by putting the tuning mechanisms at the other end of the body.

Drum Kit

The drum kit is so much a part of contemporary music that it is easy to forget it is a relatively recent invention, even though the separate elements that make it up often date to antiquity. In the 1900s, a need emerged for a way of playing various percussion instruments, ideally while sitting down; this need was driven in the main, though not exclusively, by jazz drummers.

The resulting set-up was first known as 'traps' (short for contraption – a term still used by some players) and was common by the 1920s in Dixieland and dance bands. By the 1950s the basic combination of instruments and implements had stabilized:

A typical rock band's instrumental line-up, based on the 'beat combo' established in the 1960s, might include the following:

The Voice

The human voice is our primeval musical instrument, with our earliest ancestors finding expression through their voices before thought was ever given to other sources of sound. Vocal music has been sung from the beginnings of recorded history; the Sumerians sang in their temples 5,000 years ago. In the West, traditions of singing have evolved from the plainchant of the middle ages, through seventeenth-century opera to today's various music styles.

Electric Guitar (Rhythm and Lead)

If one instrument can claim to be the twentieth century's greatest, then the electric guitar is probably it. When the early pioneers, Adolph Rickenbacker, George Beauchamp and Paul Barth, experimented with electro-magnetic pickups to amplify the sound of a guitar in the 1930s, none could have foreseen what an impact this innovation would have on all styles of popular music.

In the mid 1930s, Charlie Christian was one of the first to see the potential as a soloist of playing a guitar that could be heard properly in a jazz band. He played an early Electric Spanish' ES-150 guitar made by Gibson. For generations of jazz players, the mellow clarity of the electric-acoustic guitar became a traditional and characteristic sound.

Early rock'n'roll records, such as Bill Haley and The Comets' 1954 hit 'Rock Around The Clock' kick-started the

see The Fifties Sources & Sounds pp 34   see The Sixties Sources & Sounds pp 78

- Bass drum (smaller than in military bands), struck by a floor-pedal beater.
- Snare drum.
- Different sized tom-toms and cymbals mounted either on the drum or a floor stand.
- Hi-hat cymbal (two cymbals clashed together by a foot pedal).

Drummers can explore endless variations: double bass drums (Billy Cobham once used three!), additional instruments like wood blocks, and also a customized mix of drum heads, cymbal shapes or stick weights, so each drummer creates a blend of sounds that becomes his or her signature.

Bass Drum

Throughout the history of percussion instruments, this drum has been the mainstay of time-keeping, whether it is used for a marching army or in a late-twentieth century heavy metal band. Both sides of the drum have heads, so the marching player can strike the heads with felt-covered drumsticks with alternate hands. The resulting boom has great power, but the drum is not really suited to rapid notes or drumrolls.

In an orchestra, the bass drum is usually held in a tilting position on a stand that can be adjusted for a better angle of attack. A smaller bass drum – struck by a foot pedal – is a staple of the drum kit (ideal as an advertisement hoarding, like Ringo Starr's Ludwig bass drum for the Beatles). In the late 1960s and early 1970s there was a vogue for using a double bass drum kit inspired by Cream's Ginger Baker.

Snare Drum

The insistent rhythm of the snare drum has accompanied war, work and play since antiquity. The Romans marched to its beat, Elizabethan revellers danced to the pipe and tabor and in the days before field telephones, military messages were transmitted via drum calls. In the twentieth century the snare (or side) drum became an essential part of the standard drum kit, and provided the off-beat drive of rock'n'roll.

In its simplest form the snare drum is a small, cylindrical drum covered with parchment. What gives the drum its distinctive sound is the snare: a strip of metal wires, nylon or gut stretched across the bottom of the drum. When the drummer strikes the top skin, the snare vibrates and the high-pitched rattle is able to slice through the loudest of bands and the fiercest of battles.

The military snare drum is hung over the drummer's shoulder, with the drumhead at an angle for ease of access; rolls, flams and paradiddles support the brass or bagpipes. In jazz and rock the rim shot, a smart crack with the stick simultaneously hitting the metal rim and the drumhead, is a frequent device.

Cymbals

We know that the clashing of 'loud' and 'well-tuned' cymbals were familiar to the writers of the Psalms, but their origins are unclear: certainly they were first used in the East, possibly in Assyria or Turkey, from where they reached the orchestras of Western Europe during the eighteenth century.

Cymbals are concave plates of brass or bronze, held at the centre – either by leather handles or a pole – so that the edges

of the metal can vibrate. Their manufacture remains a craft full of closely guarded secrets and tradition: the present-day Zildjian cymbal company is descended from a long line of Turkish cymbal-makers.

There are now hundreds of varieties to select from, particularly for use on a drum kit, including:

- The crash: a bright cymbal with a fast crescendo.
- The sizzle: with half a dozen rivets set loosely in the cymbal.
- The ride: a ringing cymbal for driving the rhythm along.
- The hi-hat: two smaller cymbals clashed together by pedal action.

For alternative effects the cymbals can be played with drum sticks, timpani sticks or wire brushes – or even recorded backwards, as The Beatles did on 'Strawberry Fields Forever'.

ROCK BAND ADDITIONS

For extra colour, the following percussion and other instruments are added to the rock band's line-up, in many and varying combinations:

PERCUSSION
Congas

The rhythm sections of Latin American bands are enhanced by a range of propulsive percussion instruments, of which the largest are the congas, the single-headed drums that found their way from Africa to Cuba and beyond. The congas – also known as tumba drums – have an upright barrel shape: the body of the drum is made of hard wood or fibreglass, open at the bottom and supported by four legs. A vellum or calfskin head is held tight on to the body below the actual level of the drumhead, giving the

Above
A standard rock drum kit.

Far Top Left
The Kinks were a perfect example of the original beat combo with three guitars and standard drum.

Far Bottom Left
The Fender Telecaster is one of the classic rock guitars.

Bottom
The congas and bongos started to appear in the rock mainstream in the late 1960s with the explosion of eclectic music influenced by African and South American rhythms.

see Bill Haley pp 48   see The Kinks pp 94   see Jimi Hendrix pp 132   see Radiohead pp 386

player unencumbered access to all parts of the head. The skill lies in using all parts of the hand, including the flat palm and the fingertips.

Generally used in pairs with different pitches, the congas are frequently complemented in Latin American line-ups by:
- Timbales: a pair of high-pitched metal-shelled drums, played with sticks and mounted on a stand with a cowbell.
- Bongos: two small bucket-shaped wooden drums, joined by a metal bar and played with the thumb and fingers.

Maracas

The hustling, shaking sound of the maracas is an essential part of Cuban music (the rumba and the mambo), although rattles go back to the Egyptians and beyond, in fact predating the drum. The sound of the maracas is multi-textured, but the technology is straightforward: a pair of round or egg-shaped containers, made from gourds, wood or plastic, mounted on the end of sticks, filled with anything from beans or pebbles to buttons or lead shot to provide the necessary sizzle. Various techniques are available, including twirling both maracas to create a kind of drumroll, banging one maraca into an open hand, or flicking the shot into the top side of the maracas before letting it fall back to the bottom for a double shuffle.

Bo Diddley's right-hand man, maracas player Jerome Green, was an essential component of the distinctively syncopated sound of Diddley's singles in the 1950s. Mick Jagger was a fan of both men and was rarely without his maracas during early Rolling Stones' performances.

Tambourine

The tambourine is one of the oldest – but one of the most underrated – of all instruments. The version used today has changed little from that used thousands of years ago by the ancient Greeks (which they called the 'timpnon'). Although its construction is simple – a shallow, round wooden frame or hoop, sometimes with a single, taut, parchment head, and circular metal discs set in pairs into the hoop – the tambourine's bright, fluttering jingle can lift a piece of music on its own. The player can shake the tambourine for a constant, rhythmic pulse, use the finger pads to provide a sharp tap, or strike the tambourine on to a knee, leg or open hand; the thumb trill involves moistening the thumb and running it round the edge of the tambourine.

The tambourine has proved particularly versatile throughout its life: as appropriate to the religious rites of antiquity as it is in folk dancing (particularly in Spain), marching band, who borrowed the instrument from Turkish military music, in rock and pop line-ups, and through generations of Salvation Army bands.

Above

The tambourine is often used to add a rhythmic pulse or a more subtle texture to the percussion sounds.

Right

Violins are used live by many bands in unplugged sets, but in the studio they have largely been replaced by software and hardware samples.

Tubular Bells

The sound of a bell can carry for miles, celebrating weddings or warning of attack. Since the great foundry cast bells are weighed in tons, they are less than practical for concert use – hence the invention of the tubular bells by John Hampton of Coventry in the 1880s. The tubular bells (known in the US as 'chimes') are a portable, efficient way of reproducing the bell sound, although they can never reproduce the sheer power of a genuine belfry. The most common version uses 18 narrow tubes, of the same width but different lengths to produce an octave and a half of individual chromatic notes. They are hung on a frame, damped by a foot-operated pedal to stop the sound and struck by a wooden mallet or a drumstick at the top of the tube.

Other instruments that can be used for bell sounds include:
- Handbells, played by teams of ringers.
- Traditional sleigh bells.
- The cowbell, often mounted on top of a drum kit.
- The triangle, which although a single steel rod, has a clear ringing tone with the ability to cut through the largest of orchestras or bands.

Washboard

A staple instrument in zydeco music (black American dance music, also featuring guitar and accordian) and the skiffle bands of the late 1950s, the washboard is one of the most widely used of the instruments that produce their sound by scraping. It is a form of rhythm-making that goes way back. It is also an example of inventive recycling for musical purposes, since the washboard was adapted directly from the domestic corrugated metal board once used in washing clothes.

The washboard as an instrument is based on the same principle as the guiro, a Latin American instrument that uses a stick scraped along the serrated notches carved into a wood block or gourd, except that the washboard creates its sound from the contact between metal and metal – players place thimbles on the ends of their fingers to produce a harder-edged, more rasping sound than the gentler guiro.

Over the years musical washboards have become increasingly elaborate constructions, worn over the shoulder and round the player's neck like an apron and involving Edward Scissorhands-style industrial gloves tipped with metal talons.

STRINGS
Violin

The violin is still the dominant orchestral instrument as well as a major force in folk, country and ethnic music. Although there have been modifications to the instrument over the centuries, the violin of the 1600s is to all intents and purposes the same used today, including the f-shaped sound holes, the polished body with separate front and back, and the wooden tuning pegs. A straight and adjustable bow, the use of metal strings and the addition of a chin-rest were all in place by the nineteenth century.

see The Fifties Sources & Sounds pp 34   *see* The Sixties Sources & Sounds pp 78

WIND

Flute

Despite Wayman Carver's work with Benny Carter and Chick Webb in the 1930s, the flute was a rarity in rock and jazz, more often heard soloing in Latin dance bands, until the 1950s, when Frank Wess (also a talented saxophonist) became a featured soloist in Count Basie's band and several California-based composers began to utilize the instrument. Although several other saxophonists have doubled on flute effectively – particularly Eric Dolphy, Charles Lloyd and Jane Bunnett – it was the specialists, such as like Herbie Mann, Hubert Laws and James Newton, who legitimized the instrument as a solo voice.

Saxophone

Musicologists say, with justification, that the saxophone is a wind instrument because it combines a clarinet mouthpiece and an oboe-like body. But the instrument has always been a slightly uneasy hybrid because of its brass construction – and now sits as comfortably in a brass section as the trumpet or trombone.

In the 1840s Adolphe Sax, the prolific Belgian-born, Paris-based instrument maker, was seeking a way to fill a gap between the clarinet and tenor brass instruments. Using recent improvements in woodwind key construction he developed the instrument, including the upturned bell of the bass clarinet, and began supplying it to military bands. Eventually some classical composers saw its potential (Ravel included sax parts in Boléro) but it was the jazz- and dance-band worlds which took it to new heights.

Of the 14 members of the family the most commonly used – apart from the tenor are:

- B-flat soprano: usually in its straight version, capable of a strident or other-worldly sound.
- E-flat alto: a creamy tone, often delivered with a soulful feel.
- E-flat baritone: plenty of growling punch in the lower register.

Tenor Saxophone

The B-flat tenor saxophone is by far the best known of the saxophone family. After a sluggish start, where its appearance was limited to military bands, a move indoors ensured that its distinctive timbre would create some of the best popular music of the twentieth century – from rock'n'roll to funk, soul to jazz, for which it became a universal icon. When the tenor sax was adopted by the jazz world it was imbued with the dangerous allure the electric guitar held for a different generation.

A tenor sax can deliver both the emotional immediacy and the lack of precision in tuning and note placing which horrified many classical composers and attracted jazz performers. The mouth's direct contact with the instrument allows the saxophonist to communicate as if through speech patterns, bringing his or her personality into direct connection with the audience. The technique of circular breathing – where the player breathes in through their nose and out through the mouth and instrument simultaneously, using the cheeks like bellows – is challenging but allows long fluid lines of improvization.

Trombone

The noble sound of the trombone has changed remarkably little since its appearance in the fifteenth century, other than the later addition of a flared bell. It is the only naturally chromatic brass instrument: the slide actually predated the valves trumpeters and horn players use by some four centuries. Every note on the trombone is played by one of the seven positions of the detachable slide – valve trombones do exist, but purists believe it creates a significant loss of tone. The glissando slide up or down the scale is a unique – and sometimes deliberately comic – effect.

The trombone is available in a range of choral voices, including a soprano version, but by far the most common is the tenor, followed by the bass. It was quickly adopted by jazz line-ups (even handling the difficulties of be-bop) and has become an essential ingredient in soul, funk and rock horn sections.

Trumpet

The trumpet has, for at least 3,000 years, been an instrument of great pomp. Court trumpeters were held in high esteem through to the 1600s. The instrument experienced a decline in popularity during the Classical era but began to rise again in the twentieth century. The instrument really found its *raison d'être*, however, with the arrival of jazz.

Common to all trumpets is a cylindrical metal bore, flared at the end. In the same way as other brass instruments, the trumpet's brilliant flourish is produced through air being vibrated by the player's embouchure – like blowing a raspberry, except putting the tongue behind the front teeth. Until the fifteenth century different notes could only be produced by tightening the embouchure, but thereafter additional loops, crooks, slides and valves were gradually added to the trumpet.

Following various tunings, the B-flat trumpet had become the norm by 1900. The three valves are pushed down to divert the air into separate loops; played in combination they can create every regular note, but high ones are still difficult. A plastic or wooden mute, placed in the bell of the trumpet, technically deadens the sound, but produces a haunting, plaintive sound.

Left

As a lead instrument in a break or as part of a horn rhythm section, the sax is a vivid and powerful instrument in the rock palate.

Below

The trumpet is a more varied instrument than it seems and can often be made to sound like the human voice, with or without mutes.

🚗 *see* **Bo Diddley** pp 20   🚗 *see* **The Rolling Stones** pp 96

Beyond Rock

ROCK-SYNTH, POP, FUNK & SOUL

A different sound to that made by the typical rock-band line-up was produced by keyboard-based bands such as The Doors, where the keyboard replaced the electric guitars. By the 1970s, bands such as Kraftwerk and New Order consisted entirely of synthesizers, and the instrument dominated 1980s' music until the re-emergence of guitar-based line-ups with indie music and Britpop in the 1990s. Many of the following instruments are used to great effect in pop, soul and funk music.

Above

Moby's music is a brilliant sythesis of electronic breaks, beats and sampled human sounds. His live shows translate the computer-generated sounds with live musicians.

Above Right

The humble drum machine has moved beyond its initial incarnations and, if handled with some skill, is now a sophisticated replacement for a real drummer.

ELECTRONIC INSTRUMENTS
Sampler and Drum Machine

As with the latest synthesizers, a sampler uses digital technology to make sounds. The difference is that, instead of generating an original synthetic sound, it actually 'plays' a mini digital recording of a sound. This could be anything – a voice, a drum beat or even a milk bottle being dropped! In the late 1970s, a pioneering sampling musical instrument such as the Fairlight CMI was as expensive as a Ferrari sports car. By the mid 1990s, samplers were no more expensive than regular synthesizers. In the future, it is likely that dedicated hardware samplers will be forsaken for more versatile personal computers that can do the same thing.

Many people use samples from CDs or download them from the Internet. Others prefer to make their own, using the sampler to make a digital recording of the sound they want (often from other people's records). Either way, the sample can then be played musically by connecting a keyboard to the sampler.

Drum machines have changed the approach to providing rhythm in music. There are two types: the type that produces a continuous beat to a pre-set pattern, and those that are played in 'real time' using sticks. A key example of the first type is Roland's TR-606 Drumatix, introduced in 1981, which inspired a generation of dance-music mixers and audiences. Roger Linn's LinnDrum, launched in 1986, is an influential instrument of the second type. It makes sampled drum sounds when special pads are hit.

Synthesizer

The synthesizer has come a long way since the world's first one – the American RCA Mk I, made in 1951, whose bulk occupied a laboratory. To play it, composers such as Milton Babbitt (a fan of Mk II) had to tap in punched-tape instructions – there was no keyboard. Synthesizers became available commercially during the mid-1960s when two innovators, Donald Buchla and Robert Moog, each brought out their own designs. Robert Moog's Moog, with its new voltage-controlled oscillator, was the more influential and was played by top rock keyboard players such as Keith Emerson.

A conventional synthesizer is a keyboard instrument that generates a wide variety of sounds purely electronically, using no mechanical parts at all. With many models providing pre-programmed sounds as well as the capability of altering every aspect of a sound (e.g. pitch, timbre, attack and delay), the synthesizer player can imitate a range of instruments or invent entirely new squeaks, warbles or rumbles.

Analogue synthesizers are now regarded as classics and are collected for the unique quality of their sounds. From the late 1970s, these gave way to a new generation that used digital microcomputers, for example the Fairlight CMI (which plays sampled sounds and Yamaha's FM (frequency modulation) models.

KEYBOARDS
Clavinet

The clavinet is essentially an electric version of the clavichord. Designed in the 1960s by Ernst Zacharias of the German company, Hohner, the clavinet evolved from the Cembalet, an instrument Zacharias had developed some years earlier as an electronic counterpart to the harpsichord. The clavinet's distinctively bright percussive sound ensured that the instrument became a firm favourite with players of funk and rock music. John Paul Jones of Led Zeppelin used the instrument extensively on the *Physical Graffiti* album, but

see The Seventies Sources & Sounds pp 186   *see* The Eighties Sources & Sounds pp 270

perhaps the clavinet's defining moment was its use in Stevie Wonder's infectious 'Superstition'.

Electric Organ

The electric organ emerged in the early twentieth century, originally designed as an economical and compact substitute for the larger pipe organ. During its history, makers have employed various techniques for producing tones: vibrating reeds, spinning tone wheels, oscillator circuits and digital samplers.

The most well known is the Hammond organ, patented by its American inventor Laurens Hammond in 1934. Featuring two keyboards and a set of foot pedals, it produces its unmistakable sound through a set of rotary generators, using drawbars to produce a great variety of tone colours. The Hammond swirling through a Leslie rotating speaker cabinet was at the heart of much black American music from the 1960s onwards, especially gospel, jazz, blues and funk. By the 1960s valves in electric organs had given way to transistors, which were superseded in turn by microcircuits in the 1970s. Instead of originating notes internally, the latest types play digitally stored samples, allowing players to imitate almost any other instrument.

Electric Piano

The electric piano can sound smooth and mellow, hard and funky, or anywhere in between. Its popularity peaked in the 1970s and declined during the 1980s, only to find a new generation of fans in the worlds of acid jazz, hip-hop, and garage. Although the Yamaha CP70 electric grand became widely accepted and a new generation of digital pianos has emerged, for many players there were only two main makes to choose from: the Fender Rhodes or the Wurlitzer.

Fender Rhodes

Most influential in the 1970s, the 'Rhodes' helped define the sound of jazz-funk and jazz-fusion, and was played by many soul, funk and disco artists. Harold Rhodes developed his Army Air Corps Piano from old bits salvaged from B-17 bombers. Using no

electrics at all, he achieved a compact portable piano by using aluminium pipes instead of strings. In the late 1950s, Rhodes collaborated with guitar maker Leo Fender to make the 32-note Piano Bass model, made famous by Ray Manzarek of The Doors. The famous 72-note Suitcase model, introduced in 1965, was the first one with the unique 'real' Rhodes sound.

Wurlitze

Frequently more at home in a guitar-based rock or pop band, the 'Wurly' has enjoyed great success from the early 1960s onwards. The Wurlitzer's development started when the Everett piano company experimented with B.F. Meissner's ideas about electro-magnetic pickups. The giant American jukebox and theatre organ manufacturer, Wurlitzer, then applied this pickup technology to make an amplifiable piano in which hammers strike metal reeds and the Wurlitzer electric piano was born. The popular EP200 model was first made in the early 1960s.

BLUES & JAZZ

For blues and jazz, the following instruments might be used in addition to ones already mentioned.

BRASS
Cornet

Pitched in B-flat, or occasionally in C, the three-valved cornet was invented in 1830 and adapted by New Orleans brass bands later in the century. Manuel Perez is credited by some as the first jazz cornettist, although Buddy Bolden may have, in fact, preceded him. The dominant brass instrument in jazz until the late 1920s, the cornet has continued to be favoured by some players, including Bobby Bradford and Graham Hynes.

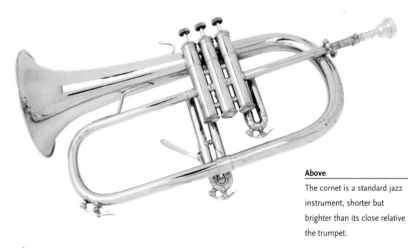

Above

The cornet is a standard jazz instrument, shorter but brighter than its close relative the trumpet.

Sousaphone

Adapted from the helicon in the 1890s, the sousaphone is a bass tuba that is being coiled in such a way that it encircles the player, resting on the left shoulder and passing under the right arm with the bell pointing forwards above the head. Adjusted and reshaped to improve the ease of carrying such a heavy bass instrument, the sousaphone is particularly suited for the American marching band. It was also a regular part of Dixieland bands, adding some beef to the bass part in the rhythm section. It is rarely seen in Europe.

Left

The Fender Rhodes has a distinctive sound that formed the core of many top rock hits in the 1970s.

🎙 *see* **The Doors** pp 140   🎙 *see* **Stevie Wonder** pp 162   🎙 *see* **Led Zeppelin** pp 200   🎙 *see* **Kraftwerk** pp 218

KEYBOARDS
Upright Piano
From honky-tonk bars to the low point of piano-smashing contests of the 1970s, the upright has been seen as the poor cousin of the grand. It can never recreate the power and tone of a grand, but its compact shape brought music into the heart of hundreds of thousands of homes at the end of the nineteenth century.

From James P. Johnson to Art Tatum to Bud Powell and Cecil Taylor to Keith Jarrett, the piano has constantly been in the vanguard of change and innovation in jazz. The diversity of major influential pianists, including Earl Hines, Duke Ellington, Oscar Peterson, Thelonious Monk and Herbie Hancock, shows the range that jazz piano can cover.

PERCUSSION
Kazoo
A kazoo is one of a family of instruments called mirlitons. They have in common a membrane which is vibrated by sound waves produced either by the player's voice or by an instrument. The distinctive sound produced has a buzzing quality, and the kazoo is the best-known member of the mirliton family. This has a membrane set into the wall of a short tube into which the player makes vocal noises. Many pop and jazz musicians have used kazoos in their music.

Vibraphone
The vibraphone, or vibes, took the metal of the glockenspiel – a small xylophone with metal bars – and added metal resonators underneath the bars, kept in motion by an electric motor to provide a quivering, breathy edge to the sound. Originally called the vibraharp, it was invented in the early twentieth century; dance and jazz bands were quick to pick up on its potential.

The glockenspiel ('bell-play' in German), struck with metal beaters, was a relatively simple instrument, and could be carried in marching bands mounted on a rod, when it was known as the bell-lyra. The vibraphone added luscious layers of sophistication: the speed of the vibrations could be varied and a sustain pedal controlled the length of the notes. Another incarnation is the tubaphone, which has metal tubes rather than bars, creating a softer sound.

The jazz world has produced the largest crop of virtuoso vibraphone players, most using a pair of mallets per hand, allowing them to play chords.

STRINGS
Double Bass
The double bass was for a long time no more than a reinforcement at the foot of orchestral string arrangements, often merely echoing the cello part. It was rarely given a chance to shine by classical composers, but thanks to jazz the double bass found its voice with a vengeance, and was free to come out of the twilight into the limelight – even helping to kick off rock'n'roll on early Elvis tracks like 'That's All Right (Mama)'.

The double bass is available in a number of sizes: for orchestral work the three-quarter size is more common than the awkward full-size version. Lower metal strings on the bass are not far off the consistency of steel hawsers, and bass players'

fingers are usually topped off by calluses. In jazz settings the bass is generally plucked rather than bowed, whereas in orchestral settings it is the other way around. Jazz players are sometimes amplified to compete with the volume of the other instruments.

WIND
Mouth Organ
The arrival of the Chinese sheng in Europe in the eighteenth century encouraged a great deal of experimentation with free-reed instruments in the early nineteenth century. One of the most popular was produced by Friedrich Buschmann of Berlin in 1821; this was the Mundäoline, now known as the mouth organ or harmonica.

From the early twentieth century, the instrument was adopted by folk and blues musicians, particularly in the US. Blues players gave it the name 'harp' and could create powerful effects by altering the shape of the mouth, making the instrument shriek and moan or even imitate a rhythmic train.

Inside the mouth organ, free metal reeds are set in slots in a small, metal-enclosed wooden frame. The notes are sounded by alternately blowing and sucking through two parallel rows of wind channels. The reeds are positioned so they respond to alternate directions of wind flow. The tongue covers channels not required. In chromatic (12-note scale) models, a finger-operated stop alternates between two sets of reeds tuned a semitone apart. They can range from two to four octaves in compass, and bass models are also played.

see Roots Sources & Sounds pp 14   see The Fifties Sources & Sounds pp 32

Right
Bill Black was a rock solid bass player in the tight band (with Scotty Moore's nifty guitarwork) that backed Elvis Presley.

Right
In the right hands, the harmonica is a powerful, soulful and expressive instrument.

Clarinet

Like saxophones, clarinets cover the musical range from the E-flat sopranino to the B-flat contrabass, but it is the B-flat soprano that is most commonly used by jazz musicians. The clarinet was the dominant woodwind in jazz until it was supplanted by the saxophone in the 1930s; however the instrument remained in the forefront because of its use by high-profile players such as Benny Goodman, Artie Shaw and Buddy DeFranco. Jimmy Giuffre and John Carter used the clarinet in more modern types of improvized music, and Anthony Braxton, Marty Ehrlich and Don Byron have ensured that it remains a highly contemporary instrument.

BLUEGRASS, COUNTRY & FOLK

These genres of music are associated with simplicity, and the instruments used have seen periods of popularity and decline. Here are some of the enduring favourites.

KEYBOARDS
Piano

A popular nineteenth-century parlour instrument in the USA, pianos have been present in country music from its inception. Old-time string bands often relied on piano for its bright rhythmic and percussive tonalities. The advent of Western-swing music in the south western USA in the early 1930s also gave rise to influential country piano players such as Al Stricklin, who played with Bob Wills And His Texas Playboys, and Moon Mullican, a member of Cliff Bruner's band and later a solo artist and Grand Ole Opry member.

Beginning in the early 1950s, piano thumper Del Wood was also a long-time favourite on The Grand Ole Opry. During that same decade, session pianist Harold Bradley enlivened many Nashville recording sessions. And in the 1960s and 1970s, Floyd Cramer played on hundreds of Nashville sessions, had several instrumental solo hits and developed a distinct 'slip-note' style that became almost synonymous with the Nashville Sound. Hargus 'Pig' Robbins was Nashville's most celebrated keyboardist in the 1970s and 1980s. Jerry Lee Lewis, Charlie Rich, Ronnie Milsap, Mickey Gilley and Gary Stewart are among the popular recording artists of the 1960s, 1970s and 1980s who accompanied themselves on piano rather than guitar.

STRINGS
Acoustic Guitar

Throughout its history, the guitar has – perhaps more than any other instrument – managed to bridge the gap between the often disconnected worlds of classical, folk and popular music. Its roots go back to Babylonian times; by the 1500s it was prevalent in Spain, and is still sometimes called the Spanish guitar.

Medieval versions – like the lute – sometimes sported rounded backs and paired strings: the 12-string guitar still exists (as heard on The Byrds' 'Mr Tambourine Man'). The standardized modern acoustic guitar has a flat back and sound board with a pronounced curved 'waist' to the body.

The acoustic guitar remained relatively unchanged until the twentieth century, when additions included steel strings for greater attack in dance-band settings, where it took over from the banjo. This marked the beginning of the guitar's rise to a major role in popular music, leading directly to the development of the semi-acoustic and fully electric versions.

Banjo

The banjo is a refinement of an instrument brought to the Americas by slaves from West Africa. Banjos were often used in early twentieth-century minstrel and vaudeville shows, but more as a comic prop than a serious musical instrument.

After the banjo's arrival in the New World, it accompanied spirituals, and thence became a regular ingredient in the Black Minstrel (and white pseudo-Minstrel) movement. In turn this led to its involvement in traditional Dixieland jazz; in the 1940s Bill Monroe introduced it to bluegrass music, from where it found its way into the 1970s country rock sound. More recently it made a return to mainstream country in The Dixie Chicks' line-up, as played by Emily Robinson. The banjo also features in the music of countries such as Malawi and Morocco.

Dobro

The dobro has often served as a bluesy supplement or substitute to the pedal steel guitar in country music. The dobro was invented in 1926 by the Dopyera brothers, who were experimenting with mechanically amplifying the acoustic guitar. The dobro was first established in country music by Cliff Carlisle, who played the instrument on some of Jimmie Rodgers' recording sessions in the late 1920s, and by Roy Acuff, the Grand Ole Opry headliner who featured dobro-players in his band during the 1930s and 1940s. It was Burkett 'Uncle Josh' Graves who largely redefined the dobro as both a lead and rhythmic instrument in bluegrass during the early 1950s when he played dobro with Flatt And Scruggs, a definitive 1950s bluegrass ensemble.

Fiddle

This ancient instrument has been popular in the USA since Colonial times and has always been at the centre of country music. In the early 1920s, the very first country records were made by old-time fiddlers John Carson and Eck Robertson.

In the 1920s and 1930s Bob Wills and other pioneers of Western-swing music in the south western USA made the fiddle (often two fiddles playing in unison, named 'twin fiddle') an essential ingredient of their sophisticated music. The fiddle was also front and centre in honky-tonk music as it emerged full-blown in the late 1940s and early 1950s. In the late 1940s, Kentuckian Bill Monroe also enlarged the fiddle's influence by making it as crucial to bluegrass music as it had been in bluegrass' antecedent, mountain string-band music.

Left and Below

Instruments on this page are a banjo (left), ovation stage guitar (bottom left) and a dobro using the resonator sound box (below).

see Moon Mullican pp 23   see Bob Wills pp 30   see Jerry Lee Lewis pp 66   see The Byrds pp 126

442

Mandolin

An off-shoot of the lute, the mandolin assumed its present-day eight-string form in early eighteenth-century Italy. The Gibson Guitar Company's early 1920s introduction of the F-series mandolin, with its enhanced tone and volume, laid the groundwork for the mandolin's rise in traditional country and bluegrass music. It was Kentucky-born Bill Monroe, often lauded as 'the father of bluegrass music', who thrust the mandolin to the forefront as a rhythmic and lead instrument when he began accompanying himself with mandolin on the Grand Ole Opry. Monroe's universally imitated, aggressive, chopping rhythmic style and flurry-like lead picking set the standards followed by more recent bluegrass mandolin virtuosos – Jesse McReynolds, Bobby Osborne, David Grisman, John Duffey and Ricky Skaggs, among them.

Pedal Steel Guitar

The modern pedal steel guitar first appeared in the late 1930s. It was the invention of Alvino Rey, a musician who invented the pedal steel as a radical enhancement of the non-pedal, lap steel guitars popular during the 1920s. The addition of pedals allowed for smooth modulation of both chords and individual strings. Speedy West, a California steel player, pioneered the pedal steel in country music using his custom-designed, three-neck, four-pedal instrument on many West Coast country recordings. Nashville session player Bud Isaacs raised the pedal steel's profile higher and inspired numerous imitators when he featured the instrument on the 1954 Webb Pierce hit, 'Slowly'. Pete Drake, Buddy Emmons, Shot Jackson, Ralph Mooney and Lloyd Green were also widely acknowledged masters of the pedal steel.

Above

A modern, Gibson-made flat back mandolin.

OTHER INSTRUMENTS

The variety of instruments used in rock, pop, funk, soul, blues, jazz, country, bluegrass and folk is staggering. The instruments already mentioned are those that are in most common use in these styles of music; there are many more, however, that are used by artists wishing to add another dimension to their playing. These are just some of those.

STRINGS
Sitar

To Western ears the sitar became the quintessential sound of Indian music following its somewhat faddish promotion by The Beatles (through their collaboration with Ravi Shankar), The Rolling Stones and Traffic in the late 1960s – though its haunting sound has been a central part of Indian classical music for centuries. Played in the lotus position, the sitar forms part of the classical Indian group, including the tabla, sarangi (a cello-like instrument) and shahnai (a relation of the oboe). Together they work around the complex improvised patterns of the raga, still alien to Western audiences: at the Concert for Bangladesh in 1971, Ravi Shankar received a rapturous ovation after several minutes, only to explain that he had in fact just been tuning up.

Right

The massed sound of steel drums can be heard in much of the music from the West Indies, its distinctive treble sound evoking the wind and the smells of the ocean.

Ukulele

The ukulele, identified so closely with Hawaii, arrived on the island literally out of the blue, on a boat that arrived in Honolulu in 1879. One of the passengers produced a 'braguinha' (a small Portuguese guitar) and the locals were smitten, adopting the instrument and calling it after a Polynesian word for a jumping flea – maybe referring to the movements of the player's fingers.

The tiny body of the braguinha was slightly enlarged – though not by much – and was strung with gut rather than steel. The native koa, an acacia, provided wood for the body. The versatile, and portable, ukulele was promoted by the Hawaiian royal family (one of whom wrote the classic 'Aloha Oe'), and then unleashed in the US after Hawaii took a stand at a San Francisco exposition in 1915. As things from the South Pacific came into vogue following the Second World War, the instrument enjoyed another burst of popularity, particularly led by Arthur Godfrey, who performed on a cheap plastic version. British audiences associate the ukulele with the toothy, winsome George 'When I'm Cleaning Windows' Formby, although he most often used a banjulele, a cross between the banjo and the ukulele.

PERCUSSION
Gong

The gong has played an important role in the theatre and in religious ceremonies – particularly in the Far East and Central Asia, where it is believed to have originated; in Malaysia gongs were long considered a valuable part of any dowry.

Essentially a large round dish of metal with an upturned edge, often with a raised boss at its centre, the gong is hit with a padded drumstick or beater, the heavier the better to build its crescendo of sound. In the classical orchestra, the instrument – about 100 cm in diameter, with a hammered surface and suspended from a frame – is technically called the 'tam-tam'.

Steel Drums

The steel drum or steelpan is a relatively recent addition to the ranks of percussion instruments. It was first created in Trinidad in the 1930s and 1940s, when a plentiful supply of 45-gallon oil drums was available; and it was found that they could be sliced in half, turned upside down and tuned. Creating a finished steel drum involves cutting the pans to size, sinking down the main pan with a sledge-hammer, defining the areas for up to 30 different notes with compass, chalk, hammer and punch, and then hammering each note back up to form a low dome. Each note is carefully tuned – usually by ear. Finally the drum is tempered and painted, or electroplated, ready for players to use sticks with rubber tips.

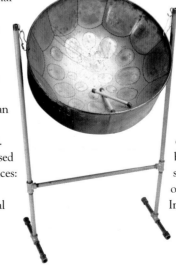

A complete range of drums form families, either called after choir voices (treble, alto, bass) or traditional instruments (guitar, cello) supported by a rhythm section. The steel orchestra, particularly in the major West Indian carnivals, can require anywhere up to 100 performers, producing a significantly uplifting volume of sound.

see The Fifties Sources & Sounds pp 34   see The Sixties Sources & Sounds pp 78

Acknowledgments

PICTURE CREDITS

Arbiter Group plc: 441 (m)

K. Billett: 433 (mr), 439 (bl).

Dorling Kindersley Ltd: 433 (tr); 441 (r)

Foundry Arts: 14 (tl), 18 (tl), 34 (t), 38 (tl), 42 (tl), 46 (tl), 48 (tl), 52 (tl), 50 (tl), 56 (tl), 74 (tl), 78 (tl), 88 (tl), 92 (tl), 94 (tl), 96 (tl), 100 (tl), 102 (tl), 120 (tl), 126 (m), 136 (tl), 134 (tl), 130 (tl), 132 (tl), 154 (tl), 156 (tl), 158 (tl), 160 (tl), 162 (tl), 166 (tl), 182 (tl), 186 (tl), 196 (tl), 198 (tl), 200 (tl), 204 (tl), 208 (tl), 210 (tl), 228 (tl), 230 (tl), 232 (tl), 234 (tl), 236 (tl), 248 (tl), 250 (tl), 252 (tl), 254 (tl), 256 (tl), 266 (tl), 270 (tl), 274 (tl), 276 (tl), 278 (tl), 280 (tl), 282 (tl), 284 (tl), 286 (tl), 324 (tl), 328 (tl), 332 (tl), 334 (tl), 336 (tl), 338 (tl), 340 (tl), 372 (tl), 376 (tl), 380 (tl), 384 (tl), 386 (tl), 390 (tl), 418 (tl), 432, 433, 434 (b), 435 (t), 436 (all), 437 (all), 438 (all), 439 (br), 440 (m), 440 (m),
441 (br), 442 (m)

Hobgoblin Music: 433 (tr), 442 (l)

Lebrecht: 435 (br)

With grateful thanks to **Redferns** and the following list of photographers: Richard E Aaron: 190, 196 (m), 199, 202, 213 (tl), 219 (l), 223, 225 (r), 228 (m), 230 (b), 237 (t), 237 (b), 254 (m), 255, 257 (tl), 265 (tl), 276 (m), 284 (m); Cyrus Andrews: 44, 94 (m), 102 (m), 105 (t), 147 (br), 167, 174, 175, 177; Jorgen Angel: 203, 205, 210 (m), 216, 217, 252 (m); Chet Atkins: 56 (b); BBC Photo Library: 20 (r), 51, 186 (m), 187 (t), 256 (b), 259 (tl), 262 (t), 286 (b), 293 (t), 294, 323, 425; Belgium: 406; Paul Bergen: 334 (m), 342 (l), 350 (bl), 351 (b), 354 (l), 361 (b), 393, 399 (b), 402 (t), 404, 407 (l), 409 (tl), 410 (bl), 412, 414 (l); Sue Bradshaw: 336 (m); Britton Barney: 417 (b); Brandon Carey: 389, 405 (b), 415 (r), 431; Fin Costello: 146 (tl), 151 (tl), 193 (l), 208 (b), 210 (br), 215, 220, 221, 222, 224, 225 (tl), 234 (m), 245, 295 (bl), 295 (tr), 302, 306 (tl), 308 (r), 321; Nigel Crane: 384 (m); Pete Cronin: 305, 315 (b); Deltahaze Corporation: 22; Ian Dickson: 24, 193 (r), 201, 250 (m), 257 (b), 259 (br), 260, 264, 311 (br), 337, 352; Earle Steve: 348 (br); Erica Echenberg: 191 (b), 263, 265 (br), 309; EMI Archives: 149; David Farrell: 88 (m), 105 (br), 122; Max Jones Files: 14; Tabatha Fireman: 367 (l), 392 (tl), 417 (t); Jeremy Fletcher: 78 (b); 369 (ml); Patrick Ford: 369 (br), 371 (tl), 371 (br), 402 (bl), 328 (b); Colin Fuller: 424 (r); Gab Archives: 42 (b), 80 (b), 289 (br), 315 (tl), 317, 426; Ross Gilmore: 396 (br), 401 (r); Mick Gold: 189 (tr); Harry Goodwin: 104, 110 (bl), 209, 233, 235; Caroline Greville: 273 (tr); Richi Havens: 142 (tl); Richi Howell: 58; Steve Hurrell: 272; Mick Hutson: 304, 329 (br), 331 (tl), 332 (m), 333, 335, 338 (m), 339, 340 (lm), 340 (br), 343 (br), 344, 345 (tl), 346, 349, 353, 355 (br), 356 (tl), 357 (l), 357 (r), 358, 363 (t), 363 (b), 364 (l), 365 (tl), 370, 377 (tl), 380 (b), 386 (m), 395; Salifu Idriss: 330; JM/Enternational: 399 (t); Ivan Keeman: 91, 109 (tl), 109 (br), 150 (t); Bob King: 280 (m), 287 (t), 347 (tl), 364 (r), 376 (m), 300 (bl); Irve Kline: 17 (b); Elliot Landy: 42 (tr), 82 (br), 329 (tr); Michael Linssen: 369 (t), 427, 429 (t); Graham Lowe: 187 (b); Hayley Madden: 387, 400, 403 (br); Harry Malone: 413 (br); Manfred Mann: 111; Michael Ochs Archive: 15 (t), 16, 19 (tl), 19 (r), 20 (tl), 21, 23 (tl), 23 (bl), 27, 28 (br), 34 (m), 34 (b), 35 (tl), 35 (b), 37 (tl), 37 (b), 38 (b), 39, 40, 42 (b), 43, 46 (b), 47, 48 (b), 49, 50 (b), 52 (b), 54, 53, 55, 57 (tl), 57 (br), 59, 60, 61(l), 61(r), 62 (tl), 63, 64 (tl), 64 (br), 65, 66 (bl), 67, 68 (tl), 68 (br), 69 (l), 70 (br), 70 (tl), 71, 72 (br), 73, 79, 80 (t), 82 (tl), 83, 84, 92 (m), 96 (b), 101, 113 (b), 114 (tl), 117 (r), 120 (m), 121, 123, 124, 126 (m), 127, 129,
130 (m), 131, 132 (m), 134 (m), 133, 135 ,137 (bl), 138 (t), 138 (br), 139, 140, 143 (tr), 143 (b), 144, 146 (r), 147 (tl), 148, 158 (m), 159, 160 (m), 161, 166 (m), 168 (tr), 169, 171, 173 (tl), 173 (br), 178 (tl), 178 (b), 181 (tl), 181 (r), 189 (bl), 190 (t), 197, 198 (m), 204 (m), 211, 213 (b), 231, 238, 242, 244 (b), 262 (br), 282 (b), 378 (tl), 422, 423; Steve Morely: 207, 218 (l), 218 (r); Leon Morris: 289 (tr); Museum of London: 271 (tl); Niemeier Petra: 112, 116, 117 (l), 229; Pakvis Peter: 368, 381, 391 (l), 409 (r); Don Paulsen: 125, 141 (br), 154 (m), 165, 170 (br), 176, 179, 180 (r); Jan Persson: 15 (b), 93, 100 (m), 107 (tl), 128, 141 (tl), 150 (bl); Martin Philbey: 361 (t), 394 (l), 397, 394 (r), 405 (t), 407 (r); Jeff Price: 378 (b); Mike Prior: 240 (b); Andrew Putler: 212; Christina Radish: 354 (r), 359 (tl), 385, 390 (m), 401 (l), 413 (tl); RB: 26, 72 (tl), 115, 142 (r), 180 (l), 241; David Redfern: 25, 29, 41, 66 (tr), 89, 90, 97, 98, 99, 95, 103 (bl), 103 (tr), 106 (tl), 106 (br), 107 (br), 110 (tr), 113 (tl), 136 (m), 145, 151 (br), 155, 156 (m), 157, 162 (m), 163, 168 (bl), 170 (tl), 172, 200 (b), 206, 226, 239 (l), 243 (t), 244, 288, 292, 297, 298 (br), 319 (tl), 348 (tl), 424 (l); Rick Richards: 36, Adam Ritchie: 78 (m); Simon Ritter: 341, 345 (r), 360, 366; Ebet Roberts: 137 (t), 188, 192, 236 (m), 248 (m), 255, 258, 270 (b), 271 (br), 274 (b), 275, 277, 278 (b), 279, 281, 283, 287 (b), 289 (l), 290 (l), 290 (r), 293 (b), 296 (l), 296 (r), 298 (t), 299, 300 (tr), 301, 303 (l), 303 (r), 308 (l), 310, 311 (tl), 313 (l), 313 (r), 314, 319 (b), 320, 322 (r), 351 (t), 356 (bl), 362 (t), 367 (r), 428; Kerstin Rodgers: 318; Lex Van Rossen: 249, 251, 430; Bill Rouda: 17 (t); Gerrit Schilp: 18 (b); Jim Sharpe: 331 (br), 379, 411, 415 (l); June Sharpe: 403 (tl); Nicky J. Simms: 350 (m), 355 (tl), 382 (m), 383, 410 (t), 416; Barbara Steinwhe: 343, 347 (br), 365 (br); Peter Still: 291; John Super: 388, 391 (r), 392 (r), 408; Gai Terrell: 28 (tl), 45; Virginia Turbett: 273 (bl), 312, 316; Michael Uhll: 306 (b); Rob Verhorst: 285, 307, 322 (l), 396 (tl), 398; Vincett Robert: 62 (br), 69 (br), 114 (bl); David Warner Ellis: 164, 214, 219 (r), 239 (tr), 240 (t), 261; Des Willie: 359 (br), 362 (b), 429 (b); Gunter Zint: 108

Topham Picturepoint: 81, 232 (m), 377 (b)

AUTHOR BIOGRAPHIES

Michael Heatley (General Editor; Chapter Openers; Sources & Sounds)
Michael Heatley edited the acclaimed *History of Rock* partwork (1981–84). He is the author of over 50 music biographies, ranging from Bon Jovi to Rolf Harris as well as books on sport and TV. He has penned liner notes to more than 100 CD reissues, and written for magazines including *Music Week, Billboard, Goldmine, Radio Times* and *The Mail on Sunday* colour supplement.

Scotty Moore (Foreword)
Winfield S. Moore III, better known as Scotty, started to learn guitar aged eight. After a stint in the US Navy he began playing around Memphis and hooked up with Sam Phillips at Sun Studios, where he also met Elvis Presley in July 1954. Moore became Elvis's guitarist and accompanied him for the next 14 years. He also became a well-respected studio engineer in Memphis and then Nashville, where he ran his own Music City Recorders studio. After his 1964 album, *The Guitar That Changed The World!*, he essentially hung up his axe, only to be persuaded back into playing by his old friend, Carl Perkins. In 1992 he returned to live performance with other Sun alumni and Elvis's favoured vocal backing group, The Jordanaires. In 1997 he released *All The King's Men*, with guest appearances from the likes of Keith Richards, Jeff Beck and Levon Helm of The Band. In 2000 he was inducted into the Rock And Roll Hall Of Fame. In 2005 *A Tribute To The King* was issued. Recorded at Abbey Road, it featured contributions from, amongst others, Mark Knopfler, Eric Clapton and Dave Gilmour. Scotty records and tours to this day.

Richard Buskin (Sixties Key Artists: UK Rock and US Rock)
Richard Buskin is the *New York Times* best-selling author of more than a dozen books on subjects ranging from record production, The Beatles and Sheryl Crow to Princess Diana, Phyllis Diller and Marilyn Monroe. His articles have appeared in newspapers such as the *New York Post, The Sydney Morning Herald, The Observer* and *The Independent*, and he also writes features and reviews for music magazines around the world. A native of London, England, he lives in Chicago.

Alan Clayson (Sixties A–Z of Artists: UK Rock and US Rock)
Musician and composer Alan Clayson has written over 30 books on musical subjects. These include the best-sellers *Backbeat: Stuart Sutcliffe - The Lost Beatle* (subject of a major film), *The Yardbirds* and *The Beatles* boxes. Moreover, as well as leading the legendary Clayson and The Argonauts, who reformed recently, his solo stage act also defies succinct description. For further information, please investigate www.alanclayson.com.

Joe Cushley (Fifties Key Artists; Eighties A–Z of Artists)
Joe Cushley has written extensively for *Mojo, Q* and *Uncut* and contributed to several books on music, including *The Rough Guide To The Beatles* and *The Mojo Collection*. He compiles albums for Union Square Music, including the acclaimed *Balling The Jack, Beyond Mississippi* and *Definitive Story of CBGB* collections. He is a respected DJ and presents a regular show on London's Resonance FM. Joe is currently Theatre and Books Editor of *What's On In London* magazine.

Rusty Cutchin (Roots)
Rusty Cutchin has been a musician, recording engineer, producer, and journalist for over 25 years. He began his journalism career in New York as editor of *Cashbox*, the music-business trade magazine. Cutchin has been Technical Editor of *Guitar One* magazine, Associate Editor of *Electronic Musician* magazine, and Editor in Chief of *Home Recording Magazine*. As a recording engineer he has worked on records by artists such as Mariah Carey, Richie Sambora, Yoko Ono, C&C Music Factory, and Queen Latifah. Most recently he has been a consulting editor and contributor to several books on home recording, guitar and music history.

Jason Draper (One-Hit Wonders)
Jason Draper is the Reviews Editor at *Record Collector*, the monthly music magazine dedicated to collecting music of all genres and on all formats. He has also written for *Uncut, Metal Hammer, Sound Nation, Big Issue Cymru* and *Buzz* magazines.

Hugh Fielder (Seventies Key Artists; Eighties Key Artists: Bon Jovi, Michael Jackson, Prince)
Hugh Fielder can remember the 1960s even though he was there. He can remember the 1970s and 1980s because he was at *Sounds* magazine (RIP) and the 1990s because he was editor of Tower Records' *TOP* magazine. He has shared a spliff with Bob Marley, a glass of wine with David Gilmour, a pint with Robert Plant, a cup of tea with Keith Richards and a frosty stare with Axl Rose. He has watched Mike Oldfield strip naked in front of him and Bobby Womack fall asleep while he was interviewing him.

Mike Gent (Seventies A–Z of Artists; Eighties Key Artists: Madonna, The Police, U2)
Nurturing an obsession with pop music which dates back to first hearing Slade's 'Gudbuy T'Jane' in 1972, Mike Gent remains fixated, despite failing to master any musical instrument, with the possible exception of the recorder. A freelance writer since 2001, he has contributed to *Writers' Forum, Book and Magazine Collector, Record Buyer, When Saturday Comes, Inside David Bowie and the Spiders* (DVD), *The Beatles 1962–1970* (DVD), Green Umbrella's *Decades* and *The Little Book of the World Cup*. Fascinated by the decade that gave the world glam, prog and punk rock, he is working on a novel set in the Seventies.

Jake Kennedy (Noughties)
Jake Kennedy is a music journalist from west London. He worked at *Record Collector* for seven years, where he was Reviews Editor. He is the author of *Joy Division & The Making Of Unknown Pleasures*. He writes for numerous magazines and fanzines, and has been a correspondent for Radio 1, BBC 6 and *NME*. He has contributed to Colin Larkin's *Encyclopedia of Popular Music* and the *1001 Albums You Must Hear Before You Die* volume. He is married but never wants kids.

Colin Salter (Sixties Soul)
Since he bought his first single – 'Reach Out I'll Be There' by The Four Tops in 1966 – Colin Salter has spent a life in music as composer, performer, promoter and researcher. His first performance, as panto dame singing ABBA and Supertramp hits in 1975, was succeeded by stints in a Glasgow punk band, a Humberside jazz-folk group and a Kendal jam collective. He worked in theatre for 15 years as a sound engineer and writer of ambient soundtracks. Since 2003 he has been developing a live-music network in rural Cumbria. He moonlights as a golden-oldies mobile DJ.

Ian Shirley (Nineties)
Ian Shirley lived and pogoed his way through British punk rock and has been buying records and watching bands ever since. He is an experienced music journalist whose feature work and reviews appear in respected magazines like *Record Collector* and *Mojo*. He was written the biographies of Bauhaus, and The Residents as well as two science-fiction novels. He has also written the definitive tome on the links between comics and music: *Can Rock And Roll Save The World*. He is currently the editor of *Record Collector's Rare Record Price Guide* and has a collection of over 2,000 vinyl albums and 5,000 CDs.

John Tobler (Fifties A–Z of Artists)
John Tobler has been writing about popular music since the late 1960s, during which time he has written books on ABBA, The Beach Boys, The Beatles, Elton John, Elvis Presley, Cliff Richard and several generic titles. He has written for numerous magazines including *ZigZag, Billboard, Music Week, Melody Maker, NME, Sounds, Country Music People* and *Folk Roots*. He has written literally thousands of sleeve notes.

Resources

FURTHER READING

Abbott, Kingsley (ed.), *Calling Out Around the World: A Motown Reader*, Helter Skelter Publishing, London, 2000

Ancelet. Barry Jean, *Cajun and Creole Music Makers*, University Press of Mississippi, Mississippi, 1999

Asbjornsen, Dag Erik, *Scented Gardens of the Mind: A Comprehensive Guide to the Golden Era of Progressive Rock: 1968–1980*, Borderline Productions, New York, 2001

Azerrad, Michael, *Our Band Could Be Your Life: Scenes from the American India Underground 1981–1991*, Little Brown & Company, New York, 2001

Bane, Michael, *The Outlaws: Revolution in Country Music*, Country Music Magazine/Doubleday/Dolphin, New York, 1978

Barr, Tim, *Rough Guide to Techno*, Rough Guide, London, 2000

Barr, Tim, *The Mini Rough Guide To Techno Music*, Rough Guides, London, 2000

Barrett, Leonard, *Rastafarians*, Beacon Press, Boston, 1997

Barrow, Steve and Dalton, Peter, *The Rough Guide To Reggae*, Rough Guides, London, 1997

Bascom, William R. and Herskovits, Melville J., *Continuity And Change In African Cultures*, University of Chicago Press, Chicago, 1962

Belle-Fortune, Brian, et al, *All Crew Muss Big Up: Some Journeys Through Jungle, Drum and Bass Culture*, London, 1999

Bennett, Joe et al, *Guitar Facts*, Flame Tree Publishing, London, 2002

Bidder, Sean, *Pump Up The Volume*, Channel 4 Books, London, 2001

Bidder, Sean, *Rough Guide to House*, Rough Guides, London, 1999

Billboard Guide to American Rock and Roll, Billboard Books, New York, 1997

Blesh, Rubi and Janis, Harriet, *They All Played Ragtime*, Oak Publishers, 1950

Blumenthal, Howard J., *The World Music CD Listener's Guide*, Billboard Books, New York, 1998

Blush, Steven, *American Hardcore: A Tribal History*, Feral House, 2001

Bogdanov, Vladimir (ed.), *All Music Guide to Electronica: The Definitive Guide to Electronic Music*, Backbeat Books, San Francisco, 2001

Bogdanov, Vladimir (ed.), *All Music Guide to the Blues: The Definitive Guide to the Blues*, Backbeat, London, 2003

Bogdanov, Vladimir (ed.), et al, *All Music Guide to Rock*, Backbeat, London, 2002

Bohlman, Philip V., *World Music: A Very Short Introduction*, Oxford Paperbacks, Oxford, 2002

Boyer, Horace Clarence, et al, *The Golden Age Of Gospel*, University of Illinois Press, Chicago, 2000

Bradley, Lloyd and Morris, Dennis, *Reggae: The Story Of Jamaican Music*, BBC Books, London, 2002

Bradley, Lloyd, *Bass Culture: When Reggae Was King*, Penguin, London, 2001

Brend, Mark, *American Troubadors: Groundbreaking Singer-Songwriters of the 60s*, Backbeat Books, San Francisco, 2001

Brewser, Bill, and Broughton, Frank, *Last Night a DJ Saved My Life*, Headline, London, 1999

Broughton, Simon (ed.), *World Music 100 Essential CDs: The Rough Guide*, Rough Guides, London, 2000

Broughton, Viv, *Black Gospel: Illustrated History of Gospel*, Blandford Press, Poole, 1985

Buskin, Richard, *Inside Tracks: A First-Hand History of Popular Music from the World's Greatest Record Producers and Engineers*, Avon, 1999

Byworth, Tony (ed.), *The Billboard Illustrated Encyclopedia of Country Music*, Billboard Books, New York, 2006

Byworth, Tony (ed.), *The Illustrated Encyclopedia of Country Music*, Flame Tree Publishing, London, 2006

Cantwell, Robert, *When We Were Good: The Folk Revival*, Harvard University Press, Harvard, 1996

Carr, Ian, *Miles Davis*, HarperCollins, New York, 1999 (new edition)

Carr, Ian, *The Rough Guide to Jazz*, Rough Guides, London, 2000

Carr, Roy, and Farren, Mick, *Elvis: The Complete Illustrated Record*, Eel Pie, London, 1982

Castro, Roy, *Bossa Nova: The Story of the Brazilian Music that Seduced The World*, A Cappella, Chicago, 2000

Chalfont, Henry and Prigoff, James, *Spraycan Art* Thames and Hudson, London, 1991

Charters, Samuel B., *The Blues Makers*, Da Capo Press, Maryland, 1991

Charters, Samuel B., *The Country Blues*, Da Capo Press, Maryland, 1959

Charters, Samuel, *Sweet As The Showers Of Rain*, Oak Publications, 1977

Chilton, John, *Let The Good Times Roll: The Story of Louis Jordan & His Music*, University of Michigan Press, 1997

Christe, Ian, *The Sound of the Beast: The Complete Headbanging History of Heavy Metal*, William Morrow, New York, 2003

Clancy, Liam, *Liam Clancy: Memoirs of an Irish Troubadour*, Virgin Books, London, 2003

Cohen, Ronald (ed.), *Alan Lomax: Selected Writings, 1934–1997*, Routledge, New York, 2003

Cohn, Nik, *Awopbopaloobopalopbamboom: The Golden Age of Rock*, Grove Press, New York, 2003

Cole, Richard, and Trubo, Richard, *Stairway to Heaven: Led Zeppelin Uncensored*, HarperEntertainment, New York, 2000

Collin, Matthew and Godfrey, John, *Altered State: The Story of Ecstasy Culture and Acid House*, Serpent's Tail, London, 1998

Cooper, Kim, *Bubblegum Music is the Naked Truth*, Feral House, 2001

Country Music Magazine (bi-monthly magazine), Nashville, Tennessee

Cuscuna, Michael and Lourie, Charlie, *The Blue Note Years*, Rizzoli, New York, 1995

Cusic, Don, *The Sound of Light: A History of Gospel and Christian Music*, Hal Leonard Publishing, Miami, 2002

Dance, Stanley, *The World of Swing*, Da Capo Press, Maryland, 1974

Davis, Stephen, *Bob Marley: Conquering Lion Of Reggae*, Plexus, London, 1993

De Koningh, Michael and Cane-Honeysett, Laurence, *Young, Gifted and Black: the Story of Trojan Records*, Sanctuary Publishing, London, 2003

Deffaa, Chip, *Traditionalists & Revivalists in Jazz*, Scarecrow Press, Maryland, 1993

Dixon, Willie, with Snowden, Don, *I Am The Blues: The Willie Dixon Story*, Da Capo Press, Maryland, 1989

DJ magazine, 1993–2003

Du Noyer, Paul (ed.), *The Billboard Illustrated Encyclopedia of Music*, Billboard Books, New York, 2003

Du Noyer, Paul (ed.), *The Illustrated Encyclopedia of Music*, Flame Tree Publishing, London, 2003

Duckworth, William, *Talking Music: Conversations with John Cage, Philip Glass, Laurie Anderson, and Five generations of American Experimental Composers*, Da Capo Press, Maryland, 1999

Ellinham, Mark, *The Rough Guide to Rock*, Rough Guides, London, 1996

Eno, Brian and Nyman, Michael, *Experimental Music: Cage and Beyond*, Cambridge University Press, Cambridge, 1999

Eno, Brian, *A Year with Swollen Appendices: the Diary of Brian Eno*, Faber and Faber, London, 1995

Erlewine, Michael et al (ed.), *All Music Guide To The Blues*, Backbeat, London, 1996

Escott, Colin, with Hawkins, Martin, *Good Rockin' Tonight: Sun Records and the Birth of Rock 'n' Roll*, St. Martin's Press, New York, 1992

Eyre, Banning, *In Griot Time: An American Guitarist in Mali*, Serpent's Tail, London, 2002

Ferris, William, *Blues From The Delta*, Anchor Press/Doubleday, New York, 1978

Fong-Torres, Ben, *The Hits Just Keep On Coming: The History of Top 40 Radio*, Backbeat Books, San Francisco, 2001

Fox, Ted, *In the Groove*, St. Martins Press, New York, 1986

Franklin, Aretha, and Ritz, David, *Aretha: From These Roots*, Villard Books, New York, 1998

Fricke, Jim, Ahearn Charlie, Nelson, George *Yes, Yes, Y'all: The Experience Music Project Oral History of Hip Hop: The First Decade*, Perseus Press, London, 2002

From Where I Stand: The Black Experience In Country Music (annotated CD collection) Country Music Foundation/Warner Bros. Records, 1998

FRoots magazine

Gaillard, Frye, *Watermelon Wine: The Spirit of Country Music*, St. Martin's, New York, 1978

Garratt, Sheryl, *Adventures In Wonderland: a Decade of Club Culture*, Headline, London, 1999

Gassen, Timothy, *The Knights Of Fuzz*, Borderline Productions, Columbia, 1996

George, Nelson, *Hip Hop America*, Penguin, London, 2000

George-Warren, Holly, et al, *The Rolling Stone Encyclopedia of Rock & Roll*, Fireside, New York, 2001

Giddins, Gary, *Celebrating Bird: The Triumph Of Charlie Parker*, Beechtree Books, New York, 1987

Gillespie, Dizzy and Fraser, Al, *To Be Or Not To Bop: Memoirs, The Autobiography Of Dizzy Gillespie*, Doubleday, New York, 1979

Gillet, Charlie, *The Sound of the City*, Da Capo Press, Maryland, 1996

Gitler, Ira, *Jazz Masters Of The Forties*, Da Capo Press, Maryland, 1966

Goff, James R. Jr., *Close Harmony: A History of Southern Gospel*, The University of North Carolina Press, 2002

Goggin, Jim and Clute, Peter, *The Great Jazz Revival: A Pictorial Celebration of Traditional Jazz*, Donna Ewald Publishing, 1994

Goldberg, Joe, *Jazz Masters Of The Fifties*, Da Capo Press, Maryland, 1965

Graff, Gary, and Durchholz, Daniel, *MusicHound Rock: The Essential Album Guide*, Gale, 1998

Gray, Michael, *Song and Dance Man III: The Art of Bob Dylan*, Continuum International Publishing Group, New York, 1999

Griffith, Nanci, and Jackson, Joe, *Nanci Griffith's Other Voices: A Personal History of Folk Music (Come From the Heart)*, Amber Waves, Maidstone, 1998

Grissim, John, *Country Music: White Man's Blues*, Paperback Library, New York, 1970

Gunst, Laurie, *Born Fi Dead: A Journey Through The Jamaican Posse Underground*, Payback Press, Edinburgh, 1999

Guralnick, Peter, *Sweet Soul Music – Rhythm and Blues and the Southern Dream of Freedom*, Mojo Books, London, 2002

Guthrie, Woody, *Bound For Glory*, Peter Smith Publisher Inc., 1985

Hagan, Chet, *The Grand Ole Opry*, Henry Holt, New York, 1989

Harper, Colin, *Dazzling Stranger: Bert Jansch and the British Folk and Blues Revival*, Bloomsbury, London, 2001

Harrison, Hank, *Kurt Cobain, Beyond Nirvana: The Legacy of Kurt Cobain*, The Archives Press, 1994

Hart, Mickey, and Kostyal, Karen, *Songcatchers: In Search of the World's Music*, National Geographic Books, 2003

Hasse, John Edward (ed.), *Jazz: The First Century*, William Morrow, New York, 2000

Heatley, Michael (ed.), *Rock & Pop: The Complete Story*, Flame Tree Publishing, London, 2006

Heilbut, Tony, *The Gospel Sound*, Limelight Editions, New York, 1973

Hildebrand, Lee, *Stars of Soul, Rhythm and Blues: Top Recording Artists and Show Stopping Performers, from Memphis and Motown to Now*, Billboard Books, New York, 1994

Hirshey, Gerri, *Nowhere to Run: The Story of Soul Music*, Macmillan, 1994

Holmes, Thomas B., *Electronic and Experimental Music*, Routledge, London, 2002

Ingham, Chris, *The Book Of Metal*, Carlton Books, London, 2002

James, Martin, *State Of Bass: Jungle – the Story so Far*, Boxtree, London, 1997)

Jeffries, Neil (ed.), *The "Kerrang!" Direktory of Heavy Metal: The Indispensable Guide to Rock Warriors and Headbangin' Heroes*, Virgin Books, London, 1993

Jenkins, Lucien (ed.), *The Billboard Illustrated Musical Instruments Handbook*, Billboard Books, New York, 2006

Jenkins, Lucien (ed.), *The Illustrated Musical Instruments Handbook*, Flame Tree Publishing, London, 2006

Jost, Ekkehard, *Free Jazz*, Da Capo Press, Maryland, 1994

Juno, Andrea, *Angry Women In Rock*, Juno Books, 2003

Katz, David, *People Funny Boy: The Genius of Lee 'Scratch' Perry*, Payback Press, London, 2000

Katz, David, *Solid Foundation: An Oral History of Reggae*, Bloomsbury, London, 2003

Kettlewell, Ben, *Electronic Music Pioneers*, Artistpro.com, California, 2001

Kingsbury, Paul, and Axelrod, Alan, (ed.), *Country: The Music and the Musicians*, Country Music Foundation/Abbeville Press, New York, 1988

Kingsbury, Paul, *Country On Compact Disc: The Essential Guide to the Music*, ed., The Country Music Foundation/Grove Press, New York, 1993

Kingsbury, Paul, *The Grand Ole Opry History of Country Music*, Villard, New York, 1995

Kirchner, Bill (ed.), *The Oxford Companion To Jazz*, Oxford University Press, Oxford, 2000

Knight, Richard, *The Blues Highway: New Orleans to Chicago*, Trailblazer Publications, London, 2001

Kozinn, Allan, *The Beatles*, Phaidon, London, 1995

Krims, Adam, *Rap Music and the Poetics of Identity*, Cambridge University Press, Cambridge, 2000

Larkin, Colin (ed.), *The Virgin Encyclopedia of Dance Music*, Virgin Books, London, 1999

Larkin, Colin, *Encyclopedia of Popular Music*, Virgin Publishing, London, 2002

Larkin, Colin, *The Guinness Who's Who of Sixties Music*, Guinness Publishing, London, 1992

Larkin, Colin, *The Virgin Encyclopedia of Heavy Rock*, Virgin Books, London, 1999

Larkin, Colin, *The Virgin Encyclopedia Of Reggae*, Virgin Books, London, 1998

Larkin, Colin, *The Virgin Illustrated Encyclopedia of Rock*, Virgin Books, London, 1999

Lee, Spike (foreword), D. Chuck, Yusuf Jah, *Fight The Power: Rap, Race & Reality*, Payback Press, Edinburgh, 1999

Leonard, Michael (ed.), *The Billboard Illustrated Complete Guitar Handbook*, Billboard Books, New York, 2005

Leonard, Michael (ed.), *The Illustrated Complete Guitar Handbook*, Flame Tree Publishing, London, 2005

Lewisohn, Mark, *The Complete Beatles Chronicle*, Harmony Books, New York, 1992

Leymarie, Isabelle, *Cuban Fire: The Saga of Salsa and Latin Jazz*, Continuum International Publishing Group, New York, 2002

Light, Alan, *The Vibe History Of Hip Hop*, Plexus, London, 1999

Lincoln Collier, James, *The Making Of Jazz: A Comprehensive History*, Houghton Mifflin Company, Boston, 1978

Logan, Nick, and Woffinden, Bob (eds.), *The Illustrated New Musical Express Encyclopedia of Rock*, Hamlyn, London, 1976

Lornell, Kip, *Happy In the Service Of The Lord*, University of Illinois Press, Chicago, 1988

Lydon, Michael, *Ray Charles: Man and Music*, Payback Press, Edinburgh, 1999

Macdonald, Ronan (ed.), *The Billboard Illustrated Home Recording Handbook*, Billboard Books, New York, 2004
Macdonald, Ronan (ed.), *The Illustrated Home Recording Handbook*, Flame Tree Publishing, London, 2004
Malone, Bill C., *Country Music U.S.A.*, University of Texas Press, Austin, Texas, 1985
Mandel, Howard (ed.), *The Billboard Illustrated Encyclopedia of Jazz & Blues*, Billboard Books, New York, 2005
Mandel, Howard (ed.), *The Illustrated Encyclopedia of Jazz & Blues*, Flame Tree Publishing, London, 2005
Marcic, Dorothy, *Respect: Women and Popular Music*, Texere, New York, 2002
Marcus, Greil, *Mystery Train: Images of America in Rock'n'Roll Music*, E P Dutton, 1975
Marsh, Dave, *For the Record: Sam and Dave*, Avon Books, New York, 1998
Marsh, Dave, *George Clinton and P-Funk (For the Record)*, Avon Books, New York, 1998
Mathieson, Kenny, *Cookin': Hard Bop and Soul Jazz, 1954-65*, Canongate Books Ltd, Edinburgh, 2002
McGowan, Chris, and Pessanha, Ricardo, *The Brazilian Sound: Samba, Bossa Nova and the Popular Music of Brazil*, Temple University Press, Philadelphia, 1998
McIver, Joel, *Nu-Metal: The Next Generation Of Rock And Punk*, Omnibus Press, London, 2002
McKay, George, *Glastonbury: A Very English Fair*, Orion, London, 2000
McNeil, Legs and McGain, Gillian (eds.), *Please Kill Me: The Uncensored Oral History of Punk*, Penguin USA, New York, 1997
McStravick, Summer and Roos, John, (eds.), *Blues-rock Explosion: From The Allman Brothers To The Yardbirds*, Old Goat Publishing, California, 2002
Mezzrow, Mezz and Wolfe, Bernard, *Really The Blues*, Doubleday, New York, 1946
Milkowski, Bill, *Jaco: Jaco Pastorius*, Backbeat, London, 1998
Milkowski, Bill, *Swing It! An Annotated History Of Jive*, Billboard Books, New York, 2001
Millard, Bob, *Country Music: 70 Years of America's Favorite Music*, HarperPerennial, New York, 1993
Moore, Allan (ed.), *The Cambridge Companion to Blues and Gospel Music*, Cambridge University Press, Cambridge, 2003
Morath, Max, and Feinstein, Michael, *The Npr Curious Listener's Guide to Popular Standards*, Perigee, New York, 2002
Morrow, Chris, *Stir It Up: Reggae Cover Art*, Thames & Hudson, London, 1999
Moynihan, Michael and Søderlind, Didrik, *Lords Of Chaos: The Bloody Rise Of The Satanic Underground*, Feral House, 2003
Mulholland, Garry, *This Is Uncool: The 500 Greatest Singles Since Punk and Disco*, Cassell, London, 2002
Nathan, David, *Soulful Divas*, Billboard Books, New York, 1999
Newman, Richard, *Blues Breaker: John Mayall And The Story Of The Blues*, Sanctuary Publishing, London, 1995
Nicholls, David (ed.), *The Cambridge Companion to John Cage*, Cambridge University Press, Cambridge, 2002
O'Brien, Karen, *Shadows and Light: Joni Mitchell: The Definitive Biography*, Virgin Books, London, 2002
O'Brien-Chang, Kevin and Chen, Wayne, *Reggae Routes: The Story Of Jamaican Music*, Temple University Press, Philadelphia, 1998
Oakley, Giles, *The Devil's Music: A History of the Blues*, Da Capo Press, Maryland, 1997
Oermann, Robert K., *America's Music: The Roots of Country*, Turner, Atlanta, 1996
Ogg, Alex, and Upshal, David, *The Hip Hop Years*, Channel 4 Books, London, 1999
Oliver, P., *The New Grove Gospel, Blues and Jazz*, Grove Publications, London, 1987
Oliver, Paul, *The Story of the Blues: The Making of a Black Music*, Pimlico, London, 1997
Olsen, Dale A., and Sheehy, Daniel (eds.), *The Garland Handbook of Latin American Music*, Garland Science, New York, 2000
Olsen, Eric et al, *The Encyclopedia of Record Producers*, Billboard, New York, 1999
Palmer, Robert, *Deep Blues*, Viking Press, 1981
Pascall, Jeremy, *The Golden Years of Rock & Roll*, Phoebus Publishing, New York, 1974
Perkins, William Eric (ed.), *Droppin' Science: Critical Essays on Rap Music and Hip Hop Culture*, Temple University Press, Philadelphia, 1996
Pessanha, Ricardo and McGowan, Chris, *The Brazilian Sound: Samba, Bossa Nova and the Popular Music of Brazil*, Temple University Press, 1998
Porter, Dick, *Rapcore: The Nu-Metal Rap Fusion*, Plexus Publishing, New Jersey, 2002
Potash, Chris (ed.) *Reggae, Rasta, Revolution: Jamaican Music from Ska to Dub*, Books With Attitude, Schirmer Books, 1997
Potter, John, *The Power of Okinawa: Roots Music from the Ryukyus*, SU Press, Selinsgrove, 2001
Prendergast, Mark, *The Ambient Century*, Bloomsbury, London, 2000
Pruter, Robert, *Chicago Soul*, University of Illinois Press, Chicago, 1992
Ramsey, Guthrie P., *Race Music: Black Cultures from Bebop to Hip-Hop*, University of California Press, Berkeley, 2003
Reuss, Richard A., and Reuss, JoAnne C., *American Folk Music and Left Wing Politics 1927–1957*, Scarecrow Press, Maryland, 2000
Reynolds, Simon, *Energy Flash: A Journey Through Rave Music and Club Culture*, Picador, London, 1997
Reynolds, Simon, *Generation Ecstasy: into the World of Techno and Rave Culture*, Routledge, London, 1999
Reynolds, Simon, *The Sex Revolts: Gender, Rebellion and Rock'n'roll*, Harvard University Press, Harvard, 1995
Ritz, David, *Divided Soul: The Life of Marvin Gaye*, Da Capo Press, Maryland, 1991
Ro, Ronin, *Have Gun Will Travel: The Spectacular Rise Of Death Row Records*, Quartet Books, London, 1998
Roberts, John Storm, *The Latin Tinge*, Oxford University Press, Philadelphia, 1998
Rosalsky, Mitch, *Encyclopedia Of Rhythm And Blues And Doo Wop Vocal Groups*, Scarecrow Press, Maryland, 2000
Rose, Tricia, *Black Noise: Rap Music and Black Culture in Contemporary America*, Wesleyan University Press, Middletown, 1994
Rosenberg, Neil V., *Bluegrass: A History*, University of Illinois Press, Urbana and Chicago, Illinois, 1985
Rosenthal, David H., *Hard Bop: Jazz and Black Music, 1955–1965*, Oxford University Press Inc., New York, 1994
Rowe, Mike, *Chicago Blues: The City And The Music*, Da Capo Press, Maryland, 1973
Rule, Greg, *Electro Shock! The Groundbreakers of Electronica*, Backbeat Books, San Francisco, 1999
Salewicz, Chris and Boot, Adrian, *Bob Marley: Songs Of Freedom*, Bloomsbury, London, 1995
Salewicz, Chris and Boot, Adrian, *Reggae Explosion*, Virgin Books, London,.2001
Sawyers, June Skinner, *The Complete Guide to Celtic Music: From the Highland Bagpipe and Riverdance to U2 and Enya*, Aurum Press, London, 2000
Schnabel, Tom, *Rhythm Planet: The Great World Music Makers*, Rizzoli Publications, New York, 1998
Schuller, Gunther, *The Swing Era*, Oxford University Press, Oxford, 1989
Schumacher, Michael, *Crossroads: The Life And Music Of Eric Clapton*, Citadel Press, Sacramento, 2003
Seeger, Pete, and Schwartz, Jo Metcalf (ed.), *The Incompleat Folksinger*, University of Nebraska Press, Lincoln, 1995
Shankar, Ravi, *Raga Mala: The Autobiography of Ravi Shankar*, Welcome Rain Publishers, New York, 2001
Shapiro, Peter, *Rough Guide to Drum N' Bass*, Rough Guides, London, 1999
Shapiro, Peter, *The Rough Guide To Hip Hop*, Rough Guides, London, 2001
Shapiro, Peter, *The Rough Guide to Soul Music*, Rough Guides, London, 2000
Shaw, Arnold, *Honkers and Shouters: The Golden Years of Rhythm and Blues*, Macmillan, London, 1978
Sheridan, Chris (ed.), *Dis Here: A Bio-discography of Julian "Cannonball" Adderley (Discographies)*, Greenwood Press, Westport, 2000
Sicko, Dan, *Techno Rebels: The Renegades of Electronic Funk*, Billboard Books, New York, 1999
Slutsky, Allen, *Standing in the Shadows of Motown*, Hal Leonard Corporation, 1991
Smith Brindle, Reginald, *The New Music: The Avant-Garde Since 1945*, Oxford University Press, Oxford, 1987
Smith, Joe, *Off the Record: An Oral History of Popular Music*, Warner Books, 1988
Songlines magazine
Southern, Eileen, *The Music Of Black Americans: A History*, Norton, New York, 1983
Spicer, Al, *The Rough Guide to Rock (100 Essential CDs)*, Rough Guides, London, 1999
Stambler, Irwin, and Stambler, Lyndon, *Folk and Blues: The Encyclopedia*, St Martin's Press, New York, 2001
Stancell, Steven, *Rap Whoz Who: The World Of Rap Music*, Schirmer Books, New York, 2001
Stone, Ruth, *The Garland Handbook of African Music*, Garland Science, New York, 1999
Strong, Martin .C., *The Great Metal Discography*, Mojo Books, London, 2002
Strong, Martin C., *The Great Rock Discography*, Canongate Publications, Edinburgh, 2002
Sudhalter, Richard M., *Lost Chords: White Musicians And Their Contributions To Jazz, 1915–1945*, Oxford University Press, Oxford, 1999
Swern, Phil, and Greenfield, Shaun, *30 Years of Number Ones*, BBC Books, London, 1990
Taylor, Marc, *A Touch of Classical Soul: Soul Singers of the Early 1970s*, Partners Publishing Group, 1999
The Rough Guide To World Music (2nd edition, Vols. 1 & 2), Rough Guides, London, 2000
Thompson, David, *Pop*, Collectors Guide Publishing, 2000
Thornton, Sarah, *Club Cultures: Music, Media and Subcultural Capital*, Polity Press, London, 1995
Tingen, Paul, *Miles Beyond: The Electric Explorations of Miles Davis, 1967-1991*, Billboard Books, 2001
Toop, David, *Ocean of Sound: Aether Talk, Ambient Sound and Imaginary Worlds*, Serpent's Tail, London, 2001
Toop, David, *The Rap Attack 3: African Jive To New York Hip Hop*, Serpent's Tail, London, 1999)
Unterberger, Richie, *The Rough Guide to Music USA*, Rough Guides, London, 1999
Unterberger, Richie, *Turn! Turn! Turn!: The 60s Folk-Rock Revolution*, Backbeat UK, London, 2002
Vallely, Fintan, *Companion to Irish Traditional Music*, Cork University Press, Cork, 1999
Veal, Michael, *Fela: The Life and Times of an African Musical Icon*, Temple University Press, Philadelphia, 2000
Vincent, Ricky, *Funk: Music, People and Rhythm of the One*, St Martin's Press, New York, 1996
Waldo, Terry, *This Is Ragtime*, Da Capo Press, Maryland, 1976
Wall, Geoff, and Hinton, Brian, *Ashley Jennings: The Guv'nor & The Rise of Folk Rock*, Helter Skelter Publishing, London, 2002
Ward, Andrew, *Dark Midnight When I Rise: The Story of the Fisk Jubilee Singers*, HarperCollins, New York, 2001
Ward, Greg, *The Rough Guide To The Blues*, Rough Guides, London, 2000
Watt, Sharon, (ed.), *Bluegrass Unlimited* (monthly magazine), Warrenton, Virginia, 2003
Weldon Johnson, James, et al, *The Books of American Negro Spirituals*, Da Capo Press, Maryland, 2003
Werkhoven, Henk N. *International Guide To New Age Music: A Comprehensive Guide to the Vast and Varied Artists and Recordings of New Age Music*, Billboard Books, New York, 1998
Westbrook, Alonzo, *The Hip Hoptionary: The Dictionary Of Hip Hop Terminology*, Harlem Moon, New York, 2002
Whitburn, Joel, *Billboard Top 1000 Singles 1955–2000*, Hal Leonard Publishing, Milwaukee, 2001
Whitburn, Joel, *Joel Whitburn's Top Country Singles*, Billboard/Record Research, Inc., Menomonee Falls, Wisconsin, 1994–2002
White, Charles, *The Life and Times of Little Richard*, Harmony Books, 1984
Whittaker, Adrian, *Be Glad: An Incredible String Band Compendium*, Helter Skelter Publishing, London, 2003
Williams, Doug, et al, *Still Standing Tall: The Story of Gospel Music's Williams Brothers*, Billboard Books, New York, 1999
Wolfe, Tom, *The Kandy-Kolored Tangerine-Flake Streamline Baby*, Simon & Schuster, New York, 1965
Wolff, Daniel, *You Send Me: The Life and Times of Sam Cooke*, Virgin Books, New York, 1995
Wyman, Bill, *Bill Wyman's Blues Odyssey: A Journey To Music's Heart And Soul*, Dorling Kindersley, London, 2001
Young Alan, *The Pilgrim Jubilees*, University Press of Mississippi, Mississippi, 2002
Young, Alan, *Woke Me Up This Morning: Black Gospel Singers and the Gospel Life*, University Press of Mississippi, Mississippi, 1997

WEBSITES

http://www.allmusic.com
http://www.allofmp3.com/
http://www.aloud.com/
http://www.apple.com/itunes/
http://www.archive.org/details/etree/
http://www.bbc.co.uk/music/
http://www.bbc.co.uk/radio/
http://www.bigmouth.co.uk/
http://www.billboard.com/
http://www.calendarlive.com/music/
http://www.channel4.com/music/
http://www.clickmusic.com/
http://www.creemmagazine.com/
http://.davidbyrne.com/radio/
http://www.downbeat.com/
http://.dustygrove.com/
http://www.efestivals.co.uk/
http://www.emusic.com/
http://www.fly.co.uk/
http://www.frootsmag.com/
http://www.getback.org/
http://www.giglist.com/
http://www.grovemusic.com/
http://www.hardradio.com/
http://www.insound.com/
http://www.jazzfm.com/
http://www.juno.co.uk/
http://www.kerang.com/
http://www.lemon-red.org/blog/
http://www.live365.com/
http://www.livedaily.com/
http://www.markprindle.com/
http://www.metracritic.com/music/
http://www.mixmag.net/
http://www.mojo4music.com/
http://www.motown.com/
http://www.mp3.com/
http://www.mtv.com/
http://.music.aol.com/
http://www.music.com/
http://.music.download.com/
http://.music.yahoo.com/
http://www.musicfirebox.com/
http://www.musicsearch.com/
http://www.musictoday.com/
http://www.musicweek.com/
http://www.myspace.com/
http://www.napster.com/
http://www.nme.com/
http://www.npr.org/
http://www.pandora.com/
http://www.pitchforkmedia.com/
http://www.play.com/
http://www.playlouder.com/
http://www.q4music.com/
http://www.reasontorock.com/
http://www.recordcollectormag.com/
http://www.rhapsody.com/
http://www.rock.com/
http://www.rockdetector.com/
http://www.rockmusiczone.com/
http://www.rock-sound.net/
http://www.rollingstone.com/
http://www.roughstock.com/
http://www.smithsonianglobalsound.org/
http://www.sonymusic.com/
http://www.sortmusic.com/
http://www.soul-sides.com/
http://www.spillonline.com/
http://www.spin.com/
http://www.stereogum.com/
http://www.stylusmagazine.com/
http://.thebluehighway.com/
http://www.thewire.co.uk/
http://www.thisdayinmusic.com/
http://.top40-charts.com/
http://www.tunes.com/
http://.turntablelab.com/
http://.uk.launch.yahoo.com/
http://www.vh1.com/
http://www.woodstock69.com/
http://www.woxy.com/

Index